EFFECTIVE TEACHING

Principles and Procedures of Applied Behavior Analysis with Exceptional Students

MARK WOLERY
University of Kentucky, Lexington

DONALD B. BAILEY, JR.
University of North Carolina at Chapel Hill

GEORGE M. SUGAI
University of Oregon, Eugene

Allyn and Bacon, Inc.
BOSTON   LONDON   SYDNEY   TORONTO

Copyright © 1988 by Allyn and Bacon, Inc.
A Division of Simon & Schuster
160 Gould Street
Needham, Massachusetts 02194-2310

Library of Congress Cataloging-in-Publication Data

Wolery, Mark.
    Effective teaching : principles and procedures of applied behavior
analysis with exceptional students / Mark Wolery, Donald B. Bailey,
Jr., George M. Sugai.
        p. cm.
    Includes bibliographies and index.
    ISBN 0-205-11308-7 (pbk.)
    1. Handicapped children—Education. 2. Teaching. 3. Behavioral
assessment of children. 4. Behavior modification. I. Bailey,
Donald B. II. Sugai, George M., 1951–. III. Title.
LC4019.W65   1988
371.9—dc 19   87–22743
                                                   CIP

Production administrator: Annette Joseph
Production coordinator: Helyn Pultz
Editorial-production service: Laura Cleveland
Cover administrator: Linda K. Dickinson
Cover designer: Hemenway Design

Printed in the United States of America

10 9 8 7 6 5 4   93 94 95 96

This book is dedicated to our wives, Ruth, Pam, and Betsy, and to our children, Steve, Tim, Lara, Rebecca, and Nathaniel.

BRIEF CONTENTS

COMPLETE CONTENTS

PART II
TECHNICAL COMPETENCIES IN APPLIED BEHAVIOR ANALYSIS

Chapter 3
Writing Behavioral Objectives   35

Chapter 6
Summarizing Behavioral Performance: Quantitative Methods   97

Chapter 7
Summarizing Behavioral Performance: Graphing Methods   110

Chapter 8
Using Data to Make Instructional Decisions   127

Chapter 9
Using Data to Identify Causal Relationships   144

Chapter 10
Using Data to Compare Treatments   169

PART III
FACILITATING ACQUISITION

Chapter 11
Structuring the Environment for Effective Teaching   187

Chapter 12
Presenting Tasks for Acquisition   214

Chapter 13
Using Reinforcers to Facilitate Skill Acquisition   234

Chapter 14
Fading Prompts to Promote Independence   253

PART IV
MOVING BEYOND ACQUISITION

Chapter 15
Building Fluency   281

Chapter 16
Thinning Reinforcement to Maintain Skills   297

Chapter 17
Generalizing Acquired Skills   313

PART V
REDUCING INAPPROPRIATE BEHAVIOR

Chapter 18
Definitional and Ethical Problems Related to
Behavior Reduction   331

Chapter 19
Decision Model for Reducing the Occurrence of Inappropriate Behaviors   349

Chapter 20
Manipulating Reinforcers to Reduce Inappropriate Behavior   383

Chapter 21
Using Timeout from Positive Reinforcement   416

Chapter 22
Aversive Techniques to Reduce Inappropriate Behaviors   445

PART VI
USING BEHAVIOR MANAGEMENT SYSTEMS AND PEERS

Chapter 23
Using Behavioral Contracts and Token Economies   471

PREFACE

About twenty years ago, Baer, Wolf, and Risley (1968) defined the dimensions of applied behavior analysis, and since then, numerous journal articles have appeared and reports of hundreds of investigations in applied behavior analysis have been published. College courses are routinely offered that provide training in the use of applied behavior analysis in schools. The purpose of this book is to provide an introduction to applied behavior analysis as it relates to teaching and managing the behavior of students with handicaps. Five elements of this purpose require comment. First, this text is an introduction to the field. Although we review current research and draw applications from it for day-to-day practice, this text is not a detailed review of the literature in applied behavior analysis. Since the text is introductory, we highlight key terms and concepts. Key terms are printed in boldface type throughout the narrative, and a definition or description of the term is included in close proximity to the highlighted term. Key terms are listed at the beginning of each chapter, and key concepts appear at the end of each chapter.

Second, this text focuses on students with handicaps. Although the principles and procedures described in the text apply to much broader populations, including nonhandicapped students, parents, and teachers, we limit the focus to students with handicaps to make the task more manageable and to communicate more directly with special education teachers.

Third, the text focuses on teaching new skills *and* managing inappropriate behaviors, both academic and social. This emphasis was taken because we believe that these functions (teaching and managing behavior) are inextricably tied to one another. Good teaching practices, in and of themselves, reduce the probability that inappropriate behavior will occur; likewise, poor teaching practices set the stage for aberrant behavior. Thus, issues related to providing and evaluating appropriate learning environments are presented. Strategies for identifying appropriate behaviors, writing objectives, collecting data, and using those data for decision making are described. Procedures are discussed for helping children acquire, become proficient in, maintain, and use new behaviors. Further, we believe that the ethical approach to reducing the occurrence of inappropriate behavior begins with a careful analysis of the environments in which students function and the relationships that exist between students' behavior and environmental variables. The text stresses teaching behaviors that will replace maladaptive responses and serve the same communicative and social functions as inappropriate behaviors.

Fourth, the text emphasizes teaching as a process rather than the application of predesigned procedures. The science of human behavior postulates several principles that govern how individuals interact with the environment and learn from it. These principles are translated into environmental manipulations (procedures or techniques) that are used to facilitate learning and reduce the occurrence of inappropriate behaviors. The translation from principle to procedure, however, is imperfect. As a result, procedures can be ineffective and, in some cases, lead to contratherapeutic outcomes. To guard against this possibility, teachers must understand the principles of behavior and continuously evaluate the effects of their treatments. In an effort to assist teachers in this task, the text describes procedures for collecting *and* using data. By monitoring the effects of instructional and behavior-management strategies, teachers can make modifications in those strategies and produce the type of behavior students need to function independently and appropriately. Numerous flowcharts and guidelines along with a behavior-reduction model for planning, implementing, and evaluating interventions are presented.

Finally, common school practices for controlling students' inappropriate behaviors are described. Examples include the use of teacher praise, suspension, and corporal punishment. These practices are evaluated on the basis of their empirical as well as logical foundations. Recommendations concerning the use of these practices are provided.

When writing this book, we had the support of numerous individuals. David L. Gast of the University of Kentucky, Peter Leone of the University of Maryland, Mark Koorland of The Florida State University, Sheila Fox of Western Washington University, and Herb Reith of Peabody College of Vanderbilt University reviewed drafts of the manuscript and provided insightful and helpful comments. In addition, several persons assisted us by collecting research articles, reading various chapter drafts, and typing the document. These persons include Cathy Alig, Debra Billings, Frances Glover, Doug Hannah, Joan Holder, Jackie Kues, Pat Red, Becky Trexel, and Annie Warberg. Finally, our wives, Ruth, Pam, and Betsy, and our children, Steve, Tim, Lara, Rebecca, and Nathaniel, have been patient and understanding about the hours spent in our offices writing this text and about the times we were mentally distracted by the task but physically present. We appreciate the support of these individuals and acknowledge their contribution to the completion of the text.

REFERENCE

Baer, D. M., Wolf, M. M., & Risley, T. R. (1968). Current dimensions of applied behavior analysis. *Journal of Applied Behavior Analysis, 1,* 91–97.

PART I

FOUNDATIONS OF APPLIED BEHAVIOR ANALYSIS

About 20 years ago, Baer, Wolf, and Risley (1968) defined and described the dimensions of applied behavior analysis. This marked the emergence of a new field based on previous research addressing how individuals learn and how individuals influence and are influenced by the environment. Chapter 1 defines learning, reviews explanations for how learning occurs, and describes different types of learning from the behavioral perspective. The development of the field of applied behavior analysis also is placed in historical context. Chapter 2 discusses the relationship between teaching and learning, and focuses on important practices in effective teaching. The dimensions and underlying assumptions of applied behavior analysis also are described. A model for teaching and controlling behavior based on applied behavior analysis is presented and includes the following steps: identify overall goals, gather specific information about the problem, specify learning objectives, plan and implement interventions, monitor student performance, and evaluate student performance. This model is used throughout the text; major steps of the model are addressed in complete chapters later in the book. Finally, Chapter 2 lists and responds to criticisms of applied behavior analysis. These criticisms and corresponding responses are provided so teachers will approach the text in a questioning manner and will be able to react to others' objections about the use of applied behavior analysis.

REFERENCE

Baer, D. M., Wolf, M. M., & Risley, T. R. (1968). Current dimensions of applied behavior analysis. *Journal of Applied Behavior Analysis, 1,* 91–97.

LEARNING AND LEARNING THEORY

Key Terms

- Learning ■ Learning Theory ■ Stimulus ■ Antecedents
- Behavior ■ Consequences ■ Respondent Conditioning
- Classical Conditioning ■ Unconditioned Stimulus ■ Conditioned
Stimulus ■ Operant Conditioning ■ Positive Reinforcement ■ Vicarious
Learning

INTRODUCTION

What does it mean to say that a student has learned something? In one respect, this is a simple question with a simple answer. Learning has occurred when a student can do something that he or she previously could not do. At another level, however, learning is an extraordinarily complex process. The actual mechanisms of learning and the internal processes it requires are unobservable events. Scientists, philosophers, and educators all have speculated about the nature of those events and how they occur. Since the facilitation of learning is the teacher's most fundamental task, an understanding of the learning process and the ability to use effective techniques to enhance it are essential.

Gagné (1985) defined *learning* as "a change in human disposition or capability that persists over a period of time and is not simply ascribable to processes of growth" (p. 2). For the purpose of this text, we define **learning** as an enduring change in behavior as a result of experience. Two aspects of the definition should be noted. First, learning is viewed as a change in behavior. Clearly, learning can occur when there is no observable change in behavior. For example, you have just read (and perhaps learned) a definition of learning. It is something you now know that you may or may not have known before. But for anyone else to know that you have learned the definition you would have to do something—write it down, say it, or apply it in some fashion. A responsible teacher needs to know whether or not learning has occurred. Therefore, it must be defined in terms of a change in behavior.

Second, learning occurs as a result of experience or interaction with the environment. Changes that occur simply as a function of maturation are not considered learned changes. However, interaction with the environment is broadly construed to include any type of experience that changes behavior, regardless of whether teaching is involved.

A **learning theory** is an attempt to explain how learning occurs. Clearly, the process of teaching (expediting learning) should be facilitated if one understands how learning occurs and the implications of that knowledge for teaching. The purpose of this chapter is first to provide a brief overview of three contrasting approaches to learning theory, and then to describe in greater detail the approach emphasized in this text.

THREE BLACK BOX THEORIES

Learning requires several steps. When presented with a given **stimulus** (e.g., math worksheet, teacher's question, or a word to read), the student first must attend to the stimulus by looking at it, hearing it, or using one of the other basic senses. Once the student has received the necessary information, he or she somehow organizes the input data, attaches meaning to it, and prepares to respond. A response is made and the student receives some form of internal or external feedback that confirms the adequacy of the response and either increases or decreases the probability of that response occurring again under similar stimulus conditions. Almost every theory of learning acknowledges, at the most basic and behavioral level, that learning has occurred when a person's response to a given stimulus has changed as a function of experience. However, theorists differ on at least two points. The first is often referred to as the *black box,* or what occurs when the individual is organizing and processing input data. It is referred to as the *black box* because we cannot see what goes on inside of it and thus must speculate as to what occurs. The second point of difference has to do with the nature and role of the feedback experience and the extent to which feedback can change understanding and behavior.

At least three broad approaches to learning theory have attempted to address the question of what goes on inside the black box: the neurophysiological approach, the information-processing approach, and the cognitive-developmental approach.

The Neurophysiological Approach

At one level, learning may be viewed as a neurophysiological process involving the brain and the central nervous system. The most comprehensive and well-developed theoretical formulation of this process was developed by D. O. Hebb (1949). According to Hebb's theory, the basic unit of the nervous system is the nerve cell, or *neuron*. Transmission of a nerve impulse is an electrochemical process in which one neuron "fires," setting off the next neuron, and so forth. In the newborn infant, these firings are not well organized or integrated with each other. Hebb argued that it is through experience that the infant's nervous system becomes integrated. Repeated exposure to the same stimulus facilitates the organization of *cell assemblies,* or groups of neurons that function as a unit. Repeated stimulation lays down these neural pathways and each exposure to a stimulus reduces the amount of stimulation required to activate a given cell assembly. Cell assemblies can be organized into larger structures referred to as *phase sequences,* which in turn can be organized into even more complex *phase cycles.* Association learning occurs as cell assemblies connect with many possible phase sequences. As children grow they are able to understand increasingly complex constructs and ideas because of the increasing complexity and refinement of neural systems organized through experience.

Others have attempted to use a different version of the neurophysiological approach by identifying parts of the brain associated with different functions, and associating certain disabilities with specific types of brain damage. For example, the left and right hemispheres of the brain control different functions. It has been suggested that language disabilities such as dyslexia may be associated with abnormalities in the left hemisphere (Levine, Hier, & Calvanio, 1981), whereas abnormalities in the right hemisphere may influence attention, affect, nonverbal or paralinguistic aspects of communication, and visual-spatial abilities (Weintraub & Mesulam, 1983). Batteries of tests have been developed to assess brain damage, such as the Halstead-Reitan Neuropsychological Battery (Reitan & Davidson, 1974) and the Luria-Nebraska Neuropsychological Battery (Golden, Hammeke, & Parisch, 1980), and significant relationships between neuropsychological, cognitive, and behavioral assessments have been reported (e.g., Klesges, 1983).

Clearly, there is a neurophysiological component to learning. Recent technological advances have made it possible to more accurately assess brain functioning, and the future is exciting in terms of the development of our understanding of the brain. It is not so clear, however, what the implications of this perspective are for teaching, since we cannot change or correct basic anomalies in the brain. Weintraub and Mesulam (1983) and others suggested the possibility that such knowledge helps us to understand why a student might behave in a certain way, and may lead us to specific nontraditional therapies that incorporate that knowledge in helping the student adapt.

The Information-Processing Approach

A number of different theorists' work can be classified under the broad rubric of information processing. Like Hebb's theory, a common thread woven through each information processing theory is an attempt to understand and explain the processes that occur between the input (sensory information) and the output (behavior). However, they differ from Hebb in that, rather than describing these processes in neurophysiological terms, they attempt to understand how the individual perceives, organizes, processes, and stores information, and how those individualized processes affect behavior. A number of these theories have been summarized by Mercer and Snell (1977). Some have been used to explain learning deficits in students labeled as mentally retarded, whereas others have been used to explain the academic difficulties of children labeled as learning disabled.

Some theorists have focused on the importance of *attention* to the effective processing of information. Clearly, for learning to occur a child must attend to a stimulus situation, particularly to the important or relevant dimensions of the stimulus. For example, in teaching a student to recognize colors it is important for him or her to learn that the shape of an object has no relevance to its color; therefore, when presented with a color discrimination task, the student must know what to attend to and what to ignore. The growing recognition of the importance of attention has led to the identification of a diagnostic category referred to as *attention deficit disorder,* described clinically by Levine and Melmed (1982). Zeaman and House (1963) conducted a number of studies of students with mental retardation and concluded that their learning problems were due to poor attention rather than retarded learning abilities. The students had a hard time sorting out and attending to the correct or relevant dimension of the task presented. The implication of this information-processing theory is that, when teaching retarded children, any extraneous cues should be eliminated during initial instruction and techniques should be used that highlight relevant dimensions to make them more distinctive. Detailed strategies for facilitating attention were described by Rinne (1984).

Other theorists have focused on the importance of *storage* and *retrieval* of information. For example, Spitz (1966) suggested seven steps in the learning process: arousal, attention, input, temporary memory, recall from temporary memory, permanent memory, and recall from permanent memory. According to Spitz, students with retardation have problems in *retrieving* information since they have not organized or filed it usefully at the time of input. One implication of this theory for teaching students with retardation is for teachers to present information in an organized fashion and to help children learn strategies for organizing and recalling information. Ellis (1970), on the other hand, focused on *memory* processes and suggested that information is stored in either primary memory (a limited-capacity, temporary storage of information that is constantly being replaced), secondary memory (storage of more meaningful memory for more than a few seconds), or tertiary memory (long-term memory). According to Ellis, the individual must incorporate *rehearsal* strategies in order for information to be stored in secondary or tertiary memory. The individual with retardation often does not use effective rehearsal strategies spontaneously, possibly because of inadequate language skills. Teaching implications suggested by this approach include teaching effective rehearsal strategies, teaching memory organizers such as mnemonics, and use of visual imagery (Mercer & Snell, 1977).

Still another information-processing approach was originally formulated by Osgood (1957) and later operationalized by others through the development of diagnostic tests and related intervention strategies. Osgood described *association* as the process by which a student relates input data to known information. This process can be disrupted because of deficits in either receiving, organizing, or storing input. The Illinois Test of Psycholinguistic Abilities (Kirk, McCarthy, & Kirk, 1968), based on a modification of Osgood's model, incorporates 12 basic components of information processing as they relate to psycholinguistic abilities. These include auditory reception, visual reception, auditory association, visual association, verbal expression, manual expression, grammatic closure, auditory closure, sound blending, visual closure, auditory sequential memory, and visual sequential memory. This approach has been suggested as useful in identifying and planning intervention programs for learning disabled students since allegedly it allows the teacher to identify specific information-processing deficits and plan for compensation or remediation. Research thus far, however, provides only limited support for the effectiveness of interventions based on this approach (Hammill & Larsen, 1978).

According to Gagné (1985), any information-processing theory must also take into account two related processes: *executive control* and *expectancy*. It is these two processes that manage, control, and select the processing of information:

> How the attention of the learner is directed, how the information is encoded, how it is retrieved, and how it is expressed in organized responses are all matters that require a choice of strategies. This choice is the function of the executive control processes, including expectancies established before learning is undertaken. (p. 79)

The Cognitive-Developmental Approach

The theoretical work of Jean Piaget is commonly referred to as the *cognitive-development approach*. Although Piaget's approach in one sense could be classified as an information-processing approach, it is unique and has had such a profound impact on psychology that it deserves separate discussion. Piaget, a biologist and an epistemologist studying the development of knowledge, did not attempt to address problems in teaching handicapped students, but others have tried to adapt his theory to do so (Dunst, 1981; Ginsberg & Opper, 1979; Kahn, 1979).

Piaget (1952) described four major stages in the development of cognitive awareness: the sensorimotor stage (approximately 0 to 2 years), the preoperational stage (approximately 2 to 7 years), the concrete operations stage (approximately 7 to 11 years), and the formal operations stage (approximately 11 years and older). The stages are descriptive in the sense that they provide information about the cognitive abilities and limitations of children of different ages, and their sequence is assumed to be invariant. Progress through these stages depends on both biological maturation and experience with the environment.

Central to Piaget's theory is the concept of *equilibration.* Just as organisms naturally and continually strive to achieve homeostasis or balance of biological functions, so too do they constantly strive to achieve a mental equilibrium or balance. Two processes are used to achieve this balance. First, through *assimilation,* the children modify the world to fit their current levels of cognitive development. For example, the child whose cognitive development has not yet reached the point at which he or she can view the world from another's perspective will always describe it from his or her own perspective. Second, through *accommodation,* children modify their behavior to more closely fit the sensory input received. According to Piaget, children and adults alike are constantly seeking equilibrium through the simultaneous processes of assimilation and accommodation. We all try to modify the world to fit our own views of it, while at the same time modifying our own perceptions as we are confronted with new information.

Several implications of Piaget's theory for teaching have been suggested. First, the four stages provide important information not only about the child's abilities, but also about the child's limitations. Teachers should not attempt to teach children skills for which they do not have the necessary cognitive prerequisites or which are too advanced given children's level of cognitive functioning. Second, growth requires active interaction with the physical environment. Children learn by *doing* rather than by being told something. Also, they learn from the natural consequences and feedback received in the process of interacting with materials and people rather than through artificial rewards or consequences imposed by teachers. Third, children learn best when the tasks, materials, and activities to which they are exposed are just challenging enough to allow for appropriate accommodation but not so difficult that learning is impossible. Thus, the teacher's role is primarily one of an environmental planner who ensures that children are provided opportunities for involvement in activities that are interesting, challenging, and facilitative of learning.

Summary Comments Regarding Black Box Theories

We have briefly reviewed three approaches to understanding what goes on inside the black box, or the mind, and have not done justice to any of them due to the brevity of coverage. The reader is encouraged to refer to the original or secondary sources cited in the References for further information.

Each approach described has logic and a limited amount of empirical data to support it. As teachers, we would be foolish to ignore the importance of any of them. It makes sense to assume that (1) learning has a neurophysiological basis; (2) when confronted with sensory input, an individual must attend to that input, organize it in some fashion, attach meaning to it, and integrate it with prior knowledge to prepare a response; (3) previously learned information must be stored and retrieved in some fashion, and (4) there are developmental aspects of learning that must be considered when planning instructional activities for students. However, it is the basic premise of this text that these theories alone or together constitute an insufficient basis for planning instructional activities for exceptional students. They do not describe or take into account a number of basic aspects of learning, a knowledge of which is necessary for good teaching to occur. An approach commonly referred to as *behavioral theory* fills this void and provides a sound basis of knowledge and skills for planning and implementing instructional activities. This approach is briefly described in the next section and elaborated on in detail throughout the remainder of this text.

BEHAVIORAL THEORY

Behavioral theory rests on three simple yet fundamental assumptions: (1) any given behavioral sequence has three basic components—antecedents, behavior, and consequences; (2) the behavioral response a person makes depends in part on the nature of the antecedent stimuli and in part on prior learning history of consequences provided when responses were previously made with similar stimuli; and (3) effective teaching involves teacher management and control of both antecedents and consequences.

Antecedents are conditions that occur just prior to a behavior, and may include the physical environment, instructional materials, teacher directions and assistance, or peer initiations. Antecedents are assumed to occasion or set the stage for certain responses. They let the individual know what is expected or demanded. Some antecedents are short and clear. For example, the teacher says, "Jeremy, what is 2 + 2?" or tells Sarah, "Sit down." Other antecedents are extended and may not be so clear. For example, the antecedents to Maria's sudden tantrum may be the accumulation of frustrating events over the entire morning. *Antecedent* is synonymous with *stimulus*.

Behavior is the response to the antecedent or stimulus situation. In behavioral theory, the response is defined in operational terms, or the specific things a person does. Thus, a behavior is an observable response such as writing, speaking, or moving rather than an inferred process such as thinking, reasoning, understanding, retrieving, or storing. Most behaviorists would not deny that inferred processes occur, only that they are unobservable and that we can only guess as to what they are. We can, however, describe the things a person does in response to a given situation. We can also identify the responses we would like a person to make.

Consequences are events that occur after the behavior and serve to affect the probability of that behavior occurring again in the future under similar stimulus conditions. Some consequences serve to increase this probability, whereas others serve to decrease it. Consequences are also stimuli.

A given individual's response is assumed to be determined in part by the clarity of the antecedent stimulus and in part by the individual's previous experiences under similar conditions, particularly the consequences he or she has received for previous responses. Moreover, it is assumed that human behavior is lawful and thus its study is a legitimate science (Grunbaum, 1952). Given the relationship between behavior and environment, effective teaching involves systematic planning and manipulation of antecedents that appropriately set the stage for learning and performance to occur and consequences that provide appropriate and effective feedback to students.

The behavioral explanation allows for the existence of the black box. However, given the uncertain nature of what goes on in the black box, it places primary emphasis on observable behavior as well as the observable antecedents and consequences to behavior. This relatively simple and straightforward conceptualization of learning actually encompasses a wide range of therapeutic interventions and teaching strategies described throughout this book.

Historical Notes on the Behavioral Explanation

To more fully appreciate the behavioral explanation and its underlying assumptions requires at least a brief discussion of its historical development. (See Hilgard and Bower (1975) and Kazdin (1978) for more detailed reviews.)

Much of the early work in developing the behavioral perspective evolved out of the psychotherapeutic field and attempts to deal with various psychological problems such as neuroses, psychoses, phobias, and addictions. The work of Freud (1949), although not behavioral in theory, was revolutionary and substantial in its impact on approaches to treating individuals with mental illness. One of his most important contributions was his emphasis on the role of experience, particularly early experience, in the development of psychological problems. Abnormal behaviors are learned, and thus have the possibility of being changed or "unlearned." This perspective differed considerably from the prevailing medical perspective that assumed such problems had a biological etiology and thus could not be changed through experience. Freud's approach to treatment, however, had several problems. First, he formulated a complex black box theory in which the id, the ego, and the superego were assumed to control behavior. Second, his intervention or therapy was predicated on the assumption that change in behavior required the individual to gain insight as to how the problem originally evolved. This insight was assumed to be a necessary condition for any meaningful treatment gains. Insight is gained through extensive psychoanalysis involving techniques such as free association and dream analysis.

Unfortunately, research has not been able to substantiate fully the effectiveness of psychoanalytic procedures. Furthermore, psychoanalysis is a time-consuming and expensive process. Thus, others turned to a more pragmatic or practical model that had direct implications for practitioners. It is impossible in a few brief paragraphs to describe all of the theorists, researchers, and events that have contributed to the behavioral explanation. However, we attempt to describe the major contributors.

One major question that had to be answered was, "How are inappropriate behaviors learned?" Freud assumed they were learned through early experiences, but did not experimentally demonstrate their acquisition. Russian physiologist Ivan Pavlov made two important contributions in this regard. His most famous experiment was his demonstration that a dog could be trained to salivate at the sound of a bell. His technique has since become known as **respondent conditioning (classical conditioning),** in which a stimulus that normally elicits a certain response is repeatedly paired with a second stimulus until the second stimulus also elicits that response. The original stimulus is referred to as the **unconditioned stimulus** (UCS) since it does not have to be learned, whereas the learned stimulus is referred to as the **conditioned stimulus** (CS). In Pavlov's experiment, a bell was paired with the presentation of food to a hungry dog. Naturally, the food (UCS) caused the dog to salivate. Eventually, however, the dog began salivating at the sound of the bell (CS) even when no food was present. This was an important experiment because it demonstrated that even reflexive behaviors, such as the secretion of digestive juices, could be modified through experience. His most important experiments, however, were those in which he demonstrated that he could experimentally induce neurotic-type behaviors in dogs, thus opening the door for the possibility that human neuroses were learned conditions.

American psychologist John Watson extended Pavlov's work by demonstrating that he could "teach" an irrational fear. He and his colleagues taught "Little Albert," an 11-month-old child, to cry whenever he saw a white furry object (Watson & Rayner, 1920). This was accomplished by ringing a loud bell behind Albert every time he reached for a white mouse. Although this study should never have been conducted for ethical reasons, it was an extremely important contribution since it provided clear evidence that at least some abnormal behaviors could be learned and, thus, possibly unlearned.

Four years after Watson's experiment, Mary Cover Jones, following Watson's advice, compared seven different techniques for eliminating fears in children: disuse (lack of exposure to the feared stimulus), verbal appeal (talking to the child and trying to associate pleasant experiences with the feared stimulus), negative adaptation (repeated exposure to the feared stimulus), repression (social ridicule by peers), distraction (diversion away from the feared stimulus), direct conditioning (pairing the feared object with a different high probability stimulus, such as food for a hungry child), and social imitation (observing others who were not afraid) (Jones, 1924). Both direct conditioning and social imitation were highly successful in eliminating fear responses.

Thus, by 1924, two major experimental demonstrations had been made. First, it had been clearly demonstrated that an irrational fear could be learned. Second, it had been demonstrated that such fears could be unlearned through the provision of specific treatment procedures. Although these conclusions may not seem tremendously exciting today, they were extremely important at the time since they differed so radically from prevailing perspectives. What followed was a tremendous growth in both the number of theorists attempting to develop and clarify the behavioral explanation, as well as a number of researchers and clinicians attempting to apply behavioral principles to the solution of social problems. Some of the more prominent theorists were Edward L. Thorndike, Edwin R. Guthrie, and Clark L. Hull.

Another important question was, "What role does feedback play in learning?" In this regard, the most well-known name associated with the behavioral explanation of learning is, of course, B. F. Skinner. His contributions are many and varied. From a theoretical perspective, he differentiated respondent and operant conditioning. **Operant conditioning** (also called *instrumental conditioning*) refers to the presentation of a consequence after a person has emitted a behavior or made a response. It differs from respondent conditioning in that there is no UCS; furthermore, there is no pairing of stimuli, but rather a sequential order of behavior and then consequences. The experimenter (or teacher) waits until the person makes a response and then provides an appropriate consequence to shape or modify that response. Much of Skinner's work focused on the application of **positive reinforcement,** or the presentation of a consequence that results in an increased likelihood of the behavior occurring again under similar conditions. Skinner clearly demonstrated the application of operant conditioning principles by changing the behavior of animals and described potential applications with people. His other contributions include a behavioral explanation of language acquisition (Skinner, 1957), a treatise on schedules of reinforcement (Ferster & Skinner, 1957), a technological approach to teaching (Skinner, 1957), a model for a utopia based on behavioral principles (Skinner, 1948), and a philosophical denial of the existence of true freedom (Skinner, 1971). Throughout his work, he has emphasized three main points. First, principles of behavior can be used to explain almost everything a person does. Second, principles of behavior can be applied to solve almost any social problem. Third, the best application of principles of behavior is wise use of positive reinforcement (positive consequences that increase the likelihood of a behavior occurring again).

These three points are emphasized in Skinner's approach to education. In his book *The Technology of Teaching* (1968), he suggested that public education has to face at least four major problems: (1) over-reliance on aversive procedures to control and motivate children, (2) the inability of teachers to give immediate feedback for student work, (3) the relative infrequency of positive reinforcement, and (4) the lack of small, well-sequenced instructional curricula. He suggested the need for major revisions in the technology of teaching to ensure that curriculum materials are well sequenced, that students receive immediate and appropriate feedback on their behavior, and that aversive control procedures are drastically reduced. One of his suggestions was that schools invest heavily in teaching machines that can be programmed in appropriately small steps and that can give immediate feedback to students regarding the accuracy of responses.

Bijou and Baer (1961, 1965, 1978) applied behavioral theory to the understanding of child development and to one explanation of mental retardation. According to Bijou (1981)

A retarded individual, from this point of view, is one who has a limited behavioral repertoire because of deficiencies in the environment and constraints imposed on the interactions that constitute his history—the more limited and restrictive the interactions, the more underdeveloped his behavioral repertoire. (p. 30)

Although Bijou recognized that "abnormal anatomical structures and physiological functioning" (p. 30) restrict learning, he also suggested that retardation is, in part, due to "deficiencies and marked deviation in the external conditions of development" (p. 31), thus explaining the importance of the environment as a mediating variable influencing the behavior of persons with retardation.

A final contributor to the development of the behavioral explanation is Albert Bandura. Bandura developed a theoretical perspective referred to as *social learning theory,* in which he argued that operant conditioning was insufficient as the sole explanation for learning (Bandura, 1969). His primary contribution was to demonstrate that learning can take place even though an individual has never before made a particular response or been reinforced for that response. Learning can occur through observing others' behavior and the consequences others receive for their behavior. This process often is referred to as **vicarious learning.** Bandura identified three distinct effects of exposure to modeling: (1) observational learning (the individual exhibits new behaviors as a function of observation), (2) inhibitory effects (the individual decreases a behavior as a function of observing a model receive negative consequences for that behavior), and (3) response facilitation effects (the frequency of using a previously acquired behavior is increased by observing a model being reinforced for that behavior).

Overview of Behavioral Interventions

Behavioral theory had led to many different treatment applications, and the research literature contains hundreds of studies documenting the effectiveness of behavioral training procedures. Although the fundamental principles remain constant across applications, two broad areas may be differentiated: the psychotherapy literature and the educational literature.

Psychotherapeutic Interventions.   Kazdin (1978) described six major behavior therapy techniques reported in the psychotherapeutic literature. *Systematic desensitization* is used with clients who exhibit high levels of anxiety or certain avoidance reactions and involves pairing relaxation techniques with a series of anxiety-producing situations. Usually, the client begins in a relaxed state and is exposed through actual presentation or imagination to a relatively mild situation. As the client maintains a relaxed state, progressively more stressful situations are presented. Relaxation and anxiety cannot occur simultaneously, and it is assumed that through systematic desensitization relaxation will emerge as the predominant state. *Flooding* also is a technique designed to be used with clients who exhibit extreme avoidance responses. However, it differs from systematic desensitization in that the client is repeatedly exposed to the feared stimulus (e.g., snakes, elevators, heights) in hopes that repeated exposure will reduce fear reactions.

Aversion therapy has been used to treat addictions such as smoking. In this technique, the behavior to be eliminated is paired with an aversive stimulus. For example, smoking may be paired with electric shock or a nausea-producing drug. The assumption is that the behavior to be eliminated will become associated with unpleasant experiences and thus will not be as appealing. *Covert conditioning* has been used both to reduce inappropriate behaviors and to increase desired behaviors. In this procedure, the client first imagines several scenes described by the therapist. These scenes focus on the targeted behavior. The client then imagines consequences to those behaviors, either covert sensitization (aversive consequences to an undesired behavior) or covert reinforcement (positive consequences for a desired behavior). Covert conditioning is potentially useful in dealing with negative behaviors (e.g., deviant sexual behaviors) in a safe fashion that does not require the client to actually perform those behaviors before aversive consequences are applied. In *modeling therapy,* the client views a model demonstrating a desired behavior. This technique has been used successfully in treating fears as well as increasing social behavior. *Biofeedback* is the process of conditioning internal physiological responses (e.g., heart rate, blood pressure) through frequent feedback and, if necessary, incentives for change.

Although each of these psychotherapeutic intervention strategies has been demonstrated to be effective, they address a limited range of problems. In general, the behaviorally oriented psychotherapist attempts to help the client define, in behavioral terms, the goal(s) for treatment. The antecedents and consequences assumed to control problem behaviors are identified and strategies for controlling them are established. Readers who are interested in more detailed information regarding the use of behavioral techniques in the therapeutic context are referred to journals such as *Behavior Therapy* and the *Journal of Behavior Therapy and Experimental Psychiatry* or sources such as Lahey and Kazdin (1981), Meyers and Craighead (1984), or Morris and Kratochwill (1983).

Educational Interventions. In educational settings, interventions have focused on manipulating both antecedents and consequences for behavior. Manipulation of antecedents for learning includes *modeling,* in which appropriate behaviors are demonstrated; *prompting,* in which teacher assistance is provided in performing a task; *stimulus modification,* in which materials are modified to facilitate correct performance; and *environmental design* or structuring the environment to maximize the likelihood of the desired response. Manipulation of consequences includes *positive reinforcement* (consequences for appropriate behavior that increase rates of behavior), *extinction* and *timeout* (removing or eliminating positive consequences for inappropriate behaviors), and *punishment* (presenting consequences for inappropriate behaviors that decrease rates of behavior). These and other techniques, such as shaping, fading, chaining, token economies, and contingency contracting, are described in detail throughout this text. In general, however, the behaviorally oriented teacher, like the psychotherapist, attempts to define, in behavioral terms, the goals for education. The antecedents and consequences assumed to control those behaviors are identified and strategies for controlling them are implemented.

Summary of Key Concepts

■ Learning is a change in behavior as a function of experience. For teachers to know whether learning has occurred, it must be defined as a change in the student's observable behavior.

■ Many theorists have attempted to explain the learning process. A behavioral approach emphasizes observable events that contribute to learning, particularly the antecedents and consequences for behavior. Although other factors mediate learning, these are most easily influenced by teachers.

REFERENCES

Bandura, A. (1969). *Principles of behavior modification.* New York: Holt, Rinehart, and Winston.

Bijou, S. W. (1981). The prevention of retarded development in disadvantaged children. In M. J. Begab, H. C. Haywood, & H. L. Garber (Eds.), *Psychosocial influences in retarded performance, Volume I: Issues and theories in development.* Baltimore: University Park Press.

Bijou, S. W., & Baer, D. M. (1961). *Child development: A systematic and empirical theory* (Vol. 1). Englewood Cliffs, NJ: Prentice-Hall.

Bijou, S. W., & Baer, D. M. (1965). *Child development: Universal stage of infancy* (Vol. 2). Englewood Cliffs, NJ: Prentice-Hall.

Bijou, S. W., & Baer, D. M. (1978). *Behavior analysis of child development.* Englewood Cliffs, NJ: Prentice-Hall.

Dunst, C. J. (1981). *Infant learning: A cognitive-linguistic intervention strategy.* Hingham, MA: Teaching Resources.

Ellis, N. R. (1970). Memory processes in retardates and normals. In N. R. Ellis (Ed.), *International review of research in mental retardation* (Vol. 4). New York: Academic Press.

Ferster, C. B., & Skinner, B. F. (1957). *Schedules of reinforcement.* New York: Appleton-Century-Crofts.

Freud, S. (1949). *An outline of psychoanalysis.* New York: Norton.

Gagné, R. M. (1985). *The conditions of learning and theory of instruction.* New York: Holt, Rinehart, and Winston.

Ginsberg, H., & Opper, S. (1979). *Piaget's theory of intellectual development* (2nd ed.). Englewood Cliffs, NJ: Prentice-Hall.

Golden, C. J., Hammeke, T. A., & Parisch, A. (1980). *The Luria-Nebraska Neuropsychological Battery: Manual.* Los Angeles: Western Psychological Services.

Grunbaum, A. (1952). Causality and the science of human behavior. *The American Scientist, 40,* 665–676.

Hammill, D. D., & Larsen, S. C. (1978). The effectiveness of psycholinguistic training: A reaffirmation of position. *Exceptional Children, 41,* 5–14.

Hebb, D. O. (1949). *The organization of behavior.* New York: Wiley.

Hilgard, E. R., & Bower, G. H. (1975). *Theories of learning* (4th ed.). Englewood Cliffs, NJ: Prentice-Hall.

Jones, M. C. (1924). The elimination of children's fears. *Journal of Experimental Psychology, 7,* 382–390.

Kahn, J. V. (1979). Applications of the Piagetian literature to severely and profoundly mentally retarded persons. *Mental Retardation, 17,* 273–280.

Kazdin, A. E. (1978). *History of behavior modification.* Baltimore: University Park Press.

Kirk, S., McCarthy, J., & Kirk, W. (1968). *Illinois Test of Psycholinguistic Abilities.* Urbana: University of Illinois Press.

Klesges, R. C. (1983). The relationship between neuropsychological, cognitive, and behavioral assessments of brain functioning in children. *Clinical Neuropsychology, 5,* 28–32.

Lahey, B. B., & Kazdin, A. E. (Eds.). (1981). *Advances in*

clinical child psychology (Vol. 4). New York: Plenum.

Levine, D. N., Hier, D. B., & Calvanio, R. (1981). Acquired learning disability for reading after left temporal lobe damage in childhood. *Neurology, 31,* 257–264.

Levine, M. D., & Melmed, R. D. (1982). The unhappy wanderers: Children with attention deficits. *Pediatric Clinics of North America, 29,* 105–120.

Mercer, C. D., & Snell, M. E. (1977). *Learning theory research in mental retardation: Implications for teaching.* Columbus, OH: Charles E. Merrill.

Meyers, A. W., & Craighead, W. E. (Eds.). (1984). *Cognitive behavior therapy with children.* New York: Plenum.

Morris, R. J., & Kratochwill, T. R. (Eds.). (1983). *The practice of child therapy.* New York: Pergamon.

Osgood, C. E. (1957). Motivational dynamics of language behavior. In M. R. Jones (Ed.), *Nebraska symposium of motivation.* Lincoln: University of Nebraska Press.

Piaget, J. (1952). *The origins of intelligence in children.* New York: W. W. Norton.

Reitan, R. M., & Davidson, L. A. (Eds.). (1974). *Clinical neuropsychology: Current status and applications.* New York: Wiley.

Rinne, C. H. (1984). *Attention: The fundamentals of classroom control.* Columbus, OH: Charles E. Merrill.

Skinner, B. F. (1948). *Walden two.* New York: Macmillan.

Skinner, B. F. (1957). *Verbal behavior.* New York: Appleton-Century-Crofts.

Skinner, B. F. (1968). *The technology of teaching.* New York: Appleton-Century-Crofts.

Skinner, B. F. (1971). *Beyond freedom and dignity.* New York: Knopf.

Spitz, H. H. (1966). The role of input organization in the learning and memory of mental retardates. In N. R. Ellis (Ed.), *International Review of Research in Mental Retardation* (Vol. 2). New York: Academic Press.

Watson, J. B., & Rayner, R. (1920). Conditioned emotional reactions. *Journal of Experimental Psychology, 3,* 1–14.

Weintraub, S., & Mesulam, M. M. (1983). Developmental learning disabilities of the right hemisphere: Emotional, interpersonal, and cognitive components. *Archives of Neurology, 40,* 463–468.

Zeaman, D., & House, B. J. (1963). The role of attention in retardate discrimination learning. In N. R. Ellis (Ed.), *Handbook of mental deficiency.* New York: McGraw-Hill.

2

EFFECTIVE TEACHING

Key Terms

- Teaching ■ Behavioral Principles ■ Behavioral Procedures
- Applied Behavior Analysis ■ Functional Relationship

Skinner (1968) defined **teaching** as "the expediting of learning" (p. 5). Of course, learning can occur in the absence of teaching; in fact, much of what we learn occurs as a result of experiences that were not intentionally designed to teach. We have schools and teachers, however, because society has determined that children need to learn certain skills which either would not be learned as a function of experiences, or which might be acquired slowly. As Skinner (1968) suggested, "the school of experience is no school at all, not because no one learns in it but because no one teaches" (p. 5). Teaching, therefore, is an active and conscious attempt to facilitate learning and thus to change behavior.

Although learning can occur in the absence of teaching, the reverse is not true. Teaching has occurred only when an effect can be demonstrated. Thus, it makes sense to say "I taught Johnny" only if Johnny has learned something.

WHAT IS EFFECTIVE TEACHING?

Traditional Views

How does one best expedite learning? Many have tried to list all of the skills necessary to become a good teacher, although some have even expressed reservations as to whether or not anyone *really* teaches another person anything of substance. This notion is represented in Kahil Gibran's *The Prophet:*

The astronomer may speak to you of his understanding of space, but he cannot give you his understanding.

The musician may sing to you of the rhythm which is in all space, but he cannot give you the ear which arrests the rhythm nor the voice that echoes it.

And he who is versed in the science of numbers can tell of the regions of weight and measure, but he cannot conduct you thither

For the vision of one man lends not its wings to another man.

However, being in the business of education, teachers must operate on the basic assumption that they can transmit knowledge and change behavior, and are obliged to determine how that task might best be accomplished.

Balassi's (1968) book *Focus on Teaching* typifies what many educators traditionally have said about good teaching. According to Balassi, an effective teacher has at least 11 basic characteristics: (1) commitment to and belief in the importance of educating children; (2) intelligence, including sound judgment, good common sense, and foresight; (3) knowledge of what to teach, how to teach, how to manage the physical environment, why we teach, knowledge of students, and knowledge of self; (4) sound character, including fairness, freedom from prejudice, integrity, and honesty; (5) good physical and mental health, with emotions under control, a generally cheerful outlook, and a healthy and wholesome view of others; (6) enthusiasm; (7) sense of humor; (8) flexibility; (9) skill in human relations; (10) pleasing appearance, and (11) effective voice and good speech habits. Unfortunately, schools of education can have an impact on only a few of these characteristics.

Current Concepts

Recently, the educational literature, Presidential commissions, and the popular media have focused on the issue of *effective teaching*. A number of papers and textbooks have reviewed the teacher effectiveness literature (e.g., White, Wyne, Stuck, & Coop, 1983) or described effective teaching strategies (Gagné, 1985; Paine, Radicchi, Rosellini, Deutchman, & Darch, 1983). In the spring of 1986, the United States Department of Education published a highly publicized document entitled *What Works: Research About Teaching and Learning* (Bennett, 1986). Forty-one effective teaching practices were specified and examples of their application were described. An entire issue of *Exceptional Children* (April 1986) was devoted to a review of effective instructional practices in special education classrooms.

Two recent reviews of effective teaching demonstrate currently accepted "best teaching practices." White et al. (1983) reviewed the literature on teaching and concluded that, while individual and isolated studies have investigated the effectiveness of a wide range of teaching practices, good research (several studies using appropriate experimental methodology) suggests that a good teacher has skills in five fundamental areas: management of instructional time, management of student behavior, instructional presentation, instructional monitoring, and

TABLE 2.1   Teaching Functions and Effective Practices Associated with Each

1. *Management of Instructional Time*
    a. Teacher is prepared to initiate instruction when class is scheduled to begin.
    b. Teacher makes full use of the time allocated for instruction.
    c. Teacher maintains a high level of student time on task.

2. *Management of Student Behavior*
    a. Teacher instructs students in a clear set of rules and procedures for classroom behavior.
    b. Teacher observes student behavior continuously and stops inappropriate behavior promptly and consistently.

3. *Instructional Presentation*
    a. Teacher presents instructionally relevant lessons that match the students' current level of understanding of the topic.
    b. Teacher reviews lesson content for the students.
    c. Teacher presents lesson content and instructional tasks clearly.
    d. Teacher makes instructional transitions quickly, smoothly, and effectively.
    e. Teacher presents instruction at an appropriately brisk rate.

4. *Instructional Monitoring*
    a. Teacher establishes reasonable work requirements and enforces them.
    b. Teacher regularly uses formal and informal assessment to determine the student's current level of understanding and progress.

5. *Instructional Feedback*
    a. Teacher provides consistent flow of performance feedback to students.
    b. Teacher gives appropriate feedback based on type of student response.

Note: From *Teaching Effectiveness Evaluation Project* (Final Report) (pp. 115–119) by K. P. White, M. D. Wyne, G. B. Stuck, and R. H. Coop, 1983, Chapel Hill, NC: School of Education, University of North Carolina at Chapel Hill.

instructional feedback. The specific skills of importance within each competency area are described in Table 2.1.

Bickel and Bickel (1986) reviewed the effective teaching literature and summarized it as follows:

> What emerges across various commentaries is the image of effective teachers taking an active, direct role in the instruction of their students. These educators give many detailed and redundant instructions and explanations when introducing a new concept (Rosenshine, 1983). They give ample opportunity for guided practice with frequent reviews of student progress (Berliner, 1984). They check for understanding, using such techniques as questioning, consistent review of homework, and review of previous day's lessons before moving on to new areas. Such teachers move among students when they are involved in practice seatwork. Feedback is provided frequently and with meaningful detail. Effective teachers use feedback strategies for positive reinforcement of student success. Feedback also provides the basis for reteaching where necessary. Effective teachers take an active role in creating a positive, expectant, and orderly classroom environment in which learning takes place. To accomplish these climate objectives, effective teachers

actively structure the learning process and the management of time, building in such things as signals for academic work and maintaining student attention by group alerting and accountability techniques and through variation in educational tasks (Berliner, 1984). (pp. 492–493)

The authors argued that these principles apply to effective special education programs as well.

Clearly, teaching is a complex activity requiring an array of personal and technical skills. This book is based on the assumption that teaching exceptional students requires fundamental knowledge in five areas. First, teachers need to have a *basic understanding of child development.* We believe this knowledge is important because it provides teachers a framework within which to understand a student's cognitive, social, and motor abilities and limitations, and to plan learning activities that are appropriately stimulating, yet not unreasonable. Second, teachers need to *know content areas* of importance for the students they are teaching. For the preschool teacher important content areas include cognitive, communication, social, self-help, and motor skills. For the elementary school teacher these content areas include reading, mathematics, spelling, social studies, and writing. The junior high- and high-school teacher must know social studies, history, English, mathematics, science, and perhaps a foreign language. Teachers of moderately and severely handicapped students need to know domestic and community living skills, vocational skills, and leisure skills. Knowledge of scope and sequence in relevant content areas is critical if teachers are to diagnose learning needs and provide a coordinated sequence of skill acquisition. Third, teachers need to *know about various handicapping conditions* and the implications of those conditions for teaching. Fourth, teachers need to *know basic principles of learning and procedures for applying those principles* with the students for whom they are responsible. Wise use of documented learning principles should maximize the probability of skill acquisition and use by students. Finally, teachers need to *be able to monitor and evaluate student learning.* This skill is important because only through careful individual monitoring can the teacher determine whether children are acquiring skills at a reasonable rate or whether a change in instructional strategies is necessary.

The five knowledge areas and specific teaching skills associated with each are displayed in Table 2.2. Knowledge of child development and curriculum content should help teachers assess student needs and plan individualized instructional objectives. Knowledge of handicapping conditions should help teachers know when to adapt or modify positions, instructional sequences, or instructional materials. Knowledge of behavioral principles and procedures provide the teacher with skills necessary to help students acquire and use new skills and behave appropriately. Knowledge of instructional monitoring and evaluation procedures should help teachers determine effective instructional strategies for individual students. In general, information regarding child development, handicapping conditions, and the scope and sequence of curriculum content areas addresses the *what* of teaching and is not the focus of this text. One

TABLE 2.2 Knowledge Areas and Skills of Importance for Teachers

Knowledge Areas	Specific Teaching Skills
Child Development	■ Assess student needs
Curriculum Content	■ Specify individualized objectives
Handicapping Conditions	■ Use positioning techniques ■ Design and use alternative communication systems ■ Modify instructional sequences ■ Modify instructional materials
Principles of Learning and Behavioral Procedures	■ Provide appropriate learning environments ■ Help students learn new skills ■ Help students perform skills independently ■ Help students behave appropriately
Instructional Monitoring and Evaluation Procedures	■ Measure behavior ■ Summarize data ■ Evaluate performance and modify instruction accordingly

exception to this statement is the text's emphasis on writing behavioral objectives. This book focuses primarily on the *process* of teaching and describes principles and procedures that are applicable across children's ages, developmental abilities, handicapping conditions, and content areas.

APPLIED BEHAVIOR ANALYSIS

As described in Chapter 1, a learning theory is an attempt to explain the mechanisms by which learning occurs. Behavioral theory is one of many possible learning theories. Behavioral theory consists of **behavioral principles** (rules governing behavior) and **behavioral procedures** (specific teaching and behavior management techniques based on behavioral principles) (Sulzer-Azaroff & Mayer, 1977). A large portion of this text is devoted to a description of behavioral procedures that are based on behavioral principles. Use of behavioral procedures alone, however, is not sufficient for effective teaching. The appropriateness of those procedures for individual students must be evaluated. **Applied behavior analysis** is the process of applying and evaluating the effects of behavioral procedures. In this section, we first provide a general overview of applied behavior analysis and then describe a model for teaching based on applied behavior analysis.

Principles of Applied Behavior Analysis

Applied behavior analysis is based on the fundamental premise that a given teaching technique may or may not work for an individual student. Students are different, each with his or her own unique learning style and learning history. Furthermore, each student may demonstrate a unique response to specific procedures. For example, it would be inappropriate to assume that all children in a class need the same amount of teacher assistance or instructional time; likewise, different children need different feedback systems for performance. The key to good teaching, therefore, is *individualization,* in which each child's individual learning needs are identified and teaching strategies are modified in accordance with those needs and student progress.

The learning needs and styles of some students are apparent. Teachers can readily identify appropriate instructional strategies and can see rapid progress from day to day. Other students may be more difficult to teach, particularly if they have learning or behavior problems. In those cases, teachers may need to be more systematic in applying teaching procedures and evaluating the effectiveness of those procedures. The need for individualization is the basis for using applied behavior analysis.

The most detailed description of applied behavior analysis was provided in an influential and thought-provoking paper written by Baer, Wolf, and Risley (1968). In that paper, applied behavior analysis was defined as follows:

> Analytic behavioral application is the process of applying sometimes tentative principles of behavior to the improvement of specific behaviors, and simultaneously evaluating whether or not any changes noted are indeed attributable to the process of application—and if so, to what parts of that process. In short, analytic behavioral application is a self-examining, discovery-oriented research procedure for studying behavior. (p. 91)

It is also a methodology for evaluating the effects of teaching.

Baer, Wolf, and Risley then went on to describe seven fundamental components of applied behavior analysis. First, it is *applied,* which means it deals with important, real-world problems. Applied behavior analysis as a field has addressed problems ranging from academic learning and behavior in school to phobias, littering, drinking, overuse of telephone directory assistance, obesity, marital problems, and driving too fast. Second, it is *behavioral,* which means it focuses on the things that people actually do. Third, it is *analytic,* which means it incorporates measurement procedures and decision-making rules for deciding whether a given procedure is effective with a given student. Fourth, it is *technological,* which means it clearly specifies the teaching strategies being used.

Fifth, it is *conceptually systematic,* which means it incorporates procedures derived from learning theory. Sixth, it seeks to find *effective* procedures, or those which produce changes large enough to have practical value for the student. Finally, it seeks to find *generalizable* effects, such that students can use the skills taught them in a variety of contexts.

Another way of describing the applied behavior analysis process is as an attempt to determine a **functional relationship** between behavior and the teaching environment. Teachers, parents, and administrators constantly ask themselves why students can or cannot do certain behaviors. Why can't Laura add? Why does Lorenzo get out of his seat so often? Many times we explain such behaviors or deficits using statements that are not instructionally useful. For example, Laura cannot add because she is learning disabled and Lorenzo gets out of his seat because he is hyperactive. Vargas (1977) described such explanations as "explanatory fictions" because they do not really explain the problem, "all they do is state the problem over again" (p. 18). Other examples of explanatory fictions include carelessness, apathy, and impulsivity. When teachers attempt to determine functional relationships, however, the focus turns to an identification of teaching procedures and environmental provisions that change behavior. A functional relationship exists when behavior change is demonstrated to occur as a function of a teaching procedure, environmental provision, or some other stimulus. In other words, the real question becomes, "What works for this student?" rather than, "Why is this student behaving in this way?"

Teaching Model for Applied Behavior Analysis

Applied behavior analysis easily lends itself to the specification of a model for teaching. Steps in this model and examples of its application are provided in Table 2.3. The first step is the identification of the overall goal. Usually, this is a problem statement regarding either the acquisition of specific skills (e.g., reading, math, self-help, time-on-task, social interactions, etc.) or the reduction of certain inappropriate behaviors (e.g., talk-outs, aggressive acts, out-of-seats, etc.). Once the initial problem statement has been made, the second step is to gather more information regarding the broad problem. For example, a skill acquisition problem would require a broad assessment of the child's skills and deficits in several developmental or academic areas in order to more precisely pinpoint the problem. A behavior reduction problem requires an analysis of the extent to which the behavior in question really is a problem. Baseline data are gathered to indicate present levels of functioning on the skill or behavior in question and provide information for later determination of teaching effect.

The third step is to specify a learning objective. As opposed to the general goal statement, an objective specifies precisely the skills the student is expected to perform, the conditions (e.g., materials, type of problem, level of reading, environmental context) under which those skills are to be demonstrated, and the level of mastery (a specific criterion that includes quantification). Fourth, an

TABLE 2.3   Applied Behavior Analysis Teaching Model

Step	Procedures	Example 1	Example 2
1	Identify overall goals by using broad problem statements.	Laura is behind in her math skills.	Lorenzo has trouble staying in his chair.
2	Gather specific information about the problem.	Laura can add single-digit problems with sums to 10, but cannot carry.	Lorenzo gets out of his seat an average of 15 times per hour.
3	Specify learning objectives.	Laura will add numerals with sums to 30, at a rate of at least 5 correct solutions per minute.	Lorenzo will stay in his seat for at least 10 minutes before getting up.
4	Plan and implement an intervention program.	Drill and practice first on sums to 20, no carrying required; then teacher instruction and modeling for carrying procedure. Bonus free choice during recess for 90% correct or better on daily work sheets.	Lorenzo loses 5 minutes of recess each time he gets out of his seat without permission.
5	Monitor student performance.	Teacher keeps daily record of accuracy on worksheets. Every Friday teacher conducts a 1-minute timing to determine rate of performance.	Teacher counts Lorenzo's out-of-seat behavior during routinely selected periods, for a total of 20 minutes of observation per day.
6	Evaluate student performance.	Teacher charts accuracy and speed data weekly and uses information to decide whether or not a change is necessary.	Teacher keeps a daily chart of out-of-seat behavior. If Lorenzo goes 3 days without any improvement, she makes a change in consequences.

intervention program is planned and implemented that meets the individual needs of the student. This plan will vary across students on a number of dimensions. For example, the student who does not know the skill at all will need to have the task broken down into small steps and the teacher will need to provide instructional assistance. The student who knows the skill but exhibits variable rates of performance may need more structure and a clear system of consequences for performance or lack thereof. Also, the intervention will differ depending upon whether the objective is to reduce a behavior, acquire a skill, become more fluent at a skill, maintain a skill over time, or generalize a skill to new situations.

Fifth, and concurrent with program implementation, is the ongoing monitoring and evaluation of child progress. This requires frequent assessment of performance over time. Finally, regular evaluation of data is conducted to determine the rate of progress and to decide whether or not instructional changes are in order. As a result of this evaluation, the teacher may decide to continue the program as is, to move back to an easier skill, to move on to a more difficult skill, or to modify the instructional procedures to facilitate attainment of the original objective.

Which Is More Important: Behavioral Procedures or Instructional Monitoring?

Two basic skills are important for teachers. The first of these is knowledge and use of principles of behavior derived from learning theory and experimental research. The second is knowledge and use of strategies for assessing student needs, specifying objectives, task-analyzing behaviors, collecting data, and monitoring progress. White (1977) suggested that all too often teacher training focuses on one or the other of these skills. For example, a course or text might be devoted to describing such fundamental principles as reinforcement, punishment, and shaping, and providing examples and guidelines for successful applications of each. This approach, referred to here as the *principles of behavior approach,* is based on the assumption that many specific procedures have been developed and field-tested over the years, and that this body of information provides a sufficient base of procedures from which teachers can choose to apply to individual students. At the other extreme, a course or text might be devoted almost exclusively to the process of analyzing and evaluating student progress. This approach, referred to here as the *measurement approach,* is based on the assumption that each student is different, and that the effective teacher is one who can accurately pinpoint individual learning needs, apply individualized teaching strategies, and evaluate the effectiveness of those strategies through careful observation and monitoring of progress.

Each approach, when used alone, has certain advantages and disadvantages. Each has been demonstrated to be effective in different ways. For example, White suggested that the principles of behavior approach generally has the greatest immediate impact on teachers. It consists of providing many specific techniques, most of which are based on large sets of data. Teachers can immediately apply those techniques and, for many children, they will be extremely effective. However, this approach has several disadvantages, the most important of which is that it ignores the unique learning needs of each individual child. If all the teacher has is a "bag of tricks," what happens when the available tricks do not work? Although this approach provides important information for teachers, used alone it can reduce independence and flexibility by encouraging reliance on specific procedures.

The applied behavior analysis approach, on the other hand, forces teachers to tailor programs to the needs of individual children and encourages high levels of independence and flexibility in teaching. Although the immediate impact on teaching is not as great, and it is time-consuming to learn to do all of the components well, a recent summary of research emphasizes the importance of these procedures. Fuchs and Fuchs (1986) reviewed 21 studies investigating the effects of formative evaluation procedures on student achievement. Each study was examined to determine whether teachers were required to record data, graph student performance data, or use systematic data-evaluation rules, and how often student performance was measured. The authors found that student achievement was significantly greater across studies when teachers graphed rather than simply recorded data, and employed data-utilization rules. Of particular importance to this discussion is the additional finding that "effect sizes connected with the use of behavior modification in addition to systematic formative evaluation were reliably higher than those representative of systematic formative evaluation only" (p. 205).

Clearly, as White suggested, the answer lies in a combination of the two approaches. In the best of both worlds, the teacher will be aware of a wide range of proven principles of learning and applications of their use, and will also be able to individualize those principles and to monitor child progress to determine whether the specific application chosen is working for a given child.

CRITICISMS OF BEHAVIORAL THEORY AND APPLIED BEHAVIOR ANALYSIS

Over the years, a number of criticisms of behavioral principles and applied behavior analysis have evolved. Prospective teachers should be aware of these criticisms for at least three reasons. First, no theory should be accepted in an unquestioning fashion. We should listen to arguments against any important theory, particularly one that has major implications for how we interact with students, and seek to determine the validity of those arguments. Second, many criticisms have grown out of highly publicized instances of inappropriate applications of behavioral theory. Teachers should be able to differentiate appropriate and inappropriate applications of behavioral theory. Third, behavioral techniques are occasionally questioned by parents, administrators, and colleagues, as well as by the general public. Teachers who incorporate systematic use of behavioral procedures and applied behavior analysis should be aware of the questions likely to be asked regarding those techniques and should be prepared to address them.

The Techniques Are Too Time-Consuming

A frequent argument against applied behavior analysis is that the process of collecting and analyzing data is too time-consuming. In today's real world of teaching, this is a valid concern. It would be impossible for the kindergarten teacher with 27 students or the learning disabilities resource teacher with 40 students to measure all skills each student is being taught. However, this does not mean teachers should not learn these techniques or use them when necessary. Frequent data collection is a key component in almost any profession where rapid decision-making is important. Data collection provides a solid basis for making instructional decisions, and is often necessary when dealing with problems in learning and behavior.

Three points are important. First, teachers should become fluent in the use of data collection and analysis techniques. This means that teacher preparation programs should not only require that teachers *know* these techniques, but should also provide sufficient opportunities for *practice* so that teachers feel comfortable with data and are able to collect and analyze it rapidly and efficiently. Also, microcomputer technology is making advances in saving the teacher time in terms of data collection and graphing. Second, many students can collect and chart their own data. In fact, self-monitoring and self-recording have been demonstrated repeatedly to be effective techniques for teaching, maintaining, and generalizing behaviors (e.g., Anderson-Inman, Paine, & Deutchman, 1984; Rhode, Morgan, & Young, 1983). Finally, not all behaviors need to be assessed frequently. However, systematic adherence to the applied behavior analysis process is important in dealing with difficult problems. Robert Pirsig (1974), in *Zen and the Art of Motorcycle Maintenance,* described the mechanic's usual intuitive approach to motorcycle repair. Often this approach is successful in dealing with routine problems. However, sometimes the intuitive approach does not work:

> When you've hit a really tough one, tried everything, racked your brain and nothing works, and you know that this time Nature has really decided to be difficult, you say, "Okay, Nature, that's the end of the *nice* guy," and you crank up the formal scientific method.
>
> For this you keep a lab notebook. Everything gets written down, formally, so that you know at all times where you are, where you've been, where you're going, and where you want to get. In scientific work and electronics technology this is necessary because otherwise the problems get so complex you get lost in them and confused and forget what you know and what you don't know and have to give up. . . . Sometimes just the act of writing down the problem straightens out your head as to what they really are. . . .
>
> The untrained observer will see only physical labor and often get the idea that physical labor is mainly what the mechanic does. Actually the physical labor is the smallest and easiest part of what the mechanic does. By far the greatest part of his work is careful observation and precise thinking. (pp. 102–103)

The process of teaching is somewhat analogous. The systematic approach to problem-solving often is necessary when dealing with difficult problems involving learning and behavior.

Association with Bribery and Food or Material Reinforcers

A second common concern addresses the emphasis of behavioral theory on positive reinforcement, or the provision of positive consequences following a desired behavior. Critics claim that use of positive reinforcers constitutes bribery of children. Clearly this is not the case since *bribery* is defined as an illegal payment. However, the underlying concern in this instance is that teachers may provide food or material reinforcers to support behaviors that students should be doing anyway. Essentially, some view this as a *payment* to students for work, and this violates their fundamental belief that students should either be self-motivated or should do what adults ask of them just because they are children and we are adults.

This concern is valid under certain conditions: when reinforcers are contrived or artificial and no attempt is made to help the student become more independent. However, many students either do not have self-control or are noncompliant. The behaviorist would argue several points. First, positive consequences for appropriate behavior are preferable to aversive consequences, even when those positive consequences initially consist of tangible material reinforcers. Second, very few adults would continue to work without pay. All of us need some positive reinforcers for performance; the teacher's task is to identify the most natural yet effective reinforcer for a student. Third, it would be unethical to use material reinforcers with a student and not implement a planned strategy for fading those reinforcers and building other, more natural feedback systems. Finally, it is more ethical to give students material reinforcers for appropriate behavior than it is to withhold them and allow students to practice inappropriate and self-defeating behavior patterns.

Association with Punishment

Although most people associate behavioral techniques with M & Ms and other positive reinforcers, some associate it with punishment techniques such as timeout or even electric shock. Hopefully this association is incorrect. Skinner's fundamental point throughout his writings was to emphasize the importance of positive behavior change procedures.

Most professionals of the behavioral orientation, however, do take a pragmatic perspective on the role of persons in the helping professions. This perspective states that the bottom line is whether or not the client or student has been helped to achieve skills, independence, and social acceptability. If (a) positive behavior change techniques have been tried and demonstrated to be ineffective, and (b) the behavior in question is of sufficient importance, then punishment or other aversive techniques may be necessary, since the clinician or teacher is ethically bound to do everything in his or her power to help the client or student.

The minimal conditions under which we find the use of punishment acceptable are described in Chapter 18, and a decision-making model for using behavior reduction procedures is described in Chapter 19.

Association with Consequences Rather than Antecedents

Most people associate consequences with behavioral techniques, whether they be positive or negative consequences. This association is probably accurate, since the majority of studies have, in fact, investigated the effects of positive and negative consequences on behavior. However, the behavioral field increasingly is recognizing the importance of manipulating antecedents, including the physical environment, in order to produce effective behavior change. Such an approach is preferable since it usually requires less teacher time, is more natural, and may result in more enduring behavior changes.

Association with Animal Research

Some critics argue that behavioral theory is based on research conducted with animals and thus is not appropriate for explaining the behavior of humans, since people are more intelligent than animals. Clearly, this could be an important argument were it not for the extensive research demonstrating applicability of the theory and procedures with children and adults. The animal research provided important insights into potential "laws" of behavior, thus encouraging other investigators to extend research to people. This process typically is followed in medical research.

Behaviorism as a Philosophy of Life

One problem for many people is that some have espoused behaviorism as a philosophy of life. Skinner's (1971) book *Beyond Freedom and Dignity* is the most comprehensive statement of this philosophical perspective. It is Skinner's belief that the laws of behavior control our every action. In his book, he stated that freedom is an illusion. There is no such thing as free will; rather, we are controlled by our environment and the contingencies that exist within it.

This view of humanity does not appeal to many people, and they reject all aspects of the behavioral explanation. It is our view, however, that one does not have to buy behaviorism as a philosophy of life in order to make use of effective behavioral change procedures with students. It *is* clear that our behavior is affected by environmental antecedents and contingencies whether we are aware of the relationships or not—otherwise, why would we be in the teaching profession if we did not believe that we could change behavior in some systematic and lawful fashion? The denial of free will, however, is not a necessary prerequisite to the effective use of behavioral techniques.

Behavioral Procedures Are Dehumanizing and Authoritarian

Some have said that use of behavioral procedures represents use of excessive force with children, is too authoritarian, and can be dehumanizing for students. This statement probably is made for at least two reasons. First, behavioral techniques are often very effective and, second, some individuals have, indeed, applied the procedures in a dehumanizing and authoritarian fashion.

Any technique, however, can be used in a demeaning and authoritarian fashion. From our perspective, this represents an unethical approach, regardless of the technique incorporated. Actually, good teachers naturally incorporate principles of behavior into their interactions with students. They do it in such a fashion that it seems a normal part of the interaction rather than as a unique and artificial technique. Thus we would argue for the ethical and natural use of behavioral procedures.

Behavioral Procedures Do Not Work in Real-World Situations

A final argument against behavioral procedures is that they may work when limited to a few small behaviors or in a relatively well-defined, well-controlled context (e.g., a resource classroom), but that either they do not work or they cannot be applied in real-world situations because it is impossible to control all aspects of the real-world environment. The classic example of this is the student who works well in a special resource room but fails to exhibit similar behavior in the regular classroom.

Several points are relevant in regard to this argument. First, behavioral procedures *can* be applied to more complex behaviors and in real-world settings. Generally speaking, however, this requires use of a technology for *chaining* and interrelating complex behaviors. Second, the concern for generalization to the real world is a legitimate concern, particularly in light of substantial research documenting that many children, especially handicapped children, often do not generalize from one setting to another. Failure to generalize simply means that the "other environment" has different controls operating on the student's behavior. Thus, teachers need to incorporate a technology for ensuring that behavior change does generalize (Stokes & Baer, 1977).

Summary of Key Concepts

- Teaching is the process by which one person facilitates learning in another person.
- Effective teaching is currently a "hot" topic. Many studies and reviews have attempted to define important aspects of effective teaching. Generally, the field agrees that effective teachers know how to manage instructional time, manage student behavior, present instructional tasks, monitor child performance, and provide instructional feedback.

- Applied behavior analysis is an approach to teaching that requires specifying learning objectives, implementing behavioral procedures, and monitoring and evaluating student performance. Its basic goal is effective, individualized instruction.

- Research suggests that effective instruction incorporates both behavioral procedures and systematic monitoring of student programs.

- Several criticisms of behavioral theory and applied behavior analysis have been offered. Teachers should be aware of those criticisms and decide how they might respond to them.

REFERENCES

Anderson-Inman, L., Paine, S. C., & Deutchman, L. (1984). Neatness counts: The effects of direct instruction and self-monitoring on the transfer of neat-paper skills to nontraining settings. *Analysis and Intervention in Development Disabilities, 4*(2), 137–155.

Baer, D. M., Wolf, M. M., & Risley, T. R. (1968). Some current dimensions of applied behavior analysis. *Journal of Applied Behavior Analysis, 1,* 91–97.

Balassi, S. J. (1968). *Focus on teaching.* New York: Odyssey Press.

Bennett, W. J. (1986). *What works: Research about teaching and learning.* Washington, DC: U.S. Department of Education.

Berliner, D. C. (1984). The half-full glass: A review of research on teaching. In P. O. Hosford (Ed.), *Using what we know about teaching* (pp. 51–77). Alexandria, VA: Association for Supervision and Curriculum Development.

Bickel, W. E., & Bickel, D. D. (1986). Effective schools, classrooms, and instruction: Implications for special education. *Exceptional Children, 52,* 489–500.

Fuchs, L. S., & Fuchs, D. (1986). Effects of systematic formative evaluation: A meta-analysis. *Exceptional Children, 53,* 199–208.

Gagne, R. M. (1985). *The conditions of learning and theory of instruction.* New York: Holt, Rinehart, and Winston.

Gibran, K. (1946). *The prophet.* New York: Knopf.

Paine, S. C., Radicchi, J., Rosellini, L. C., Deutchman, L., & Darch, C. B. (1983). *Structuring your classroom for academic success.* Champaign, IL: Research Press.

Pirsig, R. M. (1974). *Zen and the art of motorcycle maintenance.* New York: Bantam.

Rhode, G., Morgan, D. P., & Young, K. K. (1983). Generalization and maintenance of treatment gains of behaviorally handicapped students from resource rooms to regular classrooms using self-evaluation procedures. *Journal of Applied Behavior Analysis, 16,* 171–188.

Rosenshine, B. V. (1983). Teaching functions in instructional programs. *Elementary School Journal, 83,* 335–352.

Skinner, B. F. (1968). *The technology of teaching.* New York: Appleton-Century-Crofts.

Skinner, B. F. (1971). *Beyond freedom and dignity.* New York: Knopf.

Stokes, T. F., & Baer, D. M. (1977). An implicit technology of generalization. *Journal of Applied Behavior Analysis, 10,* 349–367.

Sulzer-Azaroff, B., & Mayer, G. R. (1977). *Applying behavior analysis procedures with children and youth.* New York: Holt, Rinehart, and Winston.

Vargas, J. (1977). *Behavioral psychology for teachers.* New York: Harper & Row.

White, K. P., Wyne, M. D., Stuck, G. B., & Coop, R. H. (1983). *Teaching effectiveness evaluation project* (Final report). Chapel Hill, NC: School of Education, University of North Carolina at Chapel Hill.

White, O. R. (1977). Behaviorism in special education: An arena for debate. In R. D. Kneedler & S. G. Tarver (Eds.), *Changing Perspectives in Special Education.* Columbus, OH: Charles E. Merrill.

PART II

TECHNICAL COMPETENCIES IN APPLIED BEHAVIOR ANALYSIS

To teach effectively and to control inappropriate behaviors, teachers should be skilled in specifying objectives, collecting data, and using that data. These skills are critical to applying applied behavior analysis procedures in classrooms. Chapter 3 provides a rationale for setting objectives, responds to common objections to writing objectives, and describes how to define behaviors, specify the conditions under which performance is desired, and establish criterion levels. Chapter 4 discusses issues that should be considered when writing objectives. These include considering the functional outcomes of objectives, setting realistic objectives, ensuring that students benefit from the objective, writing objectives for complex skills, and considering students' input when formulating objectives. The chapter also includes a discussion of writing objectives that correspond to different phases of learning and developing objectives for high-level skills.

Chapters 5 through 8 address issues related to data collection, summary, and use. Chapter 5 provides a rationale for collecting data on behavior, and then describes procedures for doing so. Examples of the procedures that are described include event-based sampling, time-based sampling, levels-of-assistance data collection, and task-analytic data collection. The chapter concludes with a discussion related to the importance of, and procedures for, collecting interobserver agreement data. Quantitative procedures for summarizing percentage, rate, duration, and latency data are presented in Chapter 6. Dimensions of data sets such as central tendency, variability, and trend are discussed. Emphasis is placed on using methods to summarize data that will result in appropriate decision-making. Chapter 7 describes using graphs for summarizing data. The properties of graphs, examples of different types of graphs, and instruction on developing appropriate graphs are provided. Chapter 8 focuses on using graphed data to make decisions about when changes are indicated in instructional procedures and about what changes are needed. Several different types of decisions are presented.

Chapters 9 and 10 focus on using data to identify causal relationships and to make comparisons between treatments. In both chapters, various single-subject experimental designs are discussed. Each design, as well as its advantages, disadvantages, and uses, is described. Chapter 9 also includes a discussion of internal and external validity as it relates to single-subject designs. The designs described in Chapter 10 are useful in comparing the effects of two or more treatments.

3

WRITING BEHAVIORAL
OBJECTIVES

Key Terms

■ Objectives ■ Individualized Education Plan ■ Long-Range
Goals ■ Long-Term Objectives ■ Short-Term Objectives ■ Task
Analysis ■ Operational ■ Conditions ■ Criteria

Most special educators have been told that the specification of learning objectives
for students is a part of good teaching. Public Law 94–142 mandates that an
Individualized Education Plan be developed for each handicapped student, and
the plan should include specific learning objectives. Why was this practice
considered so important that it was mandated by federal law? This chapter
examines the rationale for specifying learning outcomes as the first step in the
effective teaching model presented in Chapter 2 and describes procedures for
writing learning objectives.

RATIONALE FOR ESTABLISHING OBJECTIVES

Establishing **objectives** may be defined as the process of describing the precise
educational aims for a particular student. The general goals of education for all
children have been described by many philosophers and educators, and include
preparing good and useful citizens, training effective and knowledgeable workers
and professionals, transmitting important social values, and facilitating independent functioning in the real world outside of school. These broad goals typically
are interpreted to mean that schools should teach students skills, such as reading,

writing, computation, and evaluation, as well as facts, such as knowledge of history, politics, science, a foreign language, or philosophy. For the individual student, an objective for a given period of time might be to say the alphabet, read a book, compute double-digit addition, use the toilet appropriately, or stop hitting peers. It is assumed that the accomplishment of specific objectives will facilitate attainment of the broader goals of education.

Mager (1962) suggested that a good objective consists of four parts. First, it describes *who* is expected to perform the task. Second, it describes precisely *what* the person is expected to do. Third, it describes the *conditions* under which the task is to be performed. Finally, a good objective specifies *how well* the task is to be performed. In this chapter, each component is discussed in greater detail. First, however, what is the rationale for specifying objectives?

To Meet the Legal Requirements of Public Law 94-142

Public Law 94–142 mandates that an **Individualized Education Plan** (IEP) be developed for each handicapped child. The IEP is to be developed by a team consisting of professionals and parents, and is to contain both long-term (annual) goals as well as short-term objectives related to the annual goals. Thus, one reason for specifying objectives for handicapped students is that such specification is mandated by law. However, there are good educational reasons for specifying objectives as well.

To Provide a Focus for Instruction

Although the broad goals of education probably are the same for all students, different students will attain those goals in different ways and to varying degrees. For example, the broad goal of independent functioning in the real world translates into very different expectations for the prospective stock broker, the minister, the special education teacher, or the student with severe cerebral palsy. Special education and applied behavior analysis are predicated on the assumption that individuals have different learning needs and deserve *individualized* objectives.

Specifying learning outcomes provides focus and direction for instruction. Of course, a broad goal, such as learning to read, also provides some focus for instruction by eliminating some broad content areas such as math or social studies. However, it still does not help the teacher plan activities for the next day, since reading is comprised of many different skills. An objective such as "names letters of the alphabet," "reads CVC words containing the vowel *a*," or "recognizes name" is much more specific and provides concrete guidance for planning instructional activities.

Providing a focus for instruction appears to have positive outcomes for students. Hartley and Davies (1976), in a review of the research on preinstructional strategies, concluded that most studies have demonstrated that use of behavioral objectives results in greater student achievement. For example, McNeil (1967) found that teachers who used behavioral objectives facilitated academic growth of students. Furthermore, when observed by their supervisors, these teachers were rated as more successful in their use of learning principles in the classroom.

To Provide a Basis for Monitoring Progress

Educators typically monitor progress by noting student performance on standardized measures such as achievement tests. However, for many students with handicaps, such tests may not be appropriate for documenting the extent to which learning has occurred. The content of the tests may not reflect the student's instructional objectives; the steps between items may be too big to show what progress has occurred; or the child may be penalized on test performance due to physical handicaps, sensory handicaps, or cultural differences. For these (and perhaps all) students, an important indicator of progress is the extent to which educationally or socially significant objectives have been attained.

An objective provides a standard or marker by which progress (or lack of progress) can be evaluated. Monitoring student progress is an essential aspect of applied behavior analysis and, in fact, of all educational endeavors. However, progress can only be monitored if teachers know what it is they are trying to achieve. Precise specification of both desired behaviors and necessary levels of performance for those behaviors facilitates decision-making. For example, if a teacher sets an objective that Marty will print his first name with 100% accuracy by June 1, and at the end of April he can only write the *M*, then it is unlikely that he will reach this objective. The teacher then must decide whether to change Marty's instructional program in an effort to accelerate progress or to change her expectations for Marty's achievement.

An objective also helps the teacher decide how best to take data so that progress may be monitored efficiently. For example, Janice, who works in a sheltered workshop, has an objective to "sort nuts, bolts, and washers of varying sizes at a rate of 25 correct sorts per minute." To meet this goal, Janice must not only sort accurately, but she also must sort quickly. Janice's teacher must take rate data as well as accuracy data to monitor progress toward this objective.

To Communicate Information Regarding Expectations

Although most teachers can describe general goals for individual students, precise specification of objectives facilitates more accurate communication to others. For example, if you are sick and a substitute teacher attempts to take your place, accurate implementation of your instructional plan will be facilitated by clearly stated learning objectives. Other professionals, including resource teachers, regular class teachers, classroom aides, therapists, and administrators also need to know a child's learning objectives. If Sarah is expected to work independently for 10 consecutive minutes without getting out of her chair or asking for assistance, that skill should be expected, encouraged, and reinforced by all persons who work with Sarah. Parents also have a need to know a child's learning objectives. Not only do they have a right to such knowledge, they have a right to provide suggestions for appropriate objectives for their child. Further, they too can encourage and reinforce skills learned in school, but they must know precisely what is expected of their child and how well it is expected to be done. Finally, students need to know precisely what is expected of them. When students know what is expected, they have a concrete goal to work toward and a standard against which they can evaluate their own progress.

COMMON OBJECTIONS TO WRITING OBJECTIVES

Although many good reasons may be cited for writing objectives, not everyone agrees with the importance of specifying outcomes for children. In this section, we list some of the more common objections to writing objectives and attempt to respond to each.

Objectives Have Little Bearing on Teaching

Lovitt (1977) suggested that many teachers "treat the specification of objectives as an exercise quite apart from teaching" (p. 33). They write objectives to meet legal requirements or because supervisors say they must, but then file them away and go about the business of teaching without reference to those objectives. This practice is understandable when teachers are simply told to do something but are not convinced of its usefulness. More importantly, many teachers are not encouraged by supervisors to *use* the objectives they have written in any meaningful fashion. To have relevance to teaching, objectives must be reviewed frequently and progress toward them must be evaluated continuously. Furthermore, the attainment of objectives should be given greater weight than student performance on achievement or other standardized tests in the evaluation of student progress if they are to be ultimately useful for teachers, administrators, students, and parents alike.

Writing Objectives Imposes Values on Others

Some teachers state that it is either impossible or undesirable to decide what is right for others. Setting objectives is imposing one person's set of values on another and strips the student of any freedom of choice (Lovitt, 1977). Lovitt suggested that few parents or special education teachers would agree with this perspective. At least two responses may be made to this objection. First, when objectives are generated in an interdisciplinary team meeting in which the parents and student participate, the chances are slim that objectives that are inconsistent with student needs or family values will be specified, especially if the team carefully considers the potential benefits of each objective for both student and family. Second, the teaching profession is, by its very nature, engaged in the practice of imposing values and knowledge on others. Writing objectives simply makes it clear to all persons, including other professionals, parents, and students, what those values are, and is vastly preferable to teaching in which objectives are not stated but values still are imposed, and no one knows for sure what values are actually being taught.

Specifying Objectives Is OK but Setting Performance Criteria Is Impossible

A third objection discussed by Lovitt (1977) is that many teachers are willing to specify the behaviors they want students to perform but object to specifying performance criteria such as levels of accuracy or fluency for fear of either over- or underteaching. Admittedly, it often is difficult to predict a given student's level of attainment at the end of a specified period of time. However, it *is* possible to determine minimal levels of achievement necessary to achieve certain ends. For example, if a goal is to bring a student's reading rate close to that of his or her peers, then samples of peer reading rates could be used to identify the target range. It is important to go beyond the specification of behaviors and include performance criteria because it is the performance criteria that provide the standard against which progress can be compared and a precise goal toward which the student, the teacher, and the parents can strive. Without performance criteria, we are placed either in the position of not knowing when a goal has been reached or having two people disagree as to whether sufficient progress toward a goal has been made. Further, specific performance criteria "tell" us when to move on to other objectives.

Behavioral Objectives Are so Specific that They Become Trivial

A fourth objection to writing objectives is that the only skills that can be written in objective format are specific, trivial skills. It is impossible to write objectives for higher level behaviors such as creativity, analytic skills, or the ability to evaluate choices and make decisions. While objectives may be appropriate for handicapped students, they are not applicable for nonhandicapped or gifted and talented students.

Although it may be easier to write objectives for relatively specific behaviors, in actuality all desired goals can ultimately be translated into specific behaviors that are indicators of the extent to which those goals have been achieved. Most people who excel at a given activity, be it playing the piano, playing basketball, or making money, set specific objectives for themselves and work toward the mastery of those objectives. Creative people perform behaviors that we judge to be creative. The skills required to synthesize and evaluate information can be specified. Teachers (and other involved decision-makers) simply must decide what it is they would like the student to do. Examples and procedures for writing "higher-level" behaviors are described in Chapter 4.

Writing Objectives for Every Learning Task Would Result in Massive Management Problems

A fifth objection to writing objectives is that it is time-consuming; if a teacher wrote objectives for every learning task for every student there would be little time left for teaching. Obviously, a teacher cannot and should not write an objective for every learning task. Not all tasks are equally important nor do they all take the same amount of time. Skills that are important to learn and that require considerable time and effort by teachers and students should be specified. Skills rated as less important and that take only a very short time to learn are less important to specify formally, although teachers should always take care to communicate clearly *all* expectations to students.

Vargas (1972) responded to the concern that objectives are too time-consuming by suggesting that setting objectives actually results in time saved in teaching. Since the desired outcomes are already specified, less time is wasted in deciding what to do and the job of testing skill acquisition is simplified.

Several other points are worth mentioning. First, as with any skill, writing objectives initially is a slow and time-consuming process. However, as more objectives are written and teachers become more fluent in writing them, the process becomes much easier. Second, many teachers maintain an "objective bank" that contains a list of previously used objectives by content area. Objectives can then be pulled as needed and adapted to meet the individual needs of new students, thus saving time. Finally, many teachers are moving toward use of computer-generated objectives and IEPs. Computer-generated IEPs have tremendous potential for saving time by immediately generating objectives derived directly from assessment procedures. Teachers and other IEP team members should be cautioned, however, to validate each of those objectives in the team meeting and to add other objectives as needed.

Writing Objectives Takes the Spontaneity Out of Teaching

Some teachers insist that they should not be bound by specific assignments but should feel free to take up whatever happens to be of interest at the moment.

Behavioral objectives, they say, tie a teacher down and keep him from exploring topics that arise from the situation or from student interests. . . . Many teachers feel that objectives should be set by the student because the student is more likely to be motivated if he can choose what to study. (Vargas, 1972, pp. 14–15)

Involving students in setting objectives is a good teaching strategy documented by research reviewed in Chapter 4. However, teachers are professionals trained to know not only how to teach children, but what to teach and what the most appropriate developmental and instructional sequences for learning are. Thus, the approach of completely following students' interests is inappropriate, particularly for handicapped students, since preferred activities often are not those resulting in the greatest long-term benefit for the student. As professionals, teachers have an ethical and moral responsibility to use their skills and training to exert leadership and provide direction for learning.

This does not mean, however, that teachers should be rigid in their instructional styles or inflexible in responding to student interests. As Vargas suggested, a good objective can be mastered in many ways and, once an objective is specified, student interests should play a large part in selecting the way in which that objective is taught. For example, a student who is working on buttoning should use a preferred shirt when practicing, and a student who is working on reading should be provided highly motivating reading material.

Objectives Make All Students Alike

Vargas (1972) suggested that a final objection to writing behavioral objectives is that many teachers feel that to set similar objectives for all students is inappropriate since it forces children into the same mold. Several responses to this concern are appropriate. First, few would advocate that the same objectives are appropriate for all children. The basic assumption underlying the IEP is that each student has unique learning needs and thus requires an individualized statement of appropriate objectives. Second, some skills *are* appropriate for all students and should be emphasized in every student's instructional program. Examples of these skills include the ability to interact appropriately with peers or to work independently. Given these broad goals, however, the manner in which each student achieves them must be individualized.

WRITING OBJECTIVES

Writing good objectives is a skill that must be developed and practiced. At least two components of a good objective must be evaluated. First, does the objective meet all of the requirements for *form*? Second, is the objective *appropriate*? The steps in the process of writing objectives are displayed in Figure 3.1. In this chapter, we address the first question and describe the form that is characteristic of a good objective.

FIGURE 3.1 Steps in writing behavioral objectives.

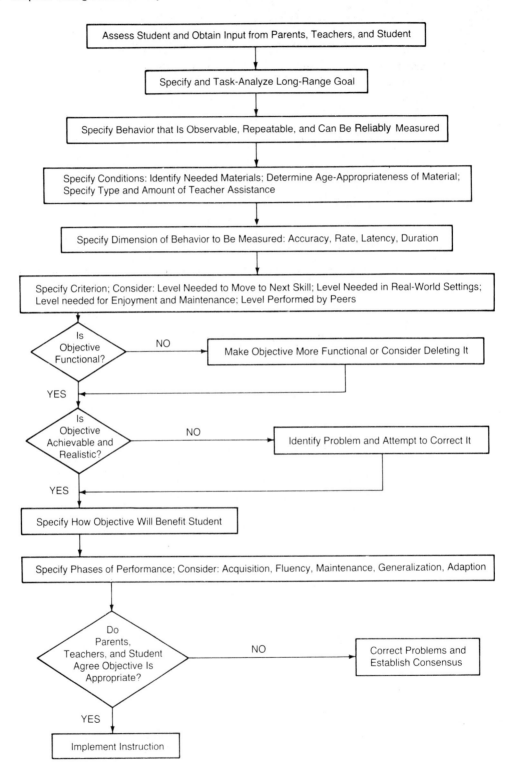

Determining Long-Range Goals and Short-Term Objectives

The first step in writing an objective is to determine **long-range educational goals.** A goal statement simply identifies the important curriculum areas for a student. An example of a long-range goal for a 12-year-old boy with learning disabilities might be to improve computational skills, whereas a goal for a 4-year-old child with spina bifida might be to improve social interaction skills with peers. A goal differs from an objective in that it represents achievement in a broad skill area and often is stated in more general terms.

Long-range goals are used as the basis for writing **long-term objectives.** These may be described as end-of-instruction statements, and usually refer to annual goals as specified in the rules and regulations for IEPs. Long-term objectives are written in objective format, examples of which are:

■ Given a verbal request by the teacher, Katie will say the letters of the alphabet without errors on each of three consecutive opportunities.

■ Using a third-grade reader and given 3 minutes, Brian will read orally at a rate of 50 words per minute on two consecutive opportunities, with no more than three errors on each occasion.

■ Given a 15-minute mealtime, Betsy will feed herself independently with a spoon without errors for three consecutive meals.

These long-range objectives are then used as a basis for writing **short-term objectives.** Usually, *short-term* is interpreted to mean quarterly objectives (every 3 months) although they may also include daily or weekly objectives. An objective is a more specific statement of learning outcome than a goal and generally represents a smaller "chunk" of behavior than does a goal. An example of a short-term objective for the above-mentioned alphabet goal is "says the letters *A-G* in correct order 100% of the opportunities requested by the teacher for three consecutive days by November 1st."

Long-range objectives, of course, are developed considering the student's present abilities (assessed through testing and/or direct observation) and comparing those abilities with present and future skill needs. Student and family input should be obtained in determining long-range objectives. Also, the feasibility of long-range objectives should be examined carefully, considering not only the student's likelihood of attaining the objective, but also the school's ability to provide the resources necessary to teach it. Resources usually include materials as well as human resources such as the teacher-student ratio, competence of adults in the environment, and the availability of expert consultation if needed.

The specification of long-range objectives is one of the most important activities in which teachers are engaged, since those objectives determine the path followed in a student's instructional program. Given the importance of this activity, a number of other factors should be considered. In Chapter 4, considerations for ensuring high-quality objectives are discussed. In Chapters 18 and 19, further considerations in planning goals and objectives for behavior reduction programs are discussed.

Once long-range objectives have been developed, short-term objectives are specified. Usually, the identification of short-term (defined here as quarterly) objectives requires the use of task analysis. **Task analysis** refers to both the *process* of breaking a task down into small teaching steps and the resulting *product,* a written sequence of student objectives. Most of us naturally conduct our own analyses of difficult tasks in order to master them. The whole task may be too complex to learn all at one time, so we master pieces of the task. Anyone who has played golf, learned to use a word-processing program, or played chess or bridge realizes the importance of mastering small steps in a long sequence of skills.

Task analysis facilitates a high success rate because the teacher presents small, manageable tasks to the student. A study by Fredericks, Anderson, and Baldwin (1979) supports the contention that effective teachers incorporate task analysis into the teaching process. Across a number of classrooms with severely handicapped students, they found that teachers of children who made high gains in their programs task-analyzed significantly more programs than did teachers of low-gain children.

Many curriculum packages include task analyses of basic skills. Teachers should refer to those skill sequences when readily available and appropriate for individual students. Teachers should also be able to construct a task analysis for objectives where skill sequences are not available. Constructing a task analysis requires at least four steps (cf., Thiagarajan, 1980; Williams & Gotts, 1977):

1. An instructional objective is identified.
2. The desired skill is broken down into its component parts. This can be accomplished by watching another person perform the skill, by performing it yourself, logically analyzing the skill, or copying sequences from normal development. Write down each separate skill.
3. Sequence the steps for teaching purposes. Sequences may reflect the temporal order for tasks, or increasing levels of response difficulty.
4. Any necessary prerequisite behaviors should be specified.

In some cases, going from long-range goals to short-term objectives involves simple identification of a "piece" of the long-range goal. For example, the goal "says the alphabet" could be divided into four sequential objectives: "says *A-F,*" "says *A-L,*" "says *A-R,*" and "says *A-Z.*" Here task analysis is simply a division process. In other cases, short-term objectives may include prerequisite skills that are not directly a part of the long-term goal, but are assumed to be necessary for successful performance of the long-term goal. For example, short-term objectives for the long-range goal of "reads time on a clock" would include skills such as "recognizes numerals 1–12," "points to long hand and short hand," and "tells common times for eating, going to bed, and watching Sesame Street."

Once a skill has been identified as a short-term objective, it must be written in proper objective format. An objective consists of three parts in addition to *who* the objective is intended for: (1) a clearly-defined behavior, (2) conditions under which the behavior is to be performed, and (3) performance criteria.

Specifying Behaviors

The first part of an objective identifies the expected behavior. This specification must be made in **operational** terms. That is, it must specify in measurable, observable terms the operations or actual behaviors that the student is to perform. To operationalize an objective means to describe what the student will actually do. It must be an observable behavior rather than an unobservable process.

For example, most would agree that statements such as "knows the alphabet," "understands carrying in addition," or "comprehends the concept of time" represent important outcomes for many students. However, they are not statements of observable behaviors, since it is not clear what is meant by knowing, understanding, or comprehending. An objective clearly specifies what is meant by each statement. For example, "knowing the alphabet" could be interpreted variously as "singing the alphabet song correctly," "pointing to letters named by the teacher," or "saying the names of letters presented by the teacher." Likewise, "comprehending the concept of time" could be interpreted variously as "telling the difference between morning and night," "reading time to the nearest hour," or "telling time to the precise minute."

A good objective is stated in operational terms by specifying the *behavior* that is expected of the student. Behaviors, of course, are acts that can be observed by two individuals who would have a high probability of agreeing whether or not those behaviors occurred. They are repeatable, have a definite beginning and end, and are measurable. Each of these characteristics must be considered in writing any objective. Examples and nonexamples of terms that describe behaviors are given in Table 3.1. Note that each nonexample could be analyzed and specific behaviors for each identified.

A behavioral statement of learning outcomes is critical for several reasons. First, the applied behavior analysis process depends on measurement and the analysis of data for decision-making. It would be impossible to take data on

TABLE 3.1 Examples and Nonexamples of Terms that Describe Behaviors

Examples of Behaviors		*Nonexamples of Behaviors*	
Says	Sorts	Understands	Comprehends
Prints	Zips	Knows	Realizes
Writes	Points	Considers	Calculates
Places	Imitates	Perceives	Discovers
Lists	Types	Believes	Is Committed
Reads Orally	Gives	Reads	Subtracts
Names	Looks	Initiates	Demonstrates
Touches	Cuts	Recognizes	Identifies

understanding or comprehending without specifying the behavioral indicators of those processes. Second, a primary purpose of writing objectives is communication of intent to students, parents, and other professionals. A general statement of a nonobservable process does not communicate sufficiently to students and does not give parents and other professionals enough information to know what skills to encourage. Finally, without specification of the precise behavior to be performed, neither student nor teacher will know when the skill has been acquired and it would be impossible to evaluate the effectiveness of various instructional strategies.

Specifying Conditions

Since behaviors are performed in specific environmental contexts, it is important to specify the **conditions** under which a behavior is to be expected. A given behavior may be appropriate under one set of conditions but not under another.

The conditions of behavioral performance are many, but include environmental considerations, materials, and amount of teacher assistance. *Environmental considerations* include the general setting and schedule within which performance is expected. For example, on-task behaviors such as keeping eyes on own work or completing math problems would be expected during certain work periods but not during transitions or outdoor play.

Materials include the instructional materials or other items used during an activity, as well as their placement or arrangement if necessary. For example, in working on the objective "tells time to the nearest hour," it would be important to specify whether that behavior should be performed with a digital clock or with a traditional clock with hands. Other examples of materials specification include the primer or book from which a student is expected to read, the scissors and paper with which a student is expected to cut, the type of math problems to be completed, or the clothing to be used in dressing. Positioning of materials may also be important. For example, how far away should the plate be from the student or should the student be sitting or standing?

Teacher assistance refers to the cues or other assistance provided by the teacher that are allowable and expected as a part of performance. Types of teacher assistance include verbal cues, physical assistance, modeling, or altering the materials to increase the probability of correct performance. For example, an objective might state that the student should "repeat a two-word sequence when presented a model by the teacher" or "bring spoon to mouth with partial physical assistance by teacher."

Specifying Criteria

To specify **criteria** for an objective means to describe how well a person should perform the desired task. Specifying criteria is important because it provides a definitive marker of when the student has met the objective. Thus, it tells us when to move on to teaching other skills or to the next step in a sequence of skills. Also, specification of criteria helps the teacher identify a relevant data-collection system to monitor progress toward the objective.

Criteria may be specified in many ways. The most basic and frequently used form is to specify an *accuracy* criterion such as percentage correct. For example, "correctly completes 90% of 20 double-digit math problems requiring carrying" or "identifies the correct color in 80% of the opportunities presented." Other types of criteria may also be important. Often the speed or *rate* at which a skill is performed contributes to its long-term usefulness to the child. For example, reading is much more fun and useful if done quickly. Thus, an example of a rate objective might be "reads from primer at a rate of 15 correct words per minute." Criteria may also include *duration* or length of performance of a task. For example, Martin may be expected to "work for a period of 15 minutes without stopping or asking for assistance." Finally, objectives may include *latency* criteria by defining the maximum time allowed between instructions and behavior. For example, "Esther will begin writing her assignment within 2 minutes of being told to begin."

A frequently asked question is, "How do you decide how well a behavior should be performed?" Examples of related questions are "Should I require 80% correct or 90% correct?" or "How many days at 80% correct should I expect before I change to another objective?" These are important questions for which few answers are available based on empirical research. Existing guidelines for data-based strategy decisions (Haring, Liberty, & White, 1980; White & Haring, 1980) are described in Chapter 8. However, in many cases we must use logic and theory to help guide our decisions. In part, the answers to these questions depend on the objectives specified. For example, in teaching Sarah to eat with a spoon, it may be acceptable for her to spill some food approximately 10% of the tries. Perfection is not essential. However, in teaching Alex to cross the street only when no traffic is coming, it is absolutely critical that he perform this task without error. At least four guidelines should be considered when specifying criteria for behavioral performance:

(1) *Consider the minimum level necessary to move on to the next skill.* Often, success at one task depends on performance levels on prerequisite or more basic tasks. For example, Ted's ability to spell words correctly and rapidly depends in part on his ability to write letters. If the eventual goal is for him to spell words correctly at a rate of 20 letters per minute, then he should be able to write letters randomly at a rate of at least 20 per minute and perhaps more. White and Haring (1980) described such behaviors as *tool movements,* referring to the basic tools required for performing later skills. For example, playing "The Blue Danube" on the piano at the proper speed first requires the ability to play random notes or scales at that speed and probably even faster. The basic point is that often prerequisite skills need to be mastered very well if the student is to be successful in performing higher-level skills.

(2) *Consider the minimum level necessary to perform the skill in the real world.* Some skills are important in and of themselves, not as prerequisites to other, more advanced skills. For these skills, it is important to ask how well they must be performed to be generally accepted by others. For example, teaching Maria to dress herself is considered important by both Maria's teachers and her parents. However, mornings are rushed at Maria's house and her parents are not willing to let her dress herself unless she can do it in 10 minutes or less. Thus, 10 minutes becomes an important performance criterion for Maria to achieve. Likewise, aggressive acts toward peers (e.g., yelling, pushing, hitting) generally are not appropriate. A student engaged in numerous aggressive acts will probably have the reduction of those behaviors stated as an IEP goal. However, since all children engage in some aggression toward peers, it is probably unrealistic to expect a child to be completely restrained at all times. Thus, the objective should specify the minimal level of aggressive acts that would be acceptable to the teacher or to peers.

(3) *Consider the minimum level necessary for enjoyment and maintenance of the skill.* We continue to practice and use acquired skills only if they are useful or enjoyable to us. Some skills, such as diagramming sentences, were learned by many of us and then promptly forgotten either because we did not enjoy the activity or because it simply was not useful. In other cases, we only use skills that we can perform at an acceptable rate. For example, if reading is a very slow process, a student is less likely to choose reading as a leisure or recreational activity. Thus, the objective should specify the minimum level of performance necessary to ensure that the skill will be useful and enjoyable for the student.

(4) *Consider peer performance levels.* Usually, we want to tailor objectives to an individual student's needs rather than the performance of other students. However, in some instances it may be important to consider peer performance levels when specifying criteria for behavioral objectives. This is particularly the case when trying to mainstream handicapped students into regular classrooms. The likelihood of successful mainstreaming is greatly increased as handicapped students' behavior begins to approximate that of peers. If the average student in third grade can independently locate assigned materials for the morning's work, with only one instruction from the teacher, that same level of independence may be a very important goal for a student with a learning disability. Also, considering peer performance levels helps teachers set realistic objectives for students. For example, Kwan needs to learn to stay in his seat and work for extended periods of time. However, it would be unreasonable to expect him to sit for 30 minutes if the other kindergartners in his class only stay in their seats for an average of 15 minutes.

Common Errors in Writing Objectives

Writing good objectives requires practice. Since errors often occur, it is important for someone else who has experience in writing objectives to read

TABLE 3.2   Common Problems in Writing Objectives

Incorrect Objectives	Problem	Possible Solutions
1. Given 10 sentences, Kim Li will copy each, putting spaces between all words, within 3 weeks.	a. Conditions not adequately specified.	a. Given a primary pencil, paper, and 10 sentences printed on the chalkboard.
	b. No criteria.	b. With 90% accuracy.
	c. Does this mean she has 3 weeks to finish the task?	c. On three consecutive trials by April 15.
2. Waylon will be able to write the letters of his name four out of five trials, 100% of the time.	a. "Be able" to is not necessary; we want him to write.	a. Waylon will write.
	b. What is a trial? Each letter or all six letters?	b. When asked to write his name, Waylon will write it.
	c. What does 100% of the time mean?	c. With no more than one error.
	d. Do the letters have to be in the correct order?	d. In the correct order.
3. Darrell will distinguish between upper- and lower-case letters.	a. "Distinguish" is not a behavior.	a. Darrell will place upper-case letters on top of the corresponding lower-case letter.
	b. Conditions not specified.	b. When given a pile of 52 letters (26 upper- and 26 lower-case).
	c. Criteria not specified.	c. Correctly place 85% of upper-case letters.

them and provide feedback. Examples of common errors are displayed in Table 3.2. The following rules should be followed in evaluating objectives:

1. Objectives should be as brief as possible. Omit phrases such as "will be able to" or "will increase" and include only the verb that describes the desired behavior (e.g., "Alonzo will write" rather than "Alonzo will be able to write").
2. Objectives should *clarify* desired outcomes rather than confuse them.
3. The three key components of an objective (target behavior, conditions, criteria) must be present.
4. Whenever possible, the objective should be stated in positive terms, describing what the student is to *do* rather than what the student is *not* to do.
5. The desired learning *must* be stated in observable, measurable terms.

Summary of Key Concepts

■ A behavioral objective is a precise description of a desired educational outcome for an individual student.

■ Behavioral objectives are important because they (a) meet legal requirements for teaching handicapped students, (b) provide a focus for instruction, (c) provide a basis for monitoring progress, and (d) communicate information about expectations.

■ A good objective specifies, in operational terms, the desired behavior, the conditions under which the behavior is expected to occur, and the criteria by which attainment of the objective will be judged.

REFERENCES

Fredericks, H. D., Anderson, R., & Baldwin, V. (1979). The identification of competency indicators of teaching of the severely handicapped. *AAESPH Review, 4,* 81–95.

Haring, N. G., Liberty, K. A., & White, O. R. (1980). Rules for data-based strategy decisions in instructional programs: Current research and instructional implications. In W. Sailor, B. Wilcox, & L. Brown (Eds.), *Methods of instruction for severely handicapped students* (pp. 159–192). Baltimore: Paul H. Brookes.

Hartley, J., & Davies, I. K. (1976). Preinstructional strategies: The role of pretests, behavioral objectives, overviews and advance organizers. *Review of Educational Research, 46,* 239–265.

Lovitt, T. C. (1977). *In spite of my resistance, I've learned from children.* Columbus, OH: Charles E. Merrill.

Mager, R. F. (1962). *Preparing instructional objectives.* Belmont, CA: Fearon.

McNeil, J. D. (1967). Concomitants of using behavioral objectives in the assessment of teacher effectiveness. *Journal of Experimental Education, 35,* 69–74.

Thiagarajan, S. (1980). Individualizing instructional objectives. *Teaching Exceptional Children, 12,* 126–127.

Vargas, J. S. (1972). *Writing worthwhile behavioral objectives.* New York: Harper & Row.

White, O. R., & Haring, N. G. (1980). *Exceptional teaching.* Columbus, OH: Charles E. Merrill.

Williams, W., & Gotts, E. A. (1977). Selected considerations in developing curriculum for severely handicapped students. In E. Sontag (Ed.), *Educational programming for the severely and profoundly handicapped* (pp. 221–236). Reston, VA: The Council for Exceptional Children.

4

ENSURING HIGH-QUALITY OBJECTIVES

Key Terms

- Functional ■ Social Validity ■ Criteria of the Next Educational Environment ■ Fair Pair Rule ■ Acquisition ■ Fluency-Building ■ Generalization ■ Maintenance ■ Adaptation ■ Knowledge ■ Comprehension ■ Application ■ Analysis ■ Synthesis ■ Evaluation ■ Critical Function

WRITING APPROPRIATE OBJECTIVES

Although the way in which an objective is written is important, the form of the objective is but one consideration. Since writing objectives in part is the imposition of one or more person's values on another, we must also examine the content and ask whether the objective is appropriate to pursue. In this section, we describe five considerations for writing appropriate objectives.

Objectives Should Be Functional

To be **functional** means to have immediate usefulness or to lead clearly to more advanced skills that will be useful for the student. Obviously, not all learning objectives will target skills the student will be able to use immediately. However, when teaching students with handicaps, it is important for teachers and other decision-makers to ask how important a given goal is for a student. If we can assume that most students with handicaps have difficulty learning or performing at least some tasks (a safe assumption), then it must be recognized that in the limited time students are in school we can only teach a finite number of skills. Thus, we must ensure that the skills we do teach are the most important. Also, children (and adults) will work harder to achieve a goal that has obvious benefits or utility for them.

Wolf (1978) introduced the concept of **social validity** (perceived worth or acceptability), one aspect of which is determining whether the behaviors specified in objectives are important for improving students' everyday functioning. Kazdin and Matson (1981) described two broad strategies for determining whether or not a given objective is socially valid. The first is referred to as *social comparison*. Here the teacher "carefully observes persons in everyday life and how they perform" (p. 41), essentially a normative approach. The purpose of social comparison is to determine how nonhandicapped students perform a certain skill so that those criteria can be used in establishing learning objectives for the students with handicaps. The second strategy is referred to as *subjective evaluation*. This procedure consists of "soliciting the opinions of others who are in a position to make meaningful decisions about [the student's] behavior by virtue of expertise in the field or relationship to the client" (p. 43). For example, Mithaug and Hagmeier (1978) asked sheltered workshop operators to identify important skills necessary for successful entrance into the workshop environment. Those skills then became the targets for instruction in their prevocational training programs.

Objectives are functional and socially valid when they improve the child's functioning in his or her present environment or when they facilitate movement to and success in the next environment. Both components are important and should be considered. Skills needed for immediate success can be determined by observing the student and identifying difficult or failure situations. Skills needed for success in future environments usually must be determined by visiting those environments. Vincent, Salisbury, Walter, Brown, Gruenwald, and Powers (1980) referred to this process as the identification of the **criteria of the next educational environment,** and described four strategies for determining needed skills: (1) place the student in the setting for a brief period of time to identify deficits that need to be taught, (2) conduct a follow-up of students you previously taught to see what successes and failures they had in that setting, (3) ask teachers or other responsible persons in the next environment to develop a list of "survival skills," and (4) observe students presently placed in the next environment to identify skills actually used.

In order to demonstrate the importance of specifying functional objectives, three examples are provided:

> Fred is a 16-year-old student with severe handicaps. It is anticipated that at age 18 he will begin some form of sheltered employment program. Presently, his teacher is engaging him in activities such as putting pegs in a pegboard, stringing beads, and sorting shapes and colors. The rationale for these activities is that they will prepare him for the work requirements in the sheltered workshop. However, upon visiting the workshop, the teacher finds out that workshop participants are engaged in activities such as assembling parts, sorting scrap materials, and painting. They also

must punch a time clock, be able to work without supervision for 30 minutes, and keep their personal belongings in their lockers. The teacher rewrites Fred's objectives and plans activities that are more directly related to the skills that will soon be required of him.

Laura is a 10-year-old child with Down syndrome. Although she recognizes letters of the alphabet, she cannot sound out the letters or put them together to sound out words. Her teachers have been working on letter sounds through a phonics approach for 3 years. The interdisciplinary team decides that a sight-word approach may be more useful for Laura and easier for her to learn. The teacher identifies 15 words that Laura would probably use frequently (e.g., girls, exit, walk) and specifies their recognition as Laura's new learning objective.

Teresa is a 6-year-old child diagnosed as having a learning disability. In particular, she has difficulty performing visual-motor tasks such as writing or copying figures. In the IEP meeting, the team suggests that one objective for Teresa should be to copy complex shapes, such as rectangles with diagonal lines in them, or other patterns. When her parents inquire as to the purpose of this objective, the initial reply is that it will help prepare her to write letters. However, team members soon realize that the shapes they would be asking Teresa to draw are not very useful ones and, in fact, many are much more difficult to write than most letters. The objective is revised to having Teresa copy 12 letters of the alphabet accurately by winter break.

These examples are intended to demonstrate situations in which objectives are made more functional or useful for students. Changes were made by observing those environments in which skills are expected to be used, or by persons interested in the student's long-term well-being sitting down and discussing the importance of individual objectives. Of course, some objectives are worthwhile, even if no immediate utility is apparent. However, given the limited time available to work with students, it is important to ask questions continually regarding the usefulness of learning objectives.

Objectives Should Be Realistic and Achievable

Specifying outcomes or aims always opens the possibility of setting objectives that are either too easy or too difficult for students. Of course, inaccurate predictions of progress will always occur since it is impossible to know ahead of time how fast students will learn or how well you will be able to conduct your instructional activities. However, realistic predictions are important for both students and parents since attainment of an objective is one indicator of competence.

Several precautions should serve to increase the likelihood of specifying realistic and achievable objectives. First, by involving other team members, parents, and the student in specifying objectives, a consensus may be reached on appropriate outcomes. Second, previous patterns of progress as well as current baseline data can be used as indicators of future progress. Third, by using practical assessment tools and identifying functional objectives, the likelihood of goals being realistic and achievable is enhanced. Finally, by monitoring progress teachers and students can identify situations in which a goal is not likely to be achieved and thus can either adjust the intervention used or change expectations for achievement.

Although it is important to set realistic and achievable goals, it may also be important to set goals that are challenging for both students and teachers. For example, Fuchs, Fuchs, and Deno (1985) studied the achievement gains of learning disabled, emotionally handicapped, and educable mentally retarded children as a function of the "ambitiousness" of goals set for them. Results indicated that students for whom ambitious goals were set achieved better than students for whom lower goals were set, even when pretreatment achievement levels were statistically controlled.

The issue of setting realistic goals becomes even more complex when resources available to achieve goals are considered. On the one hand, it may not be ethical to set goals for which human, financial, and time resources are not available. On the other hand, it is unethical (and illegal) to omit important objectives on the IEP simply because resources are limited. For example, if a child needs the help of a speech-language pathologist, and the school district does not have a therapist available, should a therapeutic objective be included in the IEP? According to Public Law 94–142, lack of resources is not sufficient justification for failing to address important learning needs of students. Teachers and other team members may need to advocate for service provision so that all objectives in the IEP are both appropriate for the child and also meet the criteria of being realistic and achievable.

Objectives Should Benefit the Student

This statement would seem to reflect the obvious. However, in many cases, objectives are specified for the convenience or benefit of schools or teachers, rather than for the student (Alberto & Troutman, 1982). For example, many teachers would probably like all of their kindergartners to sit in their seats for 2 hours at a time. This is an unreasonable expectation for 5-year-old children, however. The objective is primarily for the benefit of the teacher rather than the student.

In the case of behavior reduction objectives, reducing inappropriate behaviors such as stereotypic behaviors, aggressive behaviors, or inappropriate social behaviors has benefits for both the target student as well as teachers and peers. In such cases, many advocate use of the **fair pair rule.** According to this rule, any behavior reduction objective should be accompanied by an objective designed to teach an appropriate skill that replaces the behavior targeted for reduction. Similarly, the teacher should identify appropriate behaviors that serve the same function as the inappropriate behavior. For example, Jane frequently throws her pencil down and quits working when she cannot write the correct answer to an assignment. Although this behavior achieves the function of getting the teacher to come over and help her, teaching Jane to ask for help would achieve the same function in a more appropriate fashion.

Objectives Should Not Be Limited to Acquisition or Knowledge-Level Skills

The vast majority of objectives specified for handicapped (and other) students specify the acquisition of certain skills; that is, learning how to do something. However, acquisition often is not enough, since many students will not *generalize* (use) skills acquired in one context to other situations. Teachers must plan for generalization. Ethical objectives not only specify the acquisition of skills, but also include provisions for teaching skill use in the natural environment.

Objectives also need not be limited to the mere recall of factual information. Almost all students can and should be taught higher level skills as well. Vargas (1972) described strategies and techniques for writing "worthwhile" behavioral objectives using the taxonomical framework suggested by Bloom, Englehart, Furst, Hill, and Krathwohl (1956).

Specification of Objectives Should Incorporate Student Input When Possible

As professionals, teachers are trained to identify appropriate learning outcomes for students. As mandated by law, parents have a right to participate in that process as well, and must approve the student's written IEP. However, there are valid reasons for also including students in specifying not only the focus or content of objectives, but also desired outcome levels. Students are then aware of the objectives specified for them and perhaps become more invested in achieving objectives they have had a part in determining.

The notion of involving employees in the process of setting goals for business and industry is referred to as *management by objectives* (MBO), and there is empirical support documenting improved planning, performance, productivity, and worker satisfaction when the MBO approach is in place (McConkie, 1979). Some evidence for the effects of involving students in goal planning also has been found. Tollefson, Tracy, Johnsen, Farmer, and Buenning (1984) found that helping learning disabled junior high-school students set realistic goals resulted in improvements in the accuracy of goal-setting and increases in attribution of achievement outcomes to personal effort. Other studies with mentally retarded students have demonstrated that goal-setting with students results in improved learning and job performance (Kliebhan, 1967; Warner & De Jung, 1971; Warner & Mills, 1980). Furthermore, Kelley and Stokes (1984) found that high-school dropouts who engaged in student-teacher contracting for workbook productivity were more likely to maintain skills and independent work performance if they were subsequently required to write their own objectives for continued work.

For student involvement to be successful, at least six factors should be attended to:

1. Students should be prepared for the IEP meeting ahead of time. The purpose of the meeting should be explained and the format and sequence of activities described. Students should be told that their input during the meeting is important and desired by all team members. In particular, students should be advised of the kinds of decisions that will be made in the meeting (e.g., learning goals, procedures for accomplishing goals) so that they anticipate and plan for input.

2. Student input during the IEP meeting should be actively encouraged. For example, one or more team members should make the effort to ask the student if he or she has any comments or suggestions at several points during the meeting.

3. If a decision is made that is different from the student's wishes, reasons for the decision should be carefully explained.

4. After the meeting and throughout the school year, students should be given the opportunity to take some responsibility for decision-making regarding when they will complete their work, the materials they will use, or the manner in which goals are accomplished.

5. For most students, some objectives should be set concerning their use of leisure or recreational time. Since actual participation in such activities is frequently initiated by students, this serves as an ideal content area for teaching them to specify objectives.

6. Providing students with choices about given objectives is also a means of securing their involvement. For example, vocational preparation is an important curriculum area for secondary students. Allowing students to choose two or three jobs from five or six for which they could be trained is an appropriate practice. While the students may not select the objective, specifying the job they want to learn automatically selects objectives that must be set.

WRITING OBJECTIVES FOR DIFFERENT PHASES OF LEARNING

The first and primary goal of education is to help children *acquire* basic skills. However, the acquisition of skills is but one step in the process of skill *use*. A major characteristic differentiating the learning patterns of handicapped and nonhandicapped students is that many nonhandicapped students bridge the gap between acquisition and use, whereas many handicapped children do not (Stokes & Baer, 1977), implying that teachers of handicapped students need to specify objectives related to skill use. Unfortunately, objectives related to skill use and generalization rarely are specified in student IEPs (Billingsley, 1984).

Five phases in learning to use skills were described by Haring, White, and Liberty (1978): acquisition, fluency-building, generalization, maintenance, and adaptation. Each phase represents a different step in skill use. The phases are important for two reasons. First, they provide a helpful framework for teachers when specifying objectives beyond the initial acquisition of skills. Second, they have direct implications for the selection of effective teaching strategies, since research has documented that success in different phases of learning is facilitated by unique teaching strategies (Haring, Liberty, & White, 1980; White & Haring, 1980). In this chapter, we describe the process of writing objectives for each phase of learning. In Chapters 11 through 17, we describe teaching techniques associated with each phase.

A summary of the points to be made in this section is displayed in Table 4.1. Three skills are used as examples, and sample objectives for each phase of learning are provided. Example 1 describes a common objective for elementary-aged children: two-digit addition with carrying. Example 2 describes the preschool or kindergarten skill of name recognition. Example 3 describes a series of objectives for helping a student initiate interactions with peers.

Acquisition

Acquisition refers to the process of learning how to perform a skill. The assumption is that prior to teaching the student cannot perform the skill. At the end of the acquisition phase, the student can accurately perform the steps in a skill sequence at a high rate of accuracy (usually at least 80 to 90%); however, he or she may not be able to perform those skills quickly and may not know them well enough to adapt or modify them to apply to situations other than the teaching environment.

When writing acquisition objectives, criteria for skill performance usually are specified in terms of accuracy, such as percentage correct. The primary goal of teaching in the acquisition phase is to eliminate errors and facilitate correct performance.

Fluency-Building

Fluency-building refers to the process of learning to perform a skill rapidly, at natural rates, or for more extensive periods of time. In operational terms, the goal of fluency-building is to increase the rate of behavior, to change the duration of behavior, or to decrease the latency of behavior. Fluency-building is an important phase of learning for several reasons. First, simple acquisition of a skill is not sufficient to ensure that the student will use the skill. For example, Larry has learned the mechanics of reading accurately. However, it is a laboriously slow process for him and thus he never chooses reading as a leisure activity. Second, students may acquire skills but not perform them fluently enough so that others

TABLE 4.1 Description and Examples of Objectives at Five Phases of Learning

Learning Phase	Definition	Measurement Criteria	Example 1	Example 2	Example 3
Acquisition	Learning how to perform a specified skill or behavior	Percentage correct	Writes answers to double-digit addition problems requiring carrying, of the type $xx + x = \_\_\_$. 90% correct of problems presented in daily probe.	Points to own name on index card and selects from four other names four out of five trials.	Initiates interaction with peer during indoor dramatic play by (a) identifying target peer, (b) calling peer by name, (c) showing peer toy, (d) offering to share toy with peer by handing toy to peer. Follows steps with 100% accuracy.
Fluency-Building	Performing a skill rapidly and easily, or for extended periods of time	Rate duration; latency	Writes answers to double-digit addition problems at rate of five correct per minute, with no more than one error per minute.	Points to own name at rate of 10 per minute.	Initiates interaction with peers at least three different times during both indoor and outdoor play.
Generalization	Using the skill under conditions that differ from those in which the skill is taught (e.g. across settings, across behaviors, across persons)	Accuracy and rate; discriminates conditions for appropriate skill use; duration and latency	Writes answers to double-digit addition problems when presented by aide.	Points to name on back of chair, locker, books, and personal articles of clothing.	Initiates similar rates of interaction with at least three different peers during both indoor and outdoor play.

| Maintenance | Continuing to use a skill even after instruction has stopped | Accuracy and rate; reduced levels of assistance | Uses double-digit addition correctly after instruction; moves on to other. | Continues to use name recognition skills 3 months after instruction has ceased. | Initiates peer interactions with only one reminder from teacher per day. |
| Adaptation | Modifying the skill to meet the requirements of changing conditions | Accuracy and rate. Is desired effect achieved? | Writes answers to double-digit addition problems when presented in format $xx + x = \_\_\_$. | Points to name when printed in sizes or typeface that differ from that learned. | Initiates peer interaction by showing work to another child and commenting on peer's work. |

will let them practice those skills. For example, Jody has learned all of the skills necessary to dress herself. However, since it takes her at least 30 minutes to put on her clothes, her parents usually do it for her, with the effect that she rarely gets to practice the skill and its use is not reinforced. Finally, some skills absolutely must be performed at a minimal rate for them to be effective. For example, Terry must not only be able to cross the street only when the "Walk" light is on, but also must make it across within the time provided by the stoplight.

Fluency objectives should include criteria in addition to percentage correct. In most cases, this means that a *rate* criterion must be included. For example, Larry will read at a minimum rate of 30 words per minute. In some cases, *fluency* may be defined as performing a skill for more extended periods of time. In this case, a *duration* criterion must be included. For example, Jeremy not only must acquire the skills needed to play independently, he must also use those independent play skills for at least 15 minutes at a time. Also, *fluency* may be defined as a reduction in the time between the presentation of instructions and the performance of a behavior. In such situations, a *latency* criterion must be included. For example, Teresa not only must acquire the skills necessary to clean up the room, she also must begin cleaning up within 1 minute of being asked to do so by the teacher.

Generalization

Generalization refers to the student's use of a skill under conditions that differ from those under which the skill was taught. Four common forms of generalization exist. Generalization across *settings* means that the student uses the skill in a different setting from the one in which the skill was taught. For example, one of Ralph's present objectives is to work independently on homework at home; at present, he works independently on assignments in class, but does not do so at home. Generalization across *behaviors* means that the student applies learning to new but similar behaviors. For example, Sue Ellen displays three inappropriate behaviors in class: talking out, getting out of seat, and teasing peers. During the month of October, Sue Ellen learns to stop talking out. Her present goal is for that learning to generalize to getting out of seat and teasing peers. Generalization across *persons* means that the student demonstrates a given skill with a variety of others. For example, Christopher's teacher taught him to say "Hi!" whenever she says "Hi" to him. However, he will not greet anyone else. Christopher's present goal is to respond appropriately to "Hi" at least 75% of the occasions presented, regardless of who greets him. Generalization across *materials* means that the student demonstrates a learned skill with a variety of similar materials. For example, Rebecca has learned to read 50 words in the context of her reader. Her goal for this learning period is to read those same words when found in a newspaper or other book.

Criteria for generalization objectives usually include both rate and accuracy statements, since both are necessary for functional skill use. Also, criterion statements may describe the importance of discriminating appropriate and inappropriate conditions for skill use. For example, Christopher probably should not say "Hi" to everyone he sees on a trip to the shopping center.

Although a few skills may only be expected in the classroom environment, the primary purpose of education is to facilitate the generalized use of important skills. It is extremely frustrating to spend time and energy teaching a skill only to see it go unused or unreinforced outside of the classroom. Given the high probability that handicapped students will not generalize well, generalization of skills must be specified as learning objectives and valued as important outcomes.

Maintenance

Maintenance means that the student continues to use a skill in the same setting even after instruction has stopped. Lack of maintenance can occur if instruction or contingencies suddenly are stopped, without planning for their gradual removal. Objectives for this phase simply describe maintained skill use in the absence of instruction. Accuracy and rate criteria still apply; however, for many students it may not be realistic to expect maintenance at the original level of attainment; some reduction in performance may occur. Therefore, initial objectives for acquisition and fluency-building may need to be *higher* than the desired or expected maintenance level. Also, maintenance objectives frequently specify the maximum allowable levels of teacher assistance to maintain a skill. For example, Sue Ellen has learned not to engage in teasing, talking out, and getting out of seat. The maintenance objective might be for Sue Ellen to continue to refrain from these behaviors after instruction has ceased with no more than one reminder from the teacher per day.

Adaptation

Adaptation means that the student modifies the acquired skill to meet the requirements of changing demands or conditions. While generalization requires the student to use the *same* skill in a variety of contexts, adaptation requires the student to actually modify or change the behavior. In part, adaptation is synonymous with "flexibility" and in part with "creativity" (White & Haring, 1980). Criteria for attainment of adaptation objectives should focus on achieving the desired *function* of a behavior rather than the precise manner in which that function is achieved. In other words, the important question is whether the student can take an acquired skill and modify or adapt it to solve a new problem. Thus, the focus of evaluation should be on solving the problem, regardless of the manner in which the child chooses to solve it.

WRITING OBJECTIVES FOR HIGHER
LEVEL BEHAVIORS

Some teachers and others have suggested that, while it may be appropriate to set objectives for the acquisition and use of such basic skills as reading, math, self-help, or social skills, it is impossible to write objectives for higher level skills. Admittedly, it often *is* difficult to write such objectives. However, operationalizing higher-level goals is important for the same reasons goal-setting is important for all students. The teacher's fundamental task is to specify the behaviors or types of behaviors expected of the student. Otherwise, how would you know what to teach, whether teaching was successful, and when to teach other skills?

For example, a common educational goal is to increase children's creativity. In order to achieve that goal, or at least to work toward it, creative behaviors must be identified and then encouraged. An example of that process was provided by Glover and Gary (1976). In working with fourth- and fifth-grade students, they wanted to increase some aspects of creativity. First, they went to the literature to determine what "experts" in the area of creative behavior said was important. Torrance (1966) suggested four aspects of creativity: *fluency* (the ability to produce a large number of ideas,) *flexibility* (the ability to produce a large variety of ideas), *elaboration* (the ability to develop or expand an idea), and *originality* (the ability to generate new ideas). Drawing on this conceptual framework, Glover and Gary devised a simple task for children and developed operational definitions for each dimension of creative behavior. Each day a noun was printed on the blackboard and students were given 10 minutes to list all possible uses of the noun. Responses were scored on four dimensions:

1. Number of different responses (fluency): any response given by a student that was not identical to a previous response given by that student on any of his or her preceding lists.
2. Number of verb forms (flexibility): total of all different *forms* of responses (uses).
3. Number of words per response (elaboration): total number of words used in the list divided by the total number of responses on the list.
4. Statistical infrequency of verb forms (originality): number of verb forms per list that had not appeared in previous lists of each individual. (Glover & Gary, 1976, p. 81)

The authors demonstrated that they could improve each dimension of creative behavior through structuring activities and reinforcing student behavior. Also, students generally improved their performance on a standardized measure of creative thinking.

Other examples of operationalizing higher level behaviors are readily found. For example, Goetz and Baer (1973) wanted to increase diversity in the block-building behavior of preschoolers. Twenty block forms were defined (e.g., "RAMP: a block leaned against another, or a triangular block placed contiguous to another, to simulate a ramp," p. 211). Objectives for intervention were to increase form diversity, defined as "the number of these 20 forms appearing at least once in any session's construction(s)" (p. 210) and new forms, defined as "the number of these 20 forms appearing in a given session's construction that had not appeared in *any* prior construction by that child (in previous sessions of blockbuilding) recorded within the study" (p. 210). Social reinforcement was used to increase the number of different forms built per session; increases in the number of new forms built were also observed. Likewise, Maloney and Hopkins (1973) attempted to increase creativity ratings of stories written by elementary-aged students by improving specific aspects of composition. A large number of objectives was identified, including number of words in sentences; number of adjectives, action verbs, adverbs, and prepositional phrases; number of different adjectives and adverbs; number of different actions, number of different beginnings; and number of sentences with more than eight words. Teacher intervention served to improve individual behaviors and resulted in improvements in global ratings of creativity by others.

These studies demonstrate that behaviors related to creativity can be operationalized and subsequently taught. Furthermore, objective ratings by others after intervention indicate that products (word lists, block-building, stories) were judged to be more creative than before intervention.

However, higher-level behaviors include more than creativity. A helpful framework for identifying higher level behaviors has been provided by Bloom et al. (1956). The framework, commonly referred to as *Bloom's taxonomy*, suggests six levels of learning objectives: knowledge, comprehension, application, analysis, synthesis, and evaluation. These levels and three examples of each are summarized in Table 4.2. Example 1 describes objectives related to learning a moral, Example 2 describes objectives related to shape recognition, and Example 3 describes objectives related to story comprehension. Each level is briefly described here; however, the reader is referred to Vargas (1972), Bloom et al. (1956), and Bailey and Leonard (1977) for more complete descriptions of each level of the taxonomy and guidelines for writing objectives at each level.

Knowledge

At the **knowledge** level of learning, students simply restate what the teacher has taught them. It is the level at which most objectives are specified, and is an important level because it provides the foundation for higher level learning. However, knowledge alone does not guarantee that the student will understand or use a concept. For example, many preschoolers, particularly those with older siblings, can state "2 + 2 = 4." However, most do not comprehend the meaning of this statement nor can they apply the fact or use addition to solve problems.

Examples of common knowledge-level objectives include stating definitions verbatim (a square is a shape with four equal sides and four equal angles), stating specific facts (in 1492 Columbus sailed the ocean blue), or stating rules (*i*

TABLE 4.2 Sample Objectives Based on Bloom's Taxonomy

Level	Definition	Example 1	Example 2	Example 3
Knowledge	The student reproduces, with little or no change, what was presented.	Student repeats moral: "A bird in the hand is worth two in the bush."	Recognizes and labels three shapes—circle, square, triangle—when presented on work sheet.	Student reads or listens to stories and answers factual questions about story content.
Comprehension	Student must demonstrate "understanding" well enough to paraphrase it or state it in another form.	Student restates moral in own words.	Describes, in own words, differences between shapes (e.g., square has four sides, circle is round).	Student tells story in own words.
Application	Student uses method, rule, or principle learned to solve a new problem.	Given an incomplete story, student completes it such that it demonstrates the moral.	Identifies shapes or three-dimensional objects (ball, book, pyramid).	Given five pictures, student can sequence in order and tell a logical story to accompany pictures.
Analysis	Student identifies the component parts.	In a given story, student identifies elements that exemplify "bird in hand," etc.	Locates and outlines shapes hidden in picture.	Student identifies themes of story and describes parts reflecting those themes.
Synthesis	Student combines elements to make a unique product.	Student writes a story to illustrate moral.	Uses shapes to create a picture.	Student writes new story to logically follow first story read.
Evaluation	Student tells whether or not a given product meets specified criteria, or compares two products for some purpose and gives reasoning.	Given two stories, student tells which one best illustrates moral and why.	Given several "crazy" shapes, selects one that best approximates shape named by teacher.	Given two possible endings of a story, student chooses ending that best meets certain criteria (e.g., which ending would make Charlie sad) and tells why.

before *e* except after *c*). Bloom et al. described three categories of knowledge objectives: knowledge of specifics (terminology, specific facts), knowledge of ways and means of dealing with specifics (conventions, trends, classifications, categories, criteria, methodology), and knowledge of universals and abstractions (principles, theories, structures).

Comprehension

At the **comprehension** level, the student must show some basic level of "understanding" of acquired knowledge. Most often, this means the student must paraphrase or describe something in his or her own words. For example, what does "*i* before *e* except after *c*" mean? Bloom, et al. described three types of comprehension: translation (putting a communication in another form); interpretation (going beyond translation to show comprehension of relationships); and extrapolation (making estimates or predictions based on an understanding of the communication).

Application

Application requires the student not only to know and understand something, but to *use* it correctly. For example, the student who demonstrates knowledge and understanding of "*i* before *e* except after *c*" should be able to use the rule to spell an unfamiliar word. According to Bloom et al., comprehension shows that the student *can* use a rule whereas, in application, the question is whether the student *will* use it without prompting.

Analysis

Analysis requires the student to divide or break down information into parts and to determine how these parts are organized. Bloom et al. described three aspects of analysis: analysis of elements (identifying the parts), analysis of relationships (determining the connections and interactions between parts), and analysis of organizational principles (recognition of the principles governing those relationships).

Synthesis

The **synthesis** level is most closely associated with creativity. It requires the ability to uniquely organize ideas and materials or to discover a unique relationship that is not readily apparent.

Evaluation

The **evaluation** level requires the ability to judge or evaluate for some purpose using specified criteria or standards. Included are making comparisons and stating reasons for decisions.

ADDITIONAL ISSUES IN WRITING OBJECTIVES

A number of other topics could be discussed in regard to the specification of objectives. Three are addressed here: age-appropriate objectives, teaching behaviors versus functions, and the interdisciplinary team.

Chronological-Age-Appropriate Objectives

Anyone who teaches exceptional children almost invariably wrestles with the issue of specifying age-appropriate objectives. By definition, most exceptional children have developmental delays in one or more skill areas. The teacher's job is to build on the student's strengths in order to improve areas of deficit. However, with more severely handicapped students who have significant skill deficits, a large discrepancy often exists between their chronological age and their developmental level. Although few professionals would suggest trying to teach a student a skill for which the necessary prerequisites had not been learned, objectives that differ significantly from the student's chronological age are problematic in that they reinforce negative, childlike perceptions of handicapped students. Furthermore, these objectives often are not very functional for students. Visit almost any residential institution, for example, and you are likely to see adults with severe handicaps engaged in activities such as putting together children's puzzles, holding dolls, or stacking blocks.

Brown, Branston, Hamre-Nietupski, Pumpian, Certo, and Gruenewald (1979) argued for chronological-age-appropriate objectives, particularly for severely handicapped adolescents and young adults:

> If one goal of education is to minimize the stigmatizing discrepancies between the handicapped and their nonhandicapped peers, it is our obligation to teach the former the major functions characteristic of their chronological age using materials and tasks which do not highlight the deficiencies in their repertoires. (p. 86)

In order to meet this obligation, Brown et al. suggested six phases in developing a curriculum that contains chronological-age-appropriate objectives:

1. Identify the broad curriculum domains important for the individual student; these domains should "reflect the major life demands of nonhandicapped adults and therefore serve to organize instructional objectives for this handicapped group" (p. 88).

2. Determine the various natural environments in which students function or will need to function; these primary environments include the school, home, or community.

3. Identify subenvironments; these are defined as parts of primary environments, each of which requires different skills for success. For example, the school environment consists of the classroom(s), the cafeteria, and the outdoor play area, each with different demands for competence.

4. Define the various activities that occur in the subenvironments.

5. Identify the skills needed in order to complete or engage in those activities successfully.

6. Write objectives and provide instructional activities to teach those skills.

Although these suggestions were written for teachers of severely handicapped students, the issue of functional, age-appropriate objectives is relevant for all teachers of exceptional children. In no way is this intended to imply that all objectives *must* be age-appropriate. However, as we seek to prepare students for success in mainstreaming environments, including those outside of the school environment, these considerations become critical.

Teaching Behaviors Versus Functions

A related issue is the level of specificity necessary when identifying and writing behavioral objectives. In this chapter, we have emphasized the importance of specifying the precise behaviors expected of a student. However, as White (1980) pointed out, often the same purpose or intent can be achieved in a variety of ways. Therefore, as we write objectives for students, we should consider alternate ways for achieving long-term goals. This requires attention to the **critical function** underlying objectives.

According to White (1980), focusing on critical functions is an attempt to determine "the function or purpose a behavior is supposed to serve, rather than the specific form of the motor act used to achieve that effect" (p. 49). For example, a goal for Lucy, who is moderately retarded, is to dress herself independently. The specific way she accomplishes this task is not as important as whether or not she can do it. The point behind critical functions is that the objective should emphasize behavioral outcomes or functions. The precise manner in which those functions are achieved is only specified if it is, in fact, critical to successful performance or if it is a more normalized or efficient method.

White suggested six steps in developing a curriculum in which the function of behavior is emphasized:

1. Identify specific needs. [This is analogous to the first five steps suggested by Brown et al. (1979) to determine age-appropriate objectives.]

2. Identify the critical elements or function of each skill.

3. Rewrite each skill description to reflect critical elements.
4. Describe at least a few ways in which the skill might be demonstrated.
5. Indicate the basic parameters that should be considered when developing "nonstandard adaptations."
6. Develop a systematic way to record the results of adaptive performance. (pp. 64–65).

When drawing objectives from existing curricula or from assessment tools, the fundamental question teachers should ask is, "What is the child really learning if I teach this objective?" In either case (establishing objectives independently or drawing them from a curriculum), teachers should consider the possibility of alternate routes to the same goal. If the route taken is less important than the goal, perhaps teachers should allow students to guide them in developing their own individualized strategies or means for accomplishing specific objectives. Also, teachers may want to teach several strategies and then allow the student to choose the one he or she prefers.

Developing Objectives on the Interdisciplinary Team

A final issue to be addressed concerns the specification of objectives as a part of an interdisciplinary team. This practice is mandated by law and is good practice for several reasons. Teachers and other professionals cannot be expected to have expertise in every area of child development and education. The team serves to bring together specialists from a variety of disciplines. More ideas or solutions to a given problem can be generated by a group than by any one individual. A group is necessary if one is to get feedback on one's own suggestions. Furthermore, a meeting should help coordinate services across disciplines and facilitate generalization of skills, since everyone is aware of objectives expected of the student.

Unfortunately, the interdisciplinary team often works better in theory than in practice. Problems reported in the literature include unequal participation by many team members (Bailey, Thiele, Helsel-DeWert, & Ware, 1985), parent presence but lack of parent involvement (Goldstein, Strickland, Turnbull, & Curry, 1980; Ysseldyke, Algozzine, & Mitchell, 1982), and problems in team organization (Bailey, 1984). In a study of individual participation on interdisciplinary teams in a residential institution, Bailey, Helsel-DeWert, Thiele, and Ware (1983) found that behaviors rated lowest included (1) asking questions, (2) making suggestions for goals and objectives, (3) providing feedback on goals and objectives suggested by others, and (4) suggesting activities requiring the coordination of two or more disciplines. In many cases, the IEP is developed before the meeting, thus precluding meaningful discussion and making it difficult to change or add new objectives (Goldstein et al., 1980).

The importance of team-generated objectives must be emphasized. Ysseldyke et al. (1982) suggested several strategies to improve team meetings. First, meetings should be structured, with time devoted to each component of the decision-making process. Second, a *consensus* of all persons present is important to ensure responsible follow-through. Third, the goal or purpose of the meeting should be clear to everyone present. Fourth, decisions are best when characterized by *nonspecialized participation* (Shaw, 1964). This means that individuals act as members of a task-oriented group, rather than as members of their own professional discipline. Finally, parents (and students when appropriate) should be actively encouraged to participate in the decision-making process.

Summary of Key Concepts

■ In addition to using proper form for writing objectives, teachers must take care to ensure that objectives are of high quality. A high-quality objective is functional, realistic and achievable, benefits the student, incorporates student and parent input, and addresses more than skill acquisition or knowledge.

■ Exceptional children often need objectives specified for skill use and generalization. Two frameworks exist for writing such objectives. One focuses on phases of learning (acquisition, fluency-building, generalization, maintenance, and adaptation), whereas the other focuses on "higher-level" behaviors (knowledge, comprehension, application, analysis, synthesis, and evaluation).

■ Teachers should be sure that objectives are age-appropriate, focus on the attainment of critical functions, and are derived by an interdisciplinary team.

REFERENCES

Alberto, P. A., & Troutman, A. C. (1982). *Applied behavior analysis for teachers.* Columbus, OH: Charles E. Merrill.

Bailey, D. B. (1984). A triaxial model of the interdisciplinary team and group process. *Exceptional Children, 51,* 17–25.

Bailey, D. B., Helsel-DeWert, M. J., Thiele, J., & Ware, W. B. (1983). Measuring individual participation on the interdisciplinary team. *American Journal of Mental Deficiency, 88,* 247–254.

Bailey, D. B., Thiele, J., Helsel-DeWert, M. J., & Ware, W. B. (1985). Participation of professionals, paraprofessionals, and direct care staff in the interdisciplinary team meeting. *American Journal of Mental Deficiency, 89,* 437–440.

Bailey, D. B., & Leonard, J. L. (1977). A model for

adapting Bloom's taxonomy to a preschool curriculum. *Gifted Child Quarterly, 21,* 97–103.

Billingsley, F. (1984). Where are the generalized outcomes? (An examination of instructional objectives). *Journal of the Association for the Severely Handicapped, 9,* 186–200.

Bloom, B. S., Englehart, M. D., Furst, E. J., Hill, W. H., & Krathwohl, D. R. (1956). *A taxonomy of educational objectives: Handbook I, the cognitive domain.* New York: McKay.

Brown, L., Branston, M. B., Hamre-Nietupski, S., Pumpian, I., Certo, N., & Gruenewald, L. (1979). A strategy for developing chronological-age-appropriate and functional curricular content for severely handicapped adolescents and young adults. *Journal of Special Education, 13,* 81–90.

Fuchs, L. S., Fuchs, D., & Deno, S.L. (1985). Importance of goal ambitiousness and goal mastery to student achievement. *Exceptional Children, 52,* 63–71.

Glover, J., & Gary, A. L. (1976). Procedures to increase some aspects of creativity. *Journal of Applied Behavior Analysis, 9,* 79–84.

Goetz, E. M., & Baer, D. M. (1973). Social control of form diversity and the emergence of new forms in children's blockbuilding. *Journal of Applied Behavior Analysis, 6,* 209–217.

Goldstein, S., Strickland, B., Turnbull, A. P., & Curry, L. (1980). An observational analysis of the IEP Conference. *Exceptional Children, 46,* 278–286.

Haring, N. G., Liberty, K. A., & White, O. R. (1980). Rules for data-based strategy decisions in instructional programs: Current research and instructional implications. In W. Sailor, B. Wilcox, & L. Brown (Eds.), *Methods of instruction for severely handicapped students* (pp. 159–192). Baltimore: Paul H. Brookes.

Haring, N. G., White, O. R., & Liberty, K. A. (1978). *An investigation of phases of learning and facilitating instructional events for the severely handicapped: Annual progress report, 1977-78.* Bureau of Education for the Handicapped, Project No. 443CH70564. Seattle: University of Washington, College of Education.

Kazdin, A. E., & Matson, J. L. (1981). Social validation in mental retardation. *Applied Research in Mental Retardation, 2,* 39–53.

Kelley, M. L., & Stokes, T. F (1984). Student-teacher contracting with goal-setting for maintenance. *Behavior Modification, 8,* 223–244.

Kliebhan, J. M. (1967). Effects of goal setting and modeling on job performance of retarded adolescents. *American Journal of Mental Deficiency, 72,* 220–226.

Maloney, K. B., & Hopkins, B. L. (1973). The modification of sentence structure and its relationship to subjective judgments of creativity in writing. *Journal of Applied Behavior Analysis, 6,* 425–433.

McConkie, M. E. (1979). Classifying and reviewing the empirical work on MBO: Some implications. *Group and Organization Studies, 4,* 461–475.

Mithaug, D. E., & Hagmeier, L. D. (1978). The development of procedures to assess prevocational competencies of severely handicapped young adults. *AAESPH Review, 3,* 94–115.

Shaw, M. E. (1964). Communication networks. In N. L. Berkowitz (Ed.), *Advances in experimental psychology* (vol. 1). New York: Academic Press.

Stokes, T. F., & Baer, D. M. (1977). An implicit technology of generalization. *Journal of Applied Behavior Analysis, 10,* 349–367.

Tollefson, N., Tracy, D. B., Johnsen, E. Q., Farmer, A. W., & Buenning, M. (1984). Goal setting and personal responsibility training for LD adolescents. *Psychology in the Schools, 21,* 224–233.

Torrance, E. P. (1966). *Torrance tests of creative thinking.* Princeton: Personnel Press.

Vargas, J. S. (1972). *Writing worthwhile behavioral objectives.* New York: Harper & Row.

Vincent, L. J., Salisbury, C., Walter, G., Brown, P., Gruenwald, L. J., & Powers, M. (1980). Program evaluation and curriculum development in early childhood special education: Criteria of the next environment. In W. Sailor, B. Wilcox, & L. Brown (Eds.), *Methods of instruction for severely handicapped students* (pp. 303–328). Baltimore: Paul H. Brookes.

Warner, D. A., & DeJung, J. E. (1971). Effects of goal setting upon learning in educable retardates. *American Journal of Mental Deficiency, 75,* 681–684.

Warner, D. A., & Mills, W. D. (1980). The effects of goal setting on the manual performance rates of moderately retarded adolescents. *Education and Training of the Mentally Retarded, 15,* 143–147.

White, O. R. (1980). Adaptive performance objectives: Form versus function. In W. Sailor, B. Wilcox, & L. Brown (Eds.), *Methods of instruction for severely handicapped students* (pp. 47–70). Baltimore: Paul H. Brookes.

White, O. R., & Haring, N. G. (1980). *Exceptional teaching.* Columbus, OH: Charles E. Merrill.

Wolf, M. M. (1978). Social validity: The case for subjective measurement, or how applied behavior analysis is finding its heart. *Journal of Applied Behavior Analysis, 11,* 203–214.

Ysseldyke, J. E., Algozzine, B., & Mitchell, J. (1982). Special education team decision making: An analysis of current practice. *Personnel and Guidance Journal, 60,* 308–313.

5

DEFINING AND MEASURING BEHAVIORS

Key Terms

■ Measurement ■ Event-Based Sampling ■ Discrete ■ Permanent
Products ■ Calibration ■ Probe ■ Duration ■ Latency ■ Interrupted
Measurement ■ Time-Based Recording ■ Mutually
Exclusive ■ Exhaustive ■ Whole-Interval Method ■ Partial-Interval
Method ■ Levels-of-Assistance Recording ■ Task Analysis
Recording ■ Reliability ■ Observer Drift ■ Observer
Reactivity ■ Intrarater Reliability ■ Interrater Reliability

Once goals and objectives have been specified, the next step in effective teaching is to develop and implement a system for measuring the target behavior and monitoring progress toward the achievement of objectives.

WHY MEASURE?

Collecting data is not a favorite activity for many teachers, who consider it to be a time-consuming process with no real or practical benefit. Teachers frequently collect data such as attendance, grade sheets, or work samples because it is required, but then file it away without using it. Others may collect additional data on student performance but gather it so infrequently that the data are not useful for decision-making. However, many valid reasons exist for the frequent measurement of student behavior. Reviews by White, Wyne, Stuck, and Coop (1983) and Fuchs and Fuchs (1986) concluded that measurement and frequent monitoring of student progress are related significantly to student achievement. Why is measurement such an important aspect of effective teaching?

To Pinpoint Student Status

One reason for measuring behaviors is to determine student status on instructional objectives. How far is the student from where we would like him or her to be? Although this information can be determined in part from formal testing, test results usually are too general to be helpful. A good measurement system allows the teacher to *pinpoint* the precise level at which a student is working and identify specific problems the student might be encountering.

To Monitor Progress and Determine Effectiveness

Most professions in today's technologically oriented society rely on regular and frequent data for rapid decision-making. The stockbroker or investment counselor, for example, must attend daily to interest rates, market trends, changes in tax laws and legislation, customer desires, consumer satisfaction, and other economic indicators. Football coaches examine individual player performance in each game, rate each player on individual responsibilities (e.g., tackle, block, run), and assign a weekly overall performance rating. The neurosurgeon conducting a complicated operation relies on a host of physiological measures to determine patient status. *Most data collection occurs, however, not because it is of general interest to the professional, but because it facilitates decision-making.* The stockbroker must decide whether to buy, hold, or sell stocks. The coach must decide which players will start the next game or which should remain in the game. The surgeon must decide whether more blood or anesthesia is needed, whether the patient is going into shock, and whether or not the surgery has been completed.

Likewise, when teachers frequently monitor student instructional progress, the failure or success of instructional strategies is readily apparent. Teachers can then use data to decide whether to continue using the same instructional strategy or to make a modification such as going back to an easier skill, moving on to a more difficult skill, or changing the instructional method. Monitoring progress toward objectives helps prevent students from working on skills far beyond the point of mastery, or continuing in the same instructional pattern with no measurable change in performance.

To Provide Feedback to Students and Parents

Monitoring instructional progress facilitates communication with both parents and students. If a student asks, "How am I doing?" or a parent asks, "How is my child doing in her reader?" it is easy to give general responses such as "just fine," "real well," or "well, she's coming along." Likewise, children who ask about their performance may initially be pleased to receive general statements of praise or encouragement. However, those statements soon lose their meaning or power if not substantiated with evidence. Summaries of data on student performance, when prepared and displayed in an understandable fashion, serve an important communicative function.

To Document Efforts and Demonstrate Accountability

Finally, monitoring instructional progress is important because it demonstrates a willingness to be accountable for student progress, provides evidence of effective teaching, and is helpful when programs do not work or progress is minimal. For example, Ms. Walker has been working on Frank's reading skills and Daryl's aggressive behavior. Not much has changed in their behavior over the course of the year. At the end of April, both students' parents call the principal and complain that Ms. Walker has done little to teach reading or reduce aggression. The principal calls her in for a joint meeting. How does Ms. Walker respond? Her response is much easier if she has frequently gathered data documenting that she (a) recognized that a problem existed, (b) took data on the problem, (c) tried a number of strategies to change behavior, and (d) used data to help decide that instruction had not been effective and to change instructional strategies. Without data, she would be placed in a defensive posture of trying to recall what she had done, when she had made changes, and the effects (or noneffects) of those changes on student behavior. Data collection can be extremely helpful if the need arises to explain lack of progress or to document progress that has occurred but which may not be apparent to parents or administrators.

The term **measurement** is synonymous with counting or quantification, and is simply the assignment of numbers according to rules to represent behavior. This chapter describes various ways of counting. The first step in implementing a measurement system is to define the behaviors to be counted. Fortunately, much of the task of defining the behaviors to be counted has been accomplished once a behavioral objective has been written. An objective specifies the precise behavior, in operational terms, expected of the student. An *operational definition* describes behaviors that are both observable and measurable. Two different individuals should be able to observe those acts and agree as to whether they occurred.

Four types of recording systems are typically used in educational settings: event based, time based, levels of assistance, and task analysis.

EVENT-BASED RECORDING

Event-based recording refers to the documentation of behaviors that are relatively **discrete** in nature. The event has a clearly definable beginning and ending, and each occurrence is approximately the same. For example, the number of hits, number of corrects, or number of initiations to peers could be counted. Event recording can be used with live behavior, such as hitting, talking, oral reading, or walking, or with **permanent products,** the results of behavior. Examples of permanent products primarily include written products, such as answers to math problems, spelling activities, or written compositions. However, many responses that do not produce written products can be adapted to produce permanent products. For example, when teaching a student a pincer grasp, the teacher could have the student place small marbles in a soft drink bottle; the bottle could be put away after the lesson and counted later. Making a videotape, or having a student read into a tape recorder or enter data into a computer produces a permanent product. Finally, tasks such as making a bed, assembling an object, putting together a puzzle, or setting a table all result in products that can be evaluated. Permanent products are easier to measure than live counts because the counting can be done when the teacher chooses to do so and can be checked. Nonpermanent data must be gathered live and is susceptible to error. However, many behaviors have no permanent products and must be counted live.

Calibrating a Counting System

The term **calibration** refers to the process of determining the correct markings of a measurement instrument. We assume, for example, that a yardstick is well calibrated. We expect the length to be exactly one yard and the inches to be accurate and equal to each other. White and Haring (1980) used the term *calibration* to describe the procedures by which a behavior is defined such that meaningful assessments are facilitated. A well-calibrated behavior has the following characteristics:

1. Each repetition of the behavior must represent essentially the same amount of behavior.
2. The counting system must be directly related to instructional objectives.
3. It must be possible to assess the behavior easily.
4. The counting system must be sensitive to changes in behavior.

Representing the Same Amount of Behavior. If inches on a yardstick were of different lengths, a measurement problem would exist. Likewise, a counting system in which different counts actually represent different amounts of behavior would also result in measurement problems since comparisons would be difficult. For example, how should reading skills be counted? One system would be to count the number of pages read. However, some pages have many words on them, whereas others have few words on them. To say that Candice has improved because she read 3 pages on Monday and by Friday was reading 10 pages per day would not make sense if the pages read on Friday contained fewer words. Using "number of pages read" as a counting rule is an example of poor calibration, since each page does not necessarily represent the same amount of behavior. The same problem is encountered with using "number of paragraphs read" or "number of sentences read," since both paragraphs and sentences can vary considerably in length. White and Haring (1980) and others suggested using "number of words read" as a well-calibrated system for counting reading behaviors. Although words also can vary in their length, each represents the smallest unit that is meaningful to count.

Relating Counts to Instructional Objectives. Although a yardstick can do a good job of measuring the length of an object, it is of no use whatsoever in determining the object's weight. The system used to count behaviors should directly relate to a student's instructional objectives. If a student's reading objective is to improve reading of blends such as *br* or *st,* the counting system should be "number of blends read correctly" rather than "number of words read correctly." The blend is the target of instruction and the behavior to be changed. Likewise, the counting system used may vary depending on the phase of teaching or learning. What is counted during the acquisition phase may be different from what is counted during the generalization phase.

Assessing Behaviors Easily. The counting system should make data collection manageable. For example, reading could be counted as "number of syllables read correctly." However, the task of counting syllables and recording corrects and errors related to each syllable would be so onerous that most teachers would quickly give up on measurement.

Sensitivity to Change. Given the fact that many exceptional students make relatively small changes in behavior over time, a measurement system should be sensitive to small gains. Not only does the system of "number of pages read" have the problem of unequal amounts of behavior, it does not reflect small changes in behavior. It takes a lot of work to go from reading one page per minute to reading two pages per minute. Using "number of words read" as the unit of measurement provides a more sensitive system that can easily show change over time in most students.

Examples of Well-Calibrated Measurement Systems

Generally speaking, teachers need to develop counting systems tailored to the needs of individual children. However, some conventions exist for counting commonly taught skills.

Mathematics. When most of us were learning to perform various mathematical operations, our answers were scored either right or wrong. However, consider Bart's performance of a three-digit addition problem (no carrying) over a one-week period:

Monday	Tuesday	Wednesday	Thursday	Friday
247	247	247	247	247
+332	+332	+332	+332	+332
222	429	469	479	579

Using the right or wrong system, this student's work would be considered wrong every day except Friday. However, improvement actually began on Tuesday, when Bart added correctly in the "ones" column. This counting system violates the calibration rule related to sensitivity to change. Likewise, compare the tasks required of the following children:

Tammy	Teresa				
2 3 5 4 6	3478	4429	5973	7489	3336
+1 +2 +1 +2 +1	+9376	+2860	+4072	+2207	+8753

Using the right or wrong system, if both Tammy and Teresa added all of their problems correctly, each would receive a score or count of 5 corrects. However, Teresa clearly had to perform more behaviors than Tammy in order to receive the same count of 5. In this case, the counting system violates the calibration rule requiring that each count represent an equal amount of behavior.

In order to solve these measurement problems, many have suggested a counting system using the rule "number of digits correct in place." The teacher scores as right or wrong each possible column in the answer; the purpose of scoring is to determine accuracy at each step of the operation. Using this rule, Bart's performance over the week would be scored as follows:

Monday	Tuesday	Wednesday	Thursday	Friday
0 correct	1 correct	1 correct	2 corrects	3 corrects
3 errors	2 errors	2 errors	1 error	0 errors

Likewise, if Tammy and Teresa perform all of their problems correctly, Tammy receives a score of 5 corrects and no errors, while Teresa receives a score of 20 corrects and no errors. This counting system is well calibrated and allows the teacher to give positive feedback to students for improvement, even though perfection has not yet been attained.

Spelling. Similarly, when we were learning to spell, words were scored as either right or wrong. However, the same problems exist as in the case of measuring mathematics performance. Different words are of different length and improvement can be made in a given word over time without that improvement being recognized in the measurement system. Consider, for example, Amy's attempts to spell the word "teacher":

Monday	Tuesday	Wednesday	Thursday	Friday
trchm	teesh	teashr	teachr	teacher

Each day she improved; however, each answer, with the exception of Friday's, would be counted as one error, no corrects.

White and Haring (1980) suggested a rule similar to the mathematics rule: "number of correct letter sequences." According to this rule, written words are comprised of a series of stimulus-response sequences. Any given stimulus has a response that is expected to follow it. A scoring system is used in which a caret is placed underneath each correct sequence. For example, if Amy spells the word "teacher" correctly, her corrected paper would look like this:

$$\wedge^t \wedge^e \wedge^a \wedge^c \wedge^h \wedge^e \wedge^r \wedge$$

Her count for this word would be 8 corrects and no errors. Each mark indicates a correct *sequence* of behaviors. Going from a blank page to the *t* represents one correct sequence. Going from the *t* to the *e* is a second correct sequence, and so forth. Finally, stopping after the *r* is considered a correct sequence as well. Thus, for any word spelled correctly, the count will always equal the total number of letters in the word plus one, since credit is given for knowing when to stop.

When errors occur, they are indicated by a mark or caret above the incorrect sequence. Consider Amy's misspellings of "teacher":

Spelling	Scoring
$\wedge^t \wedge^e \vee^e \vee^c \wedge^h \wedge^e \wedge^r \wedge$	6 corrects; 2 errors
$\wedge^t \wedge^e \vee^c \wedge^h \wedge^e \wedge^r \wedge$	6 corrects; 1 error
$\wedge^t \wedge^e \wedge^a \wedge^c \wedge^h \wedge^e \vee$	6 corrects; 1 error
$\wedge^t \wedge^e \wedge^a \wedge^c \wedge^h \wedge^e \wedge^r \vee^r \wedge$	8 corrects; 1 error

In the first example, Amy substituted an extra *e* for the *a*. This counts as two errors, since the *e—e* sequence is incorrect and the *e—c* sequence is incorrect. In the second example, Amy left out the *a*. This counts as one error, since the *e—c* sequence is incorrect; all other sequences, however, are correct. In the third example, Amy left out the final *r*. Again, this counts as one error, since the *e* is not the correct ending of the word. In the final example, Amy added an extra *r* at the end. Eight correct sequences occur, with the one error being the *r—r* sequence.

Other Examples. The above examples demonstrate that an operationally defined skill does not necessarily constitute a well-calibrated measurement system. Calibration is essential to good measurement and must be considered when developing a counting system. Other examples of behaviors and ways to calibrate counts for them are displayed in Table 5.1.

Collecting Behavioral Counts

Once a behavior is defined and calibrated, observation must occur for data to be collected. Some behaviors, such as oral reading or solving math problems, can be observed using probes. **A probe** is a brief, structured presentation of a task for the

TABLE 5.1 Examples of Calibrating Behavioral Objectives

Behavior	Sample Counting Systems
Cuts with scissors	Number of snips
	Number of inches cut
	Number of snips within 1/4″ of line
Rides trike	Number of feet ridden
	Number of revolutions of pedals
	Number of seconds stays on
Draws a person	Number of body parts drawn
	Number of parts correctly placed
Matches block/bead color pattern	Number of blocks in correct sequence
Interacts with peers	Number of verbal initiations
	Number of verbal responses to peer initiations
	Number of peers with whom student interacts
Writes a story	Number of words written
	Number of different ideas expressed

purpose of collecting data. For example, a child might be asked to read orally for 2 minutes or to solve one page of math problems. If the reader or the math work sheet is representative of the words and math problems on which the student is presently working, such probes, conducted frequently, should provide an adequate measure of behavior. Other behaviors, such as social interactions, play skills, vocational skills, or language behaviors may need more extensive observation periods. Furthermore, some behaviors, such as toilet accidents or tantrums, may occur only a few times each day or less. For these events, a running count of each occurrence is necessary.

In order to collect observational data, the teacher must first prepare a data-collection sheet. According to Tawney & Gast (1984), a data form should include at least three parts. First, the form should provide space to record *situational information,* including the student's name, date and time of observation, beginning and ending times, the behaviors(s) observed, instructional strategy used, and the names of the persons conducting instruction and collecting data. Second, the form should provide adequate space to record *performance information.* Finally, the form should provide space for *summary information,* including total observation time, summaries of student performance, and comments. Examples of commonly used data collection sheets are displayed in Figures 5.1 through 5.6.

When recording a given event, at least three methods could be used: occurrence, duration, or latency.

Occurrence. Probably the most frequently used event-recording system is to code whether or not a specific behavior occurred, or whether a behavior was correct or incorrect. For example, the teacher could record each word read correctly, each problem solved, each talk-out, or each aggressive act. In all cases, the teacher makes an either-or choice: either the behavior happened or it did not. Examples of data collection sheets for occurrence data are displayed in Figure 5.1. In Figure

FIGURE 5.1 Sample data-collection sheets for occurrence data.

Name: __Barry__ Date: __11/1/88__
Behavior/Objective: __Reads CVC words__
Time: __10:00 – 10:05__

Trial	C	E	
1	✓		
2	✓		
3		✓	
4	✓		
5		✓	
6		✓	
7	✓		
8	✓		
9	✓		
10	✓		
Total	7	3	

Comments:
All errors
were on words
with "e" as
middle vowel

(a)

Student: __Scott__
Behavior: __Gets out of seat__
Week: __March 1-5, 1988__

Day	Time Observed	Record of Behaviors	Total
Monday	10:00 – 10:30	卌 ‖	7
Tuesday	10:30 – 11:00	卌 卌 ‖	11
Wednesday	10:00 – 10:30	‖‖	4
Thursday	10:10 – 10:40	卌 ‖	6
Friday	10:15 – 10:45	卌	5
Total			33

(b)

Student: __Yolinda__
Behavior: __Pants dry__
Dates: __Sept. 1-15, 1988__

Time	Checker	1	2	3	4	5	6	7	8	9	10	11	12	13	14	15
9:00	Jones	✓	✓	–	✓	✓	✓	✓	✓				–	✓	✓	✓
10:00	Jones	✓	–	–	✓	–	–	✓	✓				–	–	✓	✓
11:00	Jones	–	–	–	✓	✓	✓	✓	✓	ABSENT	ABSENT	ABSENT	✓	✓	–	✓
12:00	Smith	✓	✓	✓	✓	–	✓	✓	✓	ABSENT	ABSENT	ABSENT	✓	–	✓	✓
1:00	Smith	✓	✓	–	–	–	–	✓	✓				–	✓	✓	✓
Total Dry		4	3	1	4	2	3	5	5				2	3	4	5

✓ = dry; – = wet

(c)

Behavior: __Task Preparation__
Setting: __Small group__
Date: __4/3/88__

Student	Gets Out Workbook	Pencil Sharpened	Paper Available
Joshua	✓	✓	✓
Missy	✓	–	✓
Allison	–	–	–
Walter	✓	✓	✓
Barbara	–	✓	✓

✓ = Yes; – = No

(d)

5.1(a) Barry's teacher records his responses to CVC words. In Figure 5.1(b) Scott's teacher records the number of times he gets out of his seat during selected 30-minute observation periods. In Figure 5.1(c) Yolinda's teachers check her pants every hour as part of a toileting program. In Figure 5.1(d) the teacher records whether each of several students performs three tasks prior to initiating small-group instruction.

Duration.   **Duration** refers to the length of time an event occurs. It is determined by timing from the beginning of a behavior to the end of a behavior. Duration measures are particularly appropriate for behaviors or events that may vary in length. For example, Peggy throws temper tantrums in the preschool. Although the teacher could take data on the number of tantrums, the figure obtained each day may be misleading. For example, she could have one tantrum of 30 seconds and another of 5 minutes. Since tantrums are rarely the same length of time, duration would be a more useful measure. Other behaviors more appropriately measured using duration include length of time working in seat, amount of independent play, or amount of time spent using adaptive equipment. An example of a form for recording duration data is displayed in Figure 5.2.

Latency.   **Latency** refers to the length of time between the presentation of a cue, command, or prompt and the student's response to that cue. It is determined by timing from the end of the cue to the beginning of the response. For example, Charles takes a long time to begin cleaning up the room after his teacher asks him to do so. His teacher collects latency data each clean-up period by measuring the length of time between instructions to clean up and the commencement of clean-up behavior. An example of a form for recording latency data is displayed in Figure 5.3.

General Considerations in Event-Based Recording

The recording of events probably is the most frequently used method of counting behavior in special education. In implementing an event-based recording system, the following four factors should be considered.

Use the Appropriate Counting Procedure.   Occurrence, duration, and latency all can be appropriate measures depending on the context and the goals for instruction. The advantages and limitations described above should be considered in selecting the measurement procedure that (a) provides the greatest amount of information, (b) most accurately reflects the goals of instruction, (c) is easily collected by the teacher, and (d) is meaningful when interpreting performance.

Gather Data at the Appropriate Times.   Some behaviors (e.g., hitting) are never allowed. However, the appropriateness of many behaviors is determined by the

FIGURE 5.2 Sample data-collection sheet for duration data.

Name: _____Lorenzo_____ Date: ___3-23-88___

Behavior: _____On-task_____ Observer: ___Matthews___

Setting: __Workshop Assembly Station__ Time Observed: __10:00 - 12:00__

Start Time	Stop Time	Duration
10:00	10:20	20
10:25	10:42	18
11:10	11:45	35
11:50	12:00	10
Total Work Time		83 minutes

Comments:

_____

__11:10 - 11:45 Began yelling at coworker; had__

_____to be removed from work area__

_____for 10 minutes.__

context in which the behavior occurs. For example, talking to peers is appropriate and desirable during recess or breaks; however, it generally is not allowed during individual work time. Teachers should ensure that data are taken during representative times when desirable behavior is expected to occur, or when inappropriate behaviors are not expected to occur.

Check the Accuracy of Counts. The process of observing and counting behavior is subject to considerable error, particularly if counting is done directly while the behavior is occurring. It is important to check periodically the accuracy of counting and recording procedures.

Keep Time Records for Occurrence Data. Often teachers will want to summarize

FIGURE 5.3 Sample form for recording latency data.

Student: ___Charles___   Behavior: __Begins center clean-__
                                                      __up when requested__

Dates: ___April 1-5, 1988___   Observer: ___Fields___
Setting: _____Morning and afternoon free play_____

Date	Morning Latency	Afternoon Latency
4/1	80 seconds	120 seconds
4/2	53 seconds	97 seconds
4/3	100 seconds	135 seconds
4/4	63 seconds	99 seconds
4/5	40 seconds	105 seconds
Average Latency	67.2 seconds	111.2 seconds

occurrence data in relation to time. For example, rather than saying that Juan hit five times, the teacher could say that he hit five times in a 10-minute period. As will be described in Chapter 6, time records allow the teacher to calculate rate data. This requires the teacher to record beginning and ending times for observation. However, Billingsley and Liberty (1982) suggested that teachers need to take care to ensure that the time recorded includes only the student's behavior and not the teacher's. For example, Alex, who is severely handicapped, is learning to assemble objects in preparation for prevocational placement. His teacher, Mr. Taylor, is counting the number of parts assembled during work periods. At 9:00 he tells Alex to begin working, and begins observing his performance. At 9:05 Alex makes an assembly error. Mr. Taylor stops his work, models the correct assembly, and then tells Alex to continue. Alex makes four more errors over the next half hour and, each time an error is made, Mr. Taylor repeats the correction procedure. At 9:30 he tells Alex to take a break. In the 30-minute period, Alex assembled 60 parts correctly and 5 parts incorrectly. However, the 30-minute period includes 5 minutes of time when Alex was not able to assemble parts, since Mr. Taylor took that amount of time to point out errors and model correct performance. To be fair to Alex, the 5 minutes should be subtracted from the total time prior to computing assembly rate.

Billingsley and Liberty (1982) differentiated between interrupted and uninterrupted systems for gathering data. **Interrupted measurement** is used when "the manipulation of antecedent stimuli and/or response consequences precludes repeated uninterrupted responding by the pupil; however antecedents and/or consequences will be faded or replaced" (p. 51). In other words, if the ultimate goal is independence on a task, the counting system should reflect what happens when the student is free to work independently. Mr. Taylor should stop the stopwatch whenever he interrupts Alex's work. Once he has completed his correction procedures, the watch is started again. This is in contrast to a situation in which the student is free to respond at his or her own rate without interruption from the teacher. For example, Mr. Taylor may ask Alex to read a set of simple instructions. Alex is allowed to read for one minute without correction or interruption.

TIME-BASED RECORDING

When using event-based recording, data are recorded whenever certain events occur, such as a talk-out or a hit. The event is the stimulus for the teacher to record the behavior. An alternative is referred to as **time-based recording.** In time-based recording, the teacher records data according to specified time intervals or at specific points in time. Time, not the event, becomes the stimulus for the teacher to record the behavior. In its simplest form, time-sampling refers to the process of observing for short intervals of time (often 10 seconds or less) and coding one category of behavior for each interval. After a number of intervals have been observed, a summary of all observations is used to determine the overall picture of behavior. Three basic decisions must be made by the teacher prior to using a time-based recording strategy: (1) the behavior or set of behaviors to be observed, (2) the length of the observation interval, and (3) rules of deciding whether to record the behavior.

The Behaviors to be Recorded

Time-based recording can be used with discrete events, such as speaking, touching, and writing, as well as with behaviors for which it is difficult to obtain a single count. For example, to determine the extent of time Latisha spends engaged in "cooperative play" at recess, it may not be meaningful to count the number of cooperative events, since many play activities are extended in nature. Furthermore, within a given 5-minute period, many specific cooperative behaviors may occur. Since it would be difficult to count them all, a system that samples the amount of time spent in cooperative play often is used.

Time-based recording can take an occurrence/nonoccurrence format, in which one behavior or class of behaviors (e.g., time on task) is coded as either occurring or not occurring. Time-based recording is also used to determine the occurrence of a variety of behaviors within a given time frame. For example, the teacher may be interested in how a student spends his or her time during a one-hour work period. A time-based recording system could be used to determine the proportion of time spent in work activities, peer interactions, looking out the window, and walking around the room. To count all of these events simultaneously would be a difficult task. However, using certain rules, time-sampling can provide an accurate estimate of the distribution of activities within a given block of time.

Systems for Coding Multiple Categories of Behavior. Many systems for coding multiple categories of behavior have been reported in the published literature. An example of a coding system described by Rhode, Morgan, and Young (1983) is displayed in Table 5.2. The system includes seven categories of appropriate classroom behavior and eight categories of inappropriate classroom behavior. The purpose of the coding system was to determine the extent to which work and behavior skills learned in a resource room generalized to the regular classroom. The categories selected for inclusion were behaviors deemed appropriate and important for success by regular classroom teachers.

Although use of existing codes is preferable, it may be difficult to find a code tailored for the purpose intended. Teachers often must develop coding systems to meet individual needs for data collection. For a coding system to be manageable and provide useful information, several factors must be considered.

Clearly Defined Categories. Often, a coding system will contain categories that include a variety of behaviors. Although it can be useful to group certain behaviors together, it is important to define clearly what constitutes examples and nonexamples of behavior in each category. For example, assume that Ms. Miller develops a coding system for social behavior. One category is aggressive behavior. What behaviors should be included in that category? Certainly hitting, biting, pushing, kicking, or grabbing would be included. But how about name-calling or teasing? What if a student is trying to get another student to do something that student does not want to do? Categories must be defined such that there is little doubt in the observer's mind as to what category a given behavior should be placed.

Exhaustive and Mutually Exclusive Categories. A coding system should be **exhaustive,** which means that any behavior observed should fit into one of the categories defined. Of course, it is difficult to anticipate every possible behavior; also, the teacher may only be interested in certain behaviors. Usually, coding systems have a category referred to as "other," in which all behaviors not fitting one of the previously defined categories are placed. Use of the "other" category allows for completeness of data in that all blocks of observed time are accounted for. However, effective use of this category requires careful definition of all behaviors of interest so they do not get placed in the "other" category because no appropriate code exists.

TABLE 5.2 Sample Observation Code for Classroom Behavior

I. Appropriate Classroom Behavior	*II. Inappropriate Behavior*
1. *Attend*—The student is looking at the teacher when the teacher is talking or presenting information to the individual or class, looking at materials in the classroom that have to do with the lesson, or looking at a peer who is presenting related academic information to the class. Attending behavior is characterized by eye contact with (and head and body orientation in the direction of) the appropriate classroom objects (teacher or task).	1. *Talking Out*—The student speaks without permission or interrupts the teacher and another student who are talking to each other.
2. *Work*—The student is engaged in or is completing teacher-assigned tasks. Work responses are characterized by nonverbal, motor movements if a written response is required. If the student is reading, progressive eye movement and page turning are evidenced.	2. *Out-of-Chair*—Movement of the student from his chair when not permitted. Such movement may include leaving the chair to open the window, remove items or threaten to remove items from the teacher's or other students' desks, name-calling, and moving around the room.
3. *Volunteer*—The student raises his hand to offer information or otherwise offers an appropriate response related to the ongoing academic activity in response to a teacher's question or suggestion.	3. *Modified Out-of-Chair*—Movement of the student from his chair with some part of the body still touching the chair (excluding sitting on feet).
4. *Reading Aloud*—The student is observed to be orally reading during the reading period or when asked to do so by the teacher. The student can be reading any form of printed material ranging from books, charts, blackboard or word cards.	4. *Noise*—The student creates any audible noise other than vocalization.
5. *Answering Questions*—The student will answer questions when called on to do so by the teacher.	5. *Rocking*—The student lifts one or more of his chair legs from the floor while he is seated in his chair.
6. *Asking the Teacher a Question*—After raising his hand to gain teacher attention, the student asks the teacher a question when she calls on him.	6. *Noncompliance*—Failure by the student to initiate the appropriate response as requested by the teacher.
7. *Other*—The student exhibits appropriate classroom behavior as determined by classroom rules in operation in the classroom.	7. *Aggression*—The student makes movement toward another person so as to come into contact with him, whether directly or by using a material object as an extension of the hand.
	8. *Other*—The student clearly violates school or classroom rules or engages in behavior which prevents him from engaging in learning tasks and which are not otherwise specifically defined. Such behavior must be determined by the rules in operation in students' classrooms. Examples of such behavior may include engaging singly in activities or tasks not approved by the teacher or related to the assigned academic tasks (i.e., combing hair, writing on desk, looking at or handling objects within the immediate area surrounding the student's desk or work area, not appropriate to the academic task at hand).

Note: From "Generalization and Maintenance of Treatment Gains of Behaviorally Handicapped Students from Resource Rooms to Regular Classrooms Using Self-Evaluation Procedures" by G. Rhode, D. P. Morgan, and R. K. Young, 1983, *Journal of Applied Behavior Analysis, 16,* p. 178. Reprinted with permission.

A coding system also should be **mutually exclusive.** That is, no overlap should exist across categories. It should be impossible for an observed behavior to fit into two different categories. For example, you might define a category called "sitting at desk" and one called "looking out window," both of which are important behaviors to document. However, a given student can be doing both at the same time. Since most time-sampling systems allow only one category to be coded for a given time interval, the observer would be in a quandry as to what category to code. Variations in coding systems exist such that it is possible to code more than one behavior category in a given interval. This changes the manner in which data are summarized, but may be necessary for some behaviors.

Simple Systems. Finally, a coding system should include only as many categories as necessary to answer the question being asked. Since behavior is quite variable, large numbers of categories of behavior could be generated. However, as more categories are generated, the more difficult it becomes to use the observational system accurately and efficiently. If categories are of little interest or do not relate to the questions being asked or decisions to be made based on data, those categories should not be included. At minimum, all behaviors of interest should be included. In cases where behaviors have been targeted for elimination or reduction, the desired replacement response should be counted. With most academic responses, this condition is quite straightforward; that is, one records both correct and error responses. When attempting to count and reduce George's "looking out of the window" behaviors, a teacher also should define and include categories that measure what he is doing when he is not looking out the window, for example, eyes on work, looking at peers or teacher, or eyes closed. George may look out the window less, but if he is sleeping instead, he has failed to acquire a suitable replacement behavior.

The Observation Interval

The second decision regarding observational procedures is deciding how often to code behavior. In event sampling, the teacher makes a record of behavior whenever an event occurs. In time-based recording, the teacher takes data at prespecified points in time, and records whatever behavior is occurring at that time. For example, Ms. Siler might decide to code Zack's classroom behavior at 10-minute intervals using the scale described in Table 5.2. Ms. Farrington, on the other hand, might decide to code Dana's behavior at 30-second intervals.

The length of the interval should be determined by several factors. First, how often do the target behaviors occur? It is important that enough intervals be observed to ensure that the sample is representative of true behavioral patterns. Second, under what conditions are the behaviors expected? If the behaviors are expected for only a short or specific portion of the day, frequent counts should be made during that short period. If the behaviors are expected throughout the day, longer intervals should be incorporated. Finally, the teacher's schedule and responsibilities will, in part, determine the frequency of observation. If the period is one in which the teacher must also be instructing students, frequent observations may be impossible.

Once an interval has been determined, an observation coding form is developed. The purpose of this form is to allow easy recording of behavior at the predetermined intervals. A sample coding sheet to accompany the categories of classroom behavior described in Table 5.2 is displayed in Figure 5.4. In this example, Ms. Siler is coding Zack's classroom behavior at 10-minute intervals. At the end of each interval, she checks the category that best describes his behavior. An alternate form for collecting the same data would consist of a box for each time interval in which the teacher would write an abbreviation or code that best describes his category of behavior.

Usually, teachers need some system for reminding them when to code behavior. One simple system is to use easily identifiable times for coding—for example, every half hour, on the hour or on the half-hour mark. However, frequent coding may necessitate use of a timer or other reminder system. For

FIGURE 5.4   Sample form for category recording of classroom behavior.

Student: _Zack_   Date: _2/18/88_
Setting: _Independent Work_   Observer: _Siler_
Start Time: _9:00_   Stop Time: _12:00_

10-Minute Intervals	APPROPRIATE							INAPPROPRIATE							
	Attend	Work	Volunteer	Read Aloud	Answer Questions	Ask Questions	Other	Talking-Out	Out-of-Chair	Modified Out-of-Chair	Noise	Rocking	Non-compliance	Aggression	Other
:10		✓													
:20		✓													
:30		✓													
:40	✓														
:50	✓														
1:00								✓							
:10								✓							
:20								✓							
:30												✓			
:40												✓			
:50														✓	
2:00														✓	
:10	✓														
:20	✓														
:30	✓														
:40		✓													
:50				✓											
3:00		✓													
Total #	5	5		1				3				2		2	
% of Observations	27.8	27.8		5.6				16.7				11.1		11.1	

example, a digital watch could be programmed to beep in 10 minutes. If data are collected every 10 or 15 seconds, the teacher will either need to look at a watch almost continuously or to have a tape player or other timer that emits a sound at prespecified intervals to signal the teacher that it is time to record.

Rules for Deciding Whether to Code Behaviors

At least three techniques can be used to code behaviors (Cooper, Heron, & Heward, 1987; Powell, Martindale, & Kulp, 1975; Sulzer-Azaroff & Mayer, 1977). The first is referred to as the **whole-interval** method. Under this system, a behavior is coded only if it occurs during the entire observation interval. For example, using the code sheet displayed in Table 5.2, Zack's behavior could only be coded as "Attending" if he attended for the entire 10-minute interval. The whole interval method is problemmatic for several reasons. First, it underestimates the true occurrence of behavior, since many behaviors will not last the entire interval of observation. Second, it is a demanding system for teachers since it requires continuous observation to know whether the behavior has, in fact, occurred for the entire interval.

A second technique is referred to as the **partial-interval** method. Under this system, a behavior is coded if it occurred during any part of the observation interval. For example, if Zack attended for any portion of the 10-minute interval, it would be coded. This method is problemmatic in that it tends to overestimate the true occurrence of behavior. Furthermore, since several behaviors could occur during the interval, which one would be coded?

The third technique is referred to as the **momentary** method. Under this system, the behavior occurring at precisely the interval mark is the one that is coded. For example, after 10 minutes, Ms. Siler looks at Zack and records the behavior in which he is engaged at that time. Given a sufficient number of observations at appropriate times, this method results in the most accurate representation of true behavior. Furthermore, it is the easiest method for teachers since they can be involved in other activities between intervals. However, this method is not sensitive to behaviors of short duration, and tends to underestimate behavior if the interval is too long.

LEVELS-OF-ASSISTANCE RECORDING SYSTEMS

When exceptional children are first learning skills, they often need various forms of assistance from teachers in order to be successful. Chapters 12 and 14 are devoted to a description of techniques for using teacher assistance effectively. Since many children would exhibit *no* correct performances without some level of assistance, a data collection and counting system is needed that shows progress toward independent performance. In other words, the data should reflect

FIGURE 5.5   Two methods of recording levels-of-assistance data.

Steps	Trials 1	2	3	4	5
_____					
_____					
_____					
_____					
_____					
_____					

Prompt Level	Trials
I	1 2 3 4 5 6 7 8 9 10
VP	1 2 3 4 5 6 7 8 9 10
G	1 2 3 4 5 6 7 8 9 10
M	1 2 3 4 5 6 7 8 9 10
PP	1 2 3 4 5 6 7 8 9 10
FM	1 2 3 4 5 6 7 8 9 10

(a)   (b)

Key: FM = Full physical manipulation; PP = Partial physical prompt; M = Model; G = Gesture prompt; VP = Verbal prompt; I = Independent

decreasing levels of teacher assistance toward that first independent performance of a task.

A **levels–of–assistance recording system** is a variation of event sampling. However, instead of a binary scoring system (the student either did or did not perform the behavior), multiple levels of performance are used to indicate level of independence. For example, assume that Jeremy is learning to button his shirt. His teacher, Mr. Fogg, identifies four levels of assistance to be used: full manipulation, partial physical assistance, modeling, and verbal cues. Instead of recording correct or error performance on each trial, Mr. Fogg records the level of assistance required on that trial in order for a correct response to occur.

Two methods of recording levels-of-assistance data are displyed in Figure 5.5. In Figure 5.5(a) the teacher writes down the assistance code for each trial attempted with the student. In Figure 5.5(b) the levels of assistance are provided for 10 trials, and the teacher simply circles the level required for each trial.

TASK-ANALYTIC RECORDING SYSTEMS

Task analysis is the process of breaking a given task down into specific steps. The purpose of task analysis is to identify discrete behaviors that can be taught. For example, Gaylord-Ross, Haring, Breen, and Pitts-Conway (1984) described a task analysis for social skills training, the purpose of which is to teach an autistic youth to interact with a nonhandicapped peer in the context of playing Pac Man. The steps in the task analysis are displayed in Figure 5.6. The figure also incorporates a system suggested by Bellamy, Horner, and Inman (1979) for

FIGURE 5.6 Recording task-analytic data.

Task	Trials
18. AS says "bye."	18 18 18 18 18
17. AS offers game to NS	17 17 17 17 17
16. AS reads own score	16 16 16 16 16
15. AS plays game	15 15 15 15 15
14. AS turns game on; resets score to zero	14 14 14 14 14
13. AS turns game off	13 13 13 13 13
12. AS reads NS score	12 12 12 12 12
11. AS receives game from NS	11 11 11 11 11
10. AS watches NS play	10 10 10 10 10
9. AS hands game to NS	9 9 9 9 9
8. AS turns game on	8 8 8 8 8
7. AS waits for response; finds someone else if none	7 7 7 7 7
6. AS says "want to play?"	6 6 6 6 6
5. AS waits for response	5 5 5 5 5
4. AS says "hi"	4 4 4 4 4
3. AS establishes a face-forward orientation	3 3 3 3 3
2. AS establishes 1 meter proximity	2 2 2 2 2
1. AS approaches NS	1 1 1 1 1

Key: AS = autistic student; NS = Nonhandicapped student.

Note. Task analysis from "The Training and Generalization of Social Interaction Skills with Autistic Youth," by R. J. Gaylord-Ross, T. G. Haring, C. Breen, and O. Pitts-Conway, 1984, *Journal of Applied Behavior Analysis, 17,* pp. 229-247. Scoring format from *Vocational Habilitation of Severely Retarded Adults: A Direct Service Technology* by G. Bellamy, R. Horner, and D. Inman, 1979, Baltimore: University Park Press.

recording whether or not each step in the sequence was performed correctly. (Correct steps are circled, whereas a slash is drawn through incorrect steps.) Data are then summarized either as the number or percentage of steps performed correctly.

RELIABILITY

Reliability refers to consistency in measurement. Any time one measures something, whether it be the weight of an object or the behavior of a person, that measurement is subject to error. Error in measurement is accepted as a fact of life in education, since "live" data are difficult to collect. However, it is important that counts be as accurate and consistent as possible; otherwise, inappropriate decisions may be made due to faulty data. Teachers should be aware of common sources of error in measurement, able to assess reliability of counts, and able to describe and implement procedures that increase the likelihood of accurate data collection.

Sources of Error in Measurement

What causes error in measurement? Kazdin (1977) described four common sources.

Complexity of the Measurement System and the Behaviors to be Coded. One source of error is the measurement system itself. The accuracy of measurement decreases as (a) the observational system becomes more complex, (b) data are collected more frequently, and (c) more complex behaviors are assessed. It is relatively easy to count the number of times a student raises his or her hand to ask a question. It is much more difficult to observe every 10 seconds and code one of 12 categories of social behavior.

Observer Drift. When an observational code is first developed, the person using it either receives training in its use or studies it carefully and practices using it. However, as data collection proceeds, the observer may "drift" from the original definition of the behaviors. Kazdin (1977) described **observer drift** as "the tendency of observers to change the manner in which they apply the definitions of behavior over time" (p. 143). For example, assume that one coding category is "aggressive behavior." At first, the teacher codes slight pushing while waiting in line as aggressive behavior. However, as time passes, many instances of much more aggressive behavior, such as hitting, biting, pulling hair, or kicking, are observed. The teacher may be less likely to code pushing in line as aggressive behavior when it is compared with other more serious behaviors. Although the data over time may depict a decrease in the counts of aggressive behavior, the decrease could be due to observe drift rather than actual change in behavior.

Observer Expectancies or Bias. The person who designs and implements an instructional program generally expects that program to work. Although it is important to have a positive attitude, those expectations may affect one's perceptions of behaviors. For example, during baseline (a preintervention period) the teacher may count aggressive behaviors, describing every one that occurs in order to point out the extent of the problem to parents or administrators. Once the teacher begins the program, however, expectations for success may change, and those expectations may cause him or her, without knowing it, to be less stringent in counting aggressive acts.

Observer Reactivity. Several studies have shown that observers improve their reliability if they know that reliability is being checked (Reid, 1970; Romanczyk, Kent, Diament, & O'Leary, 1973), a phenomenon known as **observer reactivity.** This finding suggests that carelessness is also a major problem affecting accuracy of measurement.

Calculating Reliability

In order to determine the accuracy of recording procedures, teachers should occasionally conduct reliability checks. Two basic approaches could be taken. One is referred to as **intrarater reliability.** In this procedure, the teacher rechecks his or her own data. For example, permanent product data, such as a math facts work sheet, could be checked twice to see if the same score is obtained both times. Or, if the teacher has access to a videotape recorder, sample observation periods could be taped and the teacher could compare live observations with data obtained by viewing the videotape in a more leisurely fashion. However, few teachers have access to videotape equipment or the time to view and code tapes. Furthermore, intrarater reliability does not address issues of observer drift or reactivity.

The most commonly used approach in applied behavior analysis is the assessment of **interrater reliability.** In this procedure, two observers gather data at the same time or score the same permanent product data. *Reliability* is defined as the extent to which the two observers agree on the data and usually is reported as percentage of agreement. Although the calculation of reliability estimates has been and continues to be an issue in the field of applied behavior analysis (Hartmann, 1977; Kratochwill & Wetzel, 1977), simple and accurate estimates are available for use by teachers.

Occurrence Data. To determine interrater reliability of occurrence data, two formulas are generally used. The first is:

$$\frac{\text{Smaller Count}}{\text{Larger Count}} \times 100 = \% \text{ Agreement}$$

If one observer, for example, counted 8 occurrences of out-of-seat behavior and the second observer counted 9 occurrences, reliability would be 8/9 × 100 or 89%. This formula provides a global estimate of interrater agreement, although it has been criticized since it is possible that the two observers actually disagreed on specific observations. They just happened to get close to the same total. A more precise formula is:

$$\frac{\text{Number of Agreements}}{\text{Number of Agreements + Disagreements}} \times 100 = \% \text{ Agreement}$$

To determine the figures that are entered into this equation, two observers independently observe and record the occurrence of events according to intervals or blocks of time. A point-by-point (Kelly, 1977) or exact agreement (Repp, Deitz, Boles, Deitz, & Repp, 1976) method is used to determine the total number of specific notations of events recorded by both observers. This number becomes the numerator in the equation. To that figure is added the total number of specific notations made by either one or the other of the observers. That number becomes the denominator in the equation.

For example, Mr. Clemmons asked Mr. Greene to observe social initiations during outdoor play. They agreed on 21 initiations. Mr. Clemmons coded an additional 3 initiations not seen by Mr. Greene, while Mr. Greene coded 1 additional initiation not seen by Mr. Clemmons. Thus, their reliability would be calculated as follows:

$$\frac{21}{21 + 3 + 1} \times 100 = \frac{21}{25} \times 100 = 84\%$$

Duration and Latency Data. The reliability of duration and latency data is determined by the following formula:

$$\frac{\text{Shorter Duration or Latency Count}}{\text{Longer Duration or Latency Count}} \times 100 = \% \text{ Agreement}$$

For example, Mr. Clemmons and Mr. Greene also observed the duration of Emily's solitary play. Mr. Clemmons recorded 8.5 minutes while Mr. Greene recorded 10 minutes. Thus, their reliability would be calculated as follows:

$$\frac{8.5}{10} \times 100 = 85\%$$

Time-Based Data. The reliability of time-sampling data uses a similar agreement formula, calculated as follows:

$$\frac{\text{Number of Intervals of Agreement}}{\text{Number of Intervals of Agreement} + \text{Number of Disagreements}} \times 100$$

For example, Mr. Clemmons and Mr. Greene coded Sam's social behavior at 15-second intervals. They agreed on 35 intervals and disagreed on 15. Thus, their reliability would be calculated as follows:

$$\frac{35}{35 + 15} \times 100 = \frac{35}{50} \times 100 = 70\%$$

Acceptable Levels of Reliability. A frequently asked question concerns acceptable levels of reliability. Generally speaking, reliability above 90% is desirable. Reliability below 80% indicates significant measurement problems and questions the usefulness of the data collected.

Improving Reliability

Collecting reliability data is a time-consuming process and frequently is not possible. At the least, however, teachers should take care to ensure that the procedures used to gather data have a high probability of resulting in consistent counts. Guidelines to follow include:

1. Be sure to define clearly, in operational terms, the behaviors to be observed and counted.
2. Clearly describe the procedures to be followed in observing and coding behavior, and then adhere to them.
3. Practice prior to actual observations.
4. Record data immediately; do not wait to record it at a later time.
5. Use equipment, such as stopwatches, tape recorders, beepers, or videotapes to improve accuracy.

Skrtic and Sepler (1982) described strategies for simplifying the monitoring of several behaviors for several students simultaneously. Of course, when reporting data to colleagues in professional meetings or in making definitive conclusions about intervention effectiveness, reliability data must be gathered and reported.

COMPUTER-ASSISTED DATA COLLECTION

One of the most significant technological changes in America's classrooms is the use of microcomputers by students and teachers alike. As microcomputers become increasingly available, software or programs to perform many routine tasks are also being made available. Now and increasingly in the next few years, teachers can use microcomputers to facilitate data collection. The technology and programs available are growing so rapidly, we will not describe specific programs. However, teachers should be aware of several facts.

First, many student-operated programs have built-in routines for monitoring performance. For example, a reading comprehension program might automatically count the number of comprehension questions correctly answered by a student. Often, such programs can store several days of data for an entire class of students. This feature relieves the teacher of the task of rating performance and recording level of accuracy. A printout summarizing performance by a student over time can be obtained. Warren and Horn (1987), described a system for automatically monitoring the performance of toddlers with severe handicaps engaged in motor development programs.

Second, other programs exist that are not a part of an instructional software package, but rather are devoted entirely to data collection and management. One of the earliest and most comprehensive of such programs was developed by Hasselbring and Hamlett (1983). The program, known as *AIMSTAR,* allows the teacher to store and retrieve rate, duration, latency, accuracy, or task-analytic data. Entries may be made daily or at other intervals convenient for the teacher. The program also can create and print charts, as described in Chapter 6.

Third, many school systems are now employing computer specialists whose job is to facilitate the use of microcomputers in educational settings. Teachers should consult such specialists for assistance in designing data-collection procedures for their classroom. Finally, teachers should attempt to keep current on recent developments in microcomputer technology. For example, the journal *Research in Developmental Disabilities* has a regular software review section.

Summary of Key Concepts

■ Defining and measuring behaviors are important because they help to pinpoint student status, monitor progress and determine effectiveness, provide feedback to students and parents, document efforts, and demonstrate accountability.

■ The first step in developing a measurement system is to define the behaviors to be counted. Behaviors should be defined in operational terms and should be well-calibrated. That is, each repetition of the behavior should represent essentially the same amount of behavior, the counting system should be directly related to instructional objectives, it must be possible to assess the behavior easily, and the counting system must be sensitive to changes in behavior.

■ Several common techniques may be used to measure student behavior. Event-based recording describes the accuracy, frequency, rate, percentage, duration, or latency of events. Time-based recording allows for the periodic coding of discrete behaviors as well as categories of behavior. Other systems exist to document the level of assistance required to perform a behavior or to count the number of steps in a task performed correctly.

REFERENCES

Bellamy, G., Horner, R., & Inman, D. (1979). *Vocational habilitation of severely retarded adults: A* *direct service technology.* Baltimore: University Park Press.

Billingsley, F. F., & Liberty, K. A. (1982). The use of time-based data in instructional programs for the severely handicapped. *The Association for the Severely Handicapped Journal, 7*(1), 47–55.

Cooper, J. O., Heron, T. E., & Heward, W. L. (1987). *Applied behavior analysis.* Columbus, OH: Merrill.

Fuchs, L. S., & Fuchs, D. L. (1986). Effects of systematic formative evaluation: A meta-analysis. *Exceptional Children, 53,* 199–208.

Gaylord-Ross, R. J., Haring, T. G., Breen, C., & Pitts-Conway, V. (1984). The training and generalization of social interaction skills with autistic youth. *Journal of Applied Behavior Analysis, 17,* 229–247.

Hartmann, D. P. (1977). Considerations in the choice of interobserver reliability estimates. *Journal of Applied Behavior Analysis, 10,* 103–116.

Hasselbring, T. S., & Hamlett, C. L. (1983). *AIM-STAR.* Portland, OR: ASIEP Education Company.

Kazdin, A. E. (1977). Artifact, bias, and complexity of assessment: The ABC's of reliability. *Journal of Applied Behavior Analysis, 10,* 141–150.

Kelly, M. B. (1977). A review of the observational data-collection and reliability procedures reported in the Journal of Applied Behavior Analysis. *Journal of Applied Behavior Analysis, 10,* 97–101.

Kratochwill, T. R., & Wetzel, R. J. (1977). Observer agreement, credibility, and judgment: Some considerations in presenting observer agreement data. *Journal of Applied Behavior Analysis, 10,* 133–139.

Powell, J., Martindale, A., & Kulp, S. (1975). An evaluation of time-sample measures of behavior. *Journal of Applied Behavior Analysis, 8,* 463–469.

Reid, J. B. (1970). Reliability assessment of observation data: A possible methodological problem. *Child Development, 41,* 1143–1150.

Repp, A. C., Deitz, D. E. D., Boles, S. M., Deitz, S. M., & Repp, C. F. (1976). Differences among common methods for calculating interobserver agreement. *Journal of Applied Behavior Analysis, 9,* 109–113.

Romanczyk, R. G., Kent, R. N., Diament, C., & O'Leary, K. D. (1973). Measuring the reliability of observational data: A reactive process. *Journal of Applied Behavior Analysis, 6,* 175–184.

Skrtic, T. M., & Sepler, H. J. (1982). Simplifying continuous monitoring of multiple-response/multiple-subject classroom interactions. *Journal of Applied Behavior Analysis, 15,* 183–187

Sulzer-Azaroff, B., & Mayer, G. R. (1977). *Applying behavior-analysis procedures with children and youth.* New York: Holt, Rinehart, and Winston.

Tawney, J. W., & Gast, D. L. (1984). *Single subject research in special education.* Columbus, OH: Merrill.

Warren, S. F., & Horn, H. M. (1987). Microcomputer applications in early childhood special education: Problems and Possibilities. *Topics in Early Childhood Special Education, 7*(2), 72–84.

White, K. P., Wyne, M. D., Stuck, G. B., & Coop, R. H. (1983). *Teaching effectiveness evaluation project. Final report.* Chapel Hill: University of North Carolina, School of Education.

White, O. R., & Haring, N. G. (1980). *Exceptional teaching* (2nd ed.). Columbus, OH: Charles E. Merrill.

6

SUMMARIZING BEHAVIORAL PERFORMANCE: QUANTITATIVE METHODS

Key Terms

■ Frequency ■ Percentage ■ Rate ■ Duration ■ Latency ■ Central
Tendency ■ Mean ■ Median ■ Mode ■ Variability ■ Range ■
■ Standard Deviation ■ Trend

When used regularly and systematically, the procedures for collecting data described in Chapter 5 provide important information for instructional monitoring and decision-making. However, data-collection sheets accumulate quickly, and can become a mass of counts and numbers filed away in a drawer, never to be seen again. For most teachers, if these data are to be useful, they must be summarized in some meaningful fashion (Gentry & Haring, 1976; Haynes & Wilson, 1979; Sackett, 1978). Through systematic summary and analysis of data, the original goals of data collection (monitoring progress; instructional decision-making; accountability; communication to students, parents, and other professionals) can be achieved.

SUMMARIZING EVENT-BASED DATA

Daily behavioral performance can be summarized in several different ways. Each method has advantages and disadvantages. The basic rule is to use the data summary method that most accurately describes the behavior and most directly relates to the dimension of behavior targeted in the student's objective. Event-based data may be described in terms of frequency, percentage, rate, duration, or latency measures.

Frequency of Events

Frequency is defined as the number of times an event occurs. It can be used alone as data but also is a necessary first step before percentage or rate measures can be calculated. Examples of frequency data are:

- Betty read 57 words correctly.
- Andrew had 4 toilet accidents.
- Carl got out of his seat 18 times.

Frequencies provide a count of behaviors or events and as such can be very useful. However, frequency counts often are difficult to interpret without some further frame of reference. Usually, a time reference or a task reference is needed for frequency data to make sense and for data to be comparable across various sampling periods. For example, did Betty read 57 out of 57 words correctly or 57 out of 100? Did Andrew have 4 accidents in a month or in one day? Did Carl get out of his seat 18 times in one day or one week? Assuming a standard set of tasks (e.g., 100 words to read) or a standard time frame (e.g., daily assessments), frequency data are more meaningful and comparable. However, in most cases, frequency data are converted to percentage data or rate data.

Percentage of Events

Percentage describes the proportion of certain events occurring out of a total of possible opportunities. Percentage is calculated as:

$$\frac{\text{Number of Events}}{\text{Total Number of Opportunities}} \times 100$$

Percentage is used for two primary purposes. One purpose is to describe the *accuracy* of a student's performance. For example, Nancy completed a work sheet consisting of 40 addition problems. If the teacher scores each problem as right or wrong, and Nancy gets 30 right, the percentage of correct problems would be calculated as:

$$\frac{30 \text{ (Number of Corrects)}}{40 \text{ (Total Number of Problems)}} = .75 \times 100 = 75\%$$

In order to determine percentage of errors, the percentage correct is simply subtracted from 100.

A second use of percentage is to describe the *proportion of time* something occurs. For example, Ralph's teacher is interested in monitoring the proportion of recess time that Ralph spends alone in solitary play. On Wednesday, Ralph engaged in solitary play for 10 minutes out of a 30-minute recess. In this case, the percentage of solitary play time would be calculated as:

$$\frac{10 \text{ (Number of Minutes Alone)}}{30 \text{ (Total Recess Time)}} = .33 \times 100 = 33\%$$

Percentage is an extremely useful measure for the two purposes described above. It provides a procedure for converting frequency data into a standard format such that comparisons across measures are possible. If other factors related to time or number of tasks vary, frequency counts are virtually impossible to compare. For example, examine the following hypothetical data of Ralph's solitary play over a 1-week period:

Day	Number of Minutes Alone	Total Recess Time	Solitary Play, %
Monday	10	15	67
Tuesday	10	20	50
Wednesday	10	25	40
Thursday	10	30	33
Friday	10	50	20

Looking only at a frequency count (number of minutes engaged in solitary play), one would have to conclude that Ralph's solitary play was quite stable over time. However, the length of recess time varied each day; in fact, the proportion or percentage of time Ralph engaged in solitary play decreased each day of the week. Percentages provide a different perspective on Ralph's behavior and allow for more meaningful comparisons across time. Finally, percentage data are useful because most people understand them and recognize that doing something at 80% correct is better than at 50%.

Percentage data suffer two major limitations, however. The first is that they do not provide information about the absolute number of times an event was observed, the total number of opportunities, or total length of time within which events were noted. For example, a teacher may tell Ralph's parents that he spent 50% of his time in solitary play on Wednesday. The percentage may be relatively unimportant for a recess lasting 15 minutes but more relevant when compared to a 55-minute recess activity. A similar analogy can be made with number of opportunities to respond. It is important to provide setting or frame-of-reference information so proper interpretations and evaluations can be made. The second limitation is much more serious. Although percentage statements can clearly reflect the accuracy of student performance, they tell us nothing about the student's speed or fluency of performance. Percentage data have a definite ceiling; you cannot get any better than 100%. However, you can continue to improve, even after reaching 100% correct, by increasing your speed. For example, Mary can complete a page of 20 multiplication problems at 100% correct; however, it takes her 2 hours to finish. Before multiplication will be useful for her, she must work faster. To document speed of performance we need to use rate measures.

When using percentage data, two additional considerations are important. First, the calculation of percentages is greatly facilitated using easy-to-calculate denominators such as 20, 25, or 50. Designing work sheets or observational sessions to result in such denominators can save time and reduce errors. Second, teachers need to be aware that, when the denominator is very small, a change in one event will result in a large change in percentage data. For example, Rosalin's teacher gives her five single-digit math problems in a daily probe. If Rosalin gets two correct on one day and three correct on the next, her percentage correct jumps from 40% to 60% and may not reflect her true average if given more than five problems. Likewise, when students are making relatively slow progress, little change is likely to be observed if given only a small number of trials. In order to be meaningful and sensitive to change, percentage data is best used with a minimum of 10 trials, and preferably 20.

Rate of Events

A measure of **rate** describes behavioral performance in relation to some time frame. Rate could be computed based on any time frame, such as the number of hurricanes per year, wars per decade, or automobile accidents per week. In education, however, the most frequently used rate measure is *rate per minute*. It is used because it allows for common comparisons across different types of behavior, it is easy to measure, and it is sensitive to small changes in behavior. The general formula for rate is:

$$\frac{\text{Number of Events}}{\text{Time}}$$

The formula for calculating rate per minute is:

$$\frac{\text{Number of Events}}{\text{Number of Minutes}}$$

For example, Craig's teacher wants to document his aggressive acts during free play. On Thursday he engaged in 25 aggressive acts during a 10-minute free play period. His rate of aggression would be calculated as:

$$\frac{25 \text{ (Number of Aggressive Acts)}}{10 \text{ (Number of Minutes)}} = 2.5 \text{ per minute}$$

A rate measure, just as percentage data, converts frequency data into a standard format allowing comparisons over time. A rate statement is interpreted as a statement of average or relative performance rather than as absolute. For example, Craig probably did not engage in exactly 2.5 aggressive acts every minute. However, over a 10-minute period he had an *average* rate of 2.5 per minute.

Behaviors that are slow to develop, take more than a minute to complete, or occur less frequently will often result in rates of less than 1 per minute. For example, if Craig engaged in 25 aggressive acts during a 50-minute free play period, his rate of aggression would be calculated as:

$$\frac{25}{50} = 0.5 \text{ per minute}$$

This is interpreted as an average of one aggressive act every 2 minutes.

When using rate measures to quantify academic performance, both correct and error rates must be calculated in order to get a picture of both accuracy and speed of performance. For example, Sherman read orally for 2 minutes. He read 30 words correctly and made 10 errors. Separate rates would then be calculated for correct and error performance:

$$\text{Correct Rate} = \frac{30}{2} = 15 \text{ per minute} \qquad \text{Error Rate} = \frac{10}{2} = 5 \text{ per minute}$$

Calculation of both rates is important, since rate can change while accuracy remains the same; likewise, accuracy can change while rate remains the same. The importance of both measures is exemplified in Figure 6.1. Figure 6.1(a) represents 5 days of percentage correct data. As may be seen, the student steadily improved accuracy over time. Figure 6.1(b) shows how the same accuracy data would look for a student who was also increasing rate of performance. Figure 6.1(c) shows how the same accuracy data would look for a student who was decreasing rate of performance.

Finally, as with all data-summary strategies, teachers should structure their data-collection procedures so that calculation of rate data is simplified. The easiest method is to use 1-minute probes for data collection so that rate per minute requires no additional calculations. When longer probes are needed, using whole-minute samples (2,3,5) or 10-minute samples makes calculating rate per minute a relatively easy process. Calculating rate per minute for 57 behaviors in a 76-second time period is time-consuming and is more likely to result in errors.

Duration of Events

Duration refers to the length of time an event occurs. It is determined by timing from the beginning to the end of a behavior. Duration data may be summarized in

FIGURE 6.1 Comparison of percentage and rate data. In Figure 6.1(c), the student's percentage of correct responding is increasing because fewer errors are being made, but the rate of correct responding is decreasing because the student is performing more slowly.

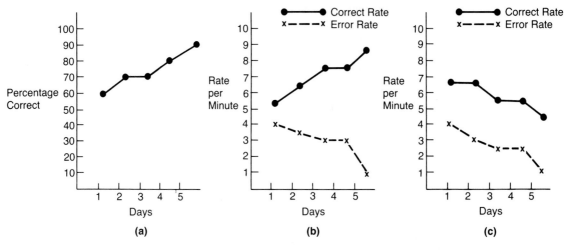

Adapted from "The Use of Time-Based Data in Instructional Programs for the Severely Handicapped" by F. F. Billingsley and K. A. Liberty, 1982, *Association for the Severely Handicapped Journal, 7* (1) p. 49. Adapted with permission.

one of two ways. Consider the following set of data for Carla, who is learning to work at her seat for longer periods of time:

Day	Work Periods	Duration in Minutes
Monday	8:30 — 8:45	15
	9:45 — 9:55	10
	10:15 — 10:20	5
	11:00 — 11:10	10
Tuesday	8:30 — 8:50	20
	9:00 — 9:15	15
	10:15 — 10:20	5
	10:30 — 10:55	25
	11:00 — 11:05	5

One method of summarizing these data is to determine the total duration of an event for a specified time period. For example, the teacher could determine the total amount of time spent working in seat per day. This would be computed by simply adding the duration of each of the separate events. On Monday, Carla worked in her seat for a total duration of 40 minutes. On Tuesday she worked for a total of 70 minutes. A second method of summarizing duration data is to determine the average duration per event. For example, Carla's teacher may be interested in how long, on the average, Carla works without stopping. This would be computed by summing the total amount of time spent working in seat and dividing that number by the number of different events observed. Carla's average duration of a given period of seatwork would be computed as:

Monday $\dfrac{40}{4}$ (Total Duration of Seatwork) = 10 minutes
              (Number of Periods of Seatwork)

Tuesday $\dfrac{70}{5}$ (Total Duration of Seatwork) = 14 minutes
              (Number of Periods of Seatwork)

Not only did Carla increase her total work time on Tuesday, she also increased the average duration of each individual work period.

Both methods of summarizing duration data can be useful. However, the first method, summing the total duration for the day, assumes that the teacher can and has observed all work periods during the day. Otherwise, the duration figure would fluctuate as a function of how often the teacher was able to gather data. If all work periods cannot be observed, or if the observation time varies from day to day, average duration per event should be used.

Latency of Events

Latency refers to the length of time between the presentation of a cue and the student's response to that cue. It is determined by timing from the end of the cue to the beginning of the response. For example, Charles takes a long time to begin cleaning up the room after his teacher asks him to do so. His teacher collects latency data each clean-up period by measuring the length of time between instructions to clean up and the commencement of clean-up behavior. The data are as follows:

Day	Period	Latency in Minutes
Monday	Block Play	3
	Dramatic Play	5
	Sand/Water Play	2
	Art	4
Tuesday	Block Play	2
	Dramatic Play	1
	Sand/Water Play	0.5
	Art	0.1

Latency data may be summarized in the same ways as duration data. Total latency for Monday, determined by summing the individual latencies obtained, would be 14 minutes, whereas for Tuesday total latency would be 3.6 minutes. However, this figure is only useful if the same number of cues is presented each day. Otherwise, the total latency might fluctuate across time depending on the number of clean-up requests. The preferred way of summarizing latency data is to determine the average latency per response by summing all observed latencies and dividing by the number of cues provided. Using this procedure, Charles' latency data would be summarized as follows:

Monday $\dfrac{14}{4}$ $\dfrac{\text{(Total Minutes Latency)}}{\text{(Number of Cues Presented)}}$ = 3.5 minutes average

Tuesday $\dfrac{3.6}{4}$ $\dfrac{\text{(Total Minutes Latency)}}{\text{(Number of Cues Presented)}}$ = .9 minutes average

On Monday it took Charles an average of 3½ minutes to begin cleaning up after teacher requests, whereas on Tuesday he began cleaning up, on the average, less than a minute after being asked.

Methods for Summarizing Time-Based Data

Time-based recording is an estimate of the duration of certain behaviors. Since time sampling most often is used to estimate the occurrence of several behaviors, the simplest and most useful technique for summarizing observational data is to determine the *proportion of time* engaged in various categories of behavior. The formula for determining proportion or percentage of time for any given category of behavior is:

$$\frac{\text{Number of Intervals Behavior Was Observed}}{\text{Total Number of Intervals Observed}} \times 100$$

Using the data in Figure 5.4, Zack's teacher observed for a total of 18 intervals on Monday. Zack's observed performance is summarized as follows:

Category	Number of Intervals	Intervals, %
Attend	5	27.8
Work	5	27.8
Answer Questions	1	5.6
Out-of-Chair	3	16.7
Rocking	2	11.1
Other Inappropriate	2	11.1

Of course, the total percentage of intervals should sum to 100. These data describe Zack's actual behavior at 25 points in time during the day. They help us estimate his general behavior throughout the day, and these data are assumed to typify his overall behavior.

STATISTICAL TECHNIQUES FOR SUMMARIZING MULTIPLE DATA POINTS

An applied behavior analysis approach to effective teaching differs from other approaches to evaluation in its emphasis on regular and frequent data collection (as opposed to, for example, simple pre- and posttesting using an achievement test or periodic tests of content for the purpose of grading students). This means that each student will have multiple data points. Three basic dimensions can be used to summarize a set of data points: central tendency, variability, and trend.

Central Tendency

Measures of **central tendency** attempt to summarize the *typical* value of a given data set. Three basic measures of central tendency are the mean, the median, and the mode. We are most familiar with the **mean,** also known as the *mathematical average*. It is calculated by summing all of the values in a data set and dividing by the total number of values available. For example, two sets of data are presented in Table 6.1. One set represents Helen's performance on math work sheets over a 2-week period; the other set represents David's talking-out behavior during individual work time over a 1-month period. Helen's mean or average percentage correct for the 2 weeks is determined by adding the values for each day (total = 825) and dividing by the total number of scores (10). Likewise, David's mean rate of talk-outs per minute is determined by summing the rates for each day (total = 142) and dividing by the total number of days (21).

A second measure of central tendency is the **median.** The median is the middle score and is determined by arranging the scores in order from lowest to highest and selecting the middle value. Data from Helen's math problems and David's talk-outs are displayed again in Table 6.2. In this table, the data for each child has been reorganized by arranging the values in order from highest to lowest. David had 21 days of data; therefore, the 11th data point would be the middle value, since 10 days fall below that value and 10 days fall above it. Thus, the median for David is 7 per minute. Helen had 10 days of data. Since this is an even number of data points, one point does not fall precisely in the middle. Thus, the average of the two middle points (the 5th and 6th values) is used to calculate the median. The median or middle score for Helen is 82.5%. Note that each score is counted when calculating the median, even if it occurs more than one time.

A third measure of central tendency for a set of values is the **mode.** The mode is the most frequently occurring score in a set of values. The mode for Helen is 70%, since that value occurred more than any other. Likewise, the mode for

TABLE 6.1   Sample Data for Computing Mean or Average Performance

Helen % Correct Math Problems		David Rate of Talk-Outs per Minute			
Day	% Correct	Day	Rate	Day	Rate
1	70	1	2	11	7
2	70	2	5	12	0
3	85	3	6	13	3
4	75	4	4	14	2
5	80	5	3	15	1
6	70	6	7	16	5
7	90	7	5	17	5
8	95	8	3	18	0
9	90	9	6	19	2
10	100	10	5	20	3
				21	5

Total = 825   Total = 79

\# data points =   10   \# data points = 21

Mean % correct = 83%   Mean talk-outs per minute = 3.76

TABLE 6.2   Sample Calculation of Median Scores for Two Sets of Data

Helen % Correct Math Problems	David Rate of Talk-Outs per Minute		
Values Ordered Lowest to Highest	Values Ordered Lowest to Highest		
70	3	6	8
70	3	6	8
70	4	6	8
75	5	7	9
80	5	8	9
85	5	8	10
90	6	8	10
90			
95			
100			

Median = 82.5   Median = 7

David is 8 per minute, since that value occurred six different times, more than any other.

The mean, median, and mode are ways of describing the central tendency of a set of values. Each has advantages and disadvantages. The mean is advantageous in that it is the most commonly used and understood. Its limitation is that one or two extremely high or low scores may significantly alter the mean, resulting in an inaccurate picture of typical performance. For example, what would happen if Helen got only 10% correct on Day 4 instead of 75%? The mean would go from 83% to 76%, which is not at all indicative of her typical performance. The median and mode are not so affected by extreme scores. In Helen's case, getting 10% correct on Day 4 would not change her median or mode at all. The mode is probably the easiest measure to calculate. However, when only a small number of values are available, the mode may be misleading. For example, Helen's most frequently occurring score is 70%. However, it is not typical of her performance. It occurred three times, but early in the first week. In David's case, the mode (8) is somewhat more representative. However, in general, the mode is rarely used as a measure of central tendency. The median is advantageous in that it provides a more stable or consistent measure of central tendency than either the mean or the mode. Its only disadvantage is that it may not communicate well to others if they do not know what a median is.

Variability

Measures of central tendency are useful because they provide a quick summary of a set of data. They perform a valuable function, since the "big picture" may not be so apparent by simply observing a set of numbers such as those displayed in Table 6.1. However, used alone, measures of central tendency provide a limited picture of the entire distribution of values. For example, Alecia and Bart both have a mean and median of seven correct spelling words over the last five spelling tests. Alecia's scores were 7, 6, 7, 8, and 7; Bart's scores were 10, 3, 5, 10, and 7. Such data lead us to a second important question: how typical is the measure of central tendency? Are the other scores close to the mean or median, or do they vary considerably? In statistical terms, these are questions of **variability:** how much variation occurs around the mean, median, or mode? Alecia's data show little variability, while Bart's data demonstrate considerable variability.

One simple measure of variability is the **range,** an indication of the distance between extreme scores in a distribution. For example, in Helen's case, the range is 30, with extremes of 70 and 100. In David's case, the range is 7, with extremes of 3 and 10. Knowing the range provides additional information regarding the interpretation of the mean, median, or mode. The larger the range, the less confidence one can place in a measure of central tendency as a sole indicator of performance status.

A more sophisticated statistical technique for describing variability is referred to as the **standard deviation.** A standard deviation can be calculated for any set of numbers and is simply a number that indicates how far a given value is from the mean of a distribution. The larger the standard deviation, the greater the variability in a set of scores. Based on the normal curve and assumptions underlying it as a theoretical model, the standard deviation is a necessary underpinning of more complex statistical analyses. The formula for its derivation is complicated, but may be found in any introductory statistics manual. With the advent of new and more sophisticated hand calculators and personal computers, computing the standard deviation is now a relatively simple task requiring the user to merely press a few buttons. However, as a tool for quickly summarizing the performance of individual children and communicating that information to others, the standard deviation is quite limited, since few people understand its use.

Trend

Although use of the range or standard deviation as measures of variability is important in summarizing a set of data, one dimension remains to be described. Of critical interest to us as teachers is whether, over time, a student's performance is getting better, getting worse, or staying the same. This question regards the **trend** in a set of data. How would you describe the trends in the data for Helen and David? Helen appears to be improving in her work over time; David seems to be on a relatively stable course in terms of daily talk-outs. However, it is difficult to determine by simply looking at the numbers.

The primary statistical technique to determine trend is known as the *regression equation*. A formula is used in which a line is drawn through the graphed data, resulting in the least amount of difference between the line and the actual data points. Known as the *least-squares line*, the formula can provide a slope for a set of data, thus providing a statistical description of trend (Parsonson & Baer, 1978). Calculators that can compute standard deviations can usually compute the slope of a data set. However, as with standard deviation, this information is limited since so few individuals understand its meaning.

Summary of Key Concepts

- The purpose of summarizing a set of data is to facilitate communication to others and to facilitate decision-making. A set of numbers, such as those displayed in Table 6.1, has limited usefulness in achieving either of these aims.

- Event-based and time-based recording may be summarized using a variety of procedures. The most common are frequency, percentage, rate, duration, and latency.

- The critical dimensions of any set of data are central tendency, variability, and trend. If these dimensions can be summarized easily and simply, the teacher has the information needed to make important decisions regarding an individual program: whether to leave it alone, try to improve or change it, or to stop a particular activity or cease work on a particular goal.

- Statistical techniques that communicate each of these pieces of information have been developed. However, their usefulness for teaching is limited by (a) the time-consuming process of calculating the values, (b) difficulty in interpreting the information obtained, and (c) difficulty in communicating its meaning to others.

REFERENCES

Gentry, D., & Haring, N. G. (1976). The essentials of performance measurement. In N. G., Haring & L. Brown (Eds.), *Teaching the severely handicapped* (Vol. 1, pp. 209–236). New York: Grune & Stratton.

Haynes, S. N., & Wilson, C. C. (1979). *Behavioral assessment.* San Francisco: Jossey-Bass.

Parsonson, B. S., & Baer, D. M. (1978). The analysis and presentation of graphic data. In T. R. Kratochwill (Ed.), *Single subject research: Strategies for evaluating change* (pp. 101–165). New York: Academic Press.

Sackett, G. P. (Ed.) (1978). *Observing behavior: Vol. II. Data collection and analysis methods.* Baltimore: University Park Press.

7

SUMMARIZING
BEHAVIORAL PERFORMANCE:
GRAPHING METHODS

Key Terms

- Time-Series Data ■ Time-Series Graphs ■ Ordinate ■ Equal-Interval
Graph ■ Abscissa ■ Sessions Format ■ Calendar Format
■ Phase-Change Line ■ Semilogarithmic Chart ■ Record Ceiling
■ Record Floor ■ Data Points

Folklore suggests that "a picture is worth a thousand words." The use of graphs to display and interpret data exemplifies this adage. Graphs can simply and efficiently communicate information about central tendency, variability, and trend in student performance. The recent meta-analysis by Fuchs and Fuchs (1986) found that, when teachers graphed data rather than simply recording it, student achievement was higher. They suggested two possible explanations for this finding. First, graphs may help teachers monitor student performance more accurately and facilitate frequent decision-making. Second, graphs may provide a vehicle for providing effective feedback to students.

Therefore, a strong argument may be made for teachers charting or graphing student performance. However, the effective use of graphs requires a basic understanding of their properties (Parsonson & Baer, 1978).

TIME-SERIES GRAPHS: BASIC PROPERTIES

Data collected as a part of the applied behavior analysis process is referred to as **time-series data** since several data points are collected over time. **A time-series**

graph simply displays that information graphically. Two simple time-series graphs in Figure 7.1 display Helen's math performance and David's talk-outs over the periods for which data were collected.

These two graphs communicate clearly and efficiently the status of each student's instructional program. Helen is making good progress on her math problems, with a rapid improvement over the 2-week period. David, on the other hand, varies in his daily talk-out rate. There does not seem to be a consistent trend over the 21-day data collection period. A quick analysis of each graph suggests that Helen's program is working and probably should continue with no changes. Since David's program to reduce talk-outs, however, does not appear to be effective, a change may be in order.

FIGURE 7.1   Sample charts displaying time-series data.

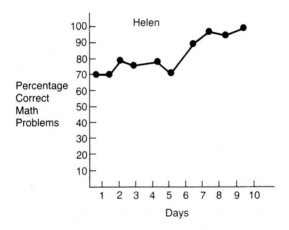

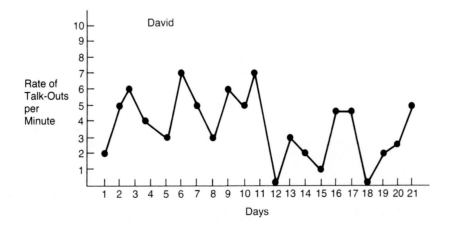

What are the basic characteristics of time-series graphs? At least four should be described: (1) the ordinate, (2) the abscissa, (3) the data points, and (4) phase-change lines.

Ordinate

The **ordinate** of a graph is the vertical axis. Almost invariably, the ordinate is a measure of the behavior of interest. The numerical values on the ordinate reflect the counting system used to measure that particular behavior. For example, Helen's math performance is documented in terms of percentage correct performance on assigned math problems. On her graph, the ordinate consists of percentage data with values ranging from 0 to 100%. David's talk-out are measured in terms of rate per minute. On his graph, the ordinate consists of rate data with values ranging from 0 to 10. The ordinate for each graph reflects the numerical value of the behavior that is counted.

Most graphs have **equal-interval** ordinates; that is, the distance between any two consecutive values is always the same. For example, on Helen's graph the distance between 10% and 20% is the same as the distance between 80% and 90%. Some charts use logarithmic intervals instead of equal intervals on the ordinate. They are explained in a later section of this chapter.

In many cases, the ordinate contains all the possible values of a variable. For example, Helen's graph could accommodate any percentage value since it ranges from 0% to 100%. However, two exceptions to this situation exist. First, many variables have no theoretical limit. For example, David's talk-outs may very well exceed 10 per minute on a given day. However, since that rate was never observed, the chart simply was drawn to accommodate the maximum rate that actually occurred. Second, for the sake of space, certain portions of a graph may not be necessary. For example, since Helen never scored below 70% on her math problems, we really do not need the bottom part of her graph. In such cases, it is possible to use a charting convention to eliminate part of the ordinate. This convention is displayed in Figure 7.2. Slash marks and a break are used to indicate that a section of the ordinate is missing.

FIGURE 7.2   Sample chart displaying deletion of a section of the ordinate.

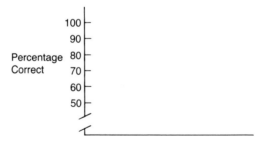

Abscissa

The **abscissa** of a graph is the horizontal axis. In time-series graphs, the abscissa represents time. The numerical values on the abscissa reflect the different times during which data were collected.

Two basic formats for the abscissa may be used: sessions and calendar. In the **sessions format,** data points are plotted sequentially as they occur. The first point on the abscissa usually represents the first session when data were collected; the second point represents the second session that data were collected, even if a 2-day period separated the two or if two sessions occurred on the same day. In the **calendar format,** each day of the week, including Saturday and Sunday, is noted on the abscissa. Data are plotted on the days in which data were actually collected.

Although many graphs use the sessions format for displaying data, as displayed in Figure 7.1, this format obscures variability in behavior explained by such events as weekends, absences, or vacation periods. The calendar format provides a more complete picture of how often data were collected and facilitates the identification of variables that may be influencing behavior. In Figure 7.3, the same data points are plotted on two separate graphs, one with a sessions format and one with a calendar format. As may be seen, the calendar format more adequately shows when data were collected. It also suggests that this student may have difficulty returning to desired levels of on-task behavior after weekends or vacation periods.

Data Points

The actual **data points** (daily performance as marked on a graph) that make up the graph or figure are plotted by finding the point at which the measured value on the ordinate intersects with the day or session on which that value occurred. At that point, a clearly defined mark or symbol should be placed. Lines are then drawn connecting successive points so that change over time can be seen easily.

In many cases, two sets of data are plotted on the same graph. One example of this situation is when rate data are used for behaviors that may be correct or incorrect. For example, Brad's prevocational instructor wants to keep data on both the rate and accuracy of Brad's work on sorting computer parts. Each sort can be correct or incorrect. Two values can be generated: correct sorts per minute and error sorts per minute. In order to plot these data, separate symbols should be used to indicate corrects and errors. While any symbol may be used, it is common practice to represent correct rates by use of solid dots and error rates by use of x's (White & Haring, 1980). A second example of the need to display two sets of data on the same graph is when the teacher wants to examine concurrently the occurrence of two separate behaviors or the same behavior at two different times. For example, Fran's teacher wanted to keep separate data on Fran's on-task behavior during reading and math periods in order to see if she was more

FIGURE 7.3   Comparison of sessions format and calendar format for abscissa.

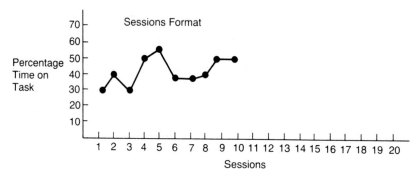

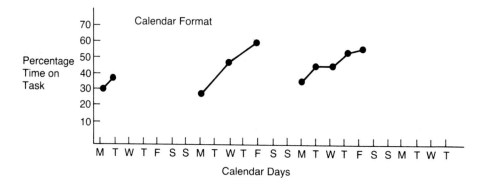

task-oriented during the reading period. Again, by using separate symbols, these two sets of data can be depicted on the same chart.

At least two guidelines pertain to drawing the connecting lines between data points. First, when two sets of data are plotted on the same graph, the connecting lines (as well as the data points themselves) should be different. For example, the connecting line for corrects could be solid and the connecting line for errors could be dashed. Second, for clarity of presentation and ease in interpretation, it is helpful to connect only those data points that occur on consecutive days (using a calendar format on the abscissa). This means that there will be breaks or gaps in a graph when weekends or absences occur. The intent of this practice is to document the effects of missed instruction. But what about days in which instruction was conducted but data were not collected? In this case, White and Haring (1980) suggested that the connecting line be used, simply crossing the missed day of data. Using this rule, any gaps in the data reflect gaps in instruction.

FIGURE 7.4   Examples of poor and appropriate formats for connecting data points.

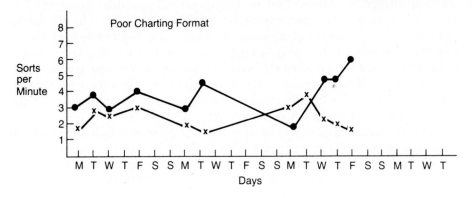

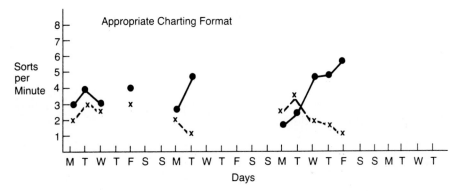

Examples of poor and appropriate graphing formats are displayed in Figure 7.4. In both figures, the same two sets of data are presented: correct rates and error rates. However, in the first figure, the data points for both sets are connected by a solid line. All data points are connected and the marks for each point are not well defined. The second figure attempts to correct this format by using, for the same data, different connecting lines, leaving gaps when days are missed and clearly marking each data point.

Phase-Change Lines

A final fundamental characteristic of time-series graphs is the use of phase-change lines. The purpose of a graph is not simply to document change or lack of change in student performance. We would also like to be able to attribute student performance to specific interventions or other environmental variables. To do this, it is necessary to show clearly on the graph when specific instructional conditions were in place and when changes in those conditions occurred.

A **phase-change line** is a vertical line on a graph drawn at the point at which a change in instructional or environmental variables occurred. For example, several phases of instruction related to Jack's aggressive behavior during 20 minutes of recess on the playground are displayed in Figure 7.5. Each time a new strategy was tried, a phase-change line was drawn and a label clearly describing the new intervention was written at the top of the phase. It is clear that none of the initial strategies was effective; aggressive behaviors were reduced only when the teacher implemented a timeout procedure requiring Jack to sit alone for 5 minutes after each aggressive act.

Phase-change lines should be drawn at the point at which any change is made that might affect performance. This could be as dramatic a change as the introduction of a token economy system, or a simpler change such as moving to a new reader. It is generally suggested that only one variable be changed at a time so that, if an effect is observed, the teacher will know the specific variable that caused the change. For example, if Nina starts a new reader and concurrently enters a new reading group, which of these variables caused the observed decrement in reading rate? Only by changing one variable at a time can the specific cause be identified. Procedures for determining causal relationships using graphed data are described in Chapter 9.

As displayed in Figure 7.5, data points should not be connected across phase-change lines. This practice more clearly differentiates behavior under different instructional conditions.

FIGURE 7.5   Sample use of phase-change lines and labels to differentiate changes in instructional or environmental variables.

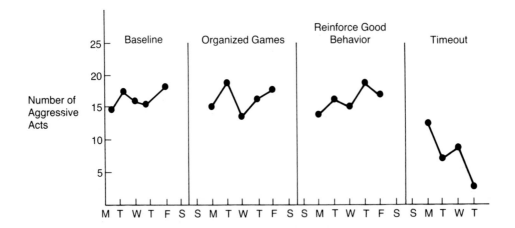

LEVELS-OF-ASSISTANCE CHARTS

Although most of the charts used by teachers are time-series charts presented in the format described above, progress for many handicapped children is documented in terms of decreased requirements for assistance by teachers. As described in Chapter 5, levels-of-assistance data can be used to describe the extent to which a student depends on external teacher support to complete a task. Charts may also be used to display progress through various levels of assistance.

The charts described thus far can be used to reflect progress under varying levels of teacher assistance if the teacher uses a given level of assistance for several days, always providing that level of assistance with every trial. When the student has mastered that level, the teacher moves to a higher level of student independence. That sequence of transitions continues until the student reaches the independent level. An example of a chart containing data collected under such conditions is displayed in Figure 7.6. The data indicate Eva's progress in learning to eat with a spoon. Data points within each phase show the percentage of correct responses given the indicated level of assistance provided.

In many cases, however, teachers may vary the level of assistance provided on a given day, according to the student's performance and progress within an instructional session. Under such conditions, other charts are needed. At least two alternatives are available. One option, displayed in Figure 7.7, is to create a chart that includes the number of trials presented and all possible levels of assistance for each day of instruction. The teacher marks or circles the level of assistance

FIGURE 7.6   Time-series chart displaying levels-of-assistance data.

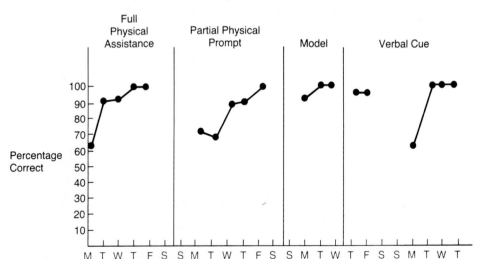

FIGURE 7.7 Chart for use with controlled presentations at varying levels of teacher assistance.

Trials

Prompt Level	Day 1	Day 2	Day 3	Day 4	Day 5	Day 6
I	1 2 3 4 5	1 2 3 4 5	1 2 3 4 5	1 2 3 4 5	1 2 3 4 5	1 2 3 4 5
VP	1 2 3 4 5	1 2 3 4 5	1 2 3 4 5	1 2 3 4 5	1 2 3 4 5	1 2 3 4 5
G	1 2 3 4 5	1 2 3 4 5	1 2 3 4 5	1 2 3 4 ⑤	①②3 ④⑤	①②③④⑤
M	1 2 3 4 5	1 2 3 ④5	1 2 ③④⑤	①②3 ④5	1 2③4 5	1 2 3 4 5
PP	1 2③④⑤	1②③4⑤	①②③3 4 5	1 2③4 5	1 2 3 4 5	1 2 3 4 5
FM	①②3 4 5	①2 3 4 5	1 2 3 4 5	1 2 3 4 5	1 2 3 4 5	1 2 3 4 5

Key: FM = Full Manipulation; M = Model; VP = Verbal Prompt; PP = Partial Physical Prompt; G = Gesture Prompt; I = Independent

Adapted from "An Instructional Interaction Pattern for the Severely Handicapped" by P. A. Alberto and P. Schofield, 1979, *Teaching Exceptional Children, 12,* pp. 16-19.

required for each trial and connects each of those marks, thus creating a time-based chart. Higher levels on the chart indicate increasing levels of independence.

An alternative to this format is to summarize the student's typical performance on a given day and use this summary statement to indicate typical level of assistance required. A sample chart following this format is displayed in Figure 7.8. Levels of assistance are arranged in order from most to least intrusive. For each day of instruction, the typical level of performance is determined. For example, if three out of five opportunities required a model from the teacher, then M would be the value for that particular day. The letter representing the typical level of assistance required is circled. Connecting lines between days are used to document direction of change over time.

FIGURE 7.8 Levels-of-assistance chart using a summary of the typical level required each day.

	Day 1	Day 2	Day 3	Day 4	Day 5	Day 6	Day 7	Day 8	Day 9	Day 10
I	I	I	I	I	I	I	I	I	I	I
VP	VP	VP	VP	VP	VP	VP	VP	VP	VP	ⓋP
G	G	G	G	G	Ⓖ	Ⓖ	G	G	G	Ⓖ
M	M	M	M	M	Ⓜ	Ⓜ	M	Ⓜ	Ⓜ	M
PP	ⓅⓅ	ⓅⓅ	ⓅⓅ	ⓅⓅ	PP	PP	ⓅⓅ	PP	PP	PP
FM	FM	FM	FM	FM	FM	FM	FM	FM	FM	FM

Key: FM = Full Manipulation; M = Model; VP = Verbal Prompt; PP = Partial Physical Prompt; G = Gesture Prompt; I = Independent

TASK-ANALYTIC CHARTS

With other behaviors, particularly those consisting of a chain of important behaviors, teachers may collect data on the number of steps correctly completed in a given task-analytic sequence. There are two ways of charting task-analytic data. One way is to use the traditional time-series chart. The ordinate represents either the number of steps completed in the chain or the percentage completed correctly. The abscissa, as usual, represents the day on which that particular level of accomplishment was observed. The actual value used for a given day is either (a) the number or percentage of steps correctly completed on a one-time probe of the behavior sometime during the day, or (b) the average number or percentage of steps completed correctly across several attempts at the behavior. A chart following such a format is displayed in Figure 7.9.

An alternative format, suggested by Bellamy, Horner, and Inman (1979), combines a data-collection sheet and chart into one system. The advantage of such an approach, in addition to its time-saving features, is that it allows the teacher to record and document performance on each step of the chain. By looking at the chart, the difficult steps become obvious. The data-collecting features of this chart were described in Chapter 5. An example of a completed chart is displayed in Figure 7.10. The steps in the task analysis are presented such that the first step is at the bottom of the chart. Numbers representing each step in the chain are displayed beside the steps. During task performance, the teacher marks each step performed correctly. Then the numeral representing the total number of correct steps is circled. The circled numeral becomes the official data point for that day, and a connecting line is drawn to other circled numerals for other days. Although the chart displayed in Figure 7.10 represents probe data for a given day, if the teacher so desires, several trials could be represented each day.

FIGURE 7.9 Time-series chart displaying task-analysis data.

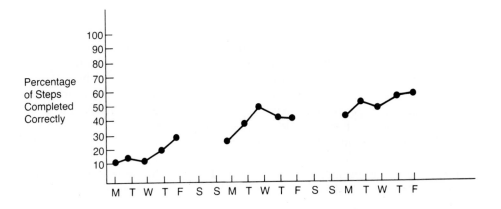

FIGURE 7.10 Task-analysis chart for learning to use a personal stereo. A slash (/) is used to indicate correct performance of a step. On each day, a circle is drawn around the numeral representing the number of steps performed correctly.

Step	Day 1	Day 2	Day 3	Day 4	Day 5
Turn off radio/remove headphones	7	7	7	7	7
Change station at commercial	6	6	6	6	6
Change station at beginning or end of song	5	5	5	5	⑤
Select rock station	4	4	4	④	4̸
Put headphones on	3	③	3̸	3̸	3̸
Adjust volume to level 6	②	2̸	②	2̸	2̸
Turn on radio	1̸	1̸	1̸	1̸	1̸

Task analysis from "The Training and Generalization of Social Interaction Skills with Autistic Youth" by R. J. Gaylord-Ross, T. G. Haring, C. Green, and V. Pitts-Conway, 1984, *Journal of Applied Behavior Analysis, 17*, p. 234.

SEMILOGARITHMIC CHARTS

Some researchers and practitioners have advocated for the use of a different kind of chart for documenting student performance. Referred to as **semilogarithmic charts,** they were developed as part of a larger approach known as *precision teaching* (Lindsley, 1964). Precision teaching may be viewed as a particular approach to applied behavior analysis that incorporates semilogarithmic charts and specific decision-making rules for interpreting charted data.

Rationale and Description

As described earlier, most charts are equal interval. The distance between any two consecutive points on either the ordinate or the abscissa is always the same. For example, the distance on the abscissa between Day 5 and Day 6 is the same as the distance between Day 11 and Day 12. Likewise, the distance on the ordinate between 20% and 25% is the same as the distance between 55% and 60%. Equal *absolute* changes are always represented by equal distances on the chart. All of the charts displayed thus far in this chapter are equal-interval charts.

On a semilogarithmic chart (referred to as a *semilog chart* or *standard behavior chart*), the abscissa (time or sessions) remains an equal-interval scale. However, the ordinate is drawn in logarithmic units. Examples of semilog charts for rate and percent measures are displayed in Figures 7.11, 7.12, and 7.14. On these charts, equal *relative* changes are represented by equal distances on the chart. Any proportionate change, such as doubling or halving, is represented by the same distance on the chart. For example, on the rate chart, the distance between 5 per minute and 10 per minute is the same as the distance between 1 per minute and 2 per minute. Both changes represent a doubling of behavior. Likewise, on the percent chart, the distance between 10% and 30% is the same as the distance between 5% and 15%, since both represent a tripling of behavior.

FIGURE 7.11 Semilogarithmic charts for rate and percentage measures.

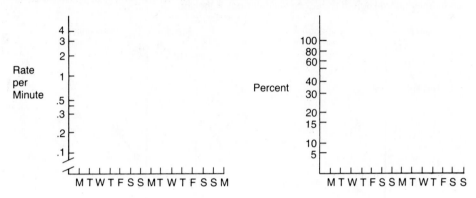

Several advantages of semilog charts have been suggested. Since the charts reflect the rate or percentage of change rather than the amount of change, they may more accurately reflect the effort involved in teaching and learning. Although going from a reading rate of 5 per minute to a rate of 10 per minute is the same absolute increase as going from 40 to 45 correct per minute, the first increase is proportionately much greater than the second and should require more effort. The distance on the chart between 5 and 10 per minute is greater than the distance between 40 and 45.

This reconfiguration of data can be particularly useful for documenting the rate of change. For example, examine Figure 7.12. These charts represent data from one phase of an intervention program reported by Favell, McGimsey, and Jones (1978). The program was an attempt to eliminate the self-injurious behavior of a profoundly retarded 15-year-old girl. Figure 7.12(a) shows baseline and intervention data plotted on a typical equal-interval chart. The intervention appears to have had a significant effect in reducing the student's rate of self-injurious behavior. Although there appears to be a slight rise in the behavior during the intervention phase, it seems insignificant. Figure 7.12(b) shows baseline and intervention behavior plotted on a semilog chart. Again, the intervention appears to have an immediate effect. However, the semilog chart clearly indicates that self-injurious behavior accelerates rapidly after the initial impact. This effect was not seen so dramatically on the equal-interval chart since the changes were small. What the semilog chart shows is that the student was actually doubling her rate of self-injury every 2 days! At that rate, she would be back at the original level within another week. Clearly, the student was adapting to the intervention (lemon juice contingent upon self-injury). In this case, using the semilog chart allows the teacher to notice this problem much earlier and make a programmatic change before the behavior gets worse.

Another advantage of semilog charts is that data usually appearing as a normal learning curve on an equal-interval chart (gradual rise at the beginning

FIGURE 7.12 Comparison of equal-interval and semilog charts in displaying the effects of an intervention designed to reduce self-injurious behavior.

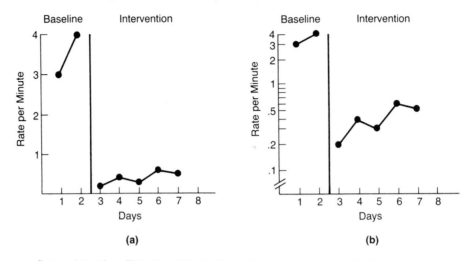

Data replotted from "The Use of Physical Restraint in the Treatment of Self-Injury and as Positive Reinforcement" by J. E. Favell, J. F. McGimsey, and M. L. Jones, 1978, *Journal of Applied Behavior Analysis, 11,* p. 229, Figure 1.

with a steeper increase over time) more closely approximate a straight line on a semilog chart. Since the learning patterns of many students actually follow this curvilinear form, transforming data to a more linear pattern through use of semilog charts should facilitate predictions about the future course of behavior. In fact, White, Billingsley, and Munson (1980) provided data relative to the increased predictive power of semilog charts. The practical benefit of this finding for teachers lies in the potential ability to determine instructional effectiveness earlier and more accurately than possible through equal-interval charts. Given the delays experienced by handicapped children, this outcome should help optimize instructional effectiveness. Bailey (1984) found that use of semilog graphs resulted in more conservative decisions about intervention effectiveness.

This is not to say that equal-interval charts are not useful; rather, it suggests that, in some cases, a semilog chart may more accurately portray student progress. White (personal communication) suggested that data patterns be examined to determine which chart most appropriately displays data and facilitates instructional decision-making. Some simple guidelines for chart selection are displayed in Figure 7.13. The assumption underlying these guidelines is that the ideal chart displays data in a linear fashion (straight line) and a relatively equal pattern of variability should be observed over time. For example, the first figure displays a curvilinear pattern plotted on equal-interval paper. If these same data were plotted on a semilog chart, they would represent a straight line.

FIGURE 7.13   Guidelines for determining whether data should be plotted on an equal-interval or semilog chart.

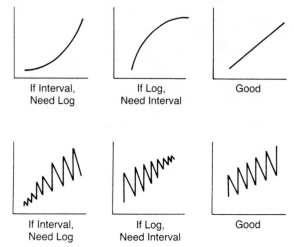

| If Interval,
Need Log | If Log,
Need Interval | Good |

| If Interval,
Need Log | If Log,
Need Interval | Good |

From O. R. White, personal communication.

Guidelines for Use

The semilog chart has many characteristics in common with other charts. However, certain guidelines and rules pertain to its use. These guidelines are described briefly in this chapter. Readers interested in more detailed guidelines for the use and interpretation of such charts should refer to McGreevy (1981), Pennypacker, Koenig, and Lindsley (1972), and White and Haring (1980). Other examples of the application of such charts for teaching purposes were described by Gaasholt (1970), Haring, Liberty, & White (1980), and Lovitt (1977).

An example of a common, commercially available version of the semilog chart, known as the *standard behavior chart,* is displayed in Figure 7.14. Sample data points have been entered to illustrate five key points:

1. The chart can hold an extraordinarily large amount of data. The abscissa is in a calendar format, with Sundays indicated by darker lines. A total of 140 calendar days are provided, which means that two charts can cover an entire school year or three can cover a calendar year.

2. The ordinate can accommodate a wide range of behaviors. Note that this chart uses rate per minute (or movements per minute) as the unit of measure. It can be used to document a count as small as one behavior per 24 hours (0.000695 movements per minute), or a count as large as 1000 movements per minute.

FIGURE 7.14 Sample semilog chart.

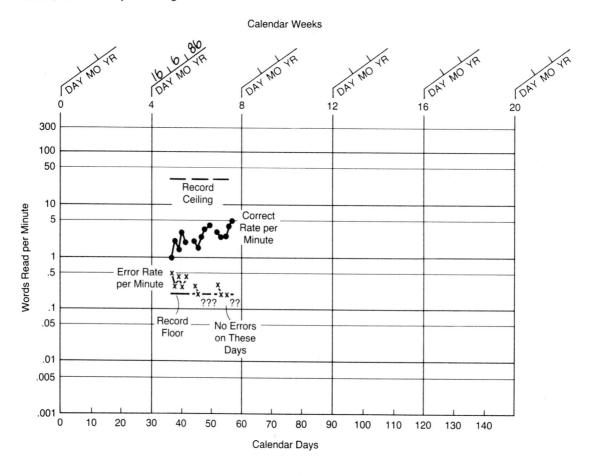

3. **A record ceiling** is noted on the chart. The record ceiling for rate measures is defined as "an upper limit on the value which a measurement can take" (White & Haring, 1980, p. 33). The rate record ceiling is calculated according to the following formula:

$$\frac{\text{Total Number of Opportunities}}{\text{Time in Minutes}}$$

For example, if Pam is given a math sheet with 50 problems on it and she has 5 minutes to complete it, the record ceiling is 10. If she cannot turn in her paper early, then the fastest correct rate she could possibly earn is 10 per minute (50 corrects ÷ 5 minutes). A line is drawn at the record ceiling to show that the student could not possibly have scored above that part of the chart. Of course, the record ceiling for percentage is always 100%.

4. **A record floor** is also noted on the chart. The record floor is defined as "that value which represents the least amount of behavior we can measure"(White & Haring, 1980, p. 34). The rate record floor is calculated according to the following formula:

$$\frac{1}{\text{Time}}$$

For example, the record floor for Pam should be 1/5, or .2. Thus the lowest possible measurement we could get (other than 0) would be 0.2 (1 correct in 5 minutes). A line is drawn at the record floor to show that the student could not possibly have scored below that part of the chart.

The percent record floor is calculated according to the following formula:

$$\frac{1}{\text{Number of Opportunities}} \times 100$$

For Pam, her percent record floor would be 1/50 × 100, or 2%. Thus, the lowest possible measurement we could get (other than 0) if we were using percent measures would be 2% (1 correct out of 50 problems).

5. You will notice that a line for 0 movements per minute is not provided on the chart. This is because the bottom of the chart could theoretically be continued forever (e.g., 1 movement per year). We do not know where below the record floor to place the 0 mark. "To remind us that the child might indeed have completed at least one movement cycle if our record floor had been lower [observation time had been longer], we chart no-count rates as little question marks just below the record floor" (White & Haring, 1980, p. 92).

These conventions are displayed in Figure 7.14. Otherwise, the charting conventions regarding data points and phase-change lines described above apply to semilog charts as well.

Summary of Key Concepts

- Research provides strong evidence to suggest that graphing student data is associated with higher levels of student achievement.
- The most frequently used graphs in educational settings are equal-interval, task-analytic, levels-of-assistance, and semilog charts.
- Effective use of graphs requires knowledge and use of appropriate plotting techniques.

REFERENCES

Bailey, D. B. (1984). Effects of lines of progress and semilogarithmic charts on ratings of charted data. *Journal of Applied Behavior Analysis, 17,* 359–365.

Bellamy, G., Horner, R., & Inman, D. (1979). *Vocational habilitation of severely retarded adults: A direct service technology.* Baltimore: University Park Press.

Favell, J. E., McGimsey, J. F., & Jones, M. L. (1978). The use of physical restraint in the treatment of self-injury and as positive reinforcement. *Journal of Applied Behavior Analysis, 11,* 225–241.

Fuchs, L. S., & Fuchs, D. (1986). Effects of systematic formative evaluation: A meta-analysis. *Exceptional Children, 53,* 199–208.

Gassholt, M. (1970). Precision techniques in the management of teacher and child behaviors. *Exceptional Children, 37,* 129–135.

Haring, N. G., Liberty, K. A., & White, O. R. (1980). Rules for data-based strategy decisions in instructional programs. In W. Sailor, B. Wilcox, & L. Brown (Eds.), *Methods of instruction for severely handicapped students* (pp. 159–192). Baltimore: Paul H. Brooks.

Lindsley, O. R. (1964). Direct measurement and prosthesis of retarded behavior. *Journal of Education, 14,* 62–81.

Lovitt, T. C. (1977). *In spite of my resistance, I've learned from children.* Columbus, OH: Charles E. Merrill.

McGreevy, P. (1981). *Teaching and learning in plain English.* Kansas City, MO: Plain English Publication.

Parsonson, B. S., & Baer, D. M. (1978). The analysis and presentation of graphic data. In T.R. Kratochwill (Ed.), *Single subject research: Strategies for evaluating change* (pp. 101–165). New York: Academic Press.

Pennypacker, H. S., Koenig, C. H., & Lindsley, O. R. (1972). *Handbook of the Standard Behavior Chart.* Kansas City, MO: Precision Media.

White, O. R., Billingsley, F., & Munson, R. (1980, October). *Evaluation of the severely and profoundly handicapped.* Paper presented at the annual meeting of The Association for the Severely Handicapped. Los Angeles.

White, O. R. & Haring, N. G. (1980). *Exceptional teaching* (2nd ed.). Columbus, OH: Charles E. Merrill.

8

USING DATA
TO MAKE
INSTRUCTIONAL DECISIONS

Key Terms

■ Slice Back ■ Step Back ■ Central Tendency Line ■ Trend
Line ■ Line of Progress ■ 'Celeration Line ■ Quickie Split-Middle
Technique ■ Minimum 'Celeration Line ■ Aim Star ■ Bounce
■ Envelope ■ Level ■ Trend

Making decisions about instructional programs requires the teacher to take a
number of variables into consideration. Does the student seem happy with his or
her work? Do you as teacher think the procedures are appropriate? However, the
most fundamental question is, "Are the instructional procedures working?"
Graphs help teachers answer this question by communicating quickly and
efficiently the nature and extent of students' progress and facilitating instructional
decision-making.

   Although, in some cases, a teacher does not need a graph to decide if a
procedure is working, an assumption underlying this chapter is that graphing
student performance and applying certain rules for instructional decision-making
should make it easier to answer this question. Fuchs and Fuchs (1986) found that,
when teachers employed specific rules for evaluating and making decisions about
student performance, student achievement was higher than when rules were not
used. Furthermore, in many cases, these procedures should allow (or encourage)
the teacher to make an instructional change earlier than might otherwise be the
case. The goal, then, is to maximize instructional effectiveness and efficiency by
frequently monitoring and evaluating student performance.

TYPES OF DECISIONS

At least eight different decisions could be made by evaluating student performance (Haring, Liberty, & White, 1980; White & Haring, 1980). In this section we briefly describe each decision; in a later section we describe data patterns suggesting each type.

Make No Change

One decision, of course, is to make no change in an instructional program. This would be the case if the student is making adequate progress toward a goal. However, teachers should continue to monitor performance even when students are successful.

Change the Goal or Aim Date

After the initiation of some instructional programs, it may become quickly apparent that the student will not achieve the goal at the expected date. If the goal is considered to be appropriate and the present instructional procedures are facilitating learning, one possible decision is to alter the time by which the objective is expected to be achieved. In other situations, it may become quickly apparent that the objective is not appropriate for a student; in such cases, the objective should be dropped and a new one substituted.

Slice Back

To **slice back** means to move back and teach an easier version or subcomponent of the same skill. For example, Blake is given a sheet of single-digit addition problems with sums to 10. He gets some but not all of them right; his rate is not improving over time. In this case, the teacher may slice back by giving him work sheets of single-digit addition problems with sums to 5. The basic skill being taught (single-digit addition) remains the same; however, the set of tasks required is more manageable. When Blake has mastered these sums, he can move on to the remaining problems.

Step Back

To **step back** means to move back and teach a prerequisite skill. It represents a more extensive change than the slice back, and is used when a task clearly is so difficult that the child needs to learn an easier skill first. For example, when Alexis is given a sheet of single-digit addition problems with sums to 10, she consistently does not get any correct, even after teacher instruction. Clearly, this task is too hard and the teacher should step back to an earlier skill such as numeral recognition, matching numerals to sets, or grouping two sets of objects together and telling how many there are all together.

Try a Different Instructional Procedure

In many instances, the teacher is confident that a particular skill or objective *is* an appropriate one for a student; however, no progress is observed. This situation calls for trying a different instructional procedure. In general, two categories of decisions could be made in this regard. One is to change the antecedent conditions. For example, the teacher could use different materials or provide more teacher assistance. The other general category is to change the consequent conditions. For example, the teacher may stop ignoring talk-outs and provide a negative consequence for them.

Move On to a New Phase of Learning

Once an objective has been met or a certain level of performance has been achieved, one possible decision is to move on to a new phase of learning. For example, Dana has learned to sound out CVC words using a phonetic approach. However, she is very slow in her reading. In this case, the teacher (and the student) would leave the acquisition phase and move on to the fluency-building phase.

Move On to a New Skill

Once a behavior can be demonstrated accurately, fluently, and under a variety of conditions, the next logical decision is to move on to a new skill. This could be the next step in a curriculum sequence or a totally new skill. For example, Bill learned to assemble a wooden chair in his prevocational program. He can do it accurately and quickly, with very little supervision. His next goal is to learn an appropriate recreational activity to engage in during break time. When moving on to new skills, teachers should periodically review and/or probe previously learned behaviors to assess and ensure continued use or maintenance of the skill.

Begin Compliance Training

Finally, some data patterns suggest the need for compliance training. This situation occurs when the teacher is confident that the objective is an appropriate one for the student and that sufficient assistance is being provided so that the student *should* be able to perform the task. Under these conditions, the teacher may decide to implement a program designed to enhance student compliance with teacher directives.

AIDS FOR INTERPRETING DATA

Interpreting data and making instructional decisions is enhanced by the use of certain visual aids or procedures. Three are discussed here: (1) lines of progress, (2) minimum 'celeration lines, and (3) analyzing variability in data. The goal of these aids is to assist the teacher in identifying the three critical aspects of any data set: central tendency, trend, and variability.

Lines of Progress

A simple procedure that often clarifies central tendency, trend, and variability in data is to draw a line through a data set that summarizes points in a phase. At least two types of lines could be used. One is referred to as the **central tendency line.** As displayed in Figure 8.1(a), the central tendency line is a horizontal line drawn through a set of data. The line represents the mean or median of the data points in a phase. In this case, the median rate per minute is 5. Although the central tendency line is helpful in determining average performance, it tells us nothing about trend. A more useful line in this regard is displayed in Figure 8.1(b). Referred to as a **trend line,** a **line of progress** (White & Haring, 1980), or a **'celeration line** (Pennypacker, Koenig, & Lindsley, 1972), the line represents a summary of both the level and trend of time-series data.

FIGURE 8.1   Comparison of a central tendency line and a line of progress to summarize time-series data.

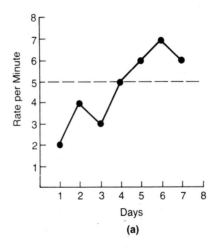
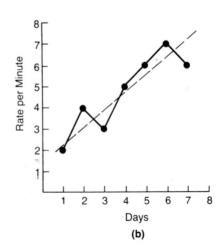

(a)   (b)

FIGURE 8.2 Steps in drawing a line of progress using the quickie split-middle technique.

(1) Divide the Data Points in Half.

(2) Divide Each Half into Halves

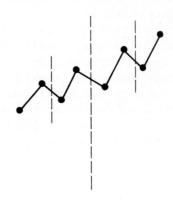

(3) Find the Median Value (Middle Rate).

(4) Draw a Line Connecting the Two Intersections.

White (1974) devised a simple method for drawing a line of progress. Known as the **quickie split-middle technique,** the procedure is an extension of the quarter-intersect method suggested by Koenig (1972). Four steps are involved, as displayed in Figure 8.2. The result is a line that best summarizes the direction and rate of progress for an individual student. By extending the line, the teacher can make a prediction as to whether or not an instructional target will be met and how long it will take. Bailey (1984) demonstrated that adding a line of progress to a set of data increases interrater agreement on the significance of changes in the data.

Minimum 'celeration Lines

A second aid for interpreting charted data is known as the **minimum 'celeration line** (White & Haring, 1980). This represents a line drawn from an initial set of baseline data points to the desired goal. The purpose of the line is to describe the rate of progress (minimum growth or 'celeration) a child would have to make in order to reach a goal. It becomes a standard or marker against which actual progress can be evaluated. If actual performance falls well below the line, a change may be in order.

A sample minimum 'celeration line is displayed in Figure 8.3. Drawing the line entails the following steps: (1) gather 3 to 5 days of baseline data to determine present levels of functioning; (2) draw a mark (often referred to as an **aim star**) at the desired rate and on the approximate date at which achievement of the goal is expected or desired (the aim star usually is taken from the student's IEP, using the criterion rate and the date at which the objective should be achieved); (3) find a "start mark" for the baseline data by locating the intersection of the median (middle) date and the median (middle) rate of those data points; (4) draw the minimum 'celeration line by connecting the start mark and the aim star. When setting the aim star, teachers should use high but reasonable expectations. It is better to have to adjust the 'celeration line because of high teacher expectations than to have a line that reflects low expectations and produces low student performance.

Haring, Liberty, and White (1980) suggested a basic rule for using the minimum 'celeration line for instructional decision-making. If the data for three consecutive days fall below the line, an instructional change should be made.

Analyzing Variability

A final note regarding visual aids relates to the analysis of variability in data. As described earlier, variability refers to day-to-day change in a given behavior.

FIGURE 8.3   Sample minimum 'celeration line.

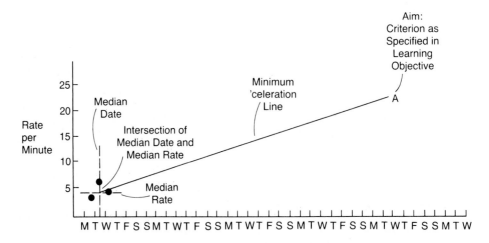

FIGURE 8.4 Drawing an envelope to describe variability or bounce.

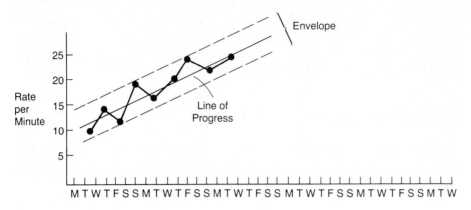

Obviously, a student's performance is not going to be constant across time. Of interest is the degree of consistency as opposed to variability. When looking at a chart, we might refer to variability as **bounce** (Pennypacker et al., 1972). Analyzing variability involves determining how much bounce occurs in the data.

Although bounce can be determined simply by looking at a chart, Pennypacker et al. (1972) suggested drawing an **envelope** as a visual aid to determining bounce. An example of such an envelope is displayed in Figure 8.4. In order to draw the envelope, a line of progress (the solid line) must first be drawn. Above the line of progress, a dotted line is drawn parallel to it such that it goes through the data point farthest from the line of progress. A similar line is drawn below the line of progress. The two dotted lines then form an envelope in which the total bounce is encased. A desirable goal, of course, is low variability in behavior, since high variability indicates a control or compliance problem.

GUIDELINES FOR DECISION-MAKING

White and Haring (1980) and Haring, Liberty, and White (1980) conducted a series of studies designed to identify and validate decision-making rules for use with charted data. Their preliminary investigations have begun to provide information on this topic, although many questions remain unanswered. In this section, we draw from these and other sources to summarize guidelines for decision-making. The use of these guidelines relies heavily on (a) setting an objective and a date by which it is to be attained, (b) using lines of progress and minimum 'celeration lines to determine real and necessary growth, (c) analyzing data frequently, and (d) implementing instruction consistently.

Data Patterns that Suggest Doing Nothing

A program is working when a student's progress toward a goal approximates or exceeds that indicated by the minimum 'celeration line. An example of such a pattern is displayed in Figure 8.5. Although some days fall below the line, progress is generally acceptable. Performance generally is stable, with few error responses.

Data Patterns that Suggest Slicing Back

Slicing back may be indicated when the data show that a student is performing some, but not all, of the tasks, yet is not making any progress. An example of such a pattern is displayed in Figure 8.6. Larry consistently performs 30 to 40% of the tasks in a sequence of assembly skills. He is not improving his performance and, in fact, is beginning to show a slight drop. This pattern suggests that the entire chain

FIGURE 8.5   Sample data pattern suggesting doing nothing.

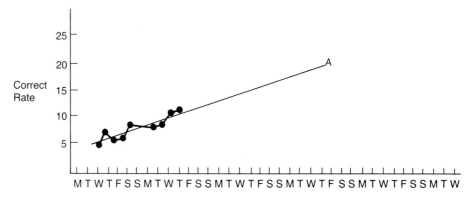

FIGURE 8.6   Sample data pattern suggesting the need to slice back.

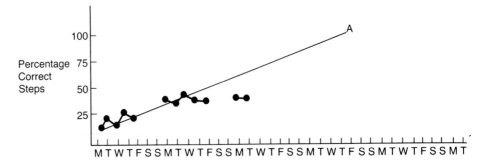

may be too difficult for him. The prevocational teacher may choose to slice back and only require him to do half of the steps. By reinforcing success, helping Larry become fluent in the skills he knows, and systematically teaching one or two new steps at a time, Larry will be able to learn the entire task. Given that he has demonstrated some initial success, it appears that the task is appropriate but needs to be divided into smaller teaching parts.

Data Patterns that Suggest Stepping Back

Stepping back is indicated when the data show that a student is not performing any part of the task correctly. The task simply is too difficult and the teacher should step back to an easier skill. An example of such a data pattern is displayed in Figure 8.7. Jennifer's teacher tried to teach her to read CVC words such as "sat" and "dog" by sounding out the words. However, she quickly realized that Jennifer was not able to do this task at all, so she decided to step back to the easier skill of recognizing letter sounds.

Data Patterns that Suggest Trying a Different Instructional Procedure

This type of pattern suggests that the student is in the acquisition phase of learning. The task is appropriate; however, the student generally needs more instructional help such as additional directions, modeling, or prompting. Patterns indicating such a change typically have a high rate of errors, but with some corrects. This pattern may be very similar to the pattern for slicing back. The difference is that the problem may not be something that is sliceable. For example, Larry's data (displayed in Figure 8.6) may indicate that Larry simply

FIGURE 8.7   Sample data pattern suggesting the need to step back.

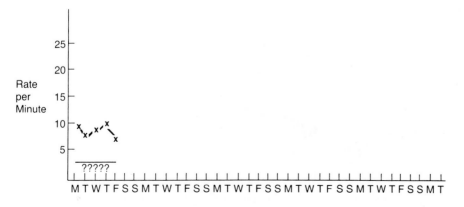

needs to observe a model performing some steps of the sequence, or may need some picture cues to remind him of the next step.

Data Patterns that Suggest Moving On to a New Phase of Learning

Moving on to a new phase of learning often is indicated when the student exhibits a high proportion of correct responses (high level of accuracy), but is not improving his or her *rate* of performance. An example of such a data pattern is displayed in Figure 8.8. At first, Danny was making the expected progress. He rapidly reduced errors until he was performing at or above 90% correct responding in reading his 6th-grade reader. However, his reading rate seemed to reach a plateau at 18 to 20 words per minute, and even his accuracy began to drop. This classic pattern suggests boredom. The student has learned the task and does not recognize the need to continue to improve rate or fluency of performance. Therefore, the teacher may need to move on to the fluency-building phase and provide additional incentives for more rapid reading.

Data Patterns that Suggest Moving On to a New Skill

When a student has met the specified criteria for skill accuracy *and* fluency, it may be time to redirect teaching efforts to a new skill. This does not mean that the teacher should totally ignore the learned skill, however. It should be reinforced whenever possible and the student should be encouraged to use it in new ways and under different conditions. Hopefully, the curriculum is sequenced such that it becomes an integral and necessary component of the next skills to be taught.

FIGURE 8.8   Sample data pattern suggesting the need to move on to fluency-building.

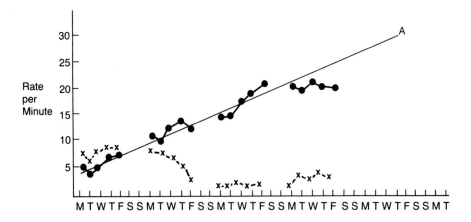

Data Patterns that Suggest the Need for Compliance Training

A compliance problem often is suggested by highly variable data patterns and by decreasing levels of performance rate and accuracy over time. An example of this pattern is displayed in Figure 8.9. Billy's math work sometimes is very good and at other times very poor. His teacher knows that he can do the work and occasionally has observed him doing it; however, his performance is sporadic at best. Thus, he does not need instruction as to how to do the work, but must learn to comply with teacher directions. Sharp drops in the percentage of correct responding also can indicate a compliance problem.

A summary of data-based instructional decisions is provided in Table 8.1.

FIGURE 8.9 Sample data pattern suggesting the need for compliance training.

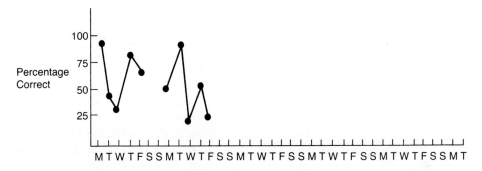

TABLE 8.1 Summary of Data-Based Decisions

Data Pattern	Interpretation	Suggested Decision
Corrects improving; errors flat or decreasing	Program is working	Continue present instructional program
Progress stalled at 20 to 50% correct	Student can perform some but not all parts of the task	Slice back or manipulate antecedents to teach difficult steps (provide teacher assistance)
Corrects at or near zero; high error rate	Task is too difficult	Step back to teach prerequisite skills
Correct rate is highly variable; correct rate drops sharply	Compliance problem	Implement compliance-management program
Corrects stalled at 80%; no increase in rate	Student is ready for fluency-building	Manipulate consequences to increase fluency and add practice time
At aim for accuracy and rate	Successful instructional program	Implement maintenance and generalization programs; move on to new task

DETERMINING WHETHER CHANGE OCCURS
ACROSS PHASES

In addition to instructional decision-making issues, another question is whether or not a change in behavior has, in fact, occurred after a change in instruction is implemented. This decision can be based on graphed data or statistical techniques. In this section, we briefly describe procedures for visually analyzing results and provide references for further information on the statistical analysis of single-subject results. These analytic techniques are used both in instructional decisions as well as in the context of experimental research, as described in Chapters 9 and 10.

Visual Analysis of Results

A detailed account of how to analyze data visually was provided by Tawney and Gast (1984). Parsonson and Baer (1978) provided an equally detailed account of how to graph various types of data. Analysis of student data is an ongoing task rather than a process that occurs at the end of a study or academic year. Wolery and Harris (1982) suggested that analysis of the effects of instructional changes should proceed through four steps. First, the reliability with which data are collected and the reliability with which the intervention is implemented should be assessed periodically. The reliability of the data collection, as discussed in Chapter 5, is usually conducted by using independent observers and calculating interobserver agreement percentages. The consistency with which the treatment is implemented is assessed through procedural reliability (Billingsley, White, & Munson, 1980). These measures should be collected and analyzed throughout the investigation rather than at its initiation or completion. If both percentages of agreement are consistently high, the analysis of the results can continue.

The second step in the process is to determine whether changes occurred in the data series. To accomplish this task, the data should be graphed and then analyzed (See Chapter 7). When scores are similar within a given condition, they are stable; when scores are not similar within a given condition, they are variable. Examples of variable and stable data patterns are shown in Figure 8.10. Data are also said to be stable when one can predict where the next few data points will be with considerable accuracy.

If data are variable, interpretation of the results will be exceedingly difficult. When variability is present, the teacher should search for explanations for the variability and attempt to reduce it. One way to do this is to standardize the conditions under which the data are collected. Ideally, variability in baseline data should become stable before beginning the intervention condition. Changes in the level and trend of the data can sometimes occur within conditions. **Level** refers to the relative position of the data on the ordinate, or value of the dependent measure. **Trend** refers to the direction in which data are going. Changes in level

FIGURE 8.10 Examples of stable and variable data patterns.

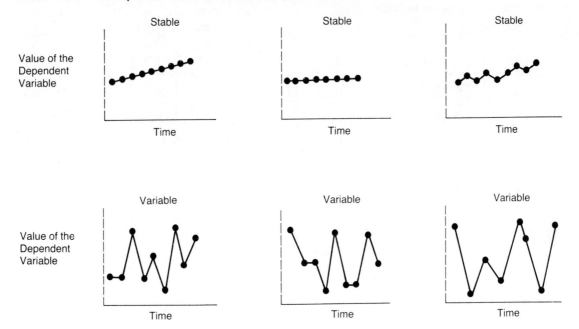

and trend are usually due to history factors or some cyclic variation in performance such as lower performance during the first part of a week. Once a stable pattern of responding is established, the teacher can proceed with the implementation of the next instructional condition.

The third step in the process of analyzing data is to determine whether changes occurred between instructional conditions. Essentially, this step asks, "Do changes in the data pattern coincide with the introduction and/or removal of the instructional variable?" A variety of changes or lack of changes are possible; common patterns are shown in Figure 8.11. One possible pattern is no observable change in the data. In such cases, the teacher would conclude that the intervention (independent variable) does not cause changes in the behavior (dependent variable). Another possible pattern is a change in variability, with a data pattern going from variable to stable, or from stable to variable. A third possible change is in the level of the data, when the relative value of the behavior on the dependent measure at the end of one condition is quite different from the value of the behavior at the beginning of the next condition. Level changes can be either increases or decreases. A change in trend involves a change in the direction in which the data are going when the condition change occurs. Finally, there can be changes in both the level and trend of the data. If it can be determined that changes in the data coincide with changes in experimental conditions, there is potential for a causal relationship to exist.

FIGURE 8.11 Examples of potential changes across conditions, including changes in level, trend, level and trend, no differences, and changes in variability.

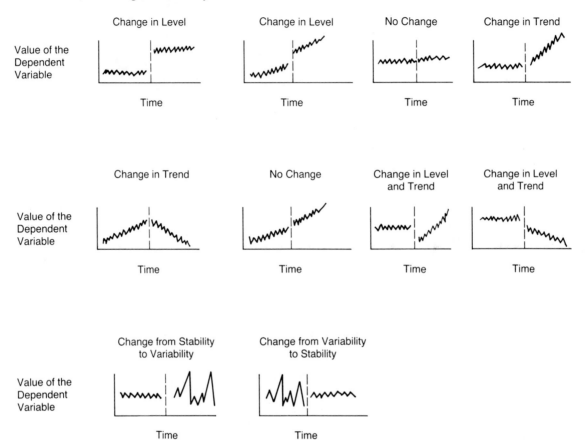

The next question to ask when interpreting data is, "Does the data pattern change each time the instructional condition changes?" This question asks whether the initial changes were repeated each time experimental conditions changed. If the major changes in the data occur *only* when the experimental conditions change, the teacher can conclude that a causal relationship exists between the intervention and behavior. This statement assumes, of course, that sufficient replications of the effects occurred and that threats to internal validity (described in the next chapter) are controlled. On the other hand, if the major changes do not consistently occur when experimental conditions change, the teacher cannot conclude that a causal relationship exists.

The final step of the interpretation process is done only when a causal relationship appears to be present. This step involves determining whether the changes were useful or worthwhile. In other words, "Are the results (effects) socially valid?" Thus, the teacher should attempt to determine whether a "meaningful" change in the student's ability to function in the environment was produced by the intervention.

Statistical Analysis of Results

Since single-subject research designs use repeated collection of data on students under standard conditions and involve the comparisons of students to themselves, the traditional statistical procedures used in group research, such as analysis of variance and t-tests, should not be used (Kazdin, 1984). In fact, some authors have argued that almost any use of statistical procedures, especially statistical significance testing, should be avoided with single-subject research (Michael, 1974). However, other researchers have suggested the need for such analyses because visual analysis may not be reliable; that is, different people may not agree as to whether experimental control has been established (e.g., Furlong & Wampold, 1982; Jones, Weinrott, & Vaught, 1978; Wampold & Furlong, 1981). As a result, a number of statistical procedures have been developed for analyzing data from single-subject research designs. Perhaps one of the simplest procedures is the split-middle-line-of-trend estimation described earlier. Bailey (1984) showed that use of this procedure will increase the agreement of raters concerning the trends in data. Other procedures also exist for analyzing trends (cf., Parsonson & Baer, 1978).

Some of the statistical procedures are designed primarily for analyzing data from given designs. Revusky (1967) described a procedure called the *Rn test* for analyzing the statistical significance of data from multiple-baseline designs. This procedure has also been applied to the analysis of trend and level changes in data from multiple-baseline designs (Wolery & Billingsley, 1982). This test requires random assignment of the order in which treatment is introduced to the baseline behaviors. Edgington (1967, 1980) developed randomization tests that can be used for alternating treatment designs given that treatments are randomly assigned to experimental sessions. Perhaps the most complex statistical test for single-subject designs is time-series analysis (Glass, Wilson, & Gottman, 1975). This procedure requires the use of a computer and it is highly unlikely that many practitioners will use it. Each of these statistical procedures is an additional "judgment aid" to help the researcher determine whether an effect has occurred. However, any reader interested in this issue should also read Carver's (1978) paper describing the pitfalls of traditional statistical significance testing. As noted above, by far the most frequently used method of assessing the effects of single-subject research is visual analysis. Our position is that this analysis should include use of trend-estimation techniques. When possible, it is desirable to also supplement the analysis with statistical procedures.

COMPUTERS AND CHARTING

As described briefly in Chapter 5, microcomputers are affecting many aspects of teaching. Numerous software programs are now available that help facilitate the charting of behaviors and the interpretation of data. Teachers should investigate those options as a time-saving alternative to charting by hand, particularly when large numbers of students are involved. One such program, AIMSTAR (Hasselbring & Hamlet, 1983), can produce both equal-interval and semilogarthmic charts for rate, duration, latency, accuracy, or task-analytic data. The program also incorporates the decision-making rules described in this chapter and indicates to the teacher the instructional strategy that has the highest probability of being successful, given the performance patterns of individual students. Fuchs, Deno, and Mirkin (1983) described the effective use of computer technology in implementing a continuous evaluation system.

Summary of Key Concepts

- Research has clearly demonstrated that, when teachers frequently analyze student performance and use data decision rules regarding instructional methodology, student performance improves.
- Three aids for instructional decision-making are lines of progress, minimum 'celeration lines, and techniques for analyzing variability.
- Specific data patterns have been identified and matched with different instructional decisions. Teachers should be aware of the possible instructional decisions to be made and data patterns that best reflect when each decision should be made.

REFERENCES

Bailey, D. B. (1984). Effects of lines of progress and semilogarithmic charts on ratings of charted data. *Journal of Applied Behavior Analysis, 17,* 359–365.

Billingsley, F. F., White, O, R., & Munson, R. (1980). Procedural reliability: A rationale and an example. *Behavioral Assessment, 2,* 229–241.

Carver, R. (1978). The case against statistical signifi-cance testing. *Harvard Educational Review, 48,* 378–399.

Edgington, E. D. (1967). Statistical inference from N = 1 experiments. *The Journal of Psychology, 65,* 195–199.

Edgington, E. D. (1980). Random assignment and statistical tests for one-subject experiments. *Behavioral Assessment, 2,* 19–28.

Fuchs, L. S., Deno, S. L., & Mirkin, P. K. (1983). Data-based program modification: A continuous evaluation system with computer technology to facilitate implementation. *Journal of Special Education Technology, 6*(2), 50–57.

Fuchs, L. S., & Fuchs, D. (1986). Effects of systematic formative evaluation: A meta-analysis. *Exceptional Children, 53,* 199–208.

Furlong, M. J., & Wampold, B. E. (1982). Intervention effects and relative variation as dimensions in experts' use of visual inference. *Journal of Applied Behavior Analysis, 15,* 415–421.

Glass, G. V., Wilson, V. L., & Gottman, J. M. (1975). *Design and analysis of time-series experiments.* Boulder, CO: Colorado Associate University Press.

Haring, N. G., Liberty, K. A., & White, O. R. (1980). Rules for data-based strategy decisions in instructional programs. In W. Sailor, B. Wilcox, & L. Brown (Eds.), *Methods of instruction for severely handicapped students* (pp. 159–192). Baltimore: Paul H. Brooks.

Hasselbring, T. S., & Hamlett, C. L. (1983). AIMSTAR. Portland, OR: ASIEP Education Company.

Jones, R. R., Weinrott, M. R., & Vaught, R. S. (1978). Effects of serial dependency on the agreement between visual and statistical inference. *Journal of Applied Behavior Analysis, 11,* 277–283.

Kazdin, A. E. (1984). Statistical analysis for single-case experimental designs. In D. H. Barlow & M. Hersen (Eds.), *Single case experimental designs: Strategies for studying behavior change* (2nd ed.). New York: Pergamon.

Koenig, C. H. (1972). *Charting the future course of behavior.* Unpublished doctoral dissertation, University of Kansas.

Michael, J. (1974). Statistical inference for individual organism research: Mixed blessing or curse? *Journal of Applied Behavior Analysis, 7,* 647–653.

Parsonson, B. S., & Baer, D. M. (1978). The analysis and presentation of graphic data. In T. R. Kratochwill (Ed.), *Single subject research: Strategies for evaluating change* (pp. 101–165). New York: Academic Press.

Pennypacker, H. S., Koenig, C. H., & Lindsley, O. R. (1972). *Handbook of the Standard Behavior Chart.* Kansas City, MO: Precision Media.

Revusky, S. (1967). Some statistical treatments compatible with individual organism methodology. *Journal of the Experimental Analysis of Behavior, 10,* 319–330.

Tawney, J. W., & Gast, D. L. (1984). *Single subject research in special education.* Columbus, OH: Charles E. Merrill.

Wampold, B. E., & Furlong, M. J. (1981). The heuristics of visual inference. *Behavioral Assessment, 5,* l55–164.

White, O. R., (1974). *The "split-middle"—a "quickie" method of trend estimation.* Seattle, WA: Experimental Education Unit, Child Development and Mental Retardation Center, University of Washington.

White, O. R., & Haring, N. G. (1980). *Exceptional teaching* (2nd ed.). Columbus, OH: Charles E. Merrill.

Wolery, M., & Billingsley, F. F. (1982). The application of Revusky's Rn test to slope and level changes. *Behavioral Assessment, 4,* 93–103.

Wolery, M., a Harris, S. R. (1982). Interpreting results of single-subject research designs. *Physical Therapy, 62,* 445–452.

9

USING DATA TO IDENTIFY
CAUSAL RELATIONSHIPS

Key Terms

■ Independent Variables ■ Antecedent Instructional Strategies ■ Setting
Events ■ Consequence or Contingency Strategies ■ Dependent
Variables ■ Causal or Functional Relationships ■ Correlational
Relationships ■ Experimental Control ■ Repeated
Measurement ■ Standard Conditions ■ Baseline
Condition ■ Stable ■ Intervention
Condition ■ Replication ■ Withdrawal Design ■ Reversible ■ Reversal
Design ■ Multiple Baseline Design ■ Multiple Probe
Design ■ Changing Criterion Design ■ Internal Validity ■ Threats to
Internal Validity ■ History ■ Maturation ■ Testing ■ Subject Selection
Bias ■ Instrumentation ■ Attrition ■ Multiple-Treatment
Interference ■ Sequence or Order Effects ■ Instability ■ Reactive
Interventions ■ Experimental Effects ■ Integrity of the
Intervention ■ Procedural Reliability ■ External Validity

The procedures for defining, counting, and charting behaviors as well as the
instructional decision-making rules described in previous chapters provide
information for monitoring instructional progress and making decisions about the
effectiveness of teaching strategies. For many teachers, these skills seem sufficient;
however, in order to be maximally effective, teachers also should be able to read
research related to effective teaching and behavior management. Further, they
should be able to engage in research if they choose to do so. This chapter describes
a rationale for teachers reading and conducting research, discusses five

experimental designs for identifying causal relationships, and describes variables that must be controlled when using single-subject research designs. The term *single-subject research* is somewhat of a misnomer. It is used for research where each subject serves as his or her own control; however, in nearly all such research, more than one subject is used and it is possible for groups to serve as a single subject (single unit of measurement). Applied behavior analysis research is a special type of single-subject research; see Baer, Wolf, and Risely (1968) for a discussion of the characteristics of applied behavior analysis research.

RATIONALE FOR TEACHERS READING AND CONDUCTING RESEARCH

Parents, teachers, and community members are concerned with the quality of public education. Numerous reports have criticized the current conditions of schooling in the United States and called for increased excellence in education (e.g., Anderson, Hiebert, Scott, & Wilkinson, 1985; National Commission on Excellence in Education, 1983). Anderson, an author of one such report, said, "We know how to effectively teach reading, but teachers don't know how." This statement implies a gap between the research literature and practice in the schools. Numerous publications in both regular and special education have identified such a gap and have attempted to translate the research literature for practitioners (e.g., Bolster, 1983; Bricker, 1982; Bricker & Filler, 1985; Haring, Lovitt, Eaton, & Hansen, 1978). Additionally, a number of journals have published articles addressing practical issues for instruction and behavior management. It is assumed that teachers who have access to this information can improve their teaching and behavior management practices and thus increase the quality of education (Prehm & McLoone, 1983). Numerous reasons exist for not reading the literature such as the daily demands on time and energy, lack of encouragement by administrators to be familiar with current developments, the nonapplied nature of some journals, and lack of access to the appropriate literature. Further, many teachers may not understand published research. Thus, in order to read the research literature, teachers need a fundamental understanding of research designs, measurement procedures, and data analysis and interpretation.

Another reason for the gap between practice and research is that many researchers are not addressing issues important to classroom teachers. Many of the problems teachers face, such as determining how best to teach a given skill or control a student's social behavior, will not go away simply because researchers have not studied them. In such cases, teachers must deal with the problem/issue without waiting for more research. They need a strategy beyond trial and error for approaching those important instructional and management questions.

Practicing teachers can and should actively participate in research. While not everyone will agree, our experience with teachers and our own teaching experience leads us to suggest that many practicing teachers can engage in systematic, scientific inquiry. This position has been suggested by numerous authors (cf., Haring & Schiefelbusch, 1976; Huling, Trang, & Correll, 1981; Strain, McConnell, & Cordisco, 1983; Tawney, 1984); in fact, many authors (e.g., Strain et al., 1983; Tawney & Gast, 1984) view teaching and research as compatible practices where both endeavors are better served. Research is more meaningful when teachers are involved, and teaching is more systematic and effective when research is involved.

This position is based in large part on two assumptions. First, "much of what we know we don't really know." This statement means many teaching practices are not substantiated by a scientific data base (Tawney, 1984). At some time, the practice may be supported by research but, at present, data simply do not exist on the issue. There is a need to identify, through systematic investigations, the most effective and efficient methods for teaching many skills and managing students' inappropriate behavior. Unfortunately, research on these applied problems may be delayed if teachers are not doing the research or getting help from others in conducting it. Many researchers simply are not faced with the need to answer those questions, and/or view teaching differently from teachers (Bolster, 1983). However, teachers face these issues daily and should be involved in investigating them. The second assumption is that education as currently practiced is an incomplete science. A partial data base exists for some of our practices but the meaningfulness of that research to real classroom situations is not known. A given procedure may work well in a laboratory school, but not in most public-school classrooms. There is a need to replicate (repeat) much of the research in classrooms to determine whether the effects of the procedures will hold true there also.

FUNDAMENTAL CONCEPTS OF RESEARCH

Two types of experimental research designs exist: traditional group research and time-series research (also called *single-subject* or *applied behavior analysis research*) (Parsonson & Baer, 1978). If implemented correctly, both types can be valid means of using the scientific method, and each is particularly useful for different kinds of research questions. They share some characteristics and are distinctly different on other dimensions. In this chapter, single-subject designs are discussed because they are more practical and useful to teachers in classroom settings. For information on group research see Kazdin (1980), Kirk (1982), and Miller and Drew (1983).

The purpose of experimental research is to identify causal relationships between independent and dependent variables. **Independent variables** are the procedures or strategies that are manipulated or compared in experiments. Synonyms for independent variable are treatment, intervention, and instruction. In single-subject research, most independent variables can be grouped into one of three categories. **Antecedent instructional strategies** refer to procedures, frequently teacher behaviors, that occur before students respond; these include the task directions teachers present, prompting procedures, and prompt-fading procedures. **Setting events** refer to changes in setting variables such as changes in room arrangement, the social environment, and materials. **Consequence or contingency strategies** refer to teacher behaviors that occur after students respond to a specific stimulus and include reinforcement, error correction, and aversive stimuli.

The **dependent variables** are the behaviors and measures that are taken to assess the effects of the independent variable. For example, if an experiment were conducted to test the effects of a new math program on students' addition skills, the percentage of correct addition problems may be an appropriate dependent variable. If another experiment were conducted on motor dexterity, students' performance on a test of motor dexterity may be the dependent variable. If an experiment compared the effects of two behavior-management procedures on students' disruptive behaviors, the number of disruptive behaviors may be the dependent variable. A synonym for *dependent variable* is *dependent measure.*

A **causal or functional relationship** is a probability statement indicating that a manipulation of the independent variable appears to cause a change in the dependent variable. For example, if a new math program produced a substantial increase in the number of correctly completed addition problems, a causal relationship may exist between the two. To determine whether a relationship exists, comparisons must be made in the data across different experimental conditions. In the simplest comparison, the independent variable is present in one condition and not present in the other. For example, in the math program experiment, comparisons are needed between students' performance before using the math program and during or after using it, or between groups of similar students—some who used it and others who did not. The systematic identification and validation of causal relationships differentiates research from monitoring student progress. For example, a teacher might use a new technique to teach Loretta to read. Baseline data are taken showing that Loretta cannot read. The teacher implements the new technique and Loretta learns to read in 6 months. From a teaching perspective, this outcome is great; however, from a research perspective, Loretta's progress might be due to a number of other reasons such as maturation or her parents teaching her to read. Research efforts must control for other potential explanations for the findings and must be replicated sufficiently before the researcher has confidence that a causal relationship exists. Causal relationships are different from correlational relationships. **Correlational relationships** exist when two or more factors appear to be related (i.e., they commonly appear together) but a casual link is not demonstrated. There is a correlational relationship between Loretta learning to read and the teacher's new technique; no demonstration exists showing that the reading program caused her to learn to read. Demonstration that the independent variable (treatment), and only the independent variable, repeatedly caused a change in the dependent variable is known as **experimental control.**

CHARACTERISTICS OF SINGLE-SUBJECT DESIGNS

The single-subject designs described here can be used with individuals or groups. When groups are used, behavior can be charted and analyzed separately or as a group. In the latter case, the entire group serves as a single organism. Single-subject designs share three characteristics. First, *the dependent variable (measure of the student's behavior) is collected repeatedly over time under standard conditions.* **Repeated measurement** means that the behaviors are assessed over time (e.g., many days or sessions). To obtain repeated measures, the behaviors must be operationally defined as described in Chapter 5. The measurement system must assess the appropriate dimension (accuracy, rate, latency) of the behavior, must happen often and long enough to get an accurate estimate of the behavior's occurrence, and must be usable during each observation. Also, the observer's recording must be checked periodically for reliability. Collecting reliability data is critical when conducting research. **Standard conditions** or important environmental variables (other than the independent variable) such as the time of day, setting (location), type of activity, difficulty of activity, number of people, etc., must remain constant or be counterbalanced throughout the experiment. Changes in these variables may result in changes in the frequency with which the behavior occurs. For example, Tony's teacher is attempting to increase the accuracy with which he writes his spelling words on a dictated test. Her independent variable is having him write each of the words he misses on a pretest five times. She needs to ensure that the difficulty of the words across lists is similar. The word difficulty would clearly influence the effectiveness of the treatment. For example, if easy words were given during the baseline condition and difficult words during the treatment (or vice versa), the results may be due to the differences in difficulty, the combined effects of word difficulty and treatment, or the treatment only. In any case, the effects of the treatment could not be determined. Steve's teacher is attempting to decrease the frequency with which he gets out of his seat by reinforcing him for completing assignments. She needs to measure this behavior at a specific time each day. His frequency may be very different in the morning as compared to the afternoon or before and after gym class. She also needs to be sure he has an equal number of assignments of equal difficulty to complete each day. Failure to keep these important environmental variables constant makes evaluation of the effects of intervention impossible.

A second characteristic is that all *single-subject designs compare the subject's performance under one experimental condition to his or her past performance under a different condition.* In many designs, the initial condition is called a **baseline condition** which, in the strictest definition, is a period of no treatment or intervention. In most cases, baseline conditions are those that exist in the classroom prior to intervention. The purpose of the baseline is to obtain a stable measure of the behavior against which the intervention performance will be compared. **Stable** refers to a consistent, predictable pattern or level of responding. For example,

Rachael's teacher wants to assess the effects of giving her extra minutes of free time if she talks less to the students sitting near her. In the past, he has reminded her not to talk at the beginning of the day, but he thinks this is not working. To make this comparison, he needs to count the number of times she talks during a specified time of class (e.g., 9:00–9:45) for several days. During this time, he needs to keep the type of activities constant, and continue to remind her at the beginning of the day not to talk. After a stable (consistent) rate of talking has been established for several days, he introduces the intervention conditions (i.e., give her extra minutes of free time if she talked less during the observation period). **Intervention conditions** occur when the independent variable is present. In this case, the baseline condition would be "reminding her not to talk at the beginning of the day" and the intervention condition would be "reminding her not to talk at the beginning of the day *plus* extra minutes of free time for talking less." When the independent variable is introduced, it is very important from a research perspective that no other variables change simultaneously. Stable data patterns during baseline are critical for making valid comparisons between baseline and intervention. If the data are not stable, the teacher is unable to build a case that the intervention made changes in the performance.

The third characteristic of all single-subject designs is that *the evidence or believability that an effect exists is established through replication* (Edgar & Billingsley, 1974). This means that a causal relationship between the independent and dependent variable can be said to exist only if it has been shown to occur repeatedly. Repeatedly implementing the different experimental conditions is known as **replication.** Experimental control is present only when an experiment has demonstrated that the dependent variable is reliably and repeatedly different when the independent variable is present compared to when it is not, and that the difference is due only to the independent variable. For example, Tim sits at a desk facing the window. His teacher notices that he looks out the window a lot and begins to collect data on the number of times he does (baseline conditions). After several days, she obtains a stable rate of looking behavior. As an intervention, she decides to place his desk so that his back is toward the window (independent variable). When his desk is positioned in this manner, there is an immediate and continuing decrease in Tim's window-looking behavior. After several days, his teacher replaces Tim's desk in the original position (second baseline condition) to see if the behavior will increase in frequency. The number of times Tim looked out the window accelerated to the levels found in the original baseline condition. To verify the effect, the teacher again rearranges Tim's desk so that his back is to the window (second intervention condition). As before, the number of times he looked out the window immediately decreased. When Tim faces the window (baseline conditions) he looks out many times each day, and when his back is to the window (intervention conditions), the number of times decreases. By counting the behavior in the original desk position, changing the position, going back to the original condition, and then changing back to the new position again, the teacher builds a believable case that the position of the desk is related to the number of times Tim looks out the window. This causal relationship would not have been demonstrated if the teacher did not return Tim's desk to its original position in the second baseline condition and then repositioned it in the second intervention condition. The change in his behavior during the first intervention could have been due to many other variables.

DESCRIPTION OF SINGLE-SUBJECT RESEARCH DESIGNS

There are at least five single-subject research designs teachers can use to identify causal relationships. Detailed descriptions and extensive guidelines for implementation of the designs are presented by Tawney and Gast (1984), Kazdin (1982), Johnston and Pennypacker (1980), Barlow and Hersen (1984), and McReynolds and Kearns (1983). These sources place their roots in Sidman's (1960) seminal book, *Tactics of Scientific Research,* and Baer, Wolf, and Risley's (1968) classic article, "Current Dimensions of Applied Behavior Analysis," in the inaugural issue of the *Journal of Applied Behavior Analysis.*

In single-subject research, upper-case letters refer to different experimental conditions; by convention, "A" refers to a baseline condition, "B" to a treatment condition, and "C" to a third condition different from either of the earlier conditions. These letters are listed in the order that each condition appears in the experiment.

A-B-A-B or A-B-A Withdrawal Design

The withdrawal design, one of the oldest and most frequently used, is also referred to as the operant design, intrasubject replication design, intraorganism replication design, or the within-subject replication design. It is sometimes called a reversal design, but that term is best suited to a different design that is described later.

The **withdrawal design** consists of a minimum of three experimental conditions: baseline (A), intervention (B), and baseline (A), a more usual pattern is baseline (A), intervention (B), baseline (A), and intervention (B). The conditions of the first and second baselines are identical, and the first and second intervention conditions are identical. The baseline conditions represent the pretreatment or prevailing conditions at the beginning of the study, and the intervention conditions are identical to the baseline with the exception that the intervention is added, all other variables remain the same. For the second baseline, the independent variable is withdrawn; thus, the name *withdrawal design.* In the final intervention condition, the independent variable is reinstated. This design requires measurement of one behavior, although measures may be taken on other behaviors to analyze the multiple effects (side effects) of the intervention. The behavior(s) that are measured (dependent variable), must be **reversible.** In other words, they must be likely to return to the original baseline levels when the intervention is withdrawn. Some behaviors are not apt to be reversible. For example, if a student learns to read a list of words using a given intervention procedure, simply removing the procedure probably will not produce a decrease in the reading performance on that list.

Experimental control, or evidence that a causal relationship exists, is demonstrated by changes in the level and/or trend of the data patterns upon introduction and removal of the treatment procedures. *Level* refers to the value of the dependent measure on the ordinate, and *trend* refers to the direction in which the data are moving over time (e.g., increasing or decreasing). A number of data patterns from withdrawal designs are shown in Figure 9.1. For example, if during baseline the data were stable and not increasing or decreasing, and during intervention the data increased over time, an effect may be possible. This would essentially be a correlational relationship. If during the second baseline condition the data decreased to the original baseline levels, performance on the dependent variable may be influenced by the independent variable. If performance under the second baseline condition was more similar to the intervention pattern than the original baseline pattern, we could not conclude that the independent variable was related to the dependent variable. The second intervention is simply another

FIGURE 9.1   Hypothetical data illustrating various data patterns with the A-B-A-B withdrawal design. In each graph, performance on the dependent variable is related to the introduction and withdrawal of the B condition.

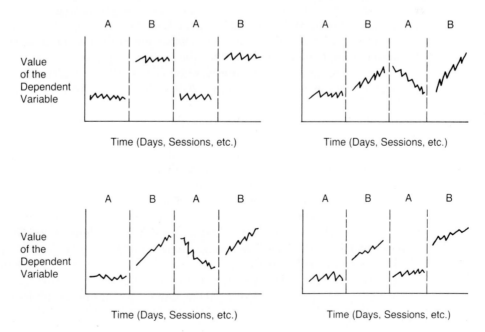

opportunity to observe whether changes in the data coincide with the introduction and removal of the independent variable. Additional repetitions of the introduction and removal of the independent variable may be conducted.

A major advantage of the withdrawal design is that only one behavior need be measured. With adequate definition, reliable measurement of the dependent variable can occur in classroom situations (cf., Hall, et al., 1971; Hall et al., 1972). Another advantage is that multiple replications may occur. A third advantage of the A-B-A-B design is that variations of the independent variable can be assessed. For example, a teacher can compare the effects of extra free time to extra free time plus daily reminders to increase task completion. This variation is discussed in Chapter 10 as a multitreatment design.

One disadvantage of the design is that the behavior must be reversible; that is, it must be likely to return to baseline levels when the treatment is withdrawn. Another disadvantage is that the intervention must be withdrawn during the second baseline condition. Sequence and/or interactive effects are possible and probable, meaning that the effects of the intervention may occur due to experience with previous conditions. For example, extra free time plus reminders may not have been effective if Josh had not experienced the baseline conditions. This is a common problem with most single-subject designs. Teachers should be sure the baseline conditions are those to which they want to generalize the results of the experiment.

The A-B-A-B design is a particularly flexible design that can be used to answer a variety of practical questions. Numerous examples exist in the literature where this design was used to assess the effects of reinforcers, reinforcement schedules, and punishment contingencies; it is particularly well suited for such investigations. The design can also be used to investigate antecedent instructional strategies. Lovitt and Curtiss (1968) used an A-B-A design to investigate the effects of having a student verbalize subtraction problems before attempting to answer them. In baseline phases (A), the student simply wrote the answer to the subtraction problems; during intervention phases (B), the student verbalized the problem prior to writing the answer. Across three types of subtraction problems, the implementation of the verbalization resulted in a rapid decrease in the error rate. Although this study illustrates the use of an antecedent instructional procedure with the withdrawal design, the inherent difficulty of studying academic behaviors with the design is also illustrated. In the second baseline condition in Lovitt and Curtiss' study, there was an increase in the error and correct rates. While an experimental effect is clear, the increase in correct rate indicates that, once the student learned to calculate a given type of problem accurately, he was not likely to stop doing so, even when the procedure he used to learn the problem type was withdrawn. When the desired comparisons are between two or more *antecedent* instructional strategies where the behavior is not likely to be reversible, the withdrawal design is a poor choice. The withdrawal design can also be used to assess the effects of setting variables. For example, some change in the classroom seating arrangement may influence students' performance. The baseline data could be collected under the original seating arrangement, and the intervention condition would be the new arrangement.

A-B-C-B or A-B-C Reversal Design

This design is an old, rarely used design that is similar to the A–B–A–B design. The **reversal design** consists of a minimum of three experimental conditions: baseline (A), intervention (B), and reversal of the intervention (C), but nearly all researchers maintain that four conditions are necessary: baseline (A), intervention (B), reversal (C), and intervention (B). When four conditions are used, the design does not end with a contratherapeutic application of the intervention. The reversal design is different from the withdrawal design in that during the second baseline (reversal, C) the intervention is not withdrawn but is reversed, applied in an opposite manner to the behaviors being studied (Leitenberg, 1973). For example, Lori talks a lot in class and her teacher wants to study the effects of teacher attention on her talking. During the baseline conditions, he collected data on how frequently she talked, and during intervention he attended to her when she was quiet. During the reversal phase, he attended to Lori when she talked, and the second intervention was identical to the first. During the reversal, the attention was given for Lori's talking. As with the withdrawal design, the reversal design requires measurement of one behavior, although measures of other behaviors are frequently taken. The behavior(s) that are measured must be reversible.

Experimental control with the reversal design is demonstrated in the same manner as with the withdrawal design. In the reversal condition, the data pattern should be similar to the initial baseline condition. An example of data from the study of Lori's in-class talking using a reversal design is shown in Figure 9.2. After taking baseline data, the teacher attended to Lori for being quiet and there was a decrease in the number of talk-outs. To determine whether the decrease was a result of the attention, he decided to reverse the contingencies—he attended to her for talking. Later he reinstated the attention for being quiet (intervention). The data show that teacher attention was functionally related to Lori's talking.

The advantages are similar to those found with the withdrawal design: only one behavior must be measured, a number of replications are possible, and variations in the independent variable can be analyzed. Similarly, disadvantages are that the behavior must be reversible and the intervention must be applied to produce contratherapeutic levels/trends in the data during the reversal condition. In the example of the teacher attending to Lori for being quiet, the attention during the reversal condition was provided for talking. Although this could dramatically document the effectiveness of teacher attention, many teachers would object to the use of this procedure. As with the withdrawal design, sequence or interactive effects also are possible and probable.

The A-B-C-B reversal design can be used to study the effects of reinforcers,

FIGURE 9.2 Hypothetical data for a reversal design illustrating the number of times Lori talked out during a 20-minute math session. Baseline (A) represents usual classroom contingencies, Intervention (B) represents reinforcement for being quiet, and Reversal (C) represents reinforcement for talking.

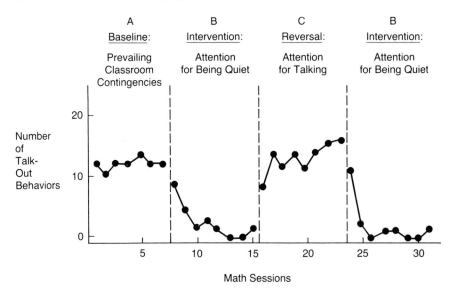

punishers, and some antecedent instructional strategies. The design is not well suited for studying setting events because of the difficulty in reversing such manipulations.

Multiple Baseline Design

The **multiple baseline design** contains two conditions: baseline and treatment. It requires repeated measures of a minimum of three simultaneous baseline conditions. Three variations of the multiple baseline design exist: (a) multiple baseline *across behaviors* such as three independent behaviors of a single student, (b) multiple baseline *across conditions,* e.g., the same behavior of a single student across three different locations (therapy room, classroom, playground) or three other stimulus conditions, and (c) multiple baseline *across students,* e.g., the same behavior of three students. The behaviors (settings/students) must be independent, meaning that changes in one will not result in changes in the others. All behaviors are monitored from the first day of the study until the completion of the study. Intervention (B) is initiated sequentially across the students, settings, or behaviors. When an effect has been demonstrated in one student (setting or behavior), the treatment is introduced to the second student (setting or behavior). Usually, an intervention remains in effect after it is initiated. For example, Nicholas frequently displays inappropriate behaviors during play times. His teacher counts the number of times he throws toys, bangs toys on the floor, or hits the toys with other toys. She collects data on each response at the same time. Her independent variable is contingent observation, which involves having him stop playing, go to the side of the play area, and watch other children play for 45 seconds. Initially, she applies the intervention to throwing toys only, and continues to collect data on all three inappropriate behaviors. When the first behavior meets a previously established criterion, contingent observation is applied to the second behavior. Finally, after the first two behaviors reach criterion, contingent observation is applied to the third behavior. Graphic display of Nicholas' data is shown in Figure 9.3. As can be seen, each behavior changed only after the treatment was applied.

Experimental control is demonstrated by introducing the intervention to each baseline series at a different time and noting the resulting changes or lack of changes in *all* behaviors. Control is established when a change in the level and/or trend of the data occurs *only* and immediately for the treated baseline behavior. Other baseline data patterns should remain stable. If changes in the level and/or trend of the data occur each time the intervention is successively introduced and if

FIGURE 9.3 Hypothetical data for a multiple baseline design illustrating the number of times Nicholas threw, banged, and hit toys. Baseline (A) represents usual contingencies; Intervention (B) represents contingent observation.

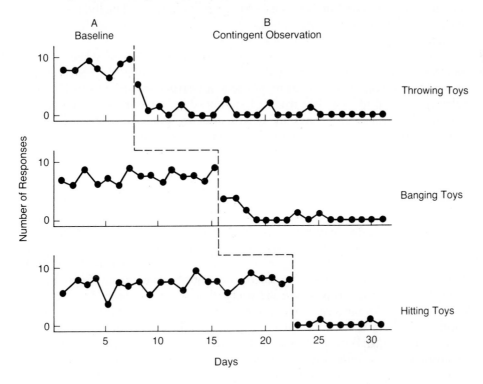

the baseline data to which the treatment is not introduced remain stable, the teacher can be confident that the treatment is effective.

The advantages of the multiple baseline design are numerous. First, no reversal or withdrawal of the intervention is required, although when one is employed, a stronger case for the existence of causal relationships can be established. Second, the design can be used with nonreversible behaviors. Third, the multiple baseline design provides information about the effectiveness of a procedure across different behaviors, settings, or students. Finally, a believable case can easily be developed with the design.

The multiple baseline design also has some disadvantages. First, to make statements about causal relationships with any confidence, a minimum of three behaviors (settings/students) should be used. When three behaviors (settings/students) are employed, a withdrawal or reversal condition should be included for at least one of the baselines (Kazdin & Kopel, 1975). This recommendation requires that the behaviors being studied are reversible. When a reversal or withdrawal condition is not used, four behaviors (setting/students) should be employed. A second disadvantage is that data must be collected for multiple behaviors, settings, or students, requiring more observational skills and time than other designs. If three or four behaviors of a single student or the same behavior of three or four students are studied, obtaining reliable measures is possible but difficult (cf., Hall, Cristler, Cranston, & Tucker, 1970). If a multiple baseline design across settings is used, the observer must collect data in each setting. Third, some behaviors must remain in baseline conditions for an extended period of time. Finally, the teacher must select behaviors (settings/students) that are independent, such that when treatment is applied to one behavior, the others will not change.

The effectiveness of different reinforcers, reinforcement schedules, and punishing stimuli can be investigated with the multiple baseline design. It can also be used to investigate the effects of antecedent instructional procedures because behaviors in multiple baseline studies do not need to be reversible. The multiple baseline designs across settings and across students (given they are in different settings) can be used to investigate the effects of environmental factors such as room arrangement or schedule changes.

Multiple-Probe Design

The **multiple-probe design** is a variation of the multiple baseline design. The major difference is that continuous (i.e., daily) measurement of the dependent variable is not required during baseline conditions (Horner & Baer, 1978; Murphey & Bryan, 1980). Rather than continuous baseline data collection, data are collected at various points in the study; these points are called *probes*. Daily data collection is done on each baseline prior to implementing the intervention to another baseline. Daily data collection also is conducted for the behavior being treated. The multiple probe design can be used across behaviors, settings (stimulus conditions), or students; however, in most publications, the design has been used across behaviors. Probes are taken on all behaviors during the first days of the study, and then the treatment is introduced to the first baseline behavior. At this point, data collection on other behaviors is suspended. Probe data are collected again on all behaviors prior to intervention with the second and each subsequent behavior. Probe data may be collected on the untreated baselines at other times as well. For example, Brian's teacher used time delay (an errorless learning procedure) to teach him to spell four lists of words. She selected four lists of words that were of equal difficulty and probed (tested) him on all four lists. After the initial probe, she used time delay to teach him List 1 and then she probed all words. After the second probe, she used time delay to teach him List 2. This process continued until she had taught him all four lists. Data from this multiple probe design example are shown Figure 9.4. As shown by the data, the percentage of

FIGURE 9.4 Hypothetical data for a multiple probe design illustrating the percentage of Brian's correct responses on spelling words. Probe (A) represents tests on each list of spelling words; Time delay (B) represents the teacher's use of time delay to teach Brian specific lists of words. Note how time delay was started at different points in time for each list of words.

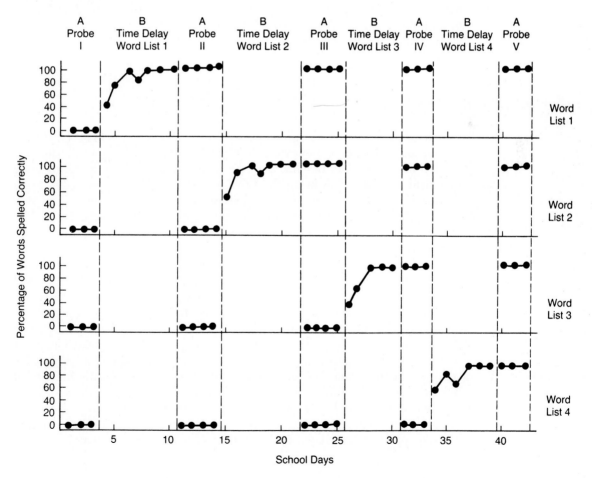

correct spelling for each list remained low until after the training was initiated for that list. After training, the percentage of correct spelling was at criterion level.

Experimental control is demonstrated in the same manner as in the multiple baseline design: by a consistent change in the level and/or trend of the data from the probe conditions to intervention conditions *and* the lack of changes in the untreated probes. The advantage of this design is that continuous data are not needed, making it more efficient than the multiple baseline design. A disadvantage is that the opportunity to analyze the effects of interventions on untreated baselines is lost.

The multiple probe design is particularly well suited for investigating antecedent instructional strategies. It can also be used when measurement of the behaviors will be reactive, that is, when simply measuring the behaviors continuously over time will result in a change in the behaviors. However, the design should only be used when there is a strong *a priori* assumption that the unmeasured baseline behaviors will occur at stable rates (Horner & Baer, 1978). Since it can be used with behaviors that are not readily reversible and that need to be learned in a sequential manner, investigations with instructional strategies are possible. The design is useful in documenting the effects of instructional procedures across different behaviors and students; thus, the design is useful in helping the teacher document accountability.

Changing Criterion Design

The **changing criterion design** was described by Hartmann and Hall (1976) and involves using the independent variable to produce sequential stepwise changes in the dependent variable. Baseline data are collected on a behavior, and then the treatment is designed to bring the behavior to a specific criterion. Once the criterion is met, a new criterion is set. This process is repeated several times over the course of the study. A minimum of four criterion changes should occur and the different criterion levels should be established before the study is started. The amount of change from one criterion level to another should vary across the different criteria. Likewise, the length of time spent at each criterion level should vary. To build a stronger case, the teacher can revert to a criterion level used earlier in the study. The design requires measurement of only one behavior, although others could be measured as side-effect measures. The design should be used with behaviors that are in students' repertoires and can be performed in a stepwise manner. No withdrawal or reversal is required. For example, Heather's teacher is attempting to decrease the number of times she gets out of her seat. He collected baseline data and for an intervention gave her a specific number of tickets each day. Heather can use a ticket to get out of her seat; the goal is for Heather to use only the number of tickets she receives. Data from Heather's program, shown in Figure 9.5., indicate that the number of times she got out of her seat appears to be related to the number of tickets she was given.

FIGURE 9.5 Hypothetical data for a changing criterion design illustrating the number of times Heather got out of her seat. During Baseline (A) no tickets were given; during Intervention (B) Heather was given progressively fewer tickets. The dashed lines (— — — — —) indicate the criterion (number of tickets she received each day).

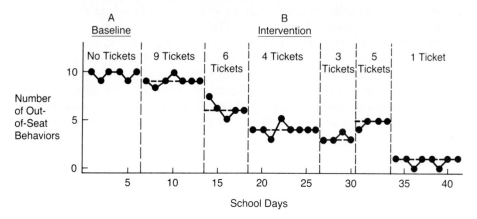

Experimental control is demonstrated by evidence that the independent variable consistently can establish performance at various criterion levels. The changes from one criterion level to another should be relatively abrupt, and the behavior should be relatively stable at each criterion level. To build a more convincing case that the independent variable is responsible for the observed changes, the number of days spent at each criterion level and the size of the criterion changes should vary throughout the investigation.

The changing criterion design requires only one behavior and no reversal or withdrawal is needed. However, it may be difficult to establish the criterion levels and there may be relatively few behaviors for which it is applicable (Tawney & Gast, 1984). Further, the design may require several weeks to complete. It can be used for either increasing or decreasing the occurrence of a behavior, but only with behaviors that are likely to be performed in a stepwise manner.

Selecting an Appropriate Design to Identify Causal Relationships

Each of these five designs can be used to identify causal relationships. When selecting from these designs, at least two issues should be considered. The primary consideration is whether a given design will answer the question being asked. A second consideration is whether a given design is practical. The teacher should select a design that allows the question to be answered and at the same time is possible to implement. For example, if a teacher wants to determine whether providing Ray with a sticker will be a reinforcer, a withdrawal design would be more appropriate than a multiple probe design. The reversal design would also be useful, but many teachers would not want to apply a potential reinforcer to some contratherapeutic behavior. If the teacher is interested in whether a particular behavior management program will be effective in changing the disruptive behavior of Chad, José, and Regina, a multiple baseline design would be the most appropriate. If the teacher is interested in whether a given instructional strategy will produce changes in students' sight-word reading, the multiple probe design would be most appropriate. If the behavior being studied is not reversible, the multiple probe design or multiple baseline design would be more appropriate than the withdrawal or reversal design. If the teacher wants to teach some behavior that is acquired in a stepwise fashion, the changing criterion design would be appropriate.

INTERNAL VALIDITY IN SINGLE-SUBJECT RESEARCH

Internal validity refers to how well a study controls for all potential explanations for the changes found in the dependent variable. Essentially, internal validity refers to how confident we can be that only the intervention is responsible for any changes noted in the behavior being studied (Tawney & Gast, 1984). Numerous **threats to internal validity** exist; these are confounding variables or flaws in the design that raise the possibility that explanations other than the treatment are responsible for the changes in the dependent variable. Probably no study can totally control for all *possible* threats to internal validity, but an adequate design must control for *plausible* or *probable* threats (Glass, Wilson, & Gottman, 1975; Kratochwill & Levin, 1978; Tawney & Gast , 1984).

History

History refers to external events occurring during or before a study that may influence the results. For example, a teacher is conducting an investigation on reading comprehension and is assessing it by asking students questions. A weekend visit from a student's grandmother probably will not influence the results; however, if the student's father begins asking his son questions about a story he reads each evening, this activity is a plausible explanation because it may influence the student's performance on the dependent variable. Likewise, if a teacher is studying procedures to decrease disruptive behaviors, and during the investigation a student teacher joins the class, the addition of another adult may influence the results. Most single-subject investigations are particularly susceptible to the history threat because they require several days, weeks, or months to complete.

To control for history threats, teachers should initiate investigations at times when confounding influences are less likely to occur. For example, an investigation should be started after the winter holidays rather than just before to prevent interrupting data collection and introducing a history threat. When uncontrolled events do occur, the teacher should describe how those events are related to the results and, when possible, study those events. In the above example, if the teacher learns a father is asking his son questions about the stories they read, she might ask the father to withhold the questions for a few days. The questions could be reinstated and the effects of the potential confounding variable could be assessed. If this is not possible, the teacher should build a logical case explaining how the history events contributed to the results.

Maturation

Maturation refers to changes in the students that are likely to occur as a result of the passage of time. It refers to physical growth as well as adaptation to a situation, habituation, or fatigue. Due to the length of many single-subject studies, maturation can easily confound the results. Although most designs control for this potential threat, studies that remain in one condition for a long time (e.g., 2 to 3 weeks) may be open to it. In addition, studies with very long or tiring sessions are susceptible to this threat. Usually, the performance at the beginning, middle, and final portions of sessions can be compared to determine whether maturation is influencing performance at the end of the session.

Testing

The **testing** threat occurs when experience with a pretest can influence posttest results. Since few single-subject studies use such measures, this is rarely a threat. The exception would be with the multiple baseline design where some behaviors remain in baseline conditions for a long time. When pre- and posttest measures are taken on the dependent variable, testing is a potential problem. Sometimes, simply the effect of being measured will influence students' behavior; such effects are discussed under the heading of "Experimental Effects."

Subject Selection Bias

Subject selection bias refers to situations where the results of an investigation may be due to differences in the students in the groups. This threat is not a problem in single-subject studies because each student serves as his or her own control. However, it is a problem with group research, and is commonly cited as a threat to internal validity.

Instrumentation

Instrumentation refers to changes in the method used to collect data on the dependent variable. When mechanical devices are used to record behavior, they can break down or lose their calibration. Human observers can also shift in their data-collection behaviors; therefore, single-subject researchers should conduct frequent reliability checks. The procedures for collecting and calculating interobserver agreement data were described in Chapter 5. These checks should occur during *each* phase of the study. It is also important that the same data-collection procedures are used throughout the study.

Changes in Experimental Unit Composition

This threat is also called *loss of subjects* or *attrition*. **Attrition** is defined as the loss of subjects due to the experimental procedures before the investigation is completed. Since many single-subject studies involve a small number of students, the loss of students for any reason can threaten the completion of the study. When groups of students (e.g., classroom) are studied as a single unit, this threat may be important. For example, a teacher is investigating the effects of a management system for decreasing the number of irrelevant comments made by her class during a daily discussion period. During baseline conditions, she conducted the daily session as usual and counted the number of irrelevant comments. When she implemented the treatment, two or three students who made the most frequent irrelevant comments were absent for 2 weeks because of illness. This short-term attrition is highly likely to influence the results. Likewise, if a couple of new students entered her class at about the point when the treatment was started and they made a large number of irrelevant comments, her results would be affected. Thus, when group behavior is being measured as a single unit, careful attention must be given to any membership changes in the group. It is always best to collect and maintain data on each student as an individual. When this is done, the teacher can analyze and respond to the data of individual students and/or the group.

Multiple-Treatment Interference

This threat is possible when students receive multiple treatments or experimental conditions. **Multiple-treatment interference** refers to the interactive and combined effects of the two or more treatments (conditions) that would not have occurred if the students had experienced only one intervention. For the designs discussed above, one primary type of multiple-treatment interference is sequence or order effects. **Sequence or order effects** refer to the order in which students receive different experimental conditions. Any second condition (e.g., treatment in a withdrawal design) occurs with the student having previous history with the previous condition (e.g., baseline). The results may occur only when the two conditions occur in that order. Any other order may result in different results.

Instability

Instability refers to data patterns seen in the dependent variable. As described in Chapters 7 and 8, when data are stable it is easy to make accurate predictions about where the next few day's datum points will fall. Several data patterns open a study to the threat of instability. When the initial data of a study are characterized by variability (lack of stability), the teacher should take the following course of action before beginning intervention. First, the investigator should search for causes of the variability. When found, the sources should be controlled or investigated. Second, the teacher should extend the initial condition until a more stable period occurs. The threat of instability is also present when the change in the data from one experimental condition to another is not greater than some of the changes that occur within conditions. In such cases, it is difficult to determine whether an effect occurs as a result of the intervention or is merely a continuation of instability. Finally, the threat of instability is also present when a dramatic intervention effect is seen, but the effect does not remain. The effect may be due to an intervention that loses its power or to some other unknown factor.

Intervening when Behavior Is Likely to Change or Reactive Interventions

The first title of this threat comes from Tawney and Gast (1984) and the second, **reactive interventions,** from Glass et al. (1975) and Kratochwill and Levin (1978). This threat can take at least three forms. First, it refers to changes in behavior that are likely to result from natural events. For example, if a student has been misbehaving, the teacher may begin baseline data collection and initiate an intervention program. Simultaneously, the student's classmates may become fed up with his behavior and independently exert influence on him. In such cases, it is impossible to determine what caused the changes. This variation of the threat is also very difficult to control. Second, it can occur when an intervention is introduced simultaneously with "changes in the system into which intervention is made" (Glass, et al., 1975, p. 55). For example, a teacher has the highest legal number of students in his class. Because of this large class size, he has a large number of behavior problems. To deal with these problems, he begins baseline data collection and implements a contingency management system. Coinciding with the implementation of the intervention, another student moves into his classroom. Because this additional student puts him over the legal class-size limit, the principal gives him a full-time teacher aide. Without further experimental manipulations, it will be impossible to tell whether the resulting decrease in behavior problems is due to the presence of the teacher aide or the contingency management system. A third variation of this effect is when a data pattern has been extreme and then comes back down to its usual level. For example, most teachers will admit that during the course of their careers there were days when the students were "just angels" or were "just wild." If an intervention were implemented after a period of days where performance was at either end of the continuum or moving toward either end, it would be impossible to conclude that the results were due to the intervention or simply the data returning to usual levels of performance. To control for this potential, changes in experimental conditions should not occur when the data are at either extreme or are moving decidedly toward either extreme.

Experimental Effects

Experimental effects result from the investigation itself rather than from the treatment (Kratochwill & Levin, 1978). For example, when students are aware that they are subjects, their performance may be altered; this is commonly referred to as a *Hawthorne effect*. Since consent from parents and at times, from students is required, students may know when they are subjects. Kratochwill and Levin cited different types of Hawthorne effects that may influence single-subject studies, including evaluation apprehension—students' performance changing because they are aware or anxious about being measured; social desirability—students altering their performance to please the teacher (experimenter); "screw you" effects—students altering their performance to make the study fail; and "John Henry" effects—students trying harder simply because the investigation is studying an innovation. It is difficult to control for these effects, beyond not reinforcing students for appearing to engage in these behaviors. Two other related experimental effects are possible. First, the introduction of an intervention may produce an effect simply because it is novel. In such cases, continuing the intervention should result in a decrease in the novelty effect. Second, an intervention could disrupt students' usual routines and be responsible for the effect. Again, continuing the intervention should allow students to adapt to the change and mitigate the influence of the disruption.

Integrity of the Independent Variable

Integrity of the intervention is a critical threat to the internal validity of single-subject studies. In most single-subject studies, the independent variable is repeatedly presented during each experimental session. When the intervention is not used as planned or is implemented inconsistently, the results are likely to be different from those that would be obtained if appropriate implementation occurred. For example, assume Debbie's teacher is attempting to increase the number of tasks she completes each day. Praise is a reinforcer for Debbie, and the teacher is using it as the treatment by praising her each time she completes an assignment. However, if during the intervention phase of the study the teacher praises Debbie inconsistently, the results of the study may be due as much to inconsistent implementation as to the praise. Billingsley, White, and Munson (1980) described a method called **procedural reliability** for assessing the consistency with which teachers implement the treatment. Frequent, periodic use of procedural reliability will control for this threat to internal validity.

In summary, a number of threats to the internal validity of single-subject studies are possible. To conclude that the intervention and only the intervention was responsible for the observed changes, the teacher must design the study to control for these threats. Such control is possible but requires consideration of these potentially confounding factors before and during the implementation of the study.

EXTERNAL VALIDITY IN SINGLE-SUBJECT RESEARCH

External validity refers to the extent to which the findings of a study apply (are generalizable) to other students, behaviors, settings, measurement differences, and situations. External validity is not something studies "have"; it is a process of applying the results from one context to another (Birnbrauer, 1981). Essentially, it asks, "Will similar results occur in situations where variations in certain conditions exist?" As such, it is always an empirical issue/question (one that requires another investigation to answer). Thus, the reliability of the findings (the extent to which findings will be consistent across variations in the context) depends on replication studies. There are at least three types of replication studies: direct, systematic, and clinical (Hersen & Barlow, 1984). Direct replication occurs when a teacher repeats one of his or her own previous studies. These can occur with the same students (intrasubject replication) or with other students (intersubject replication). In either case, the experimental procedures are identical to the study being replicated (Tawney & Gast, 1984). Systematic replication involves investigations where only slight variations of another investigation are studied. They may be conducted by the original investigator or by another researcher. Clinical replication, as defined by Hersen and Barlow, involves systematically assessing the effects of a treatment package that contains at least two separate intervention procedures.

Identifying the limits and applications of the results from an investigation is a critical task for applied researchers because it helps practitioners select interventions for their students, problem situations, and contexts (Kazdin, 1981). Further, it is important to determine whether findings will be repeated in situations where less control is exerted over nonexperimental variables than those in the original study (Kazdin, 1981). For example, will the results from a well-controlled laboratory study apply to usual practice in the classroom? Some authors have questioned the ability of single-subject designs to produce results that are generalizable (Miller & Drew, 1983); however, both Birnbrauer (1981) and Kazdin (1981) pointed out the fallacy of this position. From the research literature, it is clear that single-subject designs have been extremely successful in documenting the effectiveness of procedures with a wide range of students, situations, and problem behaviors (Kazdin, 1981; Tawney & Gast, 1984). Essentially, this text is a description of procedures and processes that have been developed, tested, and found effective by using these designs.

As stated earlier, each investigation does not inherently have or lack external validity (Birnbrauer, 1981). However, according to Birnbrauer, the application of the results to other contexts is facilitated when several things occur. First, if authors present their findings in the context of established theory or systematic knowledge, their findings are more understandable to readers. Second, simply having students or settings similar to that of another investigation is not sufficient reason to expect external validity. Third, experimenters should study more intently and report the relationships that were in effect during baseline conditions. Birnbrauer indicated that findings are apt to be more generalizable (evidence more external validity) if the relationships that exist during the baseline condition are present in the situation to which application is being questioned. Further, when a given effect fails to replicate, that case should be studied to determine why the lack of external validity occurred (Kazdin, 1981).

Summary of Key Concepts

- A gap exists between research knowledge and practice; by participating in research, teachers can help bridge that gap and improve the quality of education.
- In single-subject research designs, (a) data are collected repeatedly over time under standard conditions, (b) the subject's performance is compared to his or her past performance under different conditions, and (c) evidence that effects occurred is established through replication.
- Teachers can use several single-subject designs to identify causal relationships, including withdrawal, reversal, multiple baseline, multiple probe, and changing criterion designs.
- Internal validity refers to the confidence the teacher can have that the results are due to the treatment and only to the treatment.
- Threats to the internal validity should be controlled and include history, maturation, testing, subject selection bias, instrumentation, attrition, multiple treatment interference, instability, reactive interventions, experimental effects, and integrity of the independent variable.
- External validity refers to the application of findings to situations other than those where the study occurred.

REFERENCES

Anderson, R. C., Hiebert, E. H., Scott, J. A., & Wilkinson, I. A. G. (1985). *Becoming a nation of readers: The report of the commission on reading.* Washington, DC: U.S. Department of Education.

Baer, D. M., Wolf, M. M., & Risley, T. R. (1968). Some current dimensions of applied behavior analysis. *Journal of Applied Behavior Analysis, 1,* 91–97.

Barlow, D. H., & Hersen, M. (1984). *Single case experimental designs: Strategies for studying behavior change* (2nd ed.). New York: Pergamon.

Billingsley, F. F., White, O. R., & Munson, R. (1980). Procedural reliability: A rationale and an example. *Behavioral Assessment, 2,* 229–241.

Birnbrauer, J. S. (1981). External validity and experimental investigation of individual behavior. *Analysis and Intervention in Developmental Disabilities, 1,* 117–132.

Bolster, A. S. (1983). Toward a more effective model of research on teaching. *Harvard Educational Review, 53,* 294–308.

Bricker, D. D. (1982). *Intervention with at-risk and handicapped infants: From research to application.* Baltimore: University Park Press.

Bricker, D. D., & Filler, J. (1985). *Severe mental retardation: From theory to practice.* Lancaster, PA: Lancaster Press.

Edgar, E. B., & Billingsley, F. F. (1974). Believability when N = 1. *The Psychological Record, 24,* 147–160.

Glass, G. V., Wilson, V. L., & Gottman, J. M. (1975). *Design and analysis of time-series experiments.* Boulder, CO: Colorado Associate University Press.

Hall, R. V., Axelrod, S., Tyler, L., Grief, E., Jones, F. C., & Robertson, R. (1972). Modification of behavior problems in the home with a parent as observer and experimenter. *Journal of Applied Behavior Analysis, 5,* 53–64.

Hall, R. V., Cristler, C., Cranston, S. S., & Tucker, B. (1970). Teachers and parents as researchers using multiple baseline designs. *Journal of Applied Behavior Analysis, 2,* 247–255.

Hall, R. V., Fox, R., Willard, D., Goldsmith, L., Emerson, M., Owen, M., Davis, F., & Porcia, E. (1971). The teacher as observer and experimenter in the modification of disputing and talking out behaviors. *Journal of Applied Behavior Analysis, 4,* 141–149.

Haring, N. G., Lovitt, T. C., Eaton, M. D., & Hansen, C. L. (1978). *The fourth R: Research in the classroom.* Columbus, OH: Charles E. Merrill.

Haring, N. G., & Schiefelbusch, R. L. (1976). *Teaching special children.* New York: McGraw-Hill.

Hartmann, D. P., & Hall, R. V. (1976). The changing criterion design. *Journal of Applied Behavior Analysis, 9,* 527–532.

Horner, R. D., & Baer, D. M. (1978). Multiple-probe technique: A variation of the multiple baseline design. *Journal of Applied Behavior Analysis, 11,* 189–196.

Huling, L. L., Trang, M., & Correll, L. (1981). Interactive research and development: A promising strategy for teacher educators. *Journal of Teacher Education, 32,* 12–14.

Johnston, J., & Pennypacker, H. S. (1980). *Strategies and tactics of human behavioral research.* Hillsdale, NJ: Erlbaum.

Kazdin, A. E. (1980). *Research design in clinical psychology.* New York: Harper & Row.

Kazdin, A. E. (1981). External validity and single-case experimentation: Issues and limitations (A response to J.S. Birnbrauer). *Analysis and Intervention in Developmental Disabilities, 1,* 133–143.

Kazdin, A. E. (1982). *Single-case research designs.* New York: Oxford University Press.

Kazdin, A. E., & Kopel, S. A. (1975). On resolving ambiguities of the multiple-baseline design: Problems and recommendations. *Behavior Therapy, 6,* 601–608.

Kirk, R. E. (1982). *Experimental design: Procedures for the behavioral sciences* (2nd ed.). Belmont, CA: Brooks-Cole.

Kratochwill, T. R., & Levin, J. R. (1978). What time-series designs may have to offer educational researchers. *Contemporary Educational Psychology, 3,* 273–329.

Leitenberg, H. (1973). The use of single-case methodology in psychotherapy research. *Journal of Abnormal Psychology, 82,* 87–101.

Lovitt, T. C., & Curtiss, K. A. (1968). Effects of manipulating an antecedent event on mathematics response rate. *Journal of Applied Behavior Analysis, 1,* 329–333.

McReynolds, L. V., & Kearns, K. P. (1983). *Single-subject experimental designs in communicative disorders.* Baltimore: University Park Press.

Miller, P. M., & Drew, C. J. (1983). Group research in special education. *Exceptional Education Quarterly, 4*(3), 61-76.

Murphey, R. J., & Bryan, A. J. (1980). Multiple baseline and multiple-probe designs: Practical alternatives for special education assessment and evaluation. *Journal of Special Education, 14,* 325–335.

National Commission on Excellence in Education (1983). *A nation at risk: The imperative for educational reform.* Washington, DC: U.S. Department of Education.

Parsonson, B. S., & Baer, D. M. (1978). The analysis and presentation of graphic data. In T. R. Kratochwill (Ed.), *Single subject research: Strategies for evaluating change* (pp. 101–165). New York: Academic Press.

Prehm, H. J., & McLoone, B. B. (1983). Questions, answers and research on the education of exceptional children. *Exceptional Education Quarterly, 4*(3), 1–7.

Sidman, M. (1960). *Tactics of scientific research: Evaluating experimental data in psychology.* New York: Basic Books.

Strain, P. S., McConnell, S., & Cordisco, L. (1983). Special educators as single-subject researchers. *Exceptional Education Quarterly, 4*(3), 40–51.

Tawney, J. W. (1984). Empirical verification of instruction: A realistic goal? In W. L. Heward, T. E. Heron, D. S. Hill, & J. Trap-Porter (Eds.), *Focus on behavioral analysis in education* (pp. 246–253). Columbus, OH: Charles E. Merrill.

Tawney, J. W., & Gast, D. L. (1984). *Single subject research in special education.* Columbus, OH: Charles E. Merrill.

10

USING DATA TO COMPARE TREATMENTS

Key Terms

- Multiple-Treatment Interference ■ Sequence (Order)
Effects ■ Inhibiting Effects ■ Enhancing Effects ■ Carryover
Effects ■ Contrast ■ Induction ■ Nonreversibility
Problem ■ Separation of Treatment Effects Problem ■ Multitreatment
Design ■ Alternating Treatments Design ■ Adapted Alternating
Treatments Design ■ Independent Behaviors ■ Parallel Treatments
Design

The single-subject designs described in Chapter 9 are used to identify causal relationships. However, teachers frequently want to know which of two or more instructional or behavior management strategies is more effective. Teachers should use instructional and behavior-management strategies on the basis of several considerations. Procedures should be acceptable to students and other concerned people (e.g., parents, administrators, etc.) and should match the age and functioning level of students. Strategy selection also should be based on research literature comparing one strategy to another. This chapter describes the importance of such studies, discusses special problems faced by such investigations, and describes four designs for conducting comparison studies.

IMPORTANCE OF COMPARISON STUDIES

In the past 25 years, hundreds of studies have been conducted to identify causal relationships between different behavior management or instructional strategies and students' behavior. Wolery, Ault, Doyle and Gast (1986) reviewed nearly 300 studies where specific instructional strategies were used to teach new behaviors to students with moderate to severe handicaps. About a dozen instructional strategies were identified from the research. A clear finding from this review was that the different instructional strategies were effective in teaching a wide array of behaviors to students of a broad age range and at various functioning levels. However, very few studies systematically compared one teaching strategy to another. Ideally, the research literature should contain numerous comparison studies. If it did, a teacher who is faced with teaching a particular behavior to a specific type of student could select the strategy that was shown by research to be the best. Because of the inadequate amount of this research, teachers do not have the type of information they need when selecting between two or more instructional or behavior-management strategies. Direct comparison studies can result in the answers to questions such as:

- Which strategy will be effective?
- Which strategy will be more efficient (i.e., take less time to learn the same amount of material)?
- Which strategy will allow students to learn more incidental information?
- Which strategy will be less offensive to others in the students' environments?
- Which strategy will require less teacher effort?
- Which strategy will allow students to learn more independently or exert more self-control over their social behavior?
- Which strategy will assist students in generalizing the learned behaviors or social control to other situations?
- Which strategy can be used effectively and efficiently in less intrusive, more natural environments?

To teach effectively, teachers must consider these and similar questions as they select instructional and behavior-management strategies. Until the research literature contains the answers to such questions, teachers must select strategies on the basis of logical analysis, their experience, and their own preference. An alternative to selecting one strategy over another is to compare them directly through applied research in the classroom. When conducting such comparison studies, teachers can use the designs described in this chapter. During such comparisons, the teacher will need to understand and control for problems that are unique to such studies.

SPECIAL PROBLEMS WITH COMPARISON STUDIES

Multiple-Treatment Interference

When two or more treatments are compared, a threat to internal validity called **multiple-treatment interference** is possible. It exists when students' behavior is different from what it would be if they only had received one of the treatments. At least two types of multiple-treatment interference exist: sequence effects and carryover effects.

Sequence Effects. **Sequence (order) effects** refer to the influence that one treatment exerts over performance during a later treatment condition. For example, the research on staff supervision and training shows that teachers are more apt to apply what they learned during inservice training sessions if they receive feedback on their classroom performance related to the content of the training (Madle, 1982). The feedback can come in a variety of forms such as verbal feedback (e.g., praise and corrective statements) from supervisors, time off from work, or monetary rewards. An interesting finding was noted when the different types of feedback were compared. When verbal feedback was given first, it was effective, and when a monetary reward was given in later treatment conditions, it also was effective. However, when teachers received monetary rewards for applying new information in the classroom and later received only verbal feedback, the latter was not effective. This is an example where sequence effects inhibit performance in later treatment conditions **(inhibiting effects).** Sequence effects can also enhance performance in later treatment conditions **(enhancing effects).** For example, students who receive direct instruction from the teacher on using one rule for spelling a particular type of word (e.g., *i* before *e* except after *c* and in words where a combination of letters is said as *a* like "neighbor" and "weigh") may be able to learn other spelling rules by simply reading the rule. If the direct instruction on one rule did not occur, simply reading the second may be ineffective. This sequence effect makes the second treatment (reading the rule) appear more effective than it would have been if the students had not experienced the first treatment. Sequence effects are not unique to comparison studies; actually, they are a potential problem in all studies where one treatment follows another. Birnbrauer (1981) stated that even withdrawal designs are in reality comparison studies; the treatment is compared to the baseline conditions.

Carryover Effects. **"Carryover effects** . . . refer to the influence of one treatment on an adjacent treatment, irrespective of overall sequencing" (Barlow & Hayes, 1979, p. 204). Carryover effects are seen when one treatment appears to "rub off" on another. Two types of carryover effects have been noted: contrast and induction. **Contrast** carryover effects are seen when two treatments are so different that one makes the other treatment work very differently from how it would have worked alone. Barlow and Hayes (1979) cited White, Nielsen and Johnson's (1972) study of timeout as an example of contrast effects. *Timeout* is a procedure where students lose the opportunity to receive reinforcement for a specific period of time when the inappropriate behavior occurs. In that study, White et al. compared different durations of timeout (30 minutes, 15 minutes, and 1 minute). The 1-minute period reduced students' behavior when used first, but when it followed longer periods, students' behavior actually increased. The contrast between the long periods and short period made the 1-minute period lose its effectiveness. **Induction** carryover effects are seen when one treatment makes a second treatment work better than it would have if used alone. For example, a teacher is comparing two reinforcement procedures; one involves an extra minute of free time for each math problem completed correctly, and the second is praise for each correct problem. Because the first treatment (extra free time) is powerful, students' performance may initially be higher during the second treatment (praise). After the students learn that extra free time is not available in the praise condition, the number of problems they complete may begin to decrease.

Three statements are important. First, sequence and carryover effects can inhibit or enhance performance in one treatment condition when another intervention is used. Second, as the definitions and examples indicate, it is very difficult to determine whether a multiple-treatment effect is a result of sequence effects or carryover effects. All carryover effects occur within the context of some sequence. To have carryover, one treatment must occur prior to the other. Third, multiple-treatment interference presents a problem for teachers trying to compare two treatments. They must be aware of this problem when conducting comparison studies.

Nonreversibility Problem

If a teacher wanted to compare the effects of two treatments, and the first treatment eliminated the behavior or established the behavior at criterion levels, it would be difficult to determine what the second treatment could do. This problem, called the **nonreversibility problem,** could be solved by studying behaviors that will return to baseline levels when a treatment is withdrawn or will not reach ceiling or floor levels. However, many interesting comparison questions involve behaviors that are not easily reversible. For example, will one instructional strategy require less training time than a second instructional procedure? If a teacher used an instructional strategy to teach students a sight-word list, they probably will not stop reading that list correctly when instruction stops. If they continue to read the list correctly, the second treatment cannot be used with that word list.

Separation of Treatment Effects Problem

The **separation of treatment effects problem** is very similar to the nonreversibility problem. The purpose of conducting comparison studies is to determine which of two procedures would be better to use. We want to be able to say, "Instructional strategy X will produce criterion-level responding better than instructional strategy Z." Likewise, we want to say, "Behavior management program X will eliminate an inappropriate behavior better than behavior management program Z." When both instructional strategies or behavior management programs are applied to the same behavior, we cannot determine whether either strategy or program would produce the results we obtained if used alone; the combined effects may be responsible. It is possible that no multiple-treatment interference occurred but the teacher cannot be certain that the same results would occur when either procedure is used alone. For example, if a teacher wanted to know which procedure resulted in fewer errors to criterion and applied both instructional strategies to the same behavior, it would be impossible to calculate the number of errors each would produce if used alone.

These three problems—multiple-treatment interference, nonreversibility of behaviors, and separation of treatment effects—require careful design and analysis. Several designs exist to deal with these problems.

SINGLE-SUBJECT DESIGNS FOR COMPARING TREATMENTS

The single-subject designs described below are used to compare two or more treatments. Each of these designs enables teachers to collect data on students repeatedly over time under standard conditions, compare students' performance under one condition to their past performance under different conditions, and use replication to build a believable case that a difference exists. Traditional group designs also can be used to compare treatments, but most special education teachers do not have access to an adequate number of similar students to use group designs properly.

Multitreatment Design

The **multitreatment design** is similar to the A-B-A-B withdrawal design. The primary difference is that two or more "interventions" are compared. At a minimum, the multitreatment design has four phases: treatment 1 (A), treatment 2 (B), treatment 1 (A), and treatment 2 (B) (Birnbrauer, Peterson, & Solnick, 1974). Many variations of the design are possible, and common sequences are A-B-A-B-C-B-C or A-B-A-B-BC-B-BC (Tawney & Gast, 1984). For example, a teacher wanted to increase the number of students who returned their homework assignments and wanted to study different rewards to motivate them to do so. The rewards were a party on Friday for students who returned their homework each day, and a note sent to their parents on Friday congratulating the students for returning all of their homework. The results of this investigation are shown in Figure 10.1. Based on an analysis of the data in Figure 10.1, the note sent to the parents resulted in more homework being returned than the party did.

The study in Figure 10.1 is a simple multitreatment design. A more complex form of the multitreatment design is shown in the following example. A teacher wanted to decrease the number of talk-outs during independent work periods. The teacher used the A-B-A-B-C-B-C multitreatment design. The A condition

FIGURE 10.1 Hypothetical data for a multitreatment design illustrating the number of homework assignments returned by students under two treatment conditions: Treatment 1 (A) represents a party on Fridays for students who returned all their homework assignments; Treatment 2 (B) represents a note sent to parents on Fridays congratulating them on their child's completion of all homework assignments.

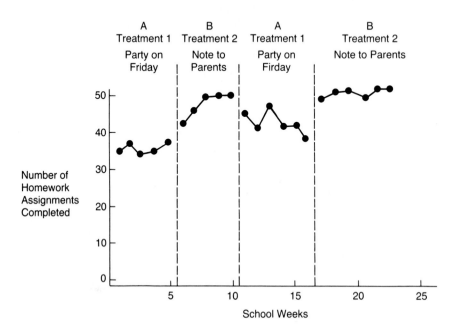

was no statement of the rule (no talking during independent work) and no extra free time for being quiet. The B treatment condition included stating the rule (no talking during independent work) and 5 minutes of free time for students who did not talk. The C treatment condition included only 5 minutes of free time for students who did not talk; the rule was not stated. Data from this study are shown in Figure 10.2. An analysis of that data indicates that the rule statement plus the 5-minute free time period resulted in fewer talk-outs than did the condition where these procedures were not in effect. Further, the data indicate that the 5-minute free time period for students who did not talk was equally effective as the rule statement plus 5-minute free time period.

Clearly, sequence effects are likely with the multitreatment design. To control for sequence effects, the study should be replicated across students using a counterbalanced order of treatment implementation. For example, one student would receive treatment *X* first and then receive treatment *Z*, another student would receive treatment *Z* first and then receive treatment *X*. The multiple-treatment design requires that the behavior be reversible; thus, it does not solve the nonreversibility problem. The multitreatment design does not deal well with

FIGURE 10.2 Hypothetical data for a multitreatment design illustrating the number of talk-out behaviors during independent work time under three different conditions: Baseline (A)—no rule stated and no free time for being quiet; Treatment 1 (B), rule stated and 5 minutes of free time awarded for being quiet; and Treatment 2 (C), rule *not* stated but 5 minutes of free time awarded for being quiet.

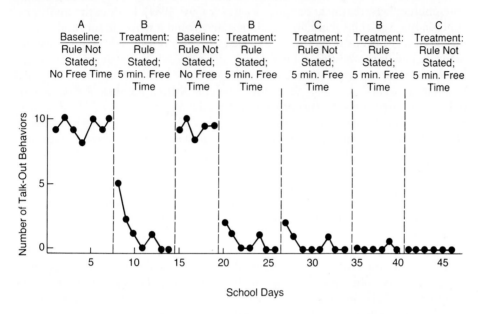

the separation of treatment effects beyond counterbalancing for order of treatment.

Experimental control is established as in the withdrawal design. However, the question of interest is usually whether one treatment is more effective than the other; thus, the differences in performance between the two treatments are analyzed. The level and trend changes in the data are analyzed across the different treatment procedures.

The advantages and disadvantages of this design are similar to those in the withdrawal design: one behavior is measured and numerous replications of the effects can occur. The primary value of the design lies in the ability to compare more than one treatment. The disadvantage of the design is that the behaviors must be reversible. Another disadvantage is that sequence effects must be controlled by counterbalancing across students.

The multitreatment design can be used to compare consequent events, such as the effects of reinforcers, reinforcement schedules, and punishment contingencies. It is less suitable for comparing the effects of antecedent instructional strategies because the behaviors must be reversible and the effects of the treatments would be difficult to separate. The design is useful for comparing setting events such as room arrangements and variations of activity schedules.

Alternating Treatments Design

The **alternating treatments design** is used to investigate the effects of two or more interventions on a single behavior (Barlow & Hayes, 1979). This design has been referred to as the multi-element baseline design, multiple-schedule design and simultaneous treatment design (Tawney & Gast, 1984). Prior to the study, any confounding variables should be counterbalanced and a schedule for implementing the interventions should be established, preferably through random assignment. A baseline condition should occur, although it is not required. After the baseline, the two or more interventions are introduced to the behavior in a rapidly alternating fashion. Usually, the study concludes with a number of days where only the more (most) effective procedure is used. Some means should be designed to ensure that the student discriminates when a given treatment is or is not in effect. This can be done by increasing the time between sessions or pairing specific discriminative stimuli with particular treatments. For example, Mark's teacher is attempting to determine which of two procedures is more effective in increasing his reading rate: previewing the material to be read or allowing him to chart his daily reading rate. After a stable reading rate is found in baseline conditions, the alternating portion of the design begins. To allow Mark to discriminate between sessions when each procedure is in effect, the teacher decides to tell him each day what he is going to do. On some days he will do the previewing and on others he will chart his data. For example, on Monday he is allowed to preview the story to be read and does not chart reading rate, but on Tuesday he does not preview the material but charts his reading rate after the reading session. On Wednesday, he again previews but does not chart, and on Thursday he charts but does not preview. When it becomes clear that one of the procedures is more effective in increasing his reading rate, that procedure should be used for a week or two to demonstrate that it alone can continue to increase his reading rate. Data from this example are shown in Figure 10.3.

Sequence effects are controlled in the alternating treatments design by the rapid alternation of treatments during the comparison phase. It is assumed that treatments that are not used for extended sessions (e.g., a maximum of 2 to 3 consecutive sessions) will produce fewer sequence problems. Carryover is not well controlled, but its potential presence can be detected if the data for one treatment move dramatically toward or away from the data for the other treatment. The design can be used with reversible or nonreversible behaviors because, during the comparison phase, no treatment remains in effect for an extended number of experimental days. It is not possible to identify the effects of any of the treatments alone because the same behavior receives both treatments.

Experimental control is demonstrated by a consistent level and/or trend difference between the interventions. Although comparisons can be made to the baseline levels and trends, this is not a requirement.

The primary advantage of the alternating treatments design is that a rapid assessment of the relative merits of two or more intervention strategies on the same behavior can be made. The major disadvantages are that sufficient controls

FIGURE 10.3 Hypothetical data for an alternating treatments design illustrating the rate of words Mark read per minute under three conditions. During Baseline (A), no previewing or self-charting occurred; during Alternating Treatments (B), previewing (o) and self-charting (□) occurred on different days; and during More Effective Treatment, previewing (o) was used.

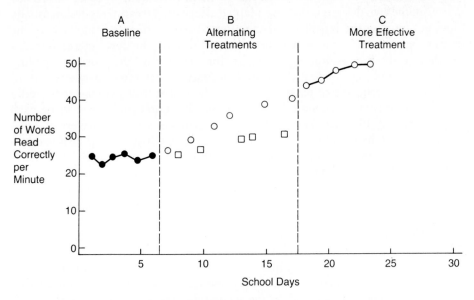

such as counterbalancing are required, and students must be able to discriminate when each treatment is being used. Another disadvantage is the inability to identify what effects the treatments alone would produce.

The alternating treatments design is quite flexible and can be used to compare reinforcement and punishment procedures. Some setting events, if rapidly alternated, can also be investigated. The design can also be used to assess the effects of antecedent instructional strategies. However, when comparing antecedent instructional strategies, the design has some weaknesses. Comparisons of the efficiency of the procedures cannot be made because each is used to teach the same behavior. Thus, measures such as sessions, trials, and errors to criterion cannot be used. The alternating treatments design can also be used as an assessment procedure. For example, if a teacher wants to determine whether a student receives information better when manual signing alone is used or when signing plus verbalizations occurs (i.e., simultaneous communication), the alternating treatments design would be appropriate.

Adapted Alternating Treatments Design

The **adapted alternating treatments design** is, as the name suggests, a variation of the alternating treatments design (Sindelar, Rosenberg, & Wilson, 1985). In the alternating treatments design, the treatments are applied to the same behavior; in the adapted alternating treatments design, the treatments are applied to different but equally difficult, independent behaviors. **Independent behaviors** are responses that do not change when one of them is treated. Another difference between the two designs is that the adapted alternating treatments design usually does not employ the last phase of the alternating treatments design where the better (best) treatment is used alone, although this may be done. For example, a teacher wants to compare strategies for increasing the correct spelling performance of two students. The first strategy is peer tutoring where a third student uses flashcards to present words to the target students who then orally spell the words. The second strategy requires the target students to write each word correctly 10 times. The teacher finds a group of words that were of equal difficulty, and then randomly assigns the words to two lists. A baseline is taken to determine that the students cannot spell each list. One list is taught using peer tutoring and the other list is taught by having students write the words 10 times. A spelling test is given on both lists each morning and during the afternoon the two treatment sessions are implemented. Data for this example are shown in Figure 10.4.

The adapted alternating treatments design controls for sequencing effects by alternating sessions when the treatments are given. If two treatments are compared, two sessions per day might occur, one with the first treatment and the other with the second treatment. If only one session per day is used, on the first day one treatment is used and on the second day the second treatment is used. Carryover is minimized by applying each treatment to different but equally difficult behaviors. The adapted alternating treatments design can be applied to

FIGURE 10.4 Hypothetical data for an adapted alternating treatments design illustrating the percentage of correctly spelled words under three conditions: Baseline (A)—no instruction on spelling these words: Comparison of Treatments (B)—peer tutoring (□) and writing each word 10 times (x).

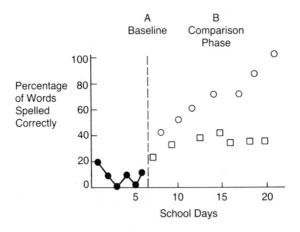

either reversible or nonreversible behaviors; thus, the nonreversibility problem is solved. In addition, it deals with the separation of treatments problem by applying the treatments to different but equally difficult behaviors.

Experimental control is shown as in the alternating treatments design. The level and trends in the data are compared during the comparison phase of the study. The adapted alternating treatments design has advantages similar to the alternating treatments design, but solves the separation of treatment effects problem. Further, the need to make the treatments discriminable is alleviated because each treatment is applied to different behaviors. The primary disadvantage of the design is that the behaviors must be independent and of equal difficulty. If the behaviors are not independent or are not equally difficult, the findings will be misleading. Another disadvantage is that the design does not have built-in replication. Thus, when the design is used, the study should be replicated with other students or across other behaviors.

The adapted alternating treatments design is primarily useful for studying antecedent instructional procedures. The design could be used to study the effects of different reinforcers or punishers, but the alternating treatments design is better for such studies. Its application to setting events is questionable.

Parallel Treatments Design

The **parallel treatments design** is used to compare the effects of antecedent instructional strategies (Gast & Wolery, in press). As with the adapted alternating treatments design, the parallel treatments design uses behaviors that are independent and of equal response difficulty. The design can be conceptualized as two multiple probe designs implemented at the same time. One treatment is applied to one group of baselines and the other treatment is applied to the other group of baselines. Counterbalancing is used to control for potential confounding variables. This design has been useful in assessing the efficiency of different instructional strategies (Bennett, Gast, Wolery, & Schuster, 1986; Godby, Gast, & Wolery, 1987). For example, Marlene's teacher is attempting to compare the effectiveness and efficiency of instructional strategy X and instructional strategy Y in teaching her to read sight words. The teacher identifies a number of sight words that are of the same difficulty. The words are randomly assigned to the two instructional strategies. The words assigned to each strategy are separated into six lists producing three baselines for each instructional strategy. All word lists are probed as in the multiple probe design, and then the first list of words *for each instructional strategy* is taught (i.e., one list with strategy X and another list with strategy Y). After the first lists meet criterion, all word lists are probed again, and instruction is initiated on the next word list for each strategy. This process is repeated until each list is acquired. The teacher needs to counterbalance variables such as time of day of instructional sessions and hold variables such as the length of the sessions and reinforcement constant across procedures. An example of data collected using a parallel treatments design is shown in Figure 10.5.

FIGURE 10.5   Hypothetical data for a parallel treatments design illustrating the effects of two different instructional strategies (Strategy *X* and Strategy *Y*) on Marlene's reading of sight-word lists. Probes or baseline conditions are indicated by BL and training conditions by "Training." Word lists 1, 3, and 5 were taught with Strategy *X*, and lists 2, 4, and 6 were taught with Strategy *Y*. In this example, Strategy *X* was more effective than Strategy *Y*.

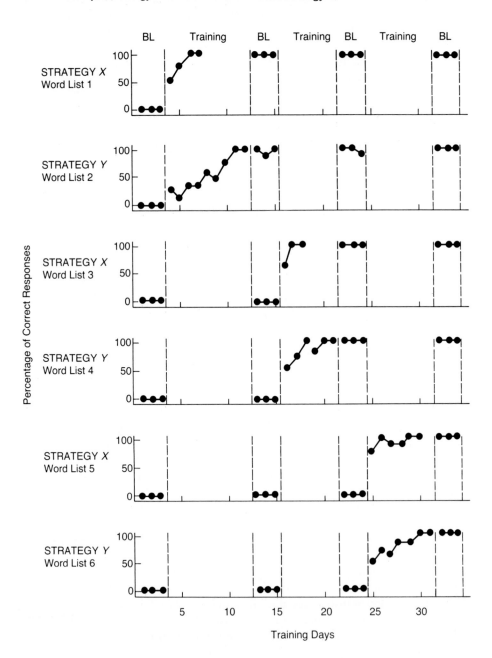

The parallel treatments design controls for sequence effects in the same manner as the adapted alternating treatments design; treatments are rapidly applied in alternating fashion. Similarly, the parallel treatments design applies each treatment to different, independent behaviors that are of equal difficulty to control, in part, for carryover effects. The design can employ behaviors that are reversible or are nonreversible. The effects of each treatment can be assessed because each is applied to separate behaviors.

Experimental control is established as in the multiple probe design. The level and trend in the data from probe conditions to training conditions are compared. In addition, comparisons are made across treatments to determine which is more effective and/or efficient. Since the design is usually implemented with three to four students who each have three to four different sets of instructional stimuli for each instructional strategy, there are a large number of opportunities to replicate the effects. These replications occur within each subject and across subjects.

The major advantage of the design is that teachers can compare two or more antecedent instructional strategies and obtain numerous replications of the results. There are at least three major disadvantages of the design. First, because of the large number of replications, the design can require several weeks or months to complete. Second, the design is complex and requires careful attention to the control of confounding variables. Third, as with the adapted alternating treatments design, it requires identification of behaviors that are independent acts of equal response difficulty.

The primary use of the design is to compare antecedent instructional strategies. Comparison of efficiency measures as well as the relative effectiveness of instructional procedures is possible and is the primary purpose of the design. The design could be used for comparing reinforcers or punishers (e.g., error-correction procedures), but is not nearly as efficient as the alternating treatments design. The design is not useful for comparing setting events such as room arrangements.

Selecting an Appropriate Design

As when selecting a design to identify causal relationships, the primary consideration is selecting a design that will answer the question(s) being asked. When the research question involves manipulation of consequent events (e.g., comparison or reinforcers, behavior management programs, or error-correction procedures), the alternating treatments design and multitreatment design are more appropriate than the adapted alternating treatments design or parallel treatments design. The alternating treatments design is more efficient than the multitreatment design, and each controls for sequence effects differently from the other. The alternating treatments design uses rapid alternation of treatments, and the multitreatment design requires counterbalancing the treatments across subjects or behaviors.

When the research question involves antecedent instructional strategies with nonreversible behaviors, the alternating treatments design, adapted alternating treatments design, and parallel treatments design are recommended over the multitreatment design. When the purpose of such a study is to assess the efficiency of the treatments, the parallel treatments design is the best choice. When instructional strategies are used, but independent behaviors of equal difficulty cannot be found, the alternating treatments design is better than any of the others.

Summary of Key Concepts

■ Teachers frequently need to select an instructional or behavior management strategy from a number of competing strategies, and must do so without the benefit of sufficient previous research.

■ Comparison studies face special problems, including multiple treatment interference, nonreversibility of some behaviors, and a need to separate the effects of each treatment.

■ Four single-subject designs can be used to evaluate the relative merits of instructional and behavior management strategies: the multitreatment design, alternating treatments design, adapted alternating-treatments design, and parallel treatments design.

■ The research question should dictate which design will be used.

REFERENCES

Barlow, D. H., & Hayes, S. C. (1979). Alternating treatments design: One strategy for comparing the effects of two treatments in a single subject. *Journal of Applied Behavior Analysis, 12,* 199–210.

Bennett, D., Gast, D. L., Wolery, M., & Schuster, J. (1986). Time delay and system of least prompts: A comparison in teaching expressive sign production. *Education and Training of the Mentally Retarded, 21,* 117–129.

Birnbrauer, J. S. (1981). External validity and experimental investigation of individual behaviour. *Analysis and Intervention in Developmental Disabilities, 1,* 117–132.

Birnbrauer, J. S., Peterson, C. R., & Solnick, J. V. (1974). Design and interpretation of studies of single subjects. *American Journal of Mental Deficiency, 79,* 191–203.

Gast, D. L., & Wolery, M. (in press). Parallel treatments design: A nested single subject design for comparing instructional procedures. *Education and Treatment of Children.*

Godby, S., Gast, D. L., & Wolery, M. (1987). A comparison of two prompting procedures: Time delay and system of least prompts in teaching object identification. *Research in Developmental Disabilities, 8,* 283–306.

Madle, R. A. (1982). Behaviorally based staff performance management. *Topics in Early Childhood Special Education, 2*(1), 73–83.

Sindelar, P. T., Rosenberg, M. S., & Wilson, R. J.

(1985). An adapted alternating treatments design for instructional research. *Education and Treatment of Children, 8,* 67–76.

Tawney, J. W., & Gast, D. L. (1984). *Single subject research in special education.* Columbus, OH: Charles E. Merrill.

White, G. D., Nielsen, G., & Johnson, S. H. (1972). Timeout duration and the suppression of deviant behavior in children. *Journal of Applied Behavior Analysis, 5,* 111–120.

Wolery, M., Ault, M. J., Doyle, P. M., & Gast, D. L. (1986). *Comparison of instructional strategies: A literature review.* (U.S. Department of Education, Grant No. G008530197). Lexington, KY: Department of Special Education.

PART III

FACILITATING ACQUISITION

The applied behavior analysis research and effective teaching research have contributed substantially to our information on how to teach. Much of this research has allowed teachers to help students learn new behaviors (i.e., acquire new skills). Chapters 11 through 14 provide information about a range of procedures for facilitating acquisition. Chapter 11 discusses issues related to structuring the learning environment. Specifically, procedures are presented for structuring the physical dimension of the environment, promoting students' engagement with learning activities, providing multiple opportunities for learning, communicating expectations to students, and facilitating student success. Chapter 12 describes procedures for presenting tasks to students; issues such as gaining students' attention, informing them of the objective, reviewing previous information, and presenting stimuli are illustrated. Various types of prompts (teacher assistance) are described as are guidelines for selecting and using prompts. The chapter concludes with a discussion of error-correction procedures and types of errors that students may exhibit.

Chapter 13 discusses the role of reinforcement in helping students learn new behaviors. Types of reinforcers are described, and procedures for identifying reinforcer preferences and guidelines for using reinforcers are discussed. Issues related to using teacher praise and employing unusual reinforcers are presented. Chapter 14 describes procedures for using and fading prompts. Antecedent prompt and test, most-to-least prompting, antecedent prompt and fade, graduated guidance, system of least prompts, and time delay are described. For each strategy, a general description, planning decisions and prerequisites, issues related to implementing the procedure, and findings when the procedure is used are provided. The chapter also includes a description of stimulus-manipulation procedures, and concludes with a discussion of guidelines for selecting instructional strategies.

11

STRUCTURING THE ENVIRONMENT FOR EFFECTIVE TEACHING

Key Terms

- Continuum of Intrusiveness ■ Least Restrictive Environment ■ Allocated Time ■ Engaged Time ■ Academic Learning Time ■ Contingency-Management Techniques ■ Massed Trials ■ Spaced Trials ■ Distributed Trials ■ Mand-Model ■ Incidental Teaching ■ Naturalistic Time Delay

The fundamentals of applied behavior analysis—specifying objectives for students, gathering data regarding student performance, and evaluating data to determine instructional effectiveness—allow the teacher to know precisely what is expected of students and to monitor student progress toward the achievement of those expectations. These fundamentals are applied to facilitate the acquisition and use of new skills and to reduce, eliminate, or control inappropriate behaviors.

Facilitating the acquisition of new skills or reducing the occurrence of inappropriate behaviors can be accomplished in many different ways. Intervention strategies may be conceptualized on a **continuum of intrusiveness.** Some teaching strategies are classified as highly intrusive, such as spanking or dismissal from school. Others, such as rearranging the classroom environment, are considered less intrusive or more natural. An important general rule is to use the most natural (least intrusive) strategy necessary to achieve an instructional outcome. For example, Helen has trouble concentrating on her work. Her teacher could use any number of strategies to help Helen, including (a) moving her desk, (b) creating a learning cubicle, (c) providing highly motivating activities, (d) providing a formal reward system for on-task behavior, or (e) punishing Helen for off-task behavior. The first three strategies are more natural, should take less teacher time and effort, should be more enjoyable for both student and teacher, and may result in more enduring changes in behavior. They are least intrusive and should be tried before more intrusive strategies are implemented.

Teachers must also provide an environment that maximizes the possibilities for learning. For many handicapped students, simply providing a stimulating learning environment will be insufficient to produce rapid and enduring changes in behavior. Effective instruction for those students will require more intrusive techniques. However, even when more intrusive techniques are used, an appropriate learning environment should exist in order to maximize the effectiveness of those techniques.

Substantial literature supports the notion of a match between the environment and the behavior expected in that environment (Barker, 1968). Furthermore, literature reviews support the importance of some aspects of the physical environment and their effects on both social and academic behavior (Semmel, Lieber, & Peck, 1986; Twardosz, 1984; Weinstein, 1979). An effective environment has at least five attributes: (1) it provides appropriate physical facilities, (2) it promotes engagement, (3) it provides multiple opportunities for learning, (4) it communicates expectations, and (5) it promotes success and reinforcement.

PROVIDING APPROPRIATE PHYSICAL FACILITIES

School environments frequently pose barriers to effective teaching and learning. Classrooms may have inadequate space, they can be noisy or distracting (e.g., located next to the cafeteria), or they can be unattractive or unpleasant because of uncomfortable furniture, drab walls, poor lighting, wrong temperatures, or outdated equipment. Special education classrooms frequently take a secondary priority in schools, and almost any teacher can recount stories of special education classrooms being located in closets, storage rooms, temporary trailers, basements, or on the stage. Although some environmental conditions will only change if school boards and citizens commit significant funds toward the renovation or expansion of facilities, many aspects of learning environments can be controlled and changed by teachers. Effective environmental planning requires an analysis of students' learning needs and a systematic study of existing environmental provisions and resources.

Planning educational environments is especially important for handicapped students. "Special" education often means the provision of special environments. In some cases, such special environments (e.g., special classes, resource rooms, low-distraction areas, modified environments to increase accessibility and mobility, Braille signs) are necessary. However, in other cases the handicapped label has served as a justification for environmental modifications that are unnecessary and often detrimental to generalized skill use, such as self-contained classrooms or barren, unstimulating rooms. Modifications of the curriculum or instructional procedures could be used instead, allowing students to learn in regular or less restricted placements.

When learning occurs in environments that are significantly different from those environments in which a behavior is expected, generalized skill performance often does not occur (Stokes & Baer, 1977). Part of this failure is due to the differences between learning and application environments. Consider a student in a prevocational program who may learn assembly skills in a quiet classroom environment, but is unsuccessful in using those skills in a noisy, busy workshop. Effective teaching of handicapped students requires that teachers carefully analyze each student's needs for a learning environment and design environments that not only maximize learning, but also facilitate students' use of those skills in other environments. Thus, the teacher in the prevocational classroom may need to introduce some levels of noise and confusion so that the classroom environment more closely approximates that of the work place.

When planning environments for all students, several principles are important. These include an environment that is comfortable, conducive to teaching and learning, adequately sized and equipped, and, for handicapped students, the least restrictive but effective.

A Comfortable Environment

A "comfortable environment" refers to the aesthetics of an environment and its physical comfort. Lighting should be adequate for reading; however, variation is important if possible. For example, Smith, Neisworth, and Greer (1978) suggested brighter lighting at reading areas and softer lighting in discussion areas. Temperature should be in a comfortable range (68 to 74 degrees F), with an adequate supply of fresh air (Smith et al., 1978). A variety of colors should be used to identify learning areas, to break up the monotony of a single color, and to brighten up the room (Olds, 1979). Sufficient furnishings must be available that are appropriate to the ages and sizes of students in the class.

An Environment Conducive to Teaching and Learning

An environment conducive to teaching and learning is one that has clearly defined learning areas, an easy and nondisruptive flow of traffic, minimal distractions, and is easily supervised and monitored by the teacher. Clearly defined learning areas serve to establish expectations for behavior. Areas should be well organized and neatly arranged to facilitate the use of materials and to provide a model for returning materials when the activity is completed.

Distractions should be reduced by separating noisy areas from quiet areas and by arranging traffic patterns so students can move quietly and directly from one area to another. Teachers should be able to observe and monitor student performance at all times. At the preschool level, activity areas should be separated by low dividers providing separate learning/activity areas for students while allowing teachers to view each area. In some cases, the practice of placing problem students near the teacher is effective. Weinstein (1979) reviewed the literature on this topic and concluded that "the weight of the evidence . . . seems to indicate that a front-center seat facilitates achievement, positive attitudes, and participation, at least for those somewhat predisposed to speak in class" (p. 580).

Many authors have suggested that noise is a primary distractor in classrooms and should be reduced at all costs. Weinstein's (1979) review, however, suggested that research to date has not provided conclusive evidence on this point. Students and teachers alike appear to adapt to noise, particularly if it is regular and predictable, such as the typical noise level in an open-space classroom. Infrequent and less predictable noisy interruptions are more distracting.

An Environment with Adequate Space and Materials

Both human and animal research suggests that crowding can have negative effects on behavior. Hutt and Viazey (1966) demonstrated increased aggressiveness in brain-damaged children as group size increased, and Kreger (1971) demonstrated that reducing overcrowding in a residential institution for severely retarded persons resulted in reduced aggression and other behavior problems. Weinstein's (1979) review suggests several undesirable effects of high-density classrooms, including increased nervousness, dissatisfaction, reduced social interactions, and increased aggression. Adequate space should be available for students to work effectively without competing with other students for space. Seats should be adequately spaced in areas where attending and individual task performance are important, since placing desks too close to each other generally increases off-task behavior and disruptiveness (Axelrod, Hall, & Tams, 1979). Likewise, adequate materials should be available to avoid arguments over toys or materials, to avoid waiting by other students, and to provide for a variety of activities. Horner (1980) found that enriching the physical environment in an institutional ward for profoundly retarded females with toys and other interesting objects reduced maladaptive behaviors, particularly stereotypic and self-injurious behaviors, and increased adaptive object-directed behavior.

A Least Restrictive Environment

Public Law 94–142 mandates that each handicapped student be placed in the **least restrictive environment** that also meets the student's educational needs. Often, restrictiveness has been defined on a continuum of placements ranging from most restrictive (residential institution) to least restrictive (regular classroom). However, any environment should be evaluated according to its restrictiveness for individual children. Edgar (1977) suggested six dimensions that must be considered in determining the restrictiveness of a given setting. First, staff expectations must not restrain student performance or opportunities. For example, a regular classroom in which the teacher had low performance expectations for a handicapped student and thus made few demands would be more restrictive than a self-contained classroom in which the teacher had high expectations for performance and provided a challenging learning environment. Second, appropriate and inclusive educational opportunities for the student must be available. An environment with poorly trained teachers and insufficient support services would be a restrictive environment. Third, the student must have opportunities to participate in experiences normally available to all students, such as music or physical education. Fourth, the physical setting must allow and facilitate a high degree of freedom and independence. It should be barrier-free and accessible to students with sensory or motor impairments, and the teacher should organize it and provide sufficient cues to promote independence. Fifth, the environment should be in close proximity to nonhandicapped peers. Finally, opportunities for interacting with nonhandicapped peers should be available.

Applications of Environmental Planning

Although a number of important principles of environmental planning may be described, two limitations should be emphasized. First, the research in this area is extremely limited. More importantly, however, environmental planning and intervention should be approached on an individual basis just as other educational interventions are implemented, especially when working with exceptional students. Often, in fact, special educators have been guilty of unnecessary and possibly inappropriate environmental modifications. For example, 15 years ago special education teachers were taught that *nothing* should be placed on the classroom walls since all special education students were highly distractible. This advice resulted (and still results) in many barren, uninviting classrooms. Although this strategy may be important for some students, no research has documented its effectiveness, and clearly it is not needed for all exceptional students.

Following an applied behavior analysis perspective, the teacher's role includes assessment of individual student needs for learning environments, planning and implementing specific environmental alterations, and evaluating the effects of those alterations on student behavior and achievement. In order to demonstrate examples of this approach to environmental planning, three published examples of environmental manipulations are described.

Student Behavior in an Open Classroom. Weinstein (1977) used time-sampling techniques to assess the behavior of students in a combination second- and third-grade open classroom. Baseline data revealed five primary problems in children's use of classroom space. First, students typically were not evenly distributed across the room, resulting in overcrowding of some areas and underutilization of other areas. Second, girls generally ignored game and science areas. Third, a limited range of activities was observed in game and science areas. Fourth, children rarely used the manipulative materials and equipment in the room. Finally, behavior in the reading area, intended to be quiet and comfortable in order to encourage concentration, often involved looking at or interacting with others as well as roughhousing.

Based on these data, an intervention plan was specified in order to achieve specific outcomes:

> Three overall goals were to encourage the use of areas that were infrequently visited, to increase their flexibility, and to facilitate the manipulation of curriculum materials. In the science area extensive shelving was built on which materials could be clearly displayed. In the games area, a low platform, table and stools provided surfaces on which to play games or write. Shelving was also added here for the storage of board games. In the reading area, a raised platform and carrels for individual study were added. The children's individual storage compartments were moved from within the area to the edge where they functioned as a partition. A small, cardboard "house" was added to the corner, which replaced the table and desk located there. It was hoped that this house would provide a quiet, private place not existing elsewhere in the room and would thus increase the use of this space. (Weinstein, 1977, p. 257)

These changes were made in part because of the messiness of game and science areas and lack of available work spaces to accommodate a variety of activities. The intervention resulted in a more equal distribution of children in the room, increased use of the game and science areas by boys and girls, increased use of manipulative behaviors, and a greater variety of behaviors in the game and science areas. The only observed change in the reading area was a decrease in instances of children looking at other children.

Toileting Skills. Siegel (1977) investigated the effects of an environmental modification on certain toileting skills. A frequent problem unique to males is "misdirected urination" or instances in which the toilet is missed during urination. This results in an unpleasant and unclean bathroom environment and makes extra work for teachers or custodial staff who are responsible for cleaning the bathroom. Siegel's study investigated the effects of small floating targets on the urination behavior of moderately retarded boys ages 8 to 14. Results indicated that the use of floating targets significantly reduced misdirected urinations in all three boys. Advantages of this procedure include the reduced amount of time needed by the teacher to modify the behavior and the decreased need to resort to more aversive techniques.

Noise and Hyperactive Behavior. Whalen, Henker, Collins, Finck, and Dotemoto (1979) studied the effects of noisy versus quiet conditions as a part of a broader study of the behavior of hyperactive boys in classroom environments. They found that in noisy conditions the hyperactive boys were less likely to attend to the task at hand and demonstrated higher levels of verbalizations, physical contact, gross motor movement, and high-energy acts. This finding reinforces the need for assessing the learning needs of individual students. Furthermore, it suggests that relatively simple strategies (e.g., quieter classroom activities) may be used to achieve the same outcomes for some students that otherwise would require the use of medication or more intrusive behavior-management techniques.

Summary

This section described physical characteristics of effective learning environments. Teachers must provide an appropriate learning environment that decreases interfering conditions, prepares students for the many similarities and differences that are present across instructional environments, and enables learning to occur. Such settings must be comfortable and reinforcing, conducive to learning and teaching, and least restrictive. When these conditions are present, effective teaching can be presented and maximum learning can occur.

Teachers should be aware, however, that for many handicapped students, environmental modification alone will not achieve desired changes in behavior. For example, Horner (1980) found that an enriched environment combined with reinforcement of adaptive behavior increased appropriate toy and object play and reduced self-stimulatory and self-injurious behavior beyond the effect observed in the enriched environment alone. Environmental provisions may constitute a necessary but insufficient intervention for many students. Furthermore, teachers should be cautioned that some environmental changes may result in temporary and seemingly effective changes, causing the teacher to believe that other needed interventions are not necessary. For example, Ms. Jones observes that Bob talks with Robin which prevents both of them from finishing their work. When the teacher separates Bob and Robin, their work completion increases and Ms. Jones is "fooled" into thinking that the problem has been eliminated. However, when Bob and Robin again sit next to one another, talking and work incompletion problems are once again observed. Environmental modifications can affect temporary improvement for some behaviors. More long-lasting and generalizable effects should be facilitated through a combination of environmental modification and systematic instruction.

PROMOTING ENGAGEMENT

One of the simplest yet most fundamental assumptions for effective teaching is that learning takes time. Furthermore, some children require more time for learning than others. This assumption was formally stated by Carroll (1963), who proposed that the amount of learning for a given student is a function of both (a) the time actually spent working on a task and (b) the time that the student needs in order to master that task. Research has consistently documented that student achievement and progress in instructional programs in part depends on the amount of time spent on school-related tasks (Emmer, 1981; Evertson, Anderson, & Brophy, 1978; Walker & Hops, 1976; Wyne & Stuck, 1979).

Several measures of time can be identified. **Allocated time** refers to the amount of time a teacher plans to devote to a given activity. For example, the daily schedule may include 45 minutes for reading, 30 minutes for math, and 30 minutes for written language. The amount of time allocated to a given activity, however, is not always the amount of time spent on that activity. Perhaps that is why research suggests that allocated time alone is not strongly related to student achievement (Berliner, 1979; Borg, 1980). **Engaged time** (also called *time-on-task*) refers to that portion of allocated time in which the student is actually engaged in the intended activity. For example, during a 45-minute reading period, the student may actually be reading for only 15 minutes. **Academic learning time** refers to that portion of engaged time in which the student is involved in an activity that actually facilitates learning. For example, during the 15 minutes of actual reading, the student may only be working on a new skill for 3 minutes. Research suggests that a strong relationship exists between engaged time and student achievement; furthermore, academic learning time accounts for additional gains in achievement (Anderson, 1976; Borg, 1980; Fisher et al., 1980). In a study of teachers of severely handicapped children, Fredericks, Anderson, and Baldwin (1979) found that the variable most likely to differentiate low-achieving from high-achieving children was the number of minutes spent on daily instruction. It appears that both the amount and quality of time spent on a given activity influence learning.

How do effective teachers maintain high levels of on-task behavior? Paine, Radicchi, Rosellini, Deutchman, and Darch (1983) suggested that the first step is for the teacher to analyze the classroom schedule to determine the total amount of time allocated to various activities. Data should be gathered over several days to determine actual amounts of engaged time within each allocated time period. Collecting data on engagement is best done through a momentary time-sampling system. Define engagement for your class and measure at least three broad categories of behavior: engaged, nonengaged (inappropriate or inattentive behavior), and waiting (appropriate behavior, but waiting for turn, materials, or directions). Samples can be gathered for each student during different times of the day and periodically throughout the year. Data should be analyzed for the class as a whole and then for individual students to determine adequacy of engaged time. Sample data from two different classes and suggested changes for each are displayed in Table 11.1.

In attempts to increase engaged time, try to limit the amount of time spent in "organizational" tasks such as lunch count, attendance, or announcements. A schedule should be established and procedures implemented to ensure that students and teachers alike adhere to it. If necessary, timers should be used as reminders of when activities begin and end.

In addition to scheduling time for instruction, at least five broad strategies for increasing engagement within the context of individual lessons should be considered: (a) providing functional, interesting, and worthwhile materials and activities; (b) being prepared for instruction; (c) pacing instruction; (d) using contingency management techniques; and (e) ensuring effective transitions.

Functional and Interesting Materials and Activities

One strategy for maintaining high levels of on-task behavior is to make the activities and materials provided to students interesting, fun, and exciting. Television shows such as *Sesame Street, Electric Company,* and *Reading Rainbow* exemplify fun learning. Although most teachers cannot approximate the multimedia, fast-paced, and varied format of these shows, they should attempt to make learning as interesting as possible. For young students, this means using manipulable, colorful materials and a gamelike format. For older students, it means teaching basic skills such as reading and math in interesting contexts that have personal meaning for the students. For example, the content of stories read could include fantasy figures, sports figures, stories students generate, or daily living activities in which students are involved.

In addition to interesting materials and activities, students are more likely to engage in activities for longer periods of time if they view those activities as important. Students should be taught that learning is worthwhile and will have some ultimate benefit for them. Teachers should not only select useful and worthwhile activities, but also should help students see the reasons why they are learning specific skills.

Preparation for Instruction

It is a mistake not to be prepared for an instructional activity (Evertson, Anderson, & Brophy, 1978; Emmer, Sanford, Clements, & Martin, 1982). Preparation means several things. First, all necessary materials (toys, pencils, work sheets, books, pictures, word cards, etc.) should be collected and placed in an organized fashion so that they are readily accessible. Second, the teacher should know the instructional objectives for each student in the group. Third, the teacher should have a procedural plan for conducting the lesson and should be sufficiently familiar with it so implementation is smooth and efficient. Finally, the teacher should have independent activities available for students to do while he or she is engaged in one-to-one or small group instruction with other students.

Pacing

A consistent research finding is that fast-paced instruction is a better facilitator of on-task behavior than slow-paced instruction. Carnine (1976) found that a

TABLE 11.1 Data from two classes for the percentage of time they spent engaged, nonengaged, and waiting. Potential changes that are needed in classroom are described.

Classroom 1

Percentage of Engaged, Nonengaged, and Waiting Time Over a 3-Day Period

Student	Day 1			Day 2			Day 3		
	Engaged	*Nonengaged*	*Waiting*	*Engaged*	*Nonengaged*	*Waiting*	*Engaged*	*Nonengaged*	*Waiting*
a	60.0	18.5	21.5	58.5	19.5	22.0	61.0	17.0	22.0
b	70.0	10.5	19.5	64.5	24.5	11.0	71.0	17.0	12.0
c	60.0	15.4	24.6	48.2	25.0	26.8	51.6	16.2	32.2
d	61.5	12.0	26.5	55.2	17.2	27.6	59.7	19.3	21.0
e	55.2	17.2	27.6	59.7	19.3	21.0	54.7	18.3	27.0
f	67.2	17.2	15.6	62.7	25.3	12.0	63.2	29.4	07.4
g	69.2	13.2	17.5	67.4	18.6	14.0	75.0	15.0	10.0
h	60.0	15.4	24.6	60.0	18.5	21.5	67.2	15.6	17.2
Mean Percentage	62.9	14.9	22.2	59.5	20.9	19.5	62.9	18.5	18.6

As a group and for each student in this class, the percentage of engaged time is lower than it should be, and the percentages of time spent nonengaged and waiting are high. Thus, the teacher needs to restructure the learning environment by using the procedures described in this section for increasing engaged time; however, targeting specific children for change as compared to the entire class is not likely to produce classwide changes.

Classroom 2

Percentage of Engaged, Nonengaged, and Waiting Time Over a 3-Day Period

Student	Day 1			Day 2			Day 3		
	Engaged	Nonengaged	Waiting	Engaged	Nonengaged	Waiting	Engaged	Nonengaged	Waiting
a	90.0	8.5	2.5	92.5	3.0	4.5	91.0	5.0	4.0
b	94.0	2.5	3.5	95.5	1.9	6.4	93.0	4.0	3.0
c	60.0	3.0	37.0	58.2	5.0	36.8	51.6	6.2	42.2
d	96.0	2.0	2.0	93.2	3.2	3.6	97.0	2.0	1.0
e	60.0	24.4	14.6	59.7	29.3	11.0	63.2	29.4	7.4
f	93.2	4.2	2.6	92.7	5.3	2.0	93.2	2.4	4.4
g	89.2	5.2	5.6	87.4	8.6	4.0	91.0	5.0	4.0
h	90.0	5.4	4.6	90.0	4.5	5.5	93.2	5.6	1.2
Mean Percentage	84.0	6.9	9.0	83.7	7.4	9.2	84.2	7.5	8.4

While most children in this class are engaged at high percentages of the time (i.e., 90% or above), student C spends much of his or her day waiting and student E spends much of his or her time nonengaged and waiting. Thus, the teacher should develop more activities for student C and perhaps develop a contingency-management program for student E. The teacher does not need to change the learning environment for other children in the classroom.

fast-paced instructional approach with first graders was superior to a slower pace as evidenced by decreased off-task behavior and increased correct responding. Koegel, Dunlap, and Dyer (1980) found similar results in a study conducted with autistic children.

What is meant by a fast-paced instructional format? Obviously, a teacher can go too fast and put too much pressure on students for rapid performance. Furst (1967) found that a moderate rate of instruction was optimal. An appropriate pace is one that keeps students actively involved in instruction, with little time spent waiting for the teacher to locate materials or for another student to respond. The studies cited thus far have focused on the interval between teacher presentation of tasks. For example, the Carnine study compared a 1-second interval with a 5-second interval. In the context of a direct-instruction format, Gersten, Carnine, and Williams (1982) defined appropriate pacing as a minimum of nine learning tasks per minute. Potentially, a fast but variable pace would be the most effective. White, Wyne, Stuck, and Coop (1983) pointed out, however, that "these findings on the negative effects of teacher pauses *following a student response* should not be confused with the positive effects of 'wait-time,' the amount of time that the teacher gives students to respond *following a question*" (p. 65).

Contingency-Management Techniques

The procedures described thus far are preferred strategies for maintaining on-task behavior since they are the most natural and least intrusive. However, these strategies will be ineffective with some students. In such cases, teachers may need to use **contingency-management techniques.** This means that the teacher sets up a system in which the availability of certain positive outcomes (e.g., tokens, free time, use of a favorite toy) is made contingent upon on-task behavior; likewise, negative consequences (e.g., loss of free time) may be made contingent upon off-task behavior. For example, White-Blackburn, Semb, and Semb (1977) established a good-behavior contract with four sixth-grade students. Students were given a list of good-conduct and assignment-completion goals along with a list of rewards and penalties. Every 15 minutes, the teacher decided whether students had earned a reward or a penalty. Results indicated that the students' on-task behavior and assignment-completion rates increased, and disruptive behavior decreased.

A cautionary note should be raised, however. Marholin and Steinman (1977) studied the behavior of fifth and sixth graders with behavior problems under three conditions: (a) an unreinforced baseline, (b) reinforcement for being on task, and (c) reinforcement for the accuracy and rate of math problems solved. Although both reinforcement conditions positively affected on-task behavior when the teacher was present, reinforcement for rate and accuracy was superior to reinforcement for being on task in reducing behavior problems and increasing the number of problems attempted when the teacher was out of the room. The authors concluded that "by providing contingencies for the products of a child's classroom activities (i.e., academic achievement), rather than for some measure of task orientation or appropriate social behavior, the child will become more independent of the teacher's continual surveillance" (p. 477).

Effective Transitions

A *transition* is a shift or change from one activity to another. It can range from simply getting out another workbook to moving to another room or teacher. Transitions are necessary to keep children involved in a variety of activities throughout the day. However, transitions can be one of the worst times of the day for teachers and students. Without careful planning, they can result in considerable time wasted or may lead to other inappropriate behaviors such as talking out or aggressive acts. For example, Kuergeleis, Deutchman, and Paine (1980) observed that transitions could last as long as 20 minutes. Given repeated transition periods throughout the day, this could result in considerable time wasted. In fact, Paine et al. (1983) suggested that the average student may spend the equivalent of one day per week on transition time alone! Arlin (1979), in an observational study in grades 1 through 9, found significantly higher rates of off-task behavior during transitions. Emmer et al. (1982) found that efficient transitions typically produced fewer disruptive behaviors and more on-task behavior.

  Effective transitions contain at least three components. First, students should be taught rules for transitions. Paine et al. (1983) suggested four basic rules:

1. Move quietly.
2. Put your books away and get what you need for the next activity. (You may need to state what that activity will be and what materials students need for it.)
3. Move your chairs quietly. (In some classes with small-group instruction, students carry their desk chairs to the group for seating there.)
4. Keep your hands and feet to yourself. (p. 85)

The teacher should introduce these rules to students and review them regularly. A preset signal (e.g., "It's transition time") coupled with specific directions for movement should always be used. Consequences for failure to follow all four rules should be in place.

  Second, teachers should avoid practices that disrupt or interfere with transitions. Kounin, Frieson, and Norton (1966) described four such practices: (a) giving confusing or conflicting directions, (b) dropping an activity or suddenly changing directions, (c) returning to an old activity after beginning a new one, and (d) providing wrong information, such as telling students to go to the wrong area or retrieve the wrong materials. Teachers with lower rates of these practices had more on-task behaviors in their classes.

  Finally, the schedule and staffing assignments should be arranged to minimize the amount of time students must spend waiting for other students. This can be accomplished by providing materials or other activities for students to do while waiting. Another is to allow students to move from station to station or from activity to activity at their own pace. This practice means that the next station or activity must be ready for students. LeLaurin and Risley (1972) demonstrated the effectiveness of such an approach by comparing "zone" versus "man-to-man" staff assignment patterns in a day care center. In the zone procedure, staff were assigned to zones or areas and stayed in those areas. Children were allowed to move from one area to another at their own pace. For example, rather than waiting for the whole group to finish lunch, children could leave as they finished and go to the bathroom to brush their teeth and then get ready for a nap. Under the man-to-man condition, all children in a group had to wait until their peers had finished one activity before moving to the next. The zone procedure resulted in more efficient transitions and higher levels of engagement than did the man-to-man procedure.

Although transitions frequently are viewed as down time or unproductive time, some learning and teaching can occur. Wolery, Doyle, Ault, Gast, and Lichtenberg (1987) presented preschoolers with a single trial on academic and language tasks as they left one activity area for another. These trials were repeated during each transition of the day. This training produced learning similar to that found in structured one-on-one training sessions. Thus, teachers should view transition times as opportunities to provide brief instruction.

PROVIDING MULTIPLE OPPORTUNITIES FOR LEARNING

Rationale for Multiple Opportunities

Research clearly supports the importance of engaged time to instructional success. The longer students work on relevant tasks, the more likely they are to achieve. A related issue is whether students have multiple opportunities to practice the same task. Assume that you are trying to learn a complicated dance step. If you only practiced the step one time each day, it probably would take a long time to master it. However, if you practiced it 20 times each day, learning would occur in a relatively short period of time. The provision of multiple opportunities for learning and practice serves to facilitate skill acquisition and fluency. The effective teacher provides such multiple opportunities for learning during each school day.

Hall, Delquadri, Greenwood, and Thurston (1982) suggested that, across students and programs, no single instructional technique appears to be clearly superior. However, in all cases, "effective procedures seemed to be those which allowed students to practice the academic task" (p. 109). Their observations suggest, however, that students may practice many skills only a few times each day. While some skills, such as math problems, may be repeated several times, others may receive practice only one time per day, or even less often. Hall et al. suggested four reasons for low academic response rates in classrooms. First, teachers may not be aware of the importance of increased student responding. Many may assume that listening and paying attention is as effective as actually responding. Second, the demands of curricula and large numbers of students may preclude multiple opportunities to practice skills. Third, increasing student responding may not be pleasant to those who are responsible for it, since it involves additional work and energy, both in terms of actually preparing and presenting the task and in grading or providing feedback to students. Finally, research suggests that students in greatest need of multiple responding often actually receive the least amount of teacher attention.

Hall et al. called for increased recognition of the importance of multiple opportunities to respond and suggested several strategies for increasing such opportunities. Among these are using grandparents or other volunteers in the classroom, asking parents to help students practice and reinforce skills at home, and using peer tutoring strategies. Self-management and self-instructional procedures (see Chapter 25) may also increase opportunities for learning. In addition, teachers can capitalize on regularly occurring classroom routines and use incidental teaching procedures (Warren & Kaiser, 1986) to create additional opportunities for responding.

Distributing Opportunities to Respond

Assuming that it is important for students to have multiple opportunities to practice a skill during the day, how should those opportunities be provided? Mulligan, Guess, Holvoet, and Brown (1980) described three possible ways in which numerous learning trials could be presented. **Massed trials** refers to the repeated presentation of several trials such that no other behavior occurs between trials. For example, the teacher might present 20 flashcards of math facts with sums under 10 to a student, one right after the other. **Spaced trials** are similar to massed trials except that a rest period or pause occurs between each trial. **Distributed trials** refers to the presentation of a program such that related or new tasks are presented between trials.

The three approaches to instruction are demonstrated in the following example. Ms. Collins is teaching Susie to recognize the color red. Being a good teacher, she realizes that Susie should have multiple opportunities to practice that skill every day and thus plans for at least 10 trials per day. Using a massed trials approach, she presents two blocks to Susie and says "Touch red." After Susie indicates her choice and is reinforced or corrected, Ms. Collins repeats the task, continuing in this manner until 10 trials have been completed. Using a spaced trials format, Ms. Collins allows for a short rest period (e.g. 15 seconds) between each trial. Using a distributed trials format, she asks Susie to touch red, then puts the red block on a tower, counts the blocks, and then starts over again. In each format, Susie eventually has to select a red block 10 times. The difference is not the number of trials, but how those trials are presented or distributed. Of course, a distributed trials format may be spread out over the entire day. For example, Ms. Collins might plan for 10 different occasions when Susie would need to select something that is red, such as red napkins for snack time, a red dress for her doll, and so forth.

In their review of the research on massed, spaced, and distributed trials, Mulligan et al. concluded that the distributed trials format is a superior instructional strategy. Students are less likely to become fatigued or bored with a given task and may increase attention to the task because of the variety of stimuli being used. When other instructional objectives are interspersed in the distributed trials format, learning is more efficient. Finally, the distributed trials format should facilitate skill generalization, since most skills are not performed repeatedly and in immediate succession in daily life. Rather, they are interspersed with other skills. In a study with young autistic children, a distributed trials condition produced higher and more stable levels of correct responding (Dunlap & Koegel, 1980). Furthermore, observers found that the distributed trials format resulted in greater interest and enthusiasm on the part of children as well as fewer behavior problems.

Holvoet, Guess, Mulligan, and Brown (1980) developed a curriculum for severely handicapped students based on the distributed trials format and extended its application to small-group instructional formats (Brown, Holvoet, Guess, & Mulligan, 1980). In Figure 11.1, a sample student schedule is presented. The same objectives are distributed throughout the day across instructional activities, in different environments, and with different persons.

Distributed trials formats are important for students of all ages and ability levels. Assume, for example, that Louise is working on the skill of following written directions. In a distributed trials format, she receives short, written

FIGURE 11.1   Sample distributed trials schedule.

MORNING SCHEDULE AND OBJECTIVES FOR BRAD

8:20–8:30 Homeroom
1. Greet teacher.
2. Locate name on coat rack.
3. Get materials from desk.
4. Sit down within 1 minute of room entry.

8:30–9:30 Reading Resource Room
1. Greet resource teacher.
2. Locate folder with name on it.
3. Put folder on desk.
4. Sit down within 1 minute of room entry.

9:30–10:30 Social Studies
1. Greet teacher.
2. Locate workbook.
3. Go to work group.
4. Be in work group within 1 minute of room entry.

10:30–11:00 Physical Education
1. Greet coach.
2. Read chart for games assignment.
3. Go to appropriate games area.
4. Be in games area within 1 minute of going outdoors.

directions for activities throughout the day, rather than a work sheet of 15 directions to read and immediately follow. Likewise, integrating reading and math instruction into the same activity can be done by presenting students with frequent word problems.

Capitalizing on Naturally Occurring Events and Routines

The distributed trials format can be implemented by capitalizing on naturally occurring events and routines in the classroom to encourage students to practice and use skills. Too often, instruction is limited to specific sessions. Reading is done between 9:00 and 9:30, self-help at 10:00, and so forth. However, in the real world, students will be required to use skills in a variety of contexts. Taking advantage of classroom events and routines to practice those skills should facilitate generalized use as well as make their function or relevance more apparent to students.

Bailey, Harms, and Clifford (1983) conducted an observational study of the social and educational aspects of mealtimes for handicapped and nonhandicapped preschoolers. The study indicated that teachers generally did not capitalize on the potential of meals for teaching and reinforcing functional skills. Children were not involved in many of the routines and were not encouraged to use language, social, or cognitive skills during meals. When asked, teachers indicated that these instructional activities occurred at other times during the day. For example, tooth-brushing activities might be held during the 10:00 self-help lesson or food labeling might occur during the 9:00 language lesson. Having children practice skills such as labeling, sorting, measuring, or pouring during the mealtime routine should facilitate skill acquisition and use and be fun as well. Mealtimes are particularly good for teaching conversational skills.

More systematic use of naturally occuring routines and activities has been advocated in the form of three specific strategies: the mand-model procedure, the incidental teaching procedure, and naturalistic time delay.

Mand-Model Procedure. The **mand-model** procedure was developed by Rogers-Warren and Warren (1980) and is graphically displayed in Figure 11.2. Its original application and purpose was to enhance children's language skills. The following description of its experimental use is provided by Warren, McQuarter, and Rogers-Warren (1984):

> The teachers were instructed to interact normally with the subjects but to intersperse their comments and instructions with the mand-model procedure. Typically, as a subject was playing with materials, a teacher would ask an open-ended question that required more than a "yes" or "no" answer (e.g., "What are you doing?") or instruct the child to verbalize about the child's activity (e.g., "Tell me what you are doing"). If the subject responded appropriately, the teacher provided positive feedback (e.g., "That's neat," or "Right"). If the subject failed to

FIGURE 11.2 Steps for the mand-model procedure.

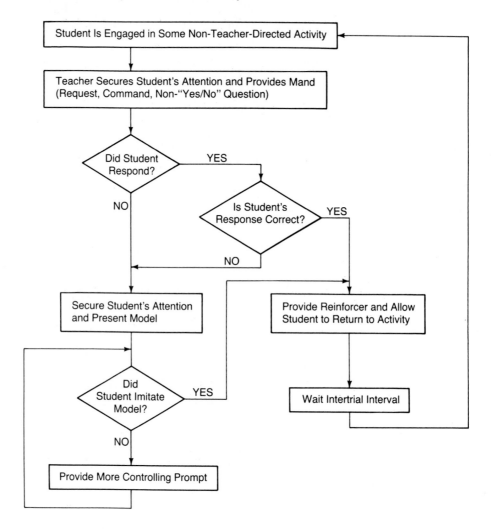

respond to the mand, the teacher then provided an appropriate verbal model (e.g., "Say, 'I'm coloring.'") and required the child's imitative response. (p. 45)

The procedure was effective in increasing verbalizations of language-delayed preschool children. It has also been useful in facilitating generalization of language skills learned in traditional structured language-training sessions (Rogers-Warren & Warren, 1980).

The mand-model procedure can be used in almost any setting because it requires only a very brief interaction between teacher and student. For example, it could be used while students are practicing a given skill and the teacher is monitoring their work. The teacher would approach one student, provide the mand (question or command), wait for the student to respond, provide a model if necessary, and acknowledge the correctness of the response.

Incidental Teaching. The **incidental teaching** procedure was developed and studied by Hart and Risley. They found it was effective in teaching preschool children from economically disadvantaged homes to acquire and generalize a number of different language behaviors (Hart & Risley, 1968, 1974, 1975). As a result of its use, a number of unanticipated effects occurred; specifically, children talked more, used more different words, and used more elaborate and complex sentences (Hart & Risley, 1980). Recently, incidental teaching has been shown to be more effective than traditional one-on-one training for teaching autistic children to use prepositions (McGee, Krantz, & McClannahan, 1985). It has also been employed when teaching autistic and autistic-like children to say "yes/no" in response to questions (Neef, Walters, & Egel, 1984). Finally, Cavallaro and Paulson (1985) used it to teach a number of different language behaviors to students with a variety of moderate to severe handicaps.

The steps in the incidental teaching procedure are shown in Figure 11.3. To use the procedure, teachers should do at least three things (Hart & Rogers-Warren, 1978). First, they should structure the classroom environment so that students need to use language. For example, materials students need can be placed so that they must ask for them, novel toys or materials can be shown to students, or parts of activities can be missing such as some pieces to a puzzle or the ending of a story. Second, teachers should be aware of the language goals for each student. Third, teachers should respond to the content of students' statements; if a student asks for materials, the materials should be provided after the student produces more complex language, rather than praising the student for asking.

Teachers must know how to use the procedure before it will be effective. As illustrated in the flowchart, the procedure requires six teacher behaviors: *focus* on the student, *verify* the topic of the student's initiation, *request an elaboration* of the student's statement, *model* an elaboration if it is not forthcoming, *confirm* the correctness of the student's statement or imitated utterance and/or praise the child, and *provide access* to the requested object, action, activity, information, or give permission. When teachers learn of incidental teaching they frequently state that they do it all the time. However, data on some Head Start teachers suggests that they use parts but not all of the procedure (Mudd & Wolery, 1987). They consistently focus on students, verify the topics of their initiations, and provide access to requested materials or activities, but rarely do they request elaborations, provide models, or confirm the correctness of students' statements. The primary difference between incidental teaching and the mand-model procedure is that incidental teaching requires a student initiation prior to teaching, whereas the mand-model can be used at any time.

Naturalistic Time Delay. The **naturalistic time delay** procedure is a variation of an errorless learning procedure called *time delay* (Touchette, 1971); it involves a brief

FIGURE 11.3 Steps for implementing incidental teaching.

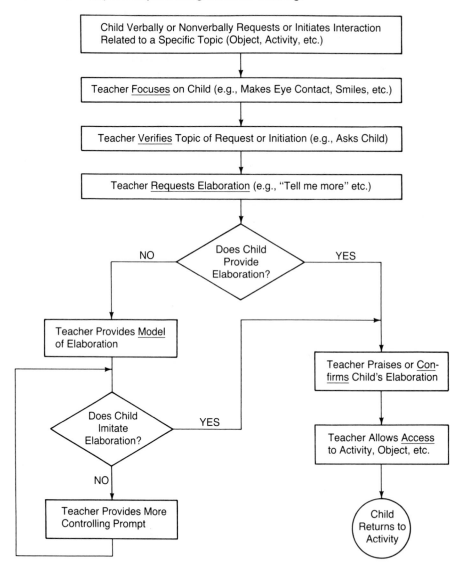

teaching interaction implemented during regularly occurring classroom routines. Initially, teachers must analyze the environment to identify specific steps of routines where instruction may be given. The most appropriate steps are those where the teacher frequently provides assistance. After a specific step in the routine is selected for instruction, the teacher delays assistance or interactions for a specified number of seconds. If the student initiates a request during that delay interval, assistance or the requested object is provided and the routine or interaction continues. If the student does not initiate, a model is provided. For example, during snack, Freda's teacher frequently pours the juice into students' glasses and he is using naturalistic time delay to teach her to make requests, such as "Juice please" or "May I have some juice." He stands near Freda with the juice container and looks at her. When she notices him, he holds the juice container in the air and looks expectantly at her for at least 5 seconds. If during those 5 seconds she requests juice, he praises her and immediately pours some juice in her glass. If she does not request during the delay interval, he provides a verbal model of a request and reinforces her if she imitates him. Naturalistic time delay is similar to the mand-model procedure and incidental teaching in that it is implemented during naturally occurring opportunities and is a brief teaching interaction.

Naturalistic time delay has been used to teach severely handicapped students to request meal trays in a cafeteria (Halle, Marshall, & Spradlin, 1979) and to teach preschoolers with developmental delays to initiate vocalizations (Halle, Baer, & Spradlin, 1981). Hale et al. (1981) also demonstrated that the procedure is relatively simple to use, and teachers can implement it in new situations after being trained to use it in other routines.

COMMUNICATING EXPECTATIONS

A fourth fundamental component of effective teaching is the provision of an organized system of classroom rules and procedures. Rules are important for at least two reasons. First, they provide students advance guidelines or expectations for behavior. Second, they provide teachers a specific standard for judging whether adherence to expectations has occurred. Studies by Emmer et al. (1981, 1982) suggest that the establishment of rules results in decreased disruptive behavior and increased on-task behavior.

Guidelines for Rules

Several authors have described characteristics of effective rules (e.g., Madsen, Becker, & Thomas, 1968; Paine et al., 1983). First, rules should be short and simple so students can remember them. Second, only a few important rules should be specified, rather than a long list. This makes the rules manageable for students and facilitates their recall. Third, when possible rules should be stated positively and in a way that tells students what they *should* do rather than what they should not do. For example, instead of "No talking" the rule could be "Be quiet during work times." Finally, a rule should be broad enough to cover a wide range of behavior, such as "Do your work without bothering others."

Effective Use of Rules

Effective use of rules first requires that students learn the rules. The rules should be written on a large poster and displayed in an easily observed place in the room.

If students cannot read, pictures should be used to give examples of positive rule application. The teachers should also conduct at least one lesson in which the rules are presented and practiced. For example, Paine et al. (1983) presented a script for introducing a set of classroom rules. Brooks (1985) emphasized the importance of presenting these rules in an organized and efficient fashion, highlighting the most important ones and giving examples of positive and negative instances of rule-related behavior. Students should be reminded of rules periodically.

Rules alone, however, are not likely to result in lasting changes in behavior unless a system of consequences for rule-following behavior exists. This point was demonstrated in a study with three elementary-aged children (Madsen, Becker, & Thomas, 1968). Three classroom conditions were studied. In the first condition, teachers generated and explained a list of classroom rules according to the principles described above. In the second condition, teachers ignored inappropriate behavior. In the third condition, teachers continued to ignore inappropriate behavior and remind students of the rules, but also praised appropriate behavior. Results indicated that rules alone had no significant effect on children's inappropriate behavior. However, when combined with ignoring inappropriate behavior and praising appropriate behavior, significant reductions in inappropriate behavior were observed. Similar results were reported by Greenwood, Hops, Delquadri, and Guild (1974) and O'Leary, Becker, Evans, and Saudargas (1969).

SUCCESSFUL AND REINFORCING ENVIRONMENTS

Finally, an effective learning environment is one in which students are usually successful and receive immediate and constructive feedback on their performance. A high success rate is believed to be important for all students in order to maintain motivation, build self-confidence, increase opportunities for reinforcement, and prevent disruptive behaviors likely to occur when tasks become too difficult. Research describing the relationship between student success in instructional tasks and subsequent achievement test scores was reported in the Beginning Teacher Evaluation Study (Fisher et al., 1978).

In special education, this practice has become a basic part of the teacher's repertoire of instructional strategies. Referred to as *errorless learning,* this approach suggests that students learn best from positive skill practice and performance, not through errors. Setting the stage for errorless learning requires three fundamental skills. First, the teacher must be able to identify and present a task appropriate to the student's current capabilities. Second, the teacher may need to use task analysis and teach only small parts of the task at one time. Finally, the teacher must be able to implement a variety of strategies, such as models, cues, and prompts, in order to facilitate student performance. These supportive strategies are described in Chapter 12; procedures for fading prompts are provided in Chapter 14.

Successful task performance often serves as its own feedback. However, for many exceptional students, success alone may be insufficient feedback for learning. An effective learning environment provides immediate and constructive feedback to student performance. As noted in Chapter 1, Skinner (1968), in *The Technology of Teaching,* suggested a number of major problems facing teachers and public education. Three of those problems related to the provision of feedback to students. First, teachers generally are not able to provide immediate feedback for the work of all students in a large classroom. Second, many teachers rely too much on aversive procedures to control and motivate students' performance. Finally, positive reinforcement for correct performance occurs relatively infrequently. Laboratory studies have repeatedly demonstrated that immediate feedback is superior to delayed feedback. This is assumed to be true because of "recency" effects as well as the fact that many events could occur between initial performance and subsequent feedback. A delay may confuse the student as to the precise behavior for which he or she is receiving feedback. A number of studies in educational settings have provided general support for the effectiveness of immediate as opposed to delayed and infrequent feedback to student performance (Gersten, Carnine, & Williams, 1982; Hughes, 1973; Webb, 1982).

The importance and effectiveness of immediate feedback for handicapped students has been demonstrated in literally hundreds of studies over the past 20 years. Often defined as providing consequences for behavior, feedback is an integral part of any special education program. Feedback may take a variety of forms; however, the three basic forms include (a) reinforcement contingencies, (b) aversive contingencies, and (c) error-correction procedures. Specific guidelines for using these feedback procedures are described in subsequent chapters.

Summary of Key Concepts

- Appropriate physical facilities should be provided for learning. The environment should be comfortable, conducive to teaching and learning, contain adequate space and material, and be least restrictive.

- The more students are engaged in learning activities, the more likely they are to learn. Engagement is enhanced by providing functional and interesting materials and activities, being prepared for instruction, using a fast pace, implementing contingency management, and using effective transitions.

- Students should be provided multiple opportunities for learning, distributed throughout the school day. Teachers should especially capitalize on naturally occurring events and routines.

- Teachers should clearly communicate expectations to students. A system of rules and classroom procedures is essential.

- Students need a successful and reinforcing environment.

■ Effective environmental planning must be individualized and should be evaluated for effectiveness.

REFERENCES

Anderson, L. W. (1976). An empirical investigation of individual differences in time to learn. *Journal of Educational Psychology, 68,* 226–233.

Arlin, M. (1979). Teacher transitions can disrupt time flow in classrooms. *American Educational Research Journal, 16,* 42–56.

Axelrod, S., Hall, R. V., & Tams, A. (1979). Comparison of two common classroom seating arrangements. *Academic Therapy, 15,* 29–36.

Bailey, D. B., Harms, T., & Clifford, R. M. (1983). Social and educational aspects of mealtimes for handicapped and nonhandicapped preschoolers. *Topics in Early Childhood Special Education, 3*(2), 19–32.

Barker, R. G. (1968). *Ecological psychology.* Stanford, CA: Stanford University Press.

Berliner, D. C. (1979). Tempus educare. In P. L. Peterson & H. J. Walberg (Eds.), *Research on teaching: Concepts, findings, and implications.* Berkeley, CA: McCutchan.

Borg, W. R. (1980). Time and school learning. In C. Denham & A. Lieberman (Eds.), *Time to learn.* Washington, DC: U.S. Department of Education.

Brooks, D. M. (1985). The teacher's communicative competence: The first day of school. *Theory Into Practice, 24,* 63–70.

Brown, F., Holvoet, J., Guess, D., & Mulligan, M. (1980). The individualized curriculum sequencing model (III): Small group instruction. *Journal of the Association for the Severely Handicapped, 5,* 352–367.

Carnine, D. W. (1976). Effects of two teacher-presentation rates on off-task behavior, answering correctly, and participation. *Journal of Applied Behavior Analysis, 9,* 199–206.

Carroll, J. B. (1963). A model of school learning. *Teacher's College Record, 64,* 723–733.

Cavallaro, C. C., & Paulson, C. L. (1985). Teaching language to handicapped children in natural settings. *Education and Treatment of Children, 8,* 1–24.

Dunlap, G., & Keogel, R. L. (1980). Motivating autistic children through stimulus variation. *Journal of Applied Behavior Analysis, 13,* 619–627.

Edgar, E. (1977). *Least restrictive educational alternatives for the severely/profoundly handicapped.* Unpublished paper, University of Washington, Seattle.

Emmer, E. T. (1981). *Effective management in junior high mathematics classrooms.* Austin, TX: University of Texas, Research and Development Center for Teacher Education, 1981. (R&D Report No. 6111).

Emmer, E. T., Sanford, J. P., Clements, B. S., & Martin, J. (1982). *Improving classroom management and organization in junior high schools: An experimental investigation.* Austin, TX: University of Texas, Research and Development Center for Teacher Education. (R&D Report No. 6153)

Evertson, C. M., Anderson, L. M., & Brophy, J. E. (1978). *Process-outcome relationships in the Texas junior high school study: Compendium.* Washington, DC: National Institute of Education. (ERIC Document Reproduction Service No. ED 166 192)

Fisher, C. W., Filby, N. M., Marlowe, R. S., Cahen, L. S., Dishaw, N. M., Moore, J. E., & Berliner, D. C. (1978). *Teaching behaviors, academic learning time, and student achievement: Final report of Phase IIIB. Beginning teacher evaluation study* (Technical Report V-I). In *Beginning teacher evaluation study.* San Francisco: Far West Laboratory for Educational Research.

Fisher, C. W., Filby, N. M., Marlowe, R., Cahen, L. S., Dishaw, N. M., Moore, J. E., & Berliner, D. C. (1980). Teaching behaviors, academic learning time, and student achievement: An overview. In C. Denham & A. Liebman (Eds.), *Time to learn*. Washington, DC: U.S. Government Printing Office.

Fredericks, H. D. B., Anderson, R., & Baldwin, V. (1979). The identification of competency indicators of teaching of the severely handicapped. *AAESPH Review, 4*, 81–95.

Furst, N. F. (1967). *The multiple languages of the classroom: A further analysis and a synthesis of meanings communicated in high school teaching* (Doctoral dissertation, Temple University). *Dissertation Abstracts, 28*, 1A–1150A. (University Microfilms No. 67–11, 421)

Gersten, R. M., Carnine, D .W., & Williams, P. B. (1982). Measuring implementation of a structural educational model in an urban school district: An observational approach. *Education Evaluation and Policy Analysis, 4*, 67–79.

Greenwood, C., Hops, H., Delquadri, J., & Guild, J. (1974). Group contingencies for group consequences in classroom management: A further analysis. *Journal of Applied Behavior Analysis, 7*, 413–425.

Hall, R. V., Delquadri, J., Greenwood, C. R., & Thurston, L. (1982). The importance of opportunity to respond in children's academic success. In E. B. Edgar, N. G. Haring, J. R. Jenkins, & C. G. Pious (Eds.), *Mentally handicapped children: Education and training* (pp. 107–149). Baltimore: University Park Press.

Halle, J. W., Baer, D. M., & Spradlin, J.E. (1981). Teachers' generalized use of delay as a stimulus control procedure to increase language use in handicapped children. *Journal of Applied Behavior Analysis, 14*, 389–409.

Halle, J. W., Marshall, A. M., & Spradlin, J. E. (1979). Time delay: A technique to increase language use and facilitate generalization in retarded children. *Journal of Applied Behavior Analysis, 12*, 431–439.

Hart, B., & Risley, T. (1968). Establishing use of descriptive adjectives in the spontaneous speech of disadvantaged preschool children. *Journal of Applied Behavior Analysis, 1*, 109–120.

Hart, B., & Risley, T. (1974). Using preschool materials to modify the language of disadvantaged children. *Journal of Applied Behavior Analysis, 7*, 243–256.

Hart, B., & Risley, T. (1975). Incidental teaching of language in the preschool. *Journal of Applied Behavior Analysis, 8*, 411–420.

Hart, B., & Risley, T. (1980). In vivo language intervention: Unanticipated general effects. *Journal of Applied Behavior Analysis, 12*, 407–432.

Hart, B., & Rogers-Warren, A. (1978). A milieu approach to teaching language. In R. L. Schiefelbush (Ed.), *Language intervention strategies* (pp. 193–235). Baltimore: University Park Press.

Holvoet, J., Guess, D., Mulligan, M., & Brown, F. (1980). The Individualized Curriculum Sequencing Model (II): A teaching strategy for severely handicapped students. *Journal of the Association for the Severely Handicapped, 5*, 337–351.

Horner, R. D. (1980). The effects of an environmental "enrichment" program on the behavior of institutionalized profoundly retarded children. *Journal of Applied Behavior Analysis, 13*, 473–491.

Hughes, D. C. (1973). An experimental investigation of the effects of pupil responding and teacher reacting on pupil achievement. *American Educational Research Journal, 10*, 21–37.

Hutt, C., & Viazey, J. J. (1966). Differential effects of group density on social behavior. *Nature, 209*, 1371–1372.

Koegel, R. L., Dunlap, G., & Dyer, K. (1980). Intertrial interval duration and learning in autistic children. *Journal of Applied Behavior Analysis, 13*, 91–99.

Kounin, J. S., Frieson, W. V., & Norton, A. E. (1966). Managing emotionally disturbed children in regular classrooms. *Journal of Educational Psychology, 57*, 1–13.

Kreger, K. C. (1971). Compensatory environment programming for the severely retarded behaviorally disturbed. *Mental Retardation, 9*, 29–33.

Kuergeleis, B., Deutchman, L., & Paine, S. (1980). *Effects of explicit timings on students' transitions.* Eugene, OR: Direct Instruction Follow Through Project, University of Oregon.

LeLaurin, K., & Risley, T. R. (1972). The organization of daycare environments: "Zone" versus "man-to-man" staff assignments. *Journal of Applied Behavior Analysis, 5*, 225–232.

Madsen, C. H., Becker, W. C., & Thomas, D. R. (1968). Rules, praise, and ignoring: Elements of elementary classroom control. *Journal of Applied Behavior Analysis, 1*, 139–150.

Marholin, D., & Steinman, W. M. (1977). Stimulus

control in the classroom as a function of the behavior reinforced. *Journal of Applied Behavior Analysis, 10,* 465–468.

McGee, G. G., Krantz, P. J., & McClannahan, L. E. (1985). The facilitative effects of incidental teaching on preposition use by autistic children. *Journal of Applied Behavior Analysis, 18,* 17–31.

Mudd, J., & Wolery, M. (1987). Teaching Head Start teachers to use incidental teaching. *Journal of the Division for Early Childhood, 11*(2), 124–134.

Mulligan, M., Guess, D., Holvoet, J., & Brown, F. (1980). The Individualized Curriculum Sequencing Model (I): Implications from research on massed, distributed, or spaced trial training. *Journal of the Association for the Severely Handicapped, 5,* 325–336.

Neef, N. A., Walters, J., & Egel, A. L. (1984). Establishing generative yes/no responses in developmentally disabled children. *Journal of Applied Behavior Analysis, 17,* 453–460.

Olds, A. P. (1979). Designing developmentally optimal classrooms for children with special needs. In S. J. Meisels (Ed.), *Special education and development: Perspectives on young children with special needs* (pp. 91–138). Baltimore: University Park Press.

O'Leary, K., Becker, W., Evans, M., & Saudargas, R. (1969). A token reinforcement program in a public school: A replication and systematic analysis. *Journal of Applied Behavior Analysis, 2,* 3–13.

Paine, S. C., Radicchi, J., Rosellini, L. C., Deutchman, L., & Darch, C. B. (1983). *Structuring your classroom for academic success.* Champaign, IL: Research Press.

Rogers-Warren, A., & Warren, S. F. (1980). Mands for verbalization: Facilitating the display of newly trained language in children. *Behavior Modification, 4,* 361–382.

Siegel, R. K. (1977). Stimulus selection and tracking during urination: Autoshaping directed behavior with toilet targets. *Journal of Applied Behavior Analysis, 10,* 255–265.

Semmel, M. I., Lieber, J., & Peck, C. A. (1986). Effects of special education environments: Beyond mainstreaming. In C. J. Meisel (Ed.), *Mainstreaming handicapped children: Outcome controversies, and new directions* (pp. 165–192). Hillsdale, NJ: Lawrence Erlbaum.

Skinner, B. F. (1968). *The technology of teaching.* New York: Appleton-Century-Crofts.

Smith, R. M., Neisworth, J. T., & Greer, J. G. (1978). *Evaluating educational environments.* Columbus, OH: Charles E. Merrill.

Stokes, T. F., & Baer, D. M. (1977). An implicit technology of generalization. *Journal of Applied Behavior Analysis, 10,* 349–367.

Touchette, P. E. (1971). Transfer of stimulus control: Measuring the moment of transfer. *Journal of the Experimental Analysis of Behavior, 15,* 347–354.

Twardosz, S. (1984). Environmental organization: The physical, social, and programmatic context of behavior. *Progress in Behavior Modification, 18,* 123–161.

Walker, H., & Hops, H. (1976). Increasing academic achievement by reinforcing direct academic performance and/or facilitative nonacademic responses. *Journal of Educational Psychology, 68,* 218–225.

Warren, S. F., & Kaiser, A. P. (1986). Incidental language teaching: A critical review. *Journal of Speech and Hearing Disorders, 51,* 291–299.

Warren, S. F., McQuarter, R. M., & Rogers-Warren, A. K. (1984). The effects of teacher mands and models on the speech of unresponsive language-delayed children. *Journal of Speech and Hearing Research, 49,* 43–52.

Webb, N. M. (1982). Group composition, group interaction, and achievement in cooperative small groups. *Journal of Educational Psychology, 74,* 475–484.

Weinstein, C. S. (1977). Modifying student behavior in an open classroom through changes in the physical design. *American Educational Research Journal, 14,* 249–262.

Weinstein, C. S. (1979). The physical environment of the school: A review of the research. *Review of Educational Research, 49,* 577–610.

Whalen, C. K., Henker, B., Colins, B. E., Finck, D., & Dotemoto, S. (1979). A social ecology of hyperactive boys: Medication effects in structured classroom environments. *Journal of Applied Behavior Analysis, 12,* 65–81.

White-Blackburn, G., Semb, S., & Semb, G. (1977). The effects of a good-behavior contract on the classroom behavior of sixth-grade students. *Journal of Applied Behavior Analysis, 10,* 312.

White, K. P., Wyne, M. D., Stuck, G. B., & Coop, R.

H. (1983). *Teaching effectiveness evaluation project. Final report.* Chapel Hill, NC: School of Education, University of North Carolina at Chapel Hill

Wolery, M., Doyle, P. M., Ault, M. J., Gast, D. L., & Lichtenberg, S. (1987). *Comparison of progressive time delay and incidental teaching during transitions on* *children's expressive language labeling.* Unpublished manuscript, Department of Special Education, University of Kentucky, Lexington.

Wyne, M. D., & Stuck, G. S. (1979). Time-on-task and reading performance in underachieving children. *Journal of Reading Behavior, 11,* 119–128.

12

PRESENTING TASKS FOR ACQUISITION

Key Terms

■ Attention ■ Stimulus ■ Acquisition ■ Stimulus Control ■ Errorless
Learning ■ Efficiency ■ Response Prompts ■ Controlling
Prompts ■ Noncontrolling Prompts ■ Gestural Prompts ■ Verbal
Prompts ■ Two-Dimensional Prompts ■ Models ■ Partial Physical
Prompts ■ Full Physical Manipulations ■ Error Correction ■ Errors of
Unlearned Prerequisite Skills ■ Systematic (Conceptual)
Errors ■ Random (Careless) Errors ■ Noncompliance Errors

Students frequently learn and behave acceptably when their environments are
structured appropriately. Well-structured environments promote engagement,
provide multiple opportunities for learning, communicate expectations, and
reinforce adaptive skills. These characteristics are fundamental to effective
instruction, but may not be sufficient to ensure that handicapped students will
learn new skills. Effective instruction involves careful presentation of tasks and
provision of teacher assistance. In this chapter, issues related to effective task
presentation are discussed, acquisition is defined, and various types of teacher
assistance are described.

PRESENTING TASKS EFFECTIVELY

A fundamental component of effective teaching is appropriate presentation of
learning tasks. Gagné (1985) identified four instructional events related to

presenting learning tasks: (1) gaining attention, (2) informing learners of the objective, (3) stimulating recall of prior learning, and (4) presenting the stimulus.

Gaining Attention

Gagné (1985) defined **attention** as "a sense of alertness for reception of stimuli" (p. 246). Students should be attending before tasks or directions are presented. Obviously, it would be difficult for a student who is not attending to know what was expected or to profit from a model or other information provided by the teacher.

Attending is best achieved by providing interesting activities to which students are naturally drawn. A rapid pace of instruction and planned variation in activities also are useful in securing students' attention. Sudden shifts in voice loudness or pitch also can serve as a signal to attend. Many preschool teachers have a preset signal, such as the teacher playing three notes on a xylophone, that alerts students to stop what they are doing and look at the teacher. Other teachers use environmental cues such as turning off the lights for a moment or employing a standard verbal direction such as "Okay, look up here."

Rinne (1984) differentiated between high-profile and low-profile techniques for focusing student attention on lesson content. High-profile techniques single out an individual who is not attending and interrupt the lesson or activity. For example, the teacher might stop in the middle of a sentence and say, "Natalie, you need to look at me and listen." Low-profile techniques are more likely to fit into the flow of the lesson without distracting student attention away from the activity. Low-profile techniques include voice modulation, repeated visual surveillance of the class, circulating around the room, and occasionally inserting each student's name at random into the directions. Rinne argued that teachers should use the lowest profile control techniques that are effective in establishing close to 100 % attention to activities.

Severely handicapped students may require more intensive interventions in order to establish attending behavior that will be useful in teaching. Sitting and looking upon request are the core of several curricula for severely handicapped students. For example, Bricker and Dennison (1978) suggested initially involving a student in a desired activity. Another activity is gradually introduced for a short period of time, and then the child is allowed to return to his or her preferred activity. Kent, Klein, Falk, and Guenther (1972) suggested the following strategy for facilitating attention to objects:

> The trainer places object on the table and points to it, says, "Look at this." If the child looks at the object, he is reinforced. If the child does not respond or responds incorrectly, the trainer may use a physical prompt such as turning the child's head toward the object or moving the object closer to the child's face. If prompts are not effective it may be necessary for the trainer to use small boxes containing edibles rather than the standard objects. The trainer moves a small box containing a few

edibles close to child's face and says. "Look." The trainer may tip the box slightly toward the child at first. If the child looks into the box, the trainer immediately reinforces him with an edible from the box. The trainer then places the box on the table and points to it, saying, "Look." If the child does not respond or responds incorrectly, the trainer may again use prompting procedures. Once the child looks at one box on the table, the trainer introduces a second and a third box spaced about the table and teaches the child to look at them. . . . The trainer then begins to substitute the standard objects for the boxes of edibles. The objects are introduced one at a time until all three boxes have been replaced with objects. (pp. 176–177)

Once the child has mastered this task, the teacher shifts to teaching the child to respond to the signal, "Look at me." Bricker and Dennison (1978) taught this task as follows:

Take the child's face between your hands and direct his face toward yours. If the child gives you even the most fleeting glance, reward him. Gradually lessen the prompts and reward the child for longer and longer gazes. Talk to the child while you are looking at each other.

If the the child does not look at you following your verbal command or physical prompting, another method of attracting his attention should be used. For example, hold a toy which interests the child close to your eyes while saying "Look at me." If he looks at the toy or your face, reinforce this by giving him the toy. Continue this procedure, varying the toys, until the child will look at your face immediately upon request. Gradually, decrease the number of times the toy is used to establish eye contact. (pp. 166–167)

Even more intrusive techniques were used by Foxx (1977) to achieve eye contact behaviors in children with severe retardation who rarely responded to any identifiable social or tangible reinforcer. The procedure, referred to as *functional movement training*, is a variation of overcorrection which is discussed in Chapter 22.

In most cases, teachers should remember that attending is not important in and of itself, but it facilitates participation in relevant instructional and social activities. The most natural and least intrusive strategies for achieving attention should be used first, and primary emphasis should be placed on task performance, not attending alone. The exception, of course, is when initial attending skills are being taught.

Informing Learners of the Objective

In Chapters 3 and 4, the importance of student involvement in planning the Individualized Education Plan was described. The same rationale applies in individual instructional activities. Students tend to perform best when told ahead of time what performance is expected of them. Exceptions include severely handicapped or very young students who have not acquired the ability to consider a future event.

Giving learners information about an objective takes some of the mystery out of instruction. When this is done, students do not have to guess what the teacher is trying to teach and have an identifiable goal to master. Although little research has been done on this topic, particularly with handicapped students, it also makes sense that the goal for instruction be stated as clearly and specifically as possible. If possible, students should be told why the particular objective is important.

Stimulating Recall of Prior Learning

A third effective teaching practice related to task presentation is to tie the current instructional activity to previous learning. This strategy is important for at least three reasons. First, it can remind the student of previously learned information that is necessary for correct performance of the task at hand. For example, the teacher may remind the student of a rule previously learned ("Remember, hang up your coat and put your lunch box in your desk *before* you choose a center.") or have the student practice a component skill (e.g., subtraction) that is a part of a larger skill (e.g., word problems). Second, interspersing previously taught material with new material can decrease students' errors and increase the number of times they are reinforced during instructional sessions (Rowan & Pear, 1985). Frequently, when new skills are being learned, the amount of success and reinforcement students receive are decreased; thus, by reviewing previously learned behaviors, students can continue to experience success. Third, and perhaps most important, this practice helps students get an overall sense of the logic and continuity of instruction. The student learns how prerequisite skills fit into a meaningful sequence and lead to the performance of more useful or functional tasks.

Presenting the Stimulus

"A **stimulus** is any physical event or condition, including the organism's own behavior" (Ferster & Perrott, 1968, p. 531). A stimulus can be described in at least two ways: it has physical properties *and* it may have an effect on behavior (Powers & Osborne, 1976). Teachers must understand and analyze the stimuli they present to students.

Nearly all stimuli are representations (examples) of a larger set of stimuli. For example, if a student is learning to put on a coat, the coat used during training is one example of all the possible coats the student may need to put on; or, if a student is learning to write the correct answer to math problems, the format used in the problem is only one of many different formats. If the child is learning to read, the print used and the order in which words occur are only one of many possible prints and word combinations. Englemann and Carnine (1982) suggested five facts related to selecting and presenting examples when teaching concepts. First, no single presentation of an example can result in learning the concept. Experiencing one example does not tell the students what interpretation they should make from the concept. Second, even when students are presented with several different examples of a concept, they can make numerous interpretations of what is being taught. For example, if a student is learning the concept of "dog" and is shown several different dogs, he or she may conclude that all four-legged animals are dogs. Third, when students are shown examples of a concept and examples that are not members of the concept but are similar, they can eliminate some incorrect interpretations. For example, if a student is learning the concept of "dog," showing the student pictures of cats and horses and asking him or her whether those are dogs eliminates the possibility that the student will decide that all four-legged animals are dogs. Fourth, when examples are shown that are not members of the concept but share many characteristics with members of the concept, the maximum number of incorrect interpretations the student could make is reduced. Therefore, teachers should select three types of examples: (a) positive introductory examples, (b) positive confirmatory examples, and (c) negative examples (Clark, 1971). *Positive introductory examples* are clear representations of the concept being taught. They are similar to other examples of the concept, should not be similar to examples belonging to other categories, and should have obvious relevant characteristics (Hupp & Mervis, 1981). *Positive confirmatory examples* show the limits or boundaries of the concept; for example, a football shows that not all balls are round. These examples should sample the range of potential examples in the generalization settings. Selecting examples in this manner is called *general case programming,* and procedures for doing it were described by Horner, Sprague, and Wilcox (1982). *Negative examples* are not members of the concept; for example, marbles are not balls. Although negative examples are not members of the concept, they should be similar to the concept being taught.

Presenting the stimulus refers to the way in which the teacher delivers the learning task to students. The stimuli or task include the materials the student is expected to use or respond to, such as workbooks, readers, shapes, or toys, as well as the verbal and written directions accompanying those materials and any other teacher assistance. An effective stimulus presentation has the following characteristics:

1. The requirements for task performance are presented in an understandable manner.

2. Extraneous materials or information likely to distract or confuse students are not included.

3. Tasks are presented in a realistic, natural, and interesting fashion.

4. Tasks are presented only when students are attending to the teacher and/or materials.

5. Tasks are presented in a fashion likely to result in a correct response.

White, Wyne, Stuck, and Coop (1983), in their review of effective teaching practices, concluded that the empirical literature provides support for at least five elements of clear presentation: (1) use of multiple examples to explain a new concept, (2) use of precise language, (3) fluent verbal presentation, (4) speaking to students so they are able to understand, and (5) clarity in asking questions, giving directions, and making assignments.

The stimulus presentation is particularly important in working with exceptional students, since many of them have difficulty sorting out relevant and irrelevant aspects of stimuli or tasks. Teachers cannot assume that students are attending to the important aspects of the stimuli. For example, a student may be looking at the smudge mark on a flashcard rather than looking at the word written on it. A student may be looking at the teacher but listening to the birds outside, or may be looking at his or her book, but be thinking about other things. To control for this possibility, duplicate materials can be used, critical aspects of stimuli can be highlighted, and students' performance can be checked regularly. Further, students can be required to demonstrate specific behaviors requiring attention. For example, if flashcards are being used, having students point to the critical aspects of the stimulus may be better than having them look at the card; or, if students are to read and understand a passage, having them take notes or say the important points into a tape recorder may be better than having them read without responding overtly.

DEFINITION OF ACQUISITION

Acquisition refers to learning the basic requirements of a behavior or task, and roughly is a synonym for *initial learning*. Acquisition occurs when students who were unable to perform a behavior in a given situation can do so at a later date. Acquisition is the first stage of learning and, as such, has a specific definition: "Acquisition is the period of learning when if performance falters, changes designed to provide information to the learner about how to perform the desired response have a higher probability than other strategies of promoting pupil progress" (Haring, Liberty, & White, 1980, pp. 171–172). This definition of acquisition has two important implications. First, it implies that students who are not learning can be provided with changes in instruction that may help them. Second, instructional strategies that provide students with more information on how to perform the behavior help them learn otherwise difficult tasks. Two types of strategies provide students with more information: (a) those that provide the information before students respond, called *antecedent procedures* and (b) those that provide students with information after they respond, called *error-correction procedures*. These two types of strategies are presented in the following sections. Generally, antecedent prompting procedures produce fewer errors than error-correction procedures (Ault, Wolery, Doyle, & Gast, 1986).

ANTECEDENT TEACHING PROCEDURES

Description of Antecedent Teaching Procedures

Antecedent teaching procedures provide students with information (assistance or prompts) before they respond to directions. These procedures are designed to facilitate the development of stimulus control. **Stimulus control** means that students will respond predictably or reliably in the presence of some antecedent stimulus. Stimulus control is established when the student is reinforced for doing the desired behavior in the presence of the target stimulus. For example, Bart is being taught to recognize his name. If he is reinforced for saying "Bart" in response to his written name, Bart will assume stimulus control over his reading behavior. However, if he is shown the word "Bart" and he says, "Billy," he would not be reinforced. Since each error eliminates a chance to reinforce the student, antecedent procedures are designed to prevent errors from occurring when the target stimulus is presented. Antecedent procedures occur on a continuum from those that allow some errors to those that are errorless. **Errorless learning** procedures preclude students from performing an incorrect response. In reality, some errors may occur even with errorless learning procedures. The extent to which the procedures are errorless depends, in large part, on how well the teacher designs and uses them. Despite the possibility of some errors, errorless procedures produce fewer errors than strategies where no antecedent information (prompts) is provided.

Rationale for Using Errorless Learning Procedures

Several reasons exist for using errorless learning procedures. First, errorless learning procedures are *effective*. When the procedures are used correctly, students learn. Most errorless procedures can be used to teach students a wide range of behaviors, but some are more efficient than others for selected behaviors (Wolery, Ault, Doyle, & Gast, 1986). Teachers should select instructional strategies based on their efficiency as well as their effectiveness. **Efficiency** refers to the amount of time and effort required to learn a skill. For example, two different strategies could result in the student eventually learning the behavior, but one may require shorter or fewer instructional sessions, fewer trials to criterion, fewer errors, or less time devoted to establishing generalization. In such cases, the more efficient procedure should be used because nearly all students in special education classrooms have substantial skill deficits.

Second, errorless learning procedures tend to promote positive social interactions between teachers and students since students respond correctly on almost all trials. Students receive a high rate of reinforcement and rarely experience negative consequences for errors.

A third reason for using errorless learning procedures is that fewer inappropriate social behaviors may occur. Considerable research indicates some students are more likely to engage in disruptive behaviors (Carr & Durand, 1985; Weeks & Gaylord-Ross, 1981) and self-injurious or aggressive behaviors (Carr, Newsom, Binkoff, 1976; Durand, 1982; Weeks & Gaylord-Ross, 1981) when they experience frequent errors in difficult tasks. When errorless learning procedures are used, the number of errors *and* inappropriate behaviors decreases (Weeks & Gaylord-Ross, 1981). Carr and Durand (1985) described a procedure for assessing whether the difficulty of the task (i.e., those with frequent errors) is related to inappropriate behavior. They measured the amount of maladaptive behavior that occurred in difficult and easy tasks; all other variables were identical. If more maladaptive behavior occurred when difficult tasks were used than when easy tasks were presented, they assumed that task difficulty was related to the aberrant behaviors.

Fourth, errorless learning procedures should be used because students learn little from errors. Errors eliminate an opportunity for the student to be reinforced for correct responding. Further, when students perform errors, they may become more fluent in making errors because of the practice they receive.

If students are not learning effectively and efficiently with less intrusive instructional strategies, errorless learning procedures should be used. There are two types of errorless learning procedures: response prompting and stimulus modification. With response-prompting strategies, the *teacher provides a prompt* to help students do the behavior correctly, but the target stimulus remains the same throughout. With stimulus-modification procedures, *stimuli are changed* systematically to make the task initially easy and then progressively more difficult. In general, response-prompting procedures should be used before stimulus-modification strategies because they are typically easier to design and implement. Response-prompting procedures use prompts (teacher assistance) to provide information to students.

Description of Prompts

A **response prompt** is defined as any teacher assistance provided *before* a target response in order to increase the likelihood of the correct behavior occurring. Although prompts are stimuli, they are not a part of the target stimulus. For example, Jackie is learning to spell "parade." Her teacher says, "Spell parade. Remember the silent *e* rule." The command, "Spell parade" is the target stimulus. The statement, "Remember the silent *e* rule" is a prompt; it provides additional information to help her spell correctly. Her teacher's goal is for Jackie to spell "parade" without the prompt.

Prompts can either produce or fail to produce the correct response. When prompts produce correct responses, they are called **controlling prompts;** when they do not produce correct responses, they are called **noncontrolling prompts.** Controlling prompts already have stimulus control of the student's behavior. When teachers use controlling prompts, their goal is to transfer the stimulus control from those prompts to the target stimulus. If "Remember the silent *e* rule" is a controlling prompt (Jackie had learned it previously), then Jackie will spell the word correctly, and the teacher's goal would be to transfer that control to "Spell parade."

Response prompts can be classified in at least two ways. One deals with the behavior the teacher does and the other with the sensory modality through which students receive the prompt. When classified by what the teacher does, "Remember the silent *e* rule" is a *verbal prompt.* When classified by the sensory modality through which students receive the prompt, it is an *auditory stimulus.* Although both classifications are used, response prompts are generally classified by what teachers do. Common examples of prompts classified this way are gestural prompts, verbal prompts, pictorial or two-dimensional prompts, models, partial physical prompts, and full physical manipulations.

Gestural Prompts. **Gestural prompts** are hand, arm, or facial movements that communicate very specific information to students about what to do. For example, Ellen is learning to match pictures and objects. Her teacher places four objects on the table, gives Ellen a picture of one of those objects, and says, "Put it on the same." The teacher then points to the correct object; her point is a gestural prompt. Another gestural prompt is seen when a teacher says, "Don, come here," and then extends her arm toward Don with the palm facing her, and quickly moves her hand toward her own body two or three times. For gestural prompts to be effective, students must understand what is being communicated. If Don does not understand the meaning of "Don, come here" or of the hand gesture, he probably will not move toward the teacher.

Verbal Prompts. **Verbal prompts** are statements by teachers that assist the student in performing correct behaviors. These verbalizations do not include task directions but are additions to task directions. Task directions are statements that tell students *to do, not how to do,* a behavior. For example, if students are learning to use a computer, a task direction might be, "Turn on your computer"; a verbal prompt is, "Put the disk in drive 1 and push the red switch."

Teachers use several different types of verbal prompts. Some verbal prompts *tell students how to do the behavior.* For example, Linda is learning to tie her shoes. She makes the first cross tie but does not know what to do next. Her teacher provides the following verbal prompt, "Make a bow" and, as she does, he tells her the next step. A variation of this type is to *tell students how to do part of the behavior.* For example, Larry is reading silently and comes to a word he does not know and asks for help. The word is "vacation" and the teacher says, "It starts with 'va ca,' you figure out the rest." She only told him how to do part of the behavior. Another type of verbal prompt is to *tell students a rule.* For example, when Jackie was spelling "parade," the teacher's verbal prompt was a rule she could apply. When students are learning a number of behaviors that follow the same rule, verbally stating the rule may be an effective prompt. The rule should be relatively brief and easily understood. A fourth type of verbal prompt is best described as a hint, or *indirect verbal prompt*. For example, during oral reading, Kevin comes to the word "pumpkin" and does not know it. His teacher says, "It's a big orange thing you carve at Halloween." This prompt allows him to rely on past experiences to identify the word. Another type of verbal prompt is *providing options*. For example, if students cannot identify a topic to write about, the teacher could say, "Write about something you saw at the zoo, something you read about, someone you like, a funny thing that happened to you." Such prompts are vague statements giving students some options about what to do.

Verbal prompts have some advantages over other prompts: they are not intrusive and do not involve physical contact with students. They can be provided while students look at their materials, given from a distance, and given to a group of students. They also have some disadvantages: the effectiveness of verbal prompts relies on students' understanding what is said. Further, they rely on students' compliance with the prompt and may not be effective with non-compliant students.

Pictorial or Two-Dimensional Prompts. Pictorial or **two-dimensional prompts** can be models of the behavior students are to do or models of the product of a specific behavior. For example, many teachers display the letters of the alphabet in the front of the room. Students can look at these two-dimensional permanent models as they write and can compare their writing to the model. Frequently, teachers write an example of a correct response on the chalkboard (e.g., when working math problems), and then leave the problem on the board for students to use as they complete similar problems. These are examples of two-dimensional prompts that are, in fact, models.

Pictorial or two-dimensional prompts can also be used to show students how to do tasks. For example, a teacher is attempting to teach Betty to mop the floor. Rather than use models or verbal prompts, he made a series of pictures. The first picture shows the materials she will need (mop, pail, and soap), the second shows the soap being put in the pail, the third shows water being put in the pail, the fourth shows the mop in the pail, the fifth shows the mop being wrung out, and the final picture shows the floor being mopped. These pictures could be used as prompts to assist Betty in knowing what behaviors to do and the order in which they should be done.

Two-dimensional prompts can also be used to communicate rules about what to do. For example, Bill takes a long time to get to work after the bell rings. He frequently sits down, then goes to sharpen his pencil, sits down again, goes and gets his folder, then sits back down. To avoid all this movement, his teacher gives him a card that says, "Sharpen your pencil, get your folder, sit down, do your work!"

Models. **Models** are demonstrations of the behaviors teachers want students to do. Models can take many forms, depending on the behavior being learned; as noted above, some models are two-dimensional prompts. When the target behavior is verbal (involves students saying something) the model is verbal; the teacher says whatever students should say. Verbal models are frequently used in language training programs and when teaching academic behaviors. For example, Ms. Raines is teaching James to label what he is doing. When he is coloring, she walks over and says, "What are you doing?" If he does not respond correctly, she says, "I'm coloring." She repeats this when James is doing many different things. Partial models also can be used, and refer to instances when teachers do a portion of the behavior they want students to do. For example, Ms. Raines could ask James what he is doing and, when he does not answer, she should could say, "I'm col"; she expects James to imitate and say, "I'm coloring." Verbal models are different from verbal prompts because models provide exact demonstrations of the correct response. Verbal prompts give students information about making the correct response.

When the target behavior is a motor movement, the model, of course, is doing that movement. For example, when coaches show students how to swing a bat, they frequently pick up a bat and say, "Watch this" and then swing it correctly. Teachers frequently use motor models when they are teaching students to print or write letters; put things together (e.g., assembly tasks); and perform many self-care skills such as dressing, brushing teeth, tying shoes, and washing hands. For instance, Phong is learning to wash his hands and his teacher is using model prompts. The teacher and Phong go to the sink and the teacher says, "Phong, do this." The teacher then models turning on the cool water followed by the warm water. If Phong imitates the model, she says, "Good, now do this" and wets her hands, retrieves the soap, and rubs one hand with the soap. With each correct behavior she reinforces him and presents the next step by modeling it. In such instances, having duplicates of the materials, such as two sinks, makes the model more realistic.

Many social behaviors are taught by using models in two distinct ways. First, teachers and peers can model appropriate social behaviors and reinforce students for imitating those behaviors. When models are used in this manner, several factors appear to increase the likelihood of students imitating the models (Bailey & Wolery, 1984). If the model is rewarded for doing the behavior, observers are more apt to imitate the behavior. If the model is similar to the observer (e.g., similar age, same gender, similar size), imitation is more likely. If the model is a high-status person, imitation also is more likely. Likewise, students tend to imitate models who can do the behavior well as compared to those who cannot. Finally, if a model imitates the students who are observing him or her, the observers are more apt to imitate the model. Second, teachers can rehearse and role-play social situations and provide models of targeted social skills. When role-playing and rehearsal are used, considerable attention should be given to reinforcing the behaviors when they occur in more natural settings.

Obviously, models are only effective when students are imitative. If students do not imitate, other prompts should be used. However, because of the wide use of models, teaching students to imitate should be a priority objective (cf., Bailey & Wolery, 1984, Chapter 4). The advantages of using models are that they can they can be used with more than one student at a time and do not require teachers to touch students. Although teachers can touch students appropriately, touching can be a powerful reinforcer. With such students, physical prompting may interfere with learning; they do not perform independently because they are receiving reinforcement (physical contact) for not doing the behavior. Likewise, touching may be aversive for other students; they do not learn the behavior because they may attempt to avoid physical contact. Another advantage is that modeling does not carry the potential of hurting students as physical prompting does.

Partial Physical Prompts. **Partial physical prompts** involve teachers touching students but not controlling all their movements. Students must exert effort or attempt the behavior when partial physical prompts are used. Examples of partial physical prompts include tapping, nudging, and light pushing or pulling. Partial physical prompts frequently are used to get responses started and when students can do parts of a behavior but not all of it. For instance, Marsha is learning to place dirty dishes in a dishwasher tray. When Marsha does not spontaneously move her arm toward the dirty dishes, Mr. Barnes nudges her at the elbow. After she picks up a dish, he waits for her to put it in the dishwasher tray. If she does not, he pushes her slightly at the wrist to get her to place the plate in the tray slot. Partial physical prompts exert more control over students' behavior than do models and verbal, gestural, or pictorial prompts.

An advantage of partial physical prompts is that they provide considerable control over students' behaviors but do not involve extended physical contact between teachers and students. However, teachers must be careful not to push, nudge, or tap too hard or harshly; the difference between a tap and a hit is simply the intensity, not the topography of the behavior. Since partial physical prompts are usually brief, teachers can use them with two or three students at once.

Full Physical Manipulations. **Full physical manipulations** involve teachers placing their hands on students and moving students through the target behaviors. Generally, teachers place their hands directly on the back of the students' hands. The teacher is "doing the work" when using full physical manipulations and the student passively complies with the movements. For example, Scott is learning to feed himself with a spoon. The teacher places her hand directly over Scott's, moves his hand to the spoon, closes Scott's fingers around it, moves his hand with the spoon to the food, scoops some food, and moves it to Scott's mouth. In most cases, teachers should be behind or to the side of students when using full physical manipulations. This will help students learn natural movements as compared to awkward or exaggerated movements. For example, when teaching Scott to scoop with a spoon, standing behind him will allow the teacher to move his arm in generally the same pattern he will use when he does it independently.

Obviously, when using full physical manipulations, teachers must be careful not to hurt students. If students resist the prompt, holding them still is preferred to pushing or pulling. When students have motor disabilities, teachers need to provide physical support at the base of the neck, shoulders, and hips to assist them in maintaining appropriate muscle tone. Similarly, some students may find physical contact by others aversive. Teachers need to desensitize the student to physical contact, establish physical contact as a conditioned reinforcer, and find other means such as models for prompting them.

Guidelines for Selecting and Using Prompts

To teach students with learning handicaps effectively, prompts undoubtedly will be needed. The manner in which prompts are selected and used will greatly determine their effectiveness.

Select the Least Intrusive, Effective Prompt. Teachers should select the least intrusive prompt needed to get the student to perform the behavior. In many cases, several of the prompts described previously could produce the same behavior. When teachers have a choice as to which prompt to use, they should select the one that allows students to do the behavior as independently as possible. For example, if both a model and a full physical manipulation will produce the response, the model should be used.

Combine Prompts If Necessary. When needed, teachers can use more than one prompt. Many of the prompts described above can be implemented simultaneously. For example, Mike is learning to print his name. His teacher prints each letter as Mike watches (model) and then provides verbal prompts ("Now move the pencil down, go back to the top of the line.") as Mike begins to print. Combining prompts provides considerable support to students for learning new behaviors.

Select Natural Prompts and Those Related to the Behavior. Teachers should select and use prompts as naturally as possible. For example, gestural prompts should be conventional gestures. In the example where the teacher was attempting to get Don to come to her, beckoning with one hand, as compared to two hands, is more natural. Using natural prompts will allow the student to benefit from social cues when those prompts are used in nonteaching settings. Likewise, prompts that are related to the behavior should be used (Barrera, Lobato-Barrera, & Sulzer-Azaroff, 1980; Remington & Clarke, 1983). For instance, when a student needs assistance with reading a word, using verbal prompts that assist him or her to apply phonetic word attack rules is better than giving verbal hints about the word.

Provide Prompts Only after Students Are Attending. Since prompts are designed to assist students in performing the target behaviors in the presence of target stimuli, it is important that they attend to the prompt. Eye contact, absence of other behaviors, and orientation of the face toward materials or the teacher are indications that students may be attending. If students are not attending to the prompt or the teacher is not sure whether they are, the teacher should secure attention prior to giving the prompt. This can be done by using the attention-gaining procedures described earlier.

Provide Prompts in a Supportive, Instructive Manner before the Student Responds. The purpose of prompts is to give students information about how to do a behavior. Thus, the prompt should occur before the student responds to the task direction. Some students respond quickly and the teacher may need to teach them to wait for assistance (i.e., more information) (Snell & Gast, 1981). Since prompts should facilitate correct responding, they should be provided in an instructive manner. When used with antecedent procedures, prompts should be presented in a supportive instructive manner rather than a corrective fashion. When prompts are aversive to students, such as physical prompts for students who avoid tactile stimuli, the teacher should find different prompts.

Fade Prompts as Soon as Possible. To ensure that students perform target behaviors in the presence of target stimuli, teachers undoubtedly will need to use prompts. However, to perform independently, students must do target behaviors when the target stimuli are present and prompts are absent. When prompts control the student's response, that control must be transferred to the target stimulus.

> Prompting is the substitution of an effective but inappropriate stimulus for an ineffective but appropriate one. Prompts are stimuli that control the desired behavior, but that are not functionally related to the task. Unfortunately, it is often the case that students who respond appropriately when prompted, founder when the prompt is removed. They evidence persistent dependence on stimuli not intrinsic to the task. Once correct responding has been initiated by prompting, the teacher's task is to maintain the response pattern while eliminating the prompt(s). (Touchette & Howard, 1984, p. 175)

Whenever prompts are used, they must later be faded. Several strategies for fading prompts are described in Chapter 14.

Plan Fading Procedures before Using Prompts. Fading prompts requires skillful use of specific strategies. When instruction is being planned, a critical issue is determining how prompts will be faded. If prompt-fading is not planned, teachers may prompt students longer than necessary or may not provide sufficient prompts for students to learn the skill being taught. Valuable instruction time will be lost when students are prompted longer than necessary. Likewise, removing prompts too quickly will result in ineffective learning. Additional training will be required to transfer stimulus control to the target stimulus.

ERROR-CORRECTION PROCEDURES

Description of Error Correction

Error Correction refers to assistance provided by teachers after students respond incorrectly to a target stimulus or when another response should have been performed (Falvey, Brown, Lyon, Baumgart, & Schroeder, 1980). The purpose of error correction is to provide the student with information on how to perform the behavior correctly. Because error-correction procedures tell students how to perform correctly, they are different from consequent events that simply tell the students the response was incorrect. If a teacher says, "No. That is incorrect" or marks an answer wrong on a paper, the student learns that the response is wrong but does not learn why it is incorrect or how to do the behavior correctly. These are examples of error consequences that are not error-correction procedures.

The type of assistance provided during error correction can include gestural prompts, verbal prompts, models, two-dimensional prompts, partial physical prompts, full physical manipulations, and combinations of these (Doyle, Wolery, Ault, & Gast, 1986). The difference, of course, is that with error correction the prompts are presented *after* students respond; with antecedent procedures, the prompts are provided *before* students respond. Although different types of error-correction assistance have been used effectively with a wide range of students and tasks, the current research does not indicate which type of assistance is most efficient (Doyle et al., 1986). Frequently, they are used in combination; for example, a model and partial physical prompts are both provided when errors occur (Faw, Reid, Schepis, Fitzgerald, & Welty, 1981), or a consequent event plus a correction procedure can be used, such as a verbal reprimand ("No.") and a model (Palyo, Cooke, Schuler, & Apolloni, 1979). Reinforcement for correct responses used with error correction appears to be more effective than reinforcement alone or error correction alone (Foxx, 1984; Matson, Esveldt-Dawson, & Kazdin, 1982).

Types of Errors

Although specific types of errors may occur for a particular type of academic or developmental content, at least four general error types can be identified (Bailey & Wolery, 1984). Teachers should analyze students' performance data and their actual performance to determine what type of error is being displayed. This analysis is critical because different teaching procedures are needed when the different types of errors occur (Bellamy, Horner, & Inman, 1979).

Errors of Unlearned Prerequisite Skills. **Errors of unlearned prerequisite skills** refer to errors that occur during initial acquisition training, are consistent, and may be difficult to detect. Two different types exist: those due to a new indicator behavior and those due to some unlearned prerequisite concept. For example, Carlos can say the answer to addition facts with sums to 18 when they are presented orally (i.e., "What is 12 plus 3?"); however, when his teacher asks him to write the answers to the same problems, he gets none of them correct. When looking at his paper, the teacher realizes that he does not know how to write numerals. The errors he made were due to a new indicator behavior, writing rather than saying. Stacy, on the other hand, writes the answers of addition problems with sums to 18. When presented with problems such as, 18 + 6 = _____ , she consistently does not get them correct; she either writes the answer as 114 or as 15. Her answers indicate that she cannot carry when the one's column is greater than nine, an error due to an unlearned conceptual prerequisite.

For errors of unlearned indicator behaviors, teachers need to determine whether the indicator behavior is important for independent functioning. As noted in previous chapters, indicator behaviors are responses that show us whether the student "knows" the concept. Some indicator behaviors are needed frequently and others are needed less often. For example, with Carlos, teaching him to write numerals may be important because it can be used in many different situations and with different content. When the teacher determines that the prerequisite indicator behavior is important, that behavior should be taught. In cases where other indicator behaviors are sufficiently useful, they should be substituted for the less useful skill. For errors of unlearned conceptual prerequisites, teachers should teach the prerequisite skill. Thus, for Stacy, the teacher would give her instruction on carrying.

Systematic Errors. **Systematic errors,** also called **conceptual errors,** refer to incorrect responses that appear to occur because the student is applying an incorrect strategy or rule. These errors occur throughout acquisition and appear consistently. For example, Lashawnda is learning to identify nouns. She is given a passage and instructed to identify all the nouns. For the following sentence, "Jim went to the store to buy some Coke and candy," Lashawnda said that the nouns were "store," "Coke," and "candy." For the sentence, "The 'windy city' is another name for the great city of Chicago," she identified "city," "name," and "city" as the nouns. With both sentences, her errors are consistent; she appears to be applying an incorrect rule that could be stated as, "A noun is a person, place, or thing, as long as it is not the name of a specific person or place." Thus, she appears to be using an incorrect rule or strategy.

Two primary methods are used to treat conceptual errors. First, teachers should use prompts, preferably antecedent prompts to teach the student the correct rule or strategy. For example, Lashawnda's teacher could give her some sentences and say. "A noun is a person, place, or thing, and includes names of specific people, places, and things." The teacher also could show her sentences similar to those where Lashawnda had applied the incorrect rule and model the use of the correct rule. Another strategy for dealing with systematic errors is to ensure that the student is not reinforced for applying the incorrect rule or strategy. Careful selection of examples and nonexamples during teaching will also decrease the development of inaccurate rules or strategies (Englemann & Carnine, 1982).

Random Errors. **Random errors,** also called **careless errors,** occur after students have learned the basic requirements of a skill and have no apparent pattern. These errors may occur at any point in the learning process, but are most problematic when students are learning to perform skills rapidly. Generally, random errors account for a small proportion of the responses students make. For example, Curtis has learned to write the answers to multiplication tables through the 9's, but is quite slow when multiplying by 7, 8, or 9. Therefore, his teacher is giving him drills on those three sets. He consistently is correct at or above 90%, but some errors do occur. When the teacher analyzes the errors, no pattern exists. Most of the errors Curtis makes are on problems that he may have done correctly at some other time.

If random errors are infrequent, the teacher probably should simply ignore them. However, with some tasks this is not desirable. To eliminate random errors, teachers should change the consequent events for correct and error responding. Consequent event changes include (a) providing reinforcement only when the percentage or rate of correct responses has increased over the previous session, (b) providing a different reinforcer, (c) giving the reinforcer less often, (d) providing extra practice when a given rate or percentage of errors-occurs, or (e) providing loss of some privilege or reward when a given rate or percentage of errors occurs. Some of these strategies can be used simultaneously; for example, the reinforcer could be changed and the loss of a reward could be implemented if too many errors occur.

Errors Due to Noncompliance. **Noncompliance errors** occur when students have demonstrated that they can do the skill correctly and are able to do the behavior (Haring et al. , 1980). These errors are frequently evidenced by high variability in students' performance data or a sharp drop in the rate of correct responses. For example, in the past, Sunny and Terry have shown that they can read a list of sight words, but they have not met criterion. For the last five sessions, Sunny's percentage of correct responses are 85, 30, 50, 20, and 70, respectively; Terry's percentage of correct responses are 85, 70, 50, 30, and 15, respectively. Sunny's data are highly variable and Terry's data show a sharp drop in the percentage of correct responses. Both patterns indicate noncompliance; the students have demonstrated that they can respond correctly, but are not doing so consistently.

To deal with noncompliance errors, a number of strategies can be used. One strategy is to progress to a more difficult task. Some students begin to show noncompliance errors when they become bored with a skill. Rather than trying to establish compliance, moving to a more difficult task may result in the restoration of cooperative responding. Other strategies involve changes in consequent events. Some of these include (a) reinforcing students for producing progressively more correct responses; (b) changing the number of correct responses for which reinforcement is given, such as changing from reinforcing every correct response to reinforcing every other correct response; (c) eliminating inadvertent reinforcement for errors; (d) removing some previously earned reward if students make a certain number of errors; and (e) providing some negative consequence if a certain number of errors occur (Haring et al., 1980).

Summary of Key Concepts

- Effective teaching involves gaining students' attention, telling students what the objective is, stimulating recall of prior learning, and presenting the stimulus clearly.

- Acquisition is learning to do the basic requirements of skills.

- Providing students with more information on how to do the response correctly appears to solve acquisition problems.

- More information can be provided to students by using antecedent response-prompting procedures (also called errorless learning procedures) and by correcting students' errors. Antecedent prompting procedures appear to produce fewer errors than error-correction strategies.

- Numerous types of prompts exist and include verbal prompts, gestural prompts, two-dimensional prompts, models, partial physical prompts, and full physical manipulations.

- The least intrusive effective prompt should be selected. Prompts should be combined when necessary and should be natural and related to the behavior being taught. They should be provided when students are attending and should be supportive and instructive. Prompts should be faded and prompt-fading should be planned prior to implementing instruction.

- Different types of errors occur, including errors of unlearned prerequisite skills, systematic errors, random errors, and noncompliance errors.

- The types of errors students display should be identified and a specific strategy to eliminate them should be used.

REFERENCES

Ault, M. J., Wolery, M., Doyle, P. M., & Gast, D. L. (1986). Comparative studies. In M. Wolery, M. J. Ault, P. M. Doyle, & D. L. Gast (Eds.). *Comparison of instructional strategies: A literature review* (pp. 228–257). (Grant No. G008530197). Lexington: Department of Special Education, University of Kentucky.

Bailey, D. B., & Wolery, M. (1984). *Teaching infants*

and preschoolers with handicaps. Columbus, OH: Charles E. Merrill.

Barrera, R. D., Lobato-Barrera, D., & Sulzer-Azaroff, B. (1980). A simultaneous treatment comparison of three expressive language training programs with a mute autistic child. *Journal of Autism and Developmental Disorders, 10,* 21–37.

Bellamy, G. T., Horner, R. H., & Inman, D. P. (1979).

Vocational habilitation of severely retarded adults: A direct service technology. Baltimore: Paul Brookes.

Bricker, D. D., & Dennison, L. (1978). Training prerequisites to verbal behavior. In M. E. Snell (Ed.), *Systematic instruction of the moderately and severely handicapped.* Columbus, OH: Charles E. Merrill.

Carr, E. G., & Durand, V. M. (1985). Reducing behavior problems through functional communication training. *Journal of Applied Behavior Analysis, 18,* 111–126.

Carr, E. G., Newsom, C. D., & Binkoff, J. A. (1976). Stimulus control of self-destructive behavior in a psychotic child. *Journal of Abnormal Child Psychology, 4,* 139–153.

Clark, D. C. (1971). Teaching concepts in the classroom: A set of teaching prescriptions derived from experimental research. *Journal of Education Psychology, 62,* 253–278.

Doyle, P. M., Wolery, M., Ault, M. J., & Gast, D. L. (1986). Error correction. In M. Wolery, M. J. Ault, P. M. Doyle, & D. L. Gast (Eds.), *Comparison of instructional strategies: A literature review* (Grant No. (G008530197) (pp. 23–57). Lexington: Department of Special Education, University of Kentucky.

Durand, V. M. (1982). Analysis and intervention of self-injurious behavior. *Journal of the Association for the Severely Handicapped, 7,* 44–53.

Englemann, S., & Carnine, D. (1982). *Theory of instruction: Principles and applications.* New York: Irvington.

Falvey, M., Brown, L., Lyon, S., Baumgart, D., & Schroeder, J. (1980). Strategies for using cues and correction procedures. In W. Sailor, B. Wilcox, & L. Brown (Eds.), *Methods of instruction for severely handicapped students* (pp. 109–133). Baltimore: Paul Brookes.

Faw, G. D., Reid, D. H., Schepis, M. M., Fitzgerald, J. R., & Welty, P. A. (1981). Involving institutional staff in the development and maintenance of sign language skills with profoundly retarded persons. *Journal of Applied Behavior Analysis, 14,* 411–423.

Ferster, C. B., & Perrott, M. C. (1968). *Behavior principles.* New York: Appleton-Century-Crofts.

Foxx, R. M. (1977). Attention training: The use of overcorrection avoidance to increase eye contact of autistic and retarded children. *Journal of Applied Behavior Analysis, 10,* 489–499.

Foxx, R. M. (1984). The use of a negative reinforcement Procedure to increase the performance of autistic and mentally retarded children on discrimination training tasks. *Analysis and Intervention in Development Disabilities, 4,* 253–265.

Gagné, R. M. (1985). *The conditions of learning and a theory of instruction* (4th ed.). New York: Holt. Rinehart, and Winston.

Haring, N. G., Liberty, K. A., & White, O. R. (1980). Rules for data-based strategy decisions in instructional programs: Current research and instructional implications. In W. Sailor, B. Wilcox, & L. Brown (Eds.), *Methods of instruction for severely handicapped students* (pp. 159–192). Baltimore: Paul Brookes.

Horner, R., Sprague, J., & Wilcox, B. (1982). General case programming for community activities. In B. Wilcox and G. Bellamy (Eds.), *Design of high school programs for severely handicapped students.* (Baltimore: Paul H. Brookes.

Hupp, S. C., & Mervis, C. B. (1981). Development of generalized concepts by severely handicapped students. *Journal of the Association for the Severely Handicapped, 6,* 14–21.

Kent, L. R., Klein, D., Falk, A., & Guenther, H. (1972). A language acquisition program for the retarded. In J. E. McLean, D. E. Yoder, & R. L. Schiefelbusch (Eds.), *Language intervention with the retarded.* Baltimore: University Park Press.

Matson, J. L., Esveldt-Dawson, K., & Kazdin, A. E. (1982). Treatment of spelling deficits in mentally retarded children. *Mental Retardation, 20,* 76–81.

Palyo, N. J., Cooke, T. P., Schuler, A. L., & Apolloni, T. (1979). Modifying echolalic speech in preschool children: Training and generalization. *American Journal of Mental Deficiency, 83,* 480–489.

Powers, R. B., & Osborne, J. G. (1976). *Fundamentals of behavior.* St. Paul, MN: West Publishing.

Remington, B., & Clarke, S. (1983). Acquisition of expressive signing by autistic children: An evaluation of the relative effects of simultaneous communication and sign-alone training. *Journal of Applied Behavior Analysis, 16,* 315–328.

Rinne, C. H. (1984). *Attention: The fundamentals of classroom control*. Columbus, OH: Charles E. Merrill.

Rowan, V. C., & Pear, J. J. (1985). A comparison of the effects of interspersal and concurrent training sequences on acquisition, retention, and generalization of picture names. *Applied Research in Mental Retardation, 6,* 127–145.

Snell, M. E., & Gast, D. L. (1981). Applying time delay procedure to the instruction of the severely handicapped. *Journal of the Association for the Severely Handicapped, 6*(3), 3–14.

Touchette, P. E., & Howard, H. S. (1984). Errorless learning: Reinforcement contingencies and stimulus control transfer in delayed prompting.

Journal of Applied Behavior Analysis, 17, 175–188.

Weeks, M., & Gaylord-Ross, R. (1981). Task difficulty and aberrant behavior in severely handicapped students. *Journal of Applied Behavior Analysis, 14,* 449–463.

White, K. P., Wyne, M. D., Stuck, G. B., & Coop, R. H. (1983). *Teaching effectiveness evaluation project. Final Report.* Chapel Hill: School of Education, University of North Carolina at Chapel Hill.

Wolery, M., Ault, M. J., Doyle, P. M., & Gast, D. L. (1986). *Comparison of instructional strategies: A literature review* (Grant No. G008530197). Lexington: Department of Special Education, University of Kentucky.

13

USING REINFORCERS
TO FACILITATE
SKILL ACQUISITION

Key Terms

■ Reinforcement History ■ Consequence ■ Reinforcing
Consequence ■ Positive Reinforcement ■ Negative
Reinforcement ■ Unconditioned (Primary) Reinforcer ■ Deprivation
States ■ Satiation States ■ Conditioned (Secondary)
Reinforcer ■ Premack Principle ■ Generalized Conditioned
Reinforcer ■ Reinforcer Menu ■ Reinforcer Sampling ■ Stimulus
Control ■ Differential Reinforcement ■ Discriminative Stimulus ■ S
Delta ■ Contingent Reinforcement ■ Shaping ■ Continuous Schedule
of Reinforcement ■ Intermittent Schedule of Reinforcement

Skinner (1953, 1969, 1971) consistently argued that behavior is heavily dependent on one's history of reinforcement. In a broad sense, **reinforcement history** refers to the consequences previously received for a behavior in a given context. One of the most fundamental skills required of teachers of handicapped students is the effective use of consequences to facilitate learning. Consequences can take many forms: (a) acknowledgment of whether a response is right or wrong; (b) presentation of rewarding events, such as praise, money, or free time; or (c) presentation of aversive events, such as criticism, correction, or punishment for errors. Consequences are important for skill acquisition for at least two reasons. First, they *communicate* and inform the student regarding response accuracy and appropriateness. Second, they serve as *incentives* to increase correct performance and decrease errors. This chapter defines the basic principles of reinforcement (one type of consequence), discusses the role of reinforcement in skill acquisition, and describes characteristics of useful reinforcers.

PRINCIPLES OF REINFORCEMENT

Reinforcing Consequences

A **consequence** is an event that follows the performance of a behavior. Consequences can be feedback presented contingently after a behavior has been emitted (performed). Depending on the consequence and how it is applied, future performance can be affected. A **reinforcing consequence** results in an increase in the future probability of a behavior. In order for the consequence to be called a reinforcer, there must be a functional relationship between its use and subsequent rates of behavior. If an increase in behavior is not observed, reinforcement has not occurred. For example, Ms. Thompson was overheard saying, "I tried reinforcement to get my child toilet-trained, but those M & Ms did not work. Reinforcement was not useful to me at all." In this case, the candy was not a reinforcer for Ms. Thompson's child since its use did not result in a behavior change. This should not be construed to mean that reinforcement does not work, however, only that Ms. Thompson was not able to identify a reinforcing consequence.

Since what is reinforcing for one student may have no effect on another, reinforcers must be individually defined. There are two types of reinforcing consequences: positive reinforcement and negative reinforcement.

Positive Reinforcement.   **Positive reinforcement** is the contingent presentation of a stimulus following a response that results in an increase in the future occurrence of the response. This definition contains two critical components. First, the procedure involves the *presentation* of a consequence that is assumed to be desired by the student. Second, as with any reinforcement, the observed effect of such a presentation is an increase in the future probability of the behavior occurring under similar stimulus conditions. Both conditions must be met if a procedure is to be described accurately as positive reinforcement.

Positive reinforcement explains both the acquisition and persistence of many behaviors. For example, Jerry has learned that he is much more likely to get his teacher to attend to him if he raises his hand and waits for her to approach him. He also has learned that whenever he does his imitations of the principal or the school custodian, his peers are likely to pay attention to him and laugh. Now his impersonations are quite frequent. Both appropriate and inappropriate behaviors have increased and been maintained by positive reinforcement. Teachers should always be aware that their own behaviors and the behaviors of their students are being maintained by a variety of environmental reinforcers. A consequence may be maintaining a behavior, even when no one is aware of that relationship. For example, a teacher has a number of students who get out of their seats. Each time they stand up, she calls their name and tells them to sit down. Her attention and verbal behaviors may actually be reinforcing the standing-up behaviors.

Negative Reinforcement. Negative reinforcement is similar to positive reinforcement in that its use results in an increase in responding. However, it differs because the consequence manipulation involves the removal of a stimulus contingent upon the behavior. Negative reinforcement explains those days when Jerry completes all of his academic assignments. Ms. Fernandez tells Jerry that he has to stay after school unless he completes all his assignments. As soon as he has finished his work, she takes away the after-school consequence. In this example, the consequence is the contingent removal of staying after school when assignments are completed; the resulting effect is an increase in academic assignment completion. Thus, **negative reinforcement** is the contingent removal of a stimulus following a response that is associated with an observed increase in the future occurrence of the response (Skinner, 1953).

Although the effective implementation of negative reinforcement produces an increase in responding, it is generally not recommended as a teaching strategy since it requires the presence of an aversive condition. Negative reinforcement has more utility as a means of explaining many everyday occurrences. When parents nag a child to do something, the child complies in order to terminate the aversive nagging. Children who have been sent to their rooms until they apologize are also responding to negative reinforcement contingencies. A student being teased by peers may produce a desired behavior in order to terminate the teasing. Negative reinforcement also explains how many adult behaviors are shaped. For example, if yelling at a group of noisy students quiets them, the teacher may be more likely to yell at them again when they are noisy.

Kinds of Reinforcing Stimuli

There are two kinds of reinforcing stimuli: (a) unconditioned or primary reinforcers and (b) conditioned or secondary reinforcers.

Unconditioned Reinforcers. An **unconditioned (primary) reinforcer** is a consequence that does not rely on previous learning to acquire reinforcing value (Kazdin, 1975). The most common examples are food, water, warmth, shelter, air, physical support (e.g., from falling), sex, physical movement, and some forms of tactile stimulation. Unconditioned reinforcers are most often used with young children, students who have severe developmental delays, or other students for whom more conventional social reinforcers are ineffective. The effectiveness of unconditioned reinforcers is easily influenced by **deprivation states** (a state in which the person has been deprived of the reinforcer so that its use is likely to be highly reinforcing) or **satiation states** (a state in which the person has had too much of the reinforcer so that its use is not likely to be reinforcing). For example, food would likely be reinforcing at 11:00 a.m. for a student who ate breakfast at 6:00 a.m. However, using food as a reinforcer immediately after lunch is not likely to be as effective. Many people view the use of primary reinforcers negatively. Therefore, unconditioned reinforcers usually are used only when necessary, and should be replaced by other learned consequences as soon as possible.

Conditioned Reinforcers. A **conditioned (secondary) reinforcer** is a learned reinforcing consequence (Skinner, 1953). Although not initially reinforcing, a conditioned reinforcer is developed by repeatedly and contingently pairing a neutral consequence with another stimulus that is already reinforcing. For example, money has no inherent reinforcing value. However, through association with the things money can buy, it quickly becomes a powerful behavioral motivator. Conditioned reinforcers are advantageous since they are (a) less affected by satiation, (b) easily controlled and manipulated by teachers and other change agents, and (c) more commonly used in everyday activities. Common examples of conditioned reinforcers used with students include verbal feedback and praise, tokens, grades, the opportunity to engage in preferred activities, and privileges such as being first in line, taking a note to the principal, or erasing the chalkboard.

When a preferred activity is used to reinforce behavior, the procedure is known as the **Premack Principle** (Premack, 1959, 1965). The application of this principle is commonly associated with "if...then..." statements where a high-frequency or high-probability behavior is used to increase the occurrence of a low-frequency or probability response. For example, Mr. Warren knows that Ellen dislikes cleaning up her study area, but enjoys working on the computer. Making Ellen's access to the computer contingent upon her cleaning up her study area is an example of using the Premack Principle.

When a consequence has been paired with several unconditioned or conditioned reinforcers, it is called a **generalized conditioned reinforcer** (Kazdin, 1975). Because they are associated with many different reinforcing stimuli, generalized reinforcers are particularly useful for avoiding satiation. For example, when Sandy has a particularly good day at school, his parents give him a coupon that he can use to "buy" some television watching time, a visit to the local video arcade, or a weekend field trip. Earning the coupon enables him to access a wide variety of reinforcers. If he becomes satiated with any one of these conditioned reinforcers, others are available.

In many settings, a single generalized conditioned reinforcer can be used to access other *back-up reinforcers.* This type of learned consequence is called a *token reinforcer.* Tokens may be anything that can be easily dispensed, such as checkmarks, poker chips, tickets, paper punches, points, etc. A *token economy* is a structured system that uses tokens, back-up reinforcers, and token-earning rules to manage a variety of behaviors. A more detailed discussion of token economies is presented in Chapter 23.

DETERMINING REINFORCER PREFERENCES

Individual learning histories and varied settings cause consequences to have different reinforcing values across as well as within individuals. Consequences that are reinforcing for one individual may have no reinforcing value for another. Likewise, a consequence that was once reinforcing for a student may have no reinforcing qualities at a later time or in a different setting. A variety of strategies may be used to identify effective reinforcers for individual students.

Observation Strategies

The most direct method of determining reinforcer preferences is to observe the individual's behavior. By systematically recording events that follow a student's responses, teachers can identify possible reinforcers that might be used in instructional programs. Vargas (1977) suggested that observational data may be used to answer the following questions about reinforcer preferences: (a) What do students ask for? (b) What do students do? (c) In what ways are students progressing? and (d) What follows persistent undesirable behavior? The last question suggests that "persistent undesirable behavior" may be maintained by positive reinforcement. Teachers should evaluate the events that follow inappropriate behavior to determine if they can be incorporated into instructional programs designed to teach more desirable behaviors. For example, Ms. King has observed that, when Jamal calls out rather than raising his hand, his peers respond. Peer attention seems to be a positive reinforcer for calling-out behaviors. To determine whether peer attention might be used as a reinforcer for other skills, Ms. King should ask herself the following questions:

1. For whom is this a powerful reinforcer?
2. Are several students interested in this reinforcer?
3. Can I justify the use of this reinforcer?
4. Can I obtain or control this reinforcer?
5. Is this reinforcer convenient to this situation? (Kerr & Nelson, 1983, p. 127)

Direct-observation strategies also include noting (a) what behaviors are displayed frequently; (b) what antecedent, consequence, and setting conditions are present when these behaviors occur; (c) what objects, activities, and choices the student makes; and (d) how frequently and after how much of a delay the reinforcers are presented. When collecting this information, teachers should determine whether the behavior occurs in more than one setting (e.g., reading group, recess, home) or under more than one condition (e.g., in reading group with different peers or with different learning activities) in order to identify the strength of the reinforcer.

Interviewing Strategies

In addition to direct-observation procedures, interviewing strategies can provide teachers with information about reinforcer preferences. These strategies involve asking students or relevant others what they prefer, like, or enjoy doing or having.

One useful source for reinforcer preference data is the student's parents, who generally know what their child likes and dislikes or finds reinforcing. When parents are interviewed about potential reinforcers, begin with open-ended questions that address specific categories. For example, Ms. Randall identified three conditions (i.e., independent time, time with peers, time with adults) and five categories of activities (i.e., play and toys, food, activities, hobbies, sports) to use in interviewing Kim Lee's parents. She asked Kim Lee's mother to identify what kinds of sports or games Kim Lee likes to play with her friends, and she asked her father to name the kinds of hobbies Kim Lee enjoys doing by herself. Open-ended questions may be followed by more direct questions when more specific information is necessary.

Information about reinforcer preferences also can be acquired by interviewing other individuals who know the student, such as peers or other teachers. Like the interview process with parents, questions and probes should be relatively general and open-ended around specific areas of interest. For example, Kim Lee's friends could be asked what they like to do when they play with her on the playground. Her previous teachers could be asked to describe what reinforcers were effective when she was in their classes.

When interviewing target students, the most direct strategy is to ask them what they would work for or like to earn. Use of the Premack Principle and its "if...then..." statement is an appropriate questioning format. For example, Ms. Fernandez asked Jerry what he would like to do if he met his words-read-per-minute goal for the week. If students do not provide preference information, teachers can ask less direct questions about their (a) favorite games or toys, (b) favorite activities, or (c) objects they would like to have, or (d) activities they would like to try. In some cases, it may be necessary to create "what if" situations. For example, Mr. Rizzo asked Lucy what book she would choose to read if she could pick any book in the library; what she would do if she had 15 free minutes during the school day; or with whom or what she would like to play during recess. In other cases, specific examples or lists of possible reinforcers can be used. Often referred to as a **reinforcer menu,** students can select from the list or rank order the items.

Another strategy related to interviews involves asking the student to provide or produce reinforcer preferences for themselves or others. For example, Ms. James established a simple token economy that includes a classroom store from which students may trade points for a variety of objects or activities. Half of the items were placed in the store by Ms. James, including school supplies, sugarless candy, gift certificates to local fast-food restaurants, "tokens" to a local video game center, and coupons for time on the classroom computer, time in the library, or time with the vice principal. The other half of the items was supplied by students. Every two weeks they place one toy or object brought from home in the school store (with teacher and parent approval), or they write their own activity coupons. Robert wrote activity coupons that enabled other students to trade points for checker games, two-person computer competitions, and lunch swaps with him. He also brought a broken lawn mower carburetor from home, placed a price tag of 500 points on it, and put it in the classroom store. Robert, however, signed up for and got accepted into an industrial arts class during fourth period. Proudly, he began earning points to buy back his broken carburetor so he and the industrial arts teacher could rebuild it.

Regardless of who is interviewed, teachers should not assume that recommended reinforcers are actually reinforcing. The reinforcement value of a stimulus can be affected by the deprivation/satiation state of the student, setting conditions, and recent reinforcement experiences (e.g., schedule, amount, or timing of reinforcement).

Sampling and Assessment Strategies

When direct-observation and interviewing strategies do not work, reinforcer sampling and assessment procedures should be considered. With **reinforcer sampling,** students are given an opportunity to sample a specific reinforcing event when they engage in an approximation of a desired response (Kazdin, 1975). Sampling also can mean having a student use a possible reinforcer. Kazdin indicated that "the more frequently the reinforcers are used, the more the clients will engage in the appropriate target behavior required to obtain them" (p. 137). A number of studies examined the use of reinforcer sampling (e.g., Ayllon & Azrin, 1968a, 1968b). For example, the opportunity to play on the playground may not be initially reinforcing for a student who does not know how to play organized games. Instruction in game-playing and assisted participation allows the student to sample the activity, and hopefully through positive associations it will become reinforcing for him or her. The purpose of reinforcer sampling is to increase the reinforcement value of a consequence by increasing the student's familiarity and experience with it. If a student does not use a reinforcer, its function in facilitating skill acquisition is weakened.

Teachers can also select reinforcers by assessing consequences that are typical or common for a given age or group of students. For example, young children tend to find the following social consequences reinforcing: smiles, overt enthusiasm, tickles, pats, toy play, and the like. Older students, however, are more likely to respond to a different variety of social reinforcers such as "high fives" or "giving five," verbal praise (e.g., "All right," "That's cool," etc.), subtle smiles and eye contact, and even being left alone. Having identified these common age-specific reinforcers, the teacher can try them to see if they are reinforcing for an individual student. This test is a critical component of confirming the actual reinforcement value a given consequence possesses.

The identification of reinforcer preferences can also be accomplished by assessing or trying novel or hard to get stimuli. Many children find novel objects or activities reinforcing. Parents and teachers frequently report that one of their children preferred to play more with the box than the toy that came in it. Even when surrounded by a table full of crayons, access to a "special" or new crayon can be reinforcing to some students. Working toward or earning something another student already possesses can also be useful in facilitating skill acquisition.

GUIDELINES FOR USING REINFORCERS EFFECTIVELY

In technical terms, teaching may be described as the process of establishing stimulus control. **Stimulus control** is a condition in which a desired response occurs predictably in the presence of a given stimulus, but not in the presence of other stimuli. Stimulus control is achieved by effective use of reinforcers. More specifically, students learn to produce particular responses in the presence of specific antecedent stimuli because of **differential reinforcement.** Differential reinforcement is the systematic and contingent presentation of a reinforcer following a desired behavior and the withholding of reinforcers when the desired behavior does not occur. Through repeated presentation of the antecedent stimulus and reinforcement of the appropriate response, stimulus control eventually is established. The stimulus that signals the learner to perform the desired response is called a **discriminative stimulus,** often abbreviated as S^D. A stimulus that signals the student not to do the desired response is called **S Delta** and is abbreviated S^Δ.

Using this conceptualization, learning occurs when students are able to discriminate between conditions in which the performance of specific behaviors will or will not be reinforced. For example, Nathaniel initially calls all vehicles "cars." Through differential reinforcement, such as praise for correct labeling and error correction, his parents teach him to discriminate cars from trucks. Marcy learns that wildly waving her hand before the teacher finishes asking a question or while the teacher is helping another student is not likely to result in teacher attention. Because of differential reinforcement, she now waits until a question is finished and quietly raises her hand.

The effective use of reinforcers to establish stimulus control requires consideration of several factors, including the timing, amount, scheduling, and selection of appropriate reinforcers. Also, reinforcers should be used in conjunction with the various forms of teacher assistance described in Chapter 12.

Timing Reinforcement

The basic rule for timing the presentation of reinforcement is to follow the desired behavior immediately with a reinforcing stimulus. Immediate presentation allows students to associate the reinforcer with the behavior. Behaviors followed immediately by reinforcement increase in rate. If the time between the target behavior and the presentation of the reinforcer is too long, the behavior may not increase. Further, delays in the presentation of reinforcers provide opportunities for nontarget behaviors to occur and be reinforced inadvertently. This situation can facilitate the development of undesirable behavior. For example, a target behavior for Tawnya is independent completion of tasks and praise is a reinforcer for her. The teacher should praise Tawnya immediately after she completes each task. However, because the teacher has several students and is very busy, her praise is frequently delayed. When Tawnya finishes a task, she begins to "daydream" and look out the window. If praise is delivered while Tawnya is looking out the window, the looking-out-of-the-window behavior will increase rather than the behaviors intended by the teacher. Reinforcers increase the behaviors they follow, not necessarily the behaviors they are intended to increase. Similarly, delays in reinforcement can lead to the development of superstitious behavior. Students may begin to perform some irrelevant behavior they think is related to receiving reinforcement. For example, if Tawnya is consistently reinforced when she is raising her hand and holding the palm just above her head, she may think that she is only reinforced if her hand is above her head. Skinner suggested that such relationships may explain the occurrence of superstitions such as not walking under ladders, not allowing black cats to cross the path, and throwing salt over one's shoulder after breaking a mirror.

After a skill has been acquired, the presentation of reinforcers can be delayed to intervals that match those in the natural environment. The natural environment rarely provides immediate feedback like that used in educational settings. When reinforcement timing does not approximate the natural environment, the behavior may not endure or be maintained by natural consequences. Students must be taught to delay their gratification and to wait for reinforcers. For example, teachers and most other workers get paid in two-week or one-month intervals; they do not get paid immediately after each work response. However, during initial acquisition, immediate reinforcement of every response is important.

Closely related to the notion of immediacy is the contingent presentation of reinforcers. **Contingent reinforcement** means that the reinforcer is provided when the behavior occurs and only when it occurs. This process also allows an association to be established between the reinforcer and behavior. If the reinforcer is provided contingently each time the behavior occurs, the behavior has a predictable effect on the environment. These learned contingencies affect the probability that a behavior will occur again. However, when students are reinforced, many behaviors may be occurring. For example, when Marcus raises his hand to ask a question, Ms. Willis says, "Great job." Unfortunately, when Marcus raises his hand he is also looking at Ms. Willis, sitting in his chair, rolling his pencil on the desk with the other hand, and tapping his feet on the floor. He could associate the praise with any of these behaviors and perhaps with the school work he is doing rather than his appropriate hand-raising. If Ms. Willis wants to reinforce his hand-raising, then immediate, contingent praise that is more informative should be given such as "Great hand-raising! Now I can answer your question."

When establishing a contingent relationship between a behavior and a reinforcing consequence, it is important to determine how well the student must perform the behavior before a reinforcer is presented. If students know the task and the instructional goal is consistent performance, reinforcement should be presented contingent only on correct performance. However, when students are just learning a task or when their present levels of functioning differ considerably from what is eventually expected, teachers will need to reinforce less-than-perfect performance. **Shaping** is the process of reinforcing successive approximations of a behavior. The purpose of shaping is to provide students with positive feedback for small changes in behavior, and to gradually require closer approximations to the final behavior before reinforcement is provided. For example, Meghan is learning to write her name. At first, her teacher reinforces her with a happy face on her paper when she traces her name. Gradually, she requires Meghan to write more letters independently before the happy face is drawn. Through systematic reinforcement, she has "shaped" Meghan's name-writing behavior.

To use shaping effectively:

1. Start with the student's present level of performance and provide reinforcement for that level in order to establish a contingent relationship.

2. Once a contingent relationship has been established and the reinforcer has proved to be effective, decide on a better level of performance that could be reasonably expected of the student. Require the improvement before reinforcement is presented.

3. When stable levels of responding are attained at each level, require closer approximations to the final behavior before presenting reinforcing consequences.

Amount of Reinforcement

Because satiation and deprivation states affect skill acquisition, teachers should strive to maintain reinforcer debts and avoid reinforcer gluts. Unconditioned reinforcers are the most affected by these conditions. Generalized conditioned reinforcers are less affected because they can be used to access a variety of back-up reinforcers.

To identity the appropriate quantity of reinforcement, teachers should manipulate reinforcer amounts systematically and observe the effects on the behavior. The goal is to identify the least amount of a reinforcer that will facilitate skill acquisition. As a response is learned, reinforcer amounts should be reduced to match quantities normally available in the student's natural environment.

The most effective quantity of reinforcement may vary across individuals and time. Mr. Abrams found that 10 minutes of chess-playing time is suitable for Linda, but Oliver plays much slower and gets upset when he is unable to finish a game. For Oliver, an extra 5 minutes of playing time has a significant effect on the reinforcement value of a chess game. On the other hand, Oliver can finish a checker game in 5 minutes. When Mr. Abrams allows Oliver to play checkers for 10 minutes, he finishes his game and spends the remaining 5 minutes teasing and arguing with Judith.

Scheduling Reinforcement

Related to the timing and amount of reinforcement is the schedule on which reinforcers are presented. During acquisition training, reinforcers should be presented contingently after *each* occurrence of the response. When reinforcement is provided for every occurrence of a response, it is called a **continuous schedule of reinforcement** (CRF). A CRF schedule allows students to receive the maximum possible number of opportunities for feedback about the accuracy of their responses. Since the probability of errors is relatively high during acquisition training, every correct response should be reinforced.

As soon as high percentages of accurate responses occur, reinforcers should be presented on an **intermittent schedule of reinforcement,** which is less than continuous. Under an intermittent schedule, reinforcing stimuli are presented on some pre-established schedule rather than on every occurrence of the target behavior. For example, when Vivian first learned to discriminate between the letters *b* and *d*, Mr. Howard reinforced each correct discrimination. As soon as she acquired the discrimination, he presented verbal encouragement and positive feedback on every other correct response. As Vivian became more proficient, Mr. Howard continued to provide positive reinforcement, but less frequently. Eventually, Vivian will require little teacher feedback to use *b* and *d* correctly. The different kinds of intermittent schedules are discussed in Chapter 16.

Naturally Occurring Reinforcers

The acquisition of a new behavior is complete only when the skill can be applied, maintained, and generalized to the student's natural environment. Part of the solution to increasing generalization requires teachers to select and use reinforcers that are commonly available in the natural environment (e.g., classroom privileges, getting in line first). When contingent relationships are established between behaviors and environmental conditions, and between behaviors and natural reinforcers, there is an increased probability that the behavior will be generalized (Horner, Bellamy, & Colvin, 1984; Stokes & Baer, 1977). During acquisition, the most natural but effective reinforcer should be used *and,* as performance criteria are met, less artificial and more naturally occurring kinds of reinforcing consequences should be used. By systematically fading the former and adding the latter, newly learned behaviors can be brought under the control of natural contingencies.

When using less natural or unconditioned reinforcers, teachers should try to pair those reinforcers with more natural consequences. For example, presentation of food as a reinforcer could be paired with verbal praise, tokens, or happy faces. Through repeated association with a known reinforcer, praise, tokens, or happy faces should eventually attain reinforcing properties.

OTHER REINFORCEMENT CONSIDERATIONS

Teachers can facilitate the acquisition of new academic and social behaviors by carefully selecting appropriate reinforcers, timing the reinforcement appropriately, providing sufficient amounts of reinforcement, using continuous and intermittent schedules of reinforcement, and using natural reinforcement. In the remaining sections, three special reinforcement topics are discussed: (a) use of teacher praise, (b) identification and use of unusual reinforcers, and (c) the negative effects of reward.

Teacher Praise

Advantages and Disadvantages of Teacher Praise. Kazdin (1975) suggested that many reasons exist for using social reinforcers such as teacher praise. They are easily administered by a variety of individuals, including teachers, parents, paraprofessionals, and peers. Social reinforcers can be presented to students without disrupting instruction and ongoing adaptive behaviors. They can be used with a variety of other reinforcing objects or events, thus reducing possible satiation effects. Finally, social consequences are common in everyday activities and interactions and thereby facilitate maintenance of skills.

Teachers frequently include some kind of social consequences whenever they implement a reinforcement program. Social consequences can become conditioned reinforcers and may take many forms, including praise, teacher attention, physical contact (pats, "high fives"), and facial expressions (smiles, eye contact, nods of approval and winks). Whenever an unconditioned reinforcer (e.g., food, activity, etc.) is presented, the teacher should also present a social consequence such as praise and/or smiles. By pairing the social consequences with unconditioned reinforcers, the social consequences will acquire reinforcement value. Once that value is acquired, the social consequences should periodically be paired with the unconditioned reinforcers so that the value will be maintained. As the unconditioned reinforcers are thinned, naturally occurring praise or other social consequences will allow the student to receive feedback and incentives for continued performance. Social consequences should also be paired with token reinforcement. Those social consequences will help bridge the gap between the student's behavior and some later reinforcing event. When praise and other social consequences are used, newly learned behaviors are more likely to transfer or generalize (Stokes & Baer, 1977).

Unfortunately, the use of teacher praise may not be as simple and straightforward as it appears. Brophy (1981) suggested that teacher praise may be overused and inappropriately applied:

> Taken together, the data on praise from this and other studies suggest that (1) much teacher praise is not even intended as reinforcement but instead is reactive behavior elicited and reinforced by students themselves; and (2) most of the teacher praise that apparently is intended as reinforcement probably does not function very effectively as such, because it is not systematically contingent on desirable behavior, lacks specification of the behavioral elements to be reinforced, and/or lacks credibility. (p. 15)

White and Haring (1980) added that social feedback can be very subtle and its effects can vary tremendously across individual students, depending on their learning experiences. Praise frequently is treated as if it functions as a "mirror opposite" of criticism; however, recent research suggests that praise and criticism may have a more independent relationship with respect to their effects on student behavior and ratings of teacher and self (Worrall, Worrall, & Melldrum, 1983). In addition, when teacher praise is overused, the reinforcement value of praise is lost because it is not associated with unconditioned reinforcers. The quality of praise may be poor because it is not given enthusiastically or in a varied manner. Furthermore, the nonspecific nature of much teacher praise makes it ineffective.

A final problem associated with social reinforcement is inconsistent and unsystematic use (Kerr & Nelson, 1983). Many teachers do not include teacher praise with other procedures such as token economies, extinction, response cost, or timeout. Its application is less systematic; teachers rarely attend to the schedule on which they deliver praise. Teachers also frequently use an inadequate number and variety of praise statements and other social reinforcers. Actually, the number of possible praise statements is only limited by the student's learning history and by a teacher's ability to describe what he or she sees or hears. When applied appropriately, however, praise and other forms of social consequences have been shown to be effective in facilitating academic and social skill acquisition (Becker, Madsen, Arnold, & Thomas, 1967; Broden, Copeland, Beasley, & Hall, 1977; Clements & Tracey, 1977; Kazdin & Klock, 1973; Madsen, Becker, & Thomas, 1968).

Given their advantages, social reinforcers may be useful for facilitating skill acquisition, maintenance, and generalization; however, teachers must monitor the use of social reinforcement and evaluate its effects. Praise, as with all reinforcers, may be reinforcing or rewarding for one individual, but may have different values for another.

Guidelines for Effective Use of Teacher Praise. To increase the potential effectiveness and decrease the undesirable side effects, teachers should adhere to the following guidelines when using praise and other social reinforcers. When praise is presented, teachers should be genuine, warm, and spontaneous (Good & Brophy, 1984; Kerr & Nelson, 1983). Students of all ages and with all types of handicaps may see through perfunctory and insincere attempts at social reinforcement. Pairing verbal praise with smiles and physical contact (or other unconditioned reinforcers) can be much more effective than a simple "good" statement.

Second, Sulzer-Azaroff and Mayer (1977) recommended that teachers use specific, rather than general, praise when reinforcing desired behavior. Descriptive praise informs students exactly what is acceptable about their behavior and implies what needs to be changed or improved (Kerr & Nelson, 1983). For example, Ms. Lewis has learned to reinforce Ben's behavior positively by "labeling" them. Rather than a general praise statement, such as "good job. . .that was real helpful," she tells Ben exactly what behaviors are being praised; for example, "Excellent work, Ben! It is so much easier to collect papers when you wait your turn." Paine, Radicchi, Rosellini, Deutchman, and Darch (1983) also recommended that student names be included in the praise statements to strengthen the association between students and their behavior. If the statement is made publicly, the positive benefits of peer acknowledgment can be included.

> Specific praise places the emphasis on the behavior, rather than on the child, which is important. For, when praise is withheld from inappropriate behavior, it helps clients to recognize (or discriminate) that it is not they but their behavior that is inadequate. Specific praise increases the likelihood that specific aspects of behavior will be repeated in the future (Paine et al., 1983, p. 125).

In some situations and for some students, teachers should be cautious when using descriptive praise in the presence of others. Such praise may direct unwanted attention toward students or cause them to be labeled (e.g., "teacher's pet") by fellow classmates (Paine et al., 1983).

Third, teachers must take time to praise appropriate student behavior. The old adage about "catch 'em being good" applies to this guideline. Specific and descriptive praise can be very powerful if used in a contingent and immediate manner. Teachers should be aware of several desirable behaviors for each student. When those behaviors occur, immediate reinforcement should be provided. Similarly, teachers must force themselves to use praise despite their feelings toward the student's behaviors. Ross may have been interrupting others, leaving his work unfinished, and using inappropriate language all morning, but if he is eating his lunch appropriately and he helps Judy with her tray, teachers should praise him for those desired behaviors.

Paine et al. (1983) added that good praise follows the "if-then" rule:

> The "if-then rule" states that if the student is doing something you want to encourage—something you want to see the student do again or do more often in the

future (and if you are sure that that is what the student is doing)—then (and only then) you should praise the student for it (p. 46).

They also suggested that teachers reinforce during the behavior so a clear association can be made between the praise statement and the desired behavior.

Fourth, effective praise is not disruptive. That is, it does not cause the student to stop doing a desirable behavior or begin some other less acceptable response. Mr. Martinez, for example, observed that when he told Anna her handwriting was improving rapidly, she stopped writing and started showing her papers to others. Mr. Martinez found that a quiet whisper and a touch on the shoulder was just as effective in strengthening her handwriting skills without disrupting the very behavior he was trying to promote.

Lastly, praise should be varied and not overused. Teachers can present social reinforcers to individuals or groups, publicly or privately, in close proximity or from across the room, while teaching or helping students, or alone or with other forms of social reinforcement. Varied use of teacher praise will reduce possible satiation effects, increase the number of functional reinforcers, and probably will be perceived as being more sincere.

Teacher praise and other types of social reinforcement can be very useful forms of feedback to students. However, like any intervention strategy, they can be overused and inappropriately applied. Teachers should use praise contingently, immediately, consistently, and systematically. Descriptive and specific praise that is varied and not disruptive will tend to be more effective and efficient.

Unusual Reinforcers

Consequences may influence students in different ways. When working with exceptional students, teachers should select reinforcers carefully by using direct observation, interviewing the student or relevant others, and trying different reinforcers. Bassett, Blanchard, and Koshland (1977) recommended that teachers use both informal strategies and systematic procedures for determining reinforcing stimuli. Guidelines for constructing reinforcement surveys for students have been developed (Raschke, 1981). Greer, Becker, Saxe, and Mirabella (1985) described conditions and procedures for teaching new reinforcers for appropriate play behaviors as a strategy for dealing with stereotypic behavior.

Despite these methods, teachers may be unable to identify appropriate reinforcers for a few students. In some instances, competing reinforcers may be too strong; for example, the coy flirts of another student may be a stronger reinforcer than earning 10 minutes of free time. In other cases, teachers cannot provide the reinforcers identified by the student. For example, cigarettes, alcohol, and money are inappropriate in most public-school settings. For other behaviors, the reinforcers appear to be a part of the inappropriate behavior. For example, sensory consequences often appear to maintain stereotypic behaviors such as rocking, twirling hair, or thumb-sucking. When reinforcers cannot be easily identified, teachers may need to use a previously unacceptable activity as a reinforcer to gain control over severe behavior problems, such as aggressive and self-injurious behavior. For example, Bruce frequently hits and bites others when demands are made of him. Social isolation (sitting by himself) is one of Bruce's most reinforcing activities. In fact, he is quiet and nondisruptive when allowed to be alone. Thus, his teachers have allowed him to be by himself rather than deal with his aggressions. They have been unsuccessful in finding reinforcers that can compete with his solitary behaviors. Social withdrawal keeps him from participating in learning experiences. Bruce's teachers tried an unusual treatment, letting him be alone after each activity he completed without aggression. Initially, if he completed 3 minutes of work, he was allowed 20 minutes to be alone. Over time, the number of minutes he had to work to be alone was increased. Although this is an unorthodox treatment, it was defendable because the aggression was controlled and Bruce learned more adaptive acceptable behaviors. Further, by pairing social consequences with the isolated behavior, they could acquire reinforcement value.

A similar approach may be taken with students who display high rates of task-interfering stereotypic behavior. Stereotypic behaviors have reinforcing properties (Rincover, 1978; Rincover, Cook, Peoples, & Packard, 1979) that can be used in a variety of ways. Hung (1978) allowed students to trade tokens earned for spontaneous sentence production for opportunities to engage in stereotypic behavior. Wolery (1978) applied sensory stimulation similar to the students' stereotypic behavior directly and contingently for correct student responses. Devany (1979) allowed students contingent access to the objects they used in stereotypic behavior for correct task discriminations. Wolery, Kirk, and Gast (1985) provided a cue to perform a stereotypic behavior contingent upon correct responses. In another study, Sugai and White (1986) let a student hold an object used in stereotypic behavior as long as he was engaged in acceptable work behaviors. If a less desirable self-stimulatory or task-interferring behavior was produced, the student lost access to the object for a brief period of time. In all of these studies, some form of stereotypic behavior was manipulated systematically and successfully to increase desired behaviors.

In summary, teachers must go beyond the usual conditioned reinforcers when working with students who have unusual learning and reinforcement histories. The rules and guidelines presented earlier for using reinforcers still apply; however, careful attention must be given to social acceptability, parsimony, and effectiveness.

Potential Negative Effects of Reward

In this chapter, the merits associated with the consistent and proper use of reinforcement to facilitate skill acquisition are described. Challenges to the use of rewards are rarely seen because of the positive and nurturing characteristics attached to the act of giving positive social consequences for desired behaviors.

However, teachers should understand that rewards also may have undesirable side effects. Winett and Winkler (1972), for example, warned that teachers must guard against using powerful reinforcement strategies to produce docile and quiet students who only talk when spoken to, raise their hands at the proper moments, never sing or laugh in the hallways, and always remain in their seats until told to stand up. Rather, teachers should use the procedure to foster enjoyment, creativity, and productive problem-solving behaviors. Further, teachers should not allow teacher-controlled consequences to direct all student responses. Balsam and Bondy (1983) warned that presentation of rewards may be accompanied by a variety of "elecited or emotional effects" (p. 289), such as, (a) aggression and stereotypic or ritualistic responses, (b) suppression of other related or associated appropriate behavior, and (c) excessive approach to or interactive behavior with the reinforcing agent. In a like manner, Balsam and Bondy described how a student's response repertoire might be dominated by a reinforcer-producing behavior at the sacrifice of other acceptable alternative behavior.

Limited generalization and discrimination are also potential negative side effects of reward. Behavioral gains are often lost when the reward system is removed. Similarly, behavior frequently comes under the control of the reinforcing agent or of the setting, rules, and contingencies. Balsam and Bondy suggested that some associated behaviors become very problematic: "One group of responses that may increase with the advent of strong reinforcers includes lying, conniving, stealing, or cheating" (p. 291). These manipulative behaviors are emitted to access the artificial reward rather than to increase the contingent reinforcement value of more naturally occurring stimuli.

Lastly, Balsam and Bondy proposed that students may imitate teacher behaviors and use similar rewards to control peer or other adult behavior. In some cases, this may become coercive and perceived as bribery. Because of the potential negative side effects of reward, Balsam and Bondy suggested that teachers observe whether the effects occur when artificial reinforcers are used. They also recommended that close attention be given to systematic training procedures that enhance the likelihood of response and stimulus generalization.

Summary of Key Concepts

- No universal reinforcers exist; reinforcer effectiveness can vary across settings, individuals, and time.

- Positive reinforcement is defined by two critical features: (a) contingent presentation of a stimulus and (b) subsequent increase in behavior.

- Reinforcers can be identified by direct observation, interviews, and reinforcer sampling; the most efficient and useful way is to emphasize direct-observation strategies.

- When reinf rcers have been identified, their effectiveness should be systematically nd continuously assessed across stimulus conditions.

- Reinforcement should be provided during initial acquisition, contingently and immediately.

- Identify and use the least amount of a reinforcer that will facilitate skill acquisition.

- As skill acquisition is demonstrated, the schedules of reinforcement should be adjusted to intermittent reinforcement.

- During skill acquisition, the most natural but effective reinforcer should be used. As performance criteria are demonstrated, less artificial and more naturally occurring types of reinforcing consequences should be incorporated.

- Teacher praise is a frequently recommended social reinforcer; however, as with other reinforcers, it can be overused and ineffective. Teacher praise should be used contingently and systematically. Descriptive and specific praise that is varied and nondisruptive should be used.

- Although some students may present unusual learning and reinforcement histories, the results of using reinforcement remain the same. Unusual reinforcers can be considered in such situations; however, careful attention must be given to social acceptability, parsimony, and effectiveness.

- Despite the general perception that reinforcement is positive, nurturing, and important for efficient skill acquisition, teachers should be cautious to assess for potential side effects similar to those found when using aversive stimuli.

REFERENCES

Ayllon, T., & Azrin, N. H. (1968a). Reinforcer sampling: A technique for increasing the behavior of mental patients. *Journal of Applied Behavior Analysis, 1,* 13–20.

Ayllon, T., & Azrin, N. H. (1968b). *The token economy: A motivational system for therapy and rehabilitation.* New York: Appleton-Century-Crofts.

Balsam, P. D., & Bondy, A. S. (1983). The negative side effects of reward. *Journal of Applied Behavior Analysis, 16,* 283–296.

Bassett, J., Blanchard, E., & Koshland, E. (1977). On determining reinforcing stimuli: Armchair versus empirical procedures. *Behavior Therapy, 8,* 205–212.

Becker, W., Madsen, C., Arnold, C., & Thomas, D. (1967). The contingent use of teacher attention and praise in reducing classroom behavior problems. *Journal of Special Education, 1,* 287–307.

Broden, M., Copeland, G., Beasley, A., & Hall, R. (1977). Altering student responses through changes in teacher verbal behavior. *Journal of Applied Behavior Analysis, 10,* 479–487.

Brophy, J. (1981). Teacher praise: A functional analysis. *Review of Educational Research, 51,* 5–32.

Clements, J., & Tracey, D. (1977). Effects of touch and verbal reinforcement on the classroom behavior of emotionally disturbed boys. *Exceptional Children, 43,* 453–454.

Devany, J. (1979, December). *Assessment of the effects of using self-stimulation as a reinforcer.* Paper presented at the 13th Annual Convention of the Association for the Advancement of Behavior Therapy, San Francisco.

Good, T. L., & Brophy, J. E. (1984). *Looking in classrooms* (3rd ed.). New York: Harper & Row.

Greer, R. D., Becker, B. J., Saxe, C. D., & Mirabella,

R. F. (1985). Conditioning histories and setting stimuli controlling engagement in stereotypy or toy play. *Analysis and Intervention in Developmental Disabilities, 5,* 269–284.

Horner, R. H., Bellamy, G. T., & Colvin, G. T. (1984). Responding in the presence of non-trained stimuli: Implications of generalization error patterns. *The Journal of the Association of Persons with Severe Handicaps, 9,* 287–295.

Hung, D. W. (1978). Using self-stimulation as reinforcement for autistic children. *Journal of Autism and Childhood Schizophrenia, 8,* 355–366.

Kazdin, A. E. (1975). *Behavior modification in applied settings.* Homewood, IL: The Dorsey Press.

Kazdin, A. E., & Klock, J. (1973). The effect of nonverbal teacher approval on student attentive behavior. *Journal of Applied Behavior Analysis, 6,* 643–654.

Kerr, M. M., & Nelson, C. M. (1983). *Strategies for managing behavior problems in the classroom.* Columbus, OH: Charles E. Merrill.

Madsen, C., Becker, W., & Thomas, D. (1968). Rules, praise, and ignoring: Elements of elementary classroom control. *Journal of Applied Behavior Analysis, 1,* 139–150.

Paine, S. C., Radicchi, J., Rosellini, L. C., Deutchman, L., Darch, C.B. (1983). *Structuring your classroom for academic success.* Champaign, IL: Research Press.

Premack, D. (1959). Toward empirical behavior laws: I. Positive reinforcement. *Psychological Review, 66,* 219–233.

Premack, D. (1969). Reinforcement theory. In D. Levine (Ed.), *Nebraska symposium on motivation* (pp. 123–180). Lincoln: University of Nebraska Press.

Raschke, D. (1981). Designing reinforcement surveys: Let the student choose the reward. *Teaching Exceptional Children, 4,* 92–96.

Rincover, A. (1978). Sensory extinction: A procedure for eliminating self-stimulatory behavior in psychotic children. *Journal of Abnormal Child Psychology, 6,* 299–310.

Rincover, A., Cook, R., Peoples, A., & Packard, D. (1979). Sensory extinction and sensory reinforcement principles for programming multiple adaptive behavior change. *Journal of Applied Behavior Analysis, 12,* 221–233.

Skinner, B. F. (1953). *Science and human behavior.* New York: Macmillan.

Skinner, B. F. (1969). *Contingencies of reinforcement: A . theoretical analysis.* New York: Appleton-Century-Crofts.

Skinner, B. F. (1971). *Beyond freedom and dignity.* New York: Knopf.

Stokes, T. F., & Baer, D. M. (1977). An implicit technology of generalization. *Journal of Applied Behavior Analysis, 10,* 349–367.

Sugai, G., & White, W. (1986). The effect of self-stimulation as a reinforcer on the vocational work rates with severely handicapped students. *Journal of Autism and Developmental Disorders, 16,* 459–471.

Sulzer-Azaroff, B., & Mayer, G. R. (1977). *Applying Behavior analysis procedures with children and youth.* New York: Holt, Rinehart & Winston.

Vargas, J. S. (1977). *Behavioral psychology for teachers.* New York: Harper & Row.

White, O. R., & Haring, N. G. (1980). *Exceptional teaching* (2nd ed.). Columbus, OH: Charles E. Merrill.

Winett, R. A., & Winkler, R. C. (1972). Current behavior modification in the classroom: Be still, be quiet, be docile. *Journal of Applied Behavior Analysis, 5,* 499–504.

Wolery, M. (1978). Self-stimulatory behavior as a basis for devising reinforcers. *AAESPH Review, 3,* 23–29.

Wolery, M., Kirk, K., & Gast, D. L. (1985). Stereoptyic behavior as a reinforcer: Effects and side effects. *Journal of Autism and Developmental Disorders, 15,* 149–161.

Worrall, C., Worrall, N., & Meldrum, C. (1983). The consequences of verbal praise and criticism. *Educational Psychologist, 3,* 127–136.

14

FADING PROMPTS TO PROMOTE INDEPENDENCE

Key Terms

■ Response Prompting Strategies ■ Antecedent Prompt and Test Procedure ■ Trial ■ Controlling Prompt ■ Most-to-Least Prompting Procedure ■ Prompt Hierarchy ■ Intrusiveness ■ Chained Tasks ■ Probes ■ Antecedent Prompt and Fade Procedure ■ Graduated Guidance ■ Shadowing ■ System of Least Prompts ■ Response Interval ■ Time Delay ■ Progressive Time Delay ■ Constant Time Delay ■ Stimulus-Manipulation Procedures ■ Stimulus Fading ■ Stimulus Shaping ■ Superimposition and Shaping or Fading

Facilitating acquisition of new skills frequently involves providing students with assistance and reinforcing them for making correct responses. When assistance is provided, students are not responding independently to natural stimuli (task directions, materials, etc.). Several strategies for transferring stimulus control from teacher assistance to natural stimuli have been identified (Wolery, Ault, Doyle, & Gast, 1986). These strategies are categorized into two groups: response-prompting procedures and stimulus-modification procedures (Billingsley & Romer, 1983; Etzel & LeBlanc, 1979; Wolery & Gast, 1984). Response-prompting procedures include antecedent prompt and test, most-to-least prompting, antecedent prompt and fade, graduated guidance, system of least prompts, and time delay. Stimulus-modification procedures include stimulus shaping, stimulus fading, and superimposition and shaping or fading. In this chapter, these strategies are described and guidelines for selecting instructional procedures are presented.

RESPONSE-PROMPTING STRATEGIES

Response-prompting strategies involve the presentation of (a) the target stimulus, (b) a prompt, and (c) reinforcement for students' correct responses or error correction/feedback procedures for incorrect responses. The prompt is then faded and the stimulus control of that prompt is transferred to the target stimulus. As a result, when students are presented with the target stimulus, they respond correctly.

Antecedent Prompt and Test Procedure

General Description. The **antecedent prompt and test procedure** involves presenting students with prompted trials and then providing them with practice or test trials where all prompts are removed. A **trial** is an opportunity for students to respond and includes an antecedent event, the student's behavior, and a consequent event. The antecedent prompt and test procedure also has been called the model-test, model-lead-test, and prompt-practice strategy (Wolery et al., 1986). If students perform correctly on test/practice trials, the teacher assumes the stimulus control has been transferred from the prompt to the target stimuli.

Planning Decisions and Prerequisite Skills. To use the antecedent prompt and test procedure, the teacher must identify a reinforcer, a consequent event for errors, and a controlling prompt. **A controlling prompt** provides the students with sufficient information to ensure a correct response. The teacher must also determine when and how test/practice trials will be presented. To benefit from this procedure, students must be able to derive the correct response from the prompt and then perform the behavior when prompts are removed.

Implementing the Procedure. Initially, the teacher presents prompted trials to students. The number of trials and the type of prompts needed depend on the skill being taught and students' abilities. Test/practice trials can be implemented in two ways: they can be presented immediately after the prompted trials or can occur at some other time during the day. During test trials, correct responses are reinforced and error responses are corrected or feedback is provided. For example, Bob is learning a list of sight words using flashcards. The teacher shows him each card and tells him what it is (model). After he has seen and heard each word, he is presented with several test trials on each card. If he is correct, reinforcement follows; if he is incorrect, he is told, "No, this is_____; say,

_____." Teachers should collect data on students' responses to test trials so they can assess the effectiveness of the instruction and identify when students have met criterion.

Findings. This procedure may result in some errors, but if the tasks are of appropriate difficulty, relatively rapid acquisition occurs (Thompson, 1984). The antecedent prompt and test procedure has been used effectively for teaching students with mild handicaps (Sindelar, Bursuck, & Halle, 1986; Stevens & Rosenshine, 1981) and preschoolers from economically disadvantaged backgrounds (Becker & Carnine, 1981). With such students, it is a common teaching strategy and is quite efficient. The antecedent prompt and test procedure also has been used successfully with students whose handicaps are more severe (Crist, Walls, & Haught, 1984); however, the procedure may not provide sufficient assistance to some students with severe handicaps.

Most-to-Least Prompting Procedure

General Description. The **most-to-least prompting procedure** involves providing progressively less intrusive prompt levels as students demonstrate that they can perform correctly at more intrusive levels (Billingsley & Romer, 1983). Synonyms for most-to-least prompting include decreasing assistance and physical prompting and fading. With the most-to-least prompting procedures, a hierarchy of prompts is used. A **prompt hierarchy** is a number of prompts that are listed in order of **intrusiveness,** which refers to the amount of control the teacher exerts over the student's behavior. For example, a full physical manipulation is more intrusive than a verbal prompt. The most-to-least prompting procedure uses the most intrusive prompt first. When students meet criterion with this prompt, the next less intrusive prompt is used until the student meets criterion with that prompt. This process continues until the student responds independently.

Planning Decisions and Prerequisite Skills. To use the most-to-least promoting procedure, a reinforcer and a controlling prompt should be identified. To benefit from this procedure, students must be able to attend to the instructional stimuli.

Several decisions must be made before using the most-to-least procedure. First, a prompt hierarchy must be developed; three samples are shown in Table 14.1. The hierarchy should have at least two prompt levels, and students' abilities (e.g., imitative skills or compliance with verbal instructions) should be considered when selecting the prompts. Likewise, the nature of the task should be considered; if the behavior involves large motor movements, full manipulations may be used; if it involves small, precise movements, partial physical prompts, models, and gestures are preferred.

Second, the teacher must determine the criterion for moving from one

TABLE 14.1   Prompt Hierarchies Listed from Most to Least Intrusive

Level of Intrusiveness	Example 1	Example 2	Example 3
Most	Full manipulation	Full manipulation on Hand	Model
	Partial physical prompt	Full manipulation on Wrist	Partial model
	Model	Full manipulation on Forearm	Gesture prompt
	Gestural prompt	Full manipulation on Elbow	Verbal prompt
	Verbal prompt	Full manipulation on Shoulder	
Least			

prompt level to the next. The criterion should be set at a high level of accuracy. If it is set too low, students will not perform correctly when less intrusive prompt levels are used.

Third, the behavior being taught should be described in considerable detail. The most-to-least procedure is typically used with **chained tasks,** which involve a number of responses put together to form a complex skill. Examples include dressing/undressing, self-feeding, house-cleaning chores, and assembly tasks. Careful description of the behavior will ensure that each step of the chain is taught.

Implementing the Procedure.   The teacher should begin each session by securing the student's attention and initiating a trial. For example, Donald's teacher is using the second prompt hierarchy described in Table 14.1 to teach him to pull up his pants. She begins by asking Donald to put on his pants, and then *places her hands over his,* helps him grasp the pants at the waistband, puts his feet in the pants' legs, and pulls them up past his knees and over his buttocks. After he can do this without resisting the full physical manipulation, she *places her hands over his wrists* and presents additional trials. When the criterion is met at this level, she provides prompts *at his forearm,* and later at his *elbows* and *shoulders.* The teacher fades the prompts by presenting trials at the most intrusive level and then progressing to less intrusive levels. With each subsequent level, Donald's teacher exerts less control over his movements and he becomes more independent. The steps for implementing the most-to-least prompts procedure are shown in Figure 14.1.

When the most-to-least procedure is used, data should be collected on students' responses. If an entire chain of responses is being taught and the student is expected to perform on each step, the response on each step should be recorded. The prompt level being used also should be noted on the data-collection sheet. When using this procedure, the teacher should periodically probe students' performance at less intrusive prompt levels and at the independent level. **Probes** are short tests, one or two trials, where students are asked to perform with less assistance. When probe data indicate that the student can perform correctly at a less intrusive level, that prompt level should be used during instruction. For example, Melinda's teacher is using partial physical prompts to teach her to set the

FIGURE 14.1 Steps for using the most-to-least prompting procedure to transfer stimulus control from a prompt to a target stimulus.

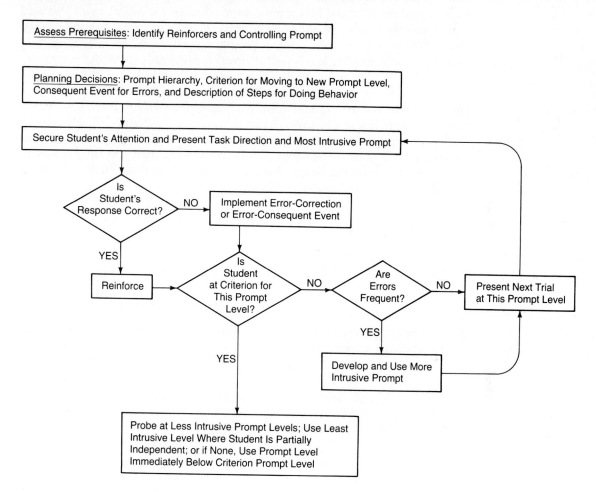

table. When he tested her at less intrusive levels, he found that she could perform many of the steps at the modeling level. As a result, he stopped the instruction at the partial physical prompt level and started at the modeling level. Sample data from a most-to-least prompting procedure are shown in Figure 14.2. An analysis of the data in Figure 14.2 indicates that initially the student could not perform the behavior correctly (baseline). The criterion for fading the prompt was set at 100% correct responding for three sessions. Full physical manipulations were introduced but unprompted responding did not increase. When partial physical prompts were introduced, prompted performance decreased but quickly came to criterion, and a couple of independent responses were noted in the probe data. When models were introduced, prompted performance dropped to near zero levels. The teacher reintroduced partial physical prompts and retained the model. During this condition, the student began to respond more correctly on unprompted probe trials. This trend continued when the model again was used alone, with the number of unprompted correct responses increasing to criterion levels. When using the most-to-least prompting procedure, teachers frequently must add new prompting levels and/or revert to previously successful prompting levels.

Findings. Most-to-least prompting has been used effectively to teach a variety of response chains. It was used to teach motor imitation (Striefel, 1974), self-feeding (Nelson, Cone, & Hanson, 1975), dressing (Ball, Seric, & Payne, 1971), and vocational task assembly (Zane, Walls, & Thvedt, 1981) to students with moderate to severe handicaps. Many, but not all of these studies involved secondary students and adults.

Most-to-least prompting has also been compared to other procedures. Gentry, Day, and Nakao (1980) compared the system of least prompts (increasing assistance) to most-to-least prompts (decreasing assistance) in teaching subjects with severe retardation to make a two-choice visual discrimination. They concluded that the most-to-least prompting procedure was more efficient than the system of least prompts. Glendenning, Adams, and Sternberg (1983) made a similar comparison in teaching 10 subjects with moderate retardation and 2 with severe retardation to perform a chained string-tying response. They concluded that the most-to-least prompting procedure was more effective in producing student-initiated correct responses. Walls, Crist, Sienicki, and Grant (1981)

FIGURE 14.2 Sample data for a most-to-least prompting procedure. The x's indicate the percentage of correct responses when prompted; the o's indicate the percentage of correct responses on unprompted probe trials.

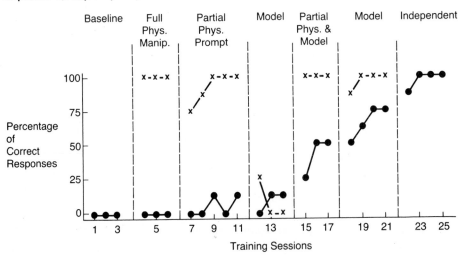

compared the two procedures in teaching 7 subjects with mild retardation and 7 with moderate retardation to perform chained responses (e.g., folding a shirt, setting a table). They found that both procedures were effective, and no statistically significant differences were found on efficiency measures (i.e., errors to criterion and seconds of instruction).

In summary, the most-to-least procedure has some definite advantages over some other prompting procedures. It can be used with students who do not wait for assistance and with those who are not imitative. The procedure is most useful for teaching response chains; however, teachers must probe students' performance to avoid providing unnecessary prompts.

Antecedent Prompt and Fade Procedure

General Description. The **antecedent prompt and fade procedure** involves providing a controlling prompt on initial trials and then fading the prompt in some systematic manner. The intensity or force of prompts can be faded, and the frequency with which prompts are provided can be reduced.

Planning Decisions and Prerequisite Skills. When using this procedure, the teacher must identify a reinforcer, a controlling prompt, and some consequent event for errors. A plan for removing the prompts must also be developed. A criterion for fading prompts usually is not specified; instead, the teacher fades the prompts based on his or her judgment that the student is ready for less assistance. To benefit from this procedure, students must attend to the instructional stimuli and assistance.

Implementing the Procedure. Initially, the teacher presents several trials at the controlling prompt level and reinforces students for being correct. The teacher then begins to fade the prompts. If the intensity of the prompts is being faded, a less intrusive form of the same prompt is presented. For example, a verbal model can be given on a continuum from very loud to very quiet. If a student is learning to name pictures, the task direction can be, "What's this?" and the prompt is the name of the picture in a normal speaking voice. Over subsequent trials, the prompt can be said more quietly. By progressively decreasing the loudness (intensity) of the model, it can be removed. Likewise, when using physical prompts, the intensity of the prompt can be faded. Initially, it could be a full manipulation, then a lighter touch, and then the teacher's hands could be moving near the student's but not touching them.

With the antecedent prompt and fade procedure, prompts also can be removed by decreasing their frequency. For example, if the teacher is using a pointing prompt in a four-choice task, she provides the task direction, and immediately points to the correct object. Initially, this occurs on every trial; on subsequent trials or sessions, progressively fewer trials have the pointing prompt; eventually no pointing is used. A flowchart describing how prompts can be removed by decreasing the frequency and intensity is shown in Figure 14.3. When using this procedure, teachers must monitor student performance to ensure that the number of errors do not increase as prompts are faded.

Findings. The antecedent prompt and fade procedure has been effective in teaching a variety of behaviors (Wolery et al., 1986). For example, Frank and Wacker (1986) used it to teach students with mild retardation to make purchases,

FIGURE 14.3 Steps for using the antecedent prompt and fade procedure to transfer stimulus control from a prompt to a target stimulus.

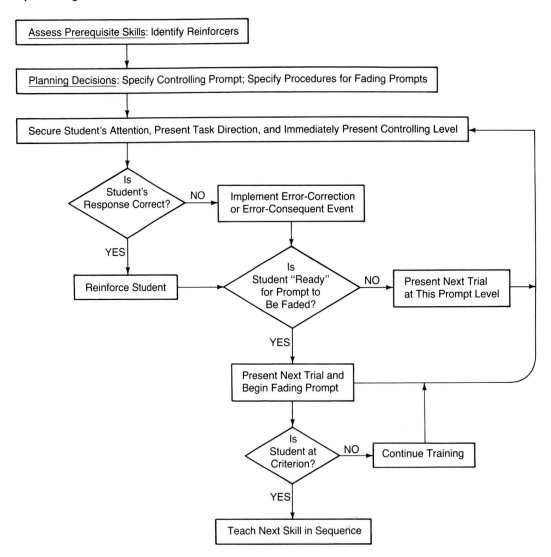

and Remington and Clarke (1983) used the procedure to teach manual signing to students with severe mental retardation. The antecedent prompt and fade procedure relies heavily on teachers' judgment of when to fade prompts; thus its effectiveness is directly related to teachers' skill in making that determination.

Graduated Guidance

General Description. **Graduated guidance** involves removing prompts by immediately withdrawing and providing them as needed by students. Synonyms for graduated guidance are physical prompting and fading and graduated prompting. The intensity and type of prompt needed to ensure correct responding are presented when needed and immediately removed as the student begins to perform correctly. For example, Eddie is learning to print his name. His teacher begins by showing him a model and then provides a full manipulation to get him to pick up his pencil, move it to the paper, and make the downward stroke of the E. As Eddie starts the downward stroke, his teacher immediately fades the full manipulation. She provides a partial physical prompt as he finishes the downward stroke to get him to move the pencil to the top of the stroke and form the first horizontal line on the E. If the partial physical prompt is not sufficient, she uses a full manipulation. As he begins to write independently, she shadows his movements with her hands. **Shadowing** means that the teacher keeps her hands near his, but does not touch him. This position allows her to implement a prompt immediately if it is needed.

Planning Decisions and Prerequisites. Graduated guidance requires identification of a reinforcer and a controlling prompt. It also requires careful description of the behavior(s) to be taught. However, it does not require a prompt hierarchy or planned consequences for errors. Students are not allowed to make errors because a controlling prompt is immediately presented if students stop or begin to respond incorrectly. Students are not required to be imitative nor do they need to wait for a prompt.

Implementing the Procedure. Graduated guidance is almost always used with chained tasks such as grooming and dressing; in most cases, all steps of the chain are taught on all trials. When instruction is provided in this manner, data collection becomes problematic. Data may be recorded on whether a given trial was prompted or unprompted. Although studies that have used graduated guidance employed physical prompts, it is possible to use other types of prompts such as verbal prompts. For example, Patsy's teacher is using graduated guidance with verbal prompts to teach her to use a calculator to add a series of numbers. The teacher begins by saying, "Patsy, add the numbers on your paper using your calculator" (task direction). The verbal prompts include, "Push the 3; push the 7; push the plus. Now push the 5, the 1, the 6, and the plus. Now push the 6, the 8, and the equals sign." In later trials, less prompts are required but, if Patsy pauses or starts

TABLE 14.2   Guidelines for using Graduated Guidance

1. Begin each trial with the type and amount of assistance (prompts) required to ensure that the student performs the behavior.
2. As the student begins to perform the behavior (within the trial), immediately fade the assistance; this can be done by (a) fading the amount of pressure (intensity) of the prompt, (b) fading the position of the prompt (e.g., from hand to wrist), or (c) stopping the prompt completely.
3. Shadow the student's movements by moving your hand near, but not touching, the student's hands.
4. If the student stops performing the behavior, immediately apply the type and amount of prompt required to ensure that the student begins doing the behavior and then fade the assistance as the student begins the response (i.e., step 2 above).
5. If the student starts to move in the wrong direction, immediately apply the amount and type of prompt required to move the student in the correct direction; fade the assistance as the student begins moving in the correct direction.
6. If a minimal amount of the final part of the task is done independently, immediately reinforce the student.
7. If the student resists assistance at the completion of the task, do not provide reinforcers.

to push the wrong number, the teacher immediately presents a prompt. Reinforcement is frequently provided as each step of a chain is done and upon completion of the sequence. Guidelines for using graduated guidance are found in Table 14.2.

Findings. Graduated guidance has been used effectively with chained tasks for students who have moderate to severe retardation, such as independent toileting (Foxx & Azrin, 1973), self-feeding (Azrin & Armstrong, 1973), and dressing (Azrin, Schaeffer, & Wesolowski, 1976). However, it also can be used for many other tasks such as academic skills, instruction-following, and play skills. Comparison studies of graduated guidance and other response-prompting procedures have not been published.

In summary, graduated guidance can be used to teach chained tasks in a nearly errorless fashion. It is used with students who are not imitative and do not wait for teacher assistance. When physical prompts are used, graduated guidance can only be used with one student at a time. Teachers must make a large number of rapid decisions as they use graduated guidance. Failure to make correct decisions may result in slower acquisition and potentially may teach students to depend on prompts. Success with the procedure depends on teachers' provision of prompts only when required.

System of Least Prompts

General Description. The **system of least prompts** involves providing students with opportunities to respond at the level of prompt they need to do the behavior correctly on each trial. Synonyms for the system of least prompts include least-to-most prompting procedure or increasing assistance (Billingsley &

Romer,1983; Snell, 1987), less-to-more direct assistance (Cuvo, Leaf, & Bora-kove, 1978), and instructional interaction model (Alberto & Schofield, 1979). As with the most-to-least prompting procedure, the system of least prompts uses a hierarchy of prompt levels. However, the prompts are presented in a sequence ranging from the least intrusive to the most intrusive, and all prompt levels could potentially be given on any single trial. For example, when Judy is learning to use a washing machine, her teacher presents a task direction, "Put the clothes in the washer" and waits a designated interval (e.g., 5 seconds) for her to begin the behavior. If she does not do the behavior, she is presented with the least intrusive prompt such as pointing to the clothing and then the washer. If she does not respond appropriately within 5 seconds, the teacher provides the next more intrusive prompt level such as a partial physical prompt. If Judy responds correctly at any prompt level, she is reinforced. If errors occur, the next intrusive prompt is provided.

Planning Decisions and Prerequisites. Before using the system of least prompts, a reinforcer, controlling prompt, and prompt hierarchy must be identified. The prompt hierarchy must include at least two prompt levels, but three to four are most common. A **response interval,** which is the amount of time the student has to begin the behavior, must also be identified. In most cases, 3 or 5 seconds is used. When setting the response interval, teachers should consider how long students usually take to begin responding. The teacher must also determine what will happen when errors occur. In most cases, teachers choose to interrupt the error and provide the next prompt but, in other cases, teachers choose to provide the controlling prompt or to terminate the trial and implement some error consequence such as a verbal reprimand.

The student must also be able to wait a few seconds for a prompt, and should use the rule, "If I don't know the correct response, I should wait for the prompt." Students should display basic attending skills (e.g., sitting, looking when asked, etc.). Students need not respond to all prompt levels, since the controlling prompt is the last prompt in the hierarchy.

Implementing the Procedure. Each trial of all sessions begins with an opportunity for the student to respond independently to the task direction alone. If a correct response occurs, the student is reinforced and that response is counted toward the criterion. If an error occurs or the student does not respond, the teacher provides the least intrusive prompt. If the response is correct after the prompt, the student is reinforced but this response does not count toward criterion. If the student responds incorrectly or does not respond, the next least intrusive prompt is provided. This process continues until the student responds correctly. As a result, students can select the level of prompt needed to ensure an accurate response. If they respond early in the sequence, the reinforcer is received more quickly. The steps for implementing the system of least prompts are shown in Figure 14.4.

Students may make four responses: *unprompted correct responses,* which occur after the task direction alone; *prompted correct responses,* which occur after a prompt;

FIGURE 14.4   Steps for using the system of least prompts to transfer stimulus control from a prompt hierarchy to a target stimulus.

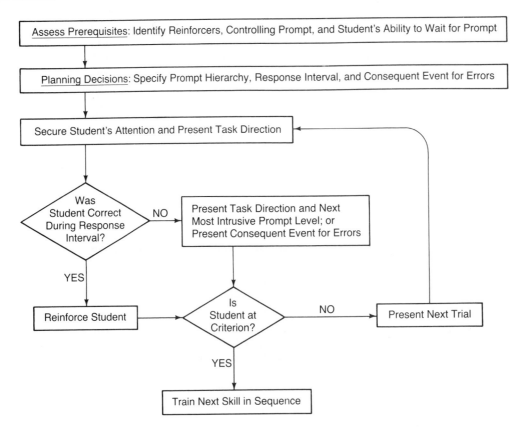

unprompted errors, which occur after the task direction before prompts; prompted errors, which occur after a prompt has been provided. When collecting data with the system of least prompts, it is important to record the level of prompt and the student's response. A sample data-collection form for the system of least prompts is shown in Figure 14.5. When using the procedure, the task direction is presented at each prompt level, more assistance is provided at each subsequent level of the prompt hierarchy, a constant delay interval follows each prompt level, and correct responses are reinforced whether they are prompted or unprompted. Data collected using the system of least prompts are shown in Figure 14.6.

Findings. The system of least prompts has been used with a variety of students and behaviors (Wolery et al., 1986). It was used effectively to teach a number of response chains, including toothbrushing (Horner & Keilitz, 1975), janitorial skills (Cuvo et al., 1978), laundry skills (Cuvo, Jacobi, & Sipko, 1981), putting on hearing aides (Tucker & Berry, 1980), mending skills (Cronin & Cuvo, 1979), and

FIGURE 14.5   Data-collection forms for the system of least prompts. For the top form, a "+" mark would be placed in the column where a correct response occurred, a "-" would be placed in columns where errors occurred, and a "o" would be placed in columns where no responses occurred, i.e., those prompt levels where the student waited for assistance. For the lower form, a slash (/) would be placed on each prompt level that was provided and the last level needed by the student would be circled.

Student Name _____ Date ___/___/____ Teacher _____
Objective _____
Setting/Materials _____

| | Task Direction Alone | Prompt Levels | | |
Trial/Stimulus		Verbal	Model	Partial Phys.
Totals				
Comments				

Key: + = Correct – + Error; and o = No response

Student Name _____ Date ___/___/____ Teacher _____
Objective _____
Setting/Materials _____

Trials

1	2	3	4	5	6	7	8	9	10	TOTAL
FM	FM	FM	FM	FM	FM	FM	FM	FM	FM	
PP	PP	PP	PP	PP	PP	PP	PP	PP	PP	
M	M	M	M	M	M	M	M	M	M	
V	V	V	V	V	V	V	V	V	V	
I	I	I	I	I	I	I	I	I	I	

Key: I = Independent; V = Verbal prompt; M = Model; PP = Partial physical; FM = Full manipulation

leisure skills (Neitupski & Svoboda, 1982). It has also been used with discrete tasks such as receptive language skills (Hupp, Mervis, Able, & Conroy-Gunter, 1986) and expressive language skills (Duker & Moonan, 1985). As noted above, comparisons between the system of least prompts and most-to-least prompts produced mixed results suggesting that, for some subjects and tasks, most-to-least prompts may be more effective.

FIGURE 14.6   Graphs of data patterns collected using the system of least prompts. The top graph indicates transfer of stimulus control. The middle graph indicates that a transfer is not occurring. The bottom graph shows data plotted by level of prompt, stimulus control occurring from one prompt level to another, and from prompt levels to independent responding.

Pattern Indicating Learning Is Occurring

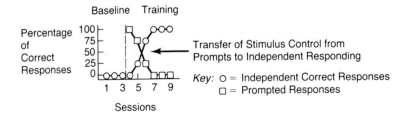

Pattern Indicating Independent Responses Are Not Occurring

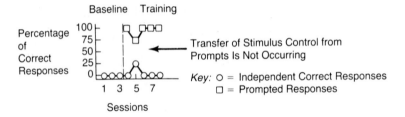

System of Least Prompts Data Graphed by Prompt Level

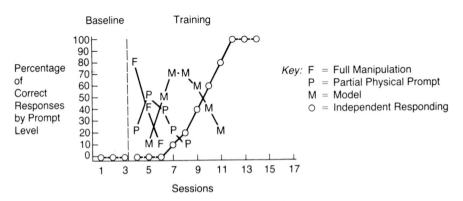

In summary, the system of least prompts is an effective procedure for transferring stimulus control and has the unique advantage of allowing students to select the amount of assistance they need to perform correctly. However, when students use prompts that are late in the hierarchy, a trial may be long and lead to inefficient instruction. The procedure does not require that students be imitative, but they must wait for a prompt if they cannot perform correctly.

Time Delay

General Description. **Time delay** involves fading prompts in time; the amount of time between the presentation of the task direction and the prompt is increased (Snell & Gast, 1981). Time delay has several synonyms including temporal transfer of stimulus control, delayed cueing, prompt delay, anticipation procedure, and stimulus delay. Two types of time delay exist: **Progressive** and **constant time delay.** With both types, the initial instructional session (or trials) involves presenting the prompt at the 0-second delay; that is, the task direction is given and the controlling prompt is immediately presented. For example, Connie is learning to name pictures. The teacher shows a picture and says, "What's this?" and immediately names the picture. On subsequent trials with progressive time delay, the delay interval between the task direction and prompt is gradually increased by specific increments. For example, with each additional session, the delay interval is increased by 1 second. During the second session, the prompt is delayed for 1 second; during the third session it is delayed for 2 seconds; during the fourth for 3 seconds; and so on. With the constant time delay procedure the 0-second trials are presented and then the prompt is delayed for a specific number of seconds that does not change. Thus, beginning with the second session and continuing in subsequent sessions, the delay interval might be 4 seconds.

Planning Decisions and Prerequisites. To use time delay, the teacher must identify a reinforcer, controlling prompt, and an error-consequent event. The number of trials at the 0-second delay interval must be identified. Usually 5 to 10 trials at 0-second delay are provided. The teacher also must determine whether progressive or constant time delay will be used. If constant time delay is used, the number of seconds the prompt will be delayed must be identified. Three or four seconds are frequently sufficient, but students' usual response latencies should be considered (Johnson, 1977). If progressive delay is used, the teacher must determine (a) how many trials will be provided at each delay interval and (b) what size the delay interval will be. Many teachers use each delay interval for one session (e.g., 10 trials), but some provide as few as 1 to 3 trials at each delay interval. Students with more severe handicaps require more trials at each delay interval. Numerous sequences for delaying the prompt have been used including: 0.5 seconds, 0.5 seconds followed by 1-second increments, and 2-second increments. Perhaps the easiest sequence for teachers is to add 1 second to the delay interval for each training session. Walls, Haught, and Dowler (1982) compared different increments (1, 3, and 5 seconds) and found 1-second delay intervals were more effective and efficient than either of the others.

To use the procedure successfully, students must be able to wait for the prompt. They should use the rule, "If I don't know the correct response, I should wait for the prompt." Some students will need to be trained to wait. Students should also display attending skills (e.g., sitting, looking when asked).

Implementing the Procedure.   Initially, the teacher presents a session or block of trials at the 0-second delay. If students respond correctly after the prompt they are reinforced. If they consistently respond incorrectly after the prompt, a more controlling prompt is used. If students do not respond after the prompt, a more powerful reinforcer is selected. After the 0-second trials, the teacher delays the presentation of the prompt. The teacher presents the task direction, waits the designated interval, and then presents the prompt. If the student responds correctly before the prompt, reinforcement is provided and that response counts toward criterion. If the student responds correctly after the prompt, reinforcement is provided but that response does not count toward criterion. If the student responds incorrectly before the prompt, the error consequence is implemented. Such performance may indicate that the student needs to be taught to wait. If the student responds incorrectly after the prompt, the controlling nature of the prompt should be assessed. If no response occurs after the prompt, the reinforcer should be changed. The steps for implementing progressive and constant time delay are shown in Figure 14.7.

On trials after the 0-second trials, students can make five different responses: correct responses before the prompt (anticipations), correct responses after the prompt (correct waits), error responses before the prompt (non-wait errors), error responses after the prompt (wait errors), and no responses. A sample data-collection forms are shown in Figure 14.8. Since five different responses are possible, each response should be recorded as it occurs. Decisions teachers should consider when progress is not being made are shown in Table 14.3. Three data patterns that may occur are shown in Figure 14.9.

Findings.   Time delay has been used effectively with a variety of students and behaviors. Primarily, it has been used with elementary and secondary students who have moderate and severe handicaps (Wolery et al., 1986). Progressive time delay has been successful in teaching communication skills, including instruction-following (Striefel, Bryan, & Aikins, 1974; Striefel, Wetherby, & Karlan, 1976), manual sign production (Kohl, Wilcox, & Karlan, 1978; Smeets & Striefel, 1976a), manual sign imitation and production (Stremel-Campbell, Cantrell, & Halle, 1977), manual sign reading (Smeets & Striefel, 1976b), and requesting (Charlop, Schriebman, & Thibodeau, 1985). In addition, it has been used in teaching sight-word reading (Browder, Hines, McCarthy, & Fees, 1984; McGee & McCoy, 1981), bed-making (Snell, 1982), task assembly (Walls, Haught, & Dowler, 1982), and visual discriminations (Touchette & Howard, 1984). Constant time delay also has been used effectively to teach communication skills, including

FIGURE 14.7 Steps for using progressive and constant time delay to transfer stimulus control from a prompt to a natural stimulus.

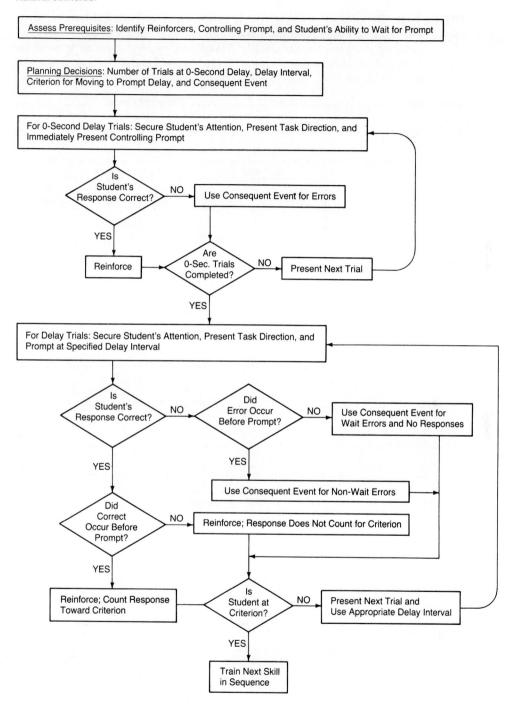

FIGURE 14.8 Data collection forms for progressive and constant time delay. On the top form, a check is placed in the column appropriate for the student's response. In the lower form, a "+" is used to indicate correct responses, a "-" is used to indicate errors, and an "o" is used to indicate no responses. These marks are placed in the "Before" column if they occurred prior to the prompt and in the "After" column if they occurred after the prompt.

Student Name _____ Date ___/___/___ Delay Interval _____
Objective _____
Setting/Materials _____ Teacher _____

Trial/Stimulus	Corrects		Errors		
	Antici-pations	Waits	Non-Waits	Waits	No Response
Totals					
Comments					

Student Name _____ Date ___/___/___ To ___/___/___
Delay Interval _____ Teacher _____
Objective _____
Setting/Materials _____

Trial/Stimulus	Date: _____		Date: _____		Date: _____	
	Before	After	Before	After	Before	After
Totals						
Comments						

FIGURE 14.9   Data patterns from time delay. Correct anticipations are denoted by triangles (△) and correct waits by circles (O). The top graph shows transfer of stimulus control as desired. The middle graph shows no transfer of stimulus control; correct waits at high percentages; therefore, differential reinforcement of correct waits and correct anticipations should be attempted. The bottom graph shows patterns where nonwait errors, wait errors, and no-responses are occurring. The data sheets should be analyzed to determine which type of error is most frequent and remediation procedures should be implemented.

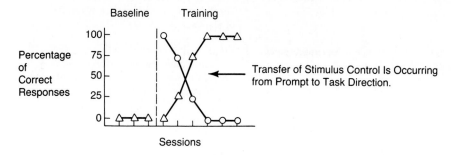

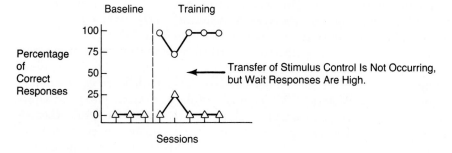

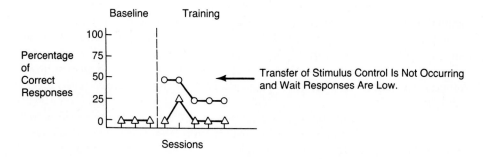

TABLE 14.3 Decisions Related to Lack of Progress with the Time Delay Procedure

Problem: Description/Pattern	Potential Solutions
Non-wait Errors: Student makes errors before the prompt; errors occur on more than 25% of the trials and persist over 2-3 sessions.	1. Use shorter delay interval. 2. Increase the number of trials at each prompt level. 3. Teach student to wait for the prompt.
Wait Errors: Student makes errors after the prompt; errors occur on more than 25% of the trials and persist over 2-3 sessions.	1. Use more controlling prompt. 2. Use more powerful reinforcers. 3. Shorten sessions if errors are at the end of session.
No-Response Errors: Student does not respond on 25% of the trials over 2-3 sessions.	1. Ensure task is appropriate. 2. Use more powerful reinforcers. 3. Shorten sessions if no-responses are at end of session.
Anticipations Do Not Appear: Student waits for prompt and responds correctly, but not before the prompt.	1. Differentially reinforce waits and anticipations. 2. Use distributed trial format.

manual sign production (Kleinert & Gast, 1982; Oliver & Halle, 1982) and manual sign imitation and production (Browder, Morris, & Snell, 1981). In addition, it has been used to teach spelling (Stevens & Schuster, 1987), sight-word reading (Precious, 1983), and visual discrimination tasks (Johnson, 1977).

Three investigations compared the effectiveness and efficiency of progressive and constant time delay. In these studies, both procedures were effective in teaching sight words to elementary-aged students with learning disabilities (Precious, Gast, & Wolery, 1985; Thomas, Wolery, & Gast, 1985) and safety words to elementary-aged students with moderate retardation (Ault, Gast, & Wolery, in press). The two procedures produced similar results in terms of efficiency when measured by the percentage of errors, number of minutes of instruction, and number of trials to criterion. Time delay also has been compared to the system of least prompts. Renzaglia and Snell (1981) concluded that essentially no differences existed between the two procedures in teaching manual sign production to students with severe handicaps. Additional comparisons with manual sign production and receptive labeling of functional objects indicated that both procedures were effective (Bennett, Gast, Wolery, & Schuster, 1986; Godby, Gast, & Wolery, in 1987); however, progressive time delay was more efficient in terms of the number of sessions, trials, errors, and instructional minutes to criterion. This was particularly true for students with severe handicaps.

In summary, time delay was effective in teaching a variety of skills to a variety of students. It has been used primarily with language and academic tasks that involve discrete responses, although it can be used with chained responses

(Snell, 1982). When used properly, errors generally occur on less than 3 to 5% of the trials. Both progressive and constant delay appear to be equally effective and efficient. Teachers report that they like to use time delay, because it promotes positive interactions with students and is easy to use. Students also report satisfaction with the procedure.

STIMULUS-MANIPULATION PROCEDURES

Response prompt-fading procedures transfer stimulus control by pairing the target stimulus with a prompt, reinforcing students for correct performance, and then fading the prompts. The prompt originates from outside the target stimulus. With **stimulus-manipulation procedures,** the stimuli to which students respond are gradually and systematically changed to transfer stimulus control. A stimulus display to which the student can initially respond is presented and students' correct responses are reinforced. Over subsequent training trials, the stimulus is changed until it resembles the target stimulus. Three types of stimulus-manipulation strategies exist: stimulus fading, stimulus shaping, and superimposition and shaping or fading (Etzel & LeBlanc, 1979).

Description of Stimulus-Manipulation Strategies

Stimulus fading "involves the gradual shifting of control from some dominant stimulus element to a different and criterion stimulus [target stimulus]. Fading uses an element of a stimulus that gradually changes along some physical dimension (e.g., intensity, size, color) to a point where the terminal discrimination is based on another dimension" (Etzel & LeBlanc, 1979, p. 369). Almost any dimension of the stimulus can be changed such as the color, shape, size, position, or surface of the stimulus (Goetz, 1982). With stimulus fading, the dimension that is changed is not a relevant or critical one needed to make the discrimination. For example, when discriminating letters, the dimension of shape is relevant. In a stimulus-fading program, the color of letters may be systematically changed. To learn the correct discrimination, students must shift from the irrelevant dimension (the one being manipulated) to the relevant one.

Stimulus shaping "involves changing the topography (configuration) of the stimulus. That is, the initial stimulus does not resemble the final or criterion level stimulus [target stimulus] on any dimension because its topography is to be gradually altered to form the criterion stimulus (Etzel & LeBlanc, 1979, p. 370). Thus, the relevant dimension on which the final discrimination must be made is manipulated. In the case of letters, the shape of the letters would be manipulated. Stimulus shaping does not require students to shift from one dimension to another.

Superimposition and shaping or fading involves placing a stimulus the student already discriminates over the target stimulus. With superimposition and shaping, the target stimulus remains present, but a stimulus the student already discriminates is superimposed upon it. The stimulus the student already discriminates is constructed to highlight the relevant dimension of the target stimulus. Little applied research has been done with superimposition and shaping or with superimposition and fading.

Evaluation of Stimulus-Manipulation Strategies

Stimulus-manipulation strategies should be used after the response prompt-fading procedures have been ineffective. When these strategies are used, stimulus shaping should be employed rather than stimulus fading. Shaping does not require the shift from an irrelevant dimension to the relevant dimension of the task. Stimulus fading and shaping can be used successfully in combination (cf., Schreibman, 1975). The primary disadvantage of stimulus-manipulation procedures is the extensive material-preparation time required (LeBlanc, Etzel, & Domash, 1978). Further, some stimuli cannot be manipulated easily or economically. As a result, systematic use of stimulus-manipulation strategies in classrooms is infrequent.

SELECTION OF INSTRUCTIONAL STRATEGIES

Since a number of response-prompting strategies and stimulus-modification procedures exist, teachers must select which one to use. Several factors should be considered such as the type of task being taught (chained or discrete trial), students' abilities (e.g., imitative abilities, ability to use verbal prompts), the teaching resources (e.g., number of students and adults in the instructional setting), and the results of previous research. Although more research is needed, some recommendations can be made. First, *students should not be exposed to strategies that may cause harm* (Zigler & Sietz, 1975). Generally, these strategies are harmless but, when physical prompts are used inappropriately, injury may result.

Second, *effective strategies should be used.* Some of the strategies have been more effective and/or efficient with certain types of skills and students than other strategies. For example, if the response is a discrete behavior (e.g., pointing to the correct object, naming items, circling the correct item, etc.) and the students will wait for a prompt and are imitative, time delay or the antecedent prompt and test strategies should be used over the other procedures. Direct comparisons of time delay to the system of least prompts indicate that both are effective but time delay is more efficient. If the behavior is a chained task and students are imitative and will wait for a prompt, the system of least prompts should be used. Although time delay has been used for chained tasks, it is complicated and the system of least prompts has a long history of effective and efficient use with such tasks. The system of least prompts provides students with more independence from the beginning of instruction than the most-to-least prompting strategy and is more systematic than the antecedent prompt and fade strategy. If the behavior is a chained task and students are not imitative or do not wait for prompts, graduated guidance or the most-to-least prompts procedure should be used. If graduated guidance is used, the teacher should be careful to ensure that students do not learn to depend on prompts. If the most-to-least prompting procedure is used, the teacher should frequently probe students' behavior at less intrusive levels of prompts.

Third, *the intrusiveness and restrictiveness of the procedures should be considered.* Although intrusiveness is difficult to judge, the system of least prompts, time delay, antecedent prompt and test appear to be minimally intrusive. Graduated guidance, antecedent prompt and fade, and the most-to-least prompting appear more intrusive. However, the type of the prompts used within each strategy will determine its intrusiveness. For example, physical prompts are more intrusive than models and verbal prompts.

Fourth, *students' response patterns should be considered.* If students respond impulsively, most-to-least prompting or antecedent prompt and test may be preferred strategies. If students wait for teachers' assistance, time delay or the system of least prompts should be used. If physical contact with the teacher appears to be a reinforcer or appears to be aversive, strategies that do not use physical prompts should be selected.

Fifth, *the principle of parsimony should be considered* (Etzel & LeBlanc, 1979). The principle of parsimony states that if two or more solutions can be used with a problem, the simplest solution should be used. Thus, if two or more of these strategies can be used to teach a student, the one that is easiest to use should be selected. For example, most-to-least prompting requires fewer decisions than the system of least prompts or graduated guidance, and constant time delay is easier than progressive time delay. The response-prompting procedures are easier to use, more economical, and require fewer materials than the stimulus-manipulation strategies.

Sixth, *the social validity of the procedures should be considered* (Wolf, 1978). Social validity of procedures refers to the acceptability of the strategies to consumers and experts. If parents object to the use of one of the strategies, another strategy should be selected and used.

Summary of Key Concepts

- Teacher assistance must be removed so students can respond correctly to only the target stimulus.

- Response-prompting and stimulus-manipulation strategies can be used to transfer stimulus control from teacher assistance to target stimuli.

- The response-prompting procedures include the antecedent prompt and test strategy, most-to-least prompting, antecedent prompt and fade procedure, graduated guidance, system of least prompts, and time delay.

■ Stimulus-manipulation strategies include stimulus shaping, stimulus fading, and superimposition and shaping or fading.

■ Selection of instructional strategies should be made on the basis of several considerations, including (a) the harm procedures could cause, (b) the effectiveness and efficiency of procedures, (c) the intrusiveness of procedures, (d) students' response patterns, (e) the principle of parsimony, and (f) the social validity of the strategies.

REFERENCES

Alberto, P., & Schofield, P. (1979). An instructional interaction pattern for the severely handicapped. *Teaching Exceptional Children, 12,* 16–19.

Ault, M., Gast, D. L., & Wolery, M. (in press). Teaching students with moderate handicaps to read safety words. *American Journal of Mental Deficiency.*

Azrin, N. H., & Armstrong, P. M. (1973). The "minimeal"—a method for teaching eating skills to the profoundly retarded. *Mental Retardation, 11,* 9–13.

Azrin, N. H., Schaeffer, R. M., & Wesolowski, M. D. (1976). A rapid method of teaching profoundly retarded persons to dress. *Mental Retardation, 14*(6), 29–33.

Ball, T. S., Seric, K., & Payne, L. E. (1971). Long-term retention of self-help skill training in the profoundly retarded. *American Journal of Mental Deficiency, 76,* 378–383.

Becker, W. C., & Carnine, D. W. (1981). Direct instruction: A behavior theory model for comprehensive educational intervention with the disadvantaged. In S. W. Bijou & R. Ruiz (Eds.), *Behavior modification: Contributions to education* (pp. 145–210). Hillsdale, NJ: Lawrence Erlbaum.

Bennett, D., Gast, D. L., Wolery, M., & Schuster, J. (1986). A comparison of two prompting procedures: Time delay and system of least prompts in teaching expressive sign labels. *Education and Training of the Mentally Retarded, 21,* 117–129.

Billingsley, F. F., & Romer, L. T. (1983). Response prompting and the transfer of stimulus control: Methods, research, and a conceptual framework. *Journal of the Association for the Severely Handicapped, 8*(2), 3–12.

Browder, D. M., Hines, C., McCarthy, L. J. & Fees, J. (1984). A treatment package for increasing sight word recognition for use in daily living skills. *Education and Training of the Mentally Retarded, 19,* 191–200.

Browder, D. M., Morris, W., & Snell, M. E. (1981). Using time delay to teach manual signs to a severely retarded student. *Education and Training of the Mentally Retarded, 16,* 252–258.

Charlop, M. H., Schreibman, L., & Thibodeau, M. G. (1985). Increasing spontaneous verbal responding in autistic children using a time delay procedure. *Journal of Applied Behavior Analysis, 18,* 155–166.

Crist, K., Walls, R. T., & Haught, P. A. (1984). Degrees of specificity in task analysis. *American Journal of Mental Deficiency, 89,* 67–74.

Cronin, K. A., & Cuvo, A. J. (1979). Teaching mending skills to retarded adolescents. *Journal of Applied Behavior Analysis, 12,* 401–406.

Cuvo, A. J., Jacobi, E., & Sipko, R. (1981). Teaching laundry skills to mentally retarded students. *Education and Training of the Mentally Retarded, 16,* 54–64.

Cuvo, A. J., Leaf, R. B., & Borakove, L. S. (1978). Teaching janitorial skills to the mentally retarded: Acquisition, generalization, and maintenance. *Journal of Applied Behavior Analysis, 11,* 345–355.

Duker, P. C., & Moonan, X. M. (1985). A program to increase manual signs, with severely/profoundly mentally retarded students in natural environments. *Applied Research in Mental Retardation, 6,* 147–158

Etzel, B. C., & LeBlanc, J. M. (1979). The simplest treatment alternative: Appropriate instructional control and errorless learning procedures for the difficult-to-teach child. *Journal of Autism and Developmental Disorders, 9,* 361–382.

Foxx, R. M., & Azrin, N. H. (1973). *Toilet training the retarded: A rapid program for day and nighttime independent toileting.* Champaign, IL: Research Press.

Frank, A. R., & Wacker, D. P. (1986). Analysis of a visual prompting procedure on acquisition and generalization of coin skills by mentally retarded children. *American Journal of Mental Deficiency, 90,* 468–472.

Gentry, D., Day, M., & Nakao, C. (1980). *The effectiveness of two prompting sequence procedures for discrimination learning with severely handicapped individuals.* Unpublished manuscript, University of Idaho.

Glendenning, N. J., Adams, G. L., & Sternberg, L. (1983). Comparison of prompt sequences. *American Journal of Mental Deficiency, 88,* 321–325.

Godby, S., Gast, O. L., & Wolery, M. (1987). A comparison of two prompting procedures: Time delay and system of least prompts in teaching object identification. *Developmental Disabilities Research, 8,* 283–306.

Goetz, E. M. (1982). Behavior principles and techniques. In K. E. Allen, & E. M. Goetz, (Eds.), *Early childhood education: Special problems, special solutions* (pp. 31–76). Rockville, MD: Aspen.

Horner, D. R., & Keilitz, I. (1975). Training mentally retarded adolescents to brush their teeth. *Journal of Applied Behavior Analysis, 8,* 301–309.

Hupp, S. C., Mervis, C. B., Able, H., & Conroy-Gunter, M. (1986). Effects of receptive and expressive training of category labels on generalized learning by severely mentally retarded children. *American Journal of Mental Deficiency, 90,* 558–565.

Johnson, C. (1977). Errorless learning in a multihandicapped adolescent. *Education and Treatment of Children, 1,* 235–239.

Kleinert, H. L., & Gast, D. L. (1982). Teaching a multihandicapped adult manual signs using a constant time delay procedure. *Journal of the Association for the Severely Handicapped, 7*(4), 25–32.

Kohl, F. L., Wilcox, B. L., & Karlan, G. R. (1978). Effects of training conditions on generalization of manual signs with moderately handicapped students. *Education and Training of the Mentally Retarded, 13,* 377–385.

LeBlanc, J. M., Etzel, B. C., & Domash, M. A. (1978). A functional curriculum for early intervention. In K. E. Allen, V. A. Holm, & R. L. Schiefelbusch (Eds.), *Early intervention—a team approach* (pp. 331–381). Austin, TX: PRO-ED.

McGee, G. G., & McCoy, J. F. (1981). Training procedures for acquisition and retention of reading in retarded youth. *Applied Research in Mental Retardation, 2,* 263–276.

Neitupski, J., & Svoboda, R. (1982). Teaching a cooperative leisure skill to severely handicapped adults. *Education and Training of the Mentally Retarded, 17,* 38–43.

Nelson, G. L., Cone, J. D., & Hanson., C. R. (1975). Training correct utensil use in retarded children: Modeling vs. physical guidance. *American Journal of Mental Deficiency, 80,* 389–399.

Oliver, C., & Halle, J. (1982). Language training in the everyday environment: Teaching functional sign use to a retarded child. *Journal of the Association for the Severely Handicapped, 8,* 50–62.

Precious, C. (1983). *Teaching sight word reading to a learning disabled student using constant time delay.* Unpublished manuscript, Department of Special Education, University of Kentucky, Lexington.

Precious, C., Gast, D. L., & Wolery, M. (1985). *Comparison of two procedures for teaching sight words.* Unpublished manuscript, Department of Special Education, University of Kentucky, Lexington.

Remington, B., & Clarke, S. (.1983). Acquisition of expressive signing by autistic children: An evaluation of the relative effects of simultaneous communication and sign-alone training. *Journal of Behavior Analysis, 16,* 315–328.

Renzaglia, A., & Snell, M. E. (1981). *Manual sign training for the severely handicapped: Time delay and system of least prompts.* Unpublished manuscript, Department of Special Education, University of Virginia, Charlottesville.

Schreibman, L. (1975). Effects of within-stimulus and extra-stimulus prompting on discrimination learning in autistic children. *Journal of Applied Behavior Analysis, 8,* 91–112.

Sindelar, P. T., Bursuck, W. D., & Halle, J. W. (1986). The effects of two variations of teacher questioning on student performance. *Education and Treatment of Children, 9,* 56–66.

Smeets, P. M., & Striefel, S. (1976a). Acquisition and cross modal generalization of receptive and expressive signing skills in a retarded deaf girl. *Journal of Mental Deficiency Research, 20,* 251–259.

Smeets, P. M., & Striefel, S. (1976b). Acquisition of sign reading by transfer of stimulus control in a retarded deaf girl. *Journal of Mental Deficiency Research, 20,* 197–205.

Snell, M. E. (1982). Analysis of time delay procedures in teaching daily living skills to retarded adults. *Analysis and intervention in Developmental Disabilities, 2,* 139–155.

Snell, M. E., (1987). *Systematic instruction of persons with severe handicaps* (3rd ed). Columbus, OH: Charles E. Merrill.

Snell, M. E., & Gast, D. L. (1981). Applying the time delay procedure to the instruction of the severely handicapped. *Journal of the Association for the Severely Handicapped, 6*(3), 3–14.

Stevens, K., & Schuster, J. (1987). Teaching spelling words using constant time delay. *Learning Disabilities Quarterly, 10,* 9-16.

Stevens, R., & Rosenshine. B. (1981). Advances in research on teaching. *Exceptional Education Quarterly, 2,* 1–9.

Stremel-Campbell, K., Cantrell, D., & Halle, J. W. (1977). Manual signing as a language system and as a speech initiator for the nonverbal severely handicapped student. In E. Sontag (Ed.). *Educational programming for the severely and profoundly handicapped* (pp. 335–347). Reston, VA: The Council for Exceptional Children.

Striefel, S. (1974). *Managing behavior: Part 7, behavior modification: Teaching a child to imitate.* Lawrence, KS: H & H Enterprises.

Striefel, S., Bryan, K., & Aikins, D. (1974). Transfer of stimulus control from motor to verbal stimuli. *Journal of Applied Behavior Analysis, 6,* 123–135.

Striefel, S., Wetherby, B., & Karlan, G, (1976). Establishing generalized verb-noun instruction following skills in retarded children. *Journal of Experimental Child Psychology, 22,* 247–260.

Thomas, T., Wolery, M., & Gast, D. L. (1985). *Comparison of constant and progressive delay in teaching sight word reading.* Unpublished manuscript, Department of Special Education, University of Kentucky, Lexington.

Thompson, A. (1984). *Comparison of the Language Master and the model-lead-test procedure for teaching sight words.* Unpublished masters thesis, University of Kentucky, Lexington.

Touchette, P. E., & Howard, J. S. (1984). Errorless learning: Reinforcement contingencies and stimulus control transfer in delayed prompting. *Journal of Applied Behavior Analysis, 17,* 175–188.

Tucker, D. J., & Berry, G. W. (1980). Teaching severely multihandicapped students to put on their own hearing aides. *Journal of Applied Behavior Analysis, 13,* 65–75.

Walls, R. T., Crist, K., Sienicki, D. A., & Grant, L. (1981). Prompting sequences in teaching independent living skills. *Mental Retardation, 19,* 243–246.

Walls, R. T., Haught, P., & Dowler, D. L. (1982). Moments of transfer of stimulus control in practical assembly tasks by mentally retarded adults. *American Journal of Mental Deficiency, 87,* 309–315.

Wolery, M., Ault, M. J., Doyle, P. M., & Gast, D. L. (1986). *Comparison of instructional strategies: A literature review.* (U. S. Department of Education. Grant No. G008530197). Lexington: Department of Special Education, University of Kentucky.

Wolery, M., & Gast, D. L. (1984). Effective and efficient procedures for the transfer of stimulus control. *Topics in Early Childhood Special Education, 4*(3), 52–77.

Wolf, M. M. (1978). Social validity: The case for subjective measurement or how applied behavior analysis is finding its heart. *Journal of Applied Behavior Analysis, 11,* 305–312.

Zane, T., Walls, R. T., & Thvedt, J. E. (1981). Prompting and fading guidance procedures: Their effect on chaining and whole task teaching strategies. *Education and Training of the Mentally Retarded, 16,* 125–135.

Zigler, E., & Sietz, V. (1975). On "an experimental evaluation of sensorimotor programming": A critique. *American Journal of Mental Deficiency, 79,* 483–492.

PART IV

MOVING BEYOND ACQUISITION

Proficient performance, maintenance, and use of skills outside of the instructional settings are critical dimensions of effective teaching. In fact, teaching should be considered effective only when students can use the behaviors when they are needed in the real world. Chapters 15 through 17 describe how to move beyond simple acquisition of behaviors to application of behaviors. Chapter 15 discusses the notion of fluency or proficiency. Fluency is defined and a rationale for addressing fluency is presented. Procedures for identifying appropriate fluency criteria are described and guidelines for promoting fluency are discussed with examples. Chapter 16 discusses the maintenance of skills. Maintenance is defined and a rationale for promoting it is presented. Procedures for promoting maintenance of responses are described and emphasis is placed on thinning reinforcement schedules. Examples of basic reinforcement schedules are provided. Guidelines for using various reinforcement schedules and their effect on response maintenance also are addressed. Chapter 17 defines generalization, provides a rationale for promoting generalization, and discusses planning issues related to generalization. Procedures for assessing generalization errors and facilitating the occurrence of generalized responding are described.

15

BUILDING FLUENCY

Key Terms

■ Fluency ■ Fluency-Building ■ Response Competition ■ Independent Level ■ Instructional Level ■ Discrepancy Analysis ■ Tool Movements ■ Practice

The goal of acquisition training is to help students respond accurately under specific stimulus conditions. High levels of accuracy, however, do not mean the student can perform the skill with the speed necessary to make it useful. Once acquisition has occurred, teachers should alter their instructional strategies to increase speed or fluency. For example, Ivan could not use a push-button phone. His teacher successfully taught him to press the buttons of his home phone number. Ivan achieved the criterion of making 10 dialings of his home phone number without an error, but each call took him an average of 90 seconds. Ivan learned the skill accurately but did not do it fast enough to be practical. His performance was not fluent. In this chapter, fluency is defined, a rationale for teaching fluency is presented, strategies for identifying appropriate fluency rates are described, and strategies for facilitating fluency are discussed.

A DEFINITION OF FLUENCY

Fluency is the "speed or ease with which a child performs a movement or series of movements" (White & Haring, 1980, p. 312). It also refers to the smoothness and naturalness of the response, and can refer to the latency and/or duration of a response. Fluency is a synonym for proficiency. **Fluency-building** refers to the process of promoting more fluent responding. Fluency-building occurs after skills have been acquired. Lack of fluency can be seen in two types of problems: (a) when performance is too slow, such as Ivan's slow dialing, or a student's slow reading and (b) when responding is inconsistent. Common examples include stuttering, erratic task completion, and writing awkward sentences when completing essays. The problem with the second type is not how fast the skill is performed, but how smoothly or consistently.

RATIONALE FOR FLUENCY-BUILDING

Achieving both accurate and fluent responding is important for a variety of reasons. First, a behavior that occurs at proficient rates is more likely to be useful. When Ivan becomes fluent at dialing his telephone number, he can contact his parents quickly. Frequently, sequences of behaviors are chained together to form more complex skills such as dressing, vocational tasks, and most academic responses. The usefulness of chained skills is directly related to the fluency with which students can perform the individual behaviors. If a student reads slowly and laboriously, the meaning, and thus the usefulness, of the passage is lost.

Second, an accurate and proficient behavior can become a prerequisite for learning more advanced skills. Erica, for example, can be taught to read CVC words, write three-word sentences, or compute basic math facts. These prerequisite behaviors can then be used to teach Erica more complex skills such as reading CCVC words, writing five-word sentences, or computing two-step math problems. If she can perform the prerequisite skills fluently, learning the more complex responses will require less effort and time.

Third, increased fluency enhances response maintenance and generalization by increasing response competition (Matlock, Billingsley, & Thompson, 1985). **Response competition** refers to two behaviors meeting the same intent or function and accessing the same reinforcer. Many lower-level skills serve the same function as more complex skills and, until the complex skill becomes fluent, the lower-level skill competes with the complex skill. For example, crawling and walking serve the same function—to get from one place to another. Beginning walkers frequently drop to their knees and crawl. Walking is not yet fluent enough to meet the child's needs but crawling is. As children become more fluent walkers, they stop crawling.

Fourth, when students perform behaviors fluently they appear more "normal" and are provided with more opportunities to receive positive social reinforcement. For example, when Ivan can fluently use the telephone, he will not delay others waiting to use the phone and will thus be perceived more favorably. Fluent responders simply look more like their peers and will be less likely to experience negative social interactions.

Fifth, accuracy and fluency are important for safety reasons. Crossing the street might be accomplished accurately but, if the student is slow, personal injury may result. Likewise, new drivers who fail to enter a crowded freeway at a speed compatible with the general traffic flow are dangers to themselves and others.

IDENTIFYING APPROPRIATE FLUENCY CRITERIA

One of the most difficult aspects in designing fluency-building programs is determining an appropriate fluency criterion for each objective. Traditionally, the focus of most instruction has been placed on accuracy and fluency research is relatively sparse. Most of the currently available fluency standards have been generated from programs that emphasize precision teaching (see *Journal of Precision Teaching*), textbooks such as White and Haring (1980), and curriculum-based assessment models (*Exceptional Children,* November 1985, *52*(3)). In general, identifying appropriate fluency rates can be accomplished by: (a) consulting published guidelines, (b) interviewing others about expected rates, and (c) conducting discrepancy analyses.

Published Guidelines

Although limited in scope, some published fluency rates are available for academic behaviors such as math, reading, spelling, and handwriting. Mercer and Mercer (1985) provided the most complete summary of published proficiency rates. A summary of research that describes suggested proficiency rates for math skills is provided in Table 15.1. Correct and error rates across problem types and grade are given for written math facts. A summary of suggested rates for reading skills is presented in Table 15.2. The behaviors listed include the students' oral reading of isolated sounds, words in lists, and words in text. Correct and error rates are given within specified and unspecified grade levels. Although the estimates vary from author to author, these general guidelines provide some focus for setting criterion statements in objectives. For some students, the higher rates may be more desirable and, for others, the lower rates may be acceptable. The teacher must use professional judgment and experience when determining the actual fluency rate for each student. If a student is taken to the lowest fluency rate listed and still maintains the behavior and uses it to acquire other more complex responses, the low fluency rate is acceptable.

Mercer and Mercer (1985) described two published guidelines for proficient rates of written spelling skills. They differentiated between the independent level and instructional level. **Independent level** refers to work completed on skills that have been mastered, whereas **instructional level** refers to skills that are being learned. Mercer and Mercer cited Starlin and Starlin (1973c) and provided the following criteria: for the independent level, kindergarten children through second graders should write 30 to 50 correct letters per minute with no more than two errors. For the instructional level, the same students should write 15 to 29 correct letters with seven or fewer errors. "For third grade through adult, the independent level is 50-70 correct letters with three to seven errors" (Mercer &

TABLE 15.1 Suggested Correct and Error Rates across Problem Type and Grade for Written Math Facts

Write Math Facts

	Digits in Simple Add. and Sub. Equations		Addition Facts 0-9 Gr. 2-3		Sub. Facts (1-5) and Facts Top Numb. 2-9 Gr. 2-3		Add. Facts Sums 10-18 and Sub. Facts Top Numb. 6-9 Gr. 3-4		Two-column Addition with Regrouping Gr. 4-5		Two-column Subtraction with Regrouping Gr. 4-6		Mult. Facts Through x9 Gr. 5-6		Division Facts Through Divisor of 9 Gr. 6	
	Cor.	Err.	Cor.	Err.	Cor.	Err.	Cor.	Err.	Cor.	Err.	Cor.	Err.	Cor.	Err.	Cor.	Err.
Koenig & Kunzelmann (1980)			60	—	60	—	90	—	60	—	60	—	90	—	60	—
Precision Teaching Project (Montana)			70-90	—	70-90	—	70-90	—	70-90	—	70-90	—	70-90	—	70-90	—
Regional Resource Center (1971a) (not grade-specific)	50	0									50	0	50	0	50	0
Smith & Lovitt (1982)			50+	0	45+	0							50+	0	45+	0
Starlin & Starlin (1973a)			20-30	0-2	20-30	0-2	40-60	0-2	40-60	0-2	40-60	0-2	40-60	0-2	40-60	0-2
Wood, Burke, Kunzelmann, & Koenig (1978)	125	0	68	0	68	0			60	0	56	0	80	0	47	0

Note: From *Teaching Students with Learning Problems* (2nd ed.) (p. 189) by C. D. Mercer and A. R. Mercer, 1985, Columbus, OH: Charles E. Merrill. Copyright © 1985 by Charles E. Merrill Publishing Company. Reprinted by permission.

TABLE 15.2 Suggested Correct and Error Oral Reading Rates within Specified and Unspecified Grade Levels

I. Grade Level Specified	Say Isolated Sounds (K–3) Cor.	Err.	Say Words in List (2–4) Cor.	Err.	Say Words in List (5–6) Cor.	Err.	Say Words in List (Adult) Cor.	Err.	Say Words in Text (1–3) Cor.	Err.	Say Words in Text (4–6) Cor.	Err.	Say Words in Text (Adult) Cor.	Err.
Koenig & Kunzelmann (1980)			140	0	120–130	0								
Starlin & Starlin (1973b)			100–126 Phonetic words; 90–128 Irregular words	0	138–148	0	198	0	50–70	2	100–200	2	100–200	2
Wolking (1973) High Achievers	36–52	0–4			134–150	0	198	0	120–132	0	156–180	0	252	0
Range:			90–140	0	120–150	0								
Mode:			100–126	0	130+	0								
Median:			115	0	136	0								

II. Grade Level Not Specified	Say Isolated Sounds Cor.	Err.	Say Words in List Cor.	Err.	Say Words in Text Cor.	Err.
Alper, Nowlin, Lemoine, Perine, & Bettencourt (1974)	80	2	60–80	2	100–120	3
Haughton (1972)	100	0				
Henderson, Clise, & Silverton (1971)	100	0				
Precision Teaching Project (Montana)	60–80 Blends	0	80–100 Sight words; 60–80 Regular words	0; 0	200+	0
Regional Resource Center (1971b)	60–80; 90–100 Blends	2; 2	80–100	2	100–120	2
Starlin (1971)	40	2	50+	0–4	100–200	2
SIMS Program (1978)			50	0	100	2
Range:	40–100	0–4	50–100	0–7	100–200	0–2
Mode:	100	0	80	2	100	2
Median:	70	2	80	2	100+	2

Note: From *Teaching Students with Learning Problems* (2nd ed.) (p. 333) by C. D. Mercer and A. R. Mercer, 1985, Columbus, OH: Charles E. Merrill. Copyright © 1985 by Charles E. Merrill Publishing Company. Reprinted by permission.

Mercer, 1985, p. 389). Koenig and Kunzelmann (1980) listed fluency rates by grade level and suggested faster responding:

1. Grade 2: 60 to 90 correct letters per minute.
2. Grade 3: 90 to 100 correct letters per minute.
3. Grade 4: 100 to 120 correct letters per minute.
4. Grade 5: 110 to 130 correct letters per minute.
5. Grade 6: 120 to 140 correct letters per minute.

Suggested handwriting fluency rates also have been identified in the published literature. The basic measurement unit is letters written per minute. The rates described by Mercer and Mercer (1985) for handwriting are listed in Table 15.3.

Interviewing Others

For many responses, such as social skills, vocational work rates, and community-based behaviors, published fluency rates are unavailable or inappropriate. In these cases, expected fluency rates can be determined by asking others who have

TABLE 15.3 Suggested Rates for Handwriting Fluency Presented in Letters Per Minute

Source	Rates
Zaner-Bloser Scales	Grade 1: 25 letters per minute
	Grade 2: 30 letters per minute
	Grade 3: 38 letters per minute
	Grade 4: 45 letters per minute
	Grade 5: 60 letters per minute
	Grade 6: 67 letters per minute
	Grade 7: 74 letters per minute
Precision Teaching	Think — write alphabet (emphasizing speed): 80 to 100 letters per minute
Project (Montana)	See — write letters (emphasizing accuracy): 75 letters per minute correct (count of three for each letter: slant, form, ending)
	See — write numerals random: 100 to 200 digits per minute
	See — write connected cursive letters: 125 letters per minute (count of three for each letter)
Koenig & Kunzelmann (1980)	See — write letters: 70 letters per minute
	See — write numerals random: 70 digits per minute

Note: From *Teaching Students with Learning Problems* (2nd ed.) (p. 418) by C. D. Mercer and A. R. Mercer, 1985, Columbus, OH: Charles E. Merrill. Copyright © 1985 by Charles E. Merrill Publishing Company. Reprinted by permission.

established acceptable or minimum levels of performance in their specific settings or for their special curriculum. This method is particularly useful when behavioral objectives are established to move students toward less restrictive environments or from one program to another. For example, if acceptable progress and change are observed, Casey will move from a self-contained special education classroom to a less restrictive resource room. To set an appropriate fluency criterion for independent working, Casey's teacher asked his new resource room teacher how many minutes he should be able to work independently in the new class. Once determined, Casey's teacher can set a criterion in an objective that will prepare him for the expectations of the new classroom. A similar strategy can be used for Kayla's dressing skills. Her parents are asked how long she has to get dressed each morning. Kayla's teacher can use this information when planning a dressing program. Interviewing others can also be useful in many other instructional or work settings. For example, vocational education programs can be established with proficiency rates that correspond to those rates designated as minimum by future employers.

Discrepancy Analysis

When interviewing is inconvenient or impossible, direct observation of others doing the behavior can be used. **Discrepancy analysis** is a comparison of the target student's performance to the performance of others doing the same skill in similar situations. To conduct a discrepancy analysis, the teacher should identify a person or group of persons who can competently do the behavior, and a situation where the behavior is needed or will be performed. A data-collection procedure should be selected that will allow measurement of the critical dimension of the behavior. For example, if the teacher is interested in the length of time students with acceptable classroom behaviors sit at their desks, a momentary time-sampling procedure or duration recording would be appropriate. If the behavior of interest is using a calculator to find answers to multiple-digit division problems, rate data may be more appropriate. Once the persons, setting/situation, and data-collection system have been identified, the teacher directly observes the competent persons performing the behavior. It is wise to observe for two or three different sessions and calculate the average across the sessions. When only one session is used, an inflated or deflated level may be identified. The average of the two or three sessions is then used as the target level, and the range as the lowest acceptable level. The teacher should then measure the target student using the same observation procedures and compare his or her performance to that of the competent persons.

Teachers can also determine appropriate fluency rates by doing the desired behavior themselves. For example, Ivan's teacher simply measured how long it took her to dial a seven-digit telephone number. She used this rate to set Ivan's criterion in the objective. Another teacher might time how long it takes her to cross the street or observe how long the light stays green. A vocational education teacher who received a subcontract for assembling instructional booklets for new cars learned to do the task himself and used his fluency rates as a guide for setting minimum criteria for his sheltered workshop employees.

Basic Tool Movements

The above procedures can be used to identify estimates of fluent responding; however, teachers must also evaluate these rates against students' use of basic tool movements (White & Haring, 1980). Each behavior has some movement cycle, or beginning and end. **Tool movements** are behaviors that are used to indicate or show that a skill has been learned. Examples of tool movements are "say" and "write." For example, Melanie can indicate her comprehension of a reading passage in a variety of ways. When a comprehension question is asked, she can answer verbally, write her response, or point to the correct answer from a list of four alternatives. Her teacher should determine whether Melanie has the basic tool movements before setting fluency rates for the target behavior. If a desired fluency rate of 20 seconds is set for a written response and it takes Melanie 25 seconds to copy the correct letters from a model, failure to accomplish the objective is confounded by Melanie's lack of fluency in performing the basic indicator or tool movement. Ideally, students should perform the tool movements fluently.

> By comparing a child's fluency on basic tool movements with his rates on more advanced probes, we are in a much better position to decide where his needs really lie. For example, Kelly's math fact rate is only 15 digits per minute and our aim for that skill is 50 per minute. At first glance, it would appear that we should start working with his basic facts. When we look at his ability to write-digits-random rate, however, we discover that he can only write 18 digits per minute, even if he doesn't have to solve any problems. (White & Haring, 1980, p. 135)

Little research is available on specific rates for fluent performance of tool movements (White & Haring, 1980). Clearly, tool-movement fluencies should be well above the criteria established for the behavior being taught. Twice the rate for the behavior in the objective is viewed as a conservative fluency for a tool movement. For example, a fluent rate for writing answers to multiplication facts through 9's is about 50 to 90 per minute (Mercer & Mercer, 1985). Currently, Thomas can copy numerals at a rate of 100 per minute, but writes answers to multiplication facts at a rate of 30 per minute. Joslynn can copy numerals at a rate of 20 per minute and write answers to multiplication facts at 8 per minute. From these data, instruction should be provided to make Thomas more fluent in multiplication facts and to make Joslynn more fluent in the basic tool movement (writing numerals).

GUIDELINES FOR FLUENCY-BUILDING

Instruction to promote fluency should occur after students have learned to perform the behavior accurately. Procedures for building fluency are relatively straightforward and include practice and manipulation of consequent events. Antecedent manipulations such as prompting strategies are not helpful because they provide more information on how to do the behavior than on doing the behavior quickly. However, during fluency-training, teachers should collect data on students' correct and error responses because attempting to increase response speed can inadvertently result in decreases in accuracy. For example, José is learning to write using cursive script. He can form all letters correctly and can join all needed combinations of letters; however, he writes slowly. The teacher provides him with practice time and also is reinforcing him for writing faster. A graph depicting his performance is shown in Figure 15.1. During baseline, he was writing about 10 letters per minute and all of them were correct; during fluency-training, Phase I, he wrote about 25 letters per minute, but only 5 were correctly formed. As a result, his teacher changed the reinforcer so that it was given only if the rate of correctly formed letters increased over the previous session. This strategy resulted in an increase in the rate of correctly formed letters and a decrease in error frequency.

Structuring Practice Sessions

Practice is defined as repeated performance of a previously acquired behavior. Practice and repetitive drill are the primary strategies used to achieve fluent responding. Since students have already acquired the skill, the teacher needs to provide practice sessions that enable them to become more fluent. White and Haring (1980) made several recommendations concerning the effective use of practice sessions. First, practice or drill sessions should be relatively short. Repetitive practice sessions can become dull and tedious. Further, students can become fatigued if practice sessions are too long. Although the length of practice sessions may vary depending upon students' ages and the skills being learned, 1 or 2 minutes is appropriate with many academic skills and tool movements. When rate data are being collected on fluency objectives, a 1-minute sample is desirable because it allows easy calculation of performance rates. Second, several practice sessions should be provided throughout the day. Scheduling short drills, called *probes,* throughout the day helps avoid boredom and fatigue. More importantly, several short sessions allow teachers the opportunity to provide reinforcement for performance several times per day rather than once or twice. Third, during each drill session, students should have as many opportunities to do the behavior as possible. Thus, individualized materials may be required.

FIGURE 15.1 Number of cursive letters per minute for José under two conditions: Baseline and Fluency Training. Fluency training consisted of Phase I (reinforcement for faster responding) and Phase II (reinforcement for increases in correct responses only). During Phase I, the number of letters written increased dramatically, but most of them were incorrectly formed; during Phase II, the number of correctly formed letters increased and the errors remained low.

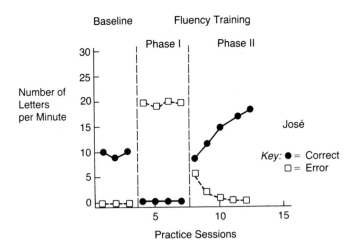

Reinforcement and Motivation

Since practice is necessary to increase fluency and because practice activities can be dull and fatiguing, motivational problems may arise. Teachers can identify motivation problems by analyzing students' performance patterns. One performance pattern that may indicate lack of motivation is a relatively stable rate of responding that is neither increasing nor decreasing. For example, Reggie is learning to unload a dishwasher in the cafeteria. He can accurately take plates from the trays and stack them in the appropriate place, so his teacher is having him practice the skill. To be fluent, he must stack plates at a rate of 30 per minute. His current rate is shown in Figure 15.2. As can be seen, he consistently stacks 8 to 10 plates per minute. When the teacher measured his performance, she noticed several interesting behaviors. When anyone entered the kitchen, he would stop and look at them, and when the cook moved from one place to another, Reggie would watch him. It appeared that Reggie was easily distracted. The teacher counted the number of times Reggie looked away from his task and found that he did so about 10 times per minute. Since his performance rates are neither increasing nor decreasing and he appears to be distracted easily, his teacher can conclude that motivational problems exist.

Another performance pattern that may indicate lack of motivation is a deterioration in the rate. For example, Denise is learning to subtract and has mastered writing the answers to problems where the top number is between 2 and 9. From Table 16.1, a fluent rate on such tasks should be at least 30, and potentially as much as 60, digits per minute. Data for Denise are shown in Figure 15.2. Those data indicate that initially her rate was about 25 correct digits per minute;

FIGURE 15.2 Performance patterns that indicate motivational problems during practice sessions. The top graph represents the number of plates Reggie stacked per minute. The targeted fluency rate was 30 plates per minute. Reggie's data indicate that he is neither increasing or decreasing, and the teacher noted that he was easily distracted during practice sessions. The middle graph represents the number of correct digits written by Denise to subtraction problems. The targeted fluency rate is 60 digits per minute. Initially, her rate was about 25 per minute, but it then decreased to slower rates; this deterioration indicates a motivational problem. The lower graph represents the number of words Lisa read out loud. The target rate was 100 per minute. Initially, her rate was stable and increasing, but then it became highly variable. This variability indicates a motivational problem.

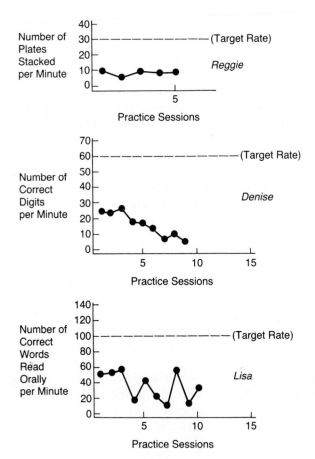

however, in the past few days, her rate has deteriorated. This decrease has been somewhat gradual but is clearly a steady drop in performance.

A final performance pattern that indicates a lack of motivation and a potential problem with compliance is a highly variable pattern. For example, Lisa is learning to read fourth-grade material and is reading words in stories (text). To be fluent, her oral reading rate should be between 100 and 200 words per minute, but her initial rate was about 50 words per minute and increasing slightly. However, as shown in Figure 15.2, the data in subsequent practice sessions became highly variable. Thus, motivation problems can be seen in (a) stable patterns of performance where additional evidence indicates the student is easily distracted or not attending to the task (e.g., Reggie), (b) deteriorating performance (e.g., Denise), or (c) highly variable data (e.g., Lisa).

To prevent these problems, teachers should consider how they present feedback to students for performance during practice sessions. Feedback should be provided after, rather than during, practice sessions (White & Haring, 1980). Feedback should emphasize the total number of correct behaviors and the consistency of the responses rather than isolated errors that may occur. Reinforcers for practice sessions should be as natural as possible (e.g., verbal praise and other social reinforcers) and should be administered contingently. Since students have already demonstrated accurate performance, few errors should occur. If feedback for errors is necessary, it should be given at some time other than immediately after the practice session.

The guidelines discussed in Chapter 13 on the effective use of reinforcement should be used during fluency-building. Fluency-training, however, requires special application of the reinforcers. As with other types of feedback, reinforcers are best provided at the end of the short practice sessions. Reinforcement can be given under at least four different contingencies when building fluent responding. First, reinforcement can be given if students master some predetermined rate. For example, Reggie's teacher decided that she would provide reinforcement if he stacked 15 plates per minute. After Reggie met this rate for three days, the teacher increased the criterion to 20 plates per minute. Data for his program are shown in Figure 15.3. When she set a new criterion, she expected that Reggie would increase his performance and be reinforced. However, his rate did not increase to higher levels. As a result, the teacher used a second manipulation of the reinforcement contingency: Reggie was reinforced only if his performance was greater than during the previous session. This contingency resulted in a steady increase in Reggie's rate until he reached the target rate of 30 plates per minute.

A third contingency for providing reinforcement is to give it only when correct rates exceed an aim line. For example, Denise's teacher decided to draw an aim line from her current subtraction rate to the target fluency rate. Reinforcement was given only when her performance was on or above the aim line. As shown in Figure 16.3, this contingency resulted in steady acceleration of the rate at which Denise wrote correct answers to subtraction problems. For practice sessions 15 and 18, she did not receive reinforcement because her rate was below the aim line.

FIGURE 15.3 Performance patterns from Figure 15.2 and application of various reinforcement contingencies to solve motivational problems. The top graph represents the number of plates Reggie stacked per minute. The targeted fluency rate was 30 plates per minute. Reggie was reinforced for stacking 15 and later 20 plates per minute; this contingency produced faster responding that did not continue to improve. Therefore, his teacher reinforced him only if the performance was higher than his previous performance. As a result, he reached the fluency target. The middle graph represents the number of correct digits written by Denise to subtraction problems. The targeted fluency rate was 60 digits per minute. The teacher reinforced her only if she was at or above the aim line. This contingency solved the motivational problem. The lower graph represents the number of words Lisa read out loud. The target rate was 100 per minute. She was reinforced only if the current correct performance was above previous performance *and* her error rate was below two per minute.

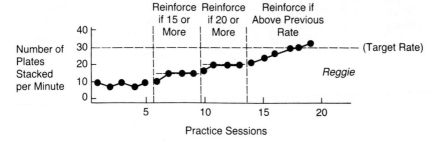

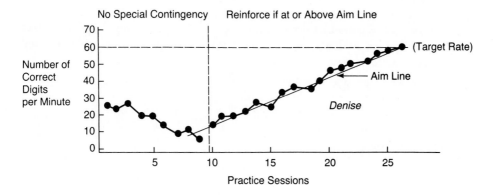

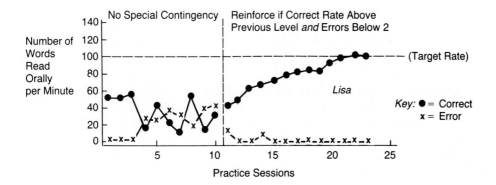

A fourth contingency for providing reinforcement is to give it only when correct rates are at or above a defined level *and* error rates are at or below a defined level. This contingency requires students to perform more quickly and ensures that the performance also will be correct. For example, when Lisa's correct oral reading rate became highly variable, the rate of errors also became variable. Her teacher decided to reinforce her only if her correct rate exceeded the rate from the previous session and if she only made two or less errors per minute. Data from this example are shown in Figure 15.3. This contingency should be used when students who were performing with low error rates begin to make frequent errors. These four contingencies should assist teachers in facilitating fluency and dealing with potential motivational problems during practice.

Since practice sessions can be tedious, gamelike contingency systems are usually effective in motivating students. A common game is to "beat the clock." Students are given an activity and told to complete it before a timer sounds or before a specific time on the clock. Frequently, a reinforcer is provided if the work is completed accurately before the time limit. Similarly, teachers can use a race format where individual students compete against each other or in teams where half the class competes against the other half. In addition to racing against others, students can also race against their previous records. Although more research is needed, microcomputers hold promise as fluency-building tools. To be useful, software must be designed to allow students to respond as rapidly as possible and feedback should be provided at the completion of the practice session. In addition to the gamelike format, microcomputer programs frequently offer data collection on students' performance, random sequences of problems, and individual practice sessions.

Self-Reinforcement as a Fluency-Facilitating Procedure

Liberty and Michael (1985) reviewed the literature dealing with teaching students with mental retardation to reinforce their own behavior. Their findings indicated that self-reinforcement can be an effective strategy in building fluency. Students, however, must be taught to use self-reinforcement. For example, after a brief period, Kim Li was taught how to use a stopwatch, count the math facts she completed accurately, and record her score on a wall chart. If she met or exceeded her previous performance, she could move a gold star to the next higher point on a progress thermometer. For more specific descriptions of self-reinforcement, see Chapter 25 of this text as well as Bandura (1976), Catania (1975), Kazdin (1978), Meichenbaum (1977, 1979), and Meichenbaum and Goodman (1971).

Summary of Key Concepts

- Procedures used to facilitate acquisition do not ensure that response proficiency will be achieved.
- Fluency is the performance of skills at rapid and/or natural rates.
- To identify acceptable fluency levels, teachers should consult published guidelines, interview other knowledgeable persons, and/or conduct a discrepancy analysis.
- Building acceptable fluency requires systematic manipulation of instructional variables, especially consequent events.
- Fluency is promoted by providing practice activities that are motivating and hold students' attention.
- Motivational problems during fluency-building practice can be identified by analyzing students' performance patterns.
- When motivation problems exist during practice activities, teachers should manipulate the reinforcement contingencies.

REFERENCES

Alper, T., Nowlin, L., Lemoine, K., Perine, M., & Bettencourt, B. (1974). The rated assessment of academic skills. *Academic Therapy, 9,* 151–164.

Bandura, A. (1976). Self-reinforcement: Theoretical and methodological considerations. *Behaviorism, 4,* 135–155.

Catania, A. (1975). The myth of self-reinforcement. *Behaviorism, 3,* 192–199.

Haughton, E. (1972). Aims—Growing and sharing. In J. B. Jordan & L. S. Robbins (Eds.), *Let's try doing something else kind of thing.* Reston, VA: The Council for Exceptional Children.

Henderson, H. H., Clise, M., & Silverton, B. (1971). *Modification of reading behavior: A phonetic program utilizing rate acceleration.* Ellensburg, WA: H. H. Henderson.

Kazdin, A. E. (1978). *History of behavior modification.* Baltimore, MD: University Park Press.

Koenig, C. H., & Kunzelmann, H. P. (1980). *Classroom learning screening manual.* Columbus, OH: Charles E. Merrill.

Liberty, K. A., & Michael, L. J. (1985). Teaching retarded students to reinforce their own behav-

ior: A review of process and operation in the current literature. In N. Haring, K. Liberty, F. Billingsley, V. Lynch, J. Kayser, & F. McCarty (Eds.), *Investigating the problem of skill generalization* (3rd ed.) (pp. 88–106). Seattle: Washington Research Organization.

Matlock, B., Billingsley, F. F., & Thompson, M. (1985). Response competition and generalization. In N. Haring, K. Liberty, F. Billingsley, V. Lynch, J. Kayser, & F. McCarthy (Eds.), *Investigating the problem of skill generalization* (3rd ed.) (pp. 80–87). Seattle: Washington Research Organization.

Meichenbaum, D. (1977). *Cognitive-behavior modification: An integrative approach.* New York: Plenum Press.

Meichenbaum, D. (1979). Teaching children self-control. In B. Lahey & A. E. Kazdin (Eds.), *Advances in clinical child psychology* (Vol. 2) (pp. 1–33). New York: Plenum Press.

Meichenbaum, D., & Goodman, J. (1971). Training impulsive children to talk to themselves: A means of developing self-control. *Journal of*

Abnormal Psychology, 77, 115–126.

Mercer, C. D., & Mercer, A. R. (1985). *Teaching students with learning problems* (2nd ed.). Columbus, OH: Charles E. Merrill.

Precision Teaching Project. Available from Skyline Center, 3300 Third Street Northeast, Great Falls, MT 59404.

Regional Resource Center. (1971a). *Diagnostic Math Inventories* (Project No. 472917, Contract No. OEC-0-9-472917 608). Eugene, OR: University of Oregon.

Regional Resource Center. (1971b). *Diagnostic Reading Inventories* (Project No. 472917, Contract No. OEC-0-9-472917 608). Eugene, OR: University of Oregon.

SIMS Reading and Spelling Program (3rd ed.). (1978). Minneapolis: Minneapolis Public Schools.

Smith, D. D., & Lovitt, T. C. (1982). *The computational arithmetic program.* Austin, TX: PRO-ED.

Starlin, C. M. (1971). *Evaluating progress toward reading proficiency.* In B. Bateman (Ed.), *Learning disorders.* Vol. 4: *Reading.* Seattle, WA: Special Child Publications.

Starlin, C. M., & Starlin, A. (1973a). *Guides to decision making in computational math.* Bemidji, MN: Unique Curriculums Unlimited.

Starlin, C. M., & Starlin, A. (1973b). *Guides to decision making in oral reading.* Bemidji, MN: Unique Curriculums Unlimited.

Starlin, C. M., & Starlin, A. (1973c). *Guides to decision making in spelling.* Bemidji, MN: Unique Curriculums Unlimited.

White, O. R., & Haring, N. G. (1980). *Exceptional teaching* (2nd ed.). Columbus, OH: Charles E. Merrill.

Wolking, W. D. (1973, October). *Rate of growth toward adult proficiency: Differences between high and low achievement children, grades 1-6.* Paper presented at the International Symposium of Learning Disabilities, Miami Beach, Florida.

Wood, S., Burke, L., Kunzelmann, H. P., Koenig, C. H. (1978). Functional criteria in basic math skill proficiency. *Journal of Special Educational Technology, 2,*(2), 29–36.

Zaner-Bloser Evaluation Scales. (1979). Columbus, OH: Zaner-Bloser.

16

THINNING REINFORCEMENT TO MAINTAIN SKILLS

Key Terms

■ Response Maintenance ■ Extinction ■ Functional Skill ■ Overlearning ■ Schedule of Reinforcement ■ Continuous Reinforcement ■ Extinction Schedule ■ Interval Schedules ■ Ratio Schedule ■ Fixed-Interval Schedules ■ Variable-Interval Schedules ■ Limited-Hold Procedure ■ Fixed-Ratio Schedules ■ Variable-Ratio Schedule ■ Ratio Strain ■ Natural Reinforcers ■ Internalized Reinforcement ■ Task-Related Reinforcement

Teachers enable students to learn new skills and perform them more accurately and fluently. Newly acquired skills, however, are useless if students fail to perform them when instruction is discontinued. **Response maintenance** is the phase of learning in which acquired and fluent skills persist over time after training or teaching has ceased. Expected behaviors occur even when teacher assistance or frequent reinforcement contingencies are not present.

Behavioral persistence and the transfer of stimulus control to nontraining settings do not occur automatically after instructional programs and behavior-change strategies have been withdrawn (Marholin & Siegel, 1978; Stokes & Baer, 1977). This finding has led to the general recommendation that instruction be designed systematically to promote maintenance and generalization (Haring, 1985; Marholin & Siegel, 1978). In this chapter, procedures and guidelines for maintaining acquired skills are described. Emphasis is placed on teaching skills that have a high probability of being maintained when instruction is discontinued and on effective use of reinforcement schedules to enhance behavioral persistence.

RATIONALE FOR TEACHING MAINTENANCE

There are a number of reasons why teachers should assess for response maintenance and implement procedures that promote behavioral persistence. First, some student-acquired behaviors are prerequisites for learning more advanced skills. For example, students must maintain accurate and fluent rates of basic multiplication facts before they can be expected to acquire more complex multiplication skills. Second, behavioral persistence is a necessary requirement for satisfactory performance in situations different from training. Before we can expect a skill to generalize to new, untrained settings, we would expect consistent skill performance from a student in the absence of teacher assistance and reinforcement and under the teaching conditions. For example, a student who learns, with teacher assistance and reinforcement, to cross a particular street corner accurately and safely should demonstrate independent crossing at that corner prior to being expected to do so at new corners or with different crossing signals. Third, one of the main goals of education is to prepare students for independent living, free from the external assists and controls provided by teachers, parents, and peers. If students do not demonstrate satisfactory and lasting use of key skills, their opportunities for more independent living are reduced. Finally, enduring appropriate behaviors increase students' access to positive reinforcement. For example, the more times and places a student can make eye contact when he or she smiles, the more opportunities he or she has for seeing and receiving another person's smile.

Response maintenance is often difficult to achieve with handicapped students who are used to receiving a considerable amount of teacher assistance and feedback. *Maintenance* actually means that a student is expected to perform a skill under **extinction** conditions, when a reinforcer once available for a given behavior is no longer accessible. Extinction is often used systematically as a procedure to *reduce* behavior (see Chapter 20). For example, a teacher may stop paying attention to a student whenever he or she swears. If swearing is being maintained by attention, terminating it should result in a decrease in swearing. For adaptive behaviors, we want response maintenance when extinction conditions are present. It is not surprising that response maintenance is often difficult to achieve.

Although a specific explanation for why some behaviors maintain under extinction conditions has not been identified, Kazdin (1975) suggested a number of possibilities. One explanation is that behavior comes under the control of other reinforcers in the instructional setting through vicarious or systematic conditioning opportunities. For example, when Erica asks for assistance, she is reinforced initially with verbal praise. However, the teacher also provides smiles and eye contact which eventually will acquire reinforcing characteristics. Similarly, effective reinforcers directly associated with or produced by the behavior begin to control the response. Whenever Erica asks for help, it is given; when Ivan dials his telephone number correctly, his call is answered and it is reinforced naturally.

A final explanation hypothesizes that increased occurrences of desirable behavior necessarily change the setting in which they occur and/or the general manner by which relevant others interact with the student. For example, when Erica does not shout or run from the room, more opportunities for positive learning and peer and adult interactions become available. Regardless of the explanation, an abundance of research suggests that responding deteriorates when training contingencies are withdrawn. This observation demands that teachers systematically plan for such change and program for response maintenance.

PROCEDURES FOR PROMOTING RESPONSE MAINTENANCE

A number of strategies should be used to enhance response maintenance. The first and most important consideration is to teach skills that are functional. A **functional skill** is one that is expected or demanded frequently in everyday activities. It is likely to be reinforced naturally by peers or a change in the environment, or its absence may have negative consequences. A functional skill is one the student finds useful. Useful skills generally are maintained because of naturally occurring consequences. In fact, there is no point in encouraging maintenance of a skill that has little or no utility!

There are many examples of student maintenance of functional skills; one example will suffice here. As Ricardo learns to read more fluently, he sounds less awkward and more understandable and, as a result, his peers tease him less often. Furthermore, he now can read comic books and magazines which he previously was unable to read. By becoming a more fluent reader, Ricardo has increased his opportunities to enjoy a number of naturally occurring and maintaining consequences. However, many handicapped students do not maintain skills easily, even when those skills are functional. In such cases, teachers must incorporate more systematic strategies to ensure that efforts to acquire new skills are not wasted due to lack of maintenance.

As in fluency-building (Chapter 15), White and Haring (1980) recommended that response maintenance be promoted through repeated drill beyond the accuracy and fluency criteria already achieved. This strategy is called **overlearning** (Travers, 1977) and emphasizes the manipulation of instructional consequences. These manipulations include changing reinforcement schedules, delaying reinforcement, removing reinforcement contingencies, teaching self-control strategies, using naturally occurring reinforcement, training relevant others, and varying training. In this chapter, each strategy is discussed; however, schedules of reinforcement are stressed.

SCHEDULES OF REINFORCEMENT

The first systematic description of the effects of reinforcement schedules on behavior was published by Ferster and Skinner (1957). They found that behavior could be predicted reliably based on the systematic manipulation of the reinforcement schedule. A **schedule of reinforcement** is a "rule denoting how many responses or which specific responses will be reinforced" (Kazdin, 1975, p. 109). Vargas (1977) added that a schedule of reinforcement "is the way in which reinforcement is contingent on behavior" (p. 144).

In Chapter 13, two basic schedules for administering reinforcement were described: **continuous** and **intermittent.** Under an **extinction schedule,** reinforcement that usually maintains a specific response is no longer provided. Without reinforcement, we would predict that the response would occur less often.

When initially teaching a new skill, each correct response should be reinforced on a continuous schedule. Continuous differential reinforcement is necessary for achieving stimulus control rapidly and efficiently. However, a continuous schedule has at least two disadvantages. First, satiation may occur making the reinforcer ineffective. This problem is avoided by using a distributed trials approach to teaching and by ensuring that teaching occurs when students are in a deprivation state relative to the reinforcer. A more serious skill-maintenance problem is the unrealistic nature of a continuous schedule. Very few behaviors are reinforced continually in the real world; students who are expected to go from continuous reinforcement to near extinction conditions rarely demonstrate response maintenance.

To facilitate maintenance, continuous schedules of reinforcement should be replaced gradually by more intermittent schedules in which either (a) some specified number of behaviors must be observed or (b) a specific amount of time must pass before reinforcement is made available. The use of intermittent schedules of reinforcement has a number of advantages. First, they are relatively resistant to satiation effects because reinforcement occurs less frequently. Second, response maintenance is more likely, especially if the schedule is systematically and gradually thinned or made more intermittent. Figure 16.1 illustrates general response patterns observed when extinction conditions are introduced following the use of continuous versus intermittent schedules of reinforcement. Finally, although teachers must monitor time intervals or behavioral occurrences, less effort and time generally are involved in administering reinforcers.

BASIC TYPES OF INTERMITTENT SCHEDULES OF REINFORCEMENT

Two basic types of intermittent reinforcement schedules may be used. **Interval schedules** provide reinforcers based on the amount of time that has passed since delivery of the last reinforcer. The second type of intermittent schedule is based on the number of targeted responses or the **ratio** of the total number of targeted responses to the one that is actually reinforced. Both interval and ratio schedules

FIGURE 16.1   General response patterns during extinction following continuous reinforcement (top graph) and intermittent schedules of reinforcement (lower graph).

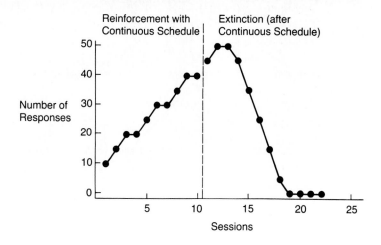

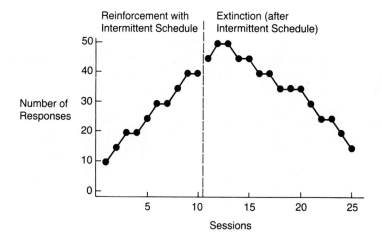

can be applied in either a fixed or variable fashion. Basic schedules of reinforcement are shown in Figure 16.2.

Interval Schedules of Reinforcement

Fixed-interval schedules specify a rule for the contingent presentation of a reinforcer based on the passage of a specific and *constant amount of time* from the last reinforced response. A reinforcer is provided for the first occurrence of a target

FIGURE 16.2   Basic variations in schedules of reinforcement.

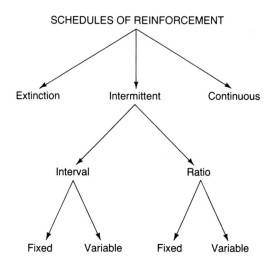

SCHEDULES OF REINFORCEMENT

Extinction   Intermittent   Continuous

Interval   Ratio

Fixed   Variable   Fixed   Variable

behavior after the specified amount of time has passed since a reinforcer was last presented. Any target responses that occur before the end of the specified time interval are not reinforced. For example, Ms. Tanaka sets a timer to ring 5 minutes after the previous reinforcer was delivered. When it rings, she looks at Jimmy to see if he is reading his book. If he appears to be reading, she goes over to him, puts her hand on his shoulder, and whispers into his ear that he is doing great work. If Jimmy is not reading when the timer rings, she waits until he has been reading for at least 30 seconds and then reinforces him. This schedule of reinforcement is called a *fixed-interval 5-minute* or FI:5 schedule. Ms. Tanaka delivers a reinforcer only if Jimmy is engaged in the appropriate response at or after the 5-minute interval. Once reinforcement is presented, she resets the timer for another 5-minute interval.

Variable-interval schedules are similar to fixed-interval schedules except that the interval size is set at a specified *average,* rather than a constant amount of time. When Ms. Tanaka uses a variable-interval 6-minute (VI:6) schedule, she sets the timer for intervals of varied sizes so that the average will be 6 minutes, e.g., 7, 5, 6, 5, 6, 6, and 7. Some additional examples of fixed- and variable-interval schedules of reinforcement are illustrated in Table 16.1.

Effects on Response Rates. Interval schedules of reinforcement tend to promote response maintenance; however, rates tend to be relatively slow as compared to ratio schedules. This slow rate of responding is due to reinforcer availability that is based on the passage of a specified amount of time. For example, whether 2 or 22 appropriate responses occur within the first 4½ minutes of a 5-minute interval schedule, a reinforcer is available only after the passage of a specified amount of

TABLE 16.1   Examples of Fixed- and Variable- Interval Schedules of Reinforcement

Interval Schedule	Reinforced Target Response
FI:8 hours	Kay works at a work-study job in which she is paid daily at 5:00 p.m. as long as she is at her work station when the checks are distributed.
VI:15 minutes	Mr. Walker checks on the students who are reading in the library on the average of every 15 minutes. If he finds that they are engaged in library-appropriate behaviors, he lets them stay an additional 5 minutes.
FI:60 minutes	Mike has a job in the school office keeping track of attendance slips. The vice-principal checks on him every hour on the hour. If she sees him writing or counting slips she tells him he is going a good job and that he is being a great help in the office.
FI:50 minutes	The bell indicating the end of the period rings every 50 minutes. When it rings, the students are allowed to talk and leave the room. As the end of the period approaches, the amount of feet-shuffling, talking, and book-closing behaviors increases. Their teacher allows them to go exactly when the bell rings when they are engaged in these behaviors.
FI:3 minutes	At the end of every 3-minute interval, the teacher looks over at Donna. If she is playing cooperatively with another student, he gives Donna a token (checkmark) that can be traded for extra play time.
VI:2 days	On the average of every 2 days, Ms. Tanaka looks in each of her student's journals. If she sees that recent entries have been made, she writes a simple praise statement and indicates that the student had earned his or her journal-writing points.
VI:10 minutes	Mr. O'Neil does not mind talking during his study hall class, just as long as there are not more than three students talking at any one time. He checks the number of students who are talking on the average of once every 10 minutes. If the class has met criterion, the whole study hall class earns 3 extra minutes at the end of class to talk as much as they like.

time from the last reinforced behavior. As interval sizes become smaller, a faster response rate is promoted and maintained.

Higher response rates also can be encouraged by using a **limited hold procedure** in which a special restriction or condition is placed on the student's performance. The "restriction requires that a primed response (the first response following termination of the required interval) must occur within a specific time limit if reinforcement is to be made available" (Sulzer-Azaroff & Mayer, 1977, p. 353). For example, Juanita's work-study employer requires that she be at her work station during at least 80% of each working hour to receive her daily paycheck. This type of contingency is more likely to increase the duration and rates of Juanita's work-station behaviors.

Effects on Maintenance. Variable-interval schedules tend to promote slightly higher rates of responding and result in more enduring performance than similar fixed-interval schedules. This difference is thought to be due to not knowing exactly when reinforcers will be available.

With interval schedules, behavior rates tend to be slower immediately following the presentation of a reinforcer up until the end of the interval, at which time responding tends to increase. Since reinforcement availability is controlled by time rather than response rate, students are more likely to respond at the end of the interval when reinforcement is more likely. For example, Ian's work rate in the attendance office tends to increase as the end of each hour approaches. After the vice-principal acknowledges his work, Ian slows down because the likelihood of receiving reinforcement is low. Response patterns tend to be slightly more consistent under variable-schedule conditions because of the increased unpredictability associated with variable intervals.

Interval schedules tend to produce performance that persists longer than when behaviors are reinforced continuously. This difference is primarily due to behaviors being controlled by time factors rather than the number of responses performed by the student. Variable-interval schedules also tend to maintain behavior longer than fixed-interval schedules under extinction conditions.

Problems and Advantages.   Interval schedules of reinforcement are easy to implement and monitor. Teachers are not required to keep track of all behavioral occurrences, only those that are present at, or occur immediately after, the interval limit. Interval schedules are easy to use with time-sample recording procedures such as those discussed in Chapter 5. Interval schedules also tend to approximate natural schedules that exist in many work, home, and community environments. For example, many salaried jobs provide paychecks at the end of some fixed interval of time. Grades for academic performance are assigned at the end of a quarter or semester. When attempting to maintain behaviors that require relatively low response rates or persistence, such as staying in seat, cooperative and independent play, or essay-writing, interval schedules are particularly advantageous.

Interval schedules, however, have the disadvantage of producing inconsistent and low rates of responding over time; therefore, they are not appropriate for all behaviors. Variable schedules and limited-hold restrictions reduce some of this disadvantage, but not sufficiently for high-rate behaviors, such as oral reading rate, certain vocational task-assembly activities, written-word spelling, or number of assignment completions.

Ratio Schedules of Reinforcement

Fixed-ratio schedules of reinforcement promote response maintenance through the contingent presentation of a reinforcer after a specific number of target responses. Ms. Tanaka reinforces Julie's toy-sharing with peers on a FR:3 schedule; that is, she receives individualized praise contingent upon every third occurrence of an appropriate behavior. On this schedule, Julie displays her toy-sharing behavior three times then looks at Ms. Tanaka for praise. To increase response maintenance, Ms. Tanaka gradually changes the schedule to FR:5, then

FR:7, FR:9, etc. These systematic changes are associated with a greater number of toy-sharing responses without the presentation of a reinforcer.

Many examples of fixed-ratio schedules can be seen in many everyday activities. Some factory workers are paid on a piecework basis and receive a specific amount of salary for the number of products produced, inspected, or packaged. Salespersons are paid additional commission if they sell more products. When a teacher reinforces a specified number of pages or assignments as correct or completed, a FR schedule is being applied.

A **variable-ratio schedule** specifies the average number of responses that must occur before reinforcement can be presented. When Ms. Tanaka finds that Julie's toy-sharing rates no longer increase under FR:7 schedule, she changes to a variable ratio of 8 schedule (VR:8). Ms. Tanaka provides verbal praise on the average of every 8 behavior occurrences. For example, she might give a reinforcer after 7 correct responses, then 9, 8, 7, 7, 8 . . . etc., but, overall, a reinforcer is presented on the average of every 8 behaviors. By increasing the unpredictability of the reinforcer presentation, she can decrease the pauses between Julie's responses. Not only will her behavior maintain longer under extinction conditions, but it will be more consistent. Additional examples of fixed- and variable-ratio schedules of reinforcement are illustrated in Table 16.2.

Effects on Response Rates.   Reinforcer availability under ratio-schedule conditions is limited primarily by the number of responses performed. The faster a student responds the sooner reinforcers become available. This condition does not exist

TABLE 16.2   Examples of Fixed- and Variable- Ratio Schedules of Reinforcement

Ratio Schedule	*Reinforced Target Response*
VR:3	Gary fills out the daily attendance slip for his teacher for each classroom period of the day. His teacher walks over to him and gives him a "special-helper" bonus token on the average of every three slips that he fills out accurately and completely.
VR:20	During reading group, Steve talks out without raising his hand. Most of the time his teachers do not call on him when he talks out; however, on the average of once out of every 20 talk-outs, a teacher will answer his question or tell him to raise his hand instead of talking out.
FR:2	There are eight periods in Karen's daily class schedule. She has worked out a special contract with her homeroom teacher that allows her to earn 15 minutes of recreational reading in the library for every two class periods in which she finishes all the assignments required.
VR:15	Jimmy serves lunch in the school cafeteria. On the average, 1 out of every 15 students who passes him says, "Thank you," when he hands them their dessert.
FR:5	Ed works in a sheltered workshop and packages plastic spoon-fork-knife and napkin combinations that are used on airlines. For every 5 packages he assembles correctly, his immediate supervisor gives him a token which can be traded in for a specified amount of his daily paycheck.

with interval schedules because a specified amount of time must past before the reinforcer is presented.

Variable-ratio schedules are associated with slightly higher rates of responding than fixed-ratio schedules. This effect is associated with not being able to predict precisely which behavior will produce reinforcement. For example, Marta receives a token for every five correct assemblies; thus, she quickly learns when a token will be presented. Generally, the ability to predict is accompanied by response pauses which in turn produce relatively slower response rates. When Marta's supervisor switches to a VR:7 schedule, her work rate increases. Since she is no longer able to predict accurately when the next reinforcer will be available, her work slow-downs become less frequent. These response pauses are similar to those observed with interval schedules but tend not to be as pronounced. Careful thinning of reinforcement schedules can maintain responding without these pauses.

Effects on Maintenance. Response patterns under ratio schedules are more consistent and regular in contrast to interval schedules. Similarly, variable-ratio schedules maintain more consistent behavior than fixed-ratio schedules. Under extinction conditions, response deterioration tends to be less pronounced when response maintenance has been promoted through ratio schedules of reinforcement. This effect is primarily due to greater consistency, higher rates of responding, and more reinforcer availability. In fact, immediately after extinction conditions are put into effect, the behavior frequently accelerates. This phenomenon, known as an *extinction burst,* is discussed in Chapter 20.

Variable-ratio schedules are the most effective in maintaining behavior under extinction conditions. This observation accounts for the difficulty experienced in eliminating some persistent and unacceptable behaviors. Eventually, all behavior will decrease and be eliminated if extinction conditions are strictly enforced. However, in most cases, inconsistent use of extinction tends to provide opportunities for variable-ratio reinforcement. The leaner the schedule of reinforcement, the easier to recover old response rates, and the more difficult to eliminate the response entirely.

Problems and Advantages. The major disadvantage associated with ratio schedules is the difficulty in counting the number of behaviors that occur. If permanent products are used, this problem can be avoided. However, high-rate behaviors demand strict teacher attention which, in turn, can interfere with other instructional activities. The problem is further compounded if more than one student or behavior must be observed and reinforced.

A second problem is **ratio strain** (Ferster, Culbertson, & Boren, 1975). When students attempt to increase their opportunities for receiving reinforcement by accelerating their rates, the accuracy of individual responses may be sacrificed. For example, Susan receives a point for every 20 words she writes in her daily journal. Since reinforcement is contingent upon the number of words written, the more she can write the more points she can acquire. However, her rapid writing rate causes the quality of her handwriting to deteriorate. Her written words can no longer be read. Solutions to the problem of ratio strain include (a) switching to a more variable schedule, (b) setting rate and accuracy criteria that approximate expected rates in the natural environment (i.e., other classroom settings), and (c) systematically adjusting the schedule based on the accuracy and rate of her responses. Careful review of the data is particularly important in the evaluation of reinforcement-schedule effects on response quality and quantity.

The advantages of ratio schedules of reinforcement are numerous. The primary advantage is that the natural environment, e.g., regular classrooms, family settings, social situations with peers, maintains many behaviors on lean ratio schedules. The systematic use of ratio schedules can increase the probability that students' behaviors will come under the control of natural schedules of reinforcement. However, it should be noted that thin schedules can also maintain inappropriate as well as appropriate behaviors. Teachers should use variable-ratio schedules to maintain desired behaviors, and be sure they do not respond to inappropriate behaviors with this schedule.

A second major advantage of ratio schedules is the promotion of high and consistent rates of responding. Because the delivery of reinforcers is affected primarily by the number of behaviors produced, students can access greater numbers of reinforcers by responding faster. These high rates are required for successful functioning in many settings. As indicated earlier, accuracy is important, but so are fluency and proficiency.

GUIDELINES FOR USING SCHEDULES OF REINFORCEMENT TO FACILITATE RESPONSE MAINTENANCE

Maintenance, fluency-building (Chapter 15), and generalization (Chapter 17) represent interrelated instructional activities. Since students with handicaps are less likely to demonstrate enduring and generalized use of skills, an interrelated plan should be developed for each student to ensure that skills taught are actually used. When developing the maintenance component of this plan, a number of factors need to be considered: (a) when to begin maintenance training, (b) guidelines for changing schedules, (c) use of overlearning, (d) use of natural antecedents, (e) use of natural reinforcers, and (f) delaying contingencies.

When to Begin Maintenance Training

Initial instruction of students with handicaps is facilitated by various forms of teacher assistance and by immediate and continuous feedback on task performance. Both teacher assistance and feedback should be considered in planning for enduring skill use. In general, teacher assistance such as prompts, models, cues, physical assists, or other forms should be removed prior to initiating a maintenance program. Strategies for fading teacher assistance were described in Chapter 14. If not completely removed, they should be brought to the level of independence at which they will be expected under maintenance conditions. For example, Ralph was taught to stay in his seat through reminders every 5 minutes. The long-term maintenance objective is for Ralph to stay in his seat with no more than one reminder per hour.

In addition to removing teacher assistance, a second prerequisite for initiating maintenance training is the attainment of high levels of correct responding and low error rates in the instructional situation. Maintenance activities should not be implemented if the student demonstrates inconsistent performance or if high rates of accuracy have not been achieved. Although the level of accuracy required will vary across students and behaviors, accuracy should be at least 80 to 90%.

Changing Schedules

In building response maintenance, the student's resistance to extinction is increased by changing schedules of reinforcement. A shift is made from continuous (rich) to intermittent (thin) schedules of reinforcement. Although this process appears simple, it must be done systematically. The schedule change should be gradual and based on the student's performance, which should be used to determine whether changes are too large or too small, or if the terminal objective has been achieved.

Fixed schedules of reinforcement should be used before variable schedules because they increase the amount of responding required for reinforcement; yet, they still provide some level of predictability. As the size of fixed schedules increases, a shift to variable or less predictable schedules should be made. Decreased predictability assists response maintenance and approaches the extinction conditions likely to be experienced when training is removed.

A careful evaluation of student performance data will indicate whether a schedule change was too fast or too large. As indicated earlier, a common phenomenon associated with ratio schedules is ratio strain (Ferster, Culbertson, & Boren, 1975). When the number of responses required for reinforcement becomes too large, responding may deteriorate in accuracy or quality. A sample set of data demonstrating this effect is displayed in Figure 16.3. Ralph's teacher was able to reduce his out-of-seat behavior by giving him a reminder at the beginning of the day and reinforcing him every 5 minutes when he stays in his seat (FI:5). Later, she continued the daily reminder and reinforced him only if he stayed in his seat for 10 minutes (FI:10). This strategy was effective in maintaining a low frequency of the behavior. However, when she switched to a VI:30 schedule, he began getting out of his seat. Going to a smaller change (i.e., VI:12 reinforcement schedule) resulted in a decrease in the behavior. The switch from a FI:10 schedule to a VI:30 schedule was too large a change for Ralph.

Use of Overlearning

White and Haring (1980) indicated that strategies for fluency-building are equally useful in building response maintenance. Thus, overlearning, or repeated drill and practice, is recommended. Instead of daily or frequent practice trials, however, overlearning activities should be provided on a less regular basis, e.g., once a week or once every other week.

Since repeated drill can be dull and unmotivating, teachers must vary the practice material and the context within which it is presented. White and Haring (1980) suggested that response opportunities be as meaningful and realistic as possible.

> For example, while trying to build a child's fluency, we might use a single math-fact sheet with the same problems repeated over and over. Once the child has gained fluency in the basic facts, however, we might begin to give him sheets with only selected facts each day. The answers to the different math facts might provide the child with the combination for a "safe" in which a prize is kept or be the key to

FIGURE 16.3 Data for Ralph's out-of-seat behavior. The FI:5 minute schedule was effective in reducing his behavior, and the FI:10 schedule was effective in maintaining the reduction, but the VI:30 schedule resulted in a loss of control. The reinforcement schedule change between FI:10 and VI:30 was too large.

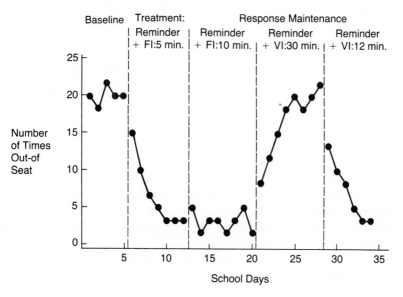

a code that lets him decipher the "secret message" for the day. Children working at the same math level could race each other to see who gets the answer first, or we might even devise equivalent sheets (in addition, subtraction, etc.) that all have the same answers, so that children at all skill levels could compete for the same prize. In any event, the child will be using the same skill in essentially the same situation but hopefully for a more useful purpose (at least in the eyes of the child) than was possible during the fluency-building phase. (p. 238)

Use of Natural Antecedents

When building response maintenance, antecedent stimuli should be similar to those the student will be required to respond to in the future. Stimuli found in the natural environment should be used during maintenance training. For example, a teacher would like Jennifer to write her name in the upper right-hand corner of her paper whenever a new assignment is started. He uses worksheets, lined paper, and task sheets that are found under normal working conditions. During his instruction, the teacher highlights relevant and common characteristics of these stimuli.

A teacher uses a simple role-playing procedure to increase the likelihood that Erica's newly acquired help-seeking skill will be learned. Erica practices with directives and questions that are common in other classroom settings, e.g., "answer comprehension question number three for us" or "read the first paragraph and tell us, in your own words, what happened." By providing successful practice opportunities with natural antecedents, the maintenance of Erica's new skill, e.g., "I don't know the answer. Will you help me," is more probable.

Use of Natural Reinforcers

Using **natural** and meaningful **reinforcers** is also important. The basic rule is to shift from artificial to natural reinforcers as soon as possible without decreasing response accuracy and fluency. For example, Harry's teacher used poker chip tokens too long and did not incorporate more desirable conditioned reinforcers, such as verbal praise and grades. She found that maintenance training was hindered by the added time required to remove tokens and to develop new reinforcers. Naturally occurring reinforcers should be developed before the shift from fluency to maintenance building occurs.

Teachers should also identify and develop reinforcing consequences that are internalizing and task-related. **Internalized reinforcement** is defined as teaching students to self-select, self-evaluate, and self-administer reinforcers. These reinforcers might take a variety of forms, e.g., self-praise statements or opportunities for a reinforcing activity. Internalized reinforcement is required when teachers or trainers are no longer available to provide reinforcement, i.e., extinction conditions. If students can be taught to provide themselves with reinforcing consequences, response endurance may be more likely. A more detailed description of self-reinforcement and other self-control strategies is provided in Chapter 25.

Task-related reinforcement provides consequences that are direct outcomes or products of the acquired behavior. Rather than providing artificial consequences (e.g., teacher attention, tokens), teachers should build reinforcement value into the behavior being taught. For example, Ms. Tanaka found that Ivan dialed telephone numbers more accurately and predictably when she arranged for someone to "answer" the calls.

Finally, when building response maintenance with natural reinforcers, teachers must attend to the amount of reinforcement. The basic guideline is to move toward amounts similar to more natural conditions. This guideline was discussed in detail in Chapter 13.

Delaying Contingencies

A final factor in facilitating the maintenance of acquired skills is varying when reinforcement is delivered. Teachers should strive to increase the delay between when reinforcement is earned and when it is actually presented. In schools, grades are presented at the end of quarters or semesters. In work settings, monetary compensation may be presented days, weeks, or even months after it has been earned. Alice may earn 12 tokens for correctly finishing her math assignments on time each day, but she does not get to trade them in for back-up reinforcers until the end of the week. In these examples, reinforcement contingencies are delayed. Maintenance training should include reinforcement contingencies that approximate those likely to be experienced under natural or extinction-like conditions; thus, the systematic delay of reinforcers is recommended.

Summary of Key Concepts

■ Behavioral persistence, called *response maintenance,* does not occur automatically after instructional programs and behavior-change strategies have been withdrawn; it must be programmed.

■ Response maintenance is a condition in which the occurrence of a behavior can be predicted reliably when extinction conditions are introduced.

■ New learning should be reinforced on a continuous basis. As acquisition is achieved, more intermittent schedules of reinforcement should be implemented.

■ Intermittent reinforcement can be based on the passage of time or the number of responses produced.

- Interval schedules tend to promote slower rates of responding than ratio schedules of reinforcement.

- In general, the less predictable the schedule of reinforcement the more likely responding will maintain under extinction conditions.

- Shift from artificial to natural reinforcers as soon as possible without decreasing response accuracy and fluency.

- The ultimate goal is to approximate the kinds of reinforcers and schedules that are likely to maintain the desired behavior in the natural environment.

REFERENCES

Ferster, C. B., Culbertson, S., & Boren, M. C. P. (1975). *Behavior principles* (2nd ed.). Englewood Cliffs, NJ: Prentice-Hall.

Ferster, C. B., & Skinner, B. F. (1957). *Schedules of reinforcement.* Englewood Cliffs, NJ: Prentice-Hall.

Haring, N. G. (Ed.), *Investigating the problem of generalization* (3rd ed.). (U.S. Department of Education, Contract No. 300–82–0364). Seattle: Area of Special Education, University of Washington.

Kazdin, A. E. (1975). *Behavior modification in applied settings.* Homewood, IL: Dorsey Press.

Marholin, D., & Siegel, L. J. (1978). Beyond the law of effect: Programming for the maintenance of behavioral change. In D. Marholin (Ed.), *Child behavior therapy* (pp. 397–415). New York: Gardner Press.

Stokes, T. F., & Baer, D. M. (1977). An implicit technology of generalization. *Journal of Applied Behavior Analysis, 10,* 349–367.

Sulzer-Azaroff, B., & Mayer, G. R. (1977). *Applying behavior analysis procedures with children and youth.* New York: Holt, Rinehart, & Winston.

Travers, R. M. (1977). *Essentials of learning: An overview for students of education* (4th ed.). New York: Macmillan.

Vargas, J. S. (1977). *Behavioral psychology for teachers.* New York: Harper & Row.

White, O. R., & Haring, N. G. (1980). *Exceptional teaching* (2nd ed.). Columbus, OH: Charles E. Merrill.

17

GENERALIZING ACQUIRED SKILLS

Key Terms

■ Stimulus Generalization   ■ Generalization   ■ Response
Generalization   ■ Error Patterns   ■ Community-Based Instruction

Instructional strategies enable teachers to produce predictable responding (i.e.,
stimulus control) within clearly defined conditions. Skill acquisition, however, is
the tip of the proverbial learning iceberg. The larger challenge consists of building
fluent skills that maintain *and* are performed in other appropriate stimulus
conditions. In previous chapters, we discussed strategies for developing fluency
and maintenance. The purpose of this chapter is to define generalization, describe
procedures for measuring its occurrence, and discuss strategies for increasing the
likelihood of generalization.

DESCRIPTION OF GENERALIZATION

Definition of Generalization

Stimulus generalization, referred to in this chapter as **generalization,** occurs
when a behavior learned in one situation (i.e., training) is observed in another
(i.e., nontraining) (Kazdin, 1975). More precisely, "generalization includes any
situation in which newly acquired responses are performed in the presence of
nontrained stimuli"(Horner, Bellamy, & Colvin, 1984, p. 287). For example, Bob
has successfully acquired an appropriate greeting response, "Hi. How are you?"
which he demonstrates in role-playing sessions with his teacher and teacher aide.

One day, Bob correctly greets a substitute teacher. In this example, Bob generalized a response across persons. Generalization also can occur across settings (e.g., to the playground, to home) and across other stimulus conditions (e.g., when different materials or directions are used). Stimulus generalization can be conceptualized as transfer of stimulus control, i.e., the stimulus control exerted by one stimulus is similar to, shared by, or transferred to other stimuli with common characteristics. For example, if Bob greets the principal in the hall, the secretary in the office, or a neighbor on the street, he has demonstrated stimulus generalization. The stimulus control developed in the role-playing sessions with the teacher and teacher aide has been transferred to other persons. This relationship is illustrated in Figure 17.1. White and Haring (1980) referred to generalization as an example of the "application phase of learning." The student has learned "when a skill will be useful and how to recognize the need for it in complex situations" (p. 239). Stimulus generalization can also be used to account for the occurrence of undesirable behaviors. For example, Katie learned that tantrum behavior could keep her from participating in a difficult academic task. Later, she used tantrums to avoid calisthenics in physical education class, standing in line in the lunchroom, and cleaning the dishes from the table at home. Although each of these situations is different, similarities existed: each required her to exert effort. The stimuli in each situation have the same effect; that is, they all set the occasion for the tantrum behaviors to occur.

A second form of generalization, **response generalization,** exists when one response influences or affects the occurrence of other responses. Skinner (1953) described response generalization as a condition in which reinforcement of a behavior increases the probability that other similar behaviors will occur. Rather than emphasizing antecedent stimuli as with stimulus generalization, response generalization focuses on the behavior. For example, when Bob meets a new person, he not only says the greeting, but he also turns his body toward the person, makes eye contact, smiles, and extends his hand for a handshake. All of these responses have a high probability of occurring and being reinforced. This relationship is illustrated in Figure 17.2.

FIGURE 17.1   Example of stimulus generalization.

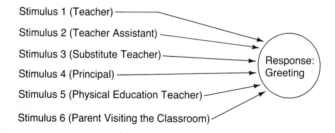

FIGURE 17.2 Example of response generalization.

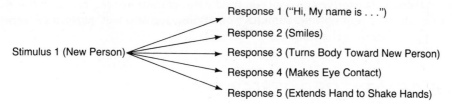

Rationale for Generalization Training

One of the primary purposes of schools and of education is to teach students skills they can use in other situations. This statement implies that schools are means, rather than ends in and of themselves. Skills are learned in school so they may be applied elsewhere. For example, students learn to read in schools, but the reading is to be used in other situations to obtain knowledge and as a leisure activity. Special education students may learn to feed themselves in school, but the true purpose is to ensure that they can use the skill wherever appropriate. College students who are preparing to become teachers attend classes so they can acquire the information and learn the skills they will use when teaching children. Thus, one of the primary purposes of schools is to facilitate stimulus generalization. Teachers frequently approach instruction with the assumption that the student, parents, other teachers, and peers will strengthen what they have already taught. Unfortunately, this train-and-hope approach is inefficient and frequently ineffective (Stokes & Baer, 1977). Perhaps one of the most consistent and startling findings from the research literature is that skills taught in school frequently do not generalize to other situations where they are needed (Stokes & Baer, 1977; Wehman, Abramson, & Norman, 1977). Students learn to perform a skill in school, become fluent in the execution of the skill, and may even maintain it after instruction stops, but they do not use or apply the skill when it is needed outside of school. The persistence of this finding has led some professionals to move instruction outside of the school and into the natural environment. However, a recent review of 115 studies where training was conducted in the natural environment produced the following finding: "A train-and-hope approach in the natural environment is not associated with a high frequency of successful skill generalization" (White, Leber, & Phifer, 1985, p. 77). In fact, about five of every six students with severe handicaps and nearly two of every three students with mild and moderate handicaps did not generalize well when only a train-and-hope approach was used in the natural environment (White et al., 1985).

Failure to obtain generalization is not restricted to learning new behaviors. Generalization also is a problem when teachers attempt to eliminate or reduce the occurrence of inappropriate social behaviors. Thus, an important educational problem is developing an instructional technology for training appropriate generalized responding. Horner et al. (1984) described this problem as developing a means "to deliver interventions that reliably and efficiently result in the acquisition of adaptive behaviors that endure over time, are performed across the full range of appropriate stimulus conditions, and are not performed across inappropriate stimulus conditions" (p. 288).

PLANNING FOR GENERALIZED RESPONDING

Planning for generalization and collecting data on whether a behavior generalizes is important for three reasons. First, the train-and-hope approach to generalization is ineffective; thus, plans to ensure its occurrence are necessary. Second, teachers need to know whether the behavior generalized to other relevant situations. Third, analyzing the data on generalization performance allows teachers to determine whether changes need to be made in their instructional procedures.

General Guidelines

Warren (1985) presented several guidelines for planning and measuring language generalization, but they are applicable to other academic and social skills as well. First, teachers should develop a "concise, detailed, realistic generalization plan" which can be integrated into students' individualized education plans (IEPs) (Warren, 1985). A specific plan for generalization training increases the probability that generalized responding will occur and will serve as a structure for measuring its occurrence. From a review of IEPs, Billingsley (1984) found that teachers rarely develop objectives addressing generalization. Based on this finding, we recommend that each acquisition objective have a corresponding generalization objective. Development of such objectives should include a listing of all the potential stimulus situations where the behavior is needed (Horner et al., 1984). Further, teachers should have a general policy that says no objective is completed until the behavior has been performed fluently (a) for someone who did not teach it, (b) in a setting different from the training setting, (c) in response to directions and/or materials other than those used in training, and (d) in response to natural situations where the behavior is appropriate and needed (i.e., used spontaneously). In addition, Stremel-Campbell and Campbell (1985) recommended thoroughly analyzing the natural environment to identify the relevant and irrelevant setting, antecedent, and consequence stimuli that will be present and may influence students' generalization. For example, Carla is learning to shop for groceries and an important skill is identifying the price of each item. In school she could read prices written by her teacher, but when they went to the grocery store, she could identify the price on only 10% of the items. The teacher had failed to analyze all the different ways in which prices are marked on items.

As a result, the teacher analyzed the natural environment and developed materials that more closely reflect the ways prices were stamped on items in stores. The training environment should also be analyzed to identify variables that may impede or facilitate generalization. A rule of thumb is to make the training setting as similar to the generalization setting as possible.

Second, a variety of individuals should be enlisted to observe the student's behaviors across different stimulus conditions. Warren (1985) suggested training parents, aides, and other teachers to observe and measure generalized responding. Persons should be selected who are likely to see the student in situations where the behavior will be needed. The teacher should determine whether those persons will cooperate with the generalization measurement and will prompt and reinforce the generalized response when it occurs. In some cases, minimal training of other persons may be necessary. Whenever others are measuring generalization, teachers should attempt to determine the accuracy of those measures.

Third, Warren (1985) recommended that generalized responding be assessed each time a training step is successfully acquired. Many skills students learn are part of a larger sequence of skills. For example, putting on a shirt is part of the larger sequence of putting on all clothing, and adding numerals with sums to 9 is part of a larger sequence of adding sums to 18 and beyond. When one step or cluster of steps is acquired, the student should be assessed for generalization. These checks should occur even when students learn the behavior easily and quickly (Warren, Rogers-Warren, Baer, & Guess, 1980). In addition, previously acquired behaviors should be assessed for maintenance and generalization.

Fourth, generalization checks should be conducted in settings or under stimulus conditions where successful responding is needed. A critical element of generalization is being able to perform acquired behaviors only when they are needed. Thus, measurement of generalization should occur in situations where it is contextually appropriate for the behaviors to occur and also where it may occur but be inappropriate. Warren et al. (1980) recommended that teachers assess students' generalization or lack thereof in the natural environment as frequently as possible.

Fifth, a consistent, reliable, and valid measurement system should be carefully maintained. The teachers should ensure that (a) responses are accurately and operationally defined, (b) observation forms are easily completed and read, (c) measurement procedures are convenient and functional with a minimum of interference to ongoing activities, and (d) the measurement system is replicable, i.e., another person could accurately implement the procedures with a minimum of training. A reliable and valid measurement system is important for objective and accurate comparison of training and generalization data and for communicating with others about students' performance. Generalization measurement may be accomplished through structured observations, informal written reports, interviews with significant others, and audio/video taping. Information obtained through formal and informal measures enables teachers to modify their training strategies so that opportunities for successful generalization can be maximized.

Generalization Error Patterns

The guidelines discussed above address planning and measurement tactics for facilitating the occurrence of generalization. Of equal importance is the analysis of generalization **error patterns,** that is, "when a learned response is performed in a nontrained, but inappropriate situation, or fails to be performed in a nontrained appropriate situation" (Horner et al., 1984, p. 288). Information obtained from an error analysis allows teachers to (a) evaluate stimulus conditions or characteristics that affect unsuccessful generalization and (b) modify their training procedures to enhance appropriate generalization.

Horner et al. (1984) described four error patterns that may be identified in an assessment of generalization and then may require instructional modifications. The first type of error involves target behaviors that have come under the control of irrelevant stimuli. The desired response is only observed when the irrelevant stimuli are present. This error is usually the outcome of training that has failed to (a) prevent the target response from occurring and being reinforced in the presence of irrelevant stimuli or (b) control for irrelevant stimuli by varying them. For example, this generalization error exists when Bob performs the correct greeting response only when he is at school. He does not do it at home, at church, on the school bus, or when he is at a neighbor's home. The greeting response is under the control of irrelevant stimuli in the school setting.

The second type of error is similar and occurs when irrelevant responses are under the control of irrelevant stimuli and are more likely to occur than the behavior being trained, even when the appropriate stimuli are present. The situation is one in which stimuli are simultaneously present for appropriate and inappropriate responses and in which the irrelevant behaviors are under more powerful stimulus control. In Bob's case, he may display the greeting response with new people but, if Tammara is present, he walks away from the new person without saying a word and talks with Tammara.

The third type of generalization error pattern, restricted stimulus control, "exists when a response that should be under the control of multiple relevant stimuli is only controlled by a subset of those stimuli" (Horner et al., 1984, p. 290). Thus, responding occurs whenever the subset of relevant stimuli are present regardless of whether other relevant stimuli are present or absent. For example, David learned to add, but when presented with subtraction problems he immediately adds the numerals. He apparently acquired a restricted rule for solving such problems (i.e., "If two numerals are close to one another, add them.") rather than learning the correct rule (i.e., "If two numerals are close to one another, identify the operation sign [+ or –] and then do what the sign indicates."). When faced with subtraction problems, he was responding to a restricted set of the relevant stimuli—the numerals rather than the numerals *and* operation sign.

The fourth type of error is associated with limited variations of the target response. This error occurs when students apply the "wrong response variation whenever a new stimulus condition is presented" (Horner et al., 1984, p. 290). For example, David can add two numerals when they are presented in columns and in line format (e.g., 23 + 120 =_____). He has learned to modify his response to different stimulus conditions. However, when presented with the same numerals in word problem format, his rate of correct responses quickly decreases. White and Haring (1980) referred to students' ability to vary their responses to solve new problems as a final phase of learning called *adaption*.

FACILITATING GENERALIZATION

In this section, guidelines for facilitating generalization are presented. Many excellent and detailed reviews of this issue appear in the literature (Baer, 1981; Drabman, Hammer, & Rosenbaum, 1979; Haring, Liberty, Billingsley, Lynch, Kayser, & McCarty, 1985; Horner et al., 1984; Marholin & Siegel, 1978; Sanders & James, 1983; Stokes & Baer, 1977; Stremel-Campbell & Campbell, 1985; Wahler, Breland, & Coe, 1979); therefore, brief guidelines are provided here. When faced with the formidable task of transferring stimulus control from the training situation to nontraining stimulus conditions, four basic instructional areas may be manipulated: (a) setting events, (b) antecedent events, (c) the targeted behaviors themselves, and (d) the consequences that follow behaviors. Although each is discussed separately, generalization training should involve manipulations of various combinations of these variables.

Setting Variables

Setting variables are general stimulus conditions that exist in the instructional setting prior to and during training and are present in the generalization setting. At least four manipulations of setting variables are possible. The most drastic is to teach in the natural environment, which is referred to as **community-based instruction.** Community-based instruction is receiving wide acceptance among teachers of the moderately to severely handicapped and is recommended by some as the teaching method of choice (cf., Snell & Grigg, 1987). The intent of community-based instruction is to eliminate the need to transfer stimulus control from the training to the natural setting. While the logic of the approach is appealing, it is clear that simply teaching in one natural environment is not sufficient to secure generalization to other natural environments (White et al., 1985). For example, students who learn to do their laundry in one laundromat may need additional training to generalize that skill to another laundromat. However, when other strategies for promoting generalization are combined with teaching in the natural environment, generalization may occur. Unfortunately, some practical and logistical factors such as transportation, high student-to-teacher ratios, and lack of liability insurance make community-based training difficult to implement.

Another setting manipulation is to make the instructional setting as similar to the generalization setting as possible. As noted earlier, the instructional and generalization environments should be analyzed prior to training. This analysis identifies variables in both settings that may facilitate or impede generalization and can be changed to make the two settings similar. Transfer of stimulus control is more likely if the stimuli in the two settings are similar. This similarity can be accomplished in a couple of ways. First, materials, routines, and requirements of the natural environment can be incorporated into the classroom. For example, if students are being prepared to work in an establishment where they will punch a time clock, a time clock should be used in the classroom. If students are learning skills that comprise a chain of behaviors (e.g., cooking, janitorial skills, etc.), those skills should be presented in the context of naturally occurring routines rather than in isolated multiple-trial training sessions (Kayser, Billingsley, & Neel, 1986). Second, teachers can use simulations of routines that occur in the natural environment (Nietupski, Hamre-Nietupski, Clancy, & Veerhusen, 1986). Nietupski et al. (1986) suggested that simulations can be used concurrently with community-based or in vivo instruction and presented guidelines for using simulations. These guidelines are displayed in Table 17.1.

The third setting manipulation is to use multiple and varied training settings (Guess, 1980). Teaching in multiple settings does not mean instruction must occur in the natural environment; teachers can change the setting within the classroom where instruction is given on particular skills. A number of other environments exist within schools such as hallways, cafeteria, playground, offices, gym, other classrooms, and bus. Students' homes and other community settings such as stores, physicians' offices, and many others are, however, also important training environments.

The fourth setting manipulation is to use multiple and varied trainers. Although no magic number of persons can be identified, Baer (1981) suggested that as few as two may be sufficient in some cases. Numerous persons can serve as trainers including teachers, teacher aides, other students, therapists (e.g., speech, occupational, and physical therapists), parents, and others who interact fre-

TABLE 17.1 Guidelines for Using Simulations

1. Analyze the community setting to identify the range of stimulus and response variations that exist.
2. Vary the simulated training systematically to provide a sufficient range of training examples.
3. Collect data on community performance to plan and implement modifications in the simulated training.
4. Use simulated training to provide intense or repeated practice in problem areas.
5. Schedule simulations so that sufficient training in the natural environment can occur and schedule simulated training in close temporal proximity to training in the natural environment.

Note: Adapted from "Guidelines for Making Simulation an Effective Adjunct to *in vivo* Community Instruction" by J. Nietupski, S. Hamre-Nietupski, P. Clancy, and K. Veerhusen, 1986, *Journal of the Association for Persons with Severe Handicaps, 11,* pp. 12–18.

quently with the student. By using multiple trainers outside of the school, training can occur in multiple settings as well. Teachers may need to train parents and other persons in the students' environment to implement instruction outside of the school. Parents should be trained to (a) expect more complex behaviors from their children, (b) reinforce those behaviors when they occur, and (c) set up situations where students can use newly learned skills. For example, if a student is learning to read, the parents could provide a brief time when the child can read at home, and should encourage him or her to read signs when they are in the community. The incidental teaching and mand-model procedures are appropriate instructional strategies for facilitating generalization (cf., Chapter 11; Hart & Risley, 1974; Rogers-Warren & Warren, 1980). These strategies allow others to teach students without providing structured instructional sessions. They can occur naturally and within the context of other activities. For example, Jan is learning to name numerals and, when shopping with her father, he shows her a price tag and asks her what numeral it is. If she answers correctly, her father reinforces her and they go about their shopping; if she answers incorrectly or says she does not know, her father gives her the answer. Such training is useful in teaching students *when* to apply newly acquired skills.

These four setting variables—teaching in the natural environment, making the instructional setting similar to the generalization setting, using multiple and varied training settings, and using multiple and varied trainers—can be used in combination to facilitate generalization. They are based, however, on a careful analysis of the instructional and generalization setting and on careful planning for generalization training.

Antecedent Variables

Antecedent variables include the examples used in instruction and the teachers' task directions or other comments, prompts, and prompt-fading procedures. As noted in Chapter 14, errorless or near errorless strategies should be used if students cannot learn readily from trial-and-error instruction. Students are more apt to generalize skills they have learned thoroughly and can perform fluently (Guess, 1980). Thus, the errorless teaching procedures should be employed to facilitate thorough learning, and fluency-building strategies should be used to establish fluent responding. However, there are two other variables for facilitating generalization: selecting and presenting examples in instruction.

Selecting Examples for Instruction. First, examples or discriminative stimuli that are likely to be present in the natural environment should be selected for use during instruction (Stokes & Baer, 1977). The systematic use of discriminative stimuli from the natural environment will facilitate generalization (Marholin & Siegel, 1978). For example, if students are being taught to order at a fast-food restaurant, the words the employee says to take the order should be used during instruction. Second, the examples selected should represent the range of possible variations in the natural environment (Sprague & Horner, 1984). For example, rather than teaching Marty to use one vending machine, he should be taught to use several machines that each require some variation in the way coins are inserted and the way selections are made. Third, examples should be selected that are "the best examples" of the concept being taught (Hupp & Mervis, 1981). *Best examples* have many attributes similar to other examples of the concept, look very different from examples of other concepts, and have relevant stimuli that are obvious. For example, if Zenus is being taught to label common objects and "ball" is one of those objects, a one-color playground ball would be better than a multicolored ball, and a completely round ball would be better than a football. Finally, multiple examples should be selected (Stokes & Baer, 1977). Using multiple examples is similar to using multiple trainers and training settings, and appears to prevent students from acquiring restricted stimulus control.

Presenting Examples for Instruction. Once examples/discriminative stimuli have been selected, teachers should present them carefully. As noted in Chapter 11, examples should be presented in distributed rather than massed practice sessions. This means that students should have numerous opportunities throughout the school day to perform the behaviors they are learning. Further, generalization appears to be facilitated when students are taught using concurrent (learning more than one concept at a time) rather than serial instruction (learning one skill and then learning another). For example, when teaching Zenus to label common objects, two or more objects should be taught at the same time rather than having him learn one label and then another. Concurrent instruction may slow initial acquisition, but appears to facilitate generalization. Another strategy is to begin teaching one concept and then introduce other concepts (Cuvo, Klevans, Borakove, Borakove, Van Landuyt, & Lutzker, 1980). Of course, multiple trainers and multiple settings should be used when presenting instruction. Finally, students should be presented with situations where generalization of newly acquired skills is not appropriate (Gelfand & Hartmann, 1984). For example, John previously had learned to boil eggs and his teacher recently taught him to fry eggs. To measure the appropriateness of generalization to other settings, his teacher asked his parents to have him boil eggs one morning and fry eggs on the next morning. To ensure that he uses appropriate materials, the pans and utensils for boiling and frying are all present each morning. Therefore, the teacher can obtain data on whether John generalizes and whether that generalization is appropriate.

Behavior Variables

Some behaviors appear to generalize more easily than others. Skills are more likely to generalize if they (a) are useful to students in other situations, (b) make students more independent, and (c) are likely to be reinforced in the natural environment (Kayser et al., 1986; Marholin & Siegel, 1978). When analyzing generalization settings, teachers should attempt to identify behaviors that meet these criteria. Frequently, two or more behaviors can be used to accomplish the same task. For example, a student who wants a drink of water can point to the sink or water fountain or can ask for a drink. Both behaviors, pointing and asking, will be successful if someone else understands the request; however, asking for a drink is more likely to be understood by more people and may be useful in more settings than pointing. Pointing in a restaurant may not be a successful way to get a glass of water. Similarly, when attempting to move students from restrictive placements to less restrictive placements, the behaviors needed to function appropriately and independently in the less restrictive environments should be identified and then be taught to the student. For example, Ms. Smith has a self-contained class and, when students need help, they get up from their seats and walk over to her. Angela, a student in Ms. Smith's class, has made good progress and is going to be placed in a regular classroom on a part-time basis. When observing the regular classroom, Ms. Smith noted that students were required to remain at their desks and raise their hands if they needed teacher assistance. To help Angela with the transition, Ms. Smith began to teach her to raise her hand when she needs help.

Related to selecting behaviors that are likely to be useful in the generalization environment, teachers should identify behaviors that will interfere with generalization. This recommendation has at least two implications. First, inappropriate social behaviors may interfere with generalization. In such cases, reduction of those inappropriate behaviors is appropriate, and the model described in Chapter 19 should be consulted. Second, some behaviors (appropriate and inappropriate) may compete with the performance of more complex behaviors (Billingsley & Neel, 1985; Matlock, Billingsley, & Thompson, 1985). For example, students who have used inappropriate behavior for communicating or have used less complex communicative responses, may continue to use these behaviors in generalization situations despite the fact that they can perform more complex behaviors in the training session. In such cases, teachers should refrain from reinforcing the less complex behaviors, build the fluency of the more complex target behaviors, and, in rare cases, use behavior-reduction strategies to reduce the occurrence of the less complex behaviors. When dealing with such situations, behaviors should be taught that serve the same function and have the same effect as the inappropriate behavior (cf., Donnellan, Mirenda, Masaros, & Fassbender, 1984). For example, Dennis was using grabbing as a means of making requests for objects. He would grab other students' toys, grab additional snacks, or grab the teacher's arm. A behavior such as patting would be incompatible with grabbing (i.e, one cannot pat and grab at the same time), but it may not serve the same function or have the same effect as grabbing. However, if Dennis were taught to say, "Toy please" or "More please," these responses would likely have the same effect as the grabbing but be more acceptable.

Consequence Variables

A number of reinforcement manipulations appear to facilitate maintenance and generalization of responses. First, natural reinforcers should be used during instruction. Skills are more likely to generalize if reinforcers used during training are similar to those found in the natural environment. Many of the naturally occurring reinforcers are social consequences such as smiles, praise, and eye contact. Thus, teachers should go to considerable lengths to develop social consequences as reinforcers. Second, reinforcement schedules used during the later phases of training should be similar to those found in the generalization environment (Koegel & Rincover, 1977; Marholin & Siegel, 1978). In most cases, the reinforcement schedule in the natural environment is quite lean; as a result, schedules of reinforcement during training should be thinned considerably. Third, delaying reinforcement is another way to facilitate generalization (Fowler & Baer, 1981). For example, reinforcement for appropriate behavior could be provided at the end of the school day rather than after each occurrence of the behavior. Also, decreasing the predictability of consequences will facilitate maintenance and generalization (Baer, Williams, Osnes, & Stokes, 1984; Dunlap & Johnson, 1985). Fourth, teachers should reinforce students when they generalize. Essentially, students should be taught the rule, "When I learn something, I should use it somewhere else." Teaching this rule or way of responding is best done by reinforcing students for generalizing behaviors from one situation to another (Stokes & Baer, 1977). Fifth, reinforcement should be provided in the natural environment when students generalize. Other teachers, parents, and therapists should be told what behaviors are likely to generalize and be encouraged to reinforce their occurrence. After the behavior has been reinforced purposefully a few times in the natural environment, the naturally occurring contingencies can be used.

Finally, Marholin and Siegel (1978) recommended that teachers help students learn to gain control over the reinforcers for their own behaviors. This can be done by teaching students to reinforce themselves or to solicit reinforcement from others. Self-instruction and self-reinforcement strategies (cf., Bandura, 1976; Lovitt & Curtiss, 1968; Meichenbaum & Goodman, 1971) have been taught to students so they control their own reinforcers. In generalization settings where schedules of reinforcement are lean, reinforcement delivery is delayed, or reinforcer strength is weak, self-management behaviors may facilitate generalization. Also, students should be taught to persist in the face of errors (Marholin & Siegel, 1978). For example, if Larry is being taught to mop floors, he should be taught to monitor the effects of his behavior. If he comes to a particularly dirty section of the floor, he must scrub longer and with more force. Simply teaching him to run the mop lightly over the entire floor will not be sufficient.

Summary of Key Concepts

- Generalization occurs when a behavior learned under one set of conditions is displayed in other conditions.

- One of the greatest challenges facing teachers is to develop effective instructional strategies that facilitate generalization.

- Although students learn to do behaviors fluently and accurately, teachers cannot assume that generalization will occur.

- By planning for and measuring generalization or lack thereof, teachers can implement instruction that will facilitate its occurrence.

- When generalization does not occur appropriately, the performance should be analyzed to determine whether (a) performance is under the control of irrelevant stimuli, (b) inappropriate behaviors under the control of irrelevant stimuli are competing with the appropriate behavior, (c) performance is controlled by only a subset of the relevant stimuli, or (d) response variation is too limited.

- To facilitate generalization, teachers can manipulate setting variables, antecedent variables, the behaviors themselves, and consequence variables.

REFERENCES

Baer, D. M. (1981). *How to plan for generalization.* Lawrence, KS: H & H Enterprises.

Baer, R. A., Williams, J. A., Osnes, P. G., & Stokes, T. F. (1984). Delayed reinforcement as an indiscriminable contingency in verbal/nonverbal correspondence training. *Journal of Applied Behavior Analysis, 17,* 429–440.

Bandura, A. (1976). Self-reinforcement: Theoretical and methodological considerations. *Behaviorism, 4,* 135–155.

Billingsley, F. F. (1984). Where are the generalized objectives? (An examination of instructional objectives). *Journal of the Association for Persons with Severe Handicaps, 9,* 186–192.

Billingsley, F. F., & Neel, R. S. (1985). Competing behaviors and their effects on skill generalization and maintenance. *Analysis and Intervention in Developmental Disabilities, 5,* 357–372.

Cuvo, A. J., Klevans, L., Borakove, S., Borakove, L. S., Van Landuyt, J., & Lutzker, J. R. (1980). A comparison of three strategies for teaching object names. *Journal of Applied Behavior Analysis, 13,* 249–257.

Donnellan, A. M., Mirenda, P. L., Mesaros, R. A., & Fassbender, L. L. (1984). Analyzing the communicative functions of aberrant behavior. *Journal of the Association for Persons with Severe Handicaps, 9,* 201–212.

Drabman, R. S., Hammer, D., & Rosenbaum, M. S. (1979). Assessing generalization, in behavior modification with children: The generalization map. *Behavioral Assessment, 1,* 203–219.

Dunlap, G., & Johnson, J. (1985). Increasing the independent responding of autistic children with unpredictable supervision. *Journal of Applied Behavior Analysis, 18,* 227–236.

Fowler, S. A., & Baer, D. M. (1981). "Do I have to be good all day?" The timing of delayed reinforcement as a factor in generalization. *Journal of Applied Behavior Analysis, 14,* 13–24.

Gelfand, D. M., & Hartmann, D. P. (1984). *Child behavior analysis and therapy* (2nd ed.). New York: Pergamon.

Guess, D. (1980). Methods in communication instruction for severely handicapped persons. In W. Sailor, B. Wilcox & L. Brown (Eds.), *Methods of instruction for severly handicapped students* (pp. 195–226). Baltimore, MD: Paul Brookes.

Haring, N., Liberty, K., Billingsley, F., Lynch, V., Kayser, J., & McCarty, F. (Eds.). (1985). *Investigating the problem of skill generalization* (3rd ed.). Seattle: Washington Research Organization.

Hart, B., & Risley, T. (1974). Incidental teaching of language in the preschool. *Journal of Applied Behavior Analysis, 8,* 411–420.

Horner, R. H., Bellamy, G. T., & Colvin, G. T. (1984). Responding in the presence of non-trained stimuli: Implications of generalization error patterns. *Journal of the Association for Persons with Severe Handicaps, 9,* 287–295.

Hupp, S. C., & Mervis, C. B. (1981). Development of generalized concepts by severely handicapped students. *The Journal of the Association for the Severely Handicapped, 6,* 14–21.

Kayser, J. E., Billingsley, F. F., & Neel, R. S. (1986). A comparison of in-context and traditional instructional approaches: Total task, single trial versus backward chaining, multiple trials. *Journal of the Association for Persons with Severe Handicaps, 11,* 28–38.

Kazdin, A. E. (1975). *Behavior modification in applied settings.* Homewood, IL: The Dorsey Press.

Koegel, R. L., & Rincover, A. (1977). Research on the difference between generalization and maintenance in extra-therapy responding. *Journal of Applied Behavior Analysis, 10,* 1–12.

Lovitt, T. C., & Curtiss, K. S. (1968). Effects of manipulating an antecedent event on mathematics response rate. *Journal of Applied Behavior Analysis, 1,* 329–333.

Marholin, D., & Siegel, L. J. (1978). Beyond the law of effect: Programming for the maintenance of behavioral change. In D. Marholin (Ed.), *Child behavior therapy* (pp. 397–415). New York: Gardner Press.

Matlock, B., Billingsley, F. F., & Thompson, M. (1985). Response competition and generalization. In N. Haring, K. Liberty, F. Billingsley, V. Lynch, J. Kayser, & F. McCarty, (Eds.), *Investigating the problem of skill generalization* (3rd ed.) (pp. 80-87). Seattle: Washington Research Organization.

Meichenbaum, D., & Goodman, J. (1971). Training impulsive children to talk to themselves: A means of developing self-control. *Journal of Abnormal Psychology, 77,* 115–126.

Nietupski, J., Hamre-Nietupski, S., Clancy, P., & Veerhusen, K. (1986). Guidelines for making simulation an effective adjunct to in vivo community instruction. *Journal of the Association for Persons with Severe Handicaps, 11,* 12–18.

Rogers-Warren, A., & Warren, S. F. (1980). Mands for verbalization: Facilitating the display of newly trained language in children. *Behavior Modification, 4,* 361–382.

Sanders, M. R., & James, J. E. (1983). The modification of parent behavior: A review of generalization and maintenance. In M. Hersen & A. S. Bellack (Eds.), *Behavior modification* (Vol. 7, No. 1). Beverly Hills, CA: Sage.

Skinner, B. F. (1953). *Science and human behavior.* New York: Macmillan.

Snell, M. E., & Grigg, N. C. (1987). Instructional assessment and curriculum development. In M. E. Snell (Ed.), *Systematic instruction of persons with severe handicaps* (3rd ed.) (pp. 64–109). Columbus, OH: Charles E. Merrill.

Sprague, J. R., & Horner, R. H. (1984). The effects of single instance, multiple instance, and general case training on generalized vending machine use by moderately and severely handicapped students. *Journal of Applied Behavior Analysis, 17,* 273–278.

Stokes, T. F., & Baer, D. M. (1977). An implicit technology of generalization. *Journal of Applied Behavior Analysis, 10,* 349–367.

Stremel-Campbell, K., & Campbell, C. R. (1985). Training techniques that may facilitate generalization. In S. F. Warren & A. K. Rogers-Warren (Eds.), *Teaching functional language: Generalization and maintenance of language skills* (pp. 251–288.) Baltimore: University Park Press.

Wahler, R. G., Breland, R. M., & Coe, T. D. (1979). Generalization processes in child behavior change. In B. Lahey & A. Kazdin (Eds.), *Advances in clinical child psychology* (Vol. 2). New York: Plenum.

Warren, S. F. (1985). Clinical strategies for the measurement of language generalization. In S. F. Warren & A. K. Rogers-Warren (Eds.), *Teaching functional language: Generalization and maintenance of language skills* (pp. 197–221). Baltimore: University Park Press.

Warren, S. F., Rogers-Warren, A., Baer, D. M., & Guess, D. (1980). Assessment and facilitation of language generalization. In W. Sailor, B. Wilcox & L. Brown (Eds.), *Methods of instruction for severely handicapped students* (pp. 227–258). Baltimore: Paul Brookes.

Wehman, P., Abramson, M., & Norman, C. (1977). Transfer of training in behavior modification programs: An evaluative review. *Journal of Special Education, 11,* 217–231.

White, O. R., & Haring, N. G. (1980). *Exceptional teaching* (2nd ed.). Columbus, OH: Charles E. Merrill.

White, O. R., Leber, B. D., & Phifer, C. E. (1985). Training in the natural environment and skill generalization: It doesn't always come naturally. In N. Haring, K. Liberty, F. Billingsley, V. Lynch, J. Kayser, & F. McCarty (Eds.), *Investigating the problem of skill generalization* (3rd ed.) (pp. 63–79). Seattle: Washington Research Organization.

PART V

REDUCING INAPPROPRIATE BEHAVIOR

Although effective teaching will prevent the occurrence of many inappropriate behaviors, some students may display problem behaviors. Applied behavior analysis research has contributed greatly to solving students' behavior problems. Many of the procedures are intrusive strategies and should be used with caution. Chapters 18 through 22 describe these procedures and their appropriate use. Chapter 18 focuses on the defintion of inappropriate behaviors and adopts a normative approach for determining whether a given student's behavior is appropriate or inappropriate in a specific situation. Chapter 18 also includes a definition of punishment and specifies the conditions under which punishment procedures can be employed legitimately.

Chapter 19 provides a decision model for reducing the occurrence of inappropriate behavior. This model is similar to the one presented in Chapter 2, and includes the steps of identifying problem situations, assessing the student and environment, specifying objectives, collecting data, developing intervention strategies, implementing the intervention plan, monitoring students' progress, and evaluating the effects of intervention. Chapter 20 describes procedures for using reinforcement to reduce the occurrence of inappropriate behaviors. This chapter focuses on various types of differential reinforcement such as differential reinforcement of other behaviors, differential reinforcement of low rates of behavior, and differential reinforcement of incompatible or alternative behaviors. The chapter also describes procedures such as vicarious reinforcement, extinction, and response cost. A definition and description, effective use, planning and implementation considerations, and advantages of each procedure are presented.

Chapter 21 defines and describes timeout from positive reinforcement. Types of timeout procedures including nonexclusionary timeout, contingent observation, exclusion timeout, and isolation/seclusion timeout are described. Guidelines for using timeout are presented; specifically, prerequisite steps, planning decisions, and implementation issues are described and illustrated. The chapter concludes with a discussion of suspension from school. A comparison to timeout, legal issues related to suspension, and recommendations concerning its use are provided. Chapter 22 describes the use of aversive stimuli. Punishment is defined and the use of direct, contingent application of aversive stimuli is presented. The types of aversive stimuli used, the findings from such use, and implications are discussed. The types, uses, and effects of overcorrection are addressed. The chapter concludes with a description of corporal punishment as it is practiced in schools. Rationale for and against its use, issues related to its use, and recommendations concerning corporal punishment are provided.

18

DEFINITIONAL AND ETHICAL PROBLEMS RELATED TO BEHAVIOR REDUCTION

Key Terms

■ Normative Approach ■ Behavioral Excesses ■ Behavioral
Deficits ■ Frequency ■ Intensity ■ Duration ■ Latency
■ Inappropriate Stimulus Control ■ Type I Punishment ■ Type II
Punishment ■ Punishment ■ Decision Model ■ Fair Pair
Rule ■ Incompatible Behaviors ■ Replacement Behaviors ■ Side
Effects ■ Informed Consent

One of the most exciting aspects of teaching is seeing students learn and apply what we have taught. Likewise, one of the most disturbing aspects is when students' behavior problems interfere with learning. This chapter defines types of behavior problems, describes general types of intervention strategies, and proposes conditions under which punishment procedures can be ethically used.

CLASSIFYING BEHAVIOR PROBLEMS

Although different perspectives exist for classifying and explaining behavior problems, a **normative approach** appears most defensible. In this approach, an individual's behavior is compared to the norms and limits of acceptable behavior for the environments in which he or she functions. Behavior problems can thus be described in three ways: *behavioral deficits, behavioral excesses,* and *inappropriate stimulus control* (Gelfand & Hartmann, 1984). Understanding each type of behavior problem should help in identifying and using the most appropriate behavior-change strategies.

Behavioral Deficits and Excesses

Some behaviors are problems because they occur too little or too much. **Behavioral excesses** are behaviors that occur too frequently, with too much force, last too long, or are delayed too long after a stimulus. **Behavioral deficits** occur infrequently, with little force, do not last a long time, or occur too quickly after a stimulus. Both excesses and deficits may be described and measured in terms of frequency (rate), intensity (magnitude), duration, or latency.

Frequency refers to how often a behavior occurs. For example, Sharon is capable of speaking, but rarely speaks to others. When teachers ask her direct questions, she looks down and remains silent. Deborah, on the other hand, talks "constantly," interrupts others when they are talking, and speaks out during tests and quiet reading times. Talking is a behavior problem for both students. Nothing is inherently inappropriate about their behavior, talking; the inappropriateness lies in how often it occurs. The literature contains many examples where behavioral excesses and deficits were treated.

Intensity refers to the amount of force with which a behavior is performed. A behavioral deficit of intensity is seen when a behavior occurs *without* sufficient force. For example, a student may not speak loudly enough or may write so lightly that his or her work is illegible. A behavioral excess related to intensity is when a behavior occurs with too much force; for example, a student speaks too loudly or presses so hard with his or her pencil that the letters blend together.

Duration refers to how long a behavior lasts per occurrence. A deficit in duration occurs when a student does not do a behavior for a sufficient length of time such as not sitting in his or her seat long enough. An example of an excess in duration is a student who stays in the bathroom too long or students who take 45 minutes to complete an assignment that should only take 15 minutes.

Latency is the amount of time between the presentation of a stimulus and the initiation of a behavior. The issue here is whether students respond too slowly or too quickly to commands, requests, or other stimuli. A deficit in latency is illustrated by a study conducted with autistic children (Dyer, Christian, & Luce, 1982). The students were taught various discrimination tasks. In one condition, they were allowed to respond as soon as the teacher gave an instruction; for example, the teacher showed them two objects and said, "Point to [and named one object]." In another condition, the teachers gave the task request, held students' hands for about 3 seconds, and then allowed them to respond. The consequent events for correct and error responding were the same in both conditions. Students produced more correct answers and fewer errors when they were required to wait before responding. Their initial responding appeared to be a deficit in latency; they were responding too quickly to attend to the task and make the correct choice. When students wait too long before responding to a stimulus, an excess in latency occurs. For example, when Ms. Barrymore asks the class to put their books away for a test, Shawn invariably waits 5 minutes before he *starts* to put his books away.

Inappropriate Stimulus Control

Deficits and excesses are not the only types of behavior problems. Consider the following examples. Betty, a 16-year-old youth, jumps out of her seat, throws her hands up in the air and claps them loudly, slaps the student next to her on the back, and yells, "All right!" John, also a 16-year-old youth, sits quietly, looks at his book, underlines some passages, writes some notes, glances up occasionally, and then returns to reading his book. Although these two descriptions demonstrate very different behaviors, neither are inherently appropriate nor inappropriate. If Betty is at a basketball game and John is in the library, their behaviors are probably appropriate. However, if the settings are switched, both may be behaving inappropriately. Many of the behaviors teachers consider maladaptive are only inappropriate in the context where they are observed, i.e., **inappropriate stimulus control.** In some other context (stimulus conditions), those behaviors would be appropriate, would not be noticed as unusual, and would seem legitimate. At least three means exist for dealing with problems of inappropriate stimulus control: (1) transferring the control of the behavior from inappropriate stimuli to those that are more appropriate, (2) changing the environment in which the inappropriate behavior is being performed to increase the likelihood of appropriate behavior, and (3) providing prompts (e.g., eye contact with a stern facial expression) to cue students that inappropriate behavior will result in punishing events and appropriate behavior will be reinforced.

Transferring stimulus control means students are taught that the behavior is acceptable under some conditions, but not under others. For example, running and yelling are appropriate on the playground but not in most classrooms. To transfer stimulus control, response prompts (described in Chapter 14) should be used. If the problem behavior is running in the classroom, a response prompt might be telling the student not to run at the beginning of class. When the student enters the room, the teacher could stop him or her, make eye contact, and state, "Don't run in the classroom, run outside on the playground." After a few days of this prompt, its intrusiveness could be faded by only making eye contact as the student enters the class and saying, "Remember, no running in the classroom" or "Remember about running." The fading would continue to the point where running is not mentioned when he or she enters the room. Naturally, the student should be reinforced for walking in the classroom and running on the playground.

Making relatively permanent changes in the classroom environment is a second strategy to increase the likelihood of appropriate behavior. The classroom might be arranged to eliminate long open areas that are conducive to running, signs could be put up that say, "Walk, don't run," and the schedule could be changed to reduce the number of opportunities students have to run.

If the third method were used, the teacher might use a warning (e.g., saying "Slow down") when students were walking too quickly or getting ready to run in the classroom. For such statements to be effective, the students would need previous experiences with either reinforcement for following directions or aversive events when they did not heed such warnings; for example, losing a few minutes of recess.

Rationale for a Normative Classification of Behavior Problems

There are at least four reasons for classifying behavior problems as behavioral excesses, behavioral deficits, or inappropriate stimulus control. First, the type of deficit or excess is one of the factors that helps determine how to measure the behavior. If the teacher wants to decrease the amount of in-class cursing, counting the number of curses (frequency) is more appropriate than timing how long each curse lasts (duration). On the other hand, if the teacher is interested in the amount of time it takes students to complete an assignment, timing the duration of their working behaviors is more appropriate than counting the number of students who completed the assignment.

The second reason for identifying the type of behavior problem is that it may help select the treatment goal and, at times, the general treatment procedure. For example, if the problem is primarily one of inappropriate stimulus control, the goal may be to transfer stimulus control to more appropriate stimuli. The type of treatment might involve response-prompting or environmental modifications. If the problem behavior is a deficit, the treatment goal may be to increase the frequency, latency, or duration of the behavior and the treatment might be to reinforce it in a systematic manner.

Third, by classifying behavior problems as deficits, excesses, and inappropriate stimulus control, we can measure the behaviors of students who do not have the particular behavior problem and set realistic goals for students who do. For example, if a teacher thinks Maria talks too often, he can measure the number of times her classmates speak. If they each talk 2 times in an hour and Maria talks 15 times, the teacher has a clear indication that she talks too often and also has an idea of how often it is appropriate for students to talk. This information allows the teacher to set an appropriate criterion for Maria's objective and also provides a standard against which to compare her performance and progress.

Fourth, by classifying problems in this manner, there is a tendency to view the behavior as a learned entity that is capable of being changed. This decreases the tendency to view maladaptive behavior as something inherent to students or due to some hypothetical, untestable cause. In other words, rather than viewing students as being inappropriate, emotionally disturbed, or "bad," we can view them as having discordant behaviors. Instead of saying Bill is an obnoxious, overbearing, disagreeable student, we can say he displays behaviors (defined specifically for a given context) that occur too frequently or not frequently enough. By viewing inappropriate behavior in this manner, we balance the responsibility for controlling it between the student, the system, and ourselves (teachers), rather than placing the responsibility totally on the student. By balancing the responsibility and recognizing that behavior can be changed, teachers can set about the task of planning interventions to teach appropriate behaviors and reduce the occurrence of inappropriate responses.

Dangers of a Normative Classification of Behavior Problems

Using a normative classification system obviously places considerable emphasis on a society's accepted mores and codes of conduct since an excess is viewed as inappropriate because it is out of keeping with the accepted norms of a given group. The inherent danger in this approach becomes obvious when we consider historical events that were considered socially acceptable and are now viewed as unacceptable. Blatant examples include German soldiers' acceptance of Hitler's treatment of Jewish persons, Americans' tolerance of the enslavement of blacks, teachers' use of excessive corporal punishment in early American education, and society's historic acceptance of inadequate treatment for retarded persons. Because of these instances, it is important for persons involved in planning behavior-reduction programs to justify clearly *why a given behavior has been targeted* and *why the selected procedures will be used* (cf., Wolf, 1978). For example, in addition to saying that a behavior is socially unacceptable and therefore inappropriate, we should ask how modifying the behavior will benefit the student. Teachers must consider many issues when deciding whether to treat a problem behavior, including whether it is developmentally appropriate, is transient, is a result of skill deficits, interferes with learning, causes injury, or poses safety problems.

Another danger of this approach is that teachers may view their responsibility as merely changing the frequency, intensity, duration, latency, or inappropriate stimulus control of maladaptive behaviors. While this is clearly part of our responsibility, students should be taught why their behavior is inappropriate (i.e., the effects or outcomes of their behaviors). They should be taught that hitting is inappropriate because it hurts others, or that yelling in class interferes with others' learning, or running in class poses safety risks. Similarly, if teachers focus only on changing the occurrence of behaviors, they may fail to teach desirable replacement behaviors.

Using a normative classification system does not negate the notion that some behaviors are inherently inappropriate. For example, in nearly all educational settings, injuring students is inappropriate. The classification presented here simply does not make judgments about a behavior being universally appropriate or inappropriate. The point is that teachers need a means of judging whether a behavior is acceptable or unacceptable in a given situation.

INTERVENTION OPTIONS

Many interventions can be used to deal with behavior problems. These interventions can be grouped into two general categories: teaching students to behave appropriately and punishing inappropriate behavior. When selecting intervention strategies, teachers should make the decision based on at least four guidelines. First, the least restrictive and least intrusive but effective strategy should be employed. Second, the procedure that is least likely to harm the student should be used. Third, the social validity or acceptability of the treatment procedure should be considered. Fourth, teachers should identify and consider the factors that appear to maintain the inappropriate behavior. These guidelines are discussed more fully in Chapter 19.

ISSUES RELATED TO REDUCING BEHAVIOR PROBLEMS

In the remainder of this chapter, punishment is defined and the issue of whether or not punishment should be used is discussed. Researchers, teachers, parents, and students hold definite and strong views about the use of punishment. The purpose of this section is to stimulate thought and discussion about its use.

Definition of Punishment

Functional Definition of Punishment. The word *punishment* has many definitions; the one used here is a technical definition. Punishment refers to a functional relationship between a stimulus or event and a decrease in the occurrence of a behavior. As with reinforcers (See Chapter 13), there are two types of punishers (Type I and Type II); both are defined by their presentation and effect on the target behavior. **Type I punishment** is the contingent presentation of an aversive stimulus that results in a decrease in the occurrence of that behavior. When the behavior decreases, the stimulus is said to be aversive. An **aversive stimulus** is one that students avoid and one that is not a positive reinforcer. Corporal punishment fits the presentation pattern of a Type I punishment. That is, it is presented contingent upon the occurrence of a problem behavior; however, before we can say paddling is punishment, it must produce a decrease in the student's behavior. **Type II punishment** is the contingent withdrawal of a reinforcer (i.e., a positive reinforcer is taken away when the behavior occurs) that results in a decrease in the occurrence of a behavior. Assuming that recess is a reinforcer for a given student, staying in at recess whenever an inappropriate behavior occurs would be a Type II punishment procedure. Response cost and timeout are both examples of Type II procedures and are described in Chapters 20 and 21, respectively.

Thus, when the word **punishment** is used in this chapter, it refers to a contingent action (presentation or withdrawal) of a stimulus or contingency *and* a decrease in the likelihood that the target behavior will occur. The public typically does not use this definition. When people discuss punishment, they only refer to the contingent presentation of aversive stimuli; its effect on behavior is not considered. Thus, when discussing punishment procedures, it is important to recognize that others may be using a different definition. Because of this definitional problem, Evans and Meyer (1985) suggested the use of the term *negative consequences* rather than *punishment;* however, this term also has multiple meanings. Since it does not solve the communication problem, we have chosen to use *punishment* in its technical and functional sense.

Individual Nature of Punishing Stimuli. As with reinforcers, punishers must be individually identified for each student. A stimulus or event that serves as a punisher for one student may have no effect on the behavior of another student and may actually be a reinforcer for yet another. For example, being made to take a puff of a cigarette contingent upon a given behavior would likely produce very different effects for people who smoke and those who do not. The cigarette may be a reinforcer for persons who smoke and a punisher for those who do not. Teachers cannot assume that a punisher that has worked with one student will automatically work with another. Further, repeated presentations of an aversive stimulus may result in students becoming desensitized to it. When this occurs, the reductive effect of the stimulus will be lost. Some stimuli (e.g., contingent electric shock), because of their extreme aversiveness, appear to be punishers for most people; however, many of the more acceptable stimuli that we assume have punishing properties (e.g., writing sentences, running laps, etc.) may in reality have very different effects for individual children.

Use of Punishment Procedures

Because of the nature of punishment procedures, it is important to question their use. Perhaps the most basic question is, "Should punishment be used?" As noted in the following quotations, this question has not been satisfactorily answered.

> We do not recognize the necessity of using intrusive interventions to modify even severe excess behaviors. (Evans, Meyer, Derer, & Hanashiro, 1985, p. 48)

> Punishment and aversive procedures continue to have a place, albeit a very narrow place, in special education programs . . . it will always be the intervention of necessity rather than choice for the educator. (Wood, 1978, p. 121–122)

> *Resolved: punishment belongs in educational programs for disturbed children and youth.* It belongs, but doesn't belong, it works, but it doesn't work, it is necessary, but it is not necessary, it is harmful, but it is not harmful, it is worth it, but it is not worth it. (Hewett, 1978, p. 116)

Answering the question, "Should punishment be used?" requires consideration of empirical (scientific), ethical/moral, and personal issues. Because experts clearly disagree on whether punishment procedures should be used, the more practical question perhaps is, "If punishment is acceptable, when and under what circumstances should it be employed?" Professionals and professional organizations have attempted to answer this question. The positions taken by two different professional organizations are shown in Tables 18.1 and 18.2. Table 18.1 gives the position of The Association for Persons with Severe Handicaps (TASH) and deals with the use of intrusive interventions, including punishment procedures. Table 18.2 lists the recommendations of the Association for the Advancement of Behavior Therapy (AABT) and deals with the treatment of self-injurious behavior.

The TASH resolution clearly limits the use of many punishment procedures; on the other hand, the AABT recommendations suggest that punishment can be used for treating self-injury if certain conditions are met.

TABLE 18.1 Recommendations on the Use of Punishment Procedures by The Association for Persons with Severe Handicaps (TASH)

Resolution by The Association for Persons with Severe Handicaps (Passed, October, 1981)

WHEREAS, in order to realize the goals and objectives of The Association for Persons with Severe Handicaps, including the right of each severely handicapped person to grow, develop, and enjoy life in integrated and normalized community environments, the following resolution is adopted:

WHEREAS, educational and other habilitative services must employ instructional and management strategies which are consistent with the right of each individual with severe handicaps to an effective treatment which does not compromise the equal important right to freedom from harm. This requires educational and habilitative procedures free from indiscriminate use of drugs, aversive stimuli, environmental deprivation, or exclusion from service; and

WHEREAS, TASH supports a cessation of the use of any treatment option which exhibits some or all of the following characteristics: (1) obvious signs of physical pain experienced by the individual; (2) potential or actual physical side effects, including tissue damage, physical illness, severe stress, and/or death, that would properly require the involvement of medical personnel; (3) dehumanization of persons with severe handicaps because the procedures are normally unacceptable for nonhandicapped persons in community environment; (4) extreme ambivalence and discomfort by family, staff, and/or caregivers regarding the necessity of such extreme strategies or their own involvement in such interventions; and (5) obvious repulsion and/or stress felt by nonhandicapped peers and community members who cannot reconcile extreme procedures with acceptable standard practice;

RESOLVED, that The Association for Persons with Severe Handicaps' resources and expertise be dedicated to the development, implementation, evaluation, dissemination, and advocacy of educational and management practices which are appropriate for use in integrated environments which are consistent with the commitment to a high quality of life for individuals with severe handicaps.

Note: From "Resolution on Intrusive Interventions" by The Association for Persons with Severe Handicaps, 1985, *TASH Newsletter, 11* (November) p. 3. Copyright 1985 by The Association for Persons with Severe Handicaps. Reprinted by permission.

TABLE 18.2 Summary of Recommendations of the Task Force Concerning Treatment of Self-Injury Sponsored by the Association for Advancement of Behavior Therapy (AABT)

■ The identification of biological and environmental conditions which may maintain the client's self-injury and the explicit inclusion of that information in the design of treatment. Such an analysis should include identification of medical conditions which may contribute to the problem, environmental situations which regularly evoke the behavior, and the consequences of self-injury which may be reinforcing it.

■ The deliberate teaching and reinforcement of noninjurious, appropriate behavior. Such behavioral alternatives to self-injury may include communication, cooperation with tasks, independent leisure, and social skills.

■ The identification and discontinuation of reinforcers for self-injurious behavior, typically by arranging conditions so that caretakers can safely and consistently minimize reactions to the behavior which might be inadvertently reinforcing it.

■ The establishment and provision of overall stimulus conditions which are associated with noninjurious behavior (such as through environmental enrichment), and the alteration or elimination of environmental conditions which are regularly associated with self-injury (such as situations which are unnecessarily frustrating or nonreinforcing).

■ In cases where the behavior is dangerous, interferes excessively with habilitative or humanizing activities, or has failed to improve when treated with the less intrusive procedures outlined above, a punishing consequence such as overcorrection, or in extremely severe cases, shock for self-injury may also be necessary.

■ The provision for generalizing improvements into all environments in which the individual lives and for maintaining improvement over time.

Note: From "The Treatment of Self-Injurious Behavior" by J. E. Favell, N. H. Azrin, A. A. Baumeister, E. G. Carr, M. F. Dorsey, R. Forehand, R. M. Foxx, O. I. Lovaas, A. Rincover, T. R. Risley, R. G. Romanczyk, D. C. Russo, S. R. Schroeder, and J. V. Solnick, 1982, *Behavior Therapy, 13,* p. 545. Copyright 1982 by The Association for Advancement of Behavior Therapy. Reprinted by permission.

Nearly all professionals agree that indiscriminate, unplanned, careless, and unmonitored use of punishment is totally unacceptable and indefensible. In our view, the minimal acceptable conditions under which punishment procedures can be considered and employed include:

1. Systematic use of a decision model.

2. Careful assessment of factors that are maintaining the behavior (Durand & Carr, 1985; Iwata, Dorsey, Slifer, Bauman, & Richman, 1982) and its communicative function (Donnellan, Mirenda, Mesaros, & Fassbender, 1984).

3. Use of assessment data in planning interventions (Evans & Meyer, 1985; Favell et al., 1982; Iwata et al., 1982).

4. Deliberate and concentrated attempts to teach and reinforce adaptive behaviors including replacement behaviors (Evans & Meyer, 1985; Favell et al., 1982; White & Haring, 1980).

5. Reliable measurement of the target behaviors (Gaylord-Ross, 1980) and of treatment implementation (Billingsley, White, & Munson, 1980).

6. Periodic monitoring of the side effects of intervention (Doke, Wolery, & Sumberg, 1983).

7. Attention to the maintenance and generalization of adaptive outcomes (Favell et al., 1982).

8. Informed consent from parents and administrative authorities (Evans & Meyer, 1985; Favell et al., 1982).

9. Prior peer review of the intervention plan (Favell et al., 1982).

10. Open implementation of the intervention (Favell et al., 1982).

11. Implementation of aversive procedures by a competent team of professionals (Wood & Braaten, 1983).

A description of each of these minimally acceptable conditions is provided in the following paragraphs.

Systematic Use of a Decision Model. **A decision model** is a series of questions and steps designed to guide teachers' actions. Use of a decision model ensures that appropriate planning, consideration of relevant issues, and objective analysis will occur prior to using punishment procedures. Evans and Meyer (1985) and Gaylord-Ross (1980) recommended decision models that include assessment of the function of the target behaviors, assessment of medical causes, implementation of environmental changes and curricular modifications prior to the use of other procedures, development of adaptive behaviors, and use of less intrusive naturalistic interventions. Implied in each model is data collection, consideration of the social validity of the procedures, and revision of the intervention if it is ineffective. Another decision model is described in Chapter 19.

Another reason for using a decision model is that potential legal or administrative action may be taken against teachers who employ aversive procedures. In such cases, the outcome frequently will be based, in large part, on whether teachers acted in a "reasonable" fashion. In fact, some laws, regulations, and guidelines related to the control of students' behavior state that professionals should use reasonable judgment in making decisions. Wood and Lakin (1978) cited Kallan's (1971) four tests of reasonableness:

1. Was the rule being enforced reasonable?

2. Was the form and extent of the force reasonable in light of the type of offense committed by the pupil?

3. Was the form and extent of the force reasonable in light of the pupil's age and known physical condition?

4. Did the teacher act without malice or personal ill will toward the pupil? (pp. 8–9)

Using a decision model will assist teachers in making a case for the reasonableness of their actions. Having to be aware of such concerns may appear distasteful but, in a litigious society, competent professionals must be aware of potential liabilities. Control of students' behavior deals with issues much greater than teacher-student interactions; it raises legal, ethical, and moral questions.

Careful Assessment of Factors that Are Maintaining the Behavior Including Its Communicative Function. Assessment of functional relationships between the target behavior, environmental stimuli, and setting events is especially important when aversive procedures are employed. If environmental stimuli and setting events appear to be causing the inappropriate behavior, changing the stimulus or setting event rather than punishing the student for responding to those events is a defensible action (Evans & Meyer, 1985). For example, LeRon is aggressive when he gets hungry and his class goes to lunch at 12:45; taking him to lunch earlier in the day is more defensible than punishing him for being aggressive. Likewise, careful assessment of the comunicative functions of aberrant behaviors is critical (cf., Donnellan et al., 1984; Durand & Carr, 1985). Punishment procedures teach students when not to do the target behavior rather than teaching them what to do. If the student consistently uses an inappropriate behavior for a specific communicative function, elimination of the behavior will not eliminate the need to communicate that function. For example, Teresa is a nonverbal student with severe handicaps. She pushes people away when she wants them to stop interacting with her (protesting function); she uses pushing to say, "Stop." Although the pushing is undesirable, using a punishment procedure may result in her using a more aberrant behavior such as self-injury to communicate her protests. Teachers should specify a hypothesis (testable explanation) about what is causing or maintaining the problem behavior, and develop an intervention strategy based on that hypothesis.

Use of Assessment Information when Planning Interventions. Hypotheses about variables that appear to maintain inappropriate behavior should be used in the selection and implementation of interventions (Donnellan et al., 1984). For example, if a maladaptive behavior is being maintained by escape from tasks (cf., Carr, Newsom, & Binkoff, 1976, 1980), the treatment should be designed to (a) teach the student an adaptive means of requesting task termination, (b) increase the reinforcement for remaining at the task, and/or (c) use instructional strategies that decrease the aversiveness of the task. Likewise, if a student's disruptive behavior is positively reinforced by peers, attempts to use planned ignoring by the teacher will be ineffective. In this case, the teacher should investigate procedures that allow peer reinforcement to be presented for adaptive behaviors or consider procedures that would successfully compete with the peer reinforcement.

Deliberate and Concentrated Attempts to Teach and Reinforce Adaptive Behavior Including Replacement Behaviors. Careful specification of both desirable and problem behaviors should occur prior to using punishment procedures. White and Haring (1980) described the simultaneous identification of objectives for adaptive and maladaptive behaviors, as the **fair pair rule.** In other words, if a behavior is going to be decreased, then another behavior should be increased. Ideally, the adaptive behavior should be incompatible with the problem behavior. **Incompatible behaviors** are those that physically cannot be done when the behavior problem is performed. For example, sitting is incompatible with standing; it is physically impossible to do both. Evans and Meyer (1985) suggested teaching "equal power" replacement behaviors. **Replacement behaviors** are responses that produce the same effect on the environment as the inappropriate behavior. In addition to replacement behaviors, other adaptive behaviors should be taught that will result in the student being more competent or independent.

Reliable Measurement of the Target Behaviors and of Treatment Implementation. Collection of data on adaptive and maladaptive behaviors is a prerequisite for the use of punishment procedures. Data collection serves at least three functions: (a) it provides a record of attempts to control the inappropriate behavior, (b) it allows teachers to determine whether the intervention is working, and (c) it can be used to make decisions about what to change if the treatment is ineffective. Data collection should be reliable. Two observers should be able to watch the student and have a high percentage of agreement about when the behavior is occurring. Although interobserver agreement data may be difficult to collect, those data are important if the teacher must present them to review or professional groups. In addition, the data must be reviewed and analyzed formatively; simply collecting the data is not sufficient. Teachers must use data to make decisions about the intervention.

Data should also be collected on how consistently the intervention is implemented. Inconsistent implementation of punishment procedures will likely produce undesirable results. Implementation measurement can be done using procedural reliability (Billingsley et al., 1980), which is assessed by observing and recording the actual implementation of the procedure and comparing that to the written implementation plan.

Periodic Monitoring of Intervention Side Effects. When punishment and other intrusive interventions (e.g., negative reinforcement) are used, numerous effects are possible; these have been referred to as *multiple effects* (Epstein, 1985; Rincover, 1981) or **side effects** (Lichstein & Schreibman, 1976). Some of these effects are adaptive and desirable, but others are maladaptive and undesirable. Balsam and Bondy (1983) divided negative side effects into three types: elicited, operant, and imitation. The *elicited effects* include (a) emotional responses such as crying (Bucher & Lovaas, 1968) or "fear reactions" (Bucher & King, 1971) when the punishment is used or the punishing stimulus is seen; (b) aggressive reactions, either toward the person administering the punishment, the punishing stimulus itself, or other persons; and (c) ritualistic, inflexible, obsessive. and/or compulsive behaviors. *Operant effects* include (a) escape, particularly from the persons who applied the punishment and frequently after a punishment episode; (b) avoidance, where the student attempts to minimize the interactions with the punisher or the situation where punishment occurred; (c) specificity of effects, where the punishment may result in a reduction of the behavior only in situations where the procedure was used; (d) general reduction effects, where the punishment results in a reduction of a number of both inappropriate and appropriate behaviors; (e) the wrong behavior effect, where, for example, students who are punished for an inappropriate interactive behavior learn that all interactions are being punished; and (f) temporary effects, where the behavior may recur (perhaps at higher rates or more intense levels) when the punishment is withdrawn. *Imitation effects* occur when teachers model behaviors they do not want students to imitate such as yelling or hitting. When implementing many punishment procedures, teachers may model behaviors that would be inappropriate if one student did them to another.

Not all intervention side effects are undesirable. Increases have been found in cooperativeness, alertness, affection-seeking (Lovaas, Freitag, Gold, & Kassorla, 1965), eye contact, smiling, and hugging (Lovaas & Simmons, 1969). Increases in participation in planned activities and decreases in untreated maladaptive behaviors also may occur (Doke et al., 1983). Further, increases in play behavior (Epstein, Doke, Sajwaj, Sorrell, & Rimmer, 1974; Koegel, Firestone, Kramme, & Dunlap, 1974) and discrimination performance have been noted when students' maladaptive behaviors were punished (Koegel & Covert, 1972).

The appropriateness or inappropriateness of side effects should be assessed in terms of their function as well as their topography. For example, Collene and Matthew are both being punished with timeout. As they are sent to timeout, they both smile—Collene in defiance and Matthew in an attempt to soften the resolve of the teacher who is administering the punishment. The manner in which these students display this side-effect behavior may influence subsequent implementations of timeout. The teacher may send Collene to timeout for more minor infractions of the rules to assert his authority and he may be more hesitant to send Matthew to timeout. In both cases, consistent implementation of the timeout intervention is at risk.

Monitoring for side effects allows teachers to reinforce positive outcomes and develop alternative plans for negative ones. While the occurrence of negative side effects is not sufficient reason to stop punishment procedures, their potential harm is sufficient to warrant careful monitoring and the development of plans to deal with them.

Attention Given to Maintenance and Generalization of Adaptive Outcomes. Although behaviors can be controlled in the treatment situation, many times control also is needed in other situations. However, a recurring finding is that generalization and maintenance of positive changes do not necessarily occur (Rutherford & Nelson, in press; Stokes & Baer, 1977). Several strategies can be devised to facilitate maintenance and generalization; these were discussed in Chapters 16 and 17.

Informed Consent from Parents and Administrative Authorities. All objectives and teaching methods on students' Individualized Education Programs (IEPs) should be developed with, and approved by, parents; punishment procedures, however, require specific consent. Parents should be told and shown how a punishment procedure will be used; they should be given sufficient opportunities to ask questions; they should give expressed written consent; and they should understand that they can stop the use of the procedure at any time. Using a problem-solving approach to involve parents increases the likelihood that they will ask questions and make relevant suggestions concerning the development of a reduction program. Barton, Brulle, and Repp (1983) stated that **informed consent** should include the following elements:

> (a) an accurate description to the client of the treatment procedure; (b) a description of and data from non-aversive treatment procedures that have been previously implemented (i.e., aversive procedures should be used only after other techniques have failed); (c) a justification for the proposed treatment program; (d) baseline data and recording procedures; (e) the anticipated behavioral outcome and the expected termination date for the program; (f) the qualifications of persons who will be implementing the procedure; and (g) the written consent and review of the Human Rights Committee, if such committee is impaneled. (p. 2)

Cook, Altman, and Haavik (1978) provided a model consent form for use in cases where aversive procedures are being considered.

In addition to obtaining parental consent, the teachers should obtain approval from the appropriate human subjects review committees. If an agency does not have such a committee, administrators should be thoroughly briefed on the proposed procedure and give their consent for its use. Prior to planning punishment interventions, the teacher should review the agency's policies related to aversive procedures. Some procedures are illegal in particular agencies and states. If policies do not exist, the agency should develop them. Wood and Braaten (1983) and Repp and Deitz (1978) raised important considerations for the development of such policies. Some agencies and organizations have elaborate policies and guidelines addressing the use of behavior-reduction procedures (e.g., May et al., 1975). Although such guidelines pose certain dangers such as long delays in the implementation of treatment and potential restriction of innovation (cf., Sajwaj, 1977; Stolz, 1977), some evidence suggests that aversive procedures may be planned more carefully and used less when workable guidelines are in place (Nolley et al., 1980).

Prior Peer Review of the Intervention Plan. It is always desirable to obtain peer review of punishment procedures prior to using them. At a minimum, use of a punishment procedure is a teacher decision. However, Evans and Meyer (1985) suggested that consultation and review be obtained from other professionals who work in similar situations with comparable populations. These persons may provide unique perspectives on the problem and suggest less intrusive procedures. Finally, peer review can be obtained by consulting with experts in the field.

Open Implementation of the Intervention. Open implementation means that parents and other responsible professionals have the right and opportunity to observe the procedure being used, are able to review the progress, and can make suggestions and evaluative comments. Conducting punishment interventions in an open fashion is important from at least two perspectives. First, others are allowed to observe the procedure, make suggestions, and express reservations, which in turn may produce more efficient implementation, less intrusive but effective alternatives, and fewer undesirable side effects. Second, it allows some measure of protection and accountability for the teacher. If procedures are implemented in the open, the teacher may be less susceptible to false accusations of abuse or maltreatment.

Implementation of Aversive Procedures by a Competent Team of Professionals. Although the public is familiar with punishment, appropriate use of punishment procedures requires more than general familiarity. Punishment is a complex functional relationship between environmental stimuli/contingencies and students' behavior. Several reasons exist for ensuring the competence of persons who use punishment procedures. First, the likelihood of the procedure being successful is increased if persons administering the program are well trained. Second, the probability that students will be abused during punishment is decreased. Third, competent persons will be better able to detect negative and positive side effects of the procedures and recognize when adjustments in the program should be made. Fourth, persons who are competent in the use of the procedures can better anticipate and explain the potential effects to others, including the student, parents, and administrative authorities. Fifth, persons with specific training and competence in teaching and learning will be better able to select effective, less intrusive procedures. Similarly, they will be more likely to identify testable explanations that appear to be causing or maintaining the occurrence of the aberrant behavior.

Summary of Key Concepts

- When classified by a normative approach, behavior problems can be identified as behavioral excesses and deficits in frequency, latency, duration, and intensity (magnitude).
- Behavior problems also can be classified by inappropriate stimulus control.
- *Punishment* is defined as the contingent action (presentation or withdrawal) of a stimulus or contingency *and* a decrease in the likelihood that the target behavior will occur.
- Two types of punishment exist—Type I and Type II. Type I is the contingent presentation of an aversive stimulus that results in a decrease in the occurrence of a behavior. Type II is the contingent withdrawal of a

positive reinforcer that results in a decrease in the occurrence of a behavior.

■ Stimuli that serve as punishers vary from one individual to another.

■ Experts do not agree on the appropriateness of punishment in educational settings.

■ The minimal acceptable conditions under which punishment can occur are as follows:

☐ Systematic use of a decision model.

☐ Careful assessment of factors that are maintaining the behavior and its communicative function.

☐ Use of assessment data in planning interventions.

☐ Deliberate and concentrated attempts to teach and reinforce adaptive behaviors including replacement behaviors.

☐ Reliable measurement of the target behaviors and of treatment implementation.

☐ Periodic monitoring of the side effects of intervention.

☐ Attention given to the maintenance and generalization of adaptive outcomes.

☐ Informed consent from parents and administrative authorities.

☐ Prior peer review of the intervention plan.

☐ Open implementation of the intervention.

☐ Implementation of aversive procedures by a competent team of professionals.

REFERENCES

Balsam, P. D., & Bondy, A. S. (1983). The negative side effects of reward. *Journal of Applied Behavior Analysis, 16,* 283–296.

Barton, L. E., Brulle, A. R., & Repp, A. C. (1983). Aversive techniques and the doctrine of the least restrictive alternative. *Exceptional Education Quarterly, 4*(3), 1–8.

Billingsley, F. F., White, O. R., & Munson, R. (1980). Procedural reliability: A rationale and an example. *Behavioral Assessment, 2,* 229–241.

Bucher, B., & King, L. W. (1971). Generalization of punishment effects in the deviant behavior of a psychotic child. *Behavior Therapy, 2,* 31–37.

Bucher, B., & Lovaas, O. I. (1968). Use of aversive stimulation in behavior modification. In M. R.

Jones (Ed.), *Miami symposium on the prediction of behavior, 1967: Aversive stimulation* (pp. 77–147). Coral Gables, FL: University of Miami Press.

Carr, E. G., Newsom, C. D., & Binkoff, J. A. (1976). Stimulus control of self-destructive behavior in a psychotic child. *Journal of Abnormal Child Psychology, 4,* 139–153.

Carr, E. G., Newsom, C. D., & Binkoff, J. A. (1980). Escape as a factor in the aggressive behavior of two retarded children. *Journal of Applied Behavior Analysis, 13,* 101–117.

Cook, J. W., Altman, K., & Haavik S. (1978). Consent for aversive treatment: A model form. *Mental Retardation, 16,* 47–51.

Doke, L. A., Wolery, M., & Sumberg, C. (1983).

Effects and side-effects of response contingent ammonia spirits in treating chronic aggression. *Behavior Modification, 7,* 531–556.

Donnellan, A. M., Mirenda, P. L., Mesaros, R. A., & Fassbender, L. L. (1984). Analyzing the communicative functions of aberrant behavior. *Journal of the Association for Persons with Severe Handicaps, 9,* 201–212.

Durand, V. M, & Carr, E. G. (1985). Self-injurious behavior: Motivating conditions and guidelines for treatment. *School Psychology Review, 14*(2) 171–176.

Dyer, K., Christian, W. P., & Luce, S. C. (1982). The role of response delay in improving the discrimination performance of autistic children. *Journal of Applied Behavior Analysis, 15,* 231–240.

Epstein, L. H., Doke, L. A., Sajwaj, T. E., Sorrell, S. & Rimmer, B. (1974). Generality and side effects of overcorrection. *Journal of Applied Behavior Analysis, 7,* 385–390.

Epstein, R. (1985). The positive side effects of reinforcement: A commentary on Balsam and Bondy (1983). *Journal of Applied Behavior Analysis, 18,* 73–78.

Evans, I., & Meyer, L. (1985). *An educative approach to behavior problems: A practical decision model for interventions with severely handicapped learners.* Baltimore: Paul Brookes.

Evans, I., Meyer, L., Derer, K. R., & Hanashiro, R. Y. (1985). An overview of the decision model. In I. Evans & L. Meyer (Eds.), *An educative approach to behavior problems: A practical decision model for interventions with severely handicapped learners* (pp. 43–61). Baltimore: Paul Brookes.

Favell, J. E., Azrin, N. H., Baumeister, A. A., Carr, E. G., Dorsey, M. F., Forehand, R., Foxx, R. M., Lovaas, O. I., Rincover, A., Risley, T. R., Romanczyk, R. G., Russo, D. C., Schroeder, S. R., & Solnick, J. V. (1982). The treatment of self-injurious behavior. *Behavior Therapy, 13,* 529–554.

Gaylord-Ross, R. (1980). A decision model for the treatment of aberrant behavior in applied settings. In W. Sailor, B. Wilcox, & L. Brown, (Eds.), *Methods of instruction for severely handicapped students* (pp. 135–158). Baltimore: Paul Brookes.

Gelfand, D. M., & Hartmann, D. P. (1984). *Child behavior analysis and therapy* (2nd ed.). (pp. 26–28). New York: Pergamon Press.

Hewett, F. M. (1978). Punishment and educational programs for behaviorally disordered and emotionally disturbed children and youth: A personal perspective. In F. H. Wood & K. C. Lakin (Eds.), *Punishment and aversive stimulation in special education: Legal, theoretical and practical issues in their use with emotionally disturbed children and youth* (pp. 119–122). Minneapolis. MN: Advanced Training Institute.

Iwata, B. A., Dorsey, M. F., Slifer, K. J., Bauman, K. E., & Richman, G. S. (1982). Toward a functional analysis of self-injury. *Analysis and Intervention in Development Disabilities, 2*(3), 3–20.

Kallan, L. (1971). *Teachers' rights and liabilities under the law.* New York: Arco Publishing.

Koegel, R. L., & Covert, A. (1972). The relationship of self-stimulation to learning in autistic children. *Journal of Applied Behavior Analysis, 5,* 381–387.

Koegel, R. L., Firestone, P. B., Kramme, K. W., & Dunlap, G. (1974). Increasing spontaneous play by suppressing self-stimulation in autistic children. *Journal of Applied Behavior Analysis, 7,* 521–528.

Lichstein, K. L., & Schreibman, L. (1976). Employing electric shock with autistic children: A review of the side effects. *Journal of Autism and Childhood Schizophrenia, 6,* 163–173.

Lovaas, O. I., Freitag, G., Gold, V. J., & Kassorla, I. C. (1965). Experimental studies in childhood schizophrenia: Analysis of self-destructive behavior. *Journal of Experimental Child Psychology, 2,* 67–84.

Lovaas, O. I., & Simmons, J. Q. (1969). Manipulation of self-destruction in three retarded children. *Journal of Applied Behavior Analysis, 2,* 143–157.

May, J. G., Risley, T. R., Twardosz, S., Friedman, P. Bijou, S. W., & Wexler, D. (1975). Guidelines for the use of behavioral procedures in state programs for retarded persons. *M. R. Research, 1.*

Nolley, D., Boelkins, D., Kocur, L., Moore, M. K., Goncalves, S., & Lewis, M. (1980). Aversive conditioning within laws and guidelines in a state facility for mentally retarded individuals. *Mental Retardation, 18,* 295–298.

Repp, A. C., & Deitz, D. E. D. (1978). Ethical issues in reducing responding of institutionalized mentally retarded persons. *Mental Retardation, 16,* 45–46.

Rincover, A. (1981). Some directions for analysis and intervention in developmental disabilities. *Analysis and Intervention in Developmental Disabilities, 1,* 109–115.

Rutherford, R. B., Jr., & Nelson, C. M. (in press). Applied behavior analysis in education: Generalization and maintenance. In J. C. Witt, S. N. Elliott, & F. M. Gresham (Eds.), *Handbook of behavior therapy in education.* New York: Plenum.

Sajwaj, T. (1977). Issues and implications of establishing guidelines for the use of behavioral techniques. *Journal of Applied Behavior Analysis, 10,* 531–540.

Stokes, T. F., & Baer, D. M. (1977). An implicit technology of generalization. *Journal of Applied Behavior Analysis, 10,* 349–367.

Stolz, S. B. (1977). Why no guidelines for behavior modification? *Journal of Applied Behavior Analysis, 10,* 541–547.

White, O. R., & Haring, N. G. (1980). *Exceptional teaching* (2nd ed.). Columbus, OH: Charles E. Merrill.

Wolf, M. M. (1978). Social validity: The case for subjective measurement or how applied behavior analysis is finding its heart. *Journal of Applied Behavior Analysis, 11,* 203-214.

Wood, F. H. (1978). Punishment and special education: Some concluding comments. In F. H. Wood & K. C. Lakin (Eds.), *Punishment and aversive stimulation in special education; Legal, theoretical and practical issues in their use with emotionally disturbed children and youth* (pp. 119–122). Minneapolis, MN: Advanced Training Institute.

Wood, F. H., & Braaten, S. (1983). Developing guidelines for the use of punishing interventions in the schools. *Exceptional Education Quarterly, 4*(3), 68–75.

Wood, F. H., & Lakin, K. C. (1978). The legal status of the use of corporal punishment and other aversive procedures in schools. In F. H. Wood & K. C. Lakin (Eds.), *Punishment and aversive stimulation in special education: Legal, theoretical and practical issues in their use with emotionally disturbed children and youth* (pp. 3–27). Minneapolis, MN: Advanced Training Institute.

19

DECISION MODEL FOR REDUCING THE OCCURRENCE OF INAPPROPRIATE BEHAVIORS

Key Terms

- Decision Model ■ Behavior ■ Incompatible Adaptive Behavior ■ Equal-Power Replacement Behaviors ■ Assessment ■ Functional Relationship ■ Testable Explanation ■ Explanatory Fiction ■ Functional Analysis ■ Setting Events ■ Discriminative Stimuli ■ Consequent Events ■ Analogue Assessment ■ Communicative Functions ■ Discrepancy Analysis ■ Restrictiveness ■ Intrusiveness ■ Parsimony ■ Least Dangerous Assumption ■ Social Validity ■ Acceptability

The process for reducing the occurrence of inappropriate behaviors is similar to systematic teaching. It includes assessment, planning, implementation, and evaluation. However, more attention must be given to the social acceptability of the goals, treatments, and outcomes as well as to the occurrence of undesirable side effects. Society is interested in whether and how teachers control behaviors as well as in what and how they teach; therefore, teachers should use a decision model to plan, implement, and evaluate their behavior-reduction interventions. A **decision model** is a series of questions and steps designed to guide teachers' actions. The model presented in this chapter is similar but not identical to other behavior reduction models (cf., Evans & Meyer, 1985; Gaylord-Ross, 1980; Lynch, McGuigan, & Shoemaker, 1983). The general model, which was described in Chapter 1, contains eight major steps which are listed in Table 19.1.

TABLE 19.1　Major Steps of the Process Model for Reducing the Occurrence of Behavior

1. Identify the Problem Situation and State It in Goal Format.
2. Assess the Student and Environment to Determine Whether a Behavior Problem Exists.
3. Specify the Objectives.
4. Plan and Collect Baseline Data.
5. Select and Plan a Suitable Intervention.
6. Implement the Intervention Plan.
7. Monitor the Student's Progress.
8. Evaluate Progress at Specific Intervals.

STEP 1: IDENTIFICATION OF PROBLEM SITUATIONS

The substeps of the first major step of the model are shown in Figure 19.1. These substeps focus on identifying problem situations, determining the type of behavior problem that exists, and stating the problem in a goal format.

Identifying Problem Situations

The first substep is to identify potential problem situations. Many behavior problems identify themselves (e.g., aggressive, self-injurious, and some disruptive behaviors). In such instances, teachers should begin to determine what type of behavior problem is present. However, not all problem situations are obvious. Teachers should systematically and regularly review their students' performance to answer the question, "Does a problem situation exist?" This question, as shown in Figure 19.1, prompts many additional questions.

An important indicator of whether a problem exists is *lack of progress on students' instructional objectives* (Etzel & LeBlanc, 1979). Although students can make progress and present behavior problems, the lack of progress suggests problems are present or may be developing. Lack of progress also may be due to poorly designed instruction; thus, it alone is insufficient evidence for concluding that a problem exists. Closely related to lack of progress is *whether students complete the tasks or assignments they receive.* Failure to complete activities may indicate a need for further assessment.

Another question is *whether students rely on adults for unnecessary assistance.* This situation is seen when students ask for another explantion, ask questions that have just been answered, ask for help, and do not complete tasks. For younger and severely handicapped students, it can take the form of waiting for teachers' prompts, not attempting new tasks, not responding after errors, doing tasks slowly, and having long latencies after instructions. Such behaviors indicate a lack of independence and may result in learned helplessness. *Learned helplessness* occurs

FIGURE 19.1 Step 1 of the decision model for behavior reduction: identifying problem situations and stating them in goal format.

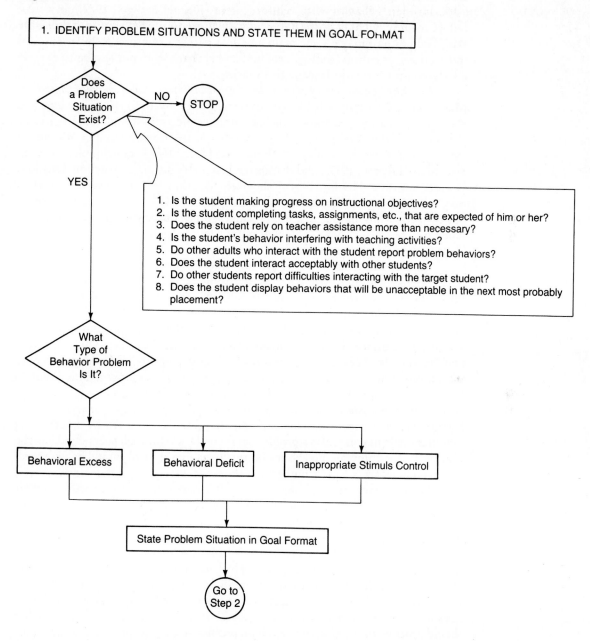

when students learn that acting helpless will result in an adult eventually doing the task or helping them do it. Learned helplessness may be due to students' failure to associate their behavior with reinforcement (Koegel & Egel, 1979), an actual failure to know what to do, or not having the prerequisite behaviors for doing the skill. Helplessness may also be maintained, in part, by reinforcement from social interactions, attention from the teacher, and perhaps from not having to expend effort to complete tasks (escape from tasks).

Another question is *whether students' behaviors interfere with teaching and learning.* Many examples of such behaviors exist and vary by the type of student and classroom situation. Examples include stereotypic (self-stimulatory) behavior (Chock & Glahn, 1983), lack of attention to instructional activities (Bryant & Budd, 1982; Koegel, Dunlap, Richman, & Dyer, 1981), noncompliance with directions (Liberty, 1977), and disruptive behaviors during instructional sessions (Carden-Smith & Fowler, 1984; Fishbein & Wasik, 1981). Disruptive behaviors may take many forms, including talking with peers, talking aloud in class, being out of seat, throwing objects, doing things to get other students to laugh, and tapping a pencil or other objects on the desk. Usually, these behaviors are identified readily by teachers.

Inappropriate social interactions with others should also be assessed when determining whether problems exist. Some students rarely initiate social interactions, have relatively brief interactions, or rarely respond to the social initiations of other students. A variety of explanations exist for social withdrawal (Gast & Wolery, 1987), and teachers must observe their students closely for social withdrawal because it does not "identify itself" as disruptive behavior does. Kerr and Nelson (1983) discussed procedures for identifying students who are socially withdrawn. On the other extreme, some students will interact with others, but do so in an inappropriate manner or do so too frequently.

Sometimes *parents, other team members, and peers report problem situations they are having with a given student.* Teachers should attend to those reports by determining whether the behavior is also a problem in their class. Although peers should not be reinforced for complaining about others, the named student should be observed. Some students are adept at bothering others and rarely being detected.

Finally, teachers should be aware of behaviors that are acceptable in their classrooms, but will be *unacceptable in future placements.* Examples of such behaviors vary depending upon the age of students, their abilities, and future placements. Some teachers, for example, allow students to seek assistance from others on in-class activities. While this is an acceptable teaching strategy, other teachers may see this behavior as inappropriate. Thus, for students who will soon be placed in such classes, the current teacher should address this potential problem.

The specific questions displayed in Figure 19.1 help answer the larger question, "Does a problem situation exist?" If the answer is "yes," the teacher should proceed to the next substep. If no problem exists, teachers should continue operating the classroom as in the past and regularly monitor students to determine whether problems develop.

Determining the Type of Problem

When a behavior problem is present, teachers should classify it as a behavioral deficit, behavioral excess, or case of inappropriate stimulus control. Determining the type of problem helps develop goals and select appropriate measures. This issue was discussed in Chapter 18.

Stating the Problem Situation in a Goal Format

A *goal* is a statement of what the teacher would like a behavior to be. If it includes a behavior to be decreased, it also should include at least one behavior to be increased. For example, if a child frequently disrupts teaching activities by talking out, the goal statement might be, "While in class, Kay will complete her assignments faster and more accurately while talking out less frequently." For a younger child who throws toys, the goal statement might be, "Laura will play with three different toys for longer periods of time with fewer throwing incidents." If the problem behavior itself is acceptable (e.g., getting drinks of water) but is occurring too frequently (behavioral excess), the goal should include the desired rate, e.g., "Brent will make no more than one trip to the drinking fountain per hour."

STEP 2: ASSESSMENT OF THE STUDENT AND ENVIRONMENT IN THE PROBLEM SITUATION

Once the goal statement is established, the second major step of the reduction process, assessment, is initiated. This step involves assessing the function of students' behavior, the adequacy of the environment, and the relationship between them. The substeps of the second general step are shown in Figure 19.2.

Defining Behaviors

The first task of the assessment is to *define the behavior.* A **behavior** is a discrete movement that has a definite beginning and end, is observable, repeatable, and can be measured reliably. Many of the descriptions used to describe students' inappropriate behaviors are not behaviors; examples are aggressive, disruptive, hyperactive, and disrespectful. These terms are classifications representing a variety of specific behaviors. For example, aggressive behavior may include acts such as pinching, hitting, kicking, biting, and stabbing others with knives. In a problem situation, the specific acts (behaviors) should be identified. Such specification will allow measurement of the problem and evaluation of the effects of intervention strategies.

FIGURE 19.2 Step 2 of the decision model for behavior reduction: assessing the student and the environment to determine whether a problem situation exists.

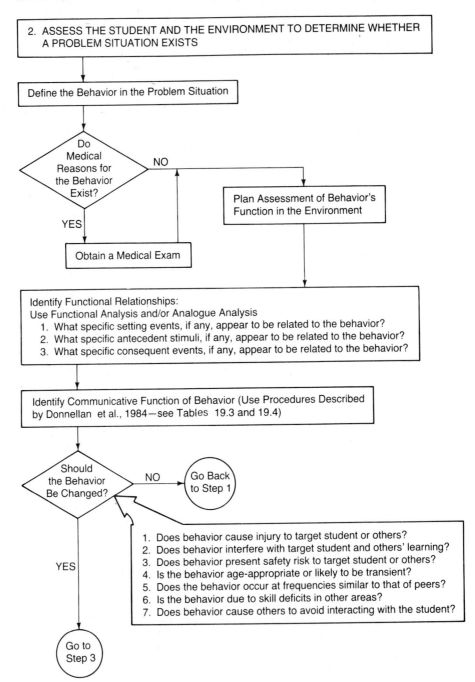

When an inappropriate behavior is identified for assessment and treatment, some adaptive, desired behaviors must also be identified. This is known as the *fair pair rule* (White & Haring, 1980). Many treatment procedures focus on increasing adaptive behaviors and thereby decreasing maladaptive behaviors. Frequently, teachers identify **incompatible adaptive behaviors** that cannot be done while doing the inappropriate behavior. Smiling is incompatible with frowning, sitting with standing, walking with running, and being quiet with talking loudly. Teachers should also identify behaviors that obtain at least the same level of reinforcement as the inappropriate behaviors. In other words, a behavior should be taught that will "get them the same thing" as the inappropriate behavior does; these are referred to as **equal-power replacement behaviors.**

Considering Medical Causes

After the behavior is defined, potential biological (medical) reasons for its occurrence should be considered (Evans & Meyer, 1985; Gaylord-Ross, 1980). When such a cause is suspected, a thorough medical examination should be obtained. Gaylord-Ross (1980) suggested that children with chronic inner-ear infections may poke and scratch their ears; in such cases, the infection should be treated rather than trying to reduce ear-poking. Other obvious examples deal with medication levels; some students may be lethargic as a result of inappropriate levels of medication. Appropriate treatment involves adjusting the medication rather than developing an intervention strategy to increase activity levels. Some environmentally caused behavior problems may exist concurrently with biologically caused disorders. For example, a student may display inappropriate social behaviors and an uncontrolled seizure condition. Controlling the seizure condition should be a high priority; however, this may not control the inappropriate social behavior.

In most cases, if problems can be treated by common medical procedures, such treatment is reasonable. The teacher's role is twofold: assisting parents in finding the appropriate medical personnel and monitoring the effects of those treatments. Teachers, however, should discriminate between problem situations that *can* and those that *should* be treated medically. Some problem situations such as hyperactive behavior can be treated with behavioral procedures, with medication (Rapport, Murphy, & Bailey, 1982), or with a combination of the two (Pelham, Schnedler, Bologna, & Contreras, 1980). Generally, psychotropic and psychostimulant medications should be used *after* behavioral procedures are shown to be unsuccessful. Further, the use of medical procedures does not mean behavioral treatments should necessarily cease. For example, medication in combination with behavioral treatment for hyperactivity may be more effective than medication alone (e.g., Pelham et al., 1980). When medical options are used, teachers should consult with parents and physicians about (a) the expected effects, (b) side effects, and (c) students' performance. See Burgio, Page, and Capriotti (1985) for a discussion of how to evaluate the effects of medications and behavioral procedures. (In the past few years, a new field of behavioral medicine has emerged; see the *Journal of Applied Behavior Analysis,* 1979, *12*(1) and frequent articles in *Behavior Therapy* and *Behavior Therapy and Experimental Psychiatry.* This field is concerned with the use of behavioral procedures to treat and prevent the occurrence of physical disease.)

Planning the Assessment

The purpose of the **assessment** is to develop hypotheses about (1) factors that may be causing and/or maintaining the inappropriate behaviors and (2) potential interventions. To do this, two issues must be addressed: the functional relationships between environmental stimuli and the behavior, and the social and communicative effects (functions) of the aberrant behavior. A **functional relationship** exists when a stimulus appears to be causally related to the occurrence of the student's behavior. A statement that describes a *possible* functional relationship between a behavior and an environmental event is called a **testable explanation** (Vargas, 1977). Many explanations have been proposed concerning the cause of behavior problems, and some of these involve high levels of inference, that is, a number of assumptions. When an explanation cannot be tested, it is known as an **explanatory fiction** (Vargas, 1977). However, to reduce the chance of making errors, teachers should search only for explanations that require low levels of inference (assumptions). Explanations with low levels of inference will lead more directly to interventions that can be implemented. The assessment should also include a determination of when, where, with whom, and under what situations the behavior occurs.

Identifying Functional Relationships. To identify functional relationships between behaviors and environmental stimuli, two types of assessment procedures may be used: a functional analysis and an analogue assessment. When conducting a **functional analysis,** also called an *ABC analysis,* information is collected on (1) setting events, (2) discriminative stimuli, (3) the student's behavior, and (4) consequent events. Immediate **setting events** are stimuli present in the physical and social environment during observation (e.g., heat in the room, lighting, number of students in the group, type of activities, etc.). Other events, called *distal setting events,* are stimuli that are not in the immediate environment. For example, events that occur in the home or on the bus ride to school may be related to students' behavior. **Discriminative stimuli** precede students' behavior and inform them about the probability of reinforcement or punishment if a given response occurs. To identify discriminative stimuli, all social initiations by others and other nonsocial events should be recorded. The student's behavior includes all the things he or she does, but attention is focused on the behavior being assessed. The **consequent events** are those things that follow the student's behavior.

Gelfand and Hartmann (1984) provided four rules for conducting functional analyses: (1) record only observable behavior and stimulus events and do not make evaluative comments or inferences about what is seen; (2) record verbal and nonverbal behavior; (3) record the time that each sequence of events occurs or make notes when a given interval of time has passed such as every 5 minutes (this information will help later when analyzing the data); and (4) use symbols, shorthand, or abbreviations to facilitate recording, taking care to make a key of any arbitrary symbols used. Generally, setting events are recorded at the beginning of the observation, and antecedent events, student's behavior, and consequent events are recorded in three columns (thus the name *ABC analysis*). Frequently, a consequent event serves as the antecedent for the student's next behavior. When this occurs, Gelfand and Hartmann suggested using a checkmark in the antecedent events column. Observational data are used to develop hypotheses about relationships between the student's behavior and setting, antecedent, and consequent events. An example of part of a functional analysis is shown in Table 19.2.

An **analogue assessment** is similar to a functional analysis, but is conducted in an artificial rather than natural environment (cf., Carr & Durand, 1985; Iwata, Dorsey, Slifer, Bauman, & Richman, 1982). In an analogue assessment, variables that may be causing or maintaining the aberrant behavior are tested. For example, if teacher attention seems to be maintaining an inappropriate behavior, the teacher could design a situation where attention is given contingent upon every occurrence of the behavior and a situation where attention is not provided contingently. The rates of the behavior would be compared between the two situations. If the rates are higher when teacher attention is provided, the behavior may be controlled, in part, by attention. These analogue-assessment sessions should be brief, relatively few in number, and free from other interfering variables. All variables other than the one being analyzed (e.g., attention) should be held constant. Analogue assessments may produce clear results and can be conducted quite efficiently.

An analogue assessment is a systematic attempt to manipulate events that may be related to the behavior. If the predictable effects are observed when the manipulations are made, the testable explanation is validated and a functional relationship is assumed. For example, the teacher who collected the data in Table 19.2 on Frank's hitting behavior might conclude that Frank hits because he is aggressive. However, this is an explanatory fiction because it does not suggest which environmental events control the frequency of the hitting. A testable explanation, on the other hand, is that Frank hits because when he does, he receives toys. This hypothesis is testable and analogue sessions can be designed where he does and does not receive toys for hitting.

Teachers also can use informal observations to identify testable explanations. For example, is the student more apt to engage in the target behavior when other students are present, when sitting with certain other students, before lunch or after lunch, or during difficult activities? Donnellan, Mirenda, Mesaros, and Fassbender (1984) identified variables to consider when identifying stimuli in the setting that may be related to students' behavior. These variables can be classified into four types: instructional, physical, and social dimensions of the environment

TABLE 19.2   Example of a Portion of a Functional Analysis of Frank's Hitting Behavior

Setting:

Observation occurred during free play in the manipulative play area (10 feet by 10 feet) of a preschool classroom. Five children — Frank, Lisa, Mary Ann, Anthony, and Peter — were present. The temperature in the room was quite comfortable and the noise level was moderate. A teacher was present and participated in their play. A large variety of toys, including duplicates of many of them, were present. Children were allowed to play with any of the toys, but were to ask the teacher for the toys they wanted.

Time	Antecedent Event	Behavior (Frank's)	Consequent Events
10:00	L (Lisa) says, "I want a puzzle."	F (Frank) looks at L.	T (Teacher) says, "Do you want a puzzle, Frank?"
	√	F says, "No, blocks."	T says, "Okay," gives F blocks.
	√	F puts blocks on floor and places six blocks in a row.	Others ignore F.
	L completes puzzle, says, "Look", and shows it to F.	F looks, hits L, and takes puzzle; dumps pieces on floor and puts it together.	L looks at F, walks to T and says, "I want a puzzle."
10:05	A (Anthony) is pushing toy car.	F crawls over to A, hits A, and takes car.	A looks at F, starts putting pieces in puzzle F had.
	P (Peter) has toy gas station.	F moves car to P, says, "Give me some gas."	P makes hissing noise, touches back of F's car.
	√	F hits P.	P moves away.
		F moves parts of gas station.	MA (Mary Ann) moves toy truck to gas station, says, "Hi."
	√	F says, "Hi. Want gas?"	MA says, "Fill 'er up." Laughs.
	√	F laughs, touches MA's truck, says, "Two dollars."	MA holds out her hand, says "Bye."
	√	F ignores MA.	MA says, "Here's two dollars" and holds out her hand.
	√	F hits MA, takes truck.	MA moves away.

Note: A check (√) indicates that a consequent event serves as an antecedent.

and changes in the environment. These types and *sample* questions for each are listed in Table 19.3; consideration of these variables may identify factors causing and/or maintaining inappropriate behaviors.

Identifying the Communicative and Social Functions of Behavior. After assessment of functional relationships, an assessment of the maladaptive behavior's social and communicative functions should occur (Donnellan et al., 1984). **Communicative functions** are the purposes or intents of communication. Behavior, including inappropriate responses, may have a purpose or effect; often that purpose is a communicative message or way to engage in social interactions. This step is particularly important for students with delayed communication abilities, but should be conducted with those who have adequate communication skills as well. Common messages communicated by inappropriate behaviors are, "Give me some attention," "I'm bored with this activity," and "I can't deal with this anymore, let me stop." For example, Carr, Newsom, and Binkoff (1980) described a student who was more aggressive in activities where demands (e.g., requirement to sit in a chair) were placed on him as compared to conditions where he could be out of the chair. The message value of the aggression could be characterized as, "I don't want to sit here." Likewise, another student engaged in yelling and grabbing behaviors at the beginning of instructional settings. A detailed analysis of the behavior indicated that the communicative function of yelling and grabbing could be characterized as, "Give me _____" (Horner & Budd, 1985).

Although many classifications of communicative functions exist (Coggins & Sandall, 1983; Dale, 1980), common functions are shown in Table 19.4. When determining what function a behavior serves, Donnellan et al. suggested listing all potential functions, observing the student, and recording which aberrant behaviors appear to be used for each. Identifying the communicative function of inappropriate behaviors is particularly helpful in identifying replacement behaviors (Carr & Durand, 1985).

The assessment procedures described above are useful for identifying the relationship between the inappropriate behavior and environmental stimuli and identifying potential treatments. In addition to these assessment strategies, teachers should, when appropriate, discuss the problem behavior with the target student. Such discussions should focus on (a) what the effects of the behavior are, (b) what may cause the inappropriate behavior to occur (using testable explanations), (c) alternatives to the inappropriate behavior, and (d) potential solutions to problem situations. We are not suggesting that teachers should assume the role of counselors, but that a frank discussion with the student about the problem situation may provide useful assessment information as well as identify potential interventions.

Developing Justification for Changing the Behavior

When the assessment is completed, the question, *"Should the behavior be changed?"* is asked. To answer this question, teachers must develop a justification for planning and implementing an intervention strategy. Frequently students' inappropriate behaviors are irritating to adults; however, this is *in*sufficient justification to engage in a behavior-reduction program. Several subquestions are shown in Figure 19.2. First, the teacher should determine whether the behavior causes

TABLE 19.3 Variables to Consider when Assessing the Relationship between Maladaptive Behavior and Setting Events

Type of Variable to Consider Specific Variables	Sample Questions about Variables
Instructional Dimension of Environment	
Nature of Materials Nature of Activity Nature of Instruction Sequence of Activities	■ Are materials/activities perceived by students as too immature (e.g., "This is baby stuff" or "This is first grade work")? ■ Are materials/activities perceived by students as too gender-specific (e.g., "This is boys/girls' work")? ■ Have the same materials/activities been used for several days in a row? ■ Do materials/activities require skills the student cannot perform? ■ Are materials/activities too easy/difficult for student? ■ Are directions for activity clearly understood by student? ■ Is the pace of instruction rapid? ■ Does student always have some activity to do? ■ Does student receive a high rate of reinforcement or other positive feedback for correct responses to instructional activities? ■ What activity preceded the activity where the problem behavior is displayed? ■ What activity immediately follows the activity where the problem behavior is displayed?
Physical Dimensions of Environment: Noninstructional Variables	
Nature of Lighting Noise Heat Physical Arrangement Time of Day	■ Is the student's area well lighted? ■ Is there a glare from the sun or other lighting? ■ Is student able to see instructional materials (e.g., blackboard)? ■ Does student appear to be bothered by too much noise? ■ Is student facing stimuli that may be distracting (e.g., corridor, window, or other students)? ■ Does student appear to react to temperature of the room? ■ Does student appear to react to noise in room? ■ Do particular odors appear to affect the student's behavior? ■ Does behavior occur at a specific time of day (e.g., after gym, before lunch, etc.)?
Social Dimension of Environment	
Number of Other Students Number of Adults Behavior of Others Toward Student Proximity of Others	■ Does the number of students in the room/area affect student's behavior? ■ Does the number of adults affect student's behavior? ■ Does inappropriate behavior occur only in the presence of specific students? ■ Does the proximity of adults influence the occurrence of the behavior? ■ Does inappropriate behavior occur only in the presence of specific adults?

TABLE 19.3   (Continued)

Type of Variable to Consider Specific Variables	Sample Questions about Variables
	■ Does inappropriate behavior occur only when others have performed a specific behavior? ■ Does inappropriate behavior occur only when close to, or away from, specific students? ■ Does student behave more/less appropriately when given persons are present/absent? ■ Does behavior appear to increase/decrease when other students or adults respond in a specific manner?
Changes in the Environment Changes in Schedule Changes in Physical Arrangement Changes at Home	■ Are transition times correlated with the occurrence of the behavior? ■ Do disruptions to the schedule appear to increase/decrease the behavior? ■ Do changes in the physical arrangement appear to increase/decrease the inappropriate behavior? ■ Do specific changes in the student's living environment appear to increase/decrease the occurrence of the inappropriate behavior?

TABLE 19.4   Common Communicative Functions

General Functions	Descriptions
Requests for attention/affection, interaction, assistance, activities and tangible objects	Behaviors that result in the performer receiving attention or social interactions. Behaviors that result in the receipt of activities or tangible objects (materials or food), etc.
Negations/Protests	Behaviors that result in the performer objecting to, showing "dissatisfaction," or refusing an activity, social initiation or request, or receipt of objects/materials.
Declarations/Comments about objects, events, activities, or others	Behaviors that result in the performer calling the attention of another to specific objects, activities, or other persons. Includes giving compliments, acknowledging the presence of others, greetings, and compliance with requests.

Note: Adapted from "Analyzing the Communicative Functions of Aberrant Behavior" by A. M. Donnellan, P. L. Mirenda, R. A. Mesaros, and L. L. Fassbender, 1984, *Journal of the Association for Persons with Severe Handicaps, 9* (3), pp. 206-207. Copyright 1984 by The Association for Persons with Severe Handicaps. Adapted by permission.

injury to the target student or others. Few reasons exist for allowing students to injure themselves or others. If the behavior is causing injury to the target student or others, justification probably exists for changing it. However, if no injury results, the teacher should determine whether the behavior interferes with learning. This can be difficult to determine. For example, stereotypic behaviors such as rocking, leg-swinging, and mouthing objects are thought to be inappropriate because they have been shown to interfere with learning (Koegel & Covert, 1972; Koegel, Firestone, Kramme, & Dunlap, 1974). However, other studies also show that some students engage in stereotypic behaviors and still learn (Chock & Glahn, 1983; Klier & Harris, 1977; Sugai & White, 1986). Furthermore, for infants and very young children, such behaviors *are,* in fact, appropriate learning experiences. Thus, the relationship between inappropriate behavior and learning may vary from student to student and may depend on a number of factors. Data can be collected on whether other students learn more when the target student is in the room or is absent. Also, data can be collected during instructional sessions when the target student is engaging in the inappropriate behavior and when he or she is not. If the behavior, based on data, appears to interfere with learning, a justification may exist for changing it. If data do not indicate this, any safety risk related to the behavior should be identified. For example, throwing some objects, climbing on shelves, and repeatedly bringing weapons to school are examples of behaviors that pose safety risks.

Another consideration is whether the behavior is chronologically age-appropriate or transient. When behaviors are age-appropriate and are likely to be transient, behavior-reduction programs probably are not warranted. When students are moderately to severely handicapped, many of their behaviors will appear inappropriate for their chronological age and body size; however, when their cognitive, social, and communicative abilities are considered, the behavior may be more age-appropriate. This presents a dilemma for making a decision concerning whether or not to change the behavior. If it does not cause injury, present safety risks, or interfere with learning, teachers should be cautious about developing behavior-reduction programs.

Teachers also should consider whether the behavior occurs at rates similar to those of peers. By collecting data on several students' behavior under similar situations, teachers can determine if the target student's behavior is discrepant with that of peers; this process is a **discrepancy analysis.** For example, talking out during class can be acceptable if it does not happen too frequently. Thus, the teacher should collect data on the frequency with which several students talk out before deciding to change the rate of a target student's talking.

Further, teachers should consider whether the inappropriate behavior is a result of skill deficits in other areas. Deficits in communication and social skills are frequently related to the occurrence of inappropriate behaviors. In such cases, the teacher should design programs to teach the social or communication skills rather than decreasing the occurrence of the aberrant behavior. Finally, the effect of the behavior on social interactions should be assessed. Ideally, frequent positive interactions should occur between students and with adults. If the maladaptive behavior causes the target student to be avoided, some justification exists for planning to change it.

   If a justification based on the above issues cannot be made for changing the behavior, the teacher should return to Step 1 and re-analyze whether a problem situation exists. If, however, a justification can be made, the third general step should be consulted.

STEP 3: SPECIFICATION OF THE OBJECTIVE

The substeps of Step 3 are illustrated in Figure 19.3. Step 3 is identical to the procedures described in Chapters 3 and 4 for specifying and writing high-quality objectives. The objective should include a behavior, the conditions under which it will be assessed, and the level at which it is to be performed. Further, the objective should be valued by persons responsible for the student. When an objective is specified for decreasing a behavior, a parallel objective must be specified for increasing adaptive behaviors. Or, one objective should be written that identifies the adaptive behavior and uses the maladaptive behavior in the criterion statement. For example, "Tim will use his hands in task-related activities or have them on his desk with no more than two occurrences of poking other children per day." The nature of the objectives will vary depending upon whether an alternative, perhaps incompatible, response or a new communicative or social response is identified.

FIGURE 19.3   Step 3 of the decision model for behavior reduction: specifying the objectives.

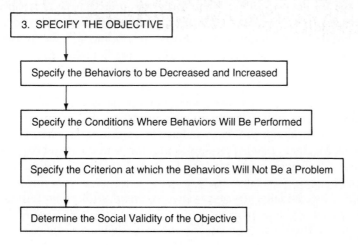

STEP 4: COLLECTION OF BASELINE DATA

The substeps for the fourth major step of the behavior-reduction process are shown in Figure 19.4. This step involves three major decisions. First, the type of behavior problem should be considered so that the appropriate behavioral dimension can be identified. For example, if the problem is a deficit or excess in frequency, frequency should be measured. The second decision concerns the type of measurement strategy to use. This decision depends on the dimension being measured. Procedures for selecting measurement strategies were described in Chapter 5. Finally, decisions about where and when data will be collected should be made. Ideally, interobserver agreement data should be collected and agreement percentages calculated. If sufficient agreement percentages exist, the fifth step of the process is initiated. If the percentages are too low, the definitions used by the observers should be checked. If this does not correct the problem, the measurement situation should be standardized to make it easier to obtain reliable data. If agreement percentages remain low, the behavior should be redefined. Although collecting such data may be difficult, teachers need some means of ensuring that the data being collected are not a result of recording errors, bias, or lack of attention during observations.

STEP 5: DEVELOPMENT OF INTERVENTION STRATEGIES

Prerequisites to Planning and Using Intervention Strategies

The fifth general step of the model is developing intervention plans; the substeps are shown in Figure 19.5. When planning intervention strategies, several considerations must be made. For example, the environment should be checked for a number of prerequisite conditions, including (1) the presence of an interesting, worthwhile curriculum, (2) a predictable sequence of events throughout the day, and (3) reinforcement for behaving appropriately.

Providing a Worthwhile Curriculum. The presence of an interesting, worthwhile curriculum is especially important in controlling inappropriate behavior. It prevents many behavior problems and can be used to treat others (Horner, 1980; Spangler & Marshall, 1983). Training communication and social skills can result in decreases in behavior problems (cf., Carr & Kologinsky, 1983; Casey, 1978). Absence of a legitimate curriculum sets the occasion for behavior problems. For example, when students are repeatedly presented with uninteresting activities, they may engage in more "interesting" behaviors, some of which may be inappropriate. If tasks are consistently too easy, they may behave as though they

FIGURE 19.4 Step 4 of the decision model for behavior reduction: collecting baseline data.

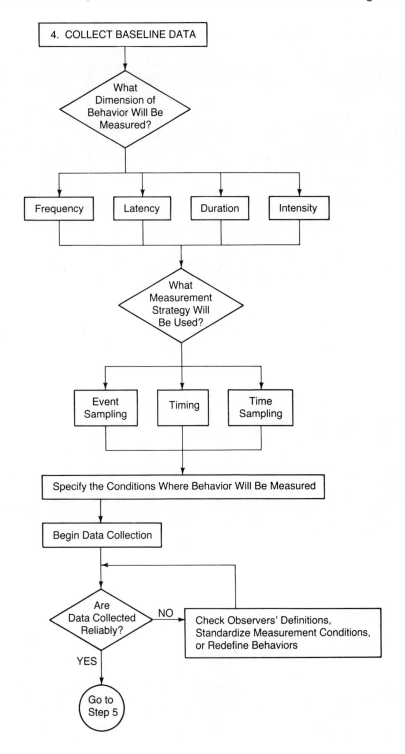

FIGURE 19.5 Step 5 of the decision model for behavior reduction: planning intervention.

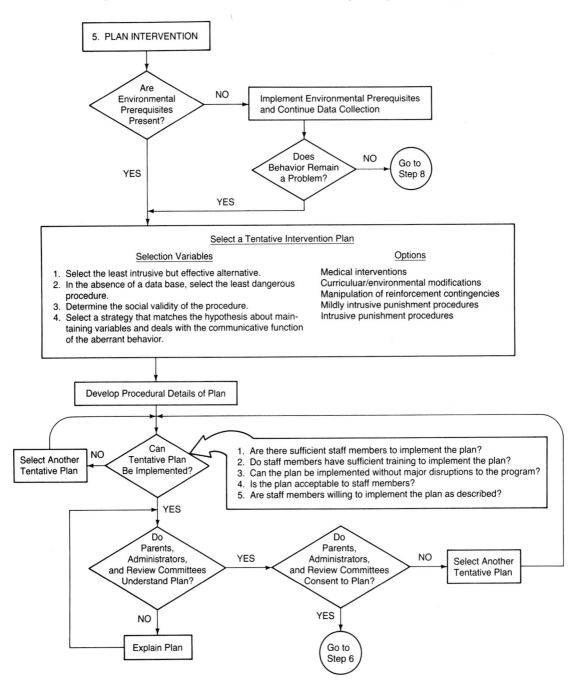

were bored and find more stimulating activities. When faced with activities that are too difficult, students may engage in inappropriate behaviors to escape the demands of the tasks (Carr & Durand, 1985; Weeks & Gaylord-Ross, 1981). If students are occupied with an interesting, worthwhile curriculum, they have less time to engage in problem behaviors. This prerequisite, however, requires time and effort from teachers. They must assess students' abilities, needs, and interests; individualize instructional objectives and activities; carefully plan activities; and monitor the results of different instructional activities. These activities are a necessary prerequisite for using more intrusive behavior-control procedures. To do otherwise is unfair to students and is "asking for trouble."

Providing Predictability. Establishing a predictable sequence of events is also important for controlling maladaptive behavior (Good & Brophy, 1984; Paine, Radicchi, Rosellini, Deutchman & Darch, 1983). Predictability is important from two perspectives. First, the sequence of activities and classroom routines should be sufficiently consistent so that students can anticipate what the day will entail. They should know when a given activity will end, when they can interact with friends, when they can expect a break, and when they will be able to go to the bathroom or eat lunch. By having a predictable schedule, students can adjust their behavior to the sequence. However, *variety* can and should be built into the classroom schedule. Time can be scheduled for a given content area, but variety should be built into that time. For example, students may have a regular math session, but the materials and format should vary considerably. When direct instruction is used, it may be desirable to teach more than one skill at the same time using a distributed-trial format (Mulligan, Guess, Holvoet & Brown, 1980; Mulligan, Lacy, & Guess, 1982). Although the instructional session should occur at the same time, the distributed-trial format will provide variety that keeps the task from becoming boring.

Second, predictability is important in terms of responding to students' behavior. Students should be able to predict what will happen if they comply or do not comply with the teacher's expectations (e.g., rules and routines). This is established by consistently applying consequent events to both compliance and lack of compliance.

Providing Reinforcement. Finally, students should be reinforced for engaging in appropriate behaviors. If students are not reinforced on at least an intermittent schedule for adaptive behaviors, they cannot be expected to continue performing them. Reinforcement should be given for appropriate social behaviors and correct responses to instructional activities. If students are being reinforced for engaging in adaptive behaviors, those responses will maintain or increase in frequency. When this occurs, students have fewer opportunities to engage in inappropriate behaviors. However, data indicate that teachers typically do not provide high rates of approval for appropriate student behavior and may provide more disapproval than approval (Heller & White, 1975; Thomas, Presland, Grant, & Glynn, 1978; White, 1975). Although teacher approval may not be a reinforcer for all students, it may be a good indication of how often teachers use positive reinforcement. Ideally, about four positive interactions should occur for each negative or corrective interaction.

If these three prerequisites (appropriate curriculum, predictability, reinforcement) are present, the next step of the behavior-reduction process is initiated. If any of these prerequisites is absent, they should be implemented and their effects evaluated. Many times, inappropriate behaviors can be controlled or prevented by implementing these prerequisite conditions. They are the starting point of effective and ethical interventions in classroom settings.

Selecting Tentative Intervention Strategies

If the behavior continues to be a problem after implementing these prerequisites, a tentative intervention plan should be selected. A wide array of strategies are listed in Table 19.5; they are grouped into the following categories: medical treatments, curricular/environmental modifications, manipulation of reinforcement contingencies, use of mildly intrusive punishment procedures, and use of intrusive punishment procedures. As used here, *punishment* refers to the contingent presentation of an aversive event or the removal of reinforcement contingencies

TABLE 19.5 Potential Intervention Strategies Listed by Intrusiveness

Type of Procedure	*Examples*
Medical Interventions	Medications
	Surgery
	Dietary changes
Curricular/Environmental Modifications	Change social dimension of the environment
	Change physical arrangement of environment
	Change schedule of activities
	Change the amount and type of materials or activities
	Change instructional methods being used
	Teach responses that fulfill same communicative function currently performed by aberrant behavior
Manipulation of Reinforcement Contingencies	Differential Reinforcement of Other Behaviors (DRO)
	Differential Reinforcement of Incompatible Behaviors (DRI)
	Differential Reinforcement of Low Rate of Behaviors (DRL)
	Contingency contracting
	Token economies
Mildly Intrusive Punishment Procedures	Extinction
	Response cost
Intrusive Punishment Procedures	Timeout
	Overcorrection
	Direct, contingent application of aversive stimuli

that *results* in a decrease in the target behavior (Neel, 1978). This is a functional definition of punishment; that is, the contingency must produce a decrease in the inappropriate behavior before it can be called punishment. At least four criteria should be used when selecting intervention strategies; however, if punishment procedures are used, the minimal acceptable conditions for implementing punishment should be considered (see Chapter 18).

The Principles of the Least Restrictive Treatment and the Least Intrusive Treatment Should Be Considered when Selecting Interventions. Although intrusiveness and restrictiveness are closely related and are sometimes used as synonyms, some differences exist. The notion of selecting the least restrictive alternative or environment has its roots in the normalization principle and the 14th Amendment to the Constitution of the United States (Barton, Brulle, & Repp, 1983). **Restrictiveness** is defined as the selection of treatments or environments that inhibit students' freedom the least, yet produce desired behavior changes (Budd & Baer, 1976). Restrictiveness refers to the degree to which environments or interventions limit, constrict, or inhibit students' freedom. Timeout would be considered more restrictive than corporal punishment because it places more limitations on students' freedom.

Intrusiveness refers to the extent to which interventions are obtrusive and intrude, impinge, or encroach on students' bodies or personal rights; intrusiveness is associated with pain, discomfort, and/or social stigma. The notion of using the least intrusive treatment is a variation of the principle of **parsimony** (Etzel & LeBlanc, 1979), which states that if two or more solutions can be used to solve a problem, the simplest procedure should be employed. Explicit in the principle of parsimony and implicit in the principle of the least intrusive alternative is the notion that only effective choices will be considered. The most appropriate wording for this principle is "Use the least intrusive *but effective* alternative" (Gast & Wolery, 1987; Keith, 1979). For example, corporal punishment is more intrusive than timeout because of the contact with the student's body and the pain that is inflicted.

Thus, interventions should be evaluated in terms of their restrictiveness, intrusiveness, and effectiveness. Some interventions will be considered restrictive but less intrusive and others intrusive and less restrictive. If two or more strategies have a data base indicating effectiveness, the least intrusive and restrictive procedure should be employed. If, however, a less intrusive or restrictive treatment has not been effective with other similar students and behaviors, the more intrusive and restrictive *but* effective procedure should be selected. It is ethically indefensible to use ineffective procedures because they are "natural" or less intrusive or restrictive than other interventions.

Some authors (e.g., Barton et al., 1983; Switzky & Miller, 1978) have questioned the wisdom of relying too heavily on the principles of the least intrusive or restrictive alternatives. Three points are pertinent. If *in*effective but less intrusive or restrictive procedures are used and their intrusiveness or restrictiveness must be increased to be successful, students may develop a tolerance for more intrusive or restrictive levels of the procedure. For example, if a 1-minute timeout procedure is used and is ineffective and the length of the timeout is gradually increased (e.g., 2 minutes, then 5, 7, and finally 10 minutes) to establish control, the length of timeout that ultimately will be effective may be greater than if the initial duration had been longer (e.g., 5 minutes). Likewise, if less intrusive or restrictive procedures take a long time before they are effective, they may be more intrusive and restrictive than an aversive procedure that produces rapid results. For example, if differential reinforcement of other behaviors (DRO), a less intrusive procedure, could establish control of a behavior in 4 weeks and overcorrection, a more intrusive procedure, could establish control in 3 days, then DRO in this instance may be more restrictive than overcorrection. Finally, if less intrusive or restrictive procedures do not have previously documented success with a specific behavior or type of student, the time, effort, and delay in treatment spent searching for effective less intrusive and restrictive procedures may constitute intrusive and restrictive treatment (cf., Repp & Deitz, 1978). Selecting intervention strategies on the basis of the notions of the least intrusive and restrictive alternatives is more difficult than it may first appear. Clearly, teachers are placed in the position of making judgments about the intrusiveness, restrictiveness, and effectiveness of strategies prior to using those procedures. They must find a balance between protecting students' rights and selecting procedures that will effectively and efficiently produce desired and needed outcomes.

The Principle of the Least Dangerous Assumption Should Be Considered when Selecting Intervention Strategies. The principle of the **least dangerous assumption** should be used when no data exist concerning the effectiveness of potential interventions (Donnellan, 1984). This principle suggests that the strategy selected should produce the least amount of harm if the procedure is ineffective. This principle may be quite important when choosing between strategies that have not been used with a particular population, behavior problem, or setting.

Social Validity Should Be Considered when Selecting Intervention Strategies. Wolf (1978) suggested that the perceived worth or acceptability (i.e., **social validity** of the goals, procedures, and effects) of intervention strategies should be evaluated by experts in the field and consumers of services. "**Acceptability** refers to judgments of lay persons, clients, and others of whether the procedures proposed for treatment are appropriate, fair, and reasonable for the problem and client" (Kazdin, French, & Sherick, 1981, p. 900). At least two reasons exist for evaluating the acceptability of interventions: (a) more acceptable treatments may be used more readily and consistently and (b) less acceptable treatments may be viewed as violating students' rights (Kazdin, 1980a). Several studies have evaluated the acceptability of various treatments for specific cases. Based on these studies, the following conclusions are possible:

1. Acceptability of different treatments can be distinguished by a variety of persons including undergraduate psychology students (Kazdin, 1980a; 1980b; 1981; Singh

& Katz, 1985), children (Kazdin, 1984; Kazdin et al., 1981), parents (Kazdin, 1984; Kazdin et al., 1981; Norton, Austen, Allen, & Hilton, 1983), teachers (Norton et al., 1983; Witt, Elliott, & Martens, 1984; Witt, Martens, & Elliott, 1984), and staff members of an inpatient psychiatric program for children (Kazdin et al., 1981).

2. Less restrictive procedures such as reinforcement of incompatible behaviors are rated as more acceptable than more restrictive procedures such as timeout (Kazdin, 1980b), positive practice (Kazdin et al., 1981), electric shock (Kazdin, 1980a), and medication (Kazdin, 1980a, 1981, 1984).

3. Teachers report using less intrusive procedures more frequently than more intrusive procedures (Salend, Esquivel, & Pine, 1984).

4. Less restrictive forms of timeout (e.g., in-class exclusion) alone and in combination with positive reinforcement are more acceptable than restrictive forms (e.g., seclusion in a locked room) (Kazdin, 1984; Norton et al., 1983).

5. More intrusive procedures are seen as more acceptable when cases are considered more severely disordered (Kazdin, 1980a).

6. Acceptability depends on the amount of teacher time and skill, amount of risks to the student, and negative effects on other students (Kazdin, 1981; Witt, Elliott, & Martens, 1984; Witt, Martens, & Elliott, 1984).

7. Ratings of acceptability can be increased by providing more information about the procedures being evaluated (Singh & Katz, 1985).

These studies provide some initial guidelines concerning acceptability; however, individual parents, other caregivers, team members, administrators, and students may view treatments differently. Thus, the acceptability of intervention strategies to persons involved with the target student should be assessed.

The Hypothesis Generated During Assessment Should Be Considered when Selecting Intervention Strategies. These hypotheses or testable explanations should suggest which variables are maintaining the occurrence of the maladaptive behavior and, when possible, the social or communicative function of the behavior. To be useful, the hypotheses must be stated as testable explanations with few assumptions being made. Several general motivational hypotheses have been generated for a variety of behavior problems (cf., Carr, 1977; Carr & Newsom, 1985; Carr & Durand, 1985; Gast & Wolery, 1987); these are illustrated in Table 19.6. Several points are noteworthy. A given behavior problem can be maintained by a number of variables across students; that is, three students may engage in talking out during class. One student's talking-out behavior may be maintained by the social attention from the teacher; another's by the social attention from peers; and the other's by escape from the demands of the academic task. Likewise, one student's behavior may be maintained by more than one variable. In Carr and Durand's (1985) study, a student's disruptive behavior appeared to be maintained by both social attention and task difficulty. The student was only disruptive when social attention was low and tasks were difficult. It is also clear that similar environmental stimuli may be related to a variety of aberrant behaviors. For

TABLE 19.6 Summary of Motivational Sources, Possible Communicative Messages, and Related Interventions

		Intervention Procedures		
Motivational Source	Possible Communi- cative Message(s)	Teach Replacement Communicative Response	Functionally Related Alt-R Procedures	Manipulation of Antecedent Conditions
I. Positive Reinforcement[a,b] Attention maintains behavior (Lovaas, Freitag, Gold, & Kassorla, 1965)	"Pay attention to me" (general) "Hello!" (greeting) "Look at me, I'm silly" (humor) "Play with me" "Look at _____" (comment) "Help me"	Teach a variety of means for requesting/soliciting attention, depending on context (e.g., tap on arm, greeting, "Play." "Help," etc.; discussed by Carr, 1981; Durand, 1982)	Use attention to reinforce already-occurring alternative responses (Hall, Lund, & Jackson, 1968; Lovaas et al., 1965) Direct instruction + social reinforcement of new alternative responses (Russo, Cataldo, & Cushing, 1981)	Alter environment to provide noncontingent attention
Material Reinforcers (e.g., food, objects) maintain behavior (Lovaas & Simmons, 1969)	"I want _____"	Teach manual sign for desired object/food (Carr, 1979; Horner & Budd, 1983)	Use desired materials to reinforce already-occurring alternative responses Direct instruction + material reinforcement of new alternative responses (Favell, McGimsey, & Jones, 1978)	Alter environment to provide noncontingent access to material reinforcers (stimulus satiation, Ayllon, 1963)
II. Negative Reinforcement [a,b] Termination of an aversive stimulus or situation maintains behavior (Carr, Newsom, & Binkoff, 1976)	"I don't want to do this anymore" "Stop!" "No!" "I don't understand; I want out!"	Teach manual/ gestural sign to terminate activity/escape (Carr, Newsom, & Binkoff, 1980; discussed by Durand, 1982)	Reinforce already occurring alternative responses with escape	Alter context to decrease/eliminate aversiveness; simplify tasks (Weeks & Gaylord-Ross 1981); increase preference value of tasks (Carr et al., 1980; Gaylord-Ross, Weeks & Lipner, 1980); decrease or alter instructional demands (Carr et al., 1976; Gaylord-Ross, et al., 1980); alter

TABLE 19.6 (Continued)

		Intervention Procedures		
Motivational Source	Possible Communicative Message(s)	Teach Replacement Communicative Response	Functionally Related Alt-R Procedures	Manipulation of Antecedent Conditions
				instructional procedures (Weeks & Gaylord-Ross, 1981)
III. Extinction/Frustration[b] Previously available reinforcers are no longer available (Baumeister & Forehand, 1971)	"Help me" "I'm frustrated" "Why can't I have ...?" "You used to give___ to me; I want it now"	Teach communicative means for obtaining desired reinforcers and/or for enlisting aid to obtain reinforcers	Reinstate previously available reinforcers contingent on occurrence of alternative response	Alter environment to provide previously available reinforcers; alter instructional procedures, provide richer reinforcement schedule, etc.
IV. Arousal induction/sensory reinforcement[a,b] Behavior provides sensory stimulation that is intrinsically reinforcing (Berkson, 1967)	"I'm not getting the input I want" "I'm bored"	Teach communicative means to obtaining sensory input, e.g., request for sensory activity (discussed by Durand, 1982)	Provide reinforcing sensory input through alternative activities (Eason, White & Newsom, 1982; Favell, McGimsey, & Schell, 1982)	Alter environment to provide more sensory input and stimulation; enrich environment and curriculum (Gaylord-Ross, 1980)
V. Arousal Reduction[b] Behavior maintained by termination of aversive overstimulation, i.e., behavior "blocks out" excess sensory input (Hutt & Hutt, 1965)	"I'm anxious/tense/excited/nervous/overwhelmed, etc." "Help me"	Teach alternative communicative means for expressing distress/enlisting aid	Provide and reinforce alternative means of removing the aversive effects of overstimulation; vigorous exercise (Ohlsen, 1978; Kern, Koegel, Dyer, Blew, & Fenton, 1982); relaxation response (Graziano & Kean, 1971)	Alter environment to decrease environmental stimulation and demands (Weeks & Gaylord-Ross, 1981)
VI. Respondent Conditioning[b] Behavior originated from association with a traumatic event (e.g., loud noise, pain) that	"I'm scared/afraid" "This is a bad habit I can't control" "I want ____ to stop" "Help!"	Teach communicative means to express distress or enlist assistance	Reinforce gradual tolerance of trigger stimulus; systematic desensitization (Wolpe, 1973; see Miranda, in press, for a review)	Alter environment to prelude occurrence of the trigger stimulus

(Continues)

TABLE 19.6 (Continued)

Motivational Source	Possible Communi- cative Message(s)	Intervention Procedures		
		Teach Replacement Communicative Response	Functionally Related Alt-R Procedures	Manipulation of Antecedent Conditions
triggers the be- havior (Wolpe, 1972)			Direct instruction + reinforcement of alternative re- sponses to trigger stimulus	
Behavior is then maintained by positive or nega- tive reinforcement			Not Applicable	Not Applicable
VII. Physiological[a,b] Behavior is the prod- uct of an aberrant physiological pro- cess (Cataldo & Harris, 1982)	"I hurt" "I'm tired"	Teach communi- cative means to express distress		

[a] — Discussed by Carr (1977).
[b] — Discussed by Romanczyk, Kistner, & Shakelford (1982).

Note: From "Analyzing the Communicative Functions of Aberrant Behavior" by A. M. Donnellan, P. L. Mirenda, R. A. Mesaros, and L. L. Fassbender, 1984, *Journal of the Association for Persons with Severe Handicaps, 9* (3), p. 209. Copyright 1984 by The Association for Persons with Severe Handicaps. Reprinted by permission.

example, aggressive, disruptive, and self-injurious behaviors have all been shown to be a function of social attention and escape from tasks (Carr, Newsom, & Binkoff, 1976; Carr & Durand, 1985; Durand, 1982; Weeks & Gaylord-Ross, 1981). Finally, some functional relationships involve setting events that are not immediately present when the behavior occurs. For example, Wahler (1980) found that when low-income mothers had aversive or negative interactions with extended family members or community agency personnel, they had more aversive interactions with their children later in the day. Wahler and Fox (1981) provided a framework for conceptualizing and studying such distal setting events. When possible, interventions should be selected that remove the control of the maintaining variable and provide acceptable replacement behaviors that fulfill the same communicative or social function currently served by the inappropriate behavior.

In summary, a number of different intervention strategies are available for decreasing the occurrence of inappropriate behaviors. Interventions should be selected based on the principles of the least intrusive and restrictive but effective alternative, principle of the least dangerous assumption, documented social validity, and an established hypothesis that identifies (a) the variables that maintain the behavior and (b) the effects of that response.

Developing a Procedural Plan

A detailed plan should be developed before implementing an intervention. This plan should include *what* will be done, *who* will do it, *how* it will be done, *when* it will be done, *when* it will be reviewed, *who* will review the effects, and *what* will happen if potential negative side effects occur. The description of how the plan will be implemented should specify exactly how staff members are to respond when the maladaptive behavior occurs. The detailed plan serves three important functions: (a) it helps anticipate and articulate how the intervention will be implemented, (b) it guides the actual implementation, and (c) it provides a model against which actual implementation can be measured and compared. After the detailed plan has been developed, it should be evaluated to determine if implementation is possible.

Evaluating the Implementation of Potential Interventions

This substep involves determining whether the tentative plan can be implemented in the situation where the problem behavior occurs. It is possible for many intervention strategies to reduce a given behavior, but not all of them will be possible to implement in every situation. Several questions, listed in Figure 19.5, address the feasibility of implementing different procedures. These questions deal with the number of available staff, their competence in implementing the procedure, the amount of disruption the procedures will cause to instruction, and the acceptability of the procedures to the staff. For example, use of differential reinforcement of other behaviors (DRO) requires that the teacher have time to monitor the student to determine whether the appropriate interval of time passes without the occurrence of the inappropriate behavior. This may not be possible if the teacher has a large number of other instructional and monitoring duties. Likewise, use of overcorrection frequently requires that one staff member be available at all times to implement the procedure. If sufficient staff members do not exist, the effectiveness of the procedure may be jeopardized. If it is determined that the procedure cannot be implemented correctly, another strategy should be selected and a tentative plan should be developed. However, if it is determined that a procedure can be used, consent should be secured from the student's parents and appropriate authorities.

Securing Informed Consent

Unlike instructional procedures, many of the behavior-reduction procedures should be used only after obtaining informed consent from parents. Clearly, the use of medical treatments, any procedure that involves aversive stimuli (e.g., negative reinforcement and punishment), or procedures that limit or exclude students from instructional opportunities (e.g., timeout) requires consent. Some of the environmental modifications and some of the procedures involving the manipulation of reinforcement contingencies (e.g., DRO) may not require informed consent. However, some agencies require consent for all goals where the intent is to reduce behaviors. Obtaining informed consent from parents involves at least two distinct steps. First, the procedure, its risks, and its implications should be explained to parents. Their understanding of this information should be confirmed. If they do not understand the procedure, it should be explained again. After they indicate that they have a clear understanding, they should be given the option of allowing the procedure to be used. If they *do not agree* to its use, another more acceptable intervention strategy should be selected. Second, if parents agree to its use, permission from any existing institutional review committees should be sought. If no review committees exist or if the intervention does not require review, parental consent should be documented and the immediate supervisor should be notified, in writing, concerning the nature and intent of the intervention plan. If, based on a review by institutional committees and/or administrators, the plan is deemed unacceptable, another intervention should be selected.

STEP 6: IMPLEMENTATION OF THE INTERVENTION PLAN

The substeps of the sixth major step in the behavior-reduction process are shown in Figure 19.6. Implementing the intervention plan primarily involves two substeps. First, the procedures are implemented. Second, the implementation is assessed continuously to determine whether it is being conducted as planned and whether adjustments are needed. Correct administration of intervention is necessary to make accurate statements about its effects (Peterson, Homer, & Wonderlich, 1982). Assessment of implementation can be done by using procedural reliability (Billingsley, White, & Munson, 1980), which involves comparing, through direct observation, the actual implementation to the detailed plan that was developed in Step 5. Based on this comparison, a percentage of agreement can be established for each step of the procedural plan. The percentage of agreement should be 90 or more. Procedural-reliability checks should occur frequently to avoid subtle unplanned changes in implementation. If lower percentages are obtained, the incorrect implementation should be changed and measurement of implementation should recur. Although teachers may find it difficult to collect procedural reliability data, the implementation of the procedures should still be monitored to determine whether it is occurring as planned. When procedural reliability estimates are sufficient, the seventh general step of the behavior-reduction process is initiated.

FIGURE 19.6   Steps 6, 7, and 8 of the decision model for behavior reduction: implementing the intervention plan, monitoring student's progress, and evaluating the effects of the intervention.

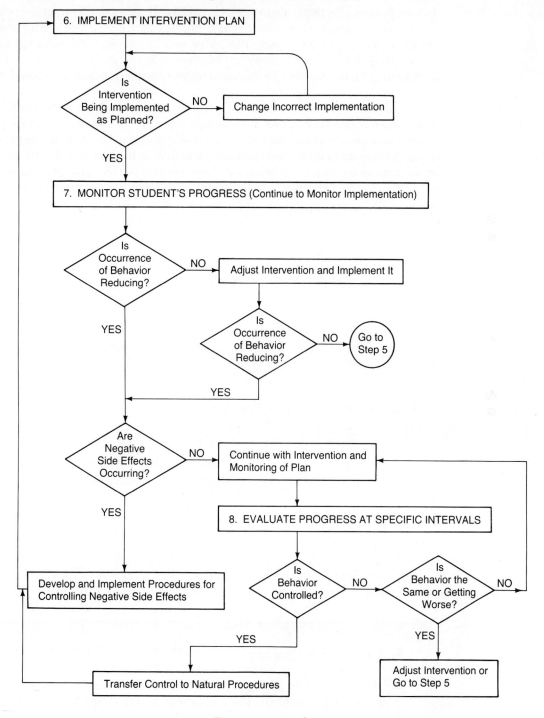

STEP 7: MONITOR STUDENT'S PROGRESS

In Step 4 of the behavior-reduction process, data collection on the target behavior began. Step 7 involves analysis of that data after starting the intervention; the substeps are shown in Figure 19.6. The procedures for summarizing and interpreting data were discussed in Chapters 6, 7, and 8. The procedures for interpreting data from single-subject designs (Chapters 9 and 10) should be employed.

Judgments about decreases in a behavior must be made on the basis of the data rather than on subjective impressions. Some procedures, such as environmental manipulations and the intrusive punishment procedures, should result in rapid changes that are noticeable within a few days or sessions (e.g., 3 to 6). With extinction, an increase in the behavior may occur prior to deceleration. The speed with which reinforcement manipulations work will vary depending on the strength of the reinforcers and the schedules on which they are implemented. However, if after several days (5 to 8), there is no substantial change in the occurrence of the behavior, adjustments should be made in the intervention. If adjustments in the intervention do not result in decreases in the behavior, another intervention plan should be selected (Step 5, Figure 19.5). If the occurrence of the behavior is reducing, the speed with which it is occurring should be evaluated. The occurrence of negative side effects should also be monitored. If negative side effects occur, a plan should be devised for dealing with them. This plan is then implemented and checked for procedural reliability. When the side effects have been controlled and the behavior is reducing, the program should be reviewed periodically (Step 8, Figure 19.6).

STEP 8: EVALUATION OF PROGRESS AT SPECIFIC INTERVALS

Assessing whether the plan is implemented appropriately and monitoring students' progress should occur on a regular basis, usually at a minimum of once per week. If the plan is poorly implemented, adjustments should be made. If the behavior is reducing sufficiently, but not yet to the level specified in the objective, intervention should continue until the behavior has been controlled. If sufficient reduction is not obtained, adjustments should be made in the intervention. After the behavior is at the level specified in the objective, transfer of the control from intervention strategies to natural conditions should occur. This withdrawal of the intervention may take many forms and should be carefully planned.

Summary of Key Concepts

■ The decision model for reducing the occurrence of behavior includes eight distinct steps: identifying problems, assessing students and the environment, specifying objectives, collecting data, selecting and planning intervention strategies, implementing the intervention, monitoring the intervention, and evaluating the progress.

■ The decision model requires:

☐ Careful identification of behavior problems.

☐ Assessment of the functional relationships between the behavior problem and environmental events.

☐ Specifying a hypothesis about variables that are maintaining the behavior.

☐ Selecting intervention strategies based on their intrusiveness, restrictiveness, effectiveness, the principle of the least dangerous assumption, social validity, and the hypothesis about maintaining variables.

☐ Careful planning, including stating the objective, measurement procedures, and intervention strategies.

☐ Careful monitoring of the effects of the intervention, the implementation of intervention, and the occurrence of side effects.

☐ Transfer of the effects to naturally occurring behaviors.

REFERENCES

Barton, L. E., Brulle, A. R., & Repp, A. C. (1983). Aversive techniques and the doctrine of least restrictive alternative. *Exceptional Educational Quarterly, 3*(4), 1–8.

Billingsley, F. F., White, O. R., & Munson, R. (1980). Procedural reliability: A rationale and an example. *Behavioral Assessment, 2,* 229–241.

Bryant, L. E., & Budd, K. S. (1982). Self-instruction training to increase independent work performance in preschoolers. *Journal of Applied Behavior Analysis, 15,* 259–271.

Budd, K. S., & Baer, D. M. (1976). Behavior modification and the law: Implications of recent judicial decisions. *Journal of Psychiatry and the Law, 4,* 171–244.

Burgio, L. D., Page, T. J., & Capriotti. R. M. (1985). Clinical behavioral pharmacology: Methods for evaluating medications and contingency management. *Journal of Applied Behavior Analysis, 18,* 45–59.

Carden-Smith, L. K., & Fowler, S. A. (1984). Positive peer pressure: The effects of peer monitoring on children's disruptive behavior. *Journal of Applied Behavior Analysis, 17,* 213–227.

Carr, E. G. (1977). The motivation of self-injurious behavior: A review of some hypotheses. *Psychological Bulletin, 84,* 800–816.

Carr, E. G., & Durand, V. M. (1985). Reducing behavior problems through functional communication training. *Journal of Applied Behavior Analysis, 18,* 111–126.

Carr, E. G., & Kologinsky, E. (1983). Acquisition of sign language by autistic children II: Spontaneity and generalization effects. *Journal of Applied Behavior Analysis, 16,* 297–314.

Carr, E. G., & Newsom, C. D. (1985). Demand-related tantrums: Conceptualization and treatment. *Behavior Modification, 9,* 403–426.

Carr, E. G., Newsom, C. D., & Binkoff, J. A. (1976). Stimulus control of self-destructive behavior in a psychotic child. *Journal of Abnormal Child Psychology, 4,* 139–153.

Carr, E. G., Newsom, C. D., & Binkoff, J. (1980). Escape as a factor in the aggressive behavior of two retarded children. *Journal of Applied Behavior Analysis, 13,* 101–117.

Casey, L. (1978). Development of communicative behavior in autistic children: A parent program using manual signs. *Journal of Autism and Childhood Schizophrenia, 8,* 45–59.

Chock, P. M., & Glahn, T. J. (1983). Learning and self-stimulation in mute and echolalic children. *Journal of Autism and Developmental Disorders, 14,* 365–381.

Coggins, T. E., & Sandall, S. (1983). The communicatively handicapped infant: Application of normal language and communication development. In S. G. Garwood & R. R. Fewell (Eds.), *Educating handicapped infants: Issues in development and intervention* (pp. 165–214). Rockville, MD: Aspen.

Dale, P. S. (1980). Is early pragmatic development measurable? *Journal of Child Language, 7,* 1–12.

Donnellan, A. M. (1984). The criterion of the least dangerous assumption. *Behavioral Disorders, 9,* 141–150.

Donnellan, A. M., Mirenda, P. L., Mesaros, R. A., & Fassbender, L. L. (1984). Analyzing the communicative functions of aberrant behavior. *Journal of the Association for Persons with Severe Handicaps, 9,* 201–212.

Durand, V. M. (1982). Analysis and intervention of self-injurious behavior. *Journal of the Association for the Severely Handicapped, 7,* 44–53.

Etzel, B C., & LeBlanc, J. M. (1979). The simplest treatment alternative: Appropriate instructional control and errorless learning procedures for the difficult-to-teach child. *Journal of Autism and Developmental Disorders, 9,* 361–382.

Evans, I., & Meyer, L. (1985). *An educative approach to behavior problems: A practical decision model for interventions with severely handicapped learners.* Baltimore: Paul Brookes.

Fishbein, J., & Wasik, B. H. (1981). Effect of the good behavior game on disruptive behavior. *Journal of Applied Behavior Analysis, 14,* 89–93.

Gast, D. L., & Wolery, M. (1987). Severe maladaptive behaviors. In M. E. Snell (Ed.), *Systematic instruction of persons with severe handicaps* (3rd ed.). (pp. 300–332). Columbus, OH: Charles E. Merrill.

Gaylord-Ross, R. (1980). A decision model for the treatment of aberrant behavior in applied settings. In W. Sailor, B. Wilcox, & L. Brown (Eds.), *Methods of instruction for severely handicapped students* (pp. 135–158). Baltimore: Paul Brookes.

Gelfand, D. M., & Hartmann, D. P. (1984). *Child*

behavior analysis and therapy (2nd ed.). New York: Pergamon Press.

Good, T. L., & Brophy, J. E. (1984). *Looking in classrooms* (3rd ed.). New York: Harper & Row.

Heller, M. S., & White, M. A. (1975). Teacher approval and disapproval on ability groupings. *Journal of Educational Psychology, 67,* 796–800.

Horner, R. D. (1980). The effects of an environmental "enrichment" program on the behavior of institutionalized profoundly retarded children. *Journal of Applied Behavior Analysis, 13,* 473–491.

Horner, R. H., & Budd, C. M. (1985). Acquisition of manual sign use: Collateral reduction of maladaptive behavior, and factors limiting generalization. *Education and Training of the Mentally Retarded, 20,* 39–47.

Iwata, B. A., Dorsey, M. F., Slifer, K. J., Bauman, K. E., & Richman, G. S. (1982). Toward a functional analysis of self-injury. *Analysis and Intervention in Developmental Disabilities, 2*(3), 3–20.

Kazdin, A. E. (1980a). Acceptability of alternative treatments for deviant child behavior. *Journal of Applied Behavior Analysis, 13,* 259–273.

Kazdin, A. E. (1980b). Acceptability of timeout from reinforcement procedures for disruptive child behavior. *Behavior Therapy, 11,* 329–344.

Kazdin, A. E. (1981). Acceptability of child treatment techniques: The influence of treatment efficacy and adverse side-effects. *Behavior Therapy, 12,* 493–506.

Kazdin, A. E. (1984). Acceptability of aversive procedures and medication as treatment alternatives for deviant child behavior. *Journal of Abnormal Child Psychology, 12,* 289–302.

Kazdin, A. E., French, N. H., & Sherick, R. B. (1981). Acceptability of alternative treatments for children: Evaluations by inpatient children, parents, and staff. *Journal of Consulting and Clinical Psychology, 49,* 900–907.

Keith, K. (1979). Behavior analysis and the principle of normalization. *AAESPH Review, 7,* 1–12.

Kerr, M. M., & Nelson, C. M. (1983). *Strategies for managing behavior problems in the classroom.* Columbus, OH: Charles E. Merrill.

Klier, J., & Harris, S. L. (1977). Self-stimulation and learning in autistic children: Physical or functional incompatibility? *Journal of Applied Behavior Analysis, 10,* 311. (Abstract)

Koegel, R. L., & Covert, A. (1972). The relationship of self-stimulation to learning in autistic children. *Journal of Applied Behavior Analysis, 5,* 381–387.

Koegel, R. L., Dunlap, G., Richman, G. S., & Dyer, K. (1981). The use of specific orienting cues for teaching discrimination tasks. *Analysis and Intervention in Developmental Disabilities, 1*(2), 187–198.

Koegel, R. L., & Egel, A. L. (1979). Motivating autistic children. *Journal of Abnormal Psychology, 88,* 418–426.

Koegel, R. L., Firestone, P. B., Kramme, K. W. & Dunlap, G. (1974). Increasing spontaneous play by suppressing self-stimulation in autistic children. *Journal of Applied Behavior Analysis, 7,* 521–528.

Liberty, K. A. (1977). *An investigation of two methods of achieving compliance with the severely handicapped in a classroom setting.* Unpublished doctoral dissertation, University of Washington, Seattle.

Lynch, V., McGuigan, C., & Shoemaker, S. (1983). An introduction to systematic instruction. *British Columbia Journal of Special Education, 7,* 1–13.

Mulligan, M., Guess, D., Holvoet, J., & Brown, F. (1980). The individualized curriculum sequencing model (1): Implications from research on massed, distributed, and spaced trial training. *Journal of the Association for the Severely Handicapped, 5,* 325–336.

Mulligan, M., Lacy, L., & Guess, D. (1982). Effects of massed, distributed, and spaced trial sequencing on severely handicapped students' performance. *Journal of the Association for the Severely Handicapped, 7*(2), 48–61.

Neel, R. S. (1978). Research findings regarding the use of punishment procedures with severely behavior disordered children. In F.H. Wood & K.C. Lakin (Eds.), *Punishment and aversive stimulation in special education: Legal, theoretical and practical issues in their use with emotionally disturbed children and youth* (pp. 65–83). Minneapolis: Advanced Training Institute.

Norton, G. R., Austen, S., Allen, G. E., & Hilton, J. (1983). Acceptability of time out from reinforcement procedures for disruptive child behavior: A further analysis. *Child and Family Behavior Therapy, 5*(2), 31–41.

Paine, S. C., Radicchi, J., Rosellini, L. C., Deutchman, L., Darch, C. B. (1983). *Structuring your classroom for academic success.* Champaign, IL: Research Press.

Pelham, W. E., Schnedler, R. B., Bologna, N. C., & Contreras, J. A. (1980). Behavioral and stimulant treatment of hyperactive children: A therapy study with methylphenidate probes in a within-subject design. *Journal of Applied Behavior Analysis, 13,* 221–236.

Peterson, L., Homer, A. L., & Wonderlich, S. A. (1982). The integrity of independent variables in behavior analysis. *Journal of Applied Behavior Analysis, 15,* 477–492.

Rapport, M. D., Murphy, H. A., & Bailey, J. S. (1982). Ritalin vs. response cost in the control of hyperactive children: A within-subject comparison. *Journal of Applied Behavior Analysis, 15,* 205–216.

Repp, A. C., & Deitz, D. E. D. (1978). On the selective use of punishment—Suggested guidelines for administrators. *Mental Retardation, 16,* 250–254.

Salend, S. J., Esquivel, L., & Pine, P. B. (1984). Regular and special education teachers' estimates of use of aversive contingencies. *Behavioral Disorders, 9,* 89–94.

Singh, N. N., & Katz, R. C. (1985). On the modification of acceptability ratings for alternative child treatments. *Behavior Modification, 9,* 375–386.

Spangler, P. F., & Marshall, A. M. (1983). The unit play manager as facilitator of purposeful activities among institutionalized profoundly and severely retarded boys. *Journal of Applied Behavior Analysis, 16,* 345–349.

Sugai, G., & White, W. J. (1986). Effects of using object self-stimulation as a reinforcer on the prevocational work rates of an autistic child. *Journal of Autism and Developmental Disorders, 16,* 459–471.

Switzky, H. N., & Miller, T. L. (1978). The least restrictive alternative. *Mental Retardation, 16*(1), 52–54.

Thomas, J. D., Presland, I. E., Grant, M. D., & Glynn, T. L. (1978). Natural rates of teacher approval and disapproval in grade 7 classrooms. *Journal of Applied Behavior Analysis, 11,* 91–94.

Vargas, J. (1977). *Behavioral psychology for teachers.* New York: Harper & Row.

Wahler, R. G. (1980). The insular mother: Her

problems in parent-child treatment. *Journal of Applied Behavior Analysis, 13,* 207–219.

Wahler, R. G., & Fox, J. J. (1981). Setting events in applied behavior analysis: Toward a conceptual and methodological expansion. *Journal of Applied Behavior Analysis, 14,* 327–338.

Weeks, M., & Gaylord-Ross, R. (1981). Task difficulty and aberrant behavior in severely handicapped students. *Journal of Applied Behavior Analysis, 14,* 449–463.

White, M. A. (1975). Natural rates of teacher approval and disapproval in the classroom. *Journal of Applied Behavior Analysis, 8,* 367–372.

White, O. R., & Haring, N. G. (1980). *Exceptional teaching.* Columbus, OH: Charles E. Merrill.

Witt, J. C., Elliott, S. N., & Martens, B. K. (1984). Acceptability of behavioral interventions used in classrooms: The influence of amount of teacher time, severity of behavior problem, and type of intervention. *Behavioral Disorders, 9,* 95–104.

Witt, J. C., Martens, B. K., & Elliott, S. N. (1984). Factors affecting teachers' judgments of the acceptability of behavioral interventions: Time involvement, behavior problem severity, and type of intervention. *Behavior Therapy, 15,* 204–209.

Wolf, M. M. (1978). Social validity: The case for subjective measurement or how applied behavior analysis is finding its heart. *Journal of Applied Behavior Analysis, 11,* 203–214.

20

MANIPULATING REINFORCERS TO REDUCE INAPPROPRIATE BEHAVIOR

Key Terms

■ Differential Reinforcement ■ Differential Reinforcement of Other Behavior (DRO) ■ Whole DRO ■ Momentary DRO ■ Inter-Response Interval ■ Differential Reinforcement of Low Rates (DRL) ■ Full-Session DRL ■ Interval DRL ■ Spaced-Responding DRL ■ Differential Reinforcement of Incompatible Behavior (DRI) ■ Differential Reinforcement of Alternative Behavior (DRA) ■ Vicarious Reinforcement ■ Extinction ■ Extinction Burst ■ Spontaneous Recovery ■ Resistance to Extinction ■ Sensory Extinction ■ Response Cost

Sometimes students' inappropriate behaviors interfere with our ability to teach and their opportunity to learn. Other behavior problems must be reduced because they are viewed as unacceptable by members of the student's social community. In this chapter, a number of behavior-reduction procedures are described that emphasize the role of reinforcement. The principle of least restrictive and most natural and effective strategy is emphasized.

Four reduction strategies are discussed: (a) procedures that emphasize the use of positive reinforcement, specifically differential reinforcement; (b) vicarious reinforcement techniques; (c) extinction; and (d) a reduction procedure called *response cost*. A thorough understanding of the behavior-reduction model discussed in Chapter 19 is an essential prerequisite for using these procedures.

DIFFERENTIAL REINFORCEMENT

One of the least aversive means of reducing troublesome behaviors is to decrease reinforcement opportunities for undesired behaviors by increasing the likelihood that more acceptable behaviors will be strengthened. We can create this condition by using positive reinforcement "differentially." **Differential reinforcement** is defined as the contingent presentation of reinforcing stimuli following desired behavior and the contingent withholding of reinforcing stimuli following undesirable behavior (Repp & Dietz, 1974; Repp & Dietz, 1979). In the following sections, three differential reinforcement procedures are described: differential reinforcement of other behavior, differential reinforcement of low rates, and differential reinforcement of alternative or incompatible behaviors.

Differential Reinforcement of Other Behavior (DRO)

One of the most common uses of differential reinforcement is the **differential reinforcement of other behavior (DRO).** Originally described by Reynolds (1961), DRO is defined as the contingent delivery of a reinforcing stimulus if the target behavior does not occur for a specified period of time. Sometimes called *omission training* (Weiher & Harman, 1975), DRO also has been described as the contingent presentation of a reinforcer for any behavior more appropriate than the response to be reduced.

Effective Use. Two time-based variations of DRO exist. In one type, **whole DRO,** a specified period of time must pass without the emission of the target behavior before the contingent presentation of a reinforcing stimulus (Repp, Barton, & Brulle, 1983). For example, Mike's teacher divides a 20-minute reading period into five 4-minute intervals. For every interval during which no hitting episodes are observed, Mike earns a point. For every four points earned, his teacher gives Mike a special certificate of merit (a previously confirmed reinforcer). In this example, reinforcement is presented contingent upon the absence of the target behavior for a specified period or interval of time.

A second variation is called **momentary DRO** (Deitz & Repp, 1983). Reinforcement is provided if the behavior is not observed at the end of the interval. Although the use of this procedure has been effective in reducing behaviors of individuals with severe retardation, Repp, Barton, and Brulle (1983) indicated stronger effects with whole rather than momentary DRO. At least initially, they suggested that whole DRO should be programmed. After acceptable levels of suppression have been achieved, programming should be shifted to momentary DRO to maintain treatment effects.

Prior to implementing DRO, the following steps should be completed: (a) identify the instructional or intervention setting where DRO will be implemented, (b) develop a clear definition of the target behavior, (c) conduct a functional analysis to determine naturally occurring discriminating and/or reinforcing stimuli, (d) collect data on the target behavior, (e) determine the inter-response interval based on baseline data, and (f) identify effective reinforcers. The **inter-response interval** is used to determine the appropriate schedule of reinforcement. It represents the average length of time between occurrences of the target response and is calculated by dividing the total number of behaviors observed by the total amount of observation time. For example, over five 20-minute observation sessions in baseline conditions, Mike's teacher observed that he hit other students 25 times. The inter-response interval is 4 minutes, or 100 minutes divided by 25 behaviors. Initially, the size of the DRO inter-response interval should be relatively short (i.e., less than the average baseline inter-response time) (Deitz & Repp, 1983). Shorter inter-response intervals will provide the student with more opportunities to earn reinforcement and to experience success.

Based on the student's progress toward the criterion set in the behavioral objective, the inter-response interval should be adjusted gradually, i.e., larger if adequate progress is demonstrated or smaller if inadequate progress is observed. Initially, these adjustments should be made so fixed-interval schedules of reinforcement are developed and then replaced by more variable schedules (e.g., FI:3 minutes, FI:4, FI:5, VI:5, VI:7. . . .). Switching from fixed to variable schedules makes the presentation of reinforcers less predictable, and student performance more consistent.

DRO should always include identification and reinforcement of appropriate replacement behaviors. From functional analysis data, Mike's teacher found that he was hitting his peers because he had not learned how to protest another student's actions in an acceptable manner and at an appropriate time and place. When he saw or heard something he did not like, Mike was taught to put his hands on his lap, turn away from the student, and talk about it with his teacher during homeroom period. Mike received an extra token reinforcer whenever he engaged in this more adaptive response. A simple representation of the DRO procedure is illustrated in Figure 20.1

Considerations. The application of DRO emphasizes positive reinforcement. However, other procedures may be required if one or more of the following conditions exist: (a) the student displays numerous inappropriate behaviors that cannot be ignored or tolerated by the social environment, (b) the student emits other inappropriate behaviors that might be reinforced, (c) reinforcers that are maintaining the target behavior cannot be controlled or removed by the teacher, and (d) teacher-controlled reinforcers are not as powerful as competing and potentially uncontrolled reinforcers available for the target behavior (e.g., laughter from peers). In these conditions, it is advisable to combine DRO with another, more intrusive procedure. For example, Hanley, Perelman, and Homan (1979) taught the mother of a 7-year-old girl with autism to use DRO in combination with timeout to reduce hand and arm waving. Gross, Farrar, and Liner (1982) reduced the self-injurious hair-pulling behaviors of a 4-year-old cerebral palsy child with a procedure consisting of DRO, overcorrection, and

FIGURE 20.1 Procedural flowchart for differential reinforcement of other behaviors (DRO).

Planning Decisions: 1. Identify intervention setting.
2. Define target behavior.
3. Conduct functional analysis.
4. Collect baseline data.
5. Determine interresponse interval.
6. Determine suitable reinforcers and schedule of reinforcement.

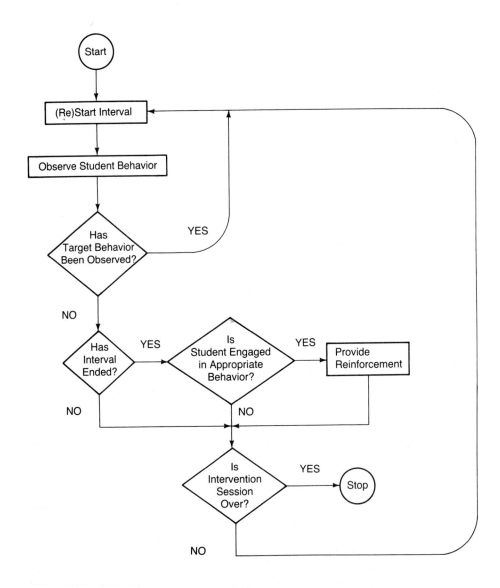

facial screening. Finally, Luce and Hall (1981) combined DRO and contingent exercise to reduce the bizarre verbal behaviors of three severely emotionally disturbed children.

Advantages. DRO is a useful behavior-reduction procedure for a number of reasons. First, DRO emphasizes the use of positive reinforcement and aversive stimuli are not used. As a result, many undesirable side effects may be avoided. DRO is also a useful procedure because target behaviors tend to reduce fairly rapidly, especially if a specific replacement response is strengthened. The focus on only one target behavior leaves many other behaviors eligible for reinforcement. Lastly, DRO has been shown to be effective with a variety of behavioral excesses: physical aggression and tantrums (Allen, Gottselig, & Boylan, 1982; Luiselli, Colozzi, & O'Toole, 1980; Rolider & Van Houten, 1984), regurgitation and rumination (O'Neil, White, King, & Carek, 1979), babbling (Olenick & Pear, 1980), stereotypy (Repp, Deitz, & Speir, 1975), and shouting (Deitz, Repp, & Deitz, 1976).

Differential Reinforcement of Low Rates (DRL)

Similar to DRO, **differential reinforcement of low rates (DRL)** also focuses on the contingent use of positive reinforcement. However, DRL is defined as the presentation of reinforcement contingent upon the emission of behavior at a specified lower rate (Deitz & Repp, 1983; Deitz & Repp, 1973, 1974). DRL is used with behaviors that must be reduced but not necessarily eliminated. For example, Carmelita raises her hand 40 times in a 20-minute period. In a reading group consisting of five students, this rate is too high. However, hand-raising is a useful and important behavior in many classrooms; thus, its total elimination is undesirable. If her teacher were to implement a DRL procedure, reinforcement would be provided for hand-raising frequencies that systematically approach more acceptable rates, e.g., 30, 15, 10, 5 hand raises.

Three variations of DRL have been described (Deitz, 1977; Deitz & Repp, 1983). In **full-session DRL,** the total number of responses observed in a session is compared to a specified criterion, and if responding is at or below that criterion, reinforcers are presented (Deitz & Repp, 1983). A second variation, **interval DRL,** is similar to full-session DRL except that the intervention session is divided into equal intervals. If responding is less than or equal to a specified limit within a given interval, reinforcement is provided. In Carmelita's case, the 20-minute period could be divided into 10 2-minute intervals, and a criterion of one hand raise per interval could be established. For each interval in which Carmelita's hand-raising does not exceed one, she receives reinforcement. The last DRL variation, **spaced-responding DRL,** is defined by the reinforcement of a response that is separated from a prior response by a specified time period. Since Carmelita raises her hand on the average of twice every minute, reinforcement would be provided whenever at least 1 minute passes between hand raises. In all three variations, response rates that exceed the specified criterion result in no reinforcement being presented.

Effective Use. As with DRO, the first steps in implementing DRL are to identify the intervention setting and define the target behavior. The next step is to assess prevailing baseline rates and specify a desired goal rate. This determination may be made by conducting a discrepancy analysis to evaluate what student rates are needed for successful responding in their present setting or in future educational placements, or by examining what rates are viewed as age- or grade-appropriate. Next, the first criterion for an acceptable low rate should be established. This determination will vary depending on which variation of DRL is selected; however, the goal is to increase the student's opportunities for success and frequent reinforcement. A specific data-decision rule for gradually adjusting this criterion also should be established (e.g., change criterion when three consecutive days are at or above criterion). Gradual and successful criterion changes allow students' opportunities to earn reinforcement. The basic steps for implementing DRL are presented in Figure 20.2.

Considerations. The success of DRL requires teachers to consider a number of issues. First, the educational or social environment must be able to tolerate initially high rates of inappropriate behavior. Second, since specific performance standards must be met and gradually adjusted over time, DRL can be time consuming; that is, achieving the target rate will require time. Third, as in DRO, the reinforcers must be powerful enough to compete with other reinforcing stimuli that might be present. If, for example, Carmelita's hand-raising responses are also being maintained by Dion and Rob's attention, teacher-controlled reinforcers will be less effective. Finally, the behavior to be reduced must have a topography or form that is considered acceptable or tolerable by the social environment. This rule limits the use of DRL to those behaviors that are acceptable in accuracy (i.e., form or topography) but are unacceptable at certain rates or frequencies. If a behavior is inaccurate and occurring at high rates, both accuracy and rate must be addressed, and DRL may be an inappropriate strategy. DRL has also been used to reduce and eliminate certain excess behaviors. Rotholz and Luce (1983) systematically eliminated the self-stimulatory behavior (i.e., object spinning and ceiling or hand staring) of an 11-year-old boy with autism to 13 or less per 15-minute interval, to 7 or less, and finally to 0. Toy play (5 minutes with a toy gyroscope) was provided contingently each time a criterion was satisfied. They also reduced the screaming and word repetitions of a 9-year-old boy with autism from a mean baseline frequency of 123 per 30-minute period to less than 15. The DRL criterion was adjusted from 61 to 29, and from 29 to 15. Music was used as a contingent reinforcer.

Advantages. DRL has a number of useful characteristics, the most appealing of which is its tolerant approach to behavior reduction. That is, DRL promotes moderation and tolerance and conveys the message that "what you are doing is

FIGURE 20.2 Procedural flowchart for differential reinforcement of low rate behaviors (DRL).

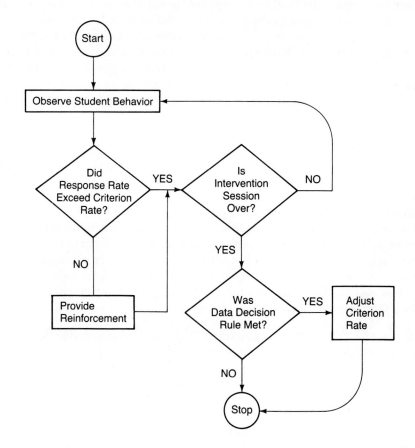

Planning Decisions: 1. Identify intervention setting.
2. Define target behavior.
3. Determine target or goal rate.
4. Specify first criterion rate.
5. Specify data decision rule for changing criterion.
6. Identify suitable reinforcers and schedule of reinforcement.

okay, as long as its not done to excess." As with DRO, DRL is a positive approach that uses regular delivery of reinforcement and does not use aversive stimuli. DRL has been applied to a variety of behaviors: talk-outs, out-of-seats, and aggressions (Deitz & Repp, 1973, 1974; Deitz, Repp, & Deitz, 1976; Deitz, Slack, Schwarzmueller, Wilander, Weatherly, & Hilliard, 1978); stereotypic responding (Singh, Dawson, & Manning, 1981); and self-stimulation (Rotholz & Luce, 1983).

Differential Reinforcement of Incompatible (DRI)
or Alternative (DRA) Behaviors

The **differential reinforcement of incompatible (DRI)** or **alternative (DRA) behaviors** are procedural variations of DRO that involve strengthening a specific behavior that is incompatible with the targeted unacceptable behavior or is an alternative response to the targeted behavior. DRI is a simple procedure that involves strengthening a specific behavior that is topographically incompatible with the undesirable behavior (Deitz & Repp, 1983). If two behaviors cannot be done simultaneously (e.g., standing and sitting), increasing the rate of the desirable behavior will probably decrease the undesirable response, and thus, replace it. For example, Billy hits Martha on the arm when he has to wait for his turn. His teacher uses DRI by having him monitor everyone's 1-minute reading timings with a stopwatch. Since this activity requires great concentration from Billy and he must hold the stopwatch in one hand and a pencil in the other, he is less likely to hit Martha. Billy could also be taught to keep his finger on the words as other students read.

DRA also consists of strengthening a replacement for unwanted behavior except that the alternative may not be topographically incompatible (Deitz & Repp, 1983). Reinforcement is provided for behaviors that are more acceptable. For example, instead of hitting Martha on the arm to get her attention, Billy can be reinforced for raising his hand and asking to talk with Martha after group. With both DRI and DRA procedures, Billy's new behaviors provide him with the opportunity to interact with Martha in a more appropriate manner; he can give information about her reading performance and he can ask her questions. Initially, the teacher provides Billy with positive reinforcement (e.g., verbal praise and token reinforcement) and, after he becomes fluent at these behaviors, he will receive systematically less reinforcement. The basic implementation steps for DRI/A are presented in Figure 20.3.

Effective Use. The first task when using DRI and DRA is to define the behavioral characteristics and communicative value of the unacceptable behavior. This information enables the teacher to select an appropriate replacement behavior. The next step is to select potential alternative or incompatible responses that may reduce the probability that the undesirable behaviors will occur. A list of replacement behaviors should be chosen that are physically incompatible (DRI), yet functionally equivalent, or that provide the student with a more acceptable response alternative (DRA). A specific replacement behavior should be selected from this list based on (a) its presence in the student's response repertoire, (b) its likelihood of being maintained in immediate and future environments, (c) its physical incompatibility or "alternativeness" with the target behavior, and (d) its practical and functional value.

Once a replacement behavior has been identified, differential reinforcement procedures should be followed. Select or identify suitable reinforcers and schedules of reinforcement. Determine data-decision rules that assist in changing

FIGURE 20.3 Procedural flowchart for differential reinforcement of alternative/incompatible behaviors (DRA/I)

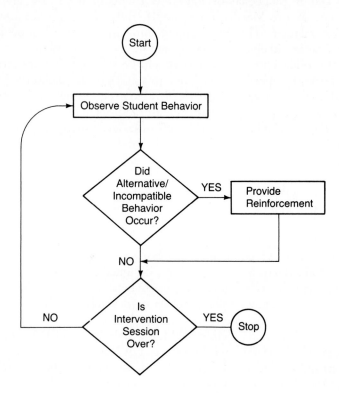

Planning Decisions: 1. Identify intervention setting.
2. Define target behavior.
3. Select and define alternative or incompatible behavior(s).
4. Identify suitable reinforcers and schedule of reinforcement.

the schedules of reinforcement to less restrictive and more natural forms (e.g., VR:12 or VI:45 min.).

Considerations. As with DRO and DRL, differential reinforcement of incompatible or alternative behaviors can be very effective procedures. However, they only can be applied when a suitable replacement behavior or behaviors are identified. *Suitable* means that the replacement behavior must be *physically* incompatible with the target behavior, or must provide a specific alternative to undesirable behaviors. With DRI, one of the most important requirements is that it must be impossible to engage in both the target and replacement behaviors simultaneously.

Alternative and incompatible responses must be functional (Matlock, Billingsley, & Thompson, 1985). This requirement emphasizes the communicative function (Donnellan, Mirenda, Mesaros, & Fassbender, 1984) or critical effect (Neel, 1983) characteristics of the student's behavior. A student may engage in an inappropriate behavior because it sets the occasion for positive or negative reinforcement. The replacement behavior must be associated with similar natural outcomes if it is to become a successfully acquired, maintained, and generalized response and if the behavior excess is to be reduced. By giving reading performance data to Martha, for example, Billy can access her attention in an appropriate manner. This requirement emphasizes the selection of practical behaviors that are likely to be maintained by the environment.

Lastly, replacement behaviors should be selected that are already in the student's response repertoire, i.e., behaviors that have been observed and that are associated with positive reinforcement. This requirement is important for a number of reasons: (a) as a familiar response, additional time will not be needed to teach the replacement behavior; (b) a schedule of reinforcement has already been established and can be incorporated into the intervention plan; and (c) as indicated earlier, the response may already have an established communicative function.

Advantages. As with other differential reinforcement procedures, DRI and DRA are constructive approaches. They emphasize the use of positive reinforcement and the development of appropriate replacement behaviors. Aversive stimuli are not presented or withdrawn with DRI or DRA. As long as a replacement response is maintained, potentially long-lasting reductive effects can be expected (Matlock et al., 1985). Many procedures designed to decrease excess behaviors have short-term effects because replacement behaviors that can be maintained by the natural environment were not identified and developed. If the alternative/incompatible behavior is adequately strengthened and maintained, the undesirable behavior is less likely to be emitted. Many applications of DRI and DRA have been described in the research literature. DRA has been applied to classroom disruptions and academic behaviors (Ayllon, Layman, & Burke, 1972; Ayllon & Roberts, 1974). DRI has been used with in- and out-of-seat behaviors (Twardosz & Sajwaj, 1972), attending and nonattending (Patterson, Jones, Whittier, & Wright, 1965), appropriate and inappropriate speech (Barton, 1970), peer interaction and isolation (Allen, Hart, Buell, Harris, & Wolf, 1964), and stereotypic and appropriate toy play (Flavell, 1973).

VICARIOUS REINFORCEMENT OF OTHERS' BEHAVIORS

Differential reinforcement strategies use direct positive reinforcement of the target student's behavior. In this section, indirect methods of decreasing behavioral excesses and increasing more adaptive responding are described. The term *vicarious reinforcement* is used; however, other common descriptors include modeling or observational learning (Bandura, 1965, 1969, 1976), imitation, incidental learning, and "ripple effect" (Kounin & Gump, 1958).

Definition and Description

Vicarious reinforcement involves the positive reinforcement of other students' behaviors in the presence of an observer whose behaviors have been targeted for modification (Bandura, 1971). The effect is a change in the observer's behaviors although they have not been directly and contingently reinforced. Vicarious reinforcement procedures are similar to DRO, DRA, or DRI in that adaptive behaviors are positively reinforced and inappropriate responses are not. More specifically, peer behaviors are reinforced and the target student is presented with the opportunity to see the reinforcement being applied. As with other forms of learning, effects associated with the use of vicarious reinforcement can be both intentional and unintentional. For example, if a teacher inadvertently reinforces a student's talk-out, other students may see talk-outs as an acceptable means of getting teacher attention.

An examination of Billy's behaviors in reading group reveals that many of them are functionally related to responses emitted by Martha and Rufus. Under these circumstances, Billy's teacher might consider using their adaptive behaviors to influence his inappropriate responses. For example, Kounin and Gump (1958) observed that, by disciplining target students, the behaviors of adjacent students can be affected. They referred to this phenomenon as the *ripple effect*. Similar findings were noted in studies of the effects of punishment on the aggressive behaviors of children. Bandura (1965), in his famous "bobo" doll experiments, found that children who saw punishment associated with aggressive behaviors displayed fewer aggressive responses themselves.

Kazdin (1973b) studied the effect of vicarious reinforcement on the attentive behaviors of four elementary-aged students with moderate mental retardation. He observed that the contingent reinforcement of appropriate attention behaviors displayed by target children affected similar behaviors in observing peers. Interestingly, when inattentive behaviors were reinforced in subsequent reversal phases, Kazdin found that the observers' attentive behaviors remained stable and did not decrease as had been predicted.

These research findings provide evidence for a number of interpretations about how the vicarious reinforcement of others' behaviors operates (Kazdin, 1973b). First, appropriate behaviors are modeled or imitated by observers and set the occasion for the same positive reinforcement received by models. A second interpretation postulates that distracting behaviors displayed by models provide increased opportunities for other students to engage in inappropriate behaviors. Similarly, when the number of distracting behaviors is reduced, the observers are also more likely to engage in acceptable behaviors. A final interpretation suggests that events associated with the delivery of reinforcement to target students function as discriminative stimuli for an observing student's behaviors. Information is provided about possible reinforcement contingencies, reinforceable behavior, and setting conditions; and the "affective expressions of models undergoing rewarding and punishing experiences" (Bandura, 1969, p. 31).

Effective Use

As in all behavior-reduction strategies, the first step in planning for the implementation of vicarious reinforcement is to identify the intervention setting. The next step is to define the problem behavior and more appropriate replacement responses. After operational definitions have been established, current baseline rates of target behaviors for *all* involved students must be determined. Data on current baseline rates allow teachers to determine (a) levels at which students are engaged in the target behavior, (b) if the behavior is really a problem for any one student, and (c) which students might serve as appropriate models. The required characteristics of the model (e.g., gender, status, response characteristics, etc.) described in the next section should be considered.

The next step involves the identification of suitable reinforcers and reinforcement schedules for all involved students. Intermittent schedules should be considered. Simple differential reinforcement procedures can be implemented for both peer and target student behaviors. Strategies should be considered for possible undesirable side-effect responses. As addressed previously, teachers should be honest and consistent in their vicarious reinforcement of student responses. If students perceive teacher behaviors as manipulative or as indicating favoritism, they are less likely to emit desired responses and more likely to engage in inappropriate behaviors. A summary of the steps involved in using vicarious reinforcement is presented in Figure 20.4.

Considerations

Vicarious reinforcement of others' behaviors is a useful reduction procedure, but specific requirements should be considered for efficient and effective implementation. These requirements can be classified into three categories: (a) characteristics of the model, (b) characteristics of the observer, and (c) nature of the outcomes associated with the modeled behavior (Clarizio, 1980).

Before vicariously reinforcing behaviors, it is important to evaluate the characteristics of the student or students who will serve as the reinforced model(s). The model should be similar to the target student with respect to age, gender, response characteristics, and interests. Although competent students who have mastered the desired behaviors can serve as good models, they may also present a picture of inaccessible success. Krumboltz and Thoresen (1969) observed that "coping" models can function as more effective models because they are faced with the same learning/change problem and can appear more similar with respect to current level of functioning. Vicariously reinforcing more than one student who displays the desired responses is also recommended. With more

FIGURE 20.4   Procedural flowchart for vicarious reinforcement of others' behaviors.

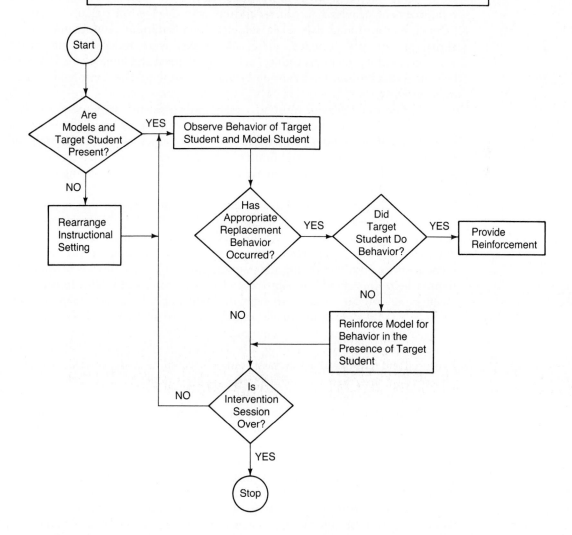

opportunities for social comparison, there is a greater probability that the target student will view the desired behaviors as appropriate.

Both the observing and modeling students should be reinforced for engaging in desirable behaviors. Ollendick, Dailey, and Shapiro (1983) concluded that target students must be reinforced on at least an intermittent basis if the effects of vicarious reinforcement are to be maintained and if counterproductive side effects are to be avoided. They observed that 4- and 5-year-old students who were observers and did not receive intermittent reinforcement made more demands for attention and reinforcement from the teacher and more frequent negative self-statements, e.g., "I quit," "You don't like me," and "I'll tell my mommy about this" (p. 490). These observations suggest that observing children were being punished vicariously, i.e., they were not receiving the same reinforcement provided to other children who engaged in similar behaviors. Ollendick et al. found that when subsequent intermittent reinforcement (i.e., verbal praise) was provided, these side effects were reduced. Thus, when vicarious reinforcement procedures are being planned and implemented, desired behaviors that are emitted by the observing student should be reinforced, at least intermittently.

The desired behavior must be present in the student's response repertoire. Although the acquisition of new behaviors can occur through vicarious reinforcement procedures (Bandura, 1969), error responses tend to be high and teacher feedback opportunities limited. Thus, desired target behaviors that are accurate (acquired) but not fluent are recommended when employing vicarious reinforcement strategies.

A third requirement addresses the kind of information that is provided when a model's responses are vicariously reinforced. Kazdin (1979) recommended that maximum information be provided to students, including (a) a clear description of the reinforced behavior; (b) a delineation of the available consequences, both reinforcing and punishing; and (c) a specification of when the desired behaviors should be emitted and will be reinforced. This information enables the student to compare and evaluate appropriate and inappropriate behaviors and the conditions under which those behaviors are reinforced (Seta, 1982). Young students, new students, and students in new situations may emit inappropriate behaviors simply because they have not learned what behaviors are expected and reinforced in the classroom. By providing students with the type of information described by Kazdin (1979), they can learn what behaviors are expected, will be reinforced, and will not be tolerated.

As discussed in previous chapters, accurate and consistent teacher behaviors are required for the successful use of vicarious reinforcement. Good and Brophy (1984) suggested that teachers must (a) be consistent in practicing what they preach, (b) establish realistic expectations, (c) be honest and reliable in their behavior toward students, and (d) display a "can do" attitude. Similarly, the teacher should be perceived as being competent and in control, and have a history of positive and nurturing relationships with both the model and the target student. Teachers should be informative when reinforcing student behaviors. Desired behaviors, setting conditions, and consequences should be clearly defined and consistently administered. Empirically validated and effective reinforcers and schedules of reinforcement should be utilized. Basic reinforcement strategies, such as the presentation of contingent reinforcement and the use of naturally occurring reinforcers, have been discussed in previous chapters and should be applied to vicarious reinforcement procedures.

Finally, vicarious reinforcement can only be effective if the classroom or social environment can tolerate possible detrimental side-effect behaviors. For example, when Martha and Rufus are contingently reinforced with verbal praise for sitting quietly as other students are reading orally, Billy's teacher must be prepared to reinforce appropriate behaviors and not attend to undesirable behaviors. If Billy cannot determine what the acceptable behaviors are, he is likely to engage in "other" behaviors that have produced reinforcing consequences in the past. These other behaviors may or may not be adaptive in the classroom setting and the teacher must be prepared to respond to them in a consistent fashion.

Advantages

Vicarious reinforcement emphasizes the use of positive reinforcement. Although the focus is placed on the indirect presentation of reinforcement, all students involved in the procedure are reinforced differentially and positively. Furthermore, the procedure is informative and instructional; that is, students can learn, as both observers and participants, about the conditions, behaviors, and consequences that are associated with appropriate and desirable functioning.

Related to its instructional value, vicarious reinforcement strategies can facilitate group functioning by shaping behaviors that enhance the smooth operation of groups. For example, when Billy sees that raising his hand for attention or waiting his turn is positively reinforced, he can learn that these behaviors are associated with cooperative learning and functioning. Another advantage of the vicarious reinforcement is the increased opportunity for students to learn social validation and comparison strategies. When Billy sees another student engage in a behavior and the consequences that follow it, he can compare his own actions to possible consequences. Having these relationships modeled decreases the probability that he will engage in socially inappropriate behavior and increases the likelihood that he will emit desirable responses.

Lastly, vicarious reinforcement procedures increase teachers' instructional efficiency. Not only can they manage the behaviors of a larger number of students, but learning opportunities are increased. The ripple effect can be a powerful means of influencing student performance without expending excessive amounts of time and energy on the implementation of individual instructional programs.

EXTINCTION

The reduction strategies discussed above involve the use of positive reinforcement, either directly or vicariously applied. In this section, another reductive technique that involves the manipulation of reinforcement is discussed.

Definition

Extinction is defined as the contingent termination or withholding of the reinforcer that maintains a target behavior. Extinction is a Type II punishment procedure because positive reinforcement is terminated contingent upon a behavior and a decrease in that behavior results. For example, during math group Ivan slouches in his chair, puts his feet on the table, and leans his head against the wall. His teacher nags him to sit up like a gentleman instead of like a wet noodle. When she uses extinction, his teacher stops nagging Ivan whenever he is slouching. At first Ivan slouches a little bit more, but she continues to withhold her attention, and eventually he starts sitting up in his chair. In this illustration, nagging is a positive reinforcer that is maintaining Ivan's slouching. Extinction consisted of removing this positive reinforcement, and the result was a decrease in slouching.

It is important to understand that a *maintaining* reinforcer is being terminated. If some other consequence is withheld, no change in responding may result. For example, the term *ignoring* is frequently and incorrectly substituted for extinction. Ignoring can be the same as extinction *only* if the attention from the person doing the ignoring is actually functioning as the maintaining reinforcer. To illustrate this point, we can examine Billy's hitting and talking-back behaviors. A functional analysis reveals that Billy's hitting behaviors are maintained and reinforced by cries of distress emitted by the *student* being struck. If the teacher were to "ignore" his behaviors, it is unlikely that hitting would be affected; in fact, we might predict an increase in hitting episodes. To decrease this behavior, the teacher needs to help Billy's peers ignore or withhold their attention. In contrast, an examination of Billy's talking-back responses reveals that they are being maintained and reinforced by the *teacher's* verbal reprimands and attention. In this case, the teacher could ignore talking-back responses and expect them to decrease.

Characteristics

Extinction is a popular and useful procedure for reducing many behavioral excesses. However, a clear understanding of its definition and its effects on behavior are important for effective implementation. Responding under extinction conditions is characterized by (a) extinction bursts, (b) tendencies toward spontaneous recovery, and (c) resistance to extinction.

Extinction Bursts. When extinction programs are first implemented, an **extinction burst,** or an immediate increase in responding, is frequently observed. Sample data for an extinction burst are shown in Figure 20.5. This increase is associated with the change in the schedule of reinforcement. Williams (1959) reported such an increase during a study designed to reduce a young boy's bedtime tantrum behaviors. The parents were instructed to remove attention for aggressive and demanding behaviors. When the extinction program was put into effect, the boy's tantrum behaviors initially escalated but were completely eliminated by the 10th session. Appropriate bedtime behaviors were maintained for about 1 week. Unfortunately, but interestingly, one night the boy's aunt put him to bed and attended to his relatively unobtrusive bedtime fussing behaviors. A full tantrum resulted and previous tantrum durations and rates were observed. By breaking from procedures outlined in the intervention program when she did, the boy's aunt inadvertently reinforced tantrum behaviors. When the extinction conditions were reinstated, Williams noted that the second extinction burst was more intense and the crying episodes overall lasted longer.

In a more recent study with two men who exhibited severe retardation, Neisworth, Hunt, Gallop, and Madle (1985) investigated the effects of extinction when immediately preceded by a continuous schedule of reinforcement (i.e., applesauce and pretzels). For one of the men, they observed a dramatic increase in self-stimulatory behavior immediately after extinction was put into effect. This extinction burst lasted about 5 days before a rapid decrease to near zero levels was observed. Interestingly, they did not observe an immediate increase in the self-stimulatory behavior of the second man. Neisworth et al. postulated that this man's learning history and higher level of functioning may have caused him to respond differently to extinction conditions.

When implementing extinction, teachers should anticipate immediate increases in the target behavior before improvement is seen. Because the probability of extinction bursts is high, teachers should be certain that (a) the schedule of reinforcement previously maintaining the behavior is analyzed, (b) the use of extinction is continued during the increase, (c) the social environment can tolerate an increase, and (d) more adaptive behaviors are being strengthened. If these conditions cannot be met, some other procedure or combination of procedures should be considered (see the decision model in Chapter 19).

FIGURE 20.5 Data illustrating the extinction burst that may occur during extinction programs.

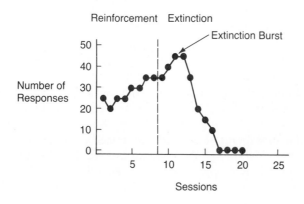

Spontaneous Recovery. The consistent application of extinction is also important to prevent the reinstatement of the problem behavior. When reinforcement for a behavior has been terminated, it is common to see a reoccurrence of that behavior. This phenomenon is called **spontaneous recovery** (Kimble, 1961). Spontaneous recovery is often short lived if the extinction conditions are maintained. However, the inadvertent reinforcement of the behavior can cause a rapid return to prior baseline rates. In the Williams' study (1959), the effect of inadvertent reinforcement was clearly demonstrated. When the boy's aunt reinforced a mild bedtime protest, tantrums were quickly reinstated. Teachers should anticipate spontaneous recovery and be prepared to continue extinction, despite the tendency to think that it is no longer effective.

Resistance to Extinction. Continued responding under extinction conditions is called **resistance to extinction.** Depending on the reinforcement history of the behavior, a considerable amount of time may be required before useful decreases are observed. Behaviors that have been maintained on intermittent schedules of reinforcement are more resistant to the effects of extinction, i.e., they tend to endure or persist longer. Skinner (1953) described responding under extinction in the following manner.

> Behavior during extinction is the result of the conditioning which has preceded it, and in this sense the extinction curve gives an additional measure of the effect of reinforcement. If only a few responses have been reinforced, extinction occurs quickly. A long history of reinforcement is followed by protracted responding. The resistance to extinction cannot be predicted from the probability of response observed at any given moment. We must know the history of reinforcement. (p. 70)

When a long history of intermittent reinforcement exists, gradual reduction may occur. As a result, teachers must be prepared to handle continued occurrences of the behavior. This can be particularly difficult with self-injurious, aggressive, or severe disruptive behaviors. For example, Lovaas and Simmons (1969) examined the effects of extinction on self-injurious behavior. They reported that one subject hit himself "9,000 times" before the behavior was eliminated. A second subject required more than 54 days to remove his self-destructive acts. Lovaas and Simmons conducted their study in a hospital setting in which student behaviors could be carefully monitored. In public schools and other less restrictive settings, gradual reductions of some behaviors (e.g., aggressions, destruction) cannot be tolerated, and more intrusive procedures may be required.

To minimize the resistance to extinction effect, each extinction consequence should continue for a time longer than the longest observed duration of the target behavior. For example, if Ivan's slouching episodes last 3 minutes, the discontinuation of nagging should be maintained for at least 4 minutes. Rolider and Van Houten (1984) taught parents to use graduated extinction to decrease bedtime tantrums. Parents were instructed to put their child in his or her bedroom and leave him or her for a specified period of time. Every two nights, 5 additional minutes were added to the ignoring time. Tantrum behaviors did not decrease until the ignoring time exceeded the duration of tantrums. Zero and near zero levels were achieved in 4 to 9 days. These findings suggest that teachers and parents must be able to apply extinction contingencies at least as long as the duration of the target behaviors being reduced.

Effective Use

The steps for implementing extinction are summarized in Figure 20.6. The first step is to define the problem behavior in operational or observable terms. Given the importance of consistent and objective implementation, it is critical that reliable definitions be developed. The next critical step involves conducting a thorough functional analysis to identify the maintaining reinforcers. Once identified, teachers must determine whether they can reliably terminate or withhold the maintaining reinforcer.

The next step consists of identifying and defining more appropriate replacement behaviors. This determination may be made from the same functional analysis conducted in the previous step, or alternative behaviors may be derived by observing other students, asking relevant others, or analyzing the setting in which the student must function. A suitable reinforcer or set of reinforcers should be identified that competes with those reinforcers that are maintaining the undesirable target behavior. In some cases, the same reinforcer can be used to strengthen replacement responses. Pinkston, Reese, LeBlanc and Baer (1973) found that teacher attention, which was previously maintaining aggressive behavior, could be withheld for low rates of aggressive behavior and could be provided to promote appropriate peer interactions. By systematically presenting and withholding teacher attention for aggressive behaviors, Pinkston et al. confirmed the functional control exerted by attention over aggression. They also used this same teacher attention to increase appropriate peer interactions.

Once reinforcing stimuli and acceptable replacement behaviors have been verified, extinction procedures can be implemented. Consistency and objectivity are essential. Formative evaluation procedures should be used to assess and interpret the effectiveness of extinction. Spontaneous recovery, extinction bursts, and other behavioral side effects should be anticipated and critically evaluated. Sajwaj, Twardosz, and Burke (1972) systematically manipulated teacher attention and observed reliable changes in both appropriate (e.g., conversation, academics, toy play) and inappropriate (e.g., disruptions) behaviors. Their findings suggest that extinction procedures may convey and affect members of a response class of behaviors "directly and/or inversely." Data-decision rules should be established to assist in making program modifications concerning how to deal with side effects.

If specific behaviors prove to be unresponsive to extinction, side effects too costly, or maintaining reinforcers difficult to identify, other interventions may be required. Miles and Cuvo (1980) compared the relative effectiveness of timeout

FIGURE 20.6 Procedural flowchart for implementing extinction programs.

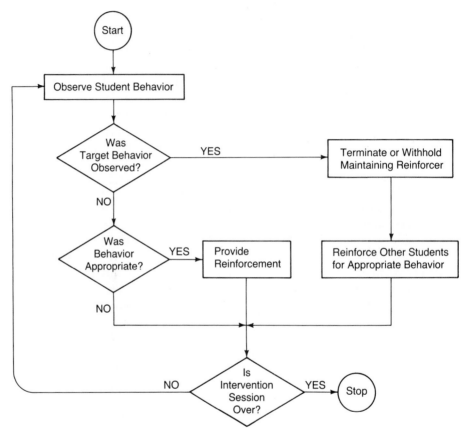

and positive reinforcement to extinction and positive reinforcement on the disruptive behavior of a 9-year-old boy with severe retardation. In the timeout condition, the boy received 2 minutes in a timeout room for each episode of disruptive behavior. During extinction, the teacher turned away from the student when a disruptive behavior occurred. Positive reinforcement consisted of physical contact and social praise for appropriate classroom behaviors and assorted backup activities and edibles for task completion. Miles and Cuvo found timeout and positive reinforcement to be more effective than extinction and positive reinforcement. They hypothesized that the boy's self-stimulatory behaviors or a failure to identify the reinforcers maintaining the boy's disruptions may explain these results.

Considerations

The effective implementation of extinction procedures is contingent upon (a) a clear identification of maintaining or reinforcing stimuli, (b) a consistent and contingent termination or withholding of these reinforcers, and (c) a thorough knowledge of response characteristics under extinction conditions.

Kazdin (1980) provided an excellent summary of these response characteristics and relationships. First, extinction strategies *cannot* be implemented if the reinforcers that are maintaining the behavior are not identifiable, manipulable, and controllable by the teacher, parent, or other change agent. If this requirement cannot be satisfied, extinction procedures cannot be effectively implemented, and a different reduction strategy should be considered. For example, a child may swear in class because of the laughter or attention it elicits from peers. Teacher ignoring of the swearing is likely to have little effect.

Second, behaviors that have been reinforced continuously rather than intermittently tend to be easier to eliminate by extinction. A simple analogy illustrates this point. When a soft drink vending machine is in good operating condition, a drink appears each time the correct money is put in. The machine provides reinforcers (soft drinks) on a continuous schedule of reinforcement. A slot machine, however, presents reinforcers (monetary payoffs) for the same response (putting money in) on an intermittent schedule. If the working components for both machines were surreptitiously manipulated so that no soft drinks or monetary payoffs were possible (extinction), the "putting money in" response would be eliminated faster and sooner in the soft drink machine than in the slot machine.

Third, every target behavior must be followed by nonreinforcement. As described earlier, occasional reinforcement can cause the behavior to be maintained for longer durations and at near baseline levels when extinction conditions are re-implemented. In our slot machine example, one winning payoff is sufficient to reinstate "putting money in" behaviors to previous levels.

Fourth, resistance to extinction is directly related to (a) the strength of the original reinforcer that maintained the behavior, (b) how long the behavior has been reinforced, and (c) the number of times extinction procedures have been attempted. In general, it is more difficult to implement extinction successfully if (a) maintaining reinforcers are very strong, (b) there is a long history or relationship between the behavior and that reinforcer, and (c) extinction has been attempted frequently. Behaviors maintained under these conditions are highly resistant to extinction.

Since extinction effects tend to be produced gradually, the fifth requirement demands that the teacher be extremely careful not to make the previously maintaining reinforcer available. One "accident" or inconsistency in program implementation can cause the behavior to recur at or above previous levels and to be more resistant in future extinction attempts.

If extinction procedures are considered, the social environment must be willing and able to tolerate (a) increases in behavior frequency and intensity, (b) spontaneous recoveries of the targeted behavioral excess, and (c) emotional reactions, such as behaviors suggesting aggression, depression, frustration, failure, etc. Matson and Dilorenzo (1984) provided the following explanation:

> If the reinforcer is withheld, the response ultimately will decrease. If, however, the increased responding is reinforced accidentally, then (1) the client realizes that sometimes increased responding is necessary to obtain the reinforcer, (2) a lean intermittent schedule is reintroduced, and (3) the behavior becomes more resistant to extinction. (p. 105)

Further, the social environment must be able to deal with peers who imitate the occurrence of inappropriate behaviors when it appears that aversive consequences are absent. For example, by ignoring Mario's talking back, the teacher may be inadvertently teaching Linda and George that there are no contingent consequences for this behavior. As a result, they may engage in the same behavior and develop new reinforcing contingencies. These side effects can be minimized by reinforcing peers who are displaying appropriate behavior. Focusing teacher attention in this manner helps the teacher not attend to the target student's disruptive behaviors.

The last and equally important requirement is to identify, teach, and reinforce a functional adaptive behavior that can serve as a replacement for the target response. If extinction procedures create a behavioral "vacuum," spontaneous recovery of undesirable behaviors is possible. The student must have a suitable alternative behavior that has the same communicative functions as those associated with behaviors being eliminated or reduced.

These requirements for using extinction clearly attest to the complexity of the procedure. It cannot be referred to as simply "ignoring."

Advantages

The cautions and limitations associated with extinction strategies have been emphasized frequently in the previous sections. However, extinction also has advantages. First, it is less aversive and more natural than procedures that are characterized as Type I punishment. It is a less aversive approach than response cost, timeout, contingent application of aversive stimuli, and overcorrection.

If its requirements are satisfied, extinction can be easy to implement. It is also a very powerful procedure that can be associated with lasting effects if the correct assessments are conducted *and* if suitable and functional replacement responses are shaped and strengthened.

Sensory Extinction

Sensory extinction is a specialized variation of extinction used to decrease behaviors that produce reinforcing sensory consequences (Rincover, 1978, 1981). Rincover first observed the effects of sensory extinction when working with a child who engaged in plate twirling as a self-stimulatory behavior. It was hypothesized that the sound of the plate on the table was functioning as the maintaining auditory reinforcer. When a piece of carpet was placed on the table, an immediate reduction in plate twirling was observed. Sensory extinction has been used to reduce a variety of self-stimulatory behavior in autistic children: object twirling, finger flapping, echolalia, light switch flipping (Devany & Rincover, 1982; Rincover, Cook, Peoples, & Packard, 1979; Rincover, Newsom, & Carr, 1979). It has also been applied to self-injury behaviors (Rincover & Devany, 1982).

In another study of auditory/sensory extinction, Day (1985) placed earplugs in the ears of a 9-year-old boy with profound retardation whenever he shrieked. Contingent 2-minute applications of earplugs following the onset of shrieks produced decreases in shrieking vocalizations. Sensory extinction has also been applied to tactile self-stimulatory behaviors. Maag, Rutherford, Wolchik, and Parks (1986) conducted a study of the relative effectiveness and generalization effects of sensory extinction and overcorrection on the self-stimulatory behavior of two autistic children. Both overcorrection (guided hand and arm movements) and sensory extinction (elastic strips for hand weaving, and pipe cleaners for string twirling) were effective in reducing self-stimulatory behaviors; however, only overcorrection produced reliable generalization from structured to unstructured settings.

The results from these studies suggest that sensory extinction may be effective for students who engage in high rates of self-stimulatory behavior, especially when more intrusive procedures such as overcorrection are not possible. A careful determination of the sensory reinforcement produced by a self-stimulatory behavior is required to ensure effective decreases. The current research, however, is inconclusive about the generalizability of sensory extinction effects.

RESPONSE COST

When differential reinforcement procedures or extinction prove to be ineffective, more intrusive and restrictive procedures may be considered. Response cost is an appropriate alternative if (a) reinforcers that are maintaining the undesirable behavior are not identifiable, (b) the dimensions (e.g., frequency, intensity) of the behavior are so extreme or severe that they must be changed immediately, (c) repeated attempts to use positive reinforcement strategies (i.e., DRO, DRI) have been unsuccessful, or (d) the long-term suppression of the response has not been achieved.

Definitions and Characteristics

Response cost is the withdrawal or removal of a reinforcer contingent upon the emission of an undesirable behavior that results in a reduction of the occurrence of the target behavior. Response cost is analogous to giving an individual a fine or penalty for inappropriate behavior. When automobile drivers exceed the posted speed limit, they may receive a ticket for which they are required to pay a specified amount of money (i.e., conditioned reinforcer). When an illegal action occurs during a football game, a loss of earned yards is assessed. When workers arrive late to their jobs, they may be docked a portion of their pay. When students engage in inappropriate classroom behaviors, they may lose minutes of recess. If future occurrences of speeding behavior, illegal sports play, and late arrivals are reduced, response cost has been implemented.

Response cost was first applied by Weiner (1962) and has been studied extensively (Kazdin, 1972; Matson & DiLorenzo, 1984; Pazulinec, Meyerrose, & Sajwaj, 1983; Rimm & Masters, 1979; Walker, 1983). Response cost is frequently confused with extinction and timeout. Extinction is the contingent *termination* or removal of reinforcers that maintain a target behavior. Response cost is similar except that it involves the contingent *removal* of reinforcers that have already been acquired and are not necessarily those that maintain the target behavior. Timeout is the contingent loss of the opportunity to access reinforcers for a specific period of time. Response cost does not involve a loss of the opportunity to earn reinforcers; previously earned reinforcers simply are removed.

Response cost procedures are commonly used in token economies. Individuals earn conditioned reinforcers for specific appropriate behaviors and are fined for specific undesirable responses (Kazdin, 1977). Elaborate systems have been developed that consist of particular rules for token gains, losses, and savings (e.g., Hops, Beickel, & Walker, 1976; Phillips, 1968; Phillips, Phillips, Fixsen, & Wolf, 1971; Walker, Hops, & Greenwood, 1981). For example, Debbie's teacher rewards appropriate social behaviors with points and punishes unacceptable responses with point fines. Debbie earns reinforcers that can be lost if inappropriate behaviors are observed.

Other variations of response cost can be developed. In one alternative, the teacher noncontingently gives students a specific number of conditioned reinforcers. When a target behavior occurs, a specified number of reinforcers are removed. For example, at the beginning of each reading group, Michael is given 15 minutes in the computer lab during lunch period. During reading, Michael's teacher removes 1 minute of his computer lab time for each talking-out episode. In this example, appropriate social behaviors are not directly reinforced; however, undesirable responses are followed by a contingent loss of reinforcers.

In another variation, a specified number of previously earned conditioned reinforcers is given to another person who then manages the response-cost consequences. For example, at the beginning of each reading group, Kyoko gives her teacher a one dollar bill that she would normally use to buy a dessert.

Whenever Kyoko is talking instead of following along, her teacher takes 25 cents and places it in a jar. This money will be sent to Kyoko's parents who will re-use it in her weekly allowance. Again, desired behaviors are not directly reinforced, but a loss of previously earned conditioned reinforcers is assessed. If talk-outs decrease to desired levels, response cost has been successfully implemented.

Effective Use

Given the considerations outlined above, response cost can be an effective behavior-reduction strategy if implemented accurately and consistently. The steps for implementing response cost are shown in Figure 20.7. The first step consists of determining if naturally occurring reinforcers are available for contingent removal. For example, minutes of recess, free reading, or independent play time are common reinforcers that can be used in response cost. If manipulatable reinforcers are not available, teachers should consider establishing a contingency-management system that employs conditioned reinforcers, e.g., token economy. This system must have effective guidelines for managing reinforcers, schedules of reinforcement, and possible side effects. More detailed descriptions of token economies and reinforcement systems are presented in Chapter 23.

After students have had the opportunity to acquire reinforcers and to establish a reinforcer reserve, response cost can be implemented. The first requirement is to provide clear definitions of those behaviors that earn positive reinforcement and those that earn penalties. Once these descriptions have been established, students must be taught rules that explain the conditions under which behaviors can be emitted and the size of rewards and fines. Based on each student's learning history, guidelines should be developed for (a) the size of each response-cost consequence, (b) the number and kind of backup reinforcers, and (c) contingency plans for undesirable side effects.

The effective use of response cost also requires specific procedures for actually collecting response-cost fines. This is especially important if tangible reinforcers are utilized. If a student refuses to "give up" her tokens, a backup contingency should be followed. Teachers should not engage in lengthy discussions or physical struggles with students over reinforcers. Instead, noncompliance should be dealt with in a standardized fashion. For example, a "lien" might be placed on other reinforcer activities or savings. Regardless of the strategy, reinforcer losses should be handled in an objective, brief, and businesslike fashion. Lengthy discussions, justifications, and arguments should be reserved for a later time and place designed for such interactions. Many of these problems can be avoided by establishing and teaching clear rules and guidelines for reinforcer earning and losses.

Walker (1983) gave three "preconditions" for the application of response cost procedures: (a) "the system should be carefully explained before applying

FIGURE 20.7   Procedural flowchart for implementing response cost.

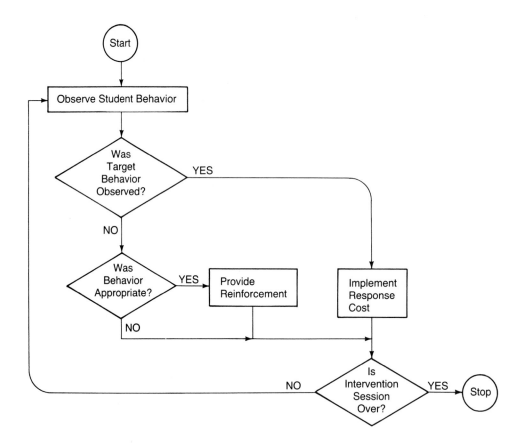

Planning Decisions: 1. Identify intervention setting.
2. Define target behaviors.
3. Identify or develop suitable conditioned reinforcers (including backup reinforcers).
4. Develop rules for reinforcer loss.
5. Develop procedures for reinforcer earning.
6. Develop rules and procedures for repeated target behaviors.
7. Explain rules to students.

it," (b) "it should be tied to a reinforcement system," and (c) "an appropriate delivery system should be developed" (p. 52). He also indicated that seven rules should be followed when implementing response cost:

1. RC should be implemented immediately after the target response or behavior occur.

2. RC should be applied each time an instance of a target behavior occurs.

3. The child should never be allowed to accumulate negative points.

4. The ratio of points earned to those lost should be controlled.

5. The implementation agent should never be intimidated out of using RC by the target child.

6. The subtraction of points should never be punitive or personalized.

7. The child's positive, appropriate behavior should be praised as frequently as opportunities permit. (p. 52)

Considerations

Like extinction, response cost is a useful procedure for managing behavioral excesses. However, the emphasis placed on the loss of previously acquired or held conditioned reinforcers demands that we view it as an aversive technique. As such, we must keep a number of implementation requirements in mind. First, the effectiveness of any response-cost procedure depends on the type and frequency of reinforcement opportunities and the individual's reinforcement history (Kazdin, 1972, 1975; Weiner, 1963). A balance must be achieved between schedules of positive reinforcement and the size of reinforcer earnings and losses. If Roger loses a relatively small amount of points compared to the number of reinforcers he has acquired, the procedure may be of limited effectiveness.

Response cost can only be implemented where manipulable reinforcers are present, or where there are regular opportunities to earn back or replenish lost reinforcers. If a deprivation state cannot be maintained, response penalties will be ineffectual. The "wealthy" person who can afford reinforcer losses will probably find response cost more a hindrance than a behavior-change incentive. On the other hand, the reinforcer-poor individual will be much more responsive to intervention consequences, at least up to the point where the debt becomes so severe that response cost and positive reinforcement become ineffective. A solution to this type of problem was reported by Doty, McInnis, and Paul (1974). Twenty-eight patients in a hospital for chronically disturbed adults were so far in debt from token fines that they were unable to access backup reinforcers. The frequency of inappropriate behavior was increasing. To remedy this problem, patients were allowed to "purchase eligibility to obtain back-up reinforcers through contingent payment on standing fines, combined with proportional payoff schedules contingent upon time without new fines" (p. 197). The effect was an increase in fine payments and purchases of consumable backup reinforcers, and a reduction in the number and kinds of behaviors that would normally result in response cost.

When considering response cost, possible side effects must be recognized. First, teachers must control the situation in which response-cost procedures are implemented. Opportunities to acquire or steal "free" reinforcers from outside sources or to escape or avoid aversive consequences must be prevented.

Contingency plans should be established for students who respond with aggressive or disruptive behaviors. Teachers should be clear and specific about what behaviors receive positive reinforcement and response cost.

Since it is a relatively simple procedure to implement, response cost can be easily abused. When teachers become frustrated with highly disruptive behaviors, they may give excessively large fines or may use response cost more frequently than necessary. With high-frequency inappropriate behaviors, fines can accumulate quickly. If backup contingencies are absent, students can be quickly placed in severe debit situations in which there is even less incentive to change. In these cases, response cost should be supplemented with a solid program of positive reinforcement. If the maximum number of fines or size of debts is exceeded, backup consequences should be given. For example, a response-cost penalty can be given for the first two occurrences of a behavior in a 30-minute period. If a third response occurs, a more intrusive consequence (e.g., timeout) is provided.

The implementation of response cost should be closely monitored. Close supervision and regular evaluation will prevent many of the above problems from getting out of control. Although conducted in a prison setting, findings by Bassett and Blanchard (1977) support the need for careful supervision and accurate implementation. They noted a deterioration and abuse of these procedures when the prison director was absent. Response-cost use and the categories of inappropriate behaviors increased dramatically when supervision was removed.

In summary, a basic requirement for the use of response cost is the presence of opportunities to earn positive reinforcers. Within this condition, individual learning histories must be considered. Response cost does not have universally reductive effects and its effectiveness may vary with an individuals' experiences, successes, and failures with reinforcement and response cost. Specific contingencies for possible side-effect behaviors must be prepared.

Advantages

When less aversive or restrictive procedures are ineffective, response cost can be a useful alternative. Response cost has been shown to be effective across a range of settings and behaviors: fire setting and aggression (Doty, McInnis, & Paul, 1974), speech difficulties (James, 1981; Kazdin, 1973; Siegel, Lenske, & Broen, 1969), head-banging and hand-biting (Woods, 1982), inappropriate verbalizations (McLaughlin & Malaby, 1972), hyperactivity (Rapport, Murphy, & Bailey, 1982), and crying (Reisinger, 1972). Furthermore, its effects tend to be relatively immediate and long lasting when paired with a strong system of reinforcement.

Response cost is relatively convenient and easy to use. Because it is similar in principle to what we experience in daily living, it is generally viewed as relatively natural and constructive. Although it can be overused and abused, response cost has its own fail-safe system; that is, it no longer functions as response cost when the individual is depleted of reinforcers.

Response cost can be administered quickly and immediately. Lengthy discussions and arguments are avoided if rules and guidelines have been clearly established. In addition, response cost does not remove the student from the existing learning or social setting as in timeout. Furthermore, response-cost procedures are quite versatile. They can be implemented with students who are young or have severe handicaps or with individuals who are older or more sophisticated.

Lastly, response cost can be easily applied to groups of students. McLaughlin and Malaby (1972) observed that a single teacher could reduce the inappropriate verbalizations of a group of approximately 25 fifth and sixth graders by making tokens (i.e., points) and teacher attention contingent on being quiet. They also reported that "the management of the token system of which control of inappropriate verbalizations was a part required only 15 minutes of time a week" (p. 332).

Summary of Key Concepts

- Behavioral excesses that interfere with teaching and learning can be decreased by systematically reinforcing more adaptive responses.

- Differential reinforcement is a useful and important procedure for strengthening adaptive behavior and decreasing undesirable behavior. It is the foundation for DRO, DRL, and DRI/A.

- Extinction is a useful strategy if the reinforcer that maintains a behavior can be identified and terminated or withheld.

- Extinction is a much more comprehensive strategy than simply ignoring a student's behaviors.

- When using extinction, we should prepare for increases in the inappropriate behavior, spontaneous recovery, and delayed decreases before desired reductions are achieved.

- Students can learn about appropriate and inappropriate behaviors by observing how teachers respond to and reinforce their peer's behaviors.

- Response cost is a simple procedure with many analogies in everyday activities; however, its effectiveness depends on the individual's learning history and experiences with reinforcement.

- Type II punishment procedures (extinction and response cost) are characterized by the contingent termination, withholding, or removal of positive reinforcement and a decrease in the target behavior.

- When implementing Type II punishment procedures (extinction and response cost), careful planning and consistent implementation are required. Failure to consider and plan for typical response patterns or side effects can cause problem behaviors to be more difficult to change. The decision model described in Chapter 19 should be used.

- The actual implementation of a Type II punishment procedure is relatively simple. The most important and difficult steps consist of (a) determining what procedure is most appropriate, (b) predicting and planning for possible side effects, and (c) strengthening suitable replacement behaviors.

REFERENCES

Allen, K. E., Hart, B., Buell, J. S., Harris, F. R., & Wolf, M. M. (1964). Effects of social reinforcement on isolate behavior of a nursery school child. *Child Development, 35,* 511–518.

Allen, L. D., Gottselig, M., & Boylan, S. (1982). A practical mechanism for using freetime as reinforcer in the classroom. *Education and Treatment of Children, 5,* 247–353.

Ayllon, T., Layman, D., & Burke, S. (1972). Disruptive behavior and reinforcement of academic performance. *Psychological Record, 22,* 315–323.

Ayllon, T., & Roberts, M. D. (1974). Eliminating discipline problems by strengthening academic performance. *Journal of Applied Behavior Analysis, 7,* 71–76.

Bandura, A. (1965). Influence of model's reinforcement contingencies on the acquisition of imitative responses. *Journal of Personality and Social Psychology, 1,* 589–595.

Bandura, A. (1969). *Principles of behavior modification.* New York: Holt, Rinehart & Winston.

Bandura, A. (1971). Vicarious and self-reinforcement processes. In R. Glaser (Ed.), *The nature of reinforcement.* New York: Academic Press.

Bandura, A. (1976). *Social learning theory.* Englewood Cliffs, NJ: Prentice-Hall.

Barton, E. S. (1970). Inappropriate speech in a severely retarded child: A case study in language conditioning and generalization. *Journal of Applied Behavior Analysis, 3,* 299–307.

Bassett, J. E., & Blanchard, E. B. (1977). The effect of the absence of close supervision on the use of response cost in a prison token economy. *Journal of Applied Behavior Analysis, 10,* 375–379.

Clarizio, H. F. (1980). *Toward positive classroom discipline* (3rd ed.). New York: John Wiley & Sons.

Day, H. M. (1985). The use of earplugs to reduce shrieking in a profoundly retarded child. *Education and Treatment of Children, 8,* 107–114.

Deitz, D. E. D., & Repp, A. C. (1983). Reducing behavior through reinforcement. *Exceptional Education Quarterly, 3,* 34–46.

Deitz, S. M. (1977). An analysis of programming DRL schedules in educational settings. *Behavior Research and Therapy, 15,* 103–111.

Deitz, S. M., & Repp, A. C. (1973). Decreasing classroom misbehavior through the use of DRL schedules of reinforcement. *Journal of Applied Behavior Analysis, 6,* 457–463.

Deitz, S. M., & Repp, A. C. (1974). Differentially reinforcing low rates of misbehavior with normal elementary school children. *Journal of Applied Behavior Analysis, 7,* 622.

Deitz, S. M., Repp, A. C., & Deitz, D. E. D. (1976). Reducing inappropriate classroom behavior of retarded students through three procedures of differential reinforcement. *Journal of Mental Deficiency Research, 20,* 155–170.

Deitz, S. M., Slack, D. J., Schwarzmueller, E. B., Wilander, A. P., Weatherly, T. J., & Hilliard, G. (1978). Reducing inappropriate behavior in special classrooms by reinforcing average interresponse times: Interval DRL. *Behavior Therapy, 9,* 37–46.

Devany, J., & Rincover, A. (1982). Self-stimulatory behavior and sensory reinforcement. In R. Koegel, A. Rincover, & A. Egel (Eds.), *Educating and understanding autistic children.* San Diego, CA: College Hill Press.

Donnellan, A. M., Mirenda, P. L., Mesaros, R. A., & Fassbender, L. L. (1984). Analyzing the communicative functions of aberrant behavior. *Journal of the Association for the Severely Handicapped, 9,* 201–212.

Doty, D. W., McInnis, T., & Paul, G. L. (1974). Remediation of negative side effects of an ongoing response-cost system with chronic mental patients. *Journal of Applied Behavior Analysis, 7,* 191–198.

Flavell, J. E. (1973). Reduction of stereotypies by

reinforcement of toy play. *Mental Retardation, 11,* 21–23.

Good, T. L., & Brophy, J. E. (1984). *Looking in classrooms* (3rd ed.). New York: Harper & Row.

Gross, A. M., Farrar, M. J., & Liner, D. (1982). Reduction of trichotillomania in a retarded cerebral palsied child using overcorrection, facial screening, and differential reinforcement of other behavior. *Education and Treatment of Children, 5,* 133–140.

Hanley, E. M., Perelman, P. E., & Homan, C. I. (1979). Parental management of a child's self-stimulation behavior through the use of timeout and DRO. *Education and Treatment of Children, 2,* 305–310.

Hops, H., Beickel, S. L., & Walker, H. M. (1976). *CLASS (Contingencies for Learning Academic and Social Skills) program consultant manual.* Center at Oregon for Research in the Behavioral Education of the Handicapped (CORBEH), University of Oregon, Eugene.

James, J. E. (1981). Behavioral self-control of stuttering using time-out from speaking. *Journal of Applied Behavior Analysis, 14,* 25–37.

Kazdin, A. E. (1972). Response cost: The removal of conditioned reinforcers for therapeutic change. *Behavior Therapy, 3,* 533–546.

Kazdin, A. E. (1973a). Effect of response cost and aversive stimulation in suppressing punished and nonpunished speech dysfluencies. *Behavior Therapy, 4,* 73–82.

Kazdin, A. E. (1973b). The effect of vicarious reinforcement on attentive behavior in the classroom. *Journal of Applied Behavior Analysis, 6,* 71–78.

Kazdin, A. E. (1975). *Behavior modification in applied settings.* Homewood, IL: Dorsey Press.

Kazdin, A. E. (1977). *The token economy: A review and evaluation.* New York: Plenum.

Kazdin, A. E. (1979). Vicarious reinforcement and punishment in operant programs for children. *Child Behavior Therapy, 1,* 13–26.

Kazdin, A. E. (1980). *Behavior modification in applied settings* (2nd ed.). Homewood, IL: Dorsey Press.

Kimble, G. A. (1961). *Hilgard and Marquis' conditioning and learning.* New York: Appleton-Century-Crofts.

Kounin, J. S., & Gump, P. V. (1958). The ripple effect in discipline. *Elementary School Journal, 59,* 158–162.

Krumboltz, J., & Thoresen, C. (Eds.) (1969). *Behavioral counseling cases and techniques.* New York: Holt, Rinehart, & Winston.

Lovaas, O. I., & Simmons, J. Q. (1969). Manipulation of self-destruction in three retarded children. *Journal of Applied Behavior Analysis, 2,* 143–157.

Luce, S. C., & Hall, V. (1981). Contingent exercise: A procedure used with differential reinforcement to reduce bizarre verbal behavior. *Education and Treatment of Children, 4,* 309–327.

Luiselli, J. K., Colozzi, G. A., & O'Toole, K. M. (1980). Programming response maintenance of differential reinforcement effects. *Child Behavior Therapy, 2,* 65–73.

Maag, J. W., Rutherford, R. B., Jr., Wolchik, S. A., & Parks, B. T. (1986). Sensory extinction and overcorrection in suppressing self-stimulation: A preliminary comparison of efficacy and generalization. *Education and Treatment of Children, 9,* 189–201.

Matlock, B., Billingsley, F. F., & Thompson, M. (1985). Response competition and generalization. In N. Haring, K. Liberty, F. Billingsley, V. Lynch, J. Kayser, & F. McCarty (Eds.), *Investigating the problem of skill generalization* (3rd ed.) (pp. 80–87). Seattle: Washington Research Organization.

Matson, J. L., & DiLorenzo, T. M. (1984). *Punishment and its alternatives: A new perspective for behavior modification.* New York: Springer.

McLaughlin, T., & Malaby, J. (1972). Reducing and measuring inappropriate verbalizations in a token classroom. *Journal of Applied Behavior Analysis, 5,* 329–333.

Miles, C. L., & Cuvo, A. J. (1980). Modification of the disruptive and productive classroom behavior of a severely retarded child: A comparison of two procedures. *Education and Treatment of Children, 3,* 113–122.

Neel, R. S. (1983). *Teaching autistic children: A functional curriculum approach (IMPACT).* Seattle: University of Washington.

Neisworth, J. T., Hunt, F. M., Gallop, H. R., & Madle, R. A. (1985). Reinforcer displacement: A preliminary study of the clinical application of the CRF/EXT effect. *Behavior Modification, 9,* 103–115.

O'Neil, P. M., White, J. L., King, C. R., & Carek, D. J. (1979). Controlling childhood rumination through differential reinforcement of other behavior. *Behavior Modification, 3,* 355–372.

Olenick, D. L., & Pear, J. J. (1980). Differential reinforcement of correct responses to probes and prompts in picture-name training with severely retarded children. *Journal of Applied Behavior Analysis, 13*, 77–89.

Ollendick, T. H., Dailey, D., & Shapiro, E. S. (1983). Vicarious reinforcement: Expected and unexpected effects. *Journal of Applied Behavior Analysis, 16*, 485–491.

Pazulinec, R., Meyerrose, M. & Sajwaj, T. (1983). Punishment via response cost. In S. Axelrod & J. Apsche (Eds.), *The effects of punishment on human behavior* (pp. 71–86). New York: Academic Press.

Patterson, G. R., Jones, R., Whittier, J., & Wright, M. A. (1965). A behavior modification technique for the hyperactive child. *Behavior Research and Therapy, 2*, 217–226.

Phillips, E. L. (1968). Achievement place: Token reinforcement procedures in a home-style rehabilitative setting for "predelinquent" boys. *Journal of Applied Behavior Analysis, 1*, 213–223.

Phillips, E. L., Phillips, E. A., Fixsen, D. L., & Wolf, M. M. (1971). Achievement place: Modification of the behaviors of predelinquent boys within a token economy. *Journal of Applied Behavior Analysis, 4*, 45–49.

Pinkston, E. M., Reese, N. M., LeBlanc, J. M., & Baer, D. M. (1973). Independent control of a preschool child's aggression and peer interaction by contingent teacher attention. *Journal of Applied Behavior Analysis, 6*, 115–124.

Rapport, M. D., Murphy, H. A., & Bailey, J. S. (1982). Ritalin vs. response cost in the control of hyperactive children: A within-subject comparison. *Journal of Applied Behavior Analysis, 15*, 205–216.

Reisinger, J. J. (1972). The treatment of anxiety-depression via positive reinforcement and response cost. *Journal of Applied Behavior Analysis, 5*, 125–130.

Repp, A. C., Barton, L. E., & Brulle, A. R. (1983). A comparison of two procedures for programming the differential reinforcement of other behavior. *Journal of Applied Behavior Analysis, 16*, 435–445.

Repp, A. C., & Deitz, D. E. D. (1979). Reinforcement based reductive procedures: Training and monitoring performance of institutional staff. *Mental Retardation, 17*, 221–226.

Repp, A. C., & Deitz, S. M. (1974). Reducing aggressive and self-injurious behavior of institutionalized retarded children through reinforcement of other behavior. *Journal of Applied Behavior Analysis, 7*, 313–325.

Repp, A. C., Deitz, S. M., & Speir, N. C. (1975). Reducing stereotypic responding of retarded persons through the differential reinforcement of other behaviors. *American Journal of Mental Deficiency, 80*, 51–56.

Reynolds, G. S. (1961). Behavioral contrast. *Journal of Experimental Analysis of Behavior, 4*, 57–71.

Rimm, D. C., & Masters, J. C. (1979). *Behavior therapy: Techniques and empirical findings.* New York: Academic Press.

Rincover, A. (1978). Sensory extinction: A procedure for eliminating self-stimulatory behavior in psychotic children. *Journal of Abnormal Child Psychology, 6*, 299–330.

Rincover, A. (1981). *How to use sensory extinction: A nonaversive treatment for self-stimulation and other behavior problems.* Lawrence, KS: H & H Enterprises.

Rincover, A., Cook, A., Peoples, A., & Packard, D. (1979). Using sensory extinction and sensory reinforcement principles to program multiple treatment gains. *Journal of Applied Behavior Analysis, 12*, 221–233.

Rincover, A., & Devany, J. (1982). The application of sensory extinction principles to self-injury in developmentally disabled children. *Analysis and Intervention in Developmental Disabilities, 1*, 67–69.

Rincover, A., Newsom, C. D., & Carr, E. G., (1979). Using sensory extinction procedures in the treatment of compulsive-like behavior of developmentally disabled children. *Journal of Consulting and Clinical Psychology, 47*, 695–701.

Rolider, A., & Van Houten, R. (1984). The effects of DRO alone and DRO plus reprimands on the undesirable behavior of three children in home settings. *Education and Treatment of Children, 7*, 17–31.

Rotholz, O. A., & Luce, S. C. (1983). Alternative reinforcement strategies for the reduction of self-stimulatory behavior in autistic youth. *Education and Treatment of Children, 6*, 363–377.

Sajwaj, T., Twardosz, S., & Burke, M. (1972). Side effects of extinction procedures in a remedial preschool. *Journal of Applied Behavior Analysis, 5*, 163–175.

Seta, J. J. (1982). The impact of comparison processes on co-actors' task performance. *Journal of Personality and Social Psychology, 42,* 281–291.

Siegel, G. M., Lenske, J., & Broen, P. (1969). Suppression of normal speech dysfluencies through response cost. *Journal of Applied Behavior Analysis, 2,* 265–276.

Singh, N. N., Dawson, M. J., & Manning, P. (1981). Effects of spaced responding DRL on the stereotyped behavior of profoundly retarded persons. *Journal of Applied Behavior Analysis, 14,* 521–526.

Skinner, B. F. (1953). *Science and human behavior.* New York: Macmillan.

Twardosz, S., & Sajwaj, T. (1972). Multiple effects of a procedure to increase sitting in a hyperactive, retarded boy. *Journal of Applied Behavior Analysis, 5,* 73–78.

Walker, H. M. (1983). Applications of response cost in school settings: Outcomes, issues, and recommendations. *Exceptional Education Quarterly, 3,* 47–55.

Walker, H. M., Hops, H., & Greenwood, C. R. (1981). RECESS: Research and development of a behavior management package for remediating social aggression in the school setting. In P. Strain (Ed.), *Utilization of classroom peers as behavior change agents (pp. 261-303).* New York: Plenum.

Weiher, R. G., & Harman, R. E. (1975). The use of omission training to reduce self-injurious behavior in a retarded child. *Behavior Therapy, 6,* 261–268.

Weiner, H. (1962). Some effects of response cost upon human development. *Journal of Experimental Analysis of Behavior, 5,* 201–208.

Weiner, H. (1963). Response cost and aversive control of human operant behavior. *Journal of Experimental Analysis of Behavior, 6,* 415–421.

Williams, C. D. (1959). The elimination of tantrum behavior by extinction procedures. *Journal of Abnormal and Social Psychology, 59,* 269.

Woods, T. S. (1982). Reducing severe aggressive and self-injurious behavior: A nonintrusive home based approach. *Behavior Disorders, 7,* 180–188.

21

USING TIMEOUT FROM POSITIVE REINFORCEMENT

Key Terms

■ Timeout from Positive Reinforcement ■ Nonexclusionary Timeout ■ Exclusionary Timeout ■ Planned Ignoring Timeout ■ Removal of Tangible Objects ■ Timeout Ribbon ■ Contingent Observation ■ Exclusion Timeout ■ Movement Suppression ■ Isolation/Seclusion ■ Timein ■ Enrichment ■ Verbal Explanation ■ Signal ■ Warnings ■ Duration of Timeout ■ Backup Contingencies ■ Schedule for Implementing Timeout ■ Criteria for Releasing Students from Timeout ■ Signaling the End of Timeout ■ Suspension ■ Expulsion

When the use of reinforcers is not effective in reducing inappropriate behavior, more intrusive strategies are needed. Timeout from positive reinforcement is one such strategy. Timeout is a well-known procedure, and many people hold strong views about its use in educational settings. Some of this difference in opinion results from its potential misuse and abuse. In this chapter, timeout is defined and different types are described. Guidelines for using timeout also are discussed. The chapter concludes with a section on suspension as practiced in many schools.

DESCRIPTION OF TIMEOUT FROM POSITIVE REINFORCEMENT

Definition of Timeout

The reinforcement principle states that if a behavior is consistently followed by reinforcement, the rate of behavior will maintain or increase. Timeout is based on the assumption that if a behavior is followed by a period of time in less reinforcing conditions, the behavior will not maintain and will decrease in frequency. **Timeout from positive reinforcement** refers to a procedure where, contingent upon a target behavior, the student experiences a period of time when less reinforcement is available (Harris, 1985; Nelson & Rutherford, 1983). In other words, timeout refers to time away from positive reinforcement; it does not necessarily refer to time away from instructional activities or from the classroom. A decrease in inappropriate behavior will occur if the procedure is implemented correctly and if the level and opportunity to receive reinforcement is substantially less than was available previously. It should be noted, however, that there are a number of ways to implement timeout. Timeout is a frequently used procedure; in fact, Zabel (1986) found that the majority of teachers in classrooms for students with mild handicaps use timeout; however, as students grow older, fewer teachers use it. In this chapter the term *timeout* is used as a shortened descriptor for "timeout from positive reinforcement."

Differentiation of Timeout from Other Punishment Procedures

As noted in Chapter 18, two types of punishment procedures exist: Type I and Type II. Both types are defined by the manner in which they are presented and the effect they have on behaviors. With Type I procedures, an aversive stimulus is presented contingent upon the occurrence of a behavior and as a result the behavior decreases. With Type II procedures, positive reinforcement is removed or withdrawn contingent upon a behavior and results in the behavior decreasing (Rutherford, 1978; Rutherford & Nelson, 1982).

Timeout is used to reduce the occurrence of behavior, but no aversive stimulus is presented; rather, the level and opportunity to gain reinforcement is removed or decreased for a period of time. Because no aversive stimulus is presented and reinforcement is lost for a period of time, timeout is a Type II punishment procedure.

Timeout is different from response cost (also a Type II procedure) in which students lose "previously awarded or earned reinforcers" (Harris, 1985, p. 282). For example, if a classroom-management system includes points for appropriate behavior and fines or point losses for inappropriate behavior, taking away previously earned points constitutes response cost. Timeout could be implemented in this system but would involve a contingent period of time when no points could be earned; previously earned points would not be taken away.

Although timeout also has been called an extinction procedure (cf., Gast & Nelson, 1977a; Polsgrove, 1982; Smith, 1981, 1982), differences in the two procedures exist. Extinction involves withdrawal of the reinforcer that maintains the target behavior while timeout involves a decrease in the general level of unspecified reinforcers for a given period of time (Harris, 1985). Timeout

TABLE 21.1 Analysis of Potential Timeout Contingencies

Punishment (& Extinction)	Extinction	Negative Reinforcement	Positive Reinforcement
Of the maladaptive behavior that results in timeout	Of continued maladaptive behaviors in timeout	Of adaptive behaviors that result in release from timeout	Of adaptive behaviors that result in release from timeout
Removal from that reinforcing setting withdrawal of response maintenance stimuli	Withdrawal of attention, etc., during timeout	Escape from aversive (nonreinforcing) setting, i.e., timeout	Return to reinforcing setting, i.e., timein

Note: From "Timeout Revisited: Guidelines for Its Use in Special Education" by C. M. Nelson and R. B. Rutherford, 1983, *Exceptional Education Quarterly, 4* (3), p. 57. Copyright 1983 by PRO-ED, Austin, Texas. Reprinted by permission.

procedures, however, may include extinction. For example, John's disruptive behavior appears to be reinforced by his classmates' reaction. If his teacher sends him to timeout contingent upon disruptive behaviors, he may not be able to experience the reinforcing reactions of his peers (extinction) and may experience a period of time where access to reinforcement in general is reduced (timeout). Thus, both extinction and timeout from positive reinforcement may be in effect.

A recent conceptual analysis of timeout indicates that a number of different contingencies may be in effect (Nelson & Rutherford, 1983). If a student is sent to timeout, the behavior that results in timeout may be punished or placed on extinction. However, if that same student must be quiet before being released from timeout, the timeout procedure may result in increases in quiet behavior due to negative reinforcement. (Being quiet while in timeout results in release from aversive conditions—the timeout area.) The contingencies that may be operating when timeout procedures are used are shown in Table 21.1. The primary point is that timeout, like other procedures, involves a number of contingencies that may produce a variety of effects on different behaviors.

TYPES OF TIMEOUT PROCEDURES

Several different procedures are used to apply timeout in classrooms. In each case, the target behavior results in a period of time where the teacher reduces access to reinforcers, either by removing reinforcing conditions from the student or by removing the student from reinforcing conditions. Removing the reinforcement from the student is considered **nonexclusionary timeout,** while removing the child from reinforcing conditions is considered **exclusionary timeout** (Harris, 1985). In general, nonexclusionary timeout is considered less intrusive and should be used before exclusionary timeout.

Removing Reinforcement from Students
(Nonexclusionary Timeout)

Numerous variations of this general type of timeout are described in the literature. Some of those variations are primarily limited to individual instruction while others can be implemented with groups of students. Some involve interruption of instructional activities while others do not.

Perhaps the least intrusive timeout procedure that removes reinforcement from students is called *planned ignoring;* the procedure is also called *withdrawal of adult social attention* and *in-seat timeout* (Rutherford & Nelson, 1982). Planned ignoring timeout is frequently used during systematic, one-on-one instruction, and an assumption is made that teacher attention has reinforcement value which, of course, may not be true for some students. **Planned ignoring timeout** involves the teacher, contingent upon the occurrence of some behavior, turning his or her face away (i.e., removing attention) from the student for a brief period of time (10 to 60 seconds). At the end of the timeout interval, the instructional session is resumed. This procedure results in an interruption of the ongoing instructional activities and has been used with socially inappropriate behaviors (cf., Miller & Kratochwill, 1979) and incorrect responses during instruction (cf., Bennett, Gast, Wolery, & Schuster, 1986; Godby, Gast, & Wolery, 1987.)

Removal of adult attention and planned ignoring almost always are used in combination with positive reinforcement for correct responses or appropriate social behavior (Rutherford & Nelson, 1982). Thus, it is difficult to identify the effects of planned ignoring alone. All programs designed to reduce the occurrence of behavior should be accompanied by reinforcement of adaptive responses and facilitation of replacement behaviors. It is important to know, however, whether such reinforcement alone is sufficient to control the behavior or whether planned ignoring is also needed. Unfortunately, too little research has occurred on this issue to make conclusive recommendations. It appears that the addition of brief planned ignoring (in-seat timeout) for error responses and reinforcement for correct responses may facilitate learning in some students, but not necessarily in others. In-seat or planned ignoring timeout have been used with other procedures such as contingent restraint from movement (Rutherford & Nelson, 1982). With this variation, the teacher holds the student so that movement is not possible. This holding and withdrawal of attention (e.g., no eye contact, no verbal interactions) is implemented contingent upon the behavior and for a specified time period. The use of restraint is based on the assumption that movement may be reinforcing. Mixed results have occurred with this combination of procedures (cf., Luiselli, Reisman, Helfen, & Pemberton, 1976; Noll & Simpson, 1979); thus, its effects must be monitored carefully.

Another variation of in-seat timeout involves the **removal of tangible objects.** This procedure involves removing materials with which students are interacting for a specified period of time contingent upon inappropriate behaviors; adult attention is also withdrawn. For example, when students who are learning to feed themselves with utensils take bites with their fingers, the food and plate are removed for short periods of time, producing decreases in sloppy eating behaviors (Barton, Guess, Garcia, & Baer, 1970; Martin, McDonald, & Omichinski, 1971). This combination of withdrawal of adult attention and removal of tangible objects can also be used with other instructional materials for students' errors or inappropriate social behaviors. For example, if Ruth were playing inappropriately with a toy, the toy and adult attention could be withdrawn for a specified period of time for each episode of inappropriate playing. Usually, this type of timeout is used with students in one-on-one or small-group instructional situations and is accompanied by reinforcement of desired behaviors. Obviously, the instructional activities are interrupted; however, the duration of the timeout is frequently quite brief (10 to 60 seconds).

Planned ignoring timeout is not always successful in eliminating target behaviors. For example, Harris and Wolchik (1979) compared the effects of overcorrection, timeout, and differential reinforcement of other behaviors for decreasing the stereotypic behaviors (e.g., repetitive tapping, stroking, or nonfunctional object movements) of four students with autism. The procedures were implemented during one-on-one sessions. When the student engaged in stereotypic behavior, the teacher said, "No hand play" and turned away from the student for 10 seconds. The results of this planned ignoring were mixed; it appeared to have no effect on the frequency of stereotypic behavior by one student, suppressive effects for two students, and reinforcing effects for the fourth. In fact, one of the students engaged in stereotypic behavior during the 10-second timeout period. These mixed results clearly indicate that planned ignoring may not be an effective procedure for removing reinforcement conditions from some students. Similarly, Plummer, Baer, and LeBlanc (1977) provided 1 minute of no teacher interactions contingent upon the disruptive behavior of one preschool student and 10 seconds of planned ignoring with another. For both students, the timeout did not result in a decrease in the targeted disruptive behaviors. These authors suggested that the timeout procedure actually functioned as a negative reinforcer; that is, teacher interactions constituted an aversive stimulus and, when it was withdrawn contingent upon inappropriate behavior, those behaviors increased.

Another variation of timeout that removes the reinforcing conditions from the student consists of turning off or reducing ongoing visual or auditory stimuli. For example, some teachers dim or turn off the lights when a certain level of inappropriate behavior is displayed by class members. While the light may not be a reinforcer, it may interfere with access to visual stimuli that are reinforcers. To be considered timeout, the lights would have to remain off for a specified time period. Ford and Veltri-Ford (1980) initially established contingent music as a reinforcer for two students with moderate and severe mental retardation and then played it continuously during baseline conditions. During the timeout conditions, they stopped the music for 30 seconds each time a target behavior occurred. This brief timeout from music decreased the target behaviors of both subjects.

Foxx and Shapiro (1978) described another method of removing reinforcing conditions: **timeout ribbon.** They initially measured the inappropriate behaviors and then provided students with ribbons to wear around their necks. The ribbons cued teachers to reinforce students and informed students that they were eligible to receive reinforcement. During these conditions, teachers increased their use of reinforcement. After high levels of reinforcement were established, the timeout procedures were implemented. Timeout consisted of removing the ribbon and not reinforcing the student for 3 minutes. After the 3-minute interval, the ribbon was given back to the student and the student was eligible to receive reinforcement. Taking the ribbon signaled teachers that reinforcement should not be provided and signaled students that they were in timeout. An isolation timeout room was available if students began to destroy materials or were extremely disruptive when the ribbon was taken away. The timeout ribbon resulted in a decrease of the inappropriate behavior for all five students in the class.

The timeout ribbon procedure holds a number of advantages. First, the teacher does not have to remove students from their work areas. Second, while in timeout, students can see other students behaving appropriately and being reinforced, although this was not required. For example, a student could put his head on his desk during timeout. Third, the teacher and other adults in the classroom can clearly see who is eligible for reinforcement, i.e., all students who are wearing a ribbon. Fourth, the ribbon clearly signals students when reinforcement is available and when they are in timeout. Foxx and Shapiro used a ribbon that students wore around their necks; this can present problems because students can resist its removal. A velcro wrist band avoids this possibility because it can be easily taken. Further, wrist bands are frequently worn by many students, making them appear more like other children for whom the procedure is not being used. McKeegan, Estill, and Campbell (1984) used a ribbon (badge) that was clipped to the subject's shirt. They successfully used procedures similar to those employed by Foxx and Shapiro to reduce stereotypic hand-slapping behaviors of an adult with profound retardation.

Removing Students from Reinforcement (Exclusionary Timeout)

Removing students from reinforcing situations is the traditional way to implement timeout. At least three different forms have been identified: contingent observation, exclusion, and isolation/seclusion. Each of these is an exclusionary procedure because students are excluded or removed from reinforcement conditions. These forms are more intrusive than those listed above because they require a change in the student's location. Signaling and prompting this change can be problematic. Therefore, exclusionary timeout should be avoided as much as possible and alternative forms of behavior control should be considered.

Contingent Observation. **Contingent observation** involves a brief period of time where the student, contingent upon an inappropriate behavior, is required to move to another location and is instructed to watch other students behave appropriately. Although instructional activities are interrupted, the student may learn some appropriate ways of behaving through imitation; he or she can observe instructional activities but cannot participate in them. This feature makes contingent observation less restrictive than other exclusionary timeout procedures.

Contingent observation has been used primarily with preschool children (Baer, Rowbury, & Baer, 1973; Tyroler & Lahey, 1980), but has also been effective with young school-aged students (Barton, Brulle, & Repp, 1987). For example, Porterfield, Herbert-Jackson, and Risley (1976) studied the reductive effects of redirection and contingent observation on the occurrence of a number of inappropriate behaviors such as aggression, crying, and material destruction performed by preschool children. The redirection consisted of teachers responding to each occurrence of inappropriate behavior by labeling it and then moving the child's attention to another toy or activity. With contingent observation, teachers labeled the inappropriate behavior, moved the child to the side of the activity, instructed him or her to watch other children play, waited until the child sat quietly (30 to 60 seconds), and then asked, "Do you know how to ask for the toys you want?" (p. 58). Permission to return to play was given if the answer was affirmative. Children who did not answer or answered negatively remained in timeout for 30 to 60 more seconds. A backup timeout area was also available if a student became so disruptive during the contingent observation that it distracted other children's play. The contingent observation resulted in substantial decreases in disruptive behavior over the redirection procedure. Although this procedure is considered less restrictive than other forms of exclusionary timeout, it has been used only with preschool children; its effectiveness with older students remains unexamined.

Exclusion Timeout. Exclusion timeout has been defined as "excluding the individual from the area of reinforcement without removing the individual from the room" (Harris, 1985, p. 280; cf. also, Gast & Nelson, 1977b, p. 459); however, other authors define it as the student being "completely removed from the time-in environment" (Nelson & Rutherford, 1983, p. 60). Given this discrepancy in definitions, the most workable solution is to consider **exclusion timeout** to be any procedure that (a) requires the student to be removed from instructional activities, (b) does not require the student to watch others (as in contingent observation), and (c) does not require the student to enter a specifically designed timeout room (as in isolation/seclusion). If students remain in the room, they are usually required to sit or stand in a corner or partitioned area of the classroom; if they are placed outside the room, they are instructed to sit or stand in the hallway or outside the classroom door.

Exclusion timeout has been used frequently (cf., Firestone, 1976; Henricksen & Doughty, 1967; Pease & Tyler, 1979). Mace, Page, Ivancic, and O'Brien (1986) used a verbal reprimand and timeout by saying, "No (naming the behavior)" and instructing the student to go to timeout. The student was then physically guided to the timeout area and told to sit in a chair that faced the corner for 2 minutes. This procedure resulted in a rapid decrease in the frequency of aggressive and disruptive behaviors.

Rolider and Van Houten (1985) used a variation of exclusion timeout called **movement suppression** with students who exhibited moderate and severe handicaps. When a target behavior occurred, the student "was positioned with his chin against the corner, both hands behind his back and with one hand on top of the other and both feet close together touching the wall" (p. 278). Firm verbal instructions consisting of "Don't move" and "Don't talk" were provided if the student moved any body part or spoke. These procedures were maintained for 2 minutes with some students and 3 minutes with others. When students were not in timeout, they were reinforced on a consistent schedule for not doing inappropriate behaviors. Movement suppression timeout resulted in rapid reduction of target behaviors and was more effective than contingent restraint alone, corner timeout without movement suppression, and isolation room timeout procedures. Luiselli, Suskin, and Slocumb (1984) successfully used a similar procedure, called *immobilization timeout,* to reduce tantrum and aggressive behaviors of two children with diagnoses of behavior disorders and mental retardation.

Isolation/Seclusion Timeout. This form of exclusionary timeout is the most restrictive, most controversial, and perhaps the most open to abuse. Isolation/seclusion timeout requires the student to leave the instructional area and enter a separate timeout room. The timeout room is usually devoid of furnishings and social stimuli. This type of timeout is frequently called *seclusion timeout* (Nelson & Rutherford, 1983; Rutherford & Nelson, 1982) and *isolation* (Harris, 1985). Consistent use of these two terms does not exist and confusion may result. Thus, the following definitions are provided. Before a treatment can be called **isolation/seclusion timeout,** it must (a) be presented contingent upon previously identified behavior(s), (b) have a definite duration that is relatively brief (e.g., 5 minutes), and (c) involve the student being in a separate room. When either term is used as a synonym for solitary confinement of an unspecified and extended duration, it is not timeout. Placement of students in rooms devoid of furnishings and social stimuli for unspecified, extended durations is unethical and in many situations illegal. Reviews of timeout all warn that isolation/seclusion timeout may be prohibited or controlled by the courts, local agencies, and/or other legal and regulative bodies (e.g., Cuenin & Harris, 1986; Gast & Nelson, 1977b; Harris, 1985; Nelson & Rutherford, 1983; Rutherford & Nelson, 1982). These warnings obviously result from potential or completed court actions (e.g., *Morales* v. *Turman,* 1973 and *Wyatt* v. *Stickney,* 1972) where timeout procedures are similar to solitary confinement without treatment. When isolation/seclusion timeout is planned, procedural safeguards should be considered and followed.

Despite potential legal issues, exclusionary timeout procedures have been used widely in residential programs and special schools for students with handicaps. Fifteen studies of this type were reviewed by Rutherford and Nelson (1982), most of which occurred during the early to mid 1970s, indicating a possible decrease in research on isolation/seclusion timeout.

DECISIONS AND GUIDELINES FOR USING TIMEOUT

Using any punishment or intrusive strategy requires careful planning and monitoring. In the following two sections, prerequisite decisions for planning and implementing timeout are described. These decisions come from those issues related to timeout that were initially described by MacDonough and Forehand (1973), but have since been reviewed and expanded by a number of authors (e.g., Brantner & Doherty, 1983; Gast & Nelson, 1977b; Harris, 1985). Based on a survey of special education teachers, it appears that these decisions are frequently used in practice (Zabel, 1986).

Prerequisite Steps to Using Timeout

Using the Behavior-Reduction Model. Before using timeout, the model described in Chapter 19 should be employed. The steps of the model include identifying problem situations, defining problem behavior(s), identifying relationships between problem behaviors and environmental stimuli, specifying objectives, specifying and implementing measurement procedures, obtaining the appropriate clearances and approvals, and implementing environmental prerequisites. The environmental prerequisites include use of appropriate, interesting, and worthwhile curriculum and curricular modifications; increasing the predictability in the daily schedule and consequences for prosocial and academic behaviors and noncompliance with rules; and reinforcement for adaptive performance including replacement behaviors. Teaching replacement behaviors should receive at least as much planning and effort as planning and implementing the timeout procedures. When these activities are completed and the teacher has decided that timeout is an appropriate intervention, he or she should proceed to steps specific to planning timeout interventions.

Enriching the Timein Environment. **Timein** refers to the time the student spends in the classroom but not in the timeout area. Since timeout requires that a meaningful difference exist in the level of reinforcement during timein and timeout, the level of reinforcement during timein is a critical issue. Solnick, Rincover, and Peterson (1977) found that a brief timeout period for the tantrums of a 6-year-old child with autism resulted in a substantial increase in tantrum behaviors. They observed that the student frequently engaged in stereotypic behaviors during timeout. Since stereotypic behavior appears to have reinforcement value, they concluded that the tantrum behaviors were being reinforced by the opportunity to engage in stereotypic behaviors. In the initial timeout conditions, the amount of reinforcement (i.e., that received from stereotypic behavior) was greater during timeout than during timein. The principle of reinforcement states that if behaviors are followed by positive reinforcers, the behaviors will maintain or increase. In this case, the student's tantrums were followed by a time when she could receive positive reinforcement rather than a period of time when access to reinforcement was restricted. When the student was physically restrained from doing stereotypic responding during timeout, the number of tantrums decreased.

Solnick et al. (1977) used a 90-second timeout procedure contingent upon the spitting and self-injurious behavior of another student with severe mental retardation. Initially, the timeout procedure resulted in an increase in these behaviors. When the timein environment was enriched by providing more materials and adult attention, the same timeout procedure was effective. If the materials and additional adult attention were removed from timein, timeout resulted in increases in spitting and self-injurious behavior. These two experiments clearly show that the effectiveness of timeout procedures is based on a decrease in the amount of reinforcement during timeout as compared to timein. Thus, when planning to use timeout, teachers must make efforts to enrich the timein setting. The **enrichment** may occur by providing more and varied materials, more interesting instructional activities, and more positive reinforcement.

If the enriched environment eliminates the target behavior, the enrichment and data collection should continue. However, if enrichment alone does not decrease the behavior, the teacher should proceed with planning the initiation of timeout. Data patterns that may occur when the timein environment is enriched are shown in Figure 21.1.

Planning Decisions for Implementing Timeout

Selecting the Type of Timeout. After assessing the effects of enrichment, teachers should make decisions related to implementing timeout. One of the first decisions deals with the type of timeout that will be used; issues related to this decision are shown in Figure 21.2. Teachers must determine whether the student will be removed from reinforcing conditions or whether the timeout conditions will be removed from the student. If the teacher attempts to remove reinforcing conditions from the student, he or she should determine whether known reinforcers exist. When no reinforcers are known for a student, it will be impossible to remove them and timeout will be unsuccessful. In such cases, the teacher should identify reinforcers and return to the beginning of the process. When reinforcers are known, the teacher's task is to determine whether those reinforcers can be removed. For example, students who engage in high rates of stereotypic behavior or who engage in high rates of isolate and "day dreaming"

FIGURE 21.1 Potential data patterns when environments are enriched prior to implementing timeout.

POTENTIAL DATA PATTERNS

ANALYSIS OF PATTERNS

This data pattern indicates stable baseline performance followed by a slight but not totally acceptable reduction of behavior during enrichment; thus, timeout was needed to establish suppression of the response to acceptable levels.

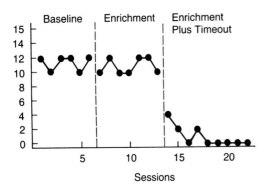

This data pattern indicates stable baseline performance followed by continued stable performance at the same levels as baseline when enrichment occurred; thus, timeout was needed to suppress the behavior to acceptable levels.

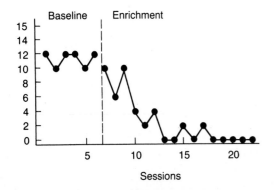

This data pattern indicates stable baseline performance followed by substantial reductions in the target behavior when the timein environment was enriched; since that reduction was to acceptable levels, timeout was not needed.

FIGURE 21.2   Planning decisions related to the type of timeout that will be used.

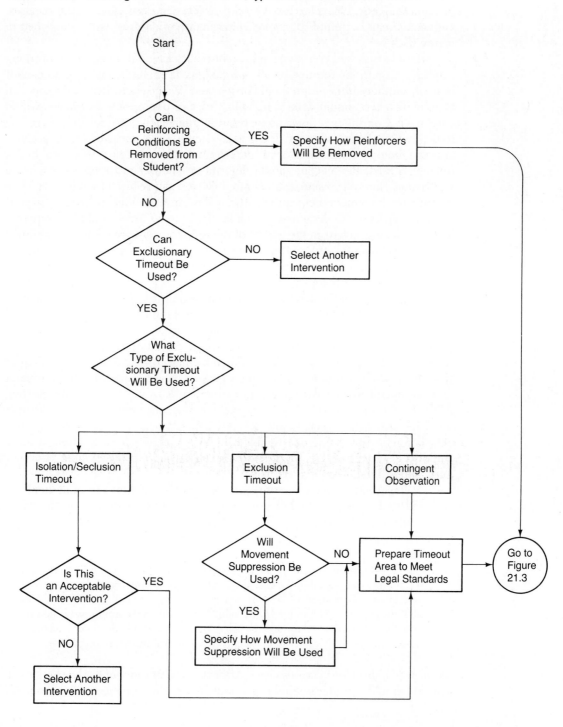

behavior may be unaffected by removal of reinforcers in the control of teachers (Cuenin & Harris, 1986; Harris & Wolchik, 1979). For cases where reinforcers are known and can be removed, the teacher is ready to address issues described in Figure 21.3.

Teachers should consider using exclusionary timeout when the reinforcing conditions cannot be removed from the student. If exclusionary timeout cannot be used, another intervention should be selected. When exclusionary timeout can be used, teachers should determine which type of exclusionary timeout will be employed. Contingent observation requires the teacher to decide where the student will sit during timeout. The area should be on the periphery of the activity area and should provide an unobstructed view of other students. When exclusion timeout is used, the teacher should determine whether movement suppression will be used (Luiselli, Suskin, & Slocumb, 1984; Rolider & Van Houten, 1985). The manner in which movement suppression will be implemented must be defined, if it is used. After these decisions are made, the timeout area should be prepared. Most studies use a chair in the corner of the room or in an area that is partitioned from other students. Any materials near the timeout area should be removed permanently to prevent students from interacting with or destroying materials while in exclusion timeout.

When isolation/seclusion timeout is chosen, the teacher should determine if it is an acceptable intervention. Some agencies prohibit the use of this timeout and the teacher should consult with the appropriate authorities to determine whether it is acceptable in their agencies. Also, parents should be consulted concerning their views. The procedures for obtaining informed consent described in Chapter 18 should be considered. In general, most persons consider other forms of timeout more acceptable than isolation/seclusion timeout (Kazdin, 1984; Norton, Austen, Allen & Hilton, 1983). However, when cases are severe, more intrusive procedures are rated as acceptable (Kazdin, 1980). For each case, the acceptability of isolation/seclusion timeout should be assessed with all teachers, administrative authorities, and parents. If isolation/seclusion is not acceptable, another intervention should be selected.

When isolation/seclusion timeout is acceptable, the timeout room should be analyzed to determine whether it is acceptable. If not, modifications should be made. Although different agencies may have specific requirements for timeout rooms, some general guidelines were provided by Gast and Nelson (1977b):

> The timeout room should: (a) be at least 6 by 6 feet in size; (b) be properly lighted (preferably recessed lights with the switch outside the room); (c) be properly ventilated; (d) be free of objects and fixtures with which a child could harm himself; (e) provide the means by which an adult can continuously monitor— visually and aurally—the student's behavior; (f) *not* be locked—a latch on the door should be used only as needed and only with careful monitoring (p. 464).

Selecting and Using Verbal Explanations. After the type of timeout has been selected, teachers should consider several other issues related to implementation; some of

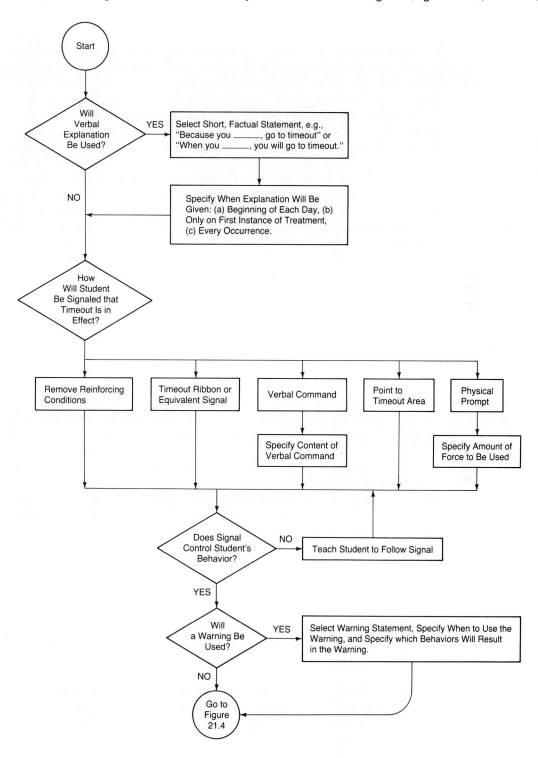

these are illustrated in Figure 21.3. One issue is whether a **verbal explanation** will be given to the student about the timeout contingencies. The verbal explanation, if used, should be businesslike, brief, specify the behavior(s) resulting in timeout, and perhaps specify the length of timeout. Although this issue has not received sufficient research attention, it appears that a verbal explanation does not facilitate the reductive effects of timeout (Gast & Nelson, 1977b). Roberts (1984a) attempted to teach preschool oppositional children about the contingencies that would be in effect during mother-child training sessions. These contingencies included praise for compliance, exclusionary timeout for noncompliance, release from timeout for being quiet, and spanking for attempting to escape from timeout. These contingencies were modeled by a therapist and another child, and the target child was questioned about his or her understanding of the contingencies. Although the child demonstrated understanding, it did not appear to result in fewer timeouts or more quiet behavior during timeouts than did the same procedures without explanations. However, when planning to use verbal explanations, teachers should determine whether students' comprehend those statements.

Facilitative effects of verbal explanations may vary across students; for example, if students have severe language deficits that preclude them from understanding the content of the statement, it may not be beneficial. Further, if students are already aware of the timeout contingencies and the behaviors that result in timeout, verbal explanations may not enhance the effects of timeout. If the student is unclear about which behaviors result in timeout, verbal explanations may be warranted. However, Roberts (1984a) suggested that experience with the contingencies of timeout may contribute to the effectiveness of verbal explanations. It also is clear that verbal interactions with students can reinforce their inappropriate behaviors; thus, verbal interactions should be brief, specific, and matter of fact. When verbal explanations are planned, the frequency with which they are delivered should be determined. Explanations can occur prior to each episode of timeout, at the beginning of each day/session, or only before the first instance of timeout is ever used. When the explanation is given for each episode of timeout, it may serve as a signal to the child that timeout is in effect.

Selecting and Using a Signal. Another planning decision involves identifying the **signal,** if any, that will be used to communicate to the student that timeout is in effect. When reinforcement conditions are being withdrawn from the student, as in planned ignoring, no signal may be necessary. The use of a timeout ribbon can signal students when reinforcement is available and when it is withdrawn. Foxx and Shapiro (1978) stated that, after the ribbons became associated with reinforcement for appropriate behaviors, students came to class, received their ribbons, and immediately began behaving appropriately. Signals such as ribbons should be selected so that they can be easily taken from and given to students, are not distracting to students, do not call undue attention to the student, and can be faded easily as students' behavior comes under control.

Other signals include verbal instructions, pointing or gesturing toward the timeout area, and physically moving the student. Brief verbal instructions or pointing are preferred to physical prompts for a number of reasons (Harris, 1985). Verbal instructions and pointing result in less interruption of instructional activities, prevent physical struggles with students which may reinforce their inappropriate behavior, avoid the chance that the student or teacher could be hurt during a struggle, and require the student to exercise more self-control (Gast & Nelson, 1977b; Nelson & Rutherford, 1983). Teachers using physical prompts should take care not to hurt the child and should systematically attempt to fade the prompts. Fading can be accomplished by pairing some other signal (e.g., verbal instruction or pointing) with the physical prompts. Graduated guidance (Chapter 14) should be used when physical prompts are employed to move the student to timeout. If the student starts to move to timeout on his or her own, the physical prompts should be removed and his or her movements followed; the prompts should be given immediately if the student stops or begins moving in the wrong direction.

After identifying the signal, teachers should determine whether it will control the student's response. If it does not, teachers should select another or establish that signal as a controlling prompt by pairing and fading more controlling prompts with the desired signal, as described above. Some teachers have students practice going to timeout; however, no research was found that supported or refuted this practice.

Selecting and Using Warnings. When decisions are made concerning verbal explanations and signals, teachers should decide whether **warnings** will be used. Little research exists on whether warnings should be used. Timeout has been effective when warnings were used and when they were not (Harris, 1985). Roberts (1984b) compared two groups of oppositional preschool children; one group received warnings and the other did not. Timeout with and without warnings was equally effective in reducing oppositional behavior, but the children in the warning group received fewer instances of timeout. Thus, it appears that using warnings may be less restrictive; that is, children who received warnings spent less time away from instructional activities. When warnings are used, (a) the content of the warning must be specified, (b) the behaviors that will receive warning should be identified, and (c) only one warning should be provided. If the warning does not result in immediate compliance, timeout should be implemented. Warnings appear appropriate when specific behaviors usually precede the inappropriate behavior. For example, Richie frequently gets out of his seat during individual work times and his teacher is using timeout to reduce this behavior. She has noticed that before he gets out of his seat he stops writing or reading, sits quietly a few seconds, looks around the room, and then gets out of his seat. A verbal warning or redirection when he stops working or is looking around the room may break the chain and prevent him from getting up and then being sent to timeout. In such cases, more justification exists for using warnings. Warnings also are sometimes used for the first occurrence of the behavior in a given day, and then timeout is implemented for each subsequent occurrence. Because of the lack of sufficient research, recommendations concerning warnings are difficult to make with confidence. Therefore, the best practice is to analyze carefully the effects of warnings when they are used.

Selecting the Duration of Timeout. Other important implementation decisions concern the duration of timeout, schedule for implementing it, and release requirements and procedures. These decisions are shown in Figure 21.4. **Duration of timeout** refers to the amount of time students are under timeout conditions, i.e., the amount of time they are away from positive reinforcement. With timeout, duration is the intensity of the punishment procedure. The intensity of any punishment procedure, including timeout, is an important consideration that may be related to its effectiveness. A minimum level of intensity for any punishment procedure is apt to be ineffective, but there may be a point at which increasing the intensity does not produce additional benefits. For example, a 3-second timeout is not likely to be effective, but a 45-minute timeout may not produce any benefits beyond those produced by a 5-minute timeout. Teachers must select a duration that will produce desirable benefits and will minimize the negative aspects of long durations. Long timeout durations should be avoided because (a) students' opportunities to learn are interrupted by timeout, (b) inappropriate behaviors are more likely during long timeouts, and (c) behavior in general may be suppressed as compared to the target behavior (Gast & Nelson, 1977b; Harris, 1985).

Several research findings relative to duration should be considered. First, a wide variety of durations (e.g., 10 seconds to 2 or 3 hours) have occurred across studies and produced reductions in target behaviors (Harris, 1985). Second, when different durations are compared, both short and long intervals produce behavior reduction but certain limitations should be noted. White, Nielsen, and Johnson (1972) compared three different durations (1, 15, and 30 minutes). All three durations were effective if the 1-minute duration was used first. If a student experienced long timeout durations and later experienced the 1-minute interval, it became ineffective. Thus, students' learning history with timeout may be an important consideration when selecting the timeout duration. Hobbs, Forehand, and Murray (1978) compared three short intervals (10 seconds, 1 and 4 minutes). The longer intervals produced more behavior reduction, and the behaviors were more likely to remain at suppressed levels when timeout was withdrawn. Third, when isolation/seclusion timeout is used, the longer the interval the longer it appears to take students to settle down in the timeout room (Benjamin, Mazzarins, & Kupfersmid, 1983). Harris (1985) stated that 5 minutes should be a sufficient duration for most populations; but, with many students, 1- and 2-minute durations are sufficient. Duration of timeout, of course, is only one of many variables that may affect the effectiveness of a given timeout procedure. Other variables include the consistency with which the procedure is used, the type of timeout, age of student, the schedule, and the conditions of the timein environment (Gast & Nelson, 1977b; Harris, 1985; Solnick, et al., 1977).

FIGURE 21.4 Planning decisions related to the duration of timeout, schedule for implementing it, and release requirements and procedures.

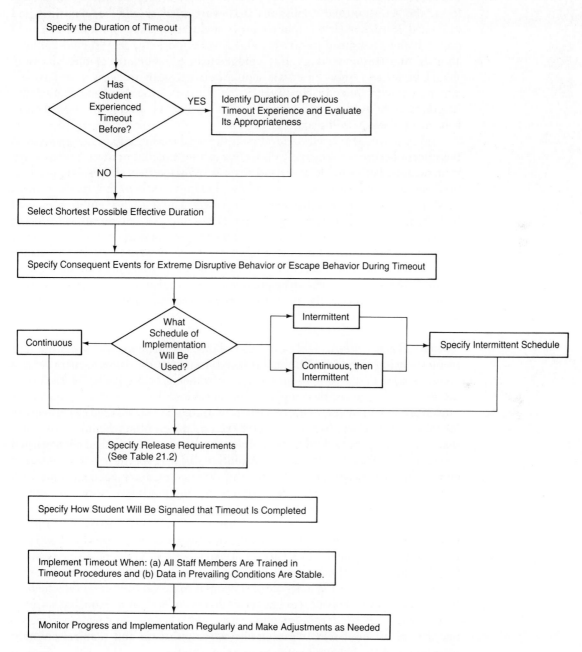

When attempting to determine the appropriate duration of timeout, teachers should determine whether timeout was used with the student in the past. If so, the duration and conditions that were used should be identified and evaluated. If teachers decide that the previous duration is appropriate, they should use it. If the previous duration is judged to be too long, they should consider another intervention strategy. If it is judged to be too short, the planned duration should be longer. Short intervals should be used with students who have no experience with timeout. However, if the interval is too short and is gradually lengthened, the student will likely learn to tolerate very long durations before behavior reduction will occur.

Another issue related to duration is the need for **backup contingencies** if the student becomes excessively disruptive during timeout or attempts to escape from timeout. For example, Foxx and Shapiro (1978) used a backup isolation/seclusion room if students became unduly disruptive when the reinforcement conditions were removed. Roberts (1984a) used spanking when children escaped from timeout. Rolider and Van Houten (1985) used verbal reprimands during movement suppression timeout for attempts to move and student verbalizations. Mace et al. (1986) "used the least amount of force necessary to guide compliance with the TO (timeout) procedure" (p. 81). These examples indicate that a wide range of consequent events can be provided when students attempt to escape from timeout or are excessively disruptive during timeout. Teachers clearly need a specific plan for such possibilities.

Selecting Timeout Schedules. Teams also should determine the **schedule for implementing timeout.** Minimal research exists on this issue. Generally, it is recommended that a continuous schedule of timeout be used. That is, each time the student engages in the inappropriate behavior, the timeout consequence is implemented. However, as noted earlier, warnings have been used extensively in the timeout literature. Barton et al. (1987) used a differential schedule of timeout; that is, students experienced timeout only when they previously had been warned for doing the behavior within a specific interval. This procedure was effective in eliminating the inappropriate behavior of three elementary-aged students with mental retardation. For example, Karen was being put in exclusion timeout for aggressive behaviors. Her teacher warned her on the first occurrence of aggression and then on the second occurrence Karen was instructed to go to timeout. She was warned again when the third aggression occurred and was sent to timeout on the fourth. This pattern of warnings put Karen on a fixed-ratio 2 (FR:2) schedule of timeout. When warnings are provided only for the first occurrence in the day, the schedule of timeout is some variable-interval schedule. If the student is warned only for behaviors that occur early in a chain, but is sent to timeout each time the target behavior occurs, the schedule would be a continuous one. Fading timeout schedules must be done with care and requires constant monitoring of the behavior rates and implementation.

Selecting and Using Release Criteria and Procedures. Teachers must identify the **criteria for releasing students from timeout.** Several possibilities exist and are shown in

Table 21.2. Mace et al. (1986) studied two different exit criteria for exclusion timeout with one typical child and two students with mental retardation. In one condition, students were allowed to leave the chair after the 2-minute duration of timeout; no behavioral criteria were set. In the second condition, students were allowed to leave timeout after 2 minutes if the last 15 seconds were free of disruptive or escape behaviors. If disruptive or escape behaviors occurred during the last 15 seconds of the 2-minute duration, the student was required to remain in timeout until 15 seconds occurred that were free of disruptive and escape behaviors. Their results suggest that both procedures reduced the target behaviors. The condition that required students to sit in timeout without being disruptive for the last 15 seconds or until 15 seconds of appropriate behavior had

TABLE 21.2   Examples and Criteria for Releasing Students from Timeout

Criteria for Release	*Example of Criteria*
Complete duration only; not contingent on behavior during timeout.	Student required to sit in a chair for 2 minutes. When the 2 minutes are completed, he or she can leave timeout.
Minimum duration plus extension until appropriate behavior occurs in timeout.	Student required to sit in a chair for 2 minutes, but he or she must be behaving appropriately (e.g., sitting quietly) at the end of the 2-minute period to be released. If he or she is not behaving appropriately, the timeout is extended until he or she displays appropriate behavior.
Minimum duration plus extension for a given interval of appropriate behavior in timeout.	Student required to sit in a chair for 2 minutes, but he or she must behave appropriately for the last 15 seconds of the 2 minutes, or for an additional 15 seconds before being released. Any inappropriate behavior requires an additional 15 seconds of appropriate behavior before being released.
Release contingent on specific interval of appropriate behavior.	Student required to behave appropriately for a specific interval of time, no minimum set. Thus, if the interval of appropriate behavior is 1 minute, the timeout would end after 1 minute of appropriate behavior.

occurred seemed to produce a slight decrease in those behaviors during the latter portion of the timeout period. However, the differences were so slight and variable that Mace et al. concluded that the practical advantages of the standard 2-minute criterion were less restrictive than requiring 15 seconds of sitting without being disruptive. However, more research of this type is needed.

Another decision that must be made relative to releasing students from timeout is **signaling the end of timeout.** In the Mace et al. (1986) study, the teacher turned the timeout chair back toward the classroom and walked away. In the Foxx and Shapiro (1978) study, students were given their ribbon and reinforcement was initiated soon thereafter. In the Roberts (1984a) study, students were told they could leave timeout. Thus, a variety of options exist. A verbal statement is probably the most accepted procedure; however, with students for whom verbal interactions may be a stimulus to engage in more disruptive behaviors or where the verbalizations may be a reinforcer, it may be wise simply to walk away.

Training Staff and Collecting and Analyzing Data. Two final tasks must be completed prior to using timeout. First, all persons who will use timeout should be thoroughly familiar with it. A written description should be developed specifying how to implement the particular timeout procedure, and staff training should occur if members are unfamiliar with the general procedures. Telling staff how to implement the procedure, modeling it for them, observing their implementation, and giving them feedback is an effective training strategy. Second, baseline data should be analyzed. Timeout should only be implemented after baseline data are stable. This is particularly important because of the mixed results that have occurred with timeout. Unstable baseline data will make it difficult to determine what effects timeout is producing.

After these two issues have been addressed and timeout is implemented, the data on students' target responses must be regularly reviewed. Potential patterns of data when timeout is used are shown in Figure 21.5. With isolation/seclusion timeout, careful records should be maintained. Gast and Nelson (1977b) recommended maintaining the following information:

> (a) the student's name; (b) the episode resulting in student's placement in timeout (behavior, activity, other students involved, staff person, etc.); (c) time of day the student was placed in timeout; (d) time of day the student was released from timeout; (e) the total time in timeout; (f) the type of timeout (contingent observation, exclusion timeout, or seclusion (isolation) timeout); the student's behavior in timeout. (pp. 264–265)

The implementation of timeout also should be assessed periodically. A procedural checklist for evaluating whether exclusionary timeout procedures are being implemented correctly is shown Figure 21.6. If timeout is not implemented consistently, it is unlikely that it will produce reductions in the target behaviors.

FIGURE 21.5   Potential data patterns when timeout procedures are implemented.

POTENTIAL DATA PATTERNS

ANALYSIS OF PATTERNS

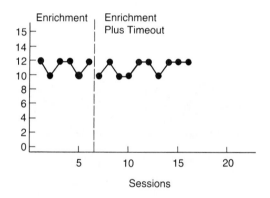

These data indicate stable performance during enrichment followed by a change in the level and trend of the data after timeout was implemented. These data indicate that timeout was effective in reducing the target response.

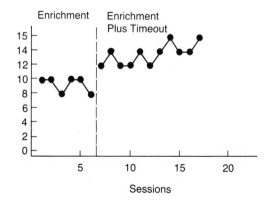

These data indicate stable performance during enrichment followed by a continuation of that pattern. Thus, in this case, timeout was not effective in reducing the frequency of the targeted behaviors. Another intervention should be selected, implemented, and evaluated.

These data indicate stable performance during enrichment followed by a change in the level and trend of the target behavior; however, the change indicates that timeout may be resulting in increases of the target behavior. This pattern indicates that timeout should be stopped and another intervention should be selected, implemented, and evaluated.

FIGURE 21.6 Sample procedural checklist for determining whether exclusionary timeout procedures are implemented appropriately.

Number of occurrences of target behavior _____
Number of times timeout was administered _____

If used, number of times verbal explanation used _____   Not in Plan
   When was verbal explanation given?
   a. Beginning of day / session
   b. Each time behavior occurred
   c. Other (describe): _____

   Verbal explanation was (circle those that apply)
   a. Brief
   b. Long
   c. Too complex
   d. Too simple

If used, number of warnings provided _____   Not in Plan

   What words were used in the warning? _____

   What behaviors resulted in warning? _____

If used, number of times a signal to go to timeout was provided _____   Not in Plan

   What signal was used? _____

   Number of times student complied with signal _____

   What occurred when student did not comply with signal? _____

Was timeout area prepared prior to student going there?   YES   NO

For each episode of timeout, record the time the student entered and was released from timeout.

Episode

	1	2	3	4	5	6	7	8	9	10
Time Entered:										
Time Released:										

What did student do during timeout? _____

What release criterion was used?

   How was student signaled that timeout was completed? _____

   How did student respond to signal? _____

SUSPENSION FROM SCHOOL

Definition and Comparison to Timeout

Suspension is a formal action by school officials that bars a student from attending school for a specified period of time (e.g., less than 10 days) contingent upon the occurrence, or perceived occurrence, of a given behavior, constellation of behaviors, or pattern of behavior. Suspension is different from **expulsion** where students are prohibited from attending school for extended periods of time.

The definition of suspension appears similar to exclusionary timeout procedures, because a student's location is changed for a specific period of time contingent upon a given behavior. Suspension as used in schools, however, is different from accepted best practice for exclusionary timeout. First, the behaviors that result in suspension frequently are ill defined. They usually are not related to property damage or aggression, but include behaviors such as tardiness, truancy, and "disrespect" (Nielsen, 1979). Acceptable practices with timeout require careful specification of target behaviors. Second, suspension, in practice, may not be implemented contingently; for example, suspensions "are used disproportionally with black, poor, and male students, and . . . are often imposed arbitrarily" (Leone, 1984, p. 84). Defensible practices with timeout require contingent use. Third, suspension may be used when administrators and teachers are presented with difficult problems that appear to require immediate action and for which the school system is not well prepared. Suspension is a quick "solution" and is frequently used before alternatives have been attempted (Dagley, 1982). Best practices with exclusionary timeout require attempts to control the behavior with less restrictive procedures and reserve intrusive procedures for severe cases (Kazdin, 1980, 1984). Fourth, behaviors that lead to suspension frequently are "the last straws" in a sequence of interactions. Thus, the behavior(s) could occur many times before the suspension consequence is used. Accepted practices with timeout involve a continuous schedule of implementation. Fifth, with suspension, the duration of the time away from school is much longer than that advocated with timeout. Finally, and perhaps most importantly, suspension may not involve time away from positive reinforcement. Students who are suspended frequently may be those for whom schools hold limited reinforcers. Thus, rather than reducing the level and opportunity for reinforcement, the suspension may provide them with an opportunity to experience many reinforcers.

Legal Issues with Suspension

Due Process Safeguards with All Students. Much of the literature related to suspension deals with its legality, particularly in terms of what due process procedures should be required. Flygare (1974) presented a detailed historical perspective of the due process issue as it relates to suspension. He discriminated between emergency suspension, short-term suspension (less than 10 days), and expulsion (until the end of the semester or school year). Emergency suspensions are short (1 or 2 days) and are reserved for "extraordinary circumstances." The need for due process is less important with these temporary and relatively infrequent emergency suspensions. For short-term suspensions, Flygare recommended that schools use the following due process procedures: "(a) notice of the charges; (b) right to present evidence and confront in some way opposing witnesses at a hearing; and (c) an impartial trier of fact (continuum of penalties for different offenses)" (p. 554). These procedures help protect schools from charges that they failed to provide due process. The school's case can be strengthened if the staff provides the student with time to prepare a defense, allows representation by counsel, attempts to determine the facts of the case, and allows appeals to other administrative authorities (Flygare, 1974).

Due Process Safeguards with Students Who Have Handicaps. Public Law 94–142 has confused the legal issue about whether and under what circumstances handicapped students can be suspended and/or expelled (Flygare, 1981; Ludlow, 1982). Leone (1985) summarized the legal difficulties with three questions:

> Is suspension or expulsion of a handicapped pupil a change in educational placement, and as such, does it entitle students to the procedural safeguards of PL 94–142?
>
> Can a handicapped student be suspended for misbehavior related to a handicapping condition?
>
> If misbehavior is related to a handicapping condition, is suspension or expulsion a denial of free appropriate public education guaranteed by PL 94–142? (p. 113)

Related unresolved issues are whether a single student can receive a series of short suspensions that essentially results in a long-term suspension and how students who are in the process of being placed in special education but are not yet "special education" students should be treated (Craft & Haussmann, 1983).

In answer to the first question, Leone (1984) stated that the courts do not consider emergency and short-term suspensions changes in students' placements. However, an informal meeting is required with the school official prior to suspension. Expulsions, on the other hand, constitute a change in students' placements and, as such, require all formal procedural safeguards that would accompany other placement changes. The issue of whether the behavior resulting in suspension is related to the handicapping condition is quite problematic. Dagley (1982) suggested that it can be a fruitless effort, but Leone (1984, 1985) maintained that analysis of students' previous and current performance may suggest patterns that will help clarify this issue. For example, when students' academic progress has slowed and results in aberrant behavior, or when students have histories of similar aberrant behavior, a relationship with the handicap is likely. The educational team is the appropriate group of persons to make this determination (Flygare, 1981; Leone, 1984; Ludlow, 1982). The courts have not ruled that suspension denies students of their rights under PL 94–142 (Leone, 1985).

Recommendations on Suspension

Although we do not wish to recommend restriction of any legal or ethical intervention, few acceptable reasons exist for schools to continue using suspension. Very little literature exists related to the effects of suspensions on students' maladaptive behaviors, but it does not appear to decrease them (Leone, 1984). If used, the behavior-reduction model presented in Chapter 19 should be followed. The model will ensure prior assessment of the target behavior, ongoing data collection, formative evaluation of the data, and use of less restrictive procedures. Any time suspension is employed, its effects on pupils' behavior and on administrators' subsequent use of suspension should be analyzed. Principals may be positively reinforced by teachers for using suspension, and principals and teachers may be negatively reinforced by the removal of the "problem" student (aversive stimulus) from the school environment. These two contingencies may (a) account for the continued use of suspension in the absence of supporting data, (b) produce increases in the frequency with which it is used, and (c) result in avoidance of more effort-producing, but effective, behavior-change strategies. Numerous alternatives to suspensions exist and include strategies described in this text: in-school suspensions (Nielsen, 1979); review and revision of school discipline codes and policies (Leone, 1984); and smaller class sizes, more individualized instruction, more meaningful instruction, and increased communication and contracting with parents (Safer, Heaton, & Parker, 1981). Given the current alternatives, the lack of data supporting suspensions, and the associated legal problems, suspension does not appear to be a viable intervention strategy.

Summary of Key Concepts

- Timeout is a Type II punishment procedure where the occurrence of the inappropriate behavior results in students receiving a given period of time in less reinforcing conditions.
- Timeout can be implemented by removing the reinforcing conditions from the student (nonexclusionary timeout) or removing the student from reinforcing conditions (exclusionary timeout).
- Nonexclusionary timeout includes planned ignoring, planned ignoring plus removal of objects, and the timeout ribbon.
- Exclusionary timeout includes contingent observation, exclusionary timeout, and isolation/seclusion.

- Exclusionary timeout is thought to be more restrictive than nonexclusionary timeout.

- The amount of reinforcement in the timein environment appears to be directly related to the effectiveness of timeout; thus, the timein environment should be enriched prior to using timeout.

- When using timeout teams must (a) select one type of timeout, (b) determine whether to use verbal explanations, (c) determine how to signal the student that timeout is to start, (d) determine whether to use warnings, (e) select an appropriate duration of timeout, (f) select an appropriate timeout schedule, (g) determine release criteria and signals, (h) monitor the implementation of timeout, and (i) collect and analyze data on target behaviors.

- Suspension of students from school is different from timeout, requires considerations of due process procedures, has little supporting data, and presents legal difficulties; thus, is not recommended as an intervention strategy.

REFERENCES

Baer, A. M., Rowbury, T., & Baer, D. M. (1973). The development of instructional control over classroom activities of deviant preschool children. *Journal of Applied Behavior Analysis, 6,* 289–298.

Barton, E. S., Guess, D., Garcia, E., & Baer, D. M. (1970). Improvements of retardates mealtime behaviors by timeout procedures using the multiple baseline technique. *Journal of Applied Behavior Analysis, 3,* 77–84.

Barton, L. E., Brulle, A. R., & Repp, A. C. (1987). Effects of differential scheduling of timeout to reduce maladaptive responding. *Exceptional Children, 53,* 351–356.

Benjamin, R., Mazzarins, H., & Kupfersmid, J. (1983). The effect of time-out (TO) duration on assaultiveness in psychiatrically hospitalized children. *Aggressive Behavior, 9*(1), 21–27.

Bennett, D., Gast, D. L., Wolery, M., & Schuster, J. (1986). Time delay and system of least prompts: A comparison in teaching manual sign production. *Education and Training of the Mentally Retarded, 21,* 117–129.

Brantner, J. P., & Doherty, M. A. (1983). A review of timeout: A conceptual and methodological analysis. In S. Axelrod & J. Apsche (Eds.), *The effects of punishment on human behavior* (pp. 87–132). New York: Academic Press.

Cuenin, L. H., & Harris, K. P. (1986). Planning, implementing, and evaluating timeout interventions with exceptional students. *TEACHING Exceptional Children, 18,* 272–276.

Craft, N., & Haussmann, S. (1983). Suspension and expulsion of handicapped individuals. *Exceptional Children, 49,* 524–527.

Dagley, D. L. (1982). Some thoughts on disciplining the handicapped. *Phi Delta Kappan, 63,* 696–697.

Firestone, P. (1976). The effects and side effects of time-out on an aggressive nursery school child. *Journal of Behavior Therapy and Experimental Psychiatry, 6,* 79–81.

Flygare, T. J. (1974). Short-term student suspension and the requirements of due process. *Journal of Law Education, 3*(4), 529–555.

Flygare, T. J. (1981). Disciplining special education students. *Phi Delta Kappan, 62,* 670–671.

Ford, J. E., & Veltri-Ford, A. (1980). Effects of timeout from auditory reinforcement on two problem behaviors. *Mental Retardation, 18,* 299–303.

Foxx, R. M., & Shapiro, S. T. (1978). The timeout ribbon: A nonexclusionary timeout procedure.

Journal of Applied Behavior Analysis, 11, 125–136.

Gast, D. L., & Nelson, C. M. (1977a). Time-out in the classroom: Implications for special education. *Exceptional Children, 43,* 461–464.

Gast, D. L., & Nelson, C. M. (1977b). Legal and ethical considerations for the use of timeout in special education settings. *Journal of Special Education, 11,* 457–467.

Godby, S., Gast, D. L., & Wolery, M. (1987). A comparison of time delay and system of least prompts in teaching object identification. *Research in Developmental Disabilities, 8,* 283–306.

Harris, K. R. (1985). Definitional, parametric, and procedural considerations in timeout interventions and research. *Exceptional Children, 51,* 279–288.

Harris, S. L., & Wolchik, S. A. (1979). Suppression of self-stimulation: Three alternative strategies. *Journal of Applied Behavior Analysis, 12,* 185–198.

Henricksen, K., & Doughty, R. (1967). Decelerating undesired mealtime behavior in a group of profoundly retarded boys. *American Journal of Mental Deficiency, 72,* 40–44.

Hobbs, S. A., Forehand, R., & Murray, R. G. (1978). Effects of various durations of timeout on the noncompliant behavior of children. *Behavior Therapy, 9,* 652–656.

Kazdin, A. E. (1980). Acceptability of timeout from reinforcement procedures for disruptive child behavior. *Journal of Applied Behavior Analysis, 13,* 259–273.

Kazdin, A. E. (1984). Acceptability of aversive procedures and medication as treatment alternatives for deviant child behavior. *Journal of Abnormal Child Psychology, 12,* 289–302.

Leone, P. E. (1984). Reconciling educational rights of handicapped pupils with the school disciplinary code. In R. B. Rutherford & C. M. Nelson (Eds.), *Monographs in behavior disorders: Severe behavior disorders of children and youth* (Vol. 7) (pp. 80–85). Reston, VA: Council for Children with Behavioral Disorders of The Council for Exceptional Children.

Leone, P. E. (1985). Suspension and expulsion of handicapped pupils. *Journal of Special Education, 19,* 111–121.

Ludlow, B. L. (1982). Handicapped students and school discipline: Guidelines for administrators. *The High School Journal, 66,* 14–17.

Luiselli, J. K., Reisman, J., Helfen, C. S., & Pemberton, B. W. (1976). Control of self-stimulatory behavior of an autistic child through brief physical restraint. *School Applications of Learning Theory, 9,* 3–13.

Luiselli, J. K., Suskin, L., Slocumb, P. R. (1984). Application of immobilization time-out in management programming with developmentally disabled children. *Child and Behavior Therapy, 6*(1), 1–15.

MacDonough, T. S., & Forehand, R. (1973). Response-contingent timeout: Important parameters in behavior modification with children. *Journal of Behavior Therapy and Experimental Psychiatry, 4,* 231–236.

Mace, F. C., Page, T. J., Ivancic, M. T., & O'Brien, S. (1986). Effectiveness of brief time-out with and without contingent delay: A comparative analysis. *Journal of Applied Behavior Analysis, 19,* 79–86.

Martin, L., McDonald, S., & Omichinski, M. (1971). An operant analysis of response interactions during meals with severely retarded girls. *American Journal of Mental Deficiency, 76,* 68–75.

McKeegan, G. F., Estill, K., & Campbell, B. M. (1984). Use of nonexclusionary timeout for the elimination of a stereotyped behavior. *Journal of Behavior Therapy and Experimental Psychiatry, 15,* 261–264.

Miller, A. J., & Kratochwill, T. R. (1979). Reduction of frequent stomachache complaints by timeout. *Behavior Therapy, 10,* 211–218.

Morales v. *Turman.* (1973). 364 Supplement, 166 E. D. Texas.

Nelson, C. M., & Rutherford, R. B. (1983). Timeout revisited: Guidelines for its use in special education. *Exceptional Education Quarterly, 4*(3), 56–67.

Nielsen, L. (1979). Let's suspend suspensions: Consequences and alternatives. *Personnel and Guidance Journal, 57,* 442–445.

Noll, M. B., & Simpson, R. L. (1979). The effects of physical time-out on the aggressive behaviors of a severely emotionally disturbed child in a public school setting. *AAESPH Review, 4,* 399–406.

Norton, G. R., Austen, S., Allen, G. E., & Hilton, J. (1983). Acceptability of timeout from reinforcement procedures for disruptive child behaviors:

A further analysis. *Child and Family Behavior Therapy, 5*(2), 31–41.

Pease, G. A., & Tyler, V. O. (1979). Self-regulation of time-out duration in the modification of disruptive classroom behavior. *Psychology in the Schools, 16,* 101–105.

Plummer, S., Baer, D. M., & LeBlanc, J. M. (1977). Functional considerations in the use of procedural timeout and an effective alternative. *Journal of Applied Behavior Analysis, 10,* 689–705.

Polsgrove, L. (1982). Return to baseline: Some comments on Smith's reinterpretation of seclusionary timeout. *Behavioral Disorders, 8,* 50–52.

Porterfield, J. K., Herbert-Jackson, E., & Risley, T. R. (1976). Contingent observation: An effective and acceptable procedure for reducing disruptive behavior of young children in a group setting. *Journal of Applied Behavior Analysis, 9,* 55–64.

Roberts, M. W. (1984a). An attempt to reduce time out resistance in young children. *Behavior Therapy, 15,* 210–216.

Roberts, M. W. (1984b). The effects of warned versus unwarned time-out procedures on child noncompliance. *Child and Family Behavior Therapy, 4*(1), 37–53.

Rolider, A., & Van Houten, R. (1985). Movement suppression time-out for undesirable behavior in psychotic and severely developmentally delayed children. *Journal of Applied Behavior Analysis, 18,* 275–288.

Rutherford, R. B. (1978). Theory and research on the use of aversive procedures in the education of moderately behaviorally disordered and emotionally disturbed children and youth. In F. H. Wood & C. K. Lakin (Eds.), *Punishment and aversive stimulation in special education: Legal, theoretical and practical issues in their use with emotionally disturbed children and youth* (pp. 41–64). Minneapolis, MN: Advanced Training Institute.

Rutherford, R. B., & Nelson, C. M. (1982). Analysis of the response contingent time-out literature with behaviorally disordered students in classroom settings. In R. B. Rutherford (Ed.), *Monographs in behavior disorders: Severe behavior disorders of children and youth* (Vol. 5). (pp. 79–105). Reston, VA: Council for Children with Behavioral Disorders of The Council for Exceptional Children.

Safer, D. J., Heaton, R. C., & Parker, F. C. (1981). A behavioral program for disruptive junior high school students: Results and follow-up. *Journal of Abnormal Child Psychology, 9,* 483–494.

Smith, D. E. P. (1981). Is isolation room time-out a punisher? *Behavioral Disorders, 6,* 247–256.

Smith, D. E. P. (1982). Timeout as reduced environmental stimulation (RES): Reply to Polsgrove. *Behavioral Disorders, 8,* 53–55.

Solnick, J. V., Rincover, A., & Peterson, C. R. (1977). Some determinants of the reinforcing and punishing effects of timeout. *Journal of Applied Behavior Analysis, 10,* 415–424.

Tyroler, M. J., & Lahey, B. B. (1980). Effects of contingent observations on the disruptive behavior of a toddler in a group setting. *Child Care Quarterly, 9,* 265–274.

White, G., Nielsen, G., & Johnson, S. (1972). Time out duration and the suppression of deviant behavior in children. *Journal of Applied Behavior Analysis, 5,* 111–120.

Wyatt v. *Stickney.* (1972). 344 F. Supplement, 387, M.D. Alabama.

Zabel, M. K. (1986). Timeout use with behaviorally disordered students. *Behavioral Disorders, 12,*(1), 15–21.

22

AVERSIVE TECHNIQUES TO REDUCE INAPPROPRIATE BEHAVIORS

Key Terms

■ Type I Punishment ■ Contingent ■ Punishment ■ Aversive Stimuli ■ Suppressive Effects ■ Restitutional Overcorrection ■ Positive Practice ■ Simple Correction ■ Corporal Punishment ■ Corporal Punishment Cycle

Previous chapters in this book addressed procedures designed to avoid the use of the strategies described in this chapter. Chapters 20 and 21 described Type II punishment procedures; this chapter focuses on Type I punishment procedures. Type I procedures are intrusive strategies and may cause discomfort and pain. They are powerful and drastic interventions with a substantial research literature. The minimal acceptable conditions for using punishment (Chapter 18) and the behavior-reduction model (Chapter 19) should be employed when these procedures are used.

Four issues are discussed in this chapter. First, the definition of Type I punishment is reviewed; second, contingent application of aversive stimuli is discussed; third, use of overcorrection is described; and fourth, corporal punishment as practiced in schools is given attention. Researchers, teachers, parents, and students hold definite and strong views about the use of Type I punishment procedures. The purpose of this chapter is to provide a context for discussions about their use.

DEFINITION OF TYPE I PUNISHMENT

As noted in Chapter 18, **Type I punishment** is defined as the contingent presentation of an aversive stimulus that results in a decrease in the target behavior. **Contingent,** of course, means that the stimulus is presented each time the target behavior occurs and only when the target behavior occurs. This is a technical and functional definition of punishment; however, the word *punishment* has many connotations and meanings. In general usage, punishment can refer to the presentation of some aversive stimulus (e.g., spanking) or withdrawal of some freedom (e.g., grounding) without reference to the effect of that contingency on the behavior. At the most, persons who use the term assume or hope that the behavior will decrease or never occur again. Punishment can also refer to retribution; that is, an aversive stimulus is presented or a freedom is suspended because some "wrong" has been committed. Punishment also can include an element of revenge or reprisal: persons who wrong society should be punished simply because the offense occurred. Similarly, many people believe that society has a responsibility to make things equal or just; they believe that when a wrong occurs, society should react by punishing the perpetrator. Because of the multiple meanings, the definition of punishment should be specified when it is discussed. As used in this chapter, **punishment** is the presentation of an aversive stimulus, contingent upon the occurrence of the target behavior, that produces a decrease in the frequency with which that behavior occurs.

DIRECT, CONTINGENT APPLICATION OF AVERSIVE STIMULI

In the education and treatment of students with handicaps, a variety of aversive stimuli have been used. **Aversive stimuli** are repugnant, disliked, and avoided when possible; they may cause pain and/or discomfort. Aversive stimuli have typically been used with students whose behavior problems are severe and, in some cases, life-threatening. The direct, contingent use of aversive stimuli fits the presentation pattern of Type I punishment; that is, when the target behavior occurs, the stimulus is applied to the student. However, the stimulus cannot be called a punisher until it produces a decrease in the occurrence of the target behavior. The range of aversive stimuli that have been investigated is staggering. Aversive stimuli have been used for each sensory modality (i.e., vision, taste, smell, hearing, touch). Also, aversive stimuli related to students' movement have been used.

Types of Aversive Stimuli Used

Stimuli Aversive to Sensory Modalities. Vision has been targeted primarily through *visual screening,* which is a procedure where students' faces are covered with a cloth or their eyes are blindfolded contingent upon the occurrence of a target behavior. Singh and Winton (1984) placed a blindfold on a profoundly retarded student for 1 minute contingent upon each episode of eating nonnutritive, inedible objects (an eating disorder called *pica*). The procedure resulted in a decrease in the target behavior. Visual screening has also been used effectively to control self-injurious behavior (Lutzker, 1978; Singh, 1980), stereotypic behaviors (McGopnigle, Duncan, Cordisco, & Barrett, 1982), and disruptive behaviors such as screaming (Singh, Winton, & Dawson, 1982) and hand-clapping (Zegiob, Jenkins, Becker, & Bristow, 1976).

The *gustatory (taste)* sense has been addressed by giving students substances that have aversive tastes. For example, Becker, Turner, and Sajwaj (1978) treated a student with profound retardation for rumination (a life-threatening behavior where food is regurgitated) by injecting lemon juice into the student's mouth contingent upon rumination or mouth movements that led to regurgitation. Fleece, O'Brien, and Drabman (1982) presented a 2:1 solution of mouthwash and water contingent upon the biting behavior of a 2½-year-old boy with moderate retardation. Similarly, Matson and Ollendick (1976) sprayed Listerine mouthwash into students' mouths contingent upon biting others. Conway and Bucher (1974) put aerosol shaving cream into the mouth of a student with retardation who engaged in tantrums. Altman, Haavik, and Higgins (1983) put a combination of Tabasco sauce and "thum" (a product designed to inhibit thumb-sucking) on a student's finger to decrease self-injurious finger biting. In another study, Tabasco sauce was sprayed into a severely retarded student's mouth to treat self-biting; this spray was used in combination with DRO, timeout, and contingent restraint (Altmeyer, Williams, & Sams, 1985). These aversive-tasting substances produced suppressive effects. **Suppressive effects** mean the target behaviors decreased in frequency.

As with visual and gustatory sensory modalities, the suppressive effects of aversive *olfactory (smell)* stimuli have been evaluated. Aromatic ammonia (not cleaning ammonia) has been used contingently to decrease self-injurious behavior (Altman, Haavik, & Cook, 1978; Baumeister & Baumeister, 1978; Tanner & Zeiler, 1975) and severe aggressive behavior (Doke, Wolery, & Sumberg, 1983). In these studies, students were required to smell the ammonia contingent upon performing the target maladaptive behaviors. It should be noted that this may cause tissue damage to the membranes of the nose; thus, aromatic ammonia should be used only when monitored by a physician.

Although less frequently investigated, the effects of aversive *auditory (hearing)* stimuli have also been studied. For example, Scagliotta (1975) presented a flat tone, at moderate amplification, through earphones to decrease the screaming behavior of a young language delayed student. Sajwaj and Hedges (1971) used contingent 105 decibel blasts from a bicycle horn to decrease a boy's disruptive behavior. Verbal reprimands also have been studied but produce variable effects. Sometimes verbal reprimands decrease the target behavior; on other occasions, verbal reprimands increase the behavior; and on still other occasions, verbal reprimands have no effect on the behavior.

Numerous types of aversive *tactile (touch)* stimuli have been used. Contingent electric shock has been used to treat severe maladaptive behaviors in clinical settings (for reviews, see Harris & Ersner-Hershfield, 1978; Lichstein & Schriebman, 1976; Neel, 1978). Other aversive tactile stimuli include contingent water mists from spray bottles (Bailey, Pokrzywinski, & Bryant, 1983; Dorsey, Iwata, Ong, & McSween, 1980; Gross, Berler, & Drabman, 1982), contingent slapping (Koegel, Firestone, Kramme, & Dunlap, 1974; Mayhew & Harris, 1978), hair tugs or pulls (Griffin, Locke, & Landers, 1975), and contingent placing of ice in a student's mouth (Drabman, Ross, Lynd, & Cordua, 1978).

Stimuli Aversive to Students' Movement. In addition to applying aversive stimuli to students' sensory receptors, required movement and restraint from movement have been used as aversive stimuli. For example, brief periods of restraint from movement (e.g., a few seconds to 1 minute) have been effective in eliminating disruptive and stereotypic behaviors (Bitgood, Peters, Jones, & Hathorn, 1982; Richmond & Bell, 1983; Tomporowski, 1983). Requiring movement has also been effective. Luce, Delquardi, and Hall (1980) reduced verbal and physical aggression of two students by requiring them to engage in exercise, standing up and sitting down 10 times, contingent upon each aggressive act. The suppressive effects of contingent exercise also have been replicated by other researchers (e.g,, Daniel, 1982; Richmond & Bennett, 1983). In addition to contingent exercise, contingent completion of chores (e.g. washing windows) served as an aversive stimulus for cursing (Fischer & Nehs, 1978).

Findings and Implications from Research on Aversive Stimuli

Based on the studies cited above and other studies using direct, contingent application of aversive stimuli, several findings are apparent. These findings are discussed in the following paragraphs. Each finding and its implications are listed in Table 22.1.

Aversiveness Is Individually Determined. As with reinforcers, stimuli that are aversive to some students will not be aversive to others. For example, contingent restraint was an aversive stimulus in the study by Bitgood et al. (1982), but Favell and her colleagues presented considerable data showing that contingent restraint can function as a positive reinforcer rather than a punishing stimulus (Favell, McGimsey, & Jones, 1978; Favell, McGimsey, Jones, & Cannon, 1981). Although a specific stimulus may be aversive to most students, there is no guarantee that it will be aversive to other students. Teachers must select aversive stimuli carefully and then evaluate the effect of those stimuli with each student.

The Intensity of the Stimulus Is Related to Effectiveness. Increased suppressive effects may occur with higher levels of the aversive stimulus; for example, longer

TABLE 22.1   Findings and Implications from Research on Direct, Contingent Application of Aversive Stimuli

Findings	Implications for Practice
Aversiveness of stimuli is individually determined.	Teachers must carefully select the stimuli used as aversive stimuli for each student. Teachers must evaluate the stimuli they select as aversive stimuli.
The intensity of the stimulus is related to effectiveness.	Teachers must select the intensity of the aversive stimulus that will be effective, but will not be too harsh.
Side effects may occur.	Teachers should plan for both desirable and undesirable side effects. Side effects should be monitored and, when appropriate, treated.
Maintenance of effects is variable.	Teachers should plan for maintenance and teach and reinforce the occurrence of desirable replacement behaviors.
Effectiveness is related to how the aversive stimuli are used.	Teachers should carefully plan the use of aversive stimuli. Teachers should periodically check the actual implementation of the aversive stimulus to ensure that it is appropriate.
Use of aversive procedures should be restricted.	Teachers should carefully consider the conditions under which punishment procedures are acceptable (Chapter 18) and use a decision model when implementing the aversive procedures (e.g., Chapter 19).

durations (i.e., 1 minute) of visual screening are more suppressive than shorter intervals (i.e., 30 seconds) (Singh, Winton, & Dawson, 1982). This finding is consistent with previous research with animal subjects. When these aversive procedures are used, teachers must determine the most appropriate level of aversive stimulation. A rule of thumb is that it should not be too intense but it should be sufficiently intense to be effective. Unfortunately, no clear empirical guidelines exist concerning what levels of a given aversive stimulus should be administered to treat a specific behavior for a particular student.

Side Effects May Occur. The occurrence of side effects or multiple effects is common. When aversive stimuli are appropriately and contingently applied to a given behavior, that response will likely be suppressed; however, a number of other behaviors may change also. Some of those changes may be positive and have educational value such as increased attention to, or participation in, tasks (e.g., Doke et al., 1983). Other side effects may be negative and actually result in the occurrence of additional aberrant behavior (e.g., Mayhew & Harris, 1978). The occurrence of positive effects is not sufficient reason to use punishment procedures. If specific positive behaviors are desired, those behaviors should be targeted and programs implemented to teach them. Likewise, the occurrence of negative side effects should not preclude the use of aversive stimuli; however, the possibility of their occurrence must be recognized and plans should be made for dealing with them. Frequently, the negative side effects may be associated with the actual application of the aversive stimulus. When the behavior is sufficiently suppressed, the aversive stimulus is used less frequently or may not be used at all, and the negative effects may decrease in frequency.

Maintenance of Effects Is Variable. Several studies report relatively long-term control of the aberrant behaviors to which aversive stimuli were applied. This finding is not likely, however, unless the environment encourages the development of adaptive responses. As noted in Chapter 18, replacement behaviors should be taught whenever punishment procedures are used. In fact, many of the studies described above also included reinforcement for adaptive responses. It is unethical and impractical to use Type I punishment procedures without also teaching and reinforcing desirable replacement behaviors.

Effectiveness Is Related to How the Aversive Stimuli Are Used. The manner in which aversive stimuli are used may have as much to do with their effectiveness as the type of aversive stimulus used. Consistent and immediate application of the stimulus is required. Inconsistent use or delayed use may not have the desired suppressive effects. Further, students should not be allowed to escape from the punishment. Teachers must select aversive procedures that can be consistently used, and should check that implementation regularly.

Use of Aversive Procedures Should Be Restricted. The Type I punishers described above are drastic procedures and in many situations may be considered child abuse; therefore, their use should be severely restricted. The 11 conditions listed in Chapter 18 concerning the use of punishment procedures should be considered carefully. Likewise, a decision model such as the one presented in Chapter 19 should be followed carefully. Another reason for restricting their use is that these procedures do not teach children what behaviors to do, but rather when and what not to do. However, in a few extreme situations, these procedures may be needed. In fact, failure to use these procedures in those situations may result in more restrictive placements, inappropriate treatment, and perhaps denial of treatment. In such cases, the procedures should be used, but used with care.

DESCRIPTION AND USE OF OVERCORRECTION

Overcorrection was first named as a part of a toilet training program for adults with retardation (Azrin & Foxx, 1971). A serendipitous observation was made during the development of that program. A resident had remained dry for a couple of hours and then openly urinated on the floor. As the trainer retrieved a mop, he realized that the offender should do the cleaning, so he required the resident to mop the floor. The resident appeared to be displeased with this consequence and it appeared to have suppressive effects (Foxx, personal communication, 1975). The procedure was systematized, named, and became a standard part of Foxx and Azrin's (1973a) toilet training program. Since that introduction, it has been applied to many different behaviors in various settings.

Types of Overcorrection

The general rationale behind overcorrection is that people are responsible for their actions. This responsibility is demonstrated by two procedures. The first is **restitutional overcorrection** in which students are required, contingent upon a disruptive act, to restore the environment to a condition better than it was at the time the behavior occurred. For example, if Randy writes on his desk, he would be required to clean his desk and also other desks in the classroom. The desks in the class are restored to a condition better than when he wrote on his own. The second type of overcorrection is **positive practice** in which students are required, contingent upon a target behavior, to perform adaptive or relevant forms of behavior that are incompatible with the maladaptive behavior. For example, when Randy wrote on his desk, he would be required to practice writing on paper. Overcorrection is different from simple correction. **Simple correction** is where students correct the results of their behaviors. For example, Randy would be required to clean only his desk.

Although overcorrection has received research only during the past 15 years, it is not a new concept in psychology. Kelly and Drabman (1977) cited Thorndike's "principle of belongingness" as a predecessor to overcorrection. This principle states that "maximally effective rewards and punishers will be situationally relevant to the behaviors they modify" (p. 469). When designing overcorrection programs, the restitutional acts and positive practice behaviors should be *related* to the maladaptive behavior. If students were overcorrected for running in the halls, they should practice walking; if they were overcorrected for throwing a toy, they should be required to pick up and put away several toys or be required or play appropriately with toys; if the inappropriate behavior was hitting, the overcorrection may be showing kindness to the victims by patting them nicely and giving them things.

Restitutional Overcorrection. Restitution is a relatively old concept as Jewish law attests: "If a man shall steal an ox, or a sheep . . . he shall restore five oxen for an ox, and four sheep for a sheep" (Exodus 22:1, *Holy Bible,* 1625). The environment of the theft victim is considerably improved because he receives additional animals for each one that is stolen. Restitution is also a common punishment procedure used in the criminal justice system. For example, youths who destroy property are required to earn money and pay damages to the owners. As such, restitution has considerable social validity with the general public, but this does not necessarily apply to school-related behaviors and interventions. However, it is important to note that unless the youths are required to pay more than the damage they cause, it would only be simple correction.

Restitution has at least six components. First, the restitution should be conceptually related to the aberrant behavior (Foxx & Azrin, 1972). That is, the restitution should correct (actually overcorrect) the aspect of the environment that was disrupted by the aberrant behavior. Second, when the aberrant behavior occurs, the student's ongoing activities and regular access to reinforcement are interrupted by verbal reprimands or physical prompts. Third, the restitution should be applied immediately after the occurrence of the aberrant behavior (Foxx & Azrin, 1972). As with other punishment and reinforcement procedures, the immediacy of the consequence is highly related to its effectiveness. Fourth, "the restitution should be extended in duration" (Foxx & Azrin, 1972, p. 16). A number of different intervals have been used; teachers should select an interval that will be suppressive yet will minimize the amount of time spent away from instructional activities. Fifth, the student should actively do the restitution without stopping (Foxx & Azrin, 1972). During the restitution, the student should be actively expending effort. This effort is different from contingent exercises because restitution requires that the effort be related to the offense. Graduated guidance is used to ensure that the student does the restitutional responses. The student should not be positively reinforced during restitutional activities. Sixth, the student is returned to the ongoing activities when the restitution is completed.

Positive Practice. Positive practice is also a relatively old notion; nearly everyone has heard the phrase "practice makes perfect." The phrase implies there is something instructive about practice; positive practice requires students to perform adaptive responses contingent upon the occurrence of the target inappropriate behavior. This procedure has been used for years in teaching academic behaviors. For example, if students misspell words on a spelling test, they may be required to write each misspelled word correctly a number of times. Research with positive practice has focused on academic errors and aberrant social behavior. Positive practice is different from negative practice because negative practice requires performance of the error or incorrect behavior and positive practice requires performance of appropriate behavior.

Five characteristics of positive practice have been identified: "(1) telling the child he behaved inappropriately; (2) stopping the child's ongoing activity; (3) providing systematic verbal instructions; (4) forcing practice of desired forms of the behavior; and (5) returning the child to his ongoing activity" (Epstein, Doke, Sajwaj, Sorrell, & Rimmer, 1974, p. 389). As with restitution, graduated guidance is used to "force" or require practice of relevant forms of adaptive behaviors, and reinforcement is not given during positive practice.

Positive practice and restitution are complex treatment packages; both include punishment procedures that have been used alone, such as response interruption, verbal reprimands, and timeout from positive reinforcement. In some applications, overcorrection also includes contingent restraint from movement and in others contingent exercise. Differential reinforcement of other behaviors is frequently combined with overcorrection. In addition, positive practice may include negative reinforcement for the practiced behaviors. When students perform the practiced behaviors independently, manual graduated guidance, which is potentially an aversive stimulus, is withdrawn (Foxx & Azrin, 1973b). Likewise, compliance training may occur since verbal instructions are frequently given and compliance is prompted if not forthcoming (Epstein et al., 1974; Measel & Alfieri, 1976). Despite this complexity, overcorrection can be implemented quite consistently. A flowchart depicting the decision points in using overcorrection is shown in Figure 22.1.

Effects of Overcorrection

Successful Use of Overcorrection. Restitution and positive practice, used separately or in combination, have been effective in reducing or eliminating a large number of behavior problems displayed by a wide array of persons in diverse situations. For example, overcorrection has been used to reduce the *self-injurious behaviors* of preschool children (Kelly & Drabman, 1977), elementary-age students (Wesolowski & Zawlocki, 1982), adolescents (Gibbs & Luyben, 1985) and adults (Azrin, Gottlieb, Hughart, Wesolowski, & Rahn, 1975). Overcorrection has been used to control *stereotypic behaviors* of preschoolers (Doke & Epstein, 1975), elementary-age students (Bierly & Billingsley, 1983), adolescents (Denny, 1980), and adults (Matson & Stephens, 1981). It has also been used effectively to treat *aggressive-disruptive behaviors* of preschoolers (Ollendick & Matson, 1976), elementary-age students (Luiselli & Rice, 1983), and adults (Matson & Stephens, 1977). Finally, overcorrection has been effective with a number of other behaviors such as manual sign errors (Linton & Singh, 1984), failure to share materials (Barton & Osborne, 1978), oral reading errors (Singh, Singh, & Winton, 1984), spelling errors (Matson, Esveldt-Dawson, Kazdin, 1982), in-class masturbation (Luiselli, Helfen, Pemberton, & Reisman, 1977), incorrect cursive letter formation (Trap, Milner-Davis, Joseph, & Cooper, 1978), and failure to make eye contact (Foxx, 1977).

Overcorrection has been effective when administered in students' homes (Ollendick & Matson, 1976), preschool programs (Doke & Epstein, 1975), special education classrooms (Bierly & Billingsley, 1983), and residential institutions (Carey & Bucher, 1983). It has been effective with students who are apparently developing normally but display problem behaviors (Ollendick & Matson, 1976); students with hearing impairments (Luiselli & Rice, 1983), visual impairments (Wesolowski & Zawlocki, 1982), mild mental retardation (Matson, Esveldt-Dawson, & Kazdin, 1982), moderate retardation (Singh et al., 1984), severe retardation (Carey & Bucher, 1983), profound retardation (Denny, 1980); autistic children (Bierly & Billingsley, 1983); chronic psychiatric patients (Matson & Stephens, 1981); and nonhandicapped college students (Young & Vogel, 1983). Thus, numerous demonstrations of the effectiveness of overcorrection exist.

FIGURE 22.1   Major decision points related to planning to use overcorrection.

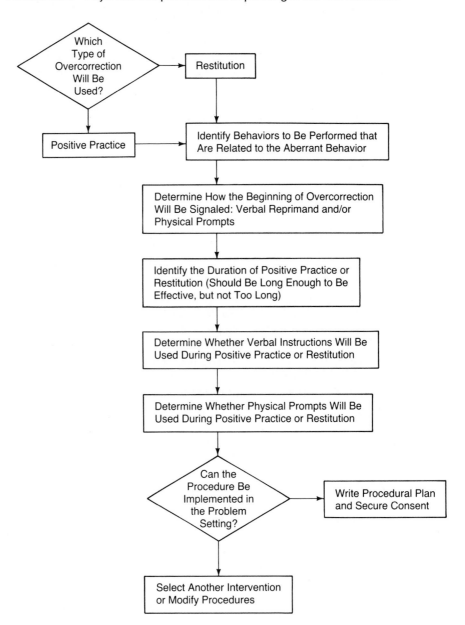

Unsuccessful Use of Overcorrection.   As with many procedures, overcorrection is not universally effective. For example, a 16-year-old student with visual impairments and profound mental retardation who was a resident of an institution engaged in self-injurious head-banging. When praise and edible reinforcers for engaging in tasks and positive practice for head-banging were implemented, the frequency of head bangs increased considerably (Measel & Alfieri, 1976). The self-injurious head-slapping of another similar subject in this study was successfully treated with reinforcement and positive practice; thus, the failure with the first subject probably was not due to incorrect implementation. Likewise, Rollings, Baumeister, and Baumeister (1977) applied positive practice to the stereotypic behavior of two adults with retardation. One student was successfully treated but the stereotypic head-weaving of the second was not eliminated. Explanations for the lack of effectiveness are numerous; for example, the physical contact of overcorrection holds reinforcement properties, positive practice on head movements is not sufficiently aversive, the social attention involved in applying overcorrection has reinforcing properties, initial assessment of the maintaining variable of the aberrant behaviors is inadequate, and the subjects have a history with more aversive procedures. It is impossible to determine whether these examples are isolated instances or whether they represent a much larger group of subjects and situations where overcorrection is ineffective. Frequently, journals do not publish studies where procedures are unsuccessful; these examples may be an indication that overcorrection is not as effective as it appears. They definitely indicate that overcorrection is not a fail-proof treatment despite considerable supporting data.

Comparative Effectiveness of Overcorrection. In a number of studies, overcorrection was successful when other procedures were not. For example, Foxx and Azrin (1973b) used overcorrection to eliminate stereotypic behaviors of two students when differential reinforcement of other behaviors (DRO), physical punishment, and noncontingent reinforcement had previously been ineffective. Overcorrection also was more effective than a verbal reprimand alone (Ollendick & Matson, 1976). Measel and Alfieri (1976) compared DRO to DRO plus positive practice in an attempt to reduce self-injurious behavior. As noted above, the combined treatment was more effective in one case and less effective in another. Trap et al. (1978) compared verbal and visual feedback to verbal and visual feedback plus immediate rewriting (positive practice) for cursive writing errors. The feedback plus immediate rewriting was more effective than feedback alone. In all of these studies, overcorrection followed the comparison procedure; thus, its superiority may be due to the sequence of training. Other studies have controlled this problem. Overcorrection was more effective than timeout or DRO for decreasing stereotypic behaviors (Harris & Wolchik, 1979). Positive practice was compared to timeout and to social punishment for treating noncompliance (Doleys, Wells, Hobbs, Roberts, & Cartelli, 1976). Positive practice appeared to be more effective than timeout but social punishment was the most effective. The latter treatment consisted of the teacher holding the student firmly by the shoulders accompanied by a loud verbal reprimand and followed by the teacher standing up and "glaring" at the student for 40 seconds. Ollendick, Shapiro, and Barrett (1981) compared positive practice to physical restraint and to a no-treatment condition. Both treatment procedures were more effective than the no-treatment condition, and each was more effective than the other for different students. Linton and Singh (1984), while teaching manual sign production, compared positive practice alone, positive practice and reinforcement, and a no-training condition. Again, both treatment procedures were more effective than the no-training condition, and positive practice plus reinforcement was the most effective. This finding has been replicated with oral reading errors (Singh et al., 1984) and spelling errors (Ollendick, Matson, Esveldt-Dawson, & Shapiro, 1980).

In general, overcorrection was superior to most treatments to which it has been compared, and its effectiveness appeared to increase when correct or adaptive responses were reinforced. Comparisons between restitution and positive practice also have been made and appear to produce similar suppressive effects (Carey & Bucher, 1981; Matson, Horne, Ollendick, & Ollendick, 1979). However, positive practice seems more likely to increase relevant (practiced) responses than restitution (Carey & Bucher, 1981).

Maintenance and Generalization Effects of Overcorrection. Maintenance of the effects has been measured and the results are quite mixed. In some cases, treated behaviors remain at zero or near zero levels for several months or as much as a year (e.g., Denny, 1980; Wesolowski & Zawlocki, 1982); in other cases, the behavior returns to baseline levels (e.g., Rollings et al., 1977). Matson, Ollendick, and Martin (1979) conducted a follow-up study of eight subjects who had participated in previous investigations using overcorrection to treat stereotypic responding. For two subjects, no stereotypic behavior occurred during follow-up assessments, but for six, the frequencies approached baseline levels. No clear explanation exists for these mixed results beyond the fact that maintenance in many cases must be systematically programmed. Such programming should involve fading the correction procedure and establishing equal-power replacement behaviors.

Generalization to novel situations has been less frequently studied than maintenance; however, in those cases where it has been studied, the results are similar: generalization sometimes occurs and at other times does not. When implementing overcorrection programs, teachers must plan strategies to increase the chances of generalization; they cannot assume it will happen automatically.

Side Effects of Overcorrection. Positive side effects have occurred when overcorrection is used. For example, when aggression during tantrums was overcorrected, inappropriate crying also decreased (Ollendick & Matson, 1976); when overcorrection was applied to stereotypic responding, appropriate movements with toys increased (Denny, 1980; Epstein et al., 1974). Increases in prosocial behaviors such as smiling, appropriate speech, and interactions with others have been noted (Singh, Manning, & Angell, 1982). In some cases, positive side effects have occurred but did not maintain when the overcorrection was no longer used (Matson & Stephens, 1981).

Negative side effects such as aggressive responses, screaming, throwing objects, and avoidance have been reported during the application of overcorrection (Carey & Bucher, 1983; Wells, Forehand, & Hickey, 1977). Increases in other aberrant behaviors such as self-injurious behavior (Rollings et al., 1977) and stereotypic behavior may occur (Epstein et al., 1974; Singh, Manning, & Angell, 1982). Both positive and negative effects are reported often enough to warrant careful planning when using overcorrection. The plans should include strategies to maximize the likelihood that the desirable effects will be maintained and the negative effects will be controlled.

Issues Related to Using Overcorrection

Topography of Positive Practice. The behaviors performed during positive practice should be related conceptually to the target aberrant behavior. If a student kicks someone, the practice should involve manipulation of the student's feet; if the student hits, the practice should involve movements of the hands. When practice related to an aberrant behavior has been effective, it can be applied to other unrelated aberrant behaviors and be effective (Epstein et al., 1974; Doke & Epstein, 1975). For example, when positive practice was successfully applied to hands for stereotypic behaviors, it was effective when applied to stereotypic feet movements. Practice unrelated to the target behavior also can be effective without previous use with a related aberrant behavior (Carey & Bucher, 1983; Roberts, Iwata, McSween, & Desmond, 1979). However, this should be called contingent exercise rather than overcorrection. Warnings concerning the use of overcorrection can maintain suppressed levels of responding (Foxx & Azrin, 1973b), decrease previously untreated behaviors (Epstein et al., 1974), and decrease similar behaviors of other untreated children (Doke & Epstein, 1975).

Duration of Overcorrection. The amount of time spent in overcorrection has varied greatly; for example, restitution has been used effectively with durations as short as 2 minutes (Foxx & Azrin, 1973b) and as long as 1 hour (Klinge, Thrasher, & Myers, 1975). Likewise, positive practice has been as short as 10 seconds (Harris & Wolchik, 1979) and as long as 2 hours (Webster & Azrin, 1973). In some cases adding to the duration of overcorrection can increase its effectiveness (Foxx & Azrin, 1973b; Ollendick & Matson, 1976). In general, longer intervals are more suppressive than shorter intervals; however, Carey and Bucher (1983) compared short positive practice (30 seconds) to long positive practice (3 minutes) and found that they had similar effects on target behaviors. They also noted that short positive practice resulted in fewer instances of negative effects (aggression and disruption) during positive practice. Although research does not dictate the most suitable duration of overcorrection, many studies employ a specific interval of practice or restitution and use intervals of 30 seconds to 3 minutes.

Educative Effects of Overcorrection. Overcorrection has been called both a punishment and educative procedure. The distinction between the two is that punishment procedures generally do not produce increases in the relevant adaptive behaviors (i.e., practiced responses or restitutional acts) and educative procedures should. Based on the current information about overcorrection, three statements are relevant. First, overcorrection clearly has suppressive effects. As noted earlier, it has been used to reduce or eliminate a large number of different behaviors in a broad array of students from a variety of settings. Second, when overcorrection was applied to stereotypic, self-injurious, and aggressive/disruptive behaviors, inconsistent effects were produced in terms of increasing the frequency of practiced responses or restitutional acts. In a few studies, increases were noted (e.g., Wells et al., 1977; Wells, Forehand, Hickey, & Green, 1977) but, in other studies, increases did not occur (e.g., Bierly & Billingsley, 1983; Denny, 1980). This may be a result of the positive practice responses not being useful to students (Carey & Bucher, 1981). Third, when overcorrection was used contingent upon errors in academic tasks, increases in practiced responses were observed frequently; however, they were more likely to occur when reinforcement also was used (Linton & Singh, 1984; Matson et al., 1982; Matson, Ollendick, & Breuning, 1983; Singh, Manning, & Angell, 1984; Trap et al., 1978).

DESCRIPTION AND USE OF CORPORAL PUNISHMENT

Corporal punishment is in many ways another example of direct, contingent application of an aversive stimulus. In fact, some of the aversive stimuli described above could be considered types of corporal punishment (e.g., aversive tasting substances, aversive tactile stimuli). Further, school administrators, teachers, other professionals, parents, and children hold strong views about its use, and the issue has been hotly debated. Corporal punishment is different, however, because of its long history in American education (Rose, 1983; Smith, Polloway, & West, 1979). In this section, the definition of corporal punishment is provided, its current use is discussed, and issues related to corporal punishment are explored.

As noted earlier, the word *punishment* has many meanings, but in this chapter it refers to a relationship between the presentation of a stimulus event and a decrease in the occurrence of a behavior. Corporal punishment has a unique meaning. *Corporal* refers to the body or things pertaining to the body. **Corporal punishment** refers to punishment that is administered to one's body. Although many definitions of corporal punishment exist, they include some common elements: pain is inflicted on the student's body, the person administering the punishment inflicts the pain intentionally, the pain is inflicted by the punisher's hand or an instrument held in the hand such as a belt or paddle, and the punisher reportedly thinks it is corrective (Smith et al., 1979; McDaniel, 1980).

Rationale For and Against the Use of Corporal Punishment

Persons who support the use of corporal punishment typically propose four reasons: Corporal punishment

1. Reduces or eliminates the occurrence of inappropriate behaviors.
2. Allows students to learn what is right and wrong and when to do given behaviors; essentially it enhances discrimination learning.
3. Prevents other students from engaging in inappropriate behaviors, i.e., it is a deterrant because they see the effects of misbehavior.
4. Is efficient, it can be easily used, and is readily available. (Rose, 1983; Smith et al., 1979)

Persons who oppose the use of corporal punishment provide a number of rationale: Corporal punishment

1. Causes negative effects such as increased avoidance, withdrawal, aggression, and emotional reactions by the punished student.
2. Provides an inappropriate model of how to interact with others.
3. May call attention to the inappropriate behavior which may increase the likelihood of it occurring at other times.
4. Produces limited generalization of reductive effects.
5. May cause peers to avoid the punished student (Rose, 1981, 1983).
6. May be a contributing factor in vandalism, delinquency, and crime (Welsh, 1978).
7. May result in permanent physical or psychological damage to punished students (Bongiovanni & Hyman, 1978).
8. Relying on corporal punishment may actually retard the development of strategies that are not punitive, are instructive, and are more acceptable to everyone involved (Smith et al., 1979).

In reality, logical and indirect scientific support exists for both arguments. The judgment cannot be made simply on the scientific evidence because the data base is incomplete. One's position must be formed on ethical, logical, and personal factors. Nonetheless, there are at least four statements on which nearly everyone can agree. First, corporal punishment is still quite common both in families (Bryan & Freed, 1982) and schools (Wood, 1978). Despite the increased attention to child abuse, the public appears to discriminate abuse from selective, infrequent use of corporal punishment (Fine & Holt, 1983). Second, the use of corporal punishment is probably maintained more on the basis of tradition, conjecture, folklore, and public opinion than on scientific fact (Rose, 1983; Smith et al., 1979). Third, corporal punishment is likely to continue in the schools because of (a) the failure of the Supreme Court to prohibit its use (Rose, 1983; Levy, 1983), (b) the "back-to-basics" movement which includes returning to "old-fashioned disci-pline" (Rose, 1983), (c) the conservative Zeitgeist or general viewpoint in the United States (Welsh, 1978), and (d) educators' belief that it works (McDaniel, 1980). Fourth, as long as corporal punishment exists, even as a restricted practice, concern and debate will be expressed about its legitimacy and efficacy. Court suits are likely to continue, and laws, regulations, and guidelines will be revised and rewritten.

Current Use of Corporal Punishment

Although the number of states that permit the use of corporal punishment may vary from year to year, only a few states prohibit school officials from using it (Wood & Lakin, 1978). Interestingly, most Western European countries, all Eastern European countries, the Soviet Union, Israel, and Japan prohibit, by law, the use of corporal punishment for students in schools (Wood & Lakin, 1978). The actual frequency with which corporal punishment is used is difficult to assess. As Wood and Lakin (1978) indicated, the legality of corporal punishment should not be equated to its use. For example, some teachers in systems where corporal punishment is permissible never use it; likewise, in some systems where it is forbidden, its use can be extensive. Corporal punishment appears to be more widely supported and perhaps more widely used in the south and southwest than in other regions of the country (Hyman & Fina, 1983).

In general, boys are more apt to receive corporal punishment than girls, and boys from economically poorer families are at greater risk (Hyman & Fina, 1983; Welsh, 1978). This may be because boys display more behaviors that are considered punishable offenses or because officials are reluctant to "hit girls." In terms of administering corporal punishment, teachers who were not paddled as children are less likely to paddle their students. For teachers who were paddled as children, their use of corporal punishment appears to be influenced by experiences in their early adult life (Hyman & Fina, 1983).

Rose (1983) presented preliminary data on the use of corporal punishment with students who have mild handicaps. Since this is the only study on the issue, the results should be considered tentative. He surveyed principals from a random sample of school districts throughout the nation. His findings include the following. Of the principals who used corporal punishment, 69% reported doing so with special education students. They reported using corporal punishment less frequently with students diagnosed as behavior disordered than those diagnosed as learning disabled and mentally retarded. Most reported infrequent use of corporal punishment, and only a few reported five or more instances in the past month. There were no gender differences among principals who used corporal punishment; however, those who reported more than five instances in the past month were exclusively male. Junior high school principals appeared to punish special education students more often than elementary or high school principals. The vast majority of corporal punishment occurred in administrative offices and with the use of a paddle. Of the principals who used corporal punishment, 97% required the presence of a witness. In about half of the cases, at least 15 minutes had elapsed between the occurrence of the behavior and administration of punishment. Fighting constituted the majority of behaviors that initiated paddling, and it was followed in order by disruptive behavior, disrespect for authority, disobedience, truancy, and miscellaneous other behaviors.

Issues Related to the Use of Corporal Punishment

Legal Issues Related to Corporal Punishment. When discussing legal issues, it is important to note that the system is variable and may change. Few states prohibit the use of corporal punishment and the courts have long maintained that schools have a right to use it. This right originated in common law where the presence of certain relationships allowed corporal punishment; for example, in the past it was legal to corporally punish wives and employees. This right is no longer recognized for wives and employees, but is recognized for children (Levy, 1983). If done reasonably, parents can legally use corporal punishment with their children. Since parents send or permit their children to go to school, they transfer this legal protection to school officials. This is known as the doctrine of *in loco parentis* (in place of a parent) (Levy, 1983; Wood & Lakin, 1978). As long as school officials act reasonably and administer the punishment to fulfill the purposes for which they were employed, i.e., maintain sufficient control to teach, they can use corporal punishment. Although suits have appeared on the basis of the Eighth Amendment (cruel and unusual punishment) and the Fourteenth Amendment (due process), the courts have been reluctant to accept these defenses (Levy, 1983; Wood & Lakin, 1978). Different states and school districts within states vary considerably on their regulations and policies on the use of corporal punishment.

Procedural Issues Related to Corporal Punishment. Rose (1981) proposed the **corporal punishment cycle** which is an explanation for the continued use of corporal punishment despite its questionable effectiveness. He analyzed an instance of corporal punishment and identified potential sources of positive and negative reinforcement for students, teachers, and principals; these sources are shown in Figure 22.2. If interactions with the teacher (regardless of the content of those interactions) are reinforcing for students, the maladaptive behavior may be positively reinforced when the teacher interrupts the class and informs a student that he or she is to be punished. Further, having the ability or power to stop the class routine may be a positive reinforcer for some students. Students may receive negative reinforcement for the inappropriate behavior because they are removed from the classroom (i.e., potential aversive stimulus). The teacher may be negatively reinforced by stopping the behavior (potential aversive stimulus) and taking the student to the principal. Because teachers and students are apt to interact on the way to the office and because the student has the teacher's undivided attention, the student may receive additional positive reinforcement. The eye contact and interactions with the principal or other office personnel may also have some positive reinforcing value for the student. The principal may provide further positive reinforcement if the student behaves in a repentant manner or "takes his punishment like a man." The principal may be positively reinforced by potential reductions in the inappropriate behavior and from teachers for dealing with the problem and giving them support. During the return to the classroom and upon the student's entry into the classroom, the student may be positively reinforced by attention from peers and/or teacher. If there is a suppressive effect on the aberrant behavior, the teacher may be negatively reinforced by its removal.

Although the student receives what is apparently an aversive stimulus (paddling), it may not have sufficient reductive power to compete with the abundance of reinforcement received throughout the cycle. Although these contingencies may not be in effect in each case, it is clear that corporal punishment as it is practiced is not a simple process. Problems inherent in its administration may severely limit the potential suppressive effects.

FIGURE 22.2 Potential sources of positive and negative reinforcement for students, teachers, and principals that may maintain the corporal punishment cycle.

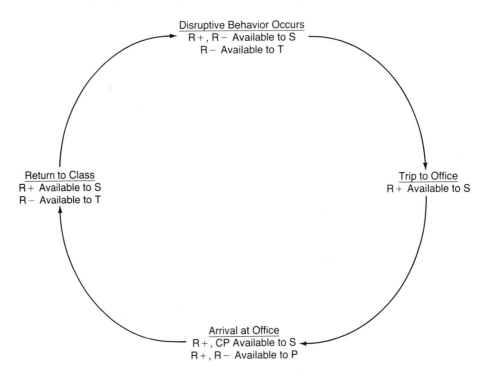

Key: S = Student; T = Teacher; P = Principal; R+ = Positive Reinforcement; R− = Negative Reinforcement; CP = Corporal Punishment

From "The Corporal Punishment Cycle: A Behavioral Analysis of the Maintenance of Corporal Punishment in Schools" by T. L. Rose, 1981, *Education and Treatment of Children, 4,* p. 160. Reprinted by permission.

Summary and Recommendations Concerning Corporal Punishment

Based on the issues discussed above, five comments are pertinent. First, consensus does not exist in the professional or public community concerning the use of corporal punishment. Teachers who plan to select corporal punishment must carefully assess the social validity of the procedure prior to its use. Second, the "legality" of corporal punishment varies from district to district and from state to state. Teachers must be aware of the guidelines and regulations governing their particular program. Third, the effectiveness of corporal punishment is questionable. The use of physical punishment and other aversive stimuli has repeatedly produced substantial reductions in behavior, at least in the short term while contingencies remain in effect (Neel, 1978); however, as practiced in schools, corporal punishment may not be a useful punishment procedure. The reductions found in laboratories and carefully controlled applied settings may not be replicated in less controlled school situations. The potential sources of reinforcement for teachers and students in the corporal punishment cycle suggest that implementation is a particular problem (Rose, 1981). Likewise, it is difficult to deliver corporal punishment immediately after the problem behavior. Fourth, all interventions including corporal punishment should meet the minimal acceptable conditions for using punishment (i.e., Chapter 18). Corporal punishment must be used and evaluated as a systematic intervention procedure rather than a crisis-intervention strategy. Fifth, corporal punishment sets the occasion for actual physical injury of students. Court cases have established that serious damage can occur; for example, some students have needed medical attention for tissue damage and broken bones and others have required hospitalization (Wood & Lakin, 1978). Professionals do *not* want to injure students, and it is wise for them to avoid, as much as possible, interventions that are open to that possibility.

Because of the above conclusions, it is difficult for us to recommend the use of corporal punishment. We do not want to limit the use of strategies that will result in students being free of their behavior problems, but the difficulties associated with corporal punishment make it a very unattractive intervention strategy. Teachers should have all intervention strategies as potential treatment options but, in our view, corporal punishment should rarely be considered or used.

Summary of Key Concepts

- ■ Type I punishment is defined as the contingent presentation of an aversive stimulus that produces a decrease in the frequency of the target behavior.
- ■ A wide variety of aversive stimuli have been used, but the aversiveness of stimuli varies from individual to individual.

- ■ Higher levels of aversiveness may be more suppressive than lower levels.
- ■ Positive and negative side effects may occur when overcorrection and direct, contingent aversive stimuli are used.
- ■ The method by which contingent aversive stimuli are presented is an important factor in determining its effectiveness.
- ■ The two forms of overcorrection, restitution and positive practice, have been used successfully to suppress a wide variety of behaviors, displayed by different students, in a range of situations.
- ■ When overcorrection and direct, contingent aversive stimuli are used, maintenance is more likely to occur when replacement behaviors are taught and reinforced.
- ■ When positive practice is used, some educative effects have been found, particularly with academic behaviors.
- ■ Corporal punishment, as practiced in schools, has supporters and opponents, and its legality varies from district to district and state to state.
- ■ The effectiveness of corporal punishment is questionable because of difficulties in implementing it.

REFERENCES

Altman, K., Haavik, S., & Cook, J. W. (1978). Punishment of self-injurious behavior in natural settings using contingent aromatic ammonia. *Behavior Research and Therapy, 16,* 85–96.

Altman, K., Haavik, S., & Higgins, S. T. (1983). Modifying the self-injurious behavior of an infant with spina bifida and diminished pain sensitivity. *Journal of Behavior Therapy and Experimental Psychiatry, 14*(2), 165–168.

Altmeyer, B. K., Williams, D. E., & Sams, V. (1985). Treatment of severe self-injurious and aggressive biting. *Journal of Behavior Therapy and Experimental Psychiatry, 16,* 159–167.

Azrin, N. H., & Foxx, R. M. (1971). A rapid method of toilet training the institutionalized retarded. *Journal of Applied Behavior Analysis, 4,* 89–99.

Azrin, N. H., Gottlieb, L., Hughart, L., Wesolowski, M. D., & Rahn, T. (1975). Eliminating self-injurious behavior by educative procedures. *Behavior Research and Therapy, 13,* 101–111.

Bailey, S. L., Pokrzywinski, J., & Bryant, L. E. (1983). Using water mist to reduce self-injurious and stereotypic behavior. *Applied Research in Mental Retardation, 4,* 229–241.

Barton, E. J., & Osborne, J. G. (1978). The development of classroom sharing by a teacher using positive practice. *Behavior Modification, 2,* 231–250.

Baumeister, A. A., & Baumeister, A. A. (1978). Suppression of repetitive self-injurious behavior by contingent inhalation of aromatic ammonia. *Journal of Autism and Childhood Schizophrenia, 8,* 71–77.

Becker, J. V., Turner, S. M., & Sajwaj, T. E. (1978). Multiple behavioral effects of the use of lemon juice with a ruminating toddler-age child. *Behavior Modification, 2,* 267–278.

Bierly, C., & Billingsley, F. F. (1983). An investigation of the educative effects of overcorrection on the behavior of an autistic child. *Behavioral Disorders, 9,* 11–21.

Bitgood, S. C., Peters, R. D., Jones, M. L., & Hathorn, N. (1982). Reducing out-of-seat behavior in developmentally disabled children through brief immobilization. *Education and Treatment of Children, 5,* 249–260.

Bongiovanni, A. F., & Hyman, I. A. (1978). Leviton is wrong on the use of corporal punishment. *Psychology in the Schools, 15,* 161–163.

Bryan, J. W., & Freed, F. W. (1982). Corporal punishment normative data and sociological and psychological correlation in a community college population. *Journal of Youth and Adolescence, 11,* 77–87.

Carey, R. G., & Bucher, B. (1981). Identifying the educative and suppressive effects of positive practice and restitutional overcorrection. *Journal of Applied Behavior Analysis, 14,* 71–80.

Carey, R. G., & Bucher, B. (1983). Positive practice overcorrection: The effects of duration of positive practice on acquisition and response reduction. *Journal of Applied Behavior Analysis, 16,* 101–109.

Conway, J. B., & Bucher, B. (1974). Soap in the mouth as an aversive consequence. *Behavior Therapy, 5,* 154–156.

Daniel, W. H. (1982). Management of chronic rumination with a contingent exercise procedure employing topographically dissimilar behavior. *Journal of Behavior Therapy and Experimental Psychiatry, 13,* 149–152.

Denny, M. (1980). Reducing self-stimulatory behavior of mentally retarded persons by alternative positive practice. *American Journal of Mental Deficiency, 84,* 610–615.

Doke, L. A., & Epstein, L. H. (1975). Oral overcorrection: Side effects and extended applications. *Journal of Experimental Child Psychology, 20,* 496–511.

Doke, L. A., Wolery, M., & Sumberg, C. (1983). Treating chronic aggression: Effects and side effects of response-contingent ammonia spirits. *Behavior Modification, 7,* 531–556.

Doleys, D. M., Wells, K. C., Hobbs, S. A., Roberts, M. W., & Cartelli, L. M. (1976). The effects of social punishment on noncompliance: A comparison with timeout and overcorrection. *Journal of Applied Behavior Analysis, 9,* 471–482.

Dorsey, M. F., Iwata, B. A., Ong, P., & McSween, T. E. (1980). Treatment of self-injurious behavior using a water mist: Initial response suppression and generalization. *Journal of Applied Behavior Analysis, 13,* 343–353.

Drabman, R. S., Ross, J. M., Lynd, R. S., & Cordua, G. D. (1978). Retarded children as observers, mediators, and generalization programmers using an icing procedure. *Behavior Modification, 2,* 371–385.

Epstein, L. H., Doke, L. A., Sajwaj, T. E., Sorrell, S., & Rimmer, B. (1974). Generality and side effects of overcorrection. *Journal of Applied Behavior Analysis, 7,* 385–390.

Exodus 22:1, (1625). *Holy Bible,* King James Version.

Favell, J. E., McGimsey, J. F., & Jones, M. L. (1978). The use of physical restraint in the treatment of self-injury and as positive reinforcement. *Journal of Applied Behavior Analysis, 11,* 225–241.

Favell, J. E., McGimsey, J. R., Jones, M. L., & Cannon, P. R. (1981). Physical restraint as positive reinforcement. *American Journal of Mental Deficiency, 85,* 425–432.

Fine, M. J., & Holt, P. (1983). Corporal punishment in the family: A systems perspective. *Psychology in the Schools, 20,* 85–92.

Fischer, J., & Nehs, R. (1978). Use of a commonly available chore to reduce a boy's rate of swearing. *Journal of Behavior Therapy and Experimental Psychiatry, 9,* 81–83.

Fleece, L., O'Brien, T., & Drabman, R. (1982). Suppression of biting behavior via contingent application of an aversive tasting liquid. *Journal of Clinical Child Psychology, 11,* 163–166.

Foxx, R. M. (1977). Attention training: The use of overcorrection avoidance to increase the eye contact of autistic and retarded children. *Journal of Applied Behavior Analysis, 10,* 489–499.

Foxx, R. M., & Azrin, N. H. (1972). Restitution: A method of eliminating aggressive-disruptive behaviors of retarded and brain-damaged patients. *Behavior Research and Therapy, 10,* 15–27.

Foxx, R. M., & Azrin, N. H. (1973a). *Toilet training the retarded: A rapid program for day and nighttime independence toileting.* Champaign, IL: Research Press.

Foxx, R. M., & Azrin, N. H. (1973b). The elimination of autistic self-stimulatory behavior by overcorrection. *Journal of Applied Behavior Analysis, 6,* 1–14.

Gibbs, J. W., & Luyben, P. D. (1985). Treatment of self-injurious behavior: Contingent versus noncontingent positive practice overcorrection. *Behavior Modification, 9,* 3–21.

Griffin, J. C., Locke, B. J., & Landers, W. F. (1975). Manipulation of potential punishment parameters in the treatment of self-injury. *Journal of Applied Behavior Analysis, 8,* 458. (Abstract)

Gross, A. M., Berler, E. S., & Drabman, R. S. (1982). Reduction of aggressive behavior in a retarded boy using a water squirt. *Journal of Behavior Therapy and Experimental Psychiatry, 13,* 95–98.

Harris, S. L., & Ersner-Herschfield, R. (1978). Behavioral suppression of seriously disruptive behavior in psychotic and retarded patients: A review of punishment and its alternatives. *Psychological Bulletin, 85,* 1352–1375.

Harris, S. L., & Wolchik, S. A. (1979). Suppression of self-stimulation: Three alternative strategies. *Journal of Applied Behavior Analysis, 12,* 185–198.

Hyman, I. A., & Fina, A. (1983). The national center for the study of corporal punishment and alternatives in the schools: Moving from policy formation to implementation. *Journal of Clinical Child Psychology, 12,* 257–260.

Kelly, J. A., & Drabman, R. S. (1977). Generalizing response suppression of self-injurious behavior through an overcorrection punishment procedure: A case study. *Behavior Therapy, 8,* 468–472.

Klinge, V., Thrasher, P., & Myers, S. (1975). Use of bed-rest overcorrection in a chronic schizophrenic. *Journal of Behavior Therapy and Experimental Psychiatry, 6,* 69–73.

Koegel, R. L., Firestone, P. B., Kramme, K. W., & Dunlap, G. (1974). Increasing spontaneous play by suppressing self-stimulation in autistic children. *Journal of Applied Behavior Analysis, 7,* 521–528.

Levy, E. R. L. (1983). The child's right to corporal integrity in the school setting: A right without a remedy under the constitution. *Journal of Clinical Child Psychology, 12,* 261–265.

Lichstein, K. L., & Schriebman, L. (1976). Employing electric shock with autistic children: A review of the side effects. *Journal of Autism and Childhood Schizophrenia, 6,* 163–173.

Linton, J. M., & Singh, N. N. (1984). Acquisition of sign language using positive practice overcorrection. *Behavior Modification, 8,* 553–566.

Luce, S. C., Delquardi, J., & Hall, R. V. (1980). Contingent exercise: A mild but powerful procedure for suppressing inappropriate verbal and aggressive behavior. *Journal of Applied Behavior Analysis, 13,* 583–594.

Luiselli, J. K., Helfen, C. S., Pemberton, B. W., & Reisman, J. (1977). The elimination of a child's in-class masturbation by overcorrection and reinforcement. *Journal of Behavior Therapy and Experimental Psychiatry, 8,* 201–204.

Luiselli, J. K., & Rice, D. M. (1983). Brief positive practice with a handicapped child: An assessment of suppressive and re-educative effects. *Education and Treatment of Children, 6*(3), 241–250.

Lutzker, J. R. (1978). Reducing self-injurious behavior by facial screening. *American Journal of Mental Deficiency, 82,* 510–513.

Matson, J. L., Esveldt-Dawson, K., & Kazdin, A. E. (1982). Treatment of spelling deficits in mentally retarded children. *Mental Retardation, 20*(2), 76–81.

Matson, J. L., Horne, A. M., Ollendick, D. G., & Ollendick, T. H. (1979). Overcorrection: A further evaluation of restitution and positive practice. *Journal of Behavior Therapy and Experimental Psychiatry, 10,* 295–298.

Matson, J. L., & Ollendick, T. H. (1976). Elimination of low frequency biting. *Behavior Therapy, 7,* 410–412.

Matson, J. L., Ollendick, T. H., & Breuning, S. E. (1983). An empirical demonstration of the random stimulus design. *American Journal of Mental Deficiency, 87,* 634–639.

Matson, J. L., Ollendick, T. H., & Martin, J. E. (1979). Overcorrection revisited: A long term follow-up. *Journal of Behavior Therapy and Experimental Psychiatry, 10*(1), 11–13.

Matson, J. L., & Stephens, R. M. (1977). Overcorrection of aggressive behavior in a chronic psychiatric patient. *Behavior Modification, 1,* 559–564.

Matson, J. L., & Stephens, R. M. (1981). Overcorrection treatment of stereotyped behaviors. *Behavior Modification, 5,* 491–502.

Mayhew, G. L., & Harris, F. C. (1978). Some negative side effects of a punishment procedure for stereotyped behavior. *Journal of Behavior Therapy and Experimental Psychiatry, 9,* 245–251.

McDaniel, T. R. (1980). Corporal punishment and teacher liability: Questions teachers ask. *Clearing House, 54,* 10–13.

McGopnigle, J. J., Duncan, D., Cordisco, L., & Barrett, R. P. (1982). Visual screening: An alternative method for reducing stereotypic behavior. *Journal of Applied Behavior Analysis, 15,* 461–467.

Measel, C. J., & Alfieri, P. A. (1976). Treatment of self-injurious behavior by a combination of reinforcement for incompatible behavior and overcorrection. *American Journal of Mental Deficiency, 81,* 147–153.

Neel, R. S. (1978). Research finding regarding the use

of punishment procedures with severely behavior disordered children. In F. H. Wood & K. C. Lakin (Eds.), *Punishment and aversive stimulation in special education: Legal, theoretical and practical issues in their use with emotionally disturbed children and youth* (pp. 65–83). Minneapolis, MN: Advanced Training Institute.

Ollendick, T. H., & Matson, J. L. (1976). An initial investigation into the parameters of overcorrection. *Psychological Reports, 39,* 1139–1142.

Ollendick, T. H., Matson, J. L., Esveldt-Dawson, K., Shapiro, E. S., (1980). Increasing spelling achievement: An analysis of treatment procedures utilizing an alternating treatments design. *Journal of Applied Behavior Analysis, 13,* 645–654.

Ollendick, T. H., Shapiro, E. S., & Barrett, R. P. (1981). Reducing stereotypic behaviors: An analysis of treatment procedures utilizing an alternating treatments design. *Behavior Therapy, 12,* 570–577.

Richmond, G., & Bell, J. C. (1983). An analysis and treatment package to reduce hand-mouthing stereotype. *Behavior Therapy, 14,* 576–581.

Richmond, G., & Bennett, G. (1983). Positive practice unrelated to the target behavior. *Psychological Reports, 52,* 350.

Roberts, P., Iwata, B. A., McSween, T. E., & Desmond, E. F. (1979). An analysis of overcorrection movements. *American Journal of Mental Deficiency, 83,* 588–594.

Rollings, J. P., Baumeister, A. A., & Baumeister, A. A. (1977). The use of overcorrection procedures to eliminate the stereotyped behavior of retarded individuals: An analysis of collateral behaviors and generalization of suppressive effects. *Behavior Modification, 1,* 29–46.

Rose, T. L. (1981). The corporal punishment cycle: A behavioral analysis of the maintenance of corporal punishment in the schools. *Education and Treatment of Children, 4,* 157–169.

Rose, T. L. (1983). A survey of corporal punishment of mildly handicapped students. *Exceptional Education Quarterly, 3*(4), 9–19.

Sajwaj, T., & Hedges, D. (1971). *Functions of parental attention in an oppositional, retarded boy.* Proceedings of the 79th Annual Convention of the American Psychological Association.

Scagliotta, E. G. (1975). Amplification as aversion therapy for screaming. *Academic Therapy, 10,* 499–452.

Singh, N. N. (1980). The effects of facial screening on infant self-injury. *Journal of Behavior Therapy and Experimental Psychiatry, 11,* 131–134.

Singh, N. N., Manning, P. J., & Angell, M. J. (1982). Effects of oral hygiene punishment procedure on chronic rumination and collateral behaviors in monozygous twins. *Journal of Applied Behavior Analysis, 15,* 309–314.

Singh, N. N., Singh, J., & Winton, A. S. (1984). Positive practice overcorrection of oral reading errors. *Behavior Modification, 8,* 23–37.

Singh, N. N., & Winton, A. S. (1984). Effects of a screening procedure on pica and collateral behaviors. *Journal of Behavior Therapy and Experimental Psychiatry, 15,* 59–65.

Singh, N. N., Winton, A. S., & Dawson, M. J. (1982). Suppression of antisocial behavior by facial screening using multiple baseline and alternating treatment designs. *Behavior Therapy, 13,* 511–520.

Smith, J. D., Polloway, E. A., & West, G. K. (1979). Corporal punishment and its implications for exceptional children. *Exceptional Children, 45,* 264–268.

Tanner, B. A., & Zeiler, M. (1975). Punishment of self-injurious behavior using aromatic ammonia as the aversive stimulus. *Journal of Applied Behavior Analysis, 8,* 53–57.

Tomporowski, P. D. (1983). Training an autistic client: The effects of brief restraint on disruptive behavior. *Journal of Behavior Therapy and Experimental Psychiatry, 14,* 169–173.

Trap, J. J., Milner-Davis, P., Joseph, S., & Cooper, J. O. (1978). The effects of feedback and consequences on transitional cursive letter formation. *Journal of Applied Behavior Analysis, 11,* 381–393.

Webster, D. R., & Azrin, N. H. (1973). Required relaxation: A method of inhibiting agitative-disruptive behavior of retardates. *Behavior Research and Therapy, 11,* 67–78.

Wells, K. C., Forehand, R., & Hickey, K. (1977). Effects of a verbal warning and overcorrection on stereotyped and appropriate behaviors. *Journal of Abnormal Child Psychology, 5,* 387–403.

Wells, K. C., Forehand, R., Hickey, K., & Green, K. (1977). Effects of a procedure derived from the overcorrection principle on manipulated and nonmanipulated behaviors. *Journal of Applied Behavior Analysis, 10,* 679–687.

Welsh, R. S. (1978). Delinquency, corporal punishment, and the schools. *Crime and Delinquency, 24,* 336–354.

Wesolowski, M. D., & Zawlocki, R. J. (1982). The differential effects of procedures to eliminate an injurious self-stimulatory behavior (digito-ocular sign) in blind retarded twins. *Behavior Therapy, 13,* 334–345.

Wood, F. H. (1978). The influence of public opinion and social custom on the use of corporal punishment in schools. In F. H. Wood & K. C. Lakin (Eds.), *Punishment and aversive stimulation in special education: Legal, theoretical and practical issues in their use with emotionally disturbed children and youth* (pp. 29–39). Minneapolis, MN: Advanced Training Institute.

Wood, F. H., & Lakin, K. C. (1978). The legal status of the use of corporal punishment and other aversive procedures in schools. In F. H. Wood & K. C. Lakin (Eds.), *Punishment and aversive stimulation in special education: Legal, theoretical and practical issues in their use with emotionally disturbed children and youth* (pp. 3–27). Minneapolis, MN: Advanced Training Institute.

Young, L. D., & Vogel, V. (1983). The use of cueing and positive practice in the treatment of tongue thrust swallowing. *Journal of Behavior Therapy and Experimental Psychiatry, 14,* 73–77.

Zegiob, L. E., Jenkins, J., Becker, J., & Bristow, A. (1976). Facial screening: Effects on appropriate and inappropriate behaviors. *Journal of Behavior Therapy and Experimental Psychiatry, 7,* 355–357.

PART VI

USING BEHAVIOR MANAGEMENT SYSTEMS AND PEERS

Applied behavior analysis has produced a number of procedures that are used separately for facilitating acquisition of behaviors or controlling inappropriate social behaviors; it also has produced a number of procedures that can best be characterized as systems. Chapters 23 through 25 describe these systems. Chapter 23 focuses on using behavioral contracts and token economies. Definitions of the two procedures are provided and issues for developing and implementing them are presented. A complete example of a token economy is provided. Chapter 24 discusses the appropriate use of peers in facilitating behavior change in students. Various group contingencies are described, procedures of using them effectively are discussed, and examples are provided. Peer-mediated management systems also are a focus of this chapter. Chapter 25 describes self-management strategies. Self-management is defined, components of self-management are presented, and issues related to their use are discussed. The chapter concludes with an explanation of some general guidelines for implementing self-management strategies.

23

USING BEHAVIORAL CONTRACTS AND TOKEN ECONOMIES

Key Terms

■ Behavior Contract ■ Contingency Contract ■ Token
Economy ■ Tokens ■ Backup Reinforcers

Two procedures, behavioral contracting and token economies, are described in this chapter. These two procedures share many similarities and incorporate a variety of applied behavior analysis principles. First, each is based on some form of positive reinforcement and emphasizes teaching and strengthening behavior. Second, each procedure may be applied to individuals or groups of students. Third, each procedure consists of several components: for example, positive reinforcement, systematic teaching, shaping and fading, measurement, behavior-reduction procedures, and a variety of other procedures. Fourth, and perhaps most important, each procedure has characteristics that are similar to those found in the natural environment. Behavioral contracting and token economies can be observed in our daily experiences. We use money or some form of credit (i.e., tokens) to buy food, services, recreational activities, and other reinforcers that enable us to function successfully and to access relaxing and pleasurable activities. We enter into many contractual agreements that specify expected behaviors, responsibilities, and consequences, and that enable us to buy automobiles and houses, hold jobs, plan academic programs, and earn teaching certificates.

BEHAVIORAL CONTRACTING

A **behavior contract,** frequently called a **contingency contract,** is an arrangement between two individuals that designates (a) how an individual's behavior is to change and (b) what the consequences are for producing such a change. "Specifically, the contract specifies the reinforcers desired by the client and the behavior desired by the individual who wishes behavior change" (Kazdin, 1975, p. 131). Frequently, the arrangement is a verbal agreement between two individuals or a "promise" made by individuals to themselves (e.g., New Year's resolutions). Informal verbal contracts, however, are difficult to monitor and frequently lack accountability; therefore, formal written agreements are recommended. For example, Mr. Hernandez and Missy wrote a contract that specified exactly the amount and type of work she will complete, the date it is to be accomplished, and the amount and type of reinforcer he will deliver when the work is completed. A copy of Missy's contract is presented in Figure 23.1.

Behavioral contracts function to control behavior and increase accountability in a variety of ways. For example, written contracts may be used to facilitate student transition from more structured behavior programs to self-management procedures (Gelfand & Hartmann, 1984). This transfer is achieved by systematically allowing the student to assume greater responsibility for the selection of behaviors and reinforcers (Homme, Csanyi, Gonzales, & Rechs, 1970). Blackburn and Powell (1976) described a task analysis of this transfer process; the steps are presented in Figure 23.2. Contracts also function to develop interpersonal relationships between teachers and students and between teachers and parents (Blechman, Olson, Schornagel, Halsdorf, & Turner, 1976). In general, contracts help make the expectations of the learning environment clear and serve as a means of "structuring reinforcement contingencies to shape or maintain adaptive behaviors in children" (Cantrell, Cantrell, Huddleston, & Woolridge, 1969, p. 215).

Contingency contracts may be written by an individual; between teacher and student; teacher and parent; teacher, parent, and student; or any other group of individuals. Behavioral contracts are useful for individuals who are capable of entering into agreements and understanding the consequences associated with their behavior. They also are helpful when working with a student's family (Stuart, 1971). Family contracts can "clarify contradictory and ambiguous communications characteristic of many dysfunctional families" (Weathers & Liberman, 1978, p. 175). However, contracts may be less effective with young, developmentally delayed students, and with some antisocial students (Gelfand & Hartmann, 1984). This is especially true when the teacher or clinician is inexperienced or the student does not understand the wording or conditions of the contract.

Elements of a Behavioral Contract

Although behavioral contracts appear simple, they consist of at least five elements (Kazdin, 1975; Stuart, 1971). First, the behaviors specified in the contract must be

FIGURE 23.1   Missy's work completion contract.

MISSY'S WORK COMPLETION CONTRACT

IF MISSY COMPLETES ALL HER WORK ACCORDING TO SCHEDULE, SHE WILL EARN TWO PICKS FROM THE ACTIVITY LIST. IF MISSY COMPLETES OVER 11 OUT OF 15 WORK ASSIGNMENTS, SHE WILL EARN ONE SELECTION.

MR. HERNANDEZ WILL VERIFY THAT HER WORK IS COMPLETED, AND MISSY WILL PLACE A "+" FOR THE DAY AND SUBJECT.

ACTIVITY LIST: 1. Lunch with Sally.
2. Classroom paper and pencil monitor for two days.
3. First choice of games during afternoon recess.
4. Extra milk during lunch for two days.
5. New binder to hold completed work.

	MATH	READING	SPELLING	WRITING
MONDAY				
TUESDAY				
WEDNESDAY				
THURSDAY				
FRIDAY				

Bonus Clause: For each 4/4 day, an extra "GOOD DAY" note will be sent home.

VALIDATIONS: _____ (Missy) _____ Date

_____ (Mr. H.) _____ Date

observable and measurable. Rosie's teacher defines "work completed" as writing accurate responses to at least 85% of the items on each assignment. With this description, both Rosie and her teacher can determine whether the behaviors have occurred. Second, contracts have clearly specified rewards or privileges that each person is to receive. For example, Rosie expects to use the classroom computer for 5 minutes when she completes her independent seatwork activities without interrupting others or getting out of her seat.

Third, behavioral contracts specify precisely what outcomes are associated with the student's failure to meet the stated expectations. With clear descriptions,

FIGURE 23.2   Sequence for transferring contractual responsibility from teacher to student.

Structured Contracts: All components are predetermined by the teacher and then are negotiated.

Partially Structured Contracts: Some components are predetermined by the teacher and some are selected by the student; then they are negotiated.

Mutually Structured Contracts: No predetermined components. All parts are cooperatively selected and negotiated.

Unstructured Contracts: No predetermined components. The student initiates and develops parts and negotiates with the teacher.

both Rosie and her teacher know what to expect when she does not complete her work accurately. The presence of an aversive consequence can be negatively reinforcing and increase the probability that the desired behaviors will occur. However, to avoid placing the student in a no-win situation in which all opportunities for success have been forfeited, opportunities to negotiate should be included. For example, Rosie is told if she does not accurately complete all five pages of her writing assignments, she will have to stay at her seat while other students use the computer. Rosie is placed in an all-or-nothing position. If one problem is incorrect or one page is not completed, Rosie has no reason to complete any portion of her work. A better arrangement provides a greater amount of computer time based on the amount of work completed. For example, 15 minutes for all work, 10 minutes for 75% of the assignments, and 5 minutes for 50%. These special clauses allow the student and teacher to avoid no-win predicaments.

Fourth, special consequences or bonuses may be used to increase a student's motivation and participation. For example, Rosie's teacher includes a bonus clause that enables her to earn an extra 5 minutes on the computer for each piece of academic work that is more than 95% accurate. Special consequences are particularly useful when new skills are being acquired or when prolonged durations of consistent responding without immediate reinforcement are desired.

Last, a reliable means of record-keeping must be in effect. Data should be collected on the occurrence of Rosie's targeted behavior and on the teacher's use of positive reinforcement, including when and how much of each occurs. These data provide feedback for students and teachers, and they make each person accountable and responsible for their own behaviors. These data also allow teachers to evaluate the effectiveness of a behavioral contract.

Behavioral contracts may take many forms ranging from simple to complex. The complexity depends on the parties involved and the conditions of the contract. Ideally, contracts should be as simple as possible. The contract illustrated in Figure 23.3 includes all basic elements of a complete behavioral

FIGURE 23.3   A prototype of a behavioral contract.

CLASSROOM CONTRACT

EFFECTIVE DATES: From _____ To _____

           Review Dates _____ , _____*

We, the undersigned parties, agree to the specified conditions that follow:

1. If _____ ,

    then _____ .

2. If _____ ,

    then _____ .

3. If _____ ,

    then _____ .

4. If _____ ,

    then _____ .

BONUS: _____

          _____

PENALTY: _____

          _____

        Signed: _____ Date: _____

        Signed: _____ Date: _____

        Signed: _____ Date: _____

        Signed: _____ Date: _____

*This contract will be reviewed at least weekly.

contract. The checklist presented in Figure 23.4 can be used to assess whether each of these components are included.

Developing a Behavioral Contract

The process of establishing a behavioral contract includes many steps found in a systematic instructional model (DeRisi & Butz, 1975). The first step is to select one or two behaviors that are functionally and socially important to the student

FIGURE 23.4　Checklist of necessary components of a complete behavioral contract.

_____ 1.　A clear statement of the target behavior.

　　　_____ defined in operational terms.

　　　_____ stated positively.

　　　_____ stated in behavioral objective form.

_____ 2.　Designation of all persons directly involved.

_____ 3.　Description of a data-collection method.

　　　_____ described in reliable and replicable terms.

　　　_____ summarized in chart or graph form.

_____ 4.　Clear identification of all reinforcers to be used.

　　　_____ specified schedule of delivery.

　　　_____ designation of who will deliver.

　　　_____ indication of how much will be delivered.

_____ 5.　Specification of behaviors, responsibilities, and/or conditions for earning or securing reinforcers.

_____ 6.　Specification of consequences for failure to meet expectations and responsibilities, or emission of inappropriate behaviors.

　　　_____ procedures for renegotiation.

_____ 7.　Specification of a bonus clause for exceptional performance.

_____ 8.　Designation of specific timeliness.

　　　_____ beginning or start date.

　　　_____ deadline for ending contract.

　　　_____ review dates for assessing progress.

_____ 9.　Signatures of all involved and dates of agreement.

and relevant others. Initially, teachers should select behaviors that have a high probability of success. If students are to learn the contracting process, they must experience initial success and reinforcement. After the behaviors have been selected, they should be defined in observable and countable terms. All parties involved in writing the contract must agree with how each behavior is defined and characterized. Kirschenbaum, Dielman, and Karoly (1982) also suggested that contract effectiveness can be improved by selecting discrete and easily identified behaviors and by setting achievable response criteria. For example, Hank writes a contract with his teacher for completing all in-class assignments to at least 85% accuracy rather than for "staying on task" for 100% of the time.

The second major step is to identify the rewards that will be associated with successful contract completion. As in any reinforcement program, these rewards or privileges should have strong reinforcing qualities and provide the student with high motivation to succeed. In addition, reinforcers should be presented as immediately and contingently as possible. For some students, small but frequent rewards may be more effective than larger but delayed reinforcers; this may be particularly true with young students, those with moderate and severe handicaps, and those with limited language skills. A careful analysis of their learning and reinforcement history should be conducted. Student input and participation in contract development should be maximized. Lovitt and Curtiss (1968), for example, observed that students who were involved actively in the design or implementation of a program tended to change their performance more than those who had similar contingencies imposed on them.

The third step is to establish a record-keeping system that will maintain participant accountability. Generally, teachers or parents maintain records of student behavior; however, peers or the student may assume this responsibility. Using peers as witnesses or participants also may increase a student's motivation to complete a contract. The intent of soliciting peers is to help the target student, not to place peers in the role of informer or contract enforcer. All involved persons should perceive the contract as fair and be included in the signature process. Only those participants who perceive the terms and process of the contract as fair and indicate their willingness to follow through should be involved. In addition to measuring contractual performance, participants also may present reinforcers or review and evaluate the contract.

The fourth step is to write the contract in terms that everyone can understand. A positively stated contract is recommended in order to increase the likelihood that the student will engage in adaptive behaviors and will attempt to gain reinforcement rather than avoid punishment. The contract should be written in a manner that minimizes punitive overtones (Clarizio, 1980). Immediately after writing the first draft of a contract, a complete review of its components and requirements should be conducted. The issues listed in Figure 23.4 can be used in this review. A careful analysis will decrease the number of implementation loopholes and problems and will increase the likelihood of a successful contract. After it has been reviewed by all concerned parties, a contract should be signed by the teacher, student, other involved persons (e.g., parents, other teachers, principal, or peers).

The fifth major step is to implement the contract and continuously monitor, review, and revise it until improvement in the targeted behaviors occurs. This formative evaluation should be based on student performance (Martin & Pear, 1983) and should actively engage the student. As behaviors are successfully changed or learned, new behaviors should be added to the contract. One or two contracts may be insufficient to mark the end of the behavior-change process. The number is likely to vary with the number of persons involved, who participates, and the nature of their motivation to change. In sequencing contracts, consequences should be employed that move the student toward increased

FIGURE 23.5 Ten basic rules for developing and implementing effective behavioral contracts.

Rule 1	The contract payoff (reward) should be immediate.
Rule 2	Initial contracts should call for and reward small approximations.
Rule 3	Reward frequently with small amounts.
Rule 4	The contract should call for and reward accomplishments.
Rule 5	Reward the performance after it occurs.
Rule 6	The contract must be fair.
Rule 7	The terms of the contract must be clear.
Rule 8	The contract must be honest.
Rule 9	The contract must be positive.
Rule 10	Contracting as a method must be used systematically.

From *How to Use Contingency Contracting in the Classroom* (pp. 18-21) by L. Homme, A. P. Csanyi, M. A. Gonzales, and J. R. Rechs, 1970, Champaign, IL: Research Press.

self-management and less external or teacher-controlled contingencies. Contracts themselves do not account for observed behavior change, but serve as a structure, or "behavioral prosthesis," for assuring that consequences are systematically delivered for the target behavior (Stuart, 1971).

The process of developing and implementing a behavioral contract is characterized by active involvement of all participants, adherence to valid instructional and behavior-change procedures, and the systematic and formative evaluation of the total process. Homme et al. (1970) have formulated 10 basic rules that efficiently summarize the contracting process; these are presented in Figure 23.5.

Behavioral contracts provide a structure and process for systematic behavior change and evaluation. The influence contracts themselves have on behavior change has not been demonstrated systematically. Little systematic and controlled research has been done to examine the specific causal factors associated with contracting (Gelfand & Hartmann, 1984; Kazdin, 1975). Much of the available research consists of clinical case studies or complex intervention packages in which contracting is only one component. Thus, the effects of contracting are difficult to identify. However, they do seem to serve an important role in structuring the development and implementation of applied behavior analysis strategies. The contracting process also maximizes positive student and teacher interaction and permits the transfer of behavior management from the teacher to the student.

TOKEN ECONOMIES

Special education programs are designed with three basic goals in mind: (a) teach individual students appropriate and useful skills, (b) remediate behavioral excesses and deficits *within* the least restrictive educational environment possible and with minimum risk, and (c) set objectives and timelines to expedite entrance into *less* restrictive settings. To accomplish these goals, a direct, systematic, and highly structured approach to teaching is employed. However, less restrictive settings, such as the regular classroom, home environment, or community, are not as externally directed; thus, special education students are frequently unsuccessful in transferring new skills to these less structured environments. Many special education classrooms use some sort of individualized or group-oriented token economy to manage academic and social behaviors and to prepare students for more natural settings. The basic components of a token economy and general guidelines for operating it are described in the following sections.

Definition and Description of the Token Economy

A **token economy** is a contingency management system that allows students to earn tokens that can be exchanged at a later time for specific backup reinforcers. **Tokens** are easily dispensed objects that are given to students contingent upon the occurrence of targeted behavior and are used to purchase other reinforcers. **Backup reinforcers** are previously identified activities, objects, events, or privileges that hold reinforcing value for students. Token economies have specific rules and guidelines that define (a) the behaviors that result in tokens, (b) procedures for delivering tokens, (c) the value of each backup reinforcer, (d) the method by which tokens are exchanged for backup reinforcers, (e) procedures for monitoring students' progress, (f) procedures for dealing with inappropriate behaviors, and (g) procedures for fading the use of the token economy.

Token economies are modeled after existing monetary systems. The tokens in real monetary systems include coins, bills, credit cards, and checks that are exchanged for specific backup reinforcers such as food, housing, clothing, educational opportunities, recreational activities, and many others. In classroom token economies, they may be objects such as cards or tickets, toy money, stickers, plastic strips, hole punches on cards, and almost any other easily delivered object. More intangible tokens include points, credits, or grades. These tokens are exchanged for objects (e.g., school supplies, trinkets, toys, games, tickets/coupons for community events, etc.), and/or activities and privileges (e.g., free time, playing games, talking with friends, being first in line, going to the library or gym, graduation, etc.).

Establishing a Token Economy

The token economy provides a useful structure for managing the learning environment; however, it requires careful planning and consistent implementation. The basic token economy consists of (a) a set of rules and procedures for earning and losing tokens, (b) backup reinforcers, and (c) rules and procedures for fading the use of tokens (Kazdin, 1977, 1985). Ayllon and McKittrick (1982) summarized the process of establishing a token economy into four steps: (a) "identify target behaviors," (b) "define tokens," (c) "identify items, privileges and other incentives for rewarding appropriate behaviors," and (d) "plan an exchange system" (p. iii). Three additional steps also should be considered: (e) plan procedures for fading the use of the token economy, (f) develop a record-keeping system, and (g) establish clear operating guidelines. Additional information about implementing token economies can be found in works by Ayllon and Azrin (1968), Kazdin (1977), O'Leary and Drabman (1971), and Walker and Buckley (1974).

Identify Target Behaviors. The first step in establishing a token economy is to define all relevant target behaviors in observable terms. Ayllon and Azrin referred to this guideline as the "Target Behavior Rule: Describe the desired performance in behavioral terms" (1968, p. 47). These behaviors generally include essential classroom expectations. Behavioral contracts are incorporated into token economies to accommodate the specific behavioral needs of individual students. Both academic and social behaviors are addressed, and students should be taught which behaviors earn token reinforcers and which result in negative consequences.

Behaviors that are characteristic of less restrictive settings should be stressed. This guideline is called the "Relevance of Behavior Rule: Teach only those behaviors that will continue to be reinforced after training" (Ayllon & Azrin, 1968, p. 49). For example, the vocational training teacher emphasizes getting to work on time, cleaning up work stations, and other work-related skills. The elementary resource room teacher stresses classroom expectations such as eyes on teacher, materials on desk or table, and raising hand for assistance.

Define Tokens. After target behaviors have been determined, an object or symbol should be selected to serve as a token reinforcer. Tokens act as a discrete stimulus that bridges the delay between a desirable behavior and the delivery of a reinforcer. Tokens should be teacher controlled and selected based on their compatibility with the demands of a specific instructional setting. Paper clips, for example, may seem like simple tokens; however, the ease with which students can obtain them decreases their utility. In a vocationally oriented program, money can serve as an appropriate token. Grades or points are more appropriate in academically based classrooms. Useful tokens are also transportable; that is, they can be carried and delivered easily across settings. Marbles or plastic strips can be more difficult for teachers and students to transport between activities (e.g., classroom to lunchroom to playground) than points written on a small card. Similarly, tokens should be easy to dispense so that students can experience immediate and contingent reinforcement. Telling students who require immediate feedback that they must wait until all students return to the classroom defeats the major purpose of a token, i.e., to bridge the delay between behavior and delivery of reinforcement.

Tokens that are resistant to satiation should be selected; that is, their reinforcing qualities are maintained as more reinforcers are acquired. Tran, for example, has earned so many coupons that he gives them away to his friends and he also engages in fewer appropriate classroom behaviors. Teachers can decrease the effects of satiation by varying the costs of backup reinforcers, decreasing the number of tokens delivered, modifying the schedule of token reinforcement, or providing more frequent opportunities to trade tokens for backup reinforcers.

Identify Items, Privileges, and Other Incentives for Rewarding Appropriate Behaviors. Points, grades, plastic strips, and paper clips have no inherent reinforcing qualities. Pennies, nickels, and dimes are reinforcing because they can be traded for other reinforcing objects and events, e.g., food and recreational activities. Tokens become useful, generalized, conditioned reinforcers when they are paired frequently with other strong reinforcers. In a token economy, these stimuli are called *backup reinforcers.* They can be identified in a number of ways. Teachers can select items in which students have expressed an interest; they can ask others (e.g., parents, peers, teachers) about possible backups; or they can provide reinforcer-sampling opportunities in which the student experiences a reinforcing object or activity.

Plan an Exchange System. Token values should be assigned to each backup reinforcer based on its relative desirability or reinforcing characteristics. Easily dispensed short-term reinforcers should be assigned relatively low values so students can earn them on a more frequent basis. For example, students might trade one token for 2 minutes of structured free time (e.g., computer time, free reading, and playing games with peers). A larger number of tokens (e.g., 50 tokens) would be required to see a special movie at the end of the week. In general, the smallest possible number of earned tokens should enable each student to access some level of backup reinforcers. For example, although Andrea has not accumulated a sufficient number of tokens to go on the field trip, she can still participate in the classroom auction.

Students can learn about tokens through role-playing activities in which tokens are earned and traded immediately for backups. For example, Mr. Gutteriz gives Marilyn a token when she raises her hand to ask a question. He immediately lets her trade her token for a raisin. Later, he introduces a second backup that costs more and allows Marilyn to select between raisins and a few minutes to read comic books. When Marilyn and other students understand the rules of the token economy, it is extended to other parts of the school day.

An exchange plan also should include rules for (a) when token exchanges occur (e.g., hourly, daily, and/or weekly), (b) how exchanges are made (e.g., write a check, withdraw the tokens from a "saving's account," exchange actual tokens), and (c) where exchanges take place (e.g., student or teacher's desk, school store). If a response-cost contingency is included, rules for returning tokens should be established. Teachers should have a planned response for students who refuse to repay token fines. When one of his students receives a penalty and declines to return tokens, Mr. Gutteriz simply notes the number of tokens lost and charges the student's token savings, or places a "lien" on his or her next purchase.

Rules should be established for dealing with "lost" or stolen tokens. Students should be taught that they are responsible for taking care of their tokens. Mr. Gutteriz has a simple rule for this problem: "If they are lost, they are gone and will not be replaced." If students are unable to take care of their own tokens, they should be taught to turn them over to the teacher. Tokens that cannot be manipulated (e.g., points, happy faces) may also be considered. Careful monitoring of token saving and spending and establishing stiff penalties will deter individuals from stealing tokens from one another or the teacher. Rules for lost or stolen tokens should be stated positively and promote individual student responsibility.

Plan Procedures for Fading the Use of the Token Economy. Special educators frequently arrange the classroom environment to maximize individual student learning. Unfortunately, many special education environments and procedures are not like those found in less restrictive environments. Procedures should be established for moving students away from token economies and toward conditions that approximate least restrictive settings. Failure to remove the controlling influence of tokens and their backups will decrease favorable maintenance and generalization. For example, when Roger discovers that plastic beads from his resource room are not used in his regular math class, his adaptive behaviors quickly decrease.

Fading the use of a token economy can be facilitated through a number of simple procedures. An emphasis should be placed on those target behaviors and expectations that are required in the least restrictive environment. Similarly, naturally occurring consequences (e.g., verbal praise, grades, public recognition) should be paired with the use of tokens and backup reinforcers. As adaptive responses are strengthened, fewer tokens can be distributed on a less frequent basis, i.e., on a more intermittent schedule. As discriminative control by stimuli from the least restrictive environment increases, rules and procedures for the token economy can be removed.

Fading students off token economies can also be facilitated by increasing the application of peer-mediated and self-management procedures. Students can be taught to assess, monitor, reinforce, or instruct themselves or their peers. By acquiring these skills, students can assume greater control over the operation of the token economy and their own behavior. In many token economies, a continuum of student participation is developed. As adaptive skills are strengthened, schedules of reinforcement thinned, and occurrences of inappropriate behaviors decreased, students become less accountable to the rules and conditions of the token economy. For example, students with greater needs may receive and exchange tokens on an hourly basis, and they may be required to trade for basic classroom privileges, e.g., pencils, paper, structured free time. Students who are more capable may be given free basic privileges, but may have to use their tokens to access special activities, e.g., movies, field trips, assemblies. The highest and most independently functioning students may not have to earn tokens at all to participate in special activities. The degree to which students can display responsible behavior dictates how accountable they are to the rules and procedures of the token economy.

Develop a Record-Keeping System. As with any instructional or behavior-management strategy, student performance data should be collected and evaluated on a continuous basis. Record-keeping in many token economies is relatively easy. The number of earned tokens can serve as an approximation of the amount of student progress. The number of tokens lost gives an indication of the occurrence of undesirable behavior. To minimize the amount of effort required, record-keeping should be integrated into the operating procedures of the token economy. Students can also be given the responsibility of maintaining their own records or the performance of their peers.

Accurate accounts of the number of earned and lost tokens, selected backups, and displayed behaviors can assist in evaluating the effectiveness of a token economy. Information about ineffective backups, token satiation, and insufficient behavior change can also be ascertained. Record-keeping strategies can be incorporated into the operating procedures of the token economy. If points are marked on a card or point sheet, a permanent product is created. If students must deposit earned tokens into a savings account, another permanent record is produced. If students must withdraw or use tokens to trade for a backup, a note can be made of the transaction. Graphs of the number of earned tokens can be developed and maintained by students. Charting one's tokens and seeing progress can be reinforcing activities for many students. Simple computer-based spreadsheet and file-management programs can be used to minimize the effort required to engage in record-keeping activities.

Establish Clear Operating Guidelines. After all the components of a token economy have been developed, clear operating guidelines should be established and followed. However, before actual implementation of a token economy, pertinent approvals should be secured (e.g., school building administrators, parents and guardians, school counselors, special education supervisor). While obtaining approvals, explanations may be required to justify the use or need for a token system or to describe its basic operating characteristics. It is advisable to secure written informed consent from parents. Approvals and informed consent will increase accountability and participation when needed.

Teachers should next engage in marketing and merchandising the token economy. Students must learn about the value and functions of tokens, what backups are available and how they are acquired, and how the token economy operates. Teachers should prepare all materials (e.g., record-keeping forms, tokens, savings and withdrawal forms) before implementing the token economy. Individual procedures and components should be field tested to decrease opportunities for student abuse or manipulation. Once the token system is intact, it can be introduced.

Teachers should avoid using their personal funds to support a classroom token economy. Free or inexpensive backup items should be obtained. Posters can be collected from local travel agencies, record stores, or movie theaters; community groups can be asked to donate items; and some local stores may provide discount coupons or reduced prices. Although many types of commercially prepared tokens can be purchased (e.g., plastic strips, paper money, linking rings), many common and inexpensive objects can serve as tokens (e.g., dried beans, holes punched in cards, buttons, teacher-made coupons). For example, Ms. Allen uses unpopped popcorn kernels as tokens. Whenever a student engages in a token-earning behavior, kernels are placed in a jar. At the end of the week, the class has a party with the popcorn that has accumulated.

The operation of a token economy should be reviewed on a continuous basis. Student performance should be evaluated to determine the effectiveness of backup reinforcers, amount of individual progress, degree of student noncompliance, and efficiency of basic operating procedures and rules. As deficiencies are identified, modifications should be made. Student performance is the best indicator of program effectiveness. Teacher implementation of token economy procedures should also be assessed. It is important to determine if (a) token reinforcers are being provided in suitable amounts and according to appropriate schedules of reinforcement, (b) varied and sufficient backup reinforcers are being maintained, (c) response-cost procedures are being used appropriately, (d) accurate records of student performance and tokens are being kept, (e) all students are being involved equally, and (f) students are being faded off the token system when appropriate. A common problem seen in many token economies is token inflation. It occurs when the relative number of tokens far exceeds the number of available backup reinforcers, resulting in a dramatic rise in the cost of backups. Token inflation can be avoided by increasing the use of other naturally occurring conditioned reinforcers (e.g., praise, social contact), controlling the frequency and number of tokens that are delivered for specific behaviors, carefully pricing backup reinforcers, and providing a variety of backup reinforcers.

Token economies should be operated within as natural a context as possible. This can be accomplished in an assortment of ways. First, the delivery of tokens and backups can be accompanied by other natural reinforcers. Second, backup reinforcers can be similar to those found in less restrictive settings. Third, behavioral expectations and rules can approximate the demands of the natural environment. Fourth, teachers can focus on increasing those adaptive behaviors that are likely to be maintained in other settings and by other individuals, and that will compete favorably for reinforcers that maintain other less desirable behaviors. Fifth, students can be encouraged to acquire useful self-management skills. Last, instructional opportunities can be incorporated into the operating procedures of token economies. For example, tokens can be maintained in accounts that require the use of deposit and withdrawal slips and written checks to purchase backups. Students would be required to practice basic math and writing skills and to learn about simple consumer concepts.

A summary of the basic guidelines for establishing and operating a token economy are included in Figure 23.6.

FIGURE 23.6   Basic guidelines for establishing and operating a token economy.

Characteristics of Useful Tokens

1. Portable, i.e., easily transported.
2. Resistant to satiation.
3. Can be given immediately.
4. Practical to setting.
5. Teacher controlled.
6. Compatible with educational or treatment program.
7. Easily dispensed.

Planning and Implementation Steps

1. Select and define target behaviors.
2. Identify possible backup reinforcers.
3. Select possible object or symbol for token.
4. Build token as conditioned reinforcer.
5. Establish exchange system and relative value of backup reinforcers.
6. Inform students of rules for token economy.
7. Develop plan for fading use of token system.
8. Establish clear record-keeping plan.

Basic Operation Guidelines

1. Deliver tokens and backup reinforcers consistently.
2. Control for token inflation.
3. Focus on increasing desirable behaviors and skills.

4. Specify rules and procedures in specific and observable terms.
5. Obtain as many free, inexpensive, and student-selected backups as possible.
6. Engage in marketing and merchandising.
7. Incorporate instructional opportunities into token economy, e.g., saving, checking, deposits, etc.
8. Pair token and backup reinforcers with social praise and other natural reinforcers.
9. Obtain approval and informed consent from administrators and parents.
10. Establish clear procedures for student noncompliance and teacher misuse.

Fading a Token Economy

1. Move from artificial to natural token and backup reinforcers.
2. Delay the presentation of reinforcement.
3. Move from continuous and predictable to more intermittent and unpredictable schedules of reinforcement.
4. Transfer stimulus control from artificial to more natural setting stimuli.
5. Teach students to self-manage the token economy.

A Token Economy Example

To illustrate the basic characteristics and procedures for operating token economies, a simple classroom application is presented. This token economy is based on a five-level continuum that provides opportunities for movement away from the token program and toward greater independence and self-management. The five levels are presented in Figure 23.7. This movement is facilitated in a number of ways. First, the use of tokens is decreased. In fact, at the "Manager" level (IV) tokens are no longer used and only general behavior ratings are given (e.g., "M" for mature, "I" for improvement needed). Second, students at the "Helper" and "Manager" levels have "free" access to "basic" privileges that are generally available in regular classroom settings, e.g., borrowing pencils, getting drinks of water, going to the restroom, or talking to neighbors. Third, the presentation of reinforcers is more delayed and intermittent at the upper levels. At the "Orientation" level, students are given points immediately and provided opportunities for frequent and regular trade-ins. "Managers" receive infrequent verbal praise and social attention and work toward letter grades and classroom placement changes. Fourth, students at higher levels spend more of their time

FIGURE 23.7   Descriptions of a five-level behavior-management example.

Level I: Orientation

Points given out immediately.

Regular and daily point trade-ins.

Continuous schedule of social reinforcement with each token.

Basic privileges must be earned with minimum number of points.

Level II: Worker

Points given out at end of each hour.

Points traded in at end of day.

VR: 3–5 (or VI:5 min) social reinforcement.

Level III: Helper

Daily rating (teacher and / or student determined) at end of day based on total number of points earned during the day.

Mature = 8+ points

Improvement needed = 5–7 points

Rowdy = less than 5 points

Level IV: Manager

Ratings given only; no points.
Privileges given with Mature and Improvement ratings.

Level V: Integrator

No longer accountable to management system.

Part or full-time in regular education programs.

outside of the special education classroom and engaged in more group-oriented activities in less restrictive settings.

The level system is designed to move students toward less frequent and more delayed natural reinforcers. To accomplish this, specific rules that specify the behaviors, conditions, and criteria for movement through the system must be developed. For example, the teacher has established rules that delineate how each student moves into the next level. Personal and individualized goals from a student's IEP are included. An example is shown in Figure 23.8.

Based on these rules, students who move up the level system from "Orientation" to "Integrator" are removed gradually from response-cost and timeout consequences except for major offenses. The teacher has established rules that indicate how a student can be "busted" to more restrictive levels. For

FIGURE 23.8   Rules and criteria for moving off the token economy and level system.

Levels I to II
Four consecutive days of 80% of possible points per day, no more than three Phase 2 and two Phase 3 timeouts (see timeout level system) and successful demonstration of all personal goals.

Levels II to III
Five consecutive days of 90% of possible points per day, no more than two Phase 2 and one Phase 3 timeouts, and successful demonstration of all personal goals.

Levels III to IV
Seven consecutive days of Mature ratings, no Phase 2 or 3 timeouts, and successful demonstration of all personal goals.

Levels IV to V
Seven consecutive days of Mature ratings, no timeouts, and successful demonstration of all personal goals.

example, (a) for every two Phase 2 timeouts earned, the student drops one level; and (b) for every Phase 3 timeout earned, the student drops one level. To permit a student the opportunity to assume greater control over his or her own behavior and to regain previous level status, special contingency contracts may be written; otherwise, a student is required to earn the next higher level according to the stated requirements.

In this particular classroom example, the teacher delivers tokens by punching a student's 3-by-5 index card with a hole-puncher. At the basic levels, each student is given a daily point card. An example of this card is presented in Figure 23.9. Each card is divided into five areas in which "punches" (tokens) are delivered: (a) academic attending behaviors (e.g., answering promptly, raising hand, waiting turn), (b) social behaviors (e.g., appropriate language, cooperation, helping others), (c) readiness (e.g., in-seat at the bell, materials ready), (d) personal goals (i.e., individualized social or academic objectives), and (e) bonus points for exceptional performance or change. Earned points can be traded for a variety of backup reinforcers, such as end-of-day short-term items or activities (e.g., small school supplies, structured free time activities such as typing, puzzles, games); end-of-week reinforcers (e.g., library time, popcorn party, larger school supplies); or end-of-month items and activities (e.g., movie, order out lunch, field trip). When needed, individualized backup reinforcers can be arranged through the behavioral contracting procedures.

The teacher and students jointly established the following token economy rules: (a) token exchanges occur once a day at 3:30 p.m., once a week every Wednesday, and once a month on the last Friday; (b) if you lose your card, that's "life in the big city"; (c) punch tokens can be withdrawn and deposited only on

FIGURE 23.9 Example of an index card used to monitor desired classroom behaviors and tokens earned.

ACADEMICS	SOCIAL
Math	Raise Hand
Reading	Waiting Turn
Science	
Spelling	
Life Skills	

BONUS: _____

_____

READINESS	PERSONAL
Materials	1. _____
In-Seat at Bell	2. _____

FIGURE 23.10 Example of deposit and withdrawal slip used to administer tokens.

DEPOSIT/WITHDRAWAL

Date _____   Name _____

Teacher Initial _____

Previous Balance	_____
Amount of Deposit	+ _____
Amount of Withdrawal	– _____
New Balance	_____

the day earned and only with classroom deposit slips (Figure 23.10); and (d) peer infringements (e.g., stealing or mutilating cards) are to be discussed only during group meetings at the end of each day. The teacher and classroom aide identified a number of social reinforcers that are paired with each delivery of a token or backup reinforcer. Social reinforcers, such as smiles, physical contact, verbal praise, compliments, and eye contact were selected because they are commonly observed in the regular classroom setting.

The teacher has carefully integrated the token economy program into his general classroom management procedures. His classroom has been arranged so social and token reinforcers contingently follow all appropriate classroom behaviors. Nuisance behaviors, such as small noises and making faces, are not reinforced or acknowledged (i.e., extinction). However, the first occurrence of minor offenses (e.g., talking back, not following simple directions) results in the loss of two points (i.e., response cost). Five points are lost for the first occurrence of a major offense (e.g., hits/touches, stealing, swearing, name-calling, throwing objects, fighting, violating the rights of others, breaking school rules). Repeated occurrences of minor and major offenses are covered in a three-phase timeout system that is illustrated in Figure 23.11. With the second occurrence of a minor offense (Phase 1), the student takes a timeout at his or her desk (i.e., head down,

FIGURE 23.11 Example of token economy response cost and timeout system.

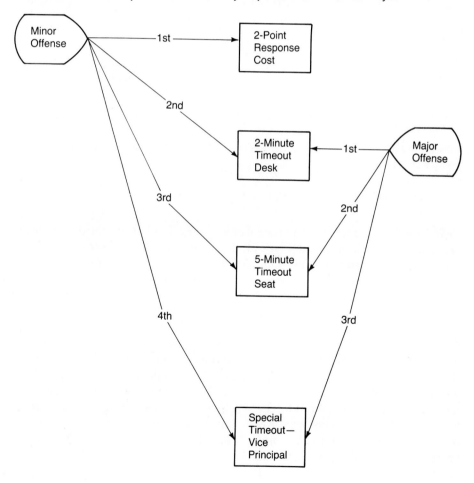

TABLE 23.1 A Sample of the Subjects and Behaviors to Which Token Economies Have Been Applied

Authors (Year)	Subjects	Behaviors
Bushell (1978)	Disadvantaged Elementary	Academic Achievement
Wolf, Phillips, Fixen, Braukmann, Kirigin, Willner, & Schumaker (1976)	Juvenile Delinquents	Variety, Academic, Social, and Personal
Wolf, Giles, & Hall (1968)	Disadvantaged Elementary	Academic Skills
Birnbrauer, Bijou, Wolf, & Kidder (1965)	Mentally Retarded	Academic Skills
Cohen & Filipczak (1971)	Delinquent Youth	Academic and Social Skills
Barrish, Saunders, & Wolf (1969)	Elementary Classroom	Appropriate Classroom Behavior
Quay, Glavin, Annesley, & Werry (1972)	Resource Room for Behavior Disordered Students	Appropriate and Inappropriate Classroom Behavior
Linscheid, Malosky, & Zimmerman (1974)	Psychiatric Patient	Appropriate Ward Behavior
O'Leary, Becker, Evans, & Saudargas (1969)	Second Graders	Following Classroom Rules

cleared desk). If the second occurrence of a major offense or the third occurrence of a minor offense is observed (Phase 2), the student receives a timeout in a special seat placed at the back of the room. At Phase 3, the student earns a trip to the vice-principal's office for a special in-school suspension procedure where preplanned arrangements have been made for the student to sit in a nonpublic place with no social attention. A Phase 3 timeout is given for the fourth occurrence of a minor offense or the third occurrence of a major offense.

Since timeout depends on the effective application of reinforcement, the teacher was careful to create a reinforcing timein environment. Two basic rules for presenting tokens (i.e, punches) and social reinforcers were used. First, whenever a student was in timeout, a token (depending upon the privilege level of a student) and/or a social reinforcer was given to at least a third of the students who were engaged in appropriate behavior. Second, during any other time and approximately once every 10 minutes (i.e., VI:10 minutes), at least one student received either a token or social reinforcement. Also, specific timeout rules were established: (a) time begins when the student engages in appropriate timeout behaviors in the timeout area, i.e., not talking or making noises, sitting with both feet on floor and chair legs touching floor; (b) timeout is not to exceed 1 minute (Phase 1), 2 minutes (Phase 2), or 5 minutes (Phase 3); and (c) special arrangements must be made for in-school suspensions that exceed 15 minutes.

This token economy is only one example from a wide range of possible variations. However, it illustrates a number of important characteristics common to all token economy systems. First, it includes a systematic structure for moving students off the token economy and into conditions that approximate less restrictive settings. Second, it uses a variety of behavior-change procedures to teach and strengthen desired behaviors, decrease or weaken undesirable forms of behavior, and facilitate the development of self-management skills. Finally, it employs specific and clear rules, criteria, and guidelines for implementing the token system.

Demonstrations and Variations of the Token Economy

It is beyond the scope of this text to review the many token economy applications. Interested readers should refer to comprehensive works by Kazdin (1977, 1985) for a review of this literature. However, it should be noted that token economies have been applied successfully across a broad range of subjects and behaviors. Table 23.1 provides a sample of this diversity.

Summary of Key Concepts

- Token economies and behavioral contracts are composed of basic applied behavior analysis procedures.

- Many of the characteristics of behavioral contracts and token economies can be seen operating in natural settings such as the home, community, and work place.

- Successful implementation of behavioral contracts and token economies is associated with systematic planning and consistent implementation.

- Behavioral contracts help students and teachers structure learning experiences and organize their behaviors. Restrictive contingencies should be faded as quickly as possible.

- Successful behavioral contracts are specific, positively stated, jointly developed, and systematically monitored.

- A basic token economy consists of tokens, backup reinforcers, rules for earning and losing tokens, and procedures for trading tokens for backups.

- Record-keeping procedures are important in maintaining accountability and evaluating the effectiveness of behavioral contracts and token economies.

■ The token economy helps teachers structure the learning environment; however, their use should be faded as quickly as possible to facilitate the maintenance and generalization of student performance.

REFERENCES

Ayllon, T., & Azrin, N. H. (1968). *The token economy: A motivational system for therapy and rehabilitation.* New York: Appleton-Century-Crofts.

Ayllon, T., & McKittrick, S. M. (1982). *How to set up a token economy.* Lawrence, KS: H & H Enterprises.

Barrish, H. H., Saunders, M., & Wolf, M.M. (1969). Good behavior game: Effects of individual contingencies for group consequences on disruptive behavior in a classroom. *Journal of Applied Behavior Analysis, 2,* 119–124.

Birnbrauer, J. S., Bijou, S. W., Wolf, M. M. & Kidder, J. D. (1965) Programmed instructions in the classroom. In L. P. Ullmann & L. Krasner (Eds.), *Case studies in behavior modification* (pp. 358–363). New York: Holt, Rinehart, & Winston.

Blackburn, J. E., & Powell, W. C. (1976). *One at a time all at once: The creative teacher's guide to individualized instruction without anarchy.* Pacific Palisades, CA: Goodyear.

Blechman, E. A., Olson, D. H. L., Schornagel, C. Y., Halsdorf, M., & Turner, A. J. (1976). The family contract game: Technique and case study. *Journal of Consulting and Clinical Psychology, 44,* 449–455.

Bushell, D., Jr. (1978). An engineering approach to the elementary classroom: The Behavior Analysis Follow Through project. In A. C. Catania & T. A. Brigham (Eds.), *Handbook of applied behavior analysis: Social and instructional processes.* (pp. 525–563). New York: Irvington.

Cantrell, R. P., Cantrell, M. L., Huddleston, C. M., & Woolridge, R. L. (1969). Contingency contracting with school problems. *Journal of Applied Behavior Analysis, 2,* 215–220.

Clarizio, H. (1980). *Toward a positive classroom discipline* (3rd ed.). New York: John Wiley & Sons.

Cohen, H., & Filipczak, J. (1971). *A new learning environment.* San Francisco: Jossey Bass.

DeRisi, W. J., & Butz, G. (1975). *Writing behavioral contracts: A case simulation practice manual.* Champaign, IL: Research Press.

Gelfand, D. M., & Hartmann, D. P. (1984). *Child behavior analysis and therapy* (2nd ed.). New York: Pergamon.

Homme, L., Csanyi, A. P., Gonzales, M. A., & Rechs, J. R. (1970). *How to use contingency contracting in the classroom.* Champaign, IL: Research Press.

Kazdin, A. E. (1975). *Behavior modification in applied settings.* Homewood, IL: Dorsey Press.

Kazdin, A. E. (1977). *The token economy: A review and evaluation.* New York: Plenum.

Kazdin, A. E. (1985). The token economy. In R. M. Turner and L. M. Ascher (Eds.), *Evaluating behavior therapy outcome* (pp. 225–253). New York: Springer Publishing.

Kirschenbaum, D. S., Dielman, J. S., & Karoly, P. (1982). Efficacy of behavioral contracting: Target behaviors, performance criteria. *Behavior Modification, 6,* 499–518.

Linscheid, T. R., Malosky, P., & Zimmerman, J. (1974). Discharge as the major consequence in a hospitalized patient's behavior management program: A case study. *Behavior Therapy, 5,* 559–564.

Lovitt, T. C., & Curtiss, K. S. (1968). Effects of manipulating an antecedent event on mathematics response rate. *Journal of Applied Behavior Analysis, 1,* 329–333.

Martin, G. & Pear, J. (1983). *Behavior modification: What it is and how to do it* (2nd ed.). Englewood Cliffs,

NJ: Prentice-Hall.

O'Leary, K. D., Becker, W. C., Evans, M. B., & Saudargas, R. A. (1969). A token reinforcement program in a public school: A replication and systematic analysis. *Journal of Applied Behavior Analysis, 2*, 3–13.

O'Leary, K. D., & Drabman, R. S. (1971). Token reinforcement programs in the classroom: A review. *Psychological Bulletin, 75*, 379–398.

Quay, H. C., Glavin, J. P., Annesley, F. R., & Werry J. S. (1972). The modification of problem behavior and academic achievement in a resource room. *Journal of School Psychology, 10*, 187–198.

Stuart, R. B. (1971). Behavioral contracting within the families of delinquents. *Journal of Behavioral Therapy & Experimental Psychiatry, 2*, 1–11.

Walker, H. M., & Buckley, N. K. (1974). *Token reinforcement techniques: Classroom applications for the hard-to-reach child.* Eugene, OR: E-B Press.

Weathers, L., & Liberman, R. P. (1978). Modification of family behavior. In D. Marholin, II (Ed.), *Child behavior therapy* (pp. 150–186). New York: Gardner Press.

Wolf, M. M., Giles, D. K., & Hall, R. V. (1968). Experiments with token reinforcement in a remedial classroom. *Behaviour Research and Therapy, 6*, 51–64.

Wolf, M. M., Phillips, E. L., Fixsen, D. G., Braukmann, C. J., Kirigin, K. A., Willner, A. G., & Schumaker, J. B. (1976). Achievement Place: The teaching-family model. *Child Care Quarterly, 5*, 92–103.

24

USING PEERS TO FACILITATE BEHAVIOR CHANGE

Key Terms

■ Group Contingency ■ Dependent-Group-Oriented ■ Independent-Group-Oriented ■ Interdependent-Group-Oriented ■ Good Behavior Game ■ Peer-Mediated Systems ■ Peer Reinforcement ■ Peer Coaching

Teaching and managing student behavior is relatively straightforward when working with two or three students on a one-to-one basis. For a number of reasons, however, teaching under those conditions is rarely possible. Classroom resources and personnel are limited, and individual instruction is difficult to schedule and present to large numbers of students. Students must learn to function successfully with other members of their natural social community. We also expect students to use many of their newly learned academic and social skills in settings outside the classroom. Furthermore, peers can be useful teaching assistants and models. Peer tutors can help teachers make more efficient use of their instructional time and can facilitate enduring behavior change outside the instructional setting.

In Chapter 23, our attention was focused on individual and group management systems that were primarily teacher directed. We discussed how token economies and behavioral contracts can help teachers structure learning and behavior-change opportunities. In this chapter, we extend our discussion to group contingency systems and emphasize the importance of peers as teaching resources.

GROUP CONTINGENCY SYSTEMS

Whenever teachers work with two or more students, they must distribute their time and resources to maximize individual learning. Teachers must have opportunities to present instruction and give feedback to students about their performance. Students must have similar opportunities to respond to instruction and to benefit from teacher feedback. **Group contingency** systems can facilitate cooperative interactions between the teacher and students and among the students themselves by making consequences either contingent on group behavior or by letting an individual student's behavior affect consequences for the entire group. For example, a class field trip might be contingent on each student finishing all assignments by 10:30 a.m. Or, the teacher might allow students an extra 5 minutes of recess if a specified student stays in his or her chair for 30 consecutive minutes.

Group Contingency Management Variations

There are many different kinds of group contingency management systems. Litow and Pumroy (1975) and Kazdin (1975) described three basic variations from which many additional modifications can be developed. One is called a **dependent-group-oriented** contingency system. The same response contingency is in effect for all group members; however, it is applied to an individual or a small subset of the larger group. It is the performance of this individual or select group that is compared to the required response criteria and that is used to determine if the group as a whole receives the reinforcer or penalty. For example, Mack has been observed to swear frequently in class. His teacher implements a dependent-group-oriented strategy in which access to computer games is dependent on Mack reducing the number of times he swears. On those mornings in which he swears no more than twice from 8:00 to 11:00 a.m., the computer game center will be opened for all students. If he exceeds two swears, the center is closed. One of the major problems with systems of this type is the undue or unreasonable pressure that might be placed on an individual student. It may be possible to defray some of this pressure by not identifying the individual or individuals on whom evaluations are being made; however, even this tactic may force teachers to assume more responsibility for group consequences than they would wish. Frequently, students can easily identify the target student. On the other hand, the target student may receive considerable spontaneous social attention when he or she earns rewards for the group.

The **independent-group-oriented** contingency system is similar except that the response contingency in effect for all group members is applied to student performance on an individual basis. The performance of an individual student does not affect the consequences associated with the behaviors of other students. For example, each student in Mack's class is expected to bring a pencil, piece of paper, and eraser to math group. Mack's teacher gives each student who comes to group prepared a token that can be used to play one computer game. Mack's individual performance does not affect what his peers might earn. This variation has the disadvantage of decreasing a student's opportunities to learn how to engage in appropriate interpersonal behaviors and how to respond to social pressure and stress.

The third variation suggested by Litow and Pumroy (1975) attempts to create a balance between individual performance and group influence, and is called an **interdependent-group-oriented** contingency system. Like the others, the same response contingency is in effect for all group members, but the final evaluation is based on a specified level of group performance. For example, Mr. Simon uses an interdependent-group-oriented strategy to reduce the number of talking-out episodes that occur in the classroom after lunch. When he hears a student talk out, he puts a check by that student's name. At the end of the day, he randomly selects five names from a box that contains cards with the names of each student written on them. If less than three of the selected students have checks for talking out, Mr. Simon adds 3 extra minutes to game day on Friday afternoon. The criterion in an interdependent-oriented strategy may be determined in a variety of ways: (a) averaging individual performance, (b) randomly selecting an individual's performance, (c) averaging the performance of a small subset of students from the larger group, (d) totaling group performance, etc. These variations have the advantage of great flexibility without forfeiting some level of social interaction. Gola, Holmes, and Holmes (1982) used an interdependent-group-oriented system with a group of students who were profoundly mentally retarded. They noted an increase in the amount of prevocational work behaviors displayed by these students. In a comparative study with 12 students with learning disabilities, Speltz, Shimamura, and McReynolds (1982) observed some individual performance differences but, in general, found group contingency systems in which reward was based on (a) group average, (b) work of low achiever, or (c) work of randomly selected student to be effective in improving arithmetic worksheet performance and social interactions.

Advantages and Disadvantages of Group Contingency Management

Group contingency strategies have many advantages. One of the most important is increased opportunities to learn appropriate skills within social contexts. In group situations, students learn from behaviors modeled by their peers. These same peers can also be taught to monitor, reinforce, and initiate extinction consequences (Carden-Smith & Fowler, 1984; Cooke & Apolloni, 1976; Hendrickson, Strain, Tremblay, & Shores, 1982; Strain, Kerr, & Ragland, 1976; Strain, Shores, & Timm, 1977). Students in group contingency situations can also observe their peers receiving reinforcement (Kazdin, 1975; Rimm & Masters, 1979). By observing such feedback, students can learn about the consequences associated with their own behaviors. A review by Hops, Finch, and McConnell (1986) revealed that early group experiences with age-similar peers may provide children with opportunities "to acquire social-affective behavior that will not be learned in interactions with their parents" (p. 544). Thus, teachers may take advantage of peer influence to produce a variety of desirable outcomes.

Another advantage of group contingency strategies is the teacher's ability to manage large numbers of students at one time. For special education students, group learning opportunities are a closer approximation to conditions existing in less restrictive settings such as large-group classrooms where appropriate group responses are required. By emphasizing group behaviors, individual students are not singled out or given excessive teacher or peer attention. Kerr and Nelson (1983) added that group-oriented contingency management systems make use of many social reinforcers that are peer-group controlled and save work for the teacher by reducing the delivery of individual reinforcers.

The systematic application of group contingency procedures also increases opportunities for building positive peer relationships. Ladd and Asher (1985) indicated that students who have difficulty in relating to their peers may be prone to learning and mental health difficulties, conduct and character disorders, and poor adult and societal adjustment. Group management systems provide excellent vehicles for systematically teaching interpersonal social skills.

Last, in a review of 20 studies that directly compared group versus individual contingencies, Pigott and Heggie (1986) found that when academic performance was reinforced, group contingencies were generally better than individual strategies. Their review also indicated that group contingency systems utilized teacher time more effectively and were associated with increases in prosocial behavior.

Group management systems, however, also have disadvantages. In some cases, students who frequently fail to meet group criteria for success or cause the group to lose privileges or rewards may become the target of excessive peer influence and ridicule. These students, in turn, may display even more uncooperative behaviors in order to reduce peer pressure, or they may remove themselves entirely from group interactions. A second problem frequently experienced is the high social status observed in students who attempt to subvert or "beat the system." The social attention attached to subversive acts can be quite reinforcing. A third problem is the issue of fairness of group contingencies, particularly when the behavior of one student causes well-behaved and compliant students to lose opportunities for reinforcement. A last disadvantage is the increased amount of supervision and administration required by the teacher. In group management arrangements, more than one student, behavior, and reinforcer may require systematic monitoring. Initially, the cost on teacher time and energy may be high, but well-prepared procedures can turn the responsibility for many of these activities over to group members.

Effective Use of Group Contingency Systems

Some of these disadvantages may be difficult to remove entirely; however, their impact can be reduced with proper planning. For example, problems can be reduced by carefully arranging the membership of a group. Teachers can select individuals who participate and attend groups on a regular and consistent basis. Arranging groups with individuals who have similar behavioral and academic characteristics is also helpful; however, some students should be more fluent at specific skills so they can serve as positive examples, be reinforced, and be taught to reinforce the behaviors of others. Similarly, all members of the group should be capable of performing the required prerequisite behaviors needed for individual and group success, for example, waiting turn and sharing. Individuals who have not acquired these skills should be placed under different contingencies or be taught necessary behaviors before being held accountable for group contingencies.

Selecting reinforcers that have some rewarding value for each member of the group will also increase individual involvement in group activities. Similarly, groups that have accepted common goals or functions tend to be more cohesive and durable. When individual subverters are exposed, attempts should be made initially to identify some reinforcing aspect of the group that will increase the subverter's appropriate involvement. If cooperative behaviors cannot be managed through group-related factors, separate contingencies (e.g., individual contracts) should be arranged. These contingencies should be strong enough to compete with reinforcers that were previously maintaining disruptive behaviors.

Specific Examples of Group Contingency Systems

Good Behavior Game. The **good behavior game** is a widely applied and studied group contingency strategy (Barrish, Saunders, & Wolf, 1969). Students are divided into teams and the level of compliance to rules established for specific behaviors is observed. The team with the highest degree of compliance "wins" access to reinforcement. Barrish et al. (1969) first applied the good behavior game format in a classroom with 24 fourth-grade students. The teacher established a set of rules and consequences for out-of-seat and talking-out behaviors (See Figure 24.1).

Barrish et al. noted significant improvement in the amount of out-of-seat and talking-out behavior displayed by these fourth graders. The rules and procedures of the good behavior game did not require the teacher to change her usual classroom rules or activities. In general, teachers, students, and the principal reported that they were pleased with the results; however, a number of problems were encountered. First, the initially large amount of time required to prepare materials and introduce the game was difficult to manage along with the teacher's regular responsibilities. Second, the teacher had to learn how to be "alert" for appropriate and inappropriate displays of behavior. Third, seven students indicated that they did not like the game because they (a) did not like being quiet, (b) wanted more involvement in making the rules, (c) did not like losing the game and receiving peer criticism, and (d) did not like it when individual students caused their team to lose. To solve the last problem, the teacher dropped two

FIGURE 24.1   Rules and consequences for the Good Behavior Game.

a. What they were about to do was a game that they would play every day during math period only.
b. The class would be divided into two teams.
c. When a team or teams won the game, the team(s) would receive certain privileges.
d. There were certain rules, however, that the teams had to follow to win (regarding appropriate and inappropriate behaviors).
e. Whenever anyone on a team was seen breaking one of these rules, that team would get a mark on the chalkboard.
f. If a team had the fewest marks, or if neither team received more than five marks, the team(s) would get to (1) wear victory tags, (2) put a star by each of its members' names on the winner's chart, (3) line up first for lunch if one team won or early if both teams won, and (4) take part at the end of the day in a 30 minute free time during which the team(s) would have special projects.
g. The team that lost would not get these privileges, would continue working on an assignment during the last half-hour of the day, and members would have to stay after school as usual if they did not do their work during the last half-hour period.
h. If a team or teams had not received more than 20 marks in a week, it would get the extra weekly privilege of going to recess 4 minutes early.

From "Good Behavior Game: Effects of Individual Contingencies for Group Consequences on Disruptive Behavior in the Classroom" by H. Barrish, M. Saunders, and M. M. Wolf, 1969, *Journal of Applied Behavior Analysis, 2*, pp. 120-121.

students from the game and made each a single-member "team." The authors suggested that social attention from peers was reinforcing disruptive behavior.

Many replications have demonstrated the effectiveness of the good behavior game (Darch & Thorpe, 1977; Fishbein & Wasik, 1981; Harris & Sherman, 1973; Medland & Stachnik, 1972). For example, Saigh and Umar (1983) used it with a group of 20 regular second graders in a rural public school in central Sudan. They noted improvements in aggressions, seat-leaving, and talking behaviors.

Other Examples. Other gamelike group contingency formats have been used to modify a variety of behaviors. Allen, Gottselig, and Boylan (1982) implemented an intervention package that consisted of (a) earned free time for the class, (b) stated and posted classroom rules, (c) a kitchen timer, and (d) flip cards indicating amount of free time earned. The disruptive classroom behaviors of eight students from a third-grade classroom ($n = 29$) were targeted. The teacher indicated that a 5-minute timer would continue to run as long as disruptive behaviors were not observed. If the bell rang at the end of the 5-minute interval, the teacher praised the class and let them know they had earned 1 minute of free time. A card indicating the total number of free-time minutes that had accumulated was displayed. Students produced a list of possible free-time activities and voted on the four they most preferred. The implementation of the DRO-5 intervention package was associated with a decrease in the rate of disruptive behaviors.

Swain, Allard, and Holborn (1982) designed a tooth-brushing game that was school based and designed to increase the tooth-brushing effectiveness of 22 first and 23 second graders. Each grade level class was divided into two teams. Eight members from each team were selected randomly to represent their team and have their teeth checked. Teams with the cleanest teeth had their names placed on a poster and winning team members were given a "scratch n' sniff" sticker. Social reinforcement and positive verbal feedback were also provided. The authors of this study observed more effective tooth-brushing behavior when the game contingencies were in effect. A 9-month follow-up indicated satisfactory maintenance of intervention gains.

The PASS (Program for Academic Survival Skills) is a group management package designed for teacher consultants and classroom teachers (Greenwood, Hops, Delquadri, & Walker, 1977; Greenwood, Hops, & Walker, 1977). It is unique in that a single measure of group survival skills (e.g., following directions, looking at the teacher, or asking questions) is used by the teacher to make contingency decisions. The teacher uses a clock which is turned on when the students, who can see a small light, are engaged in survival skills. When any individual student is behaving inappropriately during instruction, the clock is turned off. Group consequences are provided when a prespecified criterion (e.g., 80% of previous performance) is met. The PASS is a packaged group management program that also provides strategies for removing the clock contingency and facilitating response maintenance.

Gamelike contingencies also have been used effectively with parents. Muir and Milan (1982) implemented a lottery game in which the mothers of three 2-year-old children with seizure disorders and cerebral palsy "won" toys, household items, complimentary meals, and merchandise discounts whenever their children mastered a language-related skill or task. The lottery intervention was found to be effective in increasing parental participation in home intervention programs. The authors indicated that a "notable aspect of this program was that parents earned reinforcement contingent on actual improvements in their children's behavior rather than for the amount of time or 'effort' devoted to programming, which do not necessarily result in behavioral changes in their children (p. 459). Parents found the gamelike format appealing and tended to be more "creative" when the contingency was in effect.

PEER-MEDIATED MANAGEMENT SYSTEMS

While observing peer interactions, teachers frequently note the influence exerted by students on the behaviors of their classmates. Unfortunately, this influence can be both negative as well as positive. If instructed and supervised carefully, however, peers can be a valuable tool to the resourceful teacher.

Peer-mediated systems are usually designed to replace teacher-directed control with more natural forms of peer-related interactions. As with both group and individual management procedures, the focus is on promoting appropriate behavior through reinforcement and systematic teaching. There have been many demonstrations of peer-mediated strategies in the research literature. For example, academic performance has been improved through peer-tutoring procedures (Greenwood, Delquadri, & Hall, 1984; Greenwood, Dinwiddie, Terry, Wade, Stanley, Thibadeau, & Delquadri, 1984). Similarly, behavioral excesses and social skill deficits have been modified through peer-assisted procedures (Axelrod, 1973; Bailey, Timbers, Phillips, & Wolf, 1971; Odom, 1981; Patterson, Cobb, & Ray, 1972; Rosenbaum, O'Leary, & Jacob, 1975; Strain & Odom, 1986).

Peer-mediated strategies have a number of advantages. First, social reinforcement delivered by peers may be more powerful than the same reinforcer presented by the teacher (McGee, Kauffman, & Nussen, 1977). Second, peers are likely to have more opportunities than teachers to dispense feedback, present antecedent conditions, and require practice of desired behaviors, thus enhancing acquisition and promoting generalized responding and response maintenance (Johnston & Johnston, 1973; Marholin & McInnis, 1978). Delquadri, Greenwood, Whorton, Carta, and Hall (1986) suggested that classwide peer tutoring results in peer supervision which, in turn, increases active engaged time, opportunities for corrective feedback, modeling, reinforcement, and practice. Furthermore, positive outcomes may occur for students who learn peer-tutoring strategies (Cohen, Kulik, & Kulik, 1982; Dougherty, Fowler, & Paine, 1985; Marholin & McInnis, 1978; Siegel & Steinman, 1973). For example, tutors may learn how to evaluate accurately their own behaviors and the behaviors of others, how to react to the responses of others, and how to model or imitate more desirable forms of behaviors. Furthermore, by teaching certain behaviors, they themselves may become more fluent in that behavior.

In a review of the peer-mediated intervention literature, however, Kalfus (1984) also observed a number of disadvantages or side effects. First, peers may not be efficient teachers and may expend excessive amounts of time to achieve specific levels of tutee performance. Kalfus suggested that systematic and detailed training procedures must be developed to make tutors as efficient as possible. Second, the additional time required to train tutors may negate any time teachers hope to save. This disadvantage may be minimized by selecting tutors who are competent, motivated, and easily trained, and who have regular attendance and good verbal and modeling skills. Third, ethical and legal implications preclude the use of peers in certain procedures, especially where edible reinforcers, punishment, and other easily misinterpreted or abused procedures might be employed. Lastly, Kalfus warned that teachers may become less interactive and decrease their own use of best instructional practices, for example, verbal praise, room scanning, and systematic instruction. Kalfus recommended that teachers (a) implement sound instructional packages with tutors and (b) engage in the continuous monitoring and evaluation of tutee and tutor behaviors, as well as their own behaviors, to decrease the impact of these potential disadvantages.

Peers have been used as tutors, reinforcing agents, and facilitators of generalization for both academic and nonacademic behaviors. In addition, they have been trained to observe and record the behaviors of their classmates. Peer-mediated strategies have been employed across a wide range of behaviors, and even with very young children (Strain, Shores, & Timm, 1977). The following guidelines should be considered when implementing peer-oriented contingency management procedures:

1. Identify specifically the skills peer-managers and tutees must learn and perform, and where (or under what conditions) these skills should be learned and demonstrated.

2. Select students who have already acquired or can be easily taught the skills and who can maintain them with minimum teacher supervision. They should display behaviors that indicate their willingness to participate and ability to be responsible. Also, the tutor should be someone the tutee respects.

3. Develop simple and systematic training procedures that include criteria for acquisition, fluency, and generalization of desired tutor behavior. Peer tutors should be given clear instructions, provided opportunities to practice, and presented feedback on implementation accuracy.

4. Collect and evaluate data on both tutor and tutee performance. Teachers should be certain that tutors are modeling and implementing desired behaviors and that peers are progressing at adequate rates. Contingency plans or procedures may need to be developed to retrain tutor skills and to facilitate the modification of tutee behavior.

5. Systematically fade peer-oriented strategies and incorporate procedures to increase student- or self-mediated contingency management strategies or self-control.

Peer managers can be used in a variety of ways to facilitate change in their classmates' behaviors. Peers can be used as models who present a demonstration of the desired target response (Peck, Cooke, & Apolloni, 1976). In this procedure, the student may need to be prompted to imitate the peer's demonstration. In addition to prompting or cuing the student, the teacher's major responsibilities include reinforcing the peer's demonstration and the student's imitation. Teachers should select peer models who have characteristics similar to the student, hold status or prestige, and are competent and reliable at producing the behavior to be imitated.

Peers can also be used to initiate social interactions. They can be taught to make "social bids" (Kerr & Nelson, 1983) or to initiate interactions with the student. Initiations may be simple verbal or physical prompts, rules for expected behavior, or more sophisticated response chains.

Another type of peer-mediated strategy involves teaching peers to prompt and/or reinforce student behaviors (Heward, Heron, Ellis, & Cooke, 1986). For example, Lancioni (1982) taught normal children to use a variety of reinforcers (edible and social) to teach withdrawn children with mental retardation to engage in appropriate social responding. **Peer reinforcement** involves training peers to recognize when appropriate and inappropriate behaviors are being displayed and to administer reinforcement in a contingent and systematic fashion.

A final form of peer-mediated programming requires teaching the peer to train or "coach" the student in the desired behaviors. In **peer coaching,** the student and teacher verbally describe and rehearse the essential characteristics of the skill and the conditions under which it must occur. The peer coach then practices the response with the student under realistic stimulus conditions. Finally, the student, teacher, and peer review the rehearsal and practice session to reinforce correct components and prompt improvements. "Through repeated practice of the desired response, the child learns how to perform the new behaviors and the coaching sequence of instruction-practice-feedback is repeated until performance matches the desired objective" (Michelson & Mannarino, 1986, p. 385).

Regardless of the peer-mediated variation implemented, one of the critical factors is the training provided the peer. Kerr and Nelson (1983) suggested the following general guidelines for training peer tutors:

1. Pinpoint the task and analyze it before you begin.
2. Collect all needed materials.
3. Explain the goal of tutoring to the tutor.
4. Explain the task to the tutor, as much as you think is needed.
5. Instruct the tutor in the use of the materials.
6. Explain how the data are to be collected.
7. Role-play the actual tutoring procedures with the tutor.
    a. Model the teaching and the feedback/praise with the tutor and the target student.
    b. Ask the tutor to try being the student for a couple of steps.
    c. Provide feedback to the tutor.
    d. Role-play some problems the tutor may encounter.
    e. If needed, train particular phrases that the tutor can use to reinforce the student.
    f. Provide the tutor with sample data and have him record them.
    g. Meet with the tutor before the first session to review the procedures.
    h. Meet daily after the tutoring session to review the procedures. (p. 165)

Variations of these peer-training procedures should be applied when teaching peers to assist in imitation training, initiate social interactions, use prompting and reinforcement strategies, and be peer coaches. Kerr and Nelson (1983) also suggested that peer training include (a) explanations of what the tutor should expect in training and in working with students; for example, the tutee may initially reject the tutor, (b) role-playing using naturally occurring materials and setting conditions, and (c) reinforcement of peer participation and learning.

Peers have been used to modify the academic performance, classroom behaviors, and social skills of a wide variety of students. Although the use of peers to facilitate generalization has not been studied as thoroughly (Kalfus, 1984) and procedures remain to be delineated, these strategies present great potential in interpersonal, classroom, home, and community settings (Stokes & Baer, 1976). Lancioni (1982) suggested that a key variable in facilitating the effects of peer-mediated interventions might be related to response-requirement similarities and differences between training and generalization settings. Further empirical investigation is required. Barton (1986) further indicated

> Although, as aforementioned, there have been a few reports (e.g., Lancioni, 1982; Wahler, 1967) of the use of peers to instruct, model, and/or reinforce prosocial behavior, little is known about the limitations of their use with respect to types of settings, prosocial responses, and target children. Furthermore, whether the use of peers is superior (i.e., in terms of adult time and treatment potency) to the use of adults as change agents, awaits empirical verification. (p. 360)

Summary of Key Concepts

- ■ A student's peer group can be a useful learning and behavior management resource.
- ■ Group and peer-mediated management procedures can be effective if carefully preplanned, if group members are carefully selected, and if effective reinforcers are available for all participants.
- ■ Group contingency systems vary in the degree to which individual or group performance affects opportunities for individual or group reinforcement.
- ■ When managing group management procedures, teachers must be alert for appropriate and inappropriate student behaviors.
- ■ Peer-mediated systems are usually designed to fade teacher-directed control to more natural forms of peer-related interactions.
- ■ Peers can be trained to be observers, tutors, reinforcing agents, and facilitators of generalized responding.
- ■ The success of peer-mediated management systems is affected by the characteristics of peers, the quality of peer training, and the competency levels of peers.

REFERENCES

Allen, L. D., Gottselig, M., & Boylan, S. (1982). A practical mechanism for using free time as a reinforcer in classrooms. *Education and Treatment of Children, 5,* 347–353.

Axelrod, S. (1973). Comparison of individual and group contingencies in two special classes. *Behavior Therapy, 4,* 37–43.

Bailey, J. S., Timbers, G. D., Phillips, E. L., & Wolf, M. M. (1971). Modification of articulation errors of pre-delinquents by their peers. *Journal of Applied Behavior Analysis, 4,* 265–281.

Barrish, H., Saunders, M., & Wolf, M. M. (1969). Good behavior game: Effects of individual contingencies for group consequences on disruptive behavior in the classroom. *Journal of Applied Behavior Analysis, 2,* 119–124.

Barton, E. J. (1986). Modification of children's prosocial behavior. In P. S. Strain, M. J. Guralnick, & H. M. Walker (Eds.), *Children's social behavior: Development, assessment, and modification* (pp. 331–372). New York: Academic Press.

Carden-Smith, L. K., & Fowler, S. A. (1984). Positive peer pressure: The effects of peer monitoring on children's disruptive behavior. *Journal of Applied Behavior Analysis, 17,* 213–227.

Cohen, P. A., Kulik, J. A., & Kulik, L. C. (1982). Educational outcomes of tutoring: A meta-analysis of findings. *American Educational Research Journal, 19,* 237–248.

Cooke, T. P., & Apolloni, T. (1976). Developing positive social-emotional behaviors: A study of training and generalization effects. *Journal of Applied Behavior Analysis, 9,* 65–78.

Darch, C. B., & Thorpe, H. W. (1977). The principal game: A group consequence procedure to increase classroom on-task behavior. *Psychology in the Schools, 14,* 341–347.

Delquadri, J., Greenwood, C. R., Whorton, D., Carta, J. J., & Hall, R. V. (1986). Classwide peer tutoring. *Exceptional Children, 52,* 535–542.

Dougherty, B. S., Fowler, S. A., & Paine, S. C. (1985). The use of peer monitors to reduce aggressive behavior during recess. *Journal of Applied Behavior Analysis, 18,* 141–153.

Fishbein, J. E., & Wasik, B. H. (1981). Effect of the good behavior game on disruptive library behavior. *Journal of Applied Behavior Analysis, 14,* 89–93.

Gola, T. J., Holmes, P. A., & Holmes, N. K. (1982). Effectiveness of a group contingency procedure for increasing prevocational behavior of profoundly mentally retarded residents. *Mental Retardation, 20,* 26–29.

Greenwood, C. R., Delquadri, J. C., & Hall, R. V. (1984). Opportunity to respond and student academic performance. In W. L. Heward, T. E. Heron, D. S. Hill, & J. Trap-Porter (Eds.), *Focus on behavior analysis in education* (pp. 58–88). Columbus, OH: Charles E. Merrill.

Greenwood, C. R., Dinwiddie, G., Terry, B., Wade, L., Stanley, S. O., Thibadeau, S., & Delquadri, J. C. (1984). Teacher- versus peer-mediated instruction: An ecobehavioral analysis of achievement outcomes. *Journal of Applied Behavior Analysis, 17,* 521–538.

Greenwood, C. R., Hops, H., Delquadri, J., & Walker, H. M. (1977). *The program for academic survival skills (PASS): Consultant's manual.* Eugene: Center at Oregon for Research in the Behavioral Education of the Handicapped, University of Oregon.

Greenwood, C. R., Hops, H., & Walker, H. M. (1977). The program for academic survival skills (PASS): Effects on student behavior and achievement. *Journal of School Psychology, 15,* 25–35.

Harris, V. W., & Sherman, J. A. (1973). Effects of peer tutoring and consequences on the math performance of elementary classroom students. *Journal of Applied Behavior Analysis, 6,* 587–597.

Hendrickson, J. M., Strain, P. S., Tremblay, A., & Shores, R. E. (1982). Interactions of behaviorally handicapped children: Functional effects of peer social initiations. *Behavior Modification, 6,* 323–353.

Heward, W. L., Heron, T. E., Ellis, D. E., & Cooke, N. L. (1986). Teaching first grade peer tutors to use verbal praise on an intermittent schedule. *Education and Treatment of Children, 9,* 5–15.

Hops, H., Finch, M., & McConnell, S. (1986). Social skills deficits. In A. E. Kazdin & P. H. Bornstein

(Eds), *Handbook of clinical behavior therapy with children* (pp. 541–598). Homewood, IL: Dorsey Press.

Johnston, M. J., & Johnston, G. T. (1973). Modification of consonant speech-sound articulation in young children. *Journal of Applied Behavior Analysis, 7,* 233–246.

Kalfus, G. R. (1984). Peer mediated intervention: A critical review. *Child and Family Behavior Therapy, 6,* 17–43.

Kazdin, A. E. (1975). *Behavior modification in applied settings.* Homewood, IL: Dorsey Press.

Kerr, M. M., & Nelson, C. M. (1983). *Strategies for managing behavior problems in the classroom.* Columbus, OH: Charles E. Merrill.

Ladd, G. W., & Asher, S. R. (1985). Social skill training and children's peer relations. In L. L'Abate and M. A. Milan (Eds.), *Handbook of social skills training and research* (pp. 219–245). New York: John Wiley & Sons.

Lancioni, G. E. (1982). Normal children as tutors to teach social responses to withdrawn mentally retarded schoolmates: Training, maintenance, and generalization. *Journal of Applied Behavior Analysis, 15,* 17–40.

Litow, L., & Pumroy, D. K. (1975). A brief review of classroom group-oriented contingencies. *Journal of Applied Behavior Analysis, 8,* 341–347.

Marholin, D., II, & McInnis, E. T. (1978). Treating children in group settings: Techniques for individualizing behavioral programs. In D. Marholin, II (Ed.), *Child behavior therapy* (pp. 107–149). New York: Gardner Press.

McGee, C. S., Kauffman, J. M., & Nussen, T. L. (1977). Children as therapeutic change agents: Reinforcement intervention paradigm. *Review of Educational Research, 47,* 451–477.

Medland, M. B., & Stachnik, T. J. (1972). Good behavior game: A replication and systematic analysis. *Journal of Applied Behavior Analysis, 5,* 45–51.

Michelson, L., & Mannarino, A. (1986). Social skills training with children: Research and clinical applications. In P. S. Strain, M. J. Guralnick, & H. M. Walker (Eds.), *Children's social behavior: Development, assessment, and modification* (pp. 373–406). New York: Academic Press.

Muir, K. A., & Milan, M. A. (1982). Parent reinforcement for child achievement: The use of lottery to maximize parent training effects. *Journal of Applied Behavior Analysis, 15,* 455–460.

Odom, S. L. (1981). The relationship of play to developmental level in mentally retarded, preschool children. *Education and Training of Mentally Retarded, 16,* 136-141.

Patterson, G., Cobb, J., & Ray, R. (1972). Direct intervention in the classroom: A set of procedures for the aggressive child. In F. W. Clark, D. R. Evans, & L. A. Hamerlynck (Eds.), *Implementing behavioral programs for schools and clinics.* Champaign, IL: Research Press.

Peck, C. A., Cooke, T. P., & Apolloni, T. (1981). Utilization of peer imitation in therapeutic and instructional contexts. In P. S. Strain (Ed.), *The utilization of classroom peers as behavior change agents* (pp. 69–99). New York: Plenum.

Pigott, H. E., & Heggie, D. L. (1986). Interpreting the conflicting results of individual versus group contingencies in classrooms: The targeted behavior as a mediating variable. *Child and Family Behavior Therapy, 7,* 1–15.

Rimm, D. C., & Masters, J. C. (1979). *Behavior therapy: Techniques and empirical findings* (2nd ed.). New York: Academic Press.

Rosenbaum, A., O'Leary, K. D., & Jacob, R. G. (1975). Behavioral intervention with hyperactive children: Group consequences as a supplement to individual contingencies. *Behavior Therapy, 6,* 315–323.

Saigh, P. A., & Umar, A. M. (1983). The effects of a good behavior game on the disruptive behavior of Sudanese elementary school students. *Journal of Applied Behavior Analysis, 16,* 339–344.

Siegel, L. J., & Steinman, W. M. (1973). The modification of a peer-observer's classroom behavior as a function of his serving as a reinforcing agent. In E. Ramp & G. Semb (Eds.), *Behavior analysis: Areas of research and application.* (pp. 329–340). Englewood Cliffs, NJ: Prentice-Hall.

Speltz, M. L., Shimamura, W., & McReynolds, W. T. (1982). Procedural variations in group contingencies: Effects on children's academic and social behaviors. *Journal of Applied Behavior Analysis, 15,* 533-544.

Stokes, T. F., & Baer, D. M. (1976). Preschool peers as mutual generalization-facilitating agents. *Behavior Therapy, 7,* 549–556.

Strain, P. S., & Odom, S. L. (1986). Peer social initiations: Effective intervention for social skills development of exceptional children. *Exceptional Children, 52,* 543–552.

Strain, P. S., Kerr, M. M., & Ragland, E. U. (1981). The use of peer social initiations in the treatment of social withdrawal. In P. S. Strain (Ed.), *The utilization of classroom peers as behavior change agents.* (pp. 101–128). New York: Plenum Press.

Strain, P. S., Shores, R. E., & Timm, M. A. (1977). Effects of peer social initiations on the behavior of withdrawn preschool children. *Journal of Applied Behavior Analysis, 10,* 289–298.

Swain, J. J., Allard, G. B., & Holborn, S. W. (1982). The good toothbrushing game: A school-based dental hygiene program for increasing the toothbrushing effectiveness of children. *Journal of Applied Behavior Analysis, 15,* 171–176.

Wahler, R. G. (1967). Child-child interactions in free field setting: Some experimental analyses. *Journal of Experimental Child Psychology, 5,* 278–293.

25

SELF-MANAGEMENT STRATEGIES

Key Terms

- Self-Management   - Self-Monitoring   - Self-Reinforcement   - Self-Instruction   - Alternate Response Training

Ultimately, the goal of academic and social skill instruction is to enable students to function independent of external or teacher-mediated interventions and control. Achieving this end requires the fluent utilization of behaviors that are reinforced in an intermittent and delayed fashion, and are under the stimulus control of naturally occurring persons, objects, and events. However, students with poor self-management skills often are unable to access necessary levels of reinforcement under the appropriate stimulus conditions. In this chapter, we discuss procedures for facilitating self-management with a focus on self-monitoring, self-reinforcement, and self-instruction.

UNDERSTANDING SELF-MANAGEMENT

Defining Self-Management

Self-management has been defined and interpreted in a variety of ways. Kazdin (1975), for example, referred to **self-management** as "those behaviors an individual deliberately undertakes to achieve self-selected outcomes" (p. 192). Kazdin (1975) and Skinner (1953) suggested that self-management can be best understood by observing how individuals use it in everyday life to control behaviors.

508

Most of the techniques operate by having the individual perform one behavior (a controlling response) which alters the probability of another behavior (a controlled response). Thus, a person may chew gum (controlling response) to reduce the likelihood of smoking cigarettes (controlled response). (Kazdin, 1975, p. 192)

Liberty and Michael (1985) added that

the major aim of teaching self-control is to teach the student to be the agent of change of his or her own behavior, then the controlling response itself must maintain and generalize beyond the training setting and after training ceases. Therefore, we must identify methods of instruction which develop not only accurate and fluent controlling responses, but maintained and generalized self-control skills. (p. 102)

Lastly, Richards and Siegel (1978) warned that

self control is not so much identified with a particular technique as it is with a treatment strategy that endeavors to teach clients how to think and behave like therapists and how to apply these thoughts and behaviors to their self-improvement. (p. 310)

What is derived from these various interpretations is that students who are characterized as having good self-management skills display a set of learned skills that enable them to access their environment and to receive favorable evaluations. These students are frequently labeled as having good self-concepts or self-esteem, or as having "their acts together." Unfortunately, the internal states inferred by these terms are not directly or reliably measured. Thus, it is important that teachers focus on the observable and teachable aspects of self-management. It is for this same reason that we have elected to use the term *self-management* as opposed to *self-control*. The latter term is more value laden and tends to deemphasize the role of environment and its effects on behavior. In this chapter, we emphasize a description used by Rimm and Masters (1979) who indicated that, although individuals with "good" (or "bad") self-management are relatively easy to identify, it

must be stressed that what such individuals possess is not strength or moral fiber, but rather a fortunate learning history that enables them, probably without much effort, to behave in self-enhancing rather than self-defeating ways. The problem with the clients is not that they are not trying hard enough, but that they simply have not yet learned to employ the most effective tactics. (p. 424)

Student acquisition and mastery of self-management skills have many advantages. The most encompassing advantage is that students become more independent as they acquire more self-management skills. The ability to move freely and appropriately through social and community settings is stressed in our society and is viewed as a highly desirable characteristic. Second, self-management skills extend learning. Teachers cannot be available in all settings to reinforce, correct, or monitor student behaviors. Similarly, self-management tactics may function as discriminative stimuli for behaviors that are not under external stimulus control. Third, self-management strategies provide opportunities for students to bridge the gap between a behavior and delayed consequences associated with that behavior. Finally, self-management skills can serve as important tools that enable students to approach new learning or stimulus conditions in a more effective and efficient manner.

Components of Self-Management

Self-management strategies have been operationalized and characterized in a variety of ways. Although most are not taught in isolation, they include (a) stimulus control, (b) self-monitoring or recording, (c) self-reinforcement, (d) self-instruction, and (e) alternate response training.

Stimulus Control. Stimulus control approaches to teaching self-management skills are based on the assumption that students perform particular behaviors in the presence of specific antecedent stimuli (Kazdin, 1975) and that learning or behavior problems are the product of inappropriate stimulus control. These behaviors (a) are under the control of stimuli the student wishes to change, (b) are not controlled by a smaller set of stimuli when it would be more appropriate, or (c) are under inappropriate stimulus control. Teachers must instruct students in strategies that enable them to identify and change environments in which problems arise. For example, when Tracey finds that she is unable to finish her homework because of television noise coming from another room, she must be taught to move to a quieter location. She must place herself in a different situation, or in some way change her environment, and, thus, behave in a more adaptive manner (Rimm & Masters, 1979).

Rimm and Masters (1979) discussed four basic techniques for building more adaptive stimulus control. The first is called *narrowing* or *tightening* and involves the development of appropriate stimulus-response connections. This technique requires that students have effective self-assessment skills that enable them to determine the wide range of stimuli that set the occasion for troublesome or appropriate responses. Undesirable stimuli outside the desirable stimuli range are weakened by removing reinforcement, and desirable stimuli are strengthened or reinforced positively. For example, during large-group reading instruction, Julius has difficulty following along with his finger while the teacher or another student is reading. He is taught to assess his sitting arrangement and to determine which students are more or less likely to distract him from following along with the reader. Julius is also taught to move his chair away from students who reinforce him when he is off task and to sit closer to students who model appropriate following along.

The second technique is called *cue strengthening*. With this procedure, teachers provide students with favorable conditions under which the desired response is more likely to occur. Weak stimulus control can be strengthened and the stimulus-response connections can be learned by the student. Essentially, more opportunities to practice appropriate responses under the desired stimulus conditions are being provided. For example, Kelly is a good reader and follows along when other students are reading. When Julius sits next to her, his teacher praises both Kelly and Julius for being good readers. Julius' teacher also highlights the fact that he is following along with his finger while other students are reading. Appropriate behaviors are being strengthened by reinforcing the behaviors of an appropriate model and enhancing the desirable discriminative stimuli.

A third strategy involves teaching students specific *alternative or competing responses*. The goal of this technique is to decrease the number of opportunities for undesirable behaviors to occur under specific stimulus conditions (i.e., differential reinforcement of alternative or incompatible behaviors). Barbie, for example, puts her fingers in her mouth when watching a movie or other children playing. Barbie's teacher has her hold a pencil during movies and prompts her to play with her peers. During those times when her fingers are not in her mouth, the teacher praises her for watching the movie or playing with her friends in an appropriate manner.

The last stimulus control technique focuses on teaching students how to identify and *terminate sequences of chained responses* that lead to undesirable behavior. The student is taught how to disrupt predictable chains of behavior and to engage in more desirable ones. For example, Randy sometimes blurts out his answers in class before the teacher has finished asking the question. When he gives the wrong answer, other students tease and laugh at him, and then point their fingers at him. When this happens, Randy swears at them. Randy's teacher has taught him to count to two before raising his hand and volunteering an answer. If he gives the right answer, she immediately praises him. If it is the wrong response, Randy's teacher immediately asks another student to answer the question. The wait response, positive reinforcement for correct answers, and rapid question-asking strategies help to disrupt the previous chain of events that resulted in Randy swearing at his classmates. Rimm and Masters (1979) added that these self-management strategies are easiest to teach at the beginning of a response chain when competing reinforcers are relatively weak.

Self-Monitoring. Self-monitoring strategies have been used in many classrooms and have been the focus of much research because they can help the classroom teacher respond to behaviors that would be otherwise unavailable for reinforcement. For example, when Maggie goes to her regular language arts class, she takes a small 3 by 5 index card on which she notes each time she requests teacher attention or help in an appropriate manner, i.e., raised hand, waited turn to speak. When Maggie comes back to the resource room, her teacher evaluates her performance and provides appropriate reinforcement.

Simply stated, **self-monitoring** or recording requires the student to record objectively the frequency of a given behavior or class of behaviors. Broden, Hall, and Mitts (1971) combined self-recording with social reinforcement and observed improvements in the study behavior of an eighth-grade girl and the talking-out behaviors of an eighth-grade boy. Self-monitoring consisted of recording study behavior and talk-outs on pieces of paper. This strategy requires that the student be able to identify the characteristics of a behavior and determine whether or not it meets the criteria of a given response class.

Although the relative effectiveness of self-monitoring as a behavior-change strategy is unclear, it is clear that it possesses some reactive qualities that cause it to be labeled an active intervention. Polsgrove (1979) indicated that self-monitoring seems to be a useful intervention when children are motivated to change and when keeping track of their own behaviors is maintained by the social environment. Furthermore, students who self-record their behaviors learn how frequently their behaviors are occurring and what stimuli may be controlling the responses. Teachers can use student self-monitoring data to set academic and behavioral objectives and to plan teaching sequences. However, teachers may need to provide external reinforcement in order to maintain accurate self-monitoring.

Self-monitoring has been suggested as a way to organize a person's immediate behaviors such that the differences between immediate and delayed consequences may be differentiated. Rachlin (1978) indicated that undesirable behaviors may be maintained by later consequences that have the opposite effect of more immediate consequences, or that adaptive responses are inhibited by prevailing conditions and remove the opportunity for later positive reinforcement. He suggested that self-monitoring responses may reduce the controlling effects of these immediate consequences and increase the likelihood of more adaptive responding. For example, the student who displays disruptive behavior in a classroom is emitting behaviors that have immediate positive consequences (e.g., peer attention, work avoidance, interacting with peers, teacher attention). These behaviors, however, may also have delayed aversive consequences (e.g., poor evaluations on assignment, punishments for disruptive behavior, loss of privileges) that are not immediately available. In a similar manner, appropriate or socially desirable behaviors may be extinguished by immediate aversive consequences and thus become unresponsive to delayed positive reinforcement. Appropriate on-task behaviors may be punished by peers, and the resulting reduction in desirable behaviors decreases opportunities for later reinforcement.

Kazdin (1974) suggested a behaviorally oriented account for the reactive effects of self-monitoring called the *operant-consequence hypothesis*. According to this model, maladaptive behaviors often have immediate reinforcing consequences and delayed aversive consequences. Inappropriate behaviors may occur because aversive consequences are remote. The act of self-monitoring may become a discriminative stimulus "for either the thoughts about the aversive consequences or the consequences themselves" (Kazdin, 1974, p. 244). Self-monitoring a behavior may then bridge the delay between the undesirable response and the ultimate aversive consequences. Similarly, for desirable behavior, self-monitoring may serve as a conditioned reinforcer that bridges the delay between the behavior and the long-term reinforcing consequences. In this way, the monitoring of desirable behaviors may serve to reinforce target behaviors. For example, Sugai and Rowe (1984) taught a 15-year-old boy to record his out-of-seat behavior on a simple chart. Except for numerical feedback about the number of recorded in-seat and out-of-seat behaviors, no reinforcement or accuracy of recording was provided the student. Under these conditions, self-recording was found be a useful and effective self-management and behavior-change procedure.

Other models have been proposed that describe the reactive nature of self-monitoring (Kanfer, 1970; Mace & Kratochwill, 1985; Nelson & Hayes, 1981; Rachlin, 1974). Regardless of the explanation, it is important to note that the systematic use of self-monitoring is associated with predictable behavior change. It is also an important prerequisite skill to self-reinforcement because students must be able to identify what they reinforce.

Students usually need to be taught how to implement a self-recording procedure, and self-recording tends to be more effective with behaviors that have already been managed by more teacher-directed interventions (O'Leary & Dubey, 1979). When training students to use self-monitoring, the following steps should be considered:

1. Select a target behavior that has already been managed with externally directed procedures. Consider a behavior to be increased and decreased.

2. With the student, define the behavior and describe the conditions under which it is appropriate and inappropriate. The behavior should be defined in terms that both the student and teacher can agree upon.

3. Develop a useful data-recording procedure. Include directions for when during the day (e.g., all day, reading period only, beginning of each class), how often (e.g., at the end of every 5-minute interval, any time within each 15-minute interval), and what to record (i.e., what behaviors, under what conditions).

4. Train the student to use the recording procedures. A high level of accuracy should be displayed before concluding training. Training can also include how to count, summarize, and/or chart the data.

5. Implement the self-recording strategy. In the beginning, conduct relatively frequent, but random, reliability checks to ensure accurate recording.

6. Initially, conduct frequent evaluation meetings to discuss the student's performance and to provide the necessary feedback and reinforcement.

7. Consult with others in the self-recording setting about the relative accuracy of the student's recording and the relative amount of behavior change observed.

Self-recording procedures and instruments can be similar to those described in earlier chapters on data collection, e.g., event recording, interval recording, etc. As the student's level of behavior approaches criteria, plans should be established for fading self-recording procedures. For example, the size of recording intervals can be increased, recording can occur less frequently, verbal reports can be substituted for written records, teacher participation can be decreased, etc. The goal is to decrease the amount of external or teacher prompting and evaluation required to maintain satisfactory levels of student behavior.

Self-Reinforcement. Self-reinforcement is another important component of the self-management paradigm. Skinner (1953) indicated that **self-reinforcement** exists when students have the opportunity to reward or reinforce themselves regardless of whether or not they perform a particular behavior. Kazdin (1975) added that self-reinforcement consists of two basic components. The first is *self-determined reinforcement* in which the student specifies the criteria or conditions for reinforcement. The second is *self-administered reinforcement.* In this component, the student distributes reinforcement, regardless of whether or not the response criteria are satisfied. As mentioned in the previous section, self-observation or self-monitoring should also be considered in the training and implementation of self-reinforcement skills. Baer, Fowler, and Carden-Smith (1984) reported that self-reinforcement was an effective strategy for increasing the task accuracy and on-task performance of a 6-year-old boy with severe conduct disorders. In their study, self-reinforcement consisted of teaching the student to grade his daily assignments and to determine his eligibility for reinforcement (recess). It should be noted that self-reinforcement was preceded by a peer-tutoring strategy and that a "mild" response-cost procedure was needed to increase accurate grading.

Although there have been many theoretical explanations for the effects associated with self-reinforcement, most evidence suggests that behavior change is a function of the student's prior external reinforcement history and observational learning experiences (Bandura, 1969, 1971; Bandura & Perloff, 1967; Karoly & Kanfer, 1974; Rimm & Masters, 1979). In a study by Glynn, Thomas, and Shee (1973), students first earned tokens from the teacher before they were taught to self-record and self-administer free-time reinforcers. Recent work by Hayes, Rosenfarb, Wulfert, Munt, Korn, and Zettle (1985) also suggests that public goal setting is an important element in the effectiveness of self-reinforcement. When college students conducted goal setting in private so others were not informed, self-reinforcement was ineffective. However, when individual goals became public, the use of self-reinforcement was associated with increases in appropriate study behaviors.

The implementation of a self-reinforcement procedure must be systematic and consistent. Research indicates that initial steps should be teacher directed and managed. As student progress is achieved, teacher involvement is decreased and student responsibilities are increased. The following guidelines should be considered when building a self-reinforcement component into a behavior-change sequence:

1. Students should be fluent at accurate self-assessment and self-monitoring.
2. Students should be involved directly in setting criteria (i.e., goals) for receiving reinforcement, i.e., levels of acceptable behavior, and in selecting possible reinforcers.

3. Teachers should provide reinforcement for (a) target behaviors displayed by students, (b) accurate matches between teacher and student data records, and (c) accurate student determinations of whether criteria were satisfied.

4. Opportunities to evaluate and match with the teacher's data should be reduced over time.

5. Opportunities for students to (a) evaluate their own performance, (b) determine goal criteria, (c) select reinforcers, and (d) administer reinforcement should be increased in a systematic manner. Teacher participation should be decreased.

6. Naturally occurring forms of reinforcement should be used throughout the self-reinforcement training process.

Self-Instruction. Although difficult to discuss in isolation from other self-management components, self-instruction is a third self-management strategy (O'Leary & Dubey, 1979). Simply stated, **self-instruction** is language directed toward oneself (Kazdin, 1975). A student is trained to make specific self-statements or suggestions that prompt specific kinds of behaviors. These statements are structured and presented as if provided by another individual (Kazdin, 1975). Whenever we use some phrase or jingle to prompt us to do a particular behavior, we are using self-instruction, for example, "look before leaping," "take a deep breath and concentrate." Although these verbalizations are described as being both covert and overt, training should focus on the accuracy of measurable verbal statements and associated changes in performance. Burgio, Whitman, and Johnson (1980) taught two grade-school students how to "focus their attention" and "to cope" with math and printing tasks through self-instruction. This successful intervention consisted of first determining whether self-instruction was present, i.e., did the students demonstrate the following: (a) ask a question, (b) answer the question, (c) give a direction on how to accomplish the task, (d) reinforce themselves for doing the task, (e) give themselves a prompt or cue to ignore distractions, and (f) specify how they would handle task failure. If these indicators were not observed, specific training was provided to increase self-instruction.

Meichenbaum and Goodman (1971) and Bornstein and Quevillon (1976) have developed models that teach students to self-instruct on skills that were previously modeled by a teacher or some external agent. Students are first taught to define a task to be learned, verbalize a way to complete it, evaluate their performance, and to praise themselves when it is done accurately. Teaching self-instruction consists of modeling and fading external prompts systematically. More specifically, after a task model is presented by the teacher, students perform the same task with verbal prompts from the teacher. Students are then instructed to do the task and verbalize what they are doing. Next, students are told to whisper the same verbalizations and, finally, to self-instruct "covertly."

This type of self-instructional paradigm has been used to improve a variety of academic and social performance, for example, creative drawing (Baker & Winston, 1985), creative thinking (Meichenbaum, 1975), academic performance (Bryant & Budd, 1982; Swanson & Scarpati, 1984), and impulsivity (Kendall & Finch, 1979). It should be noted, however, that some research has failed to replicate the same levels of improvement for hyperactive children (Friedling & O'Leary, 1979) and disruptive preschoolers (Billings & Wasik, 1985). Bornstein (1985) indicated that the effectiveness of self-instruction strategies is unclear because the research methodology is not sophisticated enough to evaluate the numerous variables that characterize self-instruction. He concluded that training in self-instruction strategies will probably be of great assistance to some individuals and of less use to others. However, the specific conditions that would predict such outcomes have yet to be delineated.

As in most applications of self-management tactics, self-instruction is usually used in conjunction with other strategies such as self-monitoring, and self-reinforcement. In general, the following guidelines should be considered in teaching the self-instruction component:

1. Provide a clear demonstration of the desired behavior and provide distinct verbal models of the required self-instructional statement, e.g., "what does the teacher want me to do?"

2. Be certain that the student is capable of doing the target behavior, saying and understanding the self-instructional statement, and identifying when the statement is required.

3. Establish stringent criteria for student demonstrations of the desired self-instructional statement.

4. Systematically fade teacher contributions to the self-instructional sequence and increase the student's responsibilities and expectations. A simple forward (or backward) chaining procedure should be considered.

5. Provide specific and natural reinforcement for accurate and fluent (a) demonstrations of target behaviors, (b) independent completion of the self-instructional sequence, and (c) use of self-monitoring and self-reinforcement.

6. Physical prompts or aids should be used to facilitate the fading of teacher assistance and increase of student self-management; however, specific rules should be established for fading the use of these prompts.

Alternate Response Training. The last self-management component consists of a set of similar strategies and is called **alternate response training.** In this set of techniques, the student is taught some alternative or competing response that interferes with opportunities for an undesirable response to be emitted. These alternatives usually include such commonly practiced strategies as counting to 10, taking a deep breath, releasing muscle tension, etc. Workman and Williams (1980) taught a 14-year-old boy to engage in a "self-cued relaxation" response (i.e., take and expel a deep breathe, and say "relax" three times) whenever he felt tension or abdominal pain. After this strategy was implemented, the number of days absent and episodes of violent arguments decreased. It should be noted that the student had also been given "deep muscle relaxation training" just prior to being trained to use the alternate response.

Students must be taught a competing or alternate behavior. If the response already exists in the student's behavioral repertoire, it must be strengthened and brought under the appropriate stimulus control. Like all self-management strategies, alternate response training is not independent of other components; it also requires that the student be able to self-monitor, self-reinforce, and self-instruct.

GENERAL GUIDELINES FOR IMPLEMENTING SELF-MANAGEMENT STRATEGIES

Although research remains to be completed in some areas, there is sufficient evidence to recommend the use of self-management training procedures. However, it is the teacher's responsibility to train students in these skills systematically and to evaluate their effectiveness in a consistent and objective fashion. As for any good instructional or behavior-change intervention, the goals are to provide students with functional and generalizable skills that move them toward the least amount of externally controlled responding as possible. Teachers should consider the following guidelines when teaching and evaluating self-management strategies:

1. Students should be trained to administer self-managed consequences in a contingent fashion (Kazdin, 1975).
2. Teachers should engage in the direct and formative measurement of both the fidelity of a student's self-management behaviors and the effect on target responses (Baer & Fowler, 1976).
3. Self-management strategies should be applied early in the student's response chain (Rimm & Masters, 1979).
4. Response criteria and instructional manipulations should be arranged so that individuals will have a high probability of meeting their behavioral objectives (Rimm & Masters, 1979).
5. Self-determined and teacher-determined goals should be developmentally and culturally appropriate to the student (Gelfand & Hartmann, 1984).
6. All persons (student, peers, parents, teachers, etc.) involved in the training and implementation of a self-management intervention must be motivated and willing to cooperate (Gelfand & Hartmann, 1984).
7. Focus self-management strategies on students' behaviors that are not "long standing," or "overly difficult problems" (Gelfand & Hartmann, 1984).
8. Focus on naturally occurring or prevalent self-management techniques and prompts (Gelfand & Hartmann, 1984).
9. Conduct a careful and thorough assessment of the student's behavioral repertoire (Gelfand & Hartmann, 1984); that is, (a) determine whether the student has the prerequisite skills to engage in or learn self-management responses, (b) identify potentially interfering responses or counterproductive behaviors, and (c) determine the settings and other stimulus conditions under which self-management skills and target responses are observed and required.

10. Reinforce the student for engaging in accurate self-management responses and for emitting the desired target behaviors (Fowler, 1986; Gelfand & Hartmann, 1984; Kazdin, 1975; Kerr & Nelson, 1983; Rimm & Masters, 1979).

11. Systematically fade externally oriented training prompts and bring self-management responses under the stimulus control of naturally occurring stimuli based on clearly defined and achievable criteria and data-decision rules (Fowler, 1986).

12. Both self-management skills and desired target responses should be operationally defined so that both the student and teacher can accurately identify them.

13. Students should be taught the rules (stimulus conditions) that govern desired target responses and self-management behaviors (Fowler, 1986).

14. Teachers should provide ample opportunities for students to practice (behavioral rehearsal, role-playing) both the desired target behaviors and self-management skills (Fowler, 1986).

15. A direct and systematic instructional approach should be taken to teach self-management skills and desired target behaviors.

Summary of Key Concepts

■ The goal of self-management training is to enable students to use skills that increase their opportunities to function independently and successfully.

■ The successful teaching of self-management skills requires a clear understanding of the student's behavioral repertoire and the response and stimulus requirements of the setting in which the behaviors are to occur.

■ Self-management skills need to be taught in a systematic and consistent fashion. Self-management skills are the end result of fading external or teacher-directed prompts.

■ It is easy to describe the existence of internal states that motivate or drive our behaviors; however, these inferred states are very difficult to measure and confirm directly. Self-management skills focus on observable behaviors that enable the student to function successfully independent of teacher or other external assistance.

REFERENCES

Baer, D. M., &. Fowler, S. A. (1976). How should we measure the potential of self-control procedures for generalized educational outcomes? In W. L. Heward, T. E. Heron, D. S. Hill, & J. Trap-Porter (Eds.), *Focus on behavior analysis in education* (pp. 145–161). Columbus, OH: Charles E. Merrill.

Baer, M., Fowler, S. A., & Carden-Smith, L. (1984). Using reinforcement and independent-grading to promote and maintain task accuracy in a mainstreamed class. *Analysis and Intervention in Developmental Disabilities, 4,* 157–170.

Baker, J. E., & Winston, A. S. (1985). Modifying children's creative drawing: Experimental analysis and social validation of a self-instructional procedure. *Education and Treatment of Children, 8,* 115–132.

Bandura, A. (1969). *Principles of behavior modification.* New York: Holt, Rinehart, & Winston.

Bandura, A. (1971). *Social learning theory.* New York: General Learning Press.

Bandura, A., & Perloff, B. (1967). Relative efficacy of self-monitoring and externally imposed reinforcement systems. *Journal of Personality and Social Psychology, 7,* 111–116.

Billings, D. C., & Wasik, B. H. (1985). Self-instructional training with pre-schoolers: An attempt to replicate. *Journal of Applied Behavior Analysis, 18,* 61–68.

Bornstein, P. H. (1985). Self-instructional training: A commentary and state-of-the-art. *Journal of Applied Behavior Analysis, 18,* 69–72.

Bornstein, P., & Quevillon, R. (1976). The effects of self instructional packages on overactive preschool boys. *Journal of Applied Behavior Analysis, 9,* 179–188.

Broden, M., Hall, R. V., & Mitts, B. (1971). The effect of self-recording of the classroom behavior of two eighth grade students. *Journal of Applied Behavior Analysis, 4,* 191–199.

Bryant, L., & Budd, K. (1982). Self-instructional training to increase independent work performance in preschoolers. *Journal of Applied Behavior Analysis, 15,* 259–271.

Burgio, L. D., Whitman, T. L., & Johnson, M. R. (1980). A self-instructional package for increasing attending behavior in educable mentally retarded children. *Journal of Applied Behavior Analysis, 13,* 443–459.

Fowler, S. A. (1986). Peer-monitoring and self-monitoring: Alternatives to traditional teacher management. *Exceptional Children, 52,* 573–582.

Friedling, C., & O'Leary, D. (1979). Effects of self-instructional training on second and third grade children: A failure to replicate. *Journal of Applied Behavior Analysis, 12,* 211–219.

Gelfand, D. M., & Hartmann, D. P. (1984). *Child behavior analysis and therapy* (2nd ed.). New York: Pergamon.

Glynn, E. L., Thomas, J. D., & Shee, S. M. (1973). Behavioral self-control of on-task behavior in an elementary classroom. *Journal of Applied Behavior Analysis, 6,* 105–113.

Hayes, S. C., Rosenfarb, I., Wulfert, E., Munt, E. D., Korn, Z., & Zettle, R. D. (1985). Self-reinforcement effects: An artifact of social standard setting. *Journal of Applied Behavior Analysis, 18,* 201–214.

Kanfer, F. H. (1970). Self-regulation: Research, issues, and speculations. In C. Neuringer & J. L. Michael (Eds.), *Behavior modification in clinical psychology.* New York: Appleton-Century-Crofts.

Karoly, P., & Kanfer, F. H. (1974). Situational and historical determinants of self reinforcement. *Behavior Therapy, 5,* 381–390.

Kazdin, A. E. (1974). Reactive self-monitoring: The effects of response desirability, goal setting, and feedback. *Journal of Consulting and Clinical Psychology, 42,* 704–714.

Kazdin, A. E. (1975). *Behavior modification in applied settings.* Homewood, IL: Dorsey Press.

Kendall, P. C., & Finch, A. J. (1979). Developing nonimpulsive behavior in children's cognitive-behavioral strategies on self-control. In P. C. Kendall & S. D. Hollon (Eds.), *Cognitive-behavioral interventions: Theory, research, and procedures.* New York: Academic Press.

Kerr, M. M., & Nelson, C. M. (1983). *Strategies for managing behavior problems in the classroom.* Columbus, OH: Charles E. Merrill.

Liberty, K. A., & Michael, L. J. (1985). Teaching retarded students to reinforce their own behavior: A review of process and operation in the current literature. In N. Haring (Ed.), *Investigating the problem of skill generalization* (3rd ed.) (pp. 88–106). Seattle: University of Washington.

Mace, F. C., & Kratochwill, T. R. (1985). Theories of reactivity in self-monitoring: A comparison of cognitive-behavioral and operant models. *Behavior Modification, 9,* 323–344.

Meichenbaum, D. (1975). Enhancing creativity by modifying what subjects say to themselves. *American Educational Research Journal, 12,* 129–145.

Meichenbaum, D., & Goodman, J. (1971). Training impulsive children to talk to themselves: A means of developing self-control. *Journal of Abnormal Psychology, 77,* 115–126.

Nelson, R. D., & Hayes, S. C. (1981). Theoretical explanations for reactivity in self-monitoring. *Behavior Modification, 5,* 3–14.

O'Leary, S. G., & Dubey, D. R. (1979). Applications of self-control procedures by children: A review. *Journal of Applied Behavior Analysis, 12,* 449–465.

Polsgrove, L. (1979). Self-control: Methods for training. *Behavior Disorders, 4,* 116–130.

Rachlin, H. (1978). Self-control: Part I. In A. C. Catania and T. A. Brigham (Eds.), *Handbook of applied behavior analysis: Social and instructional processes.* New York: Irvington Publishers.

Rachlin, H. (1974). Self-control. *Behaviorism, 2,* 94–102.

Richards, C. S., & Siegel, L. J. (1978). Behavioral treatment of anxiety states and avoidance behaviors in children. In D. Marholin, II (Ed.), *Child behavior therapy* (pp. 274–338). New York: Gardner Press.

Rimm, D. C., & Masters, J. C. (1979). *Behavior therapy: Techniques and empirical findings* (2nd ed.). New York: Academic Press.

Skinner, B. F. (1953). *Science and human behavior.* New York: Macmillan.

Sugai, G., & Rowe, P. (1984). The effect of self-recording on out-of-seat behavior of an educable mentally retarded student. *Education and Training of the Mentally Retarded, 19,* 23–28.

Swanson, H. L., & Scarpati, S. (1984). Self-instruction training to increase academic performance of educationally handicapped children. *Child and Family Behavior Therapy, 6,* 23–40.

Workman, E. A., & Williams, R. L. (1980). Self-cued relaxation in the control of an adolescent's violent arguments and debilitating somatic complaints. *Education and Treatment of Children, 3,* 315–322.

INDEXES

SUBJECT INDEX

Aberrant behavior (*see* Behavior
    problems)
Abscissa, 113
Academic learning, 194
Acquisition
    defined, 219
    objectives for, 57
Adaptation objectives, 61
Adaptive outcomes, 343
Aim line, 292
Aim star, 132
AIMSTAR (computer program), 94
Allocated time, 194
Alternative response training
    deep muscle relaxation training, 516
    defined, 516–517
    self-cued relaxation, 516
Analogue assessment, 357
Antecedents, defined, 9
Antecedent instructional strategies (*see*
    also Interventions)
    defined, 147
Antecedent prompt and fade, 259–261
Applied behavior analysis
    criticisms of, 26–30
    defined, 21
    dimensions of, 22–23
    model for teaching, 23–25
Assessment
    analogue assessment, 357
    communicative function, 358–359
    discrepancy analysis, 362
    of environmental variables, 359–361
    functional analysis, 356–358
    identifying functional relationships,
        356
    of maintaining factors, 371–375
    purpose, 356
Attention
    defined, 215
    procedures for securing, 215–216
    role in learning, 6
Attention deficit disorder, 6
Attrition threat to validity, 162
Aversion therapy, 14
Aversive stimuli
    defined, 336, 446
    intensity of, 448–449
    results of using, 446–450
    types of, 446–448

Back-up reinforcers, 237, 479, 481
Baseline condition, defined, 148
Behavior
    defined, 9
    defining, 353, 355

inappropriate (*see* Behavior problems)
incompatible, 342, 355
independent behaviors, 178
replacement, 342
superstitious, 242
Behavioral assessment (*see* Assessment)
Behavioral contract (*see* Behavior
    contract)
Behavioral interventions (*see*
    Interventions)
Behavioral principles, 21
Behavioral procedures (*see also*
    Interventions), 21
Behavioral theory
    history of, 10–13
    principles of, 12
    of child development, 12–13
    of mental retardation, 12–13
Behavior contract
    advantages of, 472
    defined, 472
    elements of, 472–475
    procedures for developing, 475–478
    procedures for transferring to natural
        contingencies, 472, 474
    rules for using, 478
Behavior problems (*see also*
    Intervention with behavior
    problems)
    assessment of, 341, 353–363
    collecting data for, 364, 365
    communicative function of, 358–359,
        361
    deficits/excesses in duration, 332
    deficits/excesses in frequency, 332
    deficits/excesses in intensity, 332
    deficits/excesses in latency, 332
    defined, 331
    hypotheses about causes, 371–374
    identification of, 350–353
    implementing plan for, 376–377
    importance of curriculum, 363, 367
    inappropriate stimulus control, 333
    intervention options, 368
    measurement of, 342
    monitoring, 342, 378
    planning interventions for, 364–376
    procedures for classifying, 331–336
    relationship to reinforcement,
        367–368
    selecting interventions for, 368–375
    specifying objectives for, 363
Behavior reduction
    decision model, defined, 349
    decision model, described, 349–379
Behavior Therapy (journal), 14, 356

Beyond Freedom and Dignity (book), 29
Biofeedback, 14
Black box, 4, 10
Bloom's taxonomy, 63–66

Calibration, 74
Carryover effects, 171
Causal or functional relationship,
    defined, 147
'Celeration line, 130
Central tendency, 105
Central tendency line, 130
Chained tasks, 256
Classical conditioning, 11
    conditioned stimulus (CS), 11
    unconditioned stimulus (UCS), 11
Cognitive-developmental explanation
    for learning, 7–8
    accommodation, 8
    assimilation, 8
    equilibration, 8
Collecting data (*see* Data collection)
Communicative function, 358–359, 361
Community-based instruction, 319
Conditioned reinforcers, 237
Conditioned stimulus (CS), 11
Consequence or contingency strategies,
    defined, 147
Consequences
    defined, 9, 235, 356
    natural, 242
    reinforcing, 235
    types of, 234
Constant time delay, 267
Contingency contract (*see* Behavior
    contract)
Contingency management, 198–199
Contingent, defined, 446
Contingent observation timeout,
    421–422
Continuous schedule of reinforcement
    (CRF), 244, 300
Continuum of intrusiveness, 187
Contracts (*see* Behavior contract)
Contrast, 171
Controlling prompt, 254
Corporal punishment
    corporal punishment cycle, 461–462
    defined, 458
    legality of, 461
    procedural issues, 461–462
    rationale for/against use of, 458–459
    recommendations concerning, 463
    use of, 460
    use with special education students,
        460–461

NAME INDEX